Wonders

ELL Small Group Guide

Strategic Support for English Language Learners

mheducation.com/prek-12

Copyright © 2023 McGraw Hill

All rights reserved. No part of this publication may be reproduced or distributed in any form or by any means, or stored in a database or retrieval system, without the prior written consent of McGraw Hill, including, but not limited to, network storage or transmission, or broadcast for distance learning.

Send all inquiries to:
McGraw Hill
1325 Avenue of the Americas
New York, NY 10019

ISBN: 978-1-26-579570-2
MHID: 1-26-579570-3

Printed in the United States of America.

4 5 6 7 8 9 LMN 26 25 24 23 22 A

UNITS 1-2

Contents

Contents

Contents

ELL Resources

A variety of resources will help English Language Learners meet grade level expectations. The components provide scaffolded instruction and practice through integrated domains to help students tackle core content and transition to more proficient levels of English.

Component	Differentiate: N = Newcomer B = Beginning I = Intermediate A = Advanced/Advanced-High AL = All Levels	Integrated Domains Reading Writing Listening Speaking	Available Digitally
ELL Small Group Guide • Shared Read, • Anchor Text, • Differentiated Genre Passage, • Leveled Reader, • Writing	B, I, A	Reading, Writing, Listening, Speaking	●
Scaffolded Shared Read	B, I (Early-Intermediate)	Reading, Writing, Listening, Speaking	●
Shared Read Writing Frames	B, I, A	Reading, Writing, Listening, Speaking	●
ELL Anchor Text Support BLMs	AL	Reading, Writing, Listening, Speaking	●
Differentiated Genre Passages	AL	Reading, Writing, Listening, Speaking	●
Leveled Readers	AL	Reading, Writing, Listening, Speaking	●
ELL Differentiated Texts	B, I, A	Reading, Writing, Listening, Speaking	●

Component	Differentiate: N = Newcomer B = Beginning I = Intermediate A = Advanced/Advanced-High AL = All Levels	Integrated Domains Reading Writing Listening Speaking	Available Digitally
ELL Extended Writing BLMs	AL	Reading, Writing, Listening, Speaking	●
Oral Language Sentence Frames	B, I, A	Listening, Speaking	●
Visual Vocabulary Cards	AL	Reading, Writing, Listening, Speaking	●
Newcomers • Newcomer Cards • Newcomer Teacher's Guide • Newcomer Online Visuals • Newcomer Interactive Games	N	Reading, Writing, Listening, Speaking	●
Language Development Kit • Language Development Cards • Language Development Practice	B, I, A	Reading, Writing, Listening, Speaking	●
Online Games	AL	Reading, Writing, Listening, Speaking	●
Language Transfers Handbook	AL	Reading, Writing, Listening, Speaking	●
Unit Assessment	B, I, A	Reading, Writing, Listening, Speaking	●

Understanding English Language Learner Levels

The *Wonders* program provides targeted language support for all levels of English language proficiency. The English language learners in your classroom have a variety of backgrounds. Students have differences in background, first languages, and levels of education. In addition, English language learners bring diverse sets of academic knowledge and cultural perspectives that should be respected and leveraged to enrich learning.

This overview is designed to help teachers determine the appropriate level of support for their English language learners and understand students' abilities depending on their language proficiencies. It is important to note that students may be at different levels in each language domain (listening, speaking, reading, and writing). Systematic, explicit, and appropriately scaffolded instruction helps English language learners attain English proficiency and meet the high expectations defined in English Language Arts standards.

BEGINNING

At this early stage of language development, students require significant language support. As they gain experience with English, support may become moderate or light for familiar tasks and topics.

The Student...

- recognizes English phonemes that correspond to phonemes produced in primary language;
- initially demonstrates more receptive than productive English skills;
- communicates basic needs and information in social and academic settings, using familiar everyday vocabulary, gestures, learned words or phrases, and/or short sentences;
- follows one- or two-step oral directions;
- answers *wh-* questions (who, what, when, where, why, which);
- comprehends words, phrases, and basic information about familiar topics as presented through stories and conversations;
- identifies concepts about print and text features;
- reads short grade-appropriate text with familiar vocabulary and simple sentences, supported by graphics or pictures;
- draws pictures and writes labels;
- expresses ideas using visuals and short responses.

INTERMEDIATE

Students require moderate support for cognitively demanding activities and light support for familiar tasks and topics.

The Student...

- pronounces most English phonemes correctly while reading aloud;
- communicates more complex personal needs, ideas, and opinions using increasingly complex vocabulary and sentences;
- follows multi-step oral directions;
- initiates and participates in collaborative conversations about social and academic topics, with support as needed;
- asks questions, retells stories or events, and comprehends basic content-area concepts;
- comprehends information on familiar and unfamiliar topics with contextual clues;
- reads increasingly complex grade-level text supported by graphics, pictures, and context clues;
- increases correct usage of written and oral language conventions;
- uses vocabulary learned, including academic language, to provide information and extended responses in contextualized oral and written prompts.

ADVANCED/ADVANCED HIGH

While the English language proficiency of students is advanced, some language support for accessing content is still necessary. If students are requiring little to no support, exiting them from the ELL designation should be considered.

The Student...

- applies knowledge of common English morphemes in oral and silent reading;
- communicates complex feelings, needs, ideas, and opinions using increasingly complex vocabulary and sentences;
- understands more nonliteral social and academic language about concrete and abstract topics;
- initiates and sustains collaborative conversations about grade-level academic and social topics;
- reads and comprehends a wide range of complex literature and informational texts at grade level;
- writes using more standard forms of English on various academic topics;
- communicates orally and in writing with fewer grammatical errors;
- tailors language, orally and in writing, to specific purposes and audiences.

Scaffolding the Shared Read

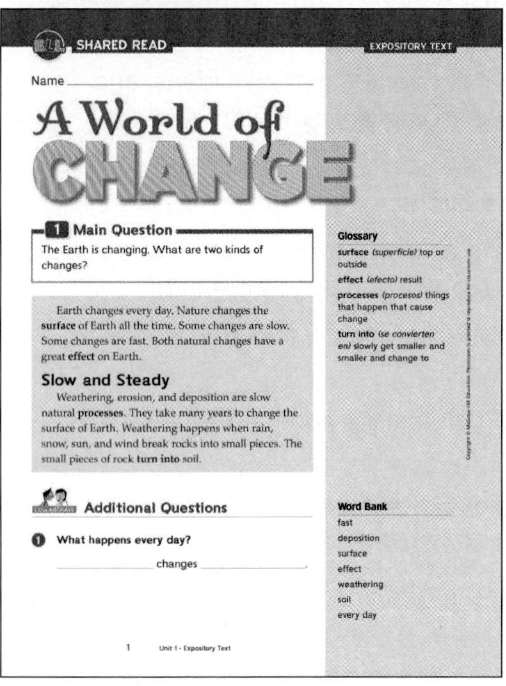

SHARED READ   EXPOSITORY TEXT

Name ____

A World of CHANGE

1 Main Question

The Earth is changing. What are two kinds of changes?

Earth changes every day. Nature changes the **surface** of Earth all the time. Some changes are slow. Some changes are fast. Both natural changes have a great **effect** on Earth.

Slow and Steady

Weathering, erosion, and deposition are slow natural **processes**. They take many years to change the surface of Earth. Weathering happens when rain, snow, sun, and wind break rocks into small pieces. The small pieces of rock **turn into** soil.

Glossary

surface *(superficie)* top or outside

effect *(efecto)* result

processes *(procesos)* things that happen that cause change

turn into *(se convierten en)* slowly get smaller and smaller and change to

Additional Questions

1. What happens every day?

____ changes ____.

Word Bank

fast
deposition
surface
effect
weathering
soil
every day

1 Unit 1 • Expository Text

Scaffolded Shared Read

Wonders provides differentiated instruction for the **Shared Read**.

- Linguistically accommodated instruction for Intermediate, Advanced and Advanced High students offers access to the grade-level text.
- Prereading strategies enhance comprehension for students from different cultural backgrounds.
- Interactive Question-Response Routine with leveled prompts focuses on the meaning of the text.
- Oral language is developed through peer interaction.
- Digital recording of the selection to listen along.

More focused instruction for Beginning and Early-Intermediate students can be found online in the **Scaffolded Shared Read**.

- Explicit instruction builds language and literacy skills by having students engage in peer and independent work.
- Integrated instruction is provided in listening, speaking, reading, and writing.
- Working with smaller chunks of text helps English Language Learners respond to Guiding and Supplementary questions.
- The Scaffolded Shared Read is a path for Beginning and Early-Intermediate students to successfully level up.

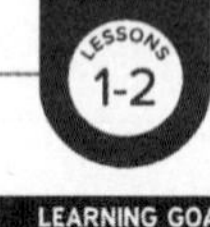

READING • SHARED READ • ACCESS THE TEXT

WEEKS 1–2

LEARNING GOALS

We can read and understand an expository text.

OBJECTIVES

Describe the overall structure of events, ideas, concepts, or information in a text or part of a text.

Review the key ideas expressed and explain their own ideas and understanding in light of the discussion.

Use context as a clue to the meaning of a word or phrase.

Observe and identify slow changes to Earth's surface caused by weathering, erosion, and deposition from water, wind, and ice. **Science**

LANGUAGE OBJECTIVES

Students will inquire by comparing and contrasting using signal words.

ELA ACADEMIC LANGUAGE

- *compare, contrast, diagrams, headings, multiple*
- Cognates: *comparar, diagrama, contrastar*

MATERIALS

Reading/Writing Companion, pp. 12-15

Online Scaffolded Shared Read, "A World of Change"

Visual Vocabulary Cards

Online ELL Visual Vocabulary Cards

DIGITAL TOOLS

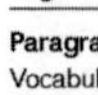

Have students read along with the audio of the selection to develop comprehension and practice fluency and pronunciation.

"A World of Change"

Prepare to Read

Build Background Discuss with students changes that happen to Earth. Have students share what they know, such as volcanic eruptions or earthquakes, erosion on a beach, or landslides. Have them describe using: I know/learned about ___. Explain that changes are happening all the time to Earth's surface.

Vocabulary Use the **Visual Vocabulary Cards** to preteach the vocabulary: *alter, collapse, substantial, hazard, destruction, crisis, severe,* and *unpredictable.* Use the online **ELL Visual Vocabulary Cards** to teach additional Vocabulary from the Shared Read: *collection, damage, location, occurs, surface,* and *warn.* (Cognates: *destrucción, crisis, colección, ocurrir;* False Cognate: *alterar*)

Set Purpose *Today we will read an expository text called "A World of Change" and focus on* ***comparing and contrasting****. As we read, think about how people respond to natural disasters.*

Read the Text

Select the online **Scaffolded Shared Read** or the Shared Read in the **Reading/Writing Companion**, based on students' language proficiency.

Scaffolded Shared Read, Lexile 580L

Beginning/ Early-Intermediate Use the online Scaffolded Shared Read to help partners work together to read and understand an expository text. Remind them to use the Glossary to help them read and the Word Bank to help them answer the Main and Additional Questions.

Intermediate/ Advanced Advanced High Read the text with students and use the Interactive Question-Response Routine to help them understand an expository text.

Reading/Writing Companion, Lexile 790L

Page 13

Paragraph 1 Read the text with students and review Vocabulary words *alter* and *surface. When do natural changes happen?* (every day) *What do fast and slow natural changes do?* (Both change Earth's surface.) Point to the word *whether* and explain that it tells that there are choices or possibilities. Have students read the last sentence. Ask: *What are the choices?* (Earth's changes are slow or fast.) Explain that *whether* sounds the same as *weather* but is spelled differently.

COLLABORATE Intermediate Have partners use the words *whether* and *weather* to generate their own sentences and indicate the spelling of the word for each sentence: The weather is rainy. We will go to the movie whether it rains or snows.

COLLABORATE Advanced/Advanced High Point to the phrase "take place" in the third and fifth sentences and explain that this phrase has **multiple meanings**. It can mean "to happen" or "substitute for." Have students identify context clues to figure out the meaning of "take place." (happen)

Paragraphs 2–5 Read the text with students and review Vocabulary words *collapse, collection, substantial, location* and *occurs. What are the three processes that change Earth's surface slowly?* (weathering, erosion, deposition) *What happens during weathering?* (Rain, snow, sun, wind break down rocks into small pieces of rock.) *What happens during erosion?* (Rivers and natural forces carry away pieces of rock.) *What happens during deposition?* (Soil and rock from erosion get dropped at a new location.)

COLLABORATE Have partners **compare and contrast** erosion and deposition using signal words, such as *both* and *in contrast.* (Possible answer: Both erosion and deposition are processes that change Earth's surface. During erosion the small pieces of rock get carried away. In contrast, during deposition the small pieces of rock get dropped in a new location.)

Page 14

Paragraphs 1–3 Read the text with students. Review Vocabulary word *hazard. How do people prevent beach erosion?* (build structures to block waves from the shore, use heavy rocks, grow plants to hold soil)

Intermediate *Does* hazard *mean something good or bad?* (bad) *How do you know?* (text tells that some types of erosion are dangerous) *Which word has a meaning similar to* hazard*?* (dangerous)

Paragraphs 4–5 Read the text with students and review Vocabulary words *destruction* and *crisis.* Read the heading. Ask: *How is this heading different from the previous heading?* (fast is the opposite of slow, powerful means "with a lot of force") *What will the section be about?* (changes that happen quickly) *What natural processes are fast and powerful?* (volcanic eruptions, landslides) *What causes a volcanic eruption?* (Pressure builds up under Earth's surface.)

Page 15

Paragraphs 1–3 Read the text with students and review Vocabulary words *severe, unpredictable, damage,* and *warn. What happens during a landslide?* (Dirt and rocks are loosened by rain and slide down the hill or mountain.) *Why is it important to have an emergency plan?* (People need to get to safe places quickly.)

Intermediate *Which words are signal words for compare and contrast?* ("Like volcanic eruptions," "In contrast") *What is the comparison in the first paragraph?* Both volcanic eruptions and landslides can happen without warning, or suddenly.

COLLABORATE Advanced/Advanced High Have partners contrast what people can do with slow- and fast-moving processes and why predicting natural disasters is important. (Unlike erosion, people cannot prevent landslides or volcanic eruptions. By predicting them, people will have time to move to safe places.)

COLLABORATE Reread the last section on page 15 with them and have students discuss why the author used the **heading** "Be Prepared."

COLLABORATE Review with students that a **diagram** text feature shows the parts of something or how a process works. Have partners retell what happens during a volcanic eruption using the diagram. (Possible answer: A volcano erupts when pressure builds under Earth's surface. Magma flows up the pipe and comes out through the vent of the crater.)

FORMATIVE ASSESSMENT

STUDENT CHECK-IN

Have partners retell the important ideas in the text. Ask them to reflect using the Check-in routine.

2 UNIT 1 TEXT SET 1

Language Development Options Using the Shared Read

Students internalize language structures and vocabulary from the reading selections to enhance their understanding about how language works and build their writing skills.

- **Text Reconstruction** The instruction focuses on a single chunk of text to support listening comprehension and language development across the four domains. The teacher reads aloud a paragraph from the selection as students listen and take notes for different purposes, such as identifying the central idea and relevant details or analyzing figurative language. Students collaborate with peers to reconstruct the text from their notes. Then they confirm understanding by comparing their reconstructed text with the original. This routine helps students to write with increasing accuracy to describe specific purposes and text structures.
- **Grammar in Context** Students identify the grammar structure in a text excerpt and review the grammar skill in context. This routine helps students enhance their understanding of the grammar skill and apply it in a short, focused writing task.
- **Independent Time** Students have an opportunity to work independently and collaboratively on a variety of activities, including glossary building, role-plays, writing tasks, and peer-to-peer instruction. The routines help students take ownership of their language development.

AUTHOR INSIGHT

"A key goal of the lessons is to provide ELLs with scaffolded opportunities to work independently or collaboratively with their peers. Engaging in productive peer or independent work is crucial for ELLs' academic language development."

—Dr. Diane August

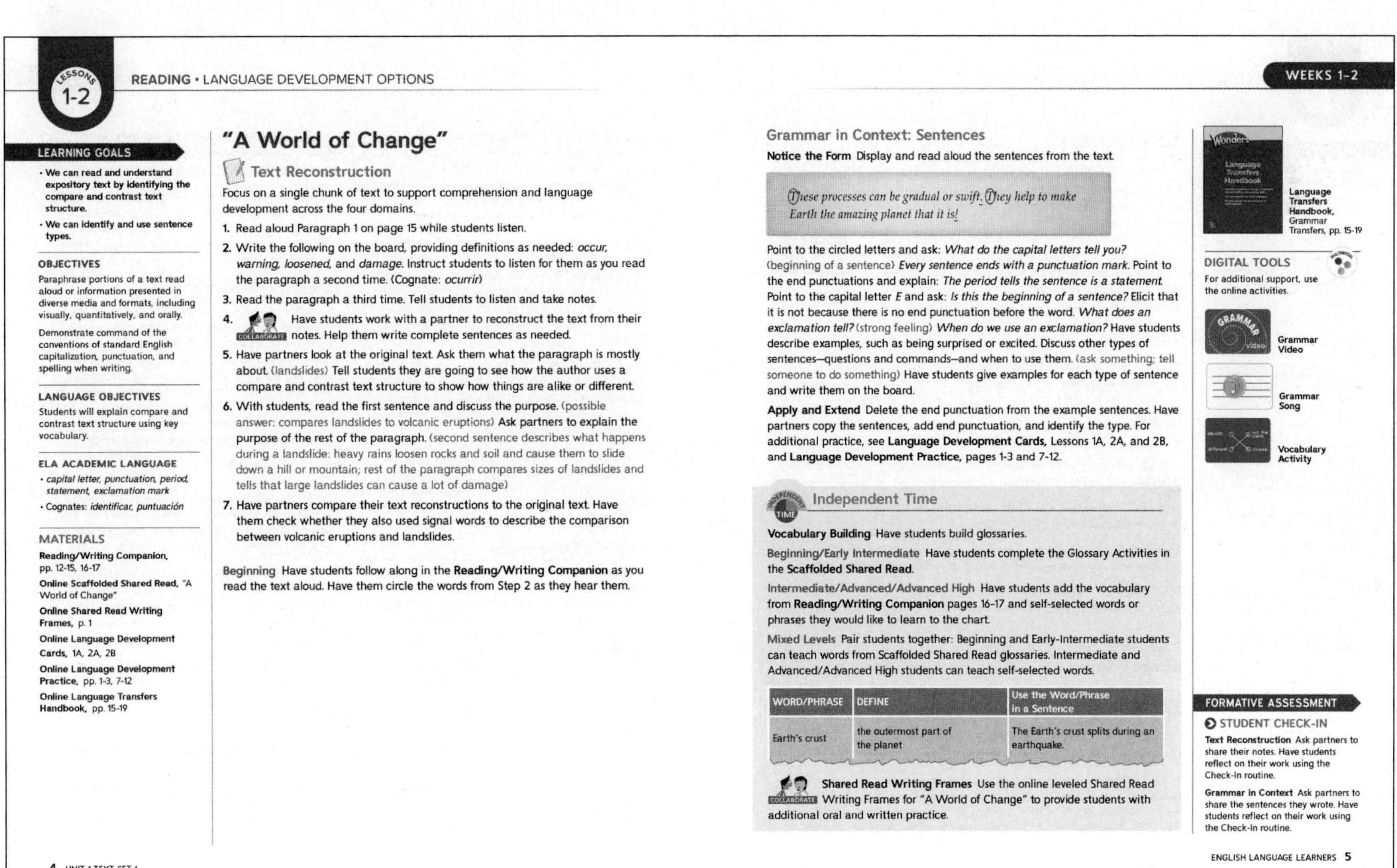

LESSONS 1-2 READING • LANGUAGE DEVELOPMENT OPTIONS

WEEKS 1–2

LEARNING GOALS

- We can read and understand expository text by identifying the compare and contrast text structure.
- We can identify and use sentence types.

OBJECTIVES

Paraphrase portions of a text read aloud or information presented in diverse media and formats, including visually, quantitatively, and orally.

Demonstrate command of the conventions of standard English capitalization, punctuation, and spelling when writing.

LANGUAGE OBJECTIVES

Students will explain compare and contrast text structure using key vocabulary.

ELA ACADEMIC LANGUAGE

- *capital letter, punctuation, period, statement, exclamation mark*
- Cognates: *identificar, puntuación*

MATERIALS

Reading/Writing Companion, pp. 12-15, 16-17

Online Scaffolded Shared Read, "A World of Change"

Online Shared Read Writing Frames, p. 1

Online Language Development Cards, 1A, 2A, 2B

Online Language Development Practice, pp. 1-3, 7-12

Online Language Transfers Handbook, pp. 15-19

"A World of Change"

Text Reconstruction

Focus on a single chunk of text to support comprehension and language development across the four domains.

1. Read aloud Paragraph 1 on page 15 while students listen.
2. Write the following on the board, providing definitions as needed: *occur, warning, loosened,* and *damage.* Instruct students to listen for them as you read the paragraph a second time. (Cognate: *ocurrir*)
3. Read the paragraph a third time. Tell students to listen and take notes.
4. COLLABORATE Have students work with a partner to reconstruct the text from their notes. Help them write complete sentences as needed.
5. Have partners look at the original text. Ask them what the paragraph is mostly about. (landslides) Tell students they are going to see how the author uses a compare and contrast text structure to show how things are alike or different.
6. With students, read the first sentence and discuss the purpose. (possible answer: compares landslides to volcanic eruptions) Ask partners to explain the purpose of the rest of the paragraph. (second sentence describes what happens during a landslide: heavy rains loosen rocks and soil and cause them to slide down a hill or mountain; rest of the paragraph compares sizes of landslides and tells that large landslides can cause a lot of damage)
7. Have partners compare their text reconstructions to the original text. Have them check whether they also used signal words to describe the comparison between volcanic eruptions and landslides.

Beginning Have students follow along in the **Reading/Writing Companion** as you read the text aloud. Have them circle the words from Step 2 as they hear them.

Grammar in Context: Sentences

Notice the Form Display and read aloud the sentences from the text.

These processes can be gradual or swift. They help to make Earth the amazing planet that it is!

Point to the circled letters and ask: *What do the capital letters tell you?* (beginning of a sentence) *Every sentence ends with a punctuation mark.* Point to the end punctuations and explain: *The period tells the sentence is a statement.* Point to the capital letter *E* and ask: *Is this the beginning of a sentence?* Elicit that it is not because there is no end punctuation before the word. *What does an exclamation tell?* (strong feeling) *When do we use an exclamation?* Have students describe examples, such as being surprised or excited. Discuss other types of sentences—questions and commands—and when to use them. (ask something; tell someone to do something) Have students give examples for each type of sentence and write them on the board.

Apply and Extend Delete the end punctuation from the example sentences. Have partners copy the sentences, add end punctuation, and identify the type. For additional practice, see **Language Development Cards,** Lessons 1A, 2A, and 2B, and **Language Development Practice,** pages 1-3 and 7-12.

Independent Time

Vocabulary Building Have students build glossaries.

Beginning/Early Intermediate Have students complete the Glossary Activities in the **Scaffolded Shared Read.**

Intermediate/Advanced/Advanced High Have students add the vocabulary from **Reading/Writing Companion** pages 16-17 and self-selected words or phrases they would like to learn to the chart.

Mixed Levels Pair students together: Beginning and Early-Intermediate students can teach words from Scaffolded Shared Read glossaries. Intermediate and Advanced/Advanced High students can teach self-selected words.

WORD/PHRASE	DEFINE	Use the Word/Phrase in a Sentence
Earth's crust	the outermost part of the planet	The Earth's crust splits during an earthquake.

COLLABORATE **Shared Read Writing Frames** Use the online leveled Shared Read Writing Frames for "A World of Change" to provide students with additional oral and written practice.

Language Transfers Handbook, Grammar Transfers, pp. 15-19

DIGITAL TOOLS

For additional support, use the online activities.

Grammar Video

Grammar Song

Vocabulary Activity

FORMATIVE ASSESSMENT

STUDENT CHECK-IN

Text Reconstruction Ask partners to share their notes. Have students reflect on their work using the Check-In routine.

Grammar in Context Ask partners to share the sentences they wrote. Have students reflect on their work using the Check-In routine.

4 UNIT 1 TEXT SET 1

ENGLISH LANGUAGE LEARNERS 5

Scaffolding the Anchor Text

AUTHOR INSIGHT

"English Language Learners benefit from exposure to grade-level text and discussions to build language and literacy skills. Learning new information, words and concepts in a new language is challenging. English Language Learners need multiple exposures to new material and benefit from opportunities to practice interacting with it in authentic ways."

—Dr. Jana Echevarria

Wonders provides linguistically accommodated instruction for all levels to access the **Anchor Text**.

- Explicit instruction helps students read grade-appropriate content area text and comprehend increasingly challenging language.
- Instruction provides more support for English Language Learners to answer deep, higher-level questions in the Reading/Writing Companion.
- Students benefit from multiple exposures to new material and opportunities to practice interacting with it in authentic ways.
- Students reinforce skills and strategies, and develop oral language by interacting with each other and practicing academic language.
- Partners use the **Anchor Text Support Blackline Masters** (BLMs) to guide them in focusing on comprehension and vocabulary while reading specific chunks of text independently.
- Students can also listen to a digital recording of the selection to develop comprehension and practice fluency and pronunciation.

LESSONS 3-8 READING • ANCHOR TEXT • ACCESS THE TEXT — WEEKS 1–2

LEARNING GOALS

Read We can read and understand an expository text.

Reread We can reread and analyze text, craft, and structure.

OBJECTIVES

Explain events, procedures, ideas, or concepts in a historical, scientific, or technical text, including what happened and why, based on specific information in the text.

Review the key ideas expressed and explain their own ideas and understanding in light of the discussion.

Observe and identify slow changes to Earth's surface caused by weathering, erosion, and deposition from water, wind, and ice. **Science**

LANGUAGE OBJECTIVES:

Students will inquire by answering questions about the text using content area vocabulary.

ELA ACADEMIC LANGUAGE

- *informational, article*
- Cognate: *informativo*

MATERIALS

Literature Anthology, pp. 10-19

Reading/Writing Companion, pp. 24-27

Online ELL Anchor Text Support BLMS pp. 1-3

DIGITAL TOOLS

Have students read along with the audio of the selection to develop comprehension and practice fluency and pronunciation.

Earthquakes

Prepare to Read

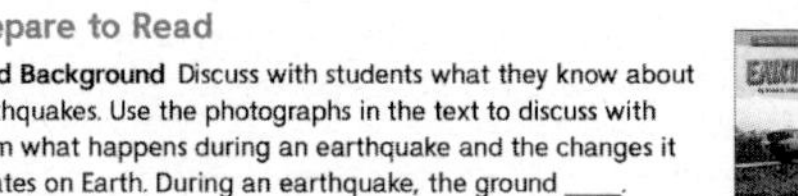

Build Background Discuss with students what they know about earthquakes. Use the photographs in the text to discuss with them what happens during an earthquake and the changes it creates on Earth. During an earthquake, the ground ____.

Vocabulary Use the **Visual Vocabulary Cards** to review the vocabulary: *alter, collapse, substantial, hazard, destruction, crisis, severe,* and *unpredictable.*

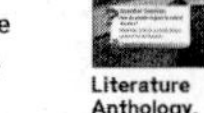

Literature Anthology, Lexile 870L

Set Purpose *Today we will read an expository text about an earthquake. As we read, think about how people respond to natural disasters.*

Have students listen to the audio summary of the text, which is available in multiple languages.

Read

Literature Anthology, pp. 10–19

Use the **Interactive Question-Response Routine** to help students read and discuss ***Earthquakes.***

Beginning Help students discuss in complete sentences. Provide sentence frames: During an earthquake the ground shakes.

Intermediate Ask students to respond in complete sentences and add details. Provide sentence starters as needed: During an earthquake, the ground shakes and splits apart.

Advanced/Advanced High Have students respond in complete sentences and add details.

Independent Reading Practice Have mixed level pairs complete Online Anchor Text Support and share their responses with the group.

Reread

Use with **Reading/Writing Companion,** pages 24-27

Literature Anthology, pages 10-11

Text Features: Photographs Read the text and restate them with students. Have them ask about words or phrases that are unfamiliar and define them for clarification, such as *jigsaw puzzle, sphere,* and *gel.* Remind them that photographs often give additional information and have students describe it using the caption. *What happens during an earthquake?* (The ground shakes.) *What are plates?* (pieces of Earth's crust) *What does the photograph show?* (large cracks on a road after an earthquake) *Where was the photograph taken?* (Myanmar) Use a map to point out Myanmar.

Beginning Read the first paragraph and restate sentences with students. *What do people feel during an earthquake?* People feel the ground shake. Help partners describe the photograph: Earthquakes make cracks on the road. Read the caption. *Where did the earthquake happen?* The earthquake happened in Myanmar.

Intermediate *What does the author compare Earth's crust to?* (jigsaw puzzle) How is Earth's crust like a jigsaw puzzle? Earth's crust is divided into pieces that fit together. *What damage did the earthquake cause?* (It damaged roads and buildings.)

Advanced/Advanced High Have partners describe what the heat inside Earth does. (It causes Earth's plates to slowly move.) *What does the photograph show?* (Possible answer: It shows damage to the road and that probably affects a lot of people.)

Literature Anthology, page 13

Genre: Informational Article Read the text and restate it with students. Explain that a seismologist studies earthquakes. Have them ask about words or phrases that are unfamiliar and define them for clarification, such as *tsunami* and *magnitude. Who experienced an earthquake?* (Dr. Cifuentes) *When did the earthquake happen?* (May 21, 1960) *How is her experience different from the rest of the selection?* (She experienced the earthquake,so she can give details about each part of the experience)

Beginning Read sentences 1-5 and restate them with students. *Where did the earthquake happen?* The earthquake happened in Santiago, Chile. *What year was it?* It was the year 1960. *Who experienced the earthquake?* Dr. Cifuentes experienced the earthquake.

Intermediate Have partners discuss what Dr. Cifuentes experienced during the earthquake: She experienced the earthquake and later a tsunami.

Advanced/Advanced High *What did she experience during the earthquakes?* (woke up from the ground shaking.; felt the earthquake and tusnami) *What happened a year later?* (She visited and saw that the land had been raised up)

Literature Anthology, pages 16-17

Author's Craft: Word Choice Read the text and restate them with students. Have them ask about words or phrases that are unfamiliar and define them for clarification, such as *tower* and *engulfed. What do underwater earthquakes cause?* (tsunamis) *What's the height of the tsunami waves at sea?* (a few feet high) *How does the author refer to the tsunami as it reaches shore?* (a towering monster) *Why is* "Tsunami Terror" *a good heading for this section?* (This section is about the destruction that tsunamis bring.)

Beginning Read paragraph 2 and restate sentences with students. Guide them to connect what they read about fast changes. *What makes a tsunami terrifying, or scary?* A tsunami can destroy shorelines.

Intermediate Have partners describe a tsunami: A tsunami is a wave that moves very fast. The wave can tower into a monster. *What does the heading tell you about this section?* This section is about the destruction that happens during a tsunami.

Advanced/Advanced High Have partners discuss why the author describes the wave as towering into a monster. Check understanding of "towering." (This metaphor shows how much bigger and scarier the waves become as they reach shore.)

FORMATIVE ASSESSMENT

STUDENT CHECK-IN

Read Have partners share their responses to the Anchor Text questions. Then have them reflect using the Check-In routine.

Reread Have partners share responses and text evidence on Reading/Writing Companion pages 24-26. Then have them reflect using the Check-In routine to fill in the bars.

6 UNIT 1 TEXT SET 1 — ENGLISH LANGUAGE LEARNERS 7

Language Development Options Using the Anchor Text

Students internalize language structures and vocabulary from authentic text to enhance their understanding about how language works and build their writing skills.

- **Text Reconstruction** The instruction focuses on a single chunk of text to support listening comprehension and language development across the four domains. The routine mirrors the Text Reconstruction for the Shared Read. This routine helps students to write with increasing accuracy to describe specific purposes and text structures.
- **Grammar in Context**: **Deconstruct a Sentence** Students deconstruct a sentence from the text through explicit instruction on how the English language works, including structure, syntax, and academic language.
- **Independent Time** Students have an opportunity to work independently and collaboratively on a variety of activities, including glossary building, role-plays, writing tasks, and peer-to-peer instruction. The routines help students take ownership of their language development.

LEARNING GOALS

- **We can read and understand expository text by identifying the compare and contrast text structure.**
- **We can identify subjects and predicates.**

OBJECTIVES

Paraphrase portions of a text read aloud or information presented in diverse media and formats, including visually, quantitatively, and orally.

Demonstrate command of the conventions of standard English grammar and usage when writing or speaking.

LANGUAGE OBJECTIVES

Students will inquire about the compare and contrast text structure using key vocabulary.

ELA ACADEMIC LANGUAGE

- *contrast, compound predicate, subject, predicate, conjunction*
- Cognates: *contrastar, sujeto, predicado, conjunción*

MATERIALS

Literature Anthology, pp. 10-19

Online Language Development Cards, 3A-3B

Online Language Development Practice pp. 13-18

Online Language Transfers Handbook, pp. 15-19

Earthquakes

Text Reconstruction

Focus on a single chunk of text to support comprehension and language development across the four domains:

1. Read aloud Paragraph 2 on page 11 in the **Literature Anthology** while students listen.
2. Write the following on the board, providing definitions as needed: *Earth's crust, jigsaw puzzle, resembles, sphere, plates, upper mantle, gel,* and *swirl.* Instruct students to listen for them as you read the paragraph a second time. (Cognate: *esfera*)
3. Read the paragraph a third time while students listen and take notes.
4. COLLABORATE Have students work with a partner to reconstruct the text from their notes. Help them write complete sentences as needed.
5. Have students look at the original text. Ask them what the paragraph is mostly about. (the Earth's crust) Tell students they are going to examine the compare and contrast text structure.
6. *In the first sentence, what does the author compare the Earth's crust to?* (a jigsaw puzzle.) *What words does the author use to show how the two are alike?* (resembles, like) *Ask students to find another comparison* (penultimate sentence). *What is the upper mantle compared to?* (thick gel)
7. Have students compare their text reconstructions to the original text. Have them check whether they also included words that compare and contrast.

Beginning Allow students to follow along in their **Literature Anthologies** as you read the text aloud. Have them point to the words from Step 2 as they hear them.

Apply Text Features: Photograph

Help students write a caption. Review: *Captions describe what is happening in a photograph and often include facts and information from the text.* Discuss with students the photograph on pages 10-11. Then have them rewrite the caption for the photograph. (Possible answer: People drive by a large crack in the road after an earthquake.)

Grammar in Context: Deconstruct a Sentence

Display this sentence from page 11: *Heat from deep inside the earth moves through the rock and causes it to slowly swirl and flow.* Deconstruct the sentence with students to help them understand subjects and predicates:

- Read the sentence with students and explain that it has a compound predicate. Help students find the subject and predicate. *Which words are the subject?* (heat from deep inside the earth) *What words are the predicates?* (moves through the rock, causes it to slowly swirl and flow)
- Circle the subject and underline the predicates. Point out that there are two predicates, and the conjunction *and* joins them. Rewrite the sentences into two, each with a simple predicate to demonstrate. *What does the conjunction* and *tell you?* (There is more than one action.) *What two things does heat do?* (moves through rock and causes rock to swirl and flow) Discuss what the sentence describes. (Possible answer: what causes rock to move)
- Write on the board: *As the mantle boils, it pushes the plates. As the mantle boils, it pulls the plates.* Have partners combine the sentences using *and.*

For more practice, see **Language Development Cards,** Lessons 3A-3B, and **Language Development Practice** pages 13-18.

Independent Time

Vocabulary Building Have students create vocabulary cards for new vocabulary they learned from the selection. Have partners copy four words onto index cards. On the back of each card, have them write a definition. Then have them take turns selecting a card, word face up, using the word in a sentence.

Beginning Allow students to write words or phrases or draw pictures.

Intermediate/Advanced/Advanced High Have students include some of the self-selected words they added to their glossaries.

COLLABORATE **Compound Subjects and Predicates** Pair students of mixed levels and have them use conjunctions and connecting words to write compound and complex sentences. Copy the chart on the board and use the first set of sentences to model combining sentences. Then have partners rewrite the sentences using conjunctions *and, but,* and *or* to describe events in *Earthquakes.* Have them copy the chart to use to rewrite their sentences:

SENTENCE	CONJUNCTION	COMPOUND SUBJECTS/ COMPOUND PREDICATES
Earth's plates crash. Earth's plates spread apart. Earth's plates slide against each other.	and	Earth's plates crash, spread apart, and slide against each other.
Earthquakes destroy buildings. Earthquakes create mountains.	but	

Language Transfers Handbook, Grammar Transfers, pp. 15-19

FORMATIVE ASSESSMENT

STUDENT CHECK-IN

Text Reconstruction Ask partners to share their notes. Have them reflect using the Check-In routine.

Grammar in Context Have students reflect on their deconstructions using the Check-In routine.

Using Genre Passages

AUTHOR INSIGHT

"Reading leveled texts provides ELLs with additional practice and exposure to the academic vocabulary found in selections in the same genre. It also enhances ELLs' understanding of the genre and helps them make connections across texts."

—Dr. Jana Echevarria

Genre Passages are online digital leveled texts with the same genre focus and Essential Question as the Shared Read and Anchor Text. The ELL Genre Passage lessons provide linguistically accommodated instruction for all levels and reinforce and apply the reading skills and text features of each genre.

- The Build Background section supports students from different cultural backgrounds.
- Prereading support includes preteaching the vocabulary and using visual and other resources.
- The Interactive Question-Response Routine is chunked by section and focuses on the meaning of the text.
- The Respond to Reading questions focus on the text features, text structure, author's purpose, and/or comprehension skills and fluency.
- Students continue to build knowledge for the Text Set by talking and writing about content.
- After reading the ELL version, some students may be ready to level-up to the On-Level Genre Passage.

LEARNING GOALS

We can apply strategies and skills to read an expository text.

OBJECTIVES

Refer to details and examples in a text when explaining what the text says explicitly and when drawing inferences from the text.

Review the key ideas expressed and explain their own ideas and understanding in light of the discussion.

Use context as a clue to the meaning of a word or phrase.

LANGUAGE OBJECTIVES

Students will inquire about the topic by comparing and contrasting using key vocabulary.

ELA ACADEMIC LANGUAGE

- *compare, contrast*
- Cognates: *comparar, contrastar*

MATERIALS

Online ELL Genre Passage, "Rising Waters"

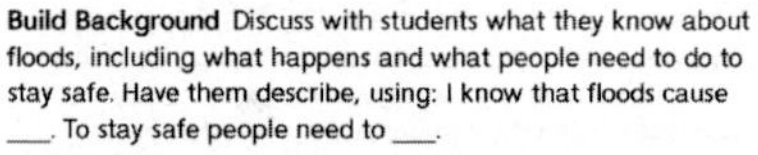

"Rising Waters"

Prepare to Read

Build Background Discuss with students what they know about floods, including what happens and what people need to do to stay safe. Have them describe, using: I know that floods cause ___. To stay safe people need to ___.

Genre Passage
Lexile 630L

Read the title and explain that "rising waters" refers to the level of water in the river and floods often happen when water flows over onto land.

Vocabulary Use the Define/Example/Ask routine to preteach difficult words or unfamiliar concepts, such as *rise/rising/rose, flood, flash flood, sewer, levees, sponge*. Invite students to add new vocabulary to their glossaries.

Set Purpose *Today we will read "Rising Waters" and focus on comparing and contrasting. As we read, think about how people respond to natural disasters.*

Read the Text

Page E1, Introduction and "Why Do Floods Happen?"

COLLABORATE **Beginning** Read the first two paragraphs. Restate the sentences as needed. *What happens to land during a flood?* (water covers land) *Are all floods the same?* (no) *Which words tell you?* Help students find the text "Not all floods are alike." *How are they different?* Some floods happen fast. Some floods happen slowly. Help partners describe elements, such as water or wind, that move fast and slowly: Water can flow fast. Water can flow slowly.

COLLABORATE **Intermediate** *How do floods happen in rivers?* (river has too much water and water flows over to land) *What type of weather causes floods?* (storms, warm weather, hurricanes, earthquakes) Have partners discuss how floods happen in warm weather, using: First, the snow melts. Next, the water flows into the river. Then, the water rises and flows on land.

Advanced/Advanced High *How can hurricanes cause floods?* (Strong winds can blow water over land.) *How can earthquakes cause floods?* (The earth shakes during an earthquake and creates big waves that cover land with water.)

Page E2, "What Happens Next?"

Beginning Read the heading and explain that it refers to what happens after a flood. Read the paragraph with students. Restate as needed. *What do floods do to plants?* Floods can kill plants. *What can happen next?* People will have less food. *What do floods do?* Floods can damage buildings and bridges.

Intermediate Read the heading with students. *What does the heading refer to?* (what happens after a flood) *How do floods make it difficult for rescue workers?* Rescue workers need bridges and roads to get to people. *What does it mean that people may be trapped by the water?* (They can't travel.)

COLLABORATE **Advanced/Advanced High** Have partners describe the effects of floods: At farms, plants can die and there will be less food to eat. If bridges and roads get damaged, then rescue workers can't travel. Then people who need help get trapped.

COLLABORATE **Multiple-Meaning Words** Have partners discuss the meanings of the multiple-meaning word *hard* and determine the meaning in sentences 6 and 7 using context clues. (difficult; do a lot of work)

Page E2, "How Do People Avoid Floods?"

COLLABORATE **Beginning** Read the heading and explain that the word *avoid* means "to keep something away or stay away from something." Read the first paragraph with them. Restate as needed. Then help partners describe what a levee is: A levee is a wall. A levee keeps away water from the land.

Intermediate Have students find clues for levee. (walls) *What is a levee?* A levee is a wall made of soil. *How does a levee protect the land?* It blocks water. *What does the author compare a wetland to? Why?* A wetland is compared to a sponge because both soak up water. Which word tells you about a comparison? (like)

Advanced/Advanced High *How do levees prevent flooding?* (Levees are walls that are made up of soil. The soil blocks and absorbs water.) *How do wetlands prevent flooding?* (Wetlands absorb water from floods.) *Why is it important to know about floods?* (to keep people safe)

COLLABORATE **Text Structure: Compare and Contrast** Have partners compare and contrast levees and wetlands: Levees and wetlands are similar because they both stop flooding. A levee is different from wetlands because levees are walls and wetlands are wet places.

Respond to Reading

Use the following instruction to help students answer the questions on page E3.

1. **Headings** *Read each heading. What is the topic of the heading?* (floods)
2. **Diagram** *What does the levee do?* (blocks or absorbs water) *Where is the levee?* (between water and land)
3. *What are effects of floods?* (Floods can kill plants that people need for food and damage buildings and roads. Floods can also make water unsafe to drink.)

Fluency Have partners take turns reading the passage.

Build Knowledge: Make Connections

Talk About the Text Have partners discuss how people respond to natural disasters.

Write About the Text Have students add their ideas to their Build Knowledge pages of their reader's notebooks.

FORMATIVE ASSESSMENT

STUDENT CHECK-IN

Have partners share their responses on page E3 and reflect using the Check-In routine.

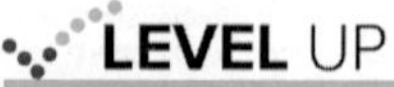

IF students read the ELL Level of the **Genre Passage** fluently and answered the questions,

THEN pair them with students who have proficiently read the On Level. Have them:

- partner read the On Level passage.
- summarize how floods happen and how to prepare for them.

Using Leveled Readers

The **Leveled Readers** for English Language Learners are scaffolded versions of the On Level Readers. They include features such as the *Language Detective, In Other Words,* and *Stop and Check* to support and enhance comprehension.

- The Build Background section supports students from different cultural backgrounds.
- Prereading support includes preteaching the vocabulary and using visuals and other resources.
- Use the Interactive Question-Response Routine to focus on meaning in chunks of text. Sample prompts are provided.
- The fluency skills for the Text Set are reinforced. Students can record themselves reading a passage several times and self-assess by submitting their best recording.
- Students continue to build knowledge for the Text Set by talking and writing about content.
- After working through the ELL version, some students may be ready to read the On Level text successfully.
- Students can also listen to a digital recording of the selection to develop comprehension and practice fluency and pronunciation.

AUTHOR INSIGHT

"Teachers must apply a wide range of effective scaffolding strategies to help ELLs process text at higher and higher levels of complexity and accelerate the development of their English proficiency. Leveled Readers with linguistically accommodated texts that also share the same genre, vocabulary, and topic as the main selection have the potential to offer just the right level of ELL support and challenge."

—Dr. Josefina V. Tinajero

READING • LEVELED READER • ACCESS THE TEXT

WEEKS 1-2

LEARNING GOALS

We can apply strategies and skills to read an expository text.

OBJECTIVES

Refer to details and examples in a text when explaining what the text says explicitly and when drawing inferences from the text.

Review the key ideas expressed and explain their own ideas and understanding in light of the discussion.

Read grade-level prose and poetry orally with accuracy, appropriate rate, and expression on successive readings.

LANGUAGE OBJECTIVES

Students will inquire by asking and answering questions about the topic.

ELA ACADEMIC LANGUAGE

- *diagram*
- Cognates: *diagrama*

MATERIALS

ELL Leveled Reader, *Changing Landscapes*

Online Differentiated Texts, "Alert! Floods and Landslides"

Visual Vocabulary Cards

DIGITAL TOOLS

Have students read along with the audio of the selections to develop comprehension and practice fluency and pronunciation.

Changing Landscapes

Prepare to Read

Build Background Have students share their experiences to discuss different types of landscapes that are near their community or other places they have been. Read the title aloud and discuss the image on the cover. Explain that the image is the Grand Canyon, and have students discuss what they know about it. Preview *Changing Landscapes* and "Students Save Wetlands" using the photographs in the text.

Leveled Reader
Lexile 740L

Vocabulary Use the routine on the **Visual Vocabulary Cards** to pre-teach ELL Vocabulary *damage* and *force* and glossary definitions on page 19. Have students add new vocabulary to their glossaries.

Set Purpose *Today we are going to read an expository text called* Changing Landscapes. *As we read, think about different changes to Earth's surface and how people respond to natural disasters.*

Read the Text

Pages 2–7, Introduction and Chapter 1

COLLABORATE **Beginning** Read the text and the diagram on page 4 with students. *What words tell you what sediment is made of?* (sand, small rocks) *What other words do you know for sediment?* (dirt, ground, soil).

Intermediate *Look at the Wetlands diagram on page 7. What things do you see that absorb water and nutrients?* (plants) *What happens to the soil in the wetlands?* (The roots of the plants hold down the soil in place.)

Advanced *How are sand dunes like wetlands?* (They protect against erosion.) *How do they differ?* (Dunes are on beaches. Wetlands are marshes or swamps.)

Pages 8–11, Chapter 2

COLLABORATE **Beginning** Help partners look for words in the text related to *damage.* (collapse, severe damage, dangerous, destruction, smash)

Intermediate *Is a landslide more likely to happen on a hill that has no trees or a hill with many trees?* (a hill with no trees) *Why?* A hill with no trees cannot slow down the soil or rocks that are going down. A landslide can damage buildings, roads, and bridges.

Advanced/Advanced High Have partners discuss what the waves of a hurricane can do. (break through storm barriers, carry away sand from beaches) Have students discuss how coastal wetlands help to protect against hurricanes. (Coastal wetlands can absorb water from rain and flooding. Also, a hurricane gets weaker when it hits land, so coastal wetlands can lessen damage from hurricanes.)

Pages 12–14, Chapter 3 and Conclusion

COLLABORATE **Reread** Have partners reread page 12 and discuss what people can do to fix damage caused by erosion.

Beginning Read page 12 with students. *How can we slow down erosion?* We can plant trees.

Intermediate *What happens when sand dunes and wetlands are lost?* Losing sand dunes and wetlands can cause erosion or landslides.

Advanced/Advanced High Have students compare the hills on page 12, discussing how stable land can prevent landslides.

COLLABORATE **Respond to Reading** Have partners discuss the questions on page 15 and answer them, using the new vocabulary.

Fluency: Intonation, Expression, Rate

Model Read page 9 with appropriate intonation, expression, and rate. Then read it aloud with students. For more practice, have students record their voices while they read a few times. Have them play their recordings and choose the best one.

Paired Read: "Students Save Wetlands"

Analytical Writing **Make Connections: Write About It**

Before students write, discuss the questions on page 18. Review the word *restoration.* Reread *the first two paragraphs on page 16. What details tell you the importance of wetlands?* Erosion is a slow change caused by wind and water. To slow down erosion, we must protect sand dunes and replant wetlands. Sand dunes trap sand brought by waves and wind. Wetlands help prevent flooding.

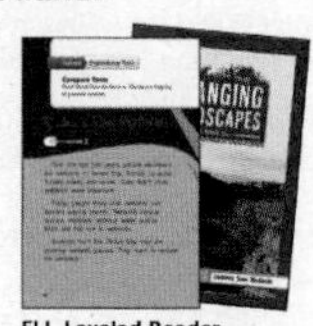

ELL Leveled Reader

Build Knowledge: Make Connections

Talk About the Text Have partners discuss different changes to Earth's surface and how people respond to natural disasters.

Write About the Text Have students add their ideas to their Build Knowledge pages of their reader's notebooks.

Self-Selected Reading

Have students choose another expository text from the online **Leveled Reader Library** or read the **Differentiated Text,** "Alert! Floods and Landslides."

FOCUS ON SCIENCE

Have students complete the activity on page 20 to research how to prepare for a natural disaster.

LITERATURE CIRCLES

Ask students to conduct a literature circle using the Thinkmark questions to guide the discussion.

FORMATIVE ASSESSMENT

STUDENT CHECK-IN

Have partners share their answers to Respond to Reading. Ask students to reflect on their learning using the Check-In routine.

LEVEL UP

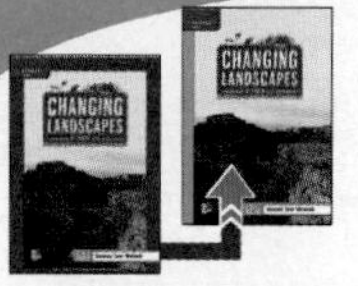

IF students read the **ELL Level** fluently and answered the questions,

THEN pair them with students who have proficiently read the On Level and have students

- read the On Level main selection aloud with their partner.
- list words they find difficult.
- discuss these words with their partners.

Access Complex Text

The On Level challenges students by including more **domain-specific words** and **complex sentence structures.**

12 UNIT 1 TEXT SET 1

ENGLISH LANGUAGE LEARNERS 13

Scaffolding Extended Writing: Write to Sources

Extended Writing Resources BLMs

Use these reproducible resources to provide additional support for reading and analyzing a student model essay.

- **Student Model** This blackline master provides comprehension support to help students read and understand a model text.
- **Analyze the Student Model** Students use this blackline master to take notes and analyze how the student model is written and organized.

Wonders provides differentiated instruction for the Write to Sources lessons in the Writing.

- Small group instruction follows the path of the whole group lessons. English Language Learners can complete the same rigorous writing projects as the rest of the class.
- Instruction focuses on scaffolding instruction for the most challenging steps in each project.
- A mixture of independent, group, and partner work provides opportunities for collaboration, oral communication, and critical thinking.
- Students set learning goals at the beginning of each lesson, and they reflect using the Check-In routine at the end.

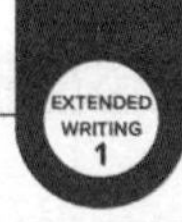

WRITING

WEEKS 1–4

LEARNING GOALS

- **We can identify a claim and relevant evidence.**
- **We can analyze a student model and student model sources.**

OBJECTIVES

Explain how an author uses reasons and evidence to support particular points of view.

Integrate information from two texts on the same topic in order to write or speak about the subject knowledgeably.

Draw evidence from literary or informational texts to support analysis, reflection, and research.

LANGUAGE OBJECTIVES

Students will discuss features of an argumentative writing using academic language.

ELA ACADEMIC LANGUAGE

- *paragraph, claim, source, relevant, evidence*
- Cognates: *párrafo, relevante, evidencia*

MATERIALS

Online ELL Extended Writing Resources BLMs:

- Maria's Model, pp. 1-3
- Analyze Maria's Model, pp. 4-5

Online Student Model Sources

Reading/Writing Companion, pp. 87-89

DIGITAL TOOLS

Have students read along with Maria's Model to develop comprehension and build fluency.

Argumentative Writing

Make a Claim

Reread the paragraph on page 87 of **Reading/Writing Companion** with the students. Review with them that a claim clearly states the writer's opinion, or what the writer thinks or believes, about the topic and that the other sentences give details to support the claim. Have students describe using: The claim tells that everyone should evacuate during a natural disaster. The sentences explain what happens if people don't evacuate.

Compare Claims Write on the board: **Strong:** *If there is a natural disaster, such as a wildfire or hurricane, everyone should evacuate.* **Weak:** *People should evacuate.* Have students compare to elicit that the strong model gives specific information about when people need to evacuate.

COLLABORATE Have partners describe what a claim tells about and compare the two claims.

Beginning Help partners describe using: The claim tells about what the writer thinks or feels about the topic. The weak model does not tell when people need to evacuate.

Intermediate Have partners describe: The claim tells about what the writer thinks or feels about a topic. The strong model is better because it tells when people should evacuate. The strong model gives specific information.

Advanced/Advanced High Have partners describe what a claim tells about and explain why the strong model is better than the weak model.

Analyze the Student Model and Sources

Analyze the Prompt Read the prompt on **Maria's Model** with students. Explain that the writer tells about his or her opinion in an argumentative essay.

Discuss the Student Model

COLLABORATE **Mixed Levels** Use Maria's Model to read with students. Before reading, discuss *hurricane* and *evacuate* with students using the Glossary. After each paragraph, have mixed pairs of language proficiency levels ask and answer the questions with each other and share responses with the group.

Paragraph 1 *Where have hurricanes in the United States hit?* (all states on the Gulf and Atlantic coasts) *What is a category 5 hurricane?* (a storm with winds over 157 mph and strong storm surges) *When do people get an evacuation order?* (when there is a category 4 or 5 hurricane)

Paragraph 2 *What can happen after a storm?* (People can be left without power and drinking water, or houses can get flooded.) *What are some reasons people stay through a storm?* (They may don't have someone to help them leave or they don't want to leave their pets.) *How does Maria use the reasons?* (as evidence)

Paragraph 3 *What happened during Hurricane Rita?* (2.5 million people tried to evacuate and there was a 100-mile traffic jam. Some people ran out of gas or left their cars.) *How many people did the Department of Emergency Management try to evacuate for Hurricane Irma?* (6.3 million) *Why was this a problem?* (not enough police officers, dangerous roads)

Paragraph 4 *What happened to the writer's grandmother during Hurricane Harvey?* (She evacuated, and her house was destroyed.) *What is an evacuation plan?* (a plan to evacuate safely during an emergency) *Why are evacuation plans necessary?* (so people can get out safely, so they are prepared for an emergency) *Which sentence retells the claim?* (first sentence) *What does it tell?* (Maria doesn't think you can force people to evacuate.)

Analyze the Student Model: Organization

Analyze Organization Use **Analyze Maria's Model** to analyze the organization as you fill in the information with students.

- Point to the first column and discuss how the essay is organized. Elicit that the claim is in the first paragraph. Explain that a claim is one sentence that clearly answers the prompt and relevant evidence supports the claim. Point out that the conclusion retells the writer's claim, or opinion.
- Review that the claim tells the focus and purpose and the relevant evidence provides support to the writer's claims.
- Discuss with them the relevant evidence in the second paragraph. *What did Maria use for relevant evidence?* (The elderly and disabled may have no one to help them leave.) *What does the relevant evidence tell us about the claim?* (tells us reasons why people won't evacuate)

Mixed Levels Have partners complete columns 1 and 2 in Analyze Maria's Model.

Beginning Help partners identify the claim and relevant evidence using: The claim tells what the writer thinks about the topic. It is in the first paragraph. The relevant evidence gives information about the claim. Relevant evidence is in all the paragraphs.

Intermediate Have partners describe the claim and relevant evidence using: The relevant evidence tells about why it's hard to get people to evacuate. It explains the claim.

Advanced/Advanced High Have partners describe the claim and the relevant evidence.

Analyze the Student Model: Sources

Read the **Online Student Model Sources** with students. Have them underline the information Maria used.

COLLABORATE Have partners complete the third column in Analyze Maria's Model. Discuss the following questions with students:

Paragraph 1 Point to paragraph 3 in Source 1 and paragraph 1 in Source 3. *What information did Maria use?* (that not everyone obeys evacuation orders and some evacuations put people in danger) Discuss with students that Maria used the information from Source 2 to explain the reasons for an evacuation order.

Paragraph 2 Discuss the information from Source 2. *What information did Maria use?* (different reasons why people stay during an evacuation) *How does she use this information?* (as support for her claim)

Paragraph 3 Discuss the information from Source 3. *What information did Maria use?* (information about the evacuation in Texas during Hurricane Rita) Elicit that Maria uses this relevant evidence to help her readers understand her claim better.

Paragraph 4 Discuss that Maria used Source 1 to remind them of her claim and identify it with them.

FORMATIVE ASSESSMENT

STUDENT CHECK-IN

Have partners share responses to Analyze Maria's Model. Ask students to reflect using the Check-in routine.

38 UNIT 1 WRITING PROJECT 1

ENGLISH LANGUAGE LEARNERS 39

Scaffolding Extended Writing: Write to Sources

During Write to Sources Part 1, students will:

- Practice and apply a rubric minilesson.
- Read a Student Model.
- Analyze the organization of the Student Model.
- Read and discuss the sources that were used in the Student Model.

During Write to Sources Part 2, students will:

- Explain the writing prompt in their own words.
- Read multiple sources that they will use in their writing.
- Take notes on the sources as they read to keep track of central ideas, claims, supporting details, and relevant evidence.
- Use the same graphic organizer as the rest of the class to plan their writing. Use the My Writing Outline BLM for additional scaffolding for planning and organization.
- Write a draft. Teacher Conferences provide individualized support for drafting and revising.
- Use a Revising Checklist with scaffolding to finalize their writing.

Extended Writing Resources BLMs

Use these reproducible resources to provide additional support for comprehension of the sources, organization, and drafting.

- **Take Notes** This blackline master provides an outline to facilitate note-taking as students read sources they will use in their writing.
- **Glossary** A glossary provides contextualized definitions to help students read sources they will use in their writing.
- **My Writing Outline** This blackline master provides organizational support to help students plan their writing.
- **Draft: Skill** This blackline master provides sentence-level language development support for the same drafting skill taught during the whole group instruction.

WRITING

WEEKS 1–4

LEARNING GOALS

- **We can synthesize information from three sources to plan and organize an argumentative essay.**
- **We can draft and revise an argumentative essay.**

OBJECTIVES

Determine the central, or main, idea of a text and explain how it is supported by relevant, or key, details.

Introduce a topic or text clearly, state an opinion, and create an organizational structure in which related ideas are grouped to support the writer's purpose.

With guidance and support from peers and adults, develop and strengthen writing as needed by planning, revising, and editing.

LANGUAGE OBJECTIVES

Students will argue a claim by describing facts.

ELA ACADEMIC LANGUAGE

- *prompt, claim, evidence*
- Cognate: *evidencia*

MATERIALS

Reading/Writing Companion, pp. 90-97

Online ELL Extended Writing Resources BLMs:

- Glossary, p. 6
- My Writing Outline, pp. 7-8
- Draft: Relevant Evidence, p. 9

Online Language Development Practice, pp. 31-36

Online Language Development Cards, 6A-6B

DIGITAL TOOLS

Have students read along with the student sources to develop comprehension and build fluency and pronunciation.

Argumentative Writing

Analyze the Sources

Review the Writing Prompt Display the prompt: *Write an argumentative essay to present to your class about whether people should build in flood zones.* Use the underlined words to discuss with students the information they will look for as they read.

Read the Sources/Take Notes Distribute the **Glossary** and read the sources on pages 91-93 in the **Reading/Writing Companion** with students. Help them identify and underline the relevant information in the text as they read.

Beginning Discuss the meaning of the words in the Glossary. Use visuals to discuss key concepts. Paraphrase challenging sentences for students. After each paragraph, help them describe: I learned about ___.

Intermediate Discuss the key concepts using the Glossary and visuals with students. Paraphrase challenging sentences with them. After each paragraph, help them retell the information.

Advanced/Advanced High Discuss the key concepts using the Glossary and visuals with students. Help them paraphrase challenging sentences. Have them retell the information after every two paragraphs.

COLLABORATE **Mixed Levels** Have pairs read **Sources 1-3** and take notes. Use the questions to discuss each source with the group.

SOURCE 1 **"How to Build in Flood Zones"** *What is the claim?* (We can't stop people from building in flood zones.) *What problem can using fill dirt cause?* (greater flooding in nearby areas and costly damage) *What is more expensive than raising a building?* (rebuilding after a flood) *Why does the author say that houses need to be built up high?* (to protect them from flooding)

SOURCE 2 **"More Wetlands Needed"** *What is the claim?* (People should not build houses in flood zones.) *What is a storm surge?* (when ocean water rises very high and winds push the water onto land) *How do natural floodplains help during a flood?* (They create a barrier from the storm.)

SOURCE 3 **"Debate on Flood Zones"** *What do developers think about building in Louisiana flood zones?* (People need more buildings for the growing population.) *What do environmentalists think about building in Louisiana flood zones?* (We need to preserve and protect wetlands.) *What does the author think?* (Developers and environmentalists need to work together.) Point out that the claim appears at the end of the essay.

Plan/Organize Ideas

Synthesize Information Guide students on how to complete the graphic organizer on pages 94-95 of the Reading/Writing Companion. Model how students can transfer their information from their graphic organizer to **My Writing Outline**. Help students figure out their claims.

Beginning Help pairs write the claim and reasons using: People should/should not build in flood zones. People need more houses for the growing population/wetlands to protect against floods.

Intermediate Have partners describe the claim and reasons: Building in flood zones is a good/bad idea because the population is growing/people need wetlands to protect against floods.

Advanced/Advanced-High Have partners describe their claims, reasons, and relevant evidence.

Draft

Review the Writing Plan. Have partners review the writing plan on their My Writing Outline.

- **Organization/My Draft** Check that the claim answers the writing prompt and appears in the first paragraph and the reasons and evidence appear in the next paragraphs. Help them paraphrase the claim for the conclusion.
- **Evidence and Sources** Check that the claim has supporting evidence and that the evidence comes from the three sources.
- **Relevant Evidence** Encourage students to choose their evidence carefully. Help them identify facts and details that support and do not support their claims.

Have students use My Writing Outline as they write their draft.

Beginning Help partners write complete sentences for their claims and reasons. Help them review that the claim answers the prompt.

Intermediate Have partners write the claim and check that it answers the prompt. Have them write the reasons and check that they support the claim. Help them check that they use relevant evidence from the sources.

Advanced/Advanced High Have partners review that their claim answers the prompt and that the reasons support the claim. Have them check for relevant evidence from the sources.

TEACHER CONFERENCES

To help students write their draft meet with each student to provide support and guidance. Discuss with students the relevant evidence in their writing and how it supports their claim.

Revise

Revising Checklist Review the Revising Checklist on page 97 of the Reading/Writing Companion.

COLLABORATE **Partner feedback** Have partners use the checklist to give feedback on each other's work. Help all students provide feedback. For example:

Beginning Help them identify sentences that describe facts and claims. Then help students use signal words in their sentences.

Intermediate Have them identify sentences that describe facts and claims. Remind them to correct for conventions.

Advanced/Advanced High Have pairs identify signal words they can use to write about facts and claims. Have them check that they only chose relevant evidence and remind them to correct for conventions.

Before they revise, have partners discuss the revisions with each other.

For additional practice see Language Development Cards, Lessons 6A-6B, and Language Development Practice, pages 31-36.

TEACHER CONFERENCES

To help students revise, meet with each student and discuss the details of the revisions students will make.

FORMATIVE ASSESSMENT

STUDENT CHECK-IN

Plan Have partners share their My Writing Outline.

Draft Have partners share an example of relevant evidence.

Revise Have partners point out two revisions in their essays.

Ask students to reflect using the Check-in routine.

40 UNIT 1 WRITING PROJECT 1

ENGLISH LANGUAGE LEARNERS 41

Scaffolding Extended Writing: Writing Process

ELL Extended Writing Resources BLMs

Use these reproducible resources to provide additional support for organization and drafting.

- **My Writing Outline** This blackline master provides an organizational structure for student writing.
- **Draft** This blackline master provides sentence-level language development support for the same draft skill taught during the whole group instruction.

Wonders provides differentiated instruction for the Writing Process lessons in the Writing.

- Small group instruction follows the path of the whole group lessons. English Language Learners can complete the same engaging writing projects as the rest of the class.
- Instruction focuses on scaffolding the most challenging steps in the writing process.
- A mixture of independent, group, and partner work provides opportunities for collaboration, oral communication, and critical thinking.

EXTENDED WRITING 1 — WRITING — WEEKS 1–4

LEARNING GOALS

- We can identify features of a personal narrative.
- We can plan a personal narrative.
- We can draft a personal narrative.

OBJECTIVES

Orient the reader by establishing a situation and introducing a narrator and/or characters; organize an event sequence that unfolds naturally.

Use a variety of transitional words and phrases to manage the sequence of events.

Use concrete words and phrases and sensory details to convey experiences and events precisely.

LANGUAGE OBJECTIVES

Students will narrate by writing a personal narrative using sequence words.

ELA ACADEMIC LANGUAGE

- *point of view, sequence, transitional, sensory*
- Cognates: *sequencia, sensorio/sensorial*

MATERIALS

Online ELL Extended Writing Resources BLMs, pp. 76–77
- My Writing Outline
- Draft: Sensory Details

Online Graphic Organizer 17

Online Language Development Cards, 13B, 83A–83B

Online Language Development Practice, pp. 76–78, 493–498

Reading/Writing Companion, pp. 86–89

Literature Anthology, p. 22

Personal Narrative

Expert Model

Features of a Personal Narrative

Review the features of a Personal Narrative. Read the story "Weathering the Storm" on page 22 of the **Literature Anthology** with students. Use it to discuss the features and identify examples together.

- *What is a personal narrative?* (a true story about the writer's life) *What does the author tell about?* (a Girl Scout camping trip during a storm)
- *A personal narrative tells the story from the author's point of view, so the writer uses first-person pronouns. What are words that show the author's point of view?* (*I, me, my, mine*)
- *The writer describes the events in a narrative in a logical order from an introduction to a conclusion. What words does the author use to tell the sequence of events?* (*same weekend, on Friday afternoon, after, that night*)
- *A personal narrative uses sensory, concrete, and figurative language to share the writer's experience. What are examples the author uses?* (She uses a metaphor; she describes "our island" because it is so flooded.)

COLLABORATE Have partners describe features of a personal narrative and tell examples to each other.

Beginning Help partners describe using: A personal narrative is a story. It tells about true events from the author's point of view. The author tells about when she was in a flood.

Intermediate Have partners describe features. For example: Writers use words to show their point of view like *me and my*. The writer also uses sequence words like *then* and *next*. The author tells about her experiences in a flood.

Advanced/Advanced High Have students describe features of a personal narrative using examples from the story on page 22.

COLLABORATE Help students learn first-person pronouns. Have partners list the first-person pronouns at the beginning of "Weathering the Storm." (me, we, us) *What do these words tell us?* They show the author's point of view. *You will use first-person pronouns in your narrative, as well.*

Plan: Choose Your Topic

Writing Prompt

COLLABORATE Confirm students understand the prompt: Write a personal narrative. Write about a time you tried your hardest to do something. Ask partners to discuss: *What does "try your hardest" mean? When did you try your hardest?* Use the discussion to help students select their writing topic.

222 UNIT 5 WRITING PROJECT 1

Plan: Sequence of Events

Signal Words for Sequence

Help students plan. Review that transitional, or signal, words such as *first, earlier, then,* and *finally* tell when events happen. Have students retell events in "Weathering the Storm" in time order. Then help students order events in their narratives using: First, my sister climbed a tree. Then, I stretched. Next, I climbed the tree and slipped. Finally, I tried my hardest and climbed the tree. Give students time to write the main events of their personal narratives in the online Sequence of Events **Graphic Organizer 17**.

Mixed Levels Have mixed-proficiency pairs create a word wall of temporal words they can use.

COLLABORATE Have partners use **My Writing Outline** to plan their writing.

Draft

Sensory Details

COLLABORATE **Add Sensory Details** Display page 89 of the **Reading/Writing Companion**. Discuss how sensory words for sight, sound, touch, taste, and feeling help readers get more engaged in the story. Ask: *What sensory words does Anna use?* (see flash floods, play in puddles, a tiny taste) Have partners use sensory words to write sentences about Anna's experience and discuss the placement of the words in each sentence.

Mixed Levels Have partners use **Draft: Sensory Details** to practice adding sensory details to sentences in their narratives.

COLLABORATE **Use Similes and Metaphors** *Writers use figurative language to help readers picture moments.* Review that a simile compares two things using *like* or *as*: *The leaf felt as soft as silk.* Review that a metaphor describes something as if it were something else: *Sam has a heart of gold.*

Language Development Practice For practice using noun phrases, see Language Development Cards, lesson 13B. For practice using figurative language, see Language Development lessons 83A–83B.

Write a Draft

COLLABORATE Have students orally share their narrative with a partner. Students should refer to My Writing Outline as they share.

Beginning My personal narrative is about the time I tried to ______. In the beginning ______. Then ______. In the end ______.

Intermediate My personal narrative is about _____. In the beginning ______. I felt ______. Then _________. In the end _______. I felt _______.

Advanced/Advanced High Have partners summarize their personal narrative and discuss how they felt.

Have students work independently to write their personal narratives.

TEACHER CONFERENCES

To help students write their drafts, meet with each student to provide support and guidance.

Beginning Help students write about the events in sequence using signal words. Discuss ways they can add sensory details throughout.

Intermediate Have students describe and read the sentences they like and sentences that are challenging. Provide suggestions to help them use signal words for sequence and add sensory details.

Advanced/Advanced High Have students discuss what they like about their draft and focus on the sequence of events and sensory details in their drafts.

FORMATIVE ASSESSMENT

STUDENT CHECK-IN

Features of a Personal Narrative Have partners name three features of a personal narrative.

Plan Have partners share My Writing Outline.

Draft Have partners point out two examples of sensory details in their drafts.

Ask students to reflect using the Check-In routine.

Scaffolding Extended Writing: Writing Process

During Process Writing Part 1, students will:

- Use an expert model to review features of the genre they will be writing in.
- Discuss the writing prompt to build knowledge and vocabulary about the topic.
- Plan the organization and content of their writing using graphic organizers.
- Learn, practice, and apply a drafting skill.
- Write a draft. Teacher Conferences provide individualized support for drafting.

During Process Writing Part 2, students will:

- Learn, practice, and apply a revising skill.
- Revise their drafts. Teacher Conferences provide individualized support for revising.
- Engage in peer conferences.
- Edit and proofread.
- Use a rubric to evaluate their writing.

ELL Extended Writing Resources BLMs

Use these reproducible resources to provide additional support for revision.

- **Revise** This blackline master provides sentence-level language development support for the same revising skill taught during the whole group instruction.

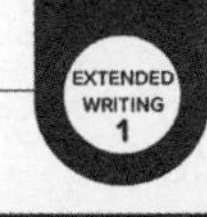

WRITING

WEEKS 1–4

LEARNING GOALS

- **We can revise a personal narrative.**
- **We can edit and proofread a personal narrative.**
- **We can publish, present, and evaluate a personal narrative.**

OBJECTIVES

Provide a conclusion that follows from the narrated experiences or events.

With guidance and support from peers and adults, develop and strengthen writing as needed by planning, revising, and editing.

Follow agreed-upon rules for discussions and carry out assigned roles.

LANGUAGE OBJECTIVES

Students will inquire about strong conclusions by revising sentences.

ELA ACADEMIC LANGUAGE

- *conclusion, purpose, peer, publish, rubric*
- Cognates: *conclusion, propósito, publicar*

MATERIALS

Literature Anthology, pp. 23

Reading/Writing Companion, pp. 90–93

Online ELL Extended Writing Resources BLMs, p. 78

- Revise: Strong Conclusions

Online Language Development Cards, 1A–3B, 62A–62B

Online Language Development Practice, 1–18, 367–372

Personal Narrative

Revise

Strong Conclusions

Remind students that good personal narratives have strong conclusions that are satisfying and support the purpose of the narrative. Discuss with students some strategies for writing strong conclusions: summing up the purpose for writing and ending with a memory or thought. Have students use these strategies as they revise their personal narratives.

COLLABORATE **Sum Up the Purpose for Writing** Review with students that a conclusion supports the purpose for writing a narrative essay. *A conclusion reminds readers why the writer wrote the narrative.* Have partners read the paragraph on **Reading/Writing Companion** page 90. Discuss with students how the author summed up the experience in the conclusion by reflecting back on events. *What was the author's purpose for writing?* (to tell about the experience of practicing every day to make the basketball team) Discuss the clear purpose of the writer explaining how he/she made the basketball team.

COLLABORATE Have partners sum up for each other the purpose for writing their personal narratives.

Beginning Help students complete sentence frames to share their purpose for writing: I wrote about this because ____. I want my audience to know ____.

Intermediate Ask questions to help students explain their purpose for writing: *What did you want to tell your audience?* Help students describe using: My purpose in writing the narrative was____.

Advanced/Advanced High Have partners ask and answer questions about their personal narratives. Then have them explain their purpose for writing them.

COLLABORATE **End with a Feeling or Observation** Review that the conclusions of personal narratives often end with a feeling or observation about the experience. Have students reread "Weathering the Storm" in **Literature Anthology** page 23. *Discuss the last line with a partner.* (Next time I go camping, though, I am going to cancel at the slightest hint of rain!) *How does the writer end this personal narrative?* (She says she hopes to go camping again, but not in the rain.) *How is this conclusion strong?* (The writer sums up the events and shares that she feels both positive and negative about her experience.) Point out the use of connecting words "Even though" in the first sentence of the conclusion. Discuss how these words help bring various experiences and feelings of the writer together as she sums them up in the conclusion.

Mixed Levels Have partners complete **Revise: Strong Conclusions** for support in improving strong conclusions.

Language Development Practice For additional practice with coordinating conjunctions, see Language Development lessons 62A and 62B.

224 UNIT 5 WRITING PROJECT 1

Revise

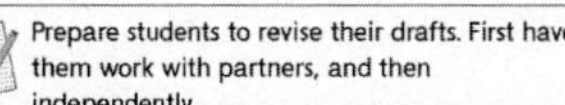

Prepare students to revise their drafts. First have them work with partners, and then independently.

Discuss features of the genre, such as using first-person pronouns and sharing their feelings about an event.

Remind students that as they revise, they should make sure the events in their narratives are in order.

Review using sensory details and figurative language in their writing.

COLLABORATE Review with students the strategies they learned to revise for a strong conclusion. Help them apply these strategies to their own writing. Have partners describe their revisions to each other.

Beginning Have partners describe their revisions. For example: I will change this sentence into a question. I will add an exclamation to show how I felt.

Intermediate Have partners describe their revisions. For example: I will change this sentence to a question. I will add an exclamation to show how I felt.

Advanced/Advanced High Invite partners to describe their revisions to each other.

Peer Conferencing

Partner Feedback

Review the Revising Checklist on page 91 of the **Reading/Writing Companion** with students. Have partners use the checklist to give feedback on each other's work. Help all students provide feedback. For example:

Beginning There is/is not a logical sequence of events in your narrative. I can/cannot tell there is a beginning, middle, and end. I like how you used the word ____ to describe ____.

Intermediate When I read your narrative, there is a logical sequence of events. I like this part because ____. You can add another detail to describe ____.

Advanced/ Advanced High After using the Revising Checklist with their partners, have students reflect on which suggestions were most helpful.

TEACHER CONFERENCES

To help students revise, meet with each student to provide support and guidance.

Beginning Help students describe the events in sequence and their revision to the conclusion.

Intermediate Have students describe and read the sentences they like and sentences that are challenging. Provide suggestions to help them.

Advanced/Advanced High Discuss with students what they like about their draft and what they want to improve. Help them find suggestions.

Edit and Proofread

Using the Editing Checklist

Discuss the items in the Editing Checklist on Reading/ Writing Companion page 92 to make sure students understand what each one means.

COLLABORATE Have partners edit and proofread each other's drafts using the Editing Checklist.

If students need more support with editing and proofreading, use **Language Development** lessons: Sentences and Fragments (1A and 1B), Punctuation (2A and 2B), Subjects and Predicates (3A and 3B). You may also wish to revisit the Language Development lessons from Draft and Revise.

Publish, Present, Evaluate

Evaluate

Have students use the rubric on Reading/Writing Companion page 93 to evaluate their own writing. Explain the language in the rubric to make sure students understand what the terms describe. Have them apply the rubric to their own writing, and then describe their thinking to a partner.

FORMATIVE ASSESSMENT

STUDENT CHECK-IN

Revise Ask partners to share ways they improved their conclusion.

Edit and Proofread Ask students to share the partner feedback they gave.

Publish, Present, Evaluate Ask partners to share the scores they gave themselves using their rubrics.

Have students reflect using the Check-In routine.

ENGLISH LANGUAGE LEARNERS 225

Instructional Routines

The instructional routines provide carefully sequenced steps to scaffold instruction and allow students to focus on learning content. Once students are familiar with a routine, the teacher can use the routine to teach new skills and content efficiently.

Interactive Question-Response

This routine was designed to provide context and opportunities for English Language Learners to learn how information builds and connects and focus on key concepts and vocabulary. The Access the Text lessons for the Shared Read, Anchor Text, Genre Passage, and Leveled Reader incorporate this routine in the instruction.

Read the Text in Chunks Read one section of text at a time so students can focus on the meaning of the text. For each text chunk:

- **Use Visuals and Text Features** Use headings to help students predict what the section will be about. Use images and other text features to aid students' comprehension.
- **Explain** As you read, explain difficult or unfamiliar concepts and words. Provide background and contextual knowledge, as needed.
- **Ask Guiding and Supplementary Questions** Help students identify the most important information or details in the text chunk, and understand how information builds and connects.
- **Scaffold Responses** Provide sentence starters/frames to help students express and communicate their ideas.
- **Reinforce Vocabulary** Reinforce the meaning and point out cognates and false cognates. Ask questions that require students to use the newly acquired vocabulary.
- **Retell** Have students retell the most important ideas in their own words.
- **Reinforce Skills and Strategies** Model using skills and strategies. Ask questions to help students apply.

Vocabulary

Use the Define/Example/Ask routine to help students learn unfamiliar, conceptually complex words they encounter in the texts. The Visual Vocabulary Cards provide this routine on the back of each card. Here is an example for the word *recent*.

1. **Define**: *Recent* means something happened a short time ago. En español, *recent* quiere decir "reciente, ocurrido hace poco." *Recent* in English and *reciente* in Spanish are cognates. They sound and mean the same thing in both languages.
2. **Example**: Mary learns about recent events from the newspaper. En español: Mary se entera de los eventos recientes por el periódico.
3. **Ask**: What word is the opposite of *recent*?
4. Now let's look at a picture that shows the word *recent*. Point to the girl. This girl likes to read the newspaper. It tells her about recent events, or events that happened a short time ago.

Partner Talk activities provide strategies to get students talking and using the new language.

This routine is available for the ELL Visual Vocabulary Cards through the online Glossary.

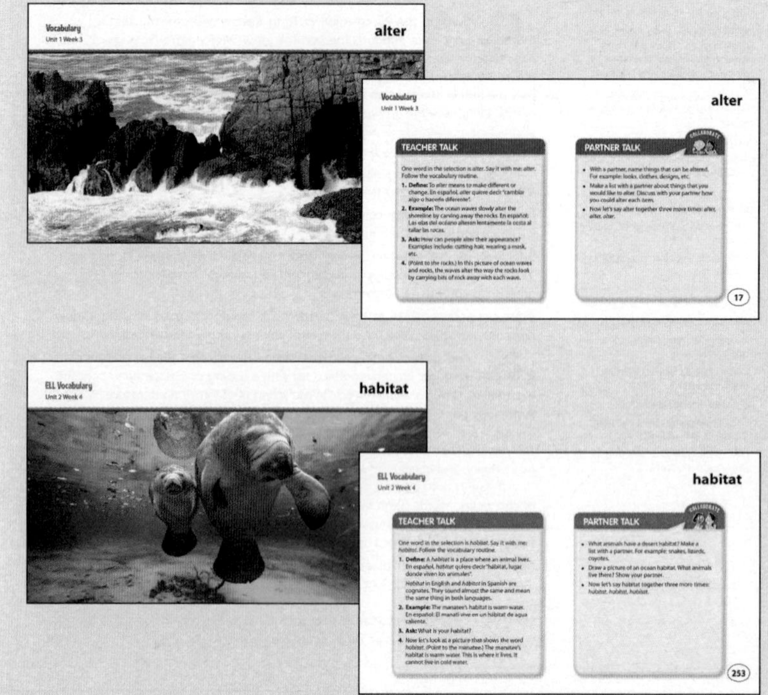

Vocabulary: Cognates

Help students transfer knowledge from their native language. Explain that cognates are words in two different languages that look similar, sound similar, and mean approximately the same thing.

Remind students to watch out for false cognates, which are words in two or more different languages that are the same or similar in sound and/or spelling, but that have different meanings; for example, *exit* (meaning in English: way out)/ *éxito* (meaning in Spanish: success).

Here is an example for the cognates *liberty/ libertad*.

1. Display cognate word pairs and images *(liberty/ libertad)*.
2. Ask a native Spanish speaker to say *liberty* and compare the sounds and appearance in *libertad*.
3. Have partners look up the words in a dictionary or try using the Spanish word in the English example sentence to see whether it makes sense. Record the meaning of the cognate word pairs.
4. Have students keep a glossary where they list the cognates they learn.

	English	Spanish	Sound (1-3)	Appearance (1-3)	Same meaning? (yes/no)	Are they cognates? (yes/no)
1.	body	boda	2	1	No	No
	The elephant has a very large body.					
2.	color	color	2	3	Yes	Yes
	My favorite color is green.					
3.	appeared	parecía				
	Laura appeared tired and ready to go to sleep.					
4.	ill	enfermo				
	Lucia is ill with a fever and a cough.					
5.	expression	expresión				
	He had a happy expression on his face.					

Vocabulary: Morphology

Use this routine to help students build vocabulary and understand how words are related. See the example below for the word *admire*.

1. Use the Define/Example/Ask routine to teach or review the word *admire*.
2. Draw a chart like the one below on the board. Discuss how the word changes when you add different endings. Invite students to complete the sentences in the last column.

Words	Spelling Changes	Part of Speech	Sentence
admire		verb	I admire my teacher.
admires	+s	verb	My sister admires her coach.
admired	+d	verb	Last night I admired the stars in the sky.
admiring	-e, +ing	verb	They are admiring the pretty flowers.
admiration	-e, +ation	noun	He showed his admiration of the musicians. He clapped loudly after the concert.

3. Have students copy the chart in their notebooks or glossaries for reference.
4. Students can work independently to continue the chart with other target words, such as:
   - contribute/ contributes/ contributed/ contributing/ contribution
   - practice/ practices/ practiced/ practicing
   - pronounce/ pronounces/ pronounced/ pronouncing/ pronunciation
   - scare/ scares/ scared/ scaring/ scary

Instructional Routines

Functional Analysis

Use this routine to help students with comprehension of complex sentences they encounter in the texts by identifying the functions of words and phrases in a sentence.

1. Identify the actor, or who/what did the action, in the sentence. See the following example:

   Sentence: *At the end of the summer, we picked enough vegetables to have a cookout.*

2. Help students break the text into sections to identify the actor and action in the sentence. Then analyze each part to extract the meaning of the sentence and analyze how they relate to each other.

   Who or What (Actor): *we*

   What happened (Action): *picked enough vegetables*

   Detail: *to have a cookout*

   When: *at the end of the summer*

At the end of the summer	In August
we picked	we took from the garden
enough vegetables	the right amount of vegetables
to have a cookout	to cook a big meal outside

Have students write the sentence in their own words.

Teacher Response Techniques

Throughout the lessons, use these techniques to motivate student participation and build oral fluency.

- **Wait for Responses** Provide enough time for students to answer a question or process their ideas to respond. Depending on their levels of proficiency, give students the option of responding in different ways, such as answering in their native language so that you can rephrase in English or answering with nonverbal cues.
- **Revise for Form** Let students know that they can respond in different ways, depending on their levels of proficiency. Repeat students' responses to model the proper form. You can model in full sentences and use academic language.
- **Repeat** Give positive confirmation to the answers that each English Language Learner offers. If the response is correct, repeat the response in a clear voice and at a slower pace to encourage others to participate.
- **Revise for Meaning** Repeating an answer offers an opportunity to clarify the meaning of a response.
- **Elaborate** If students give a one-word answer or a nonverbal cue, elaborate on the answer to model fluent speaking and grammatical patterns. Provide more examples or repeat the answer using proper academic language.
- **Elicit** Prompt students to give a more comprehensive response by asking additional questions or guiding them to get to an answer.

Collaborative Work 

The lessons in *Wonders* provide English Language Learners with opportunities for collaborative work to engage them in their learning and interact with one another in meaningful ways. The prompt and response frames below help students at different language proficiency levels work together.

- **Elaborate and Ask Questions to Request Clarification. Prompts:** Can you tell me more about it? Can you be more specific? What do you mean by ...? How/Why is that important? **Responses:** I think it means that ... In other words ... It's important because ... It's similar to when ...
- **Support Ideas with Text Evidence. Prompts:** Can you give any examples from the text or pictures? What evidence do you see for that? Can you show me where the text says that? **Responses:** The text says that ... Some evidence that supports that is ... An example from another text is ...
- **Build on and/or Challenge a partner's Idea. Prompts:** What do you think of the idea that ...? Can you add to this idea? Do you agree? What are other ideas/ perspectives? What else should we think about? How does that connect to the idea that ...? **Responses:** I want to add that ... I want to follow up on your idea ... Another way to look at it is ... What you said makes me think of ...
- **Paraphrase. Prompts:** What do we know so far? I'm not sure that was clear. How else can you say it? How can we relate what I said to the question? **Responses:** So you're saying that ... Let me see if I understand you ... Do you mean that ...? In other words ... It sounds like you're saying that ...
- **Determine the Central Idea and Relevant Details. Prompts:** What have we discussed so far? What can we agree on? What are the main points or ideas we can share? What relevant details support that idea? What are some examples? **Responses:** We can agree that ... The central idea seems to be ... An example is ... One relevant detail is ...

Planner

Customize your own lesson plans at
my.mheducation.com

Reading
Suggested Daily Time

MATERIALS

Shared Read
- Reading/Writing Companion
- Online Scaffolded Shared Read
- Online Visual Vocabulary Cards
- Online Shared Read Writing Frames

Anchor Text
- Literature Anthology
- Online ELL Anchor Text Support BLMs
- Online Visual Vocabulary Cards
- Online Oral Language Sentence Frames

Additional Texts
- ELL Genre Passage
- Leveled Reader
- Online Leveled Reader Library
- Online ELL Differentiated Text

MATERIALS

Write to Sources
- Reading/Writing Companion
- Online Student Model Sources
- Online ELL Extended Writing Resources BLMs
- Online Language Development Kit

Writing Process
- Reading/Writing Companion
- Online ELL Extended Writing Resources BLMs
- Online Language Development Kit

Reading

Shared Read

Access the Text

Prepare to Read
- Build Background
- Preteach Vocabulary
- Set Purpose

Read the Text
- Beginning/Early Intermediate: Online Scaffolded Shared Read
- Intermediate/Advance/Advanced High: Reading/Writing Companion Shared Read

Language Development Options
- Listening Comprehension: Text Reconstruction
- Grammar in Context

Independent Time Activities
- Build Vocabulary
- Grammar Practice
- Oral and Writing Practice

Writing

Write to Sources: Units 1–4
- Read and Analyze Student Model and Sources

Write to Sources: Units 1–4
- Analyze a Prompt
- Read Sources and Take Notes

Writing Process: Units 5–6
- Analyze an Expert Model

Writing Process: Units 5–6
- Plan: Choose a Topic/Organization

Learning Goals

Specific learning goals identified in every lesson make clear what students will be learning and why. These smaller goals provide stepping stones to help students meet their Text Set and Extended Writing Goals.

Reading		
Anchor Text		**Additional Texts**
Access the Text **Prepare to Read** • Build Background • Preteach Vocabulary • Set Purpose **Read the Anchor Text** **Reread** • Analyze the text, craft, and structure	**Language Development Options** • Listening Comprehension: Text Reconstruction • Grammar in Context: Deconstruct a Sentence COLLABORATE **Independent Time Activities** • Build Vocabulary • Grammar Practice • Oral and Writing Practice	**Teacher Choice:** **Skills Practice** **ELL Genre Passage** • Comprehension • Vocabulary • Genre/Text Features • Fluency **ELL Leveled Reader** • Comprehension • Vocabulary • Fluency **Self-Selected Reading** • Classroom Library • Differentiated Texts • Online Leveled Reader Library
Writing		
Write to Sources: Units 1–4 • Plan and Organize Ideas	**Write to Sources: Units 1–4** • Draft	**Write to Sources: Units 1–4** • Revise
Writing Process: Units 5–6 • Draft	**Writing Process: Units 5–6** • Revise	**Writing Process: Units 5–6** • Publish, Present, Evaluate

Check-In Routine

The Check-In Routine at the close of each lesson guides students to self-reflect on how well they understood each learning goal.

Review the lesson learning goal.

Reflect on the activity.

Self-Assess by holding up 1, 2, 3, or 4 fingers.

Share with your teacher.

Supporting Newcomers

Components: Using the Newcomer Kit

Use the online ***Wonders* Newcomer Components** for students with little or no English proficiency. These components provide newcomers with access to basic, high-utility vocabulary they can begin using right away. The kit helps students develop language skills to transition to the Beginning level of language proficiency.

Newcomer Cards

Each card introduces a topic through colorful visuals to stimulate conversation to help students develop oral language and build vocabulary.

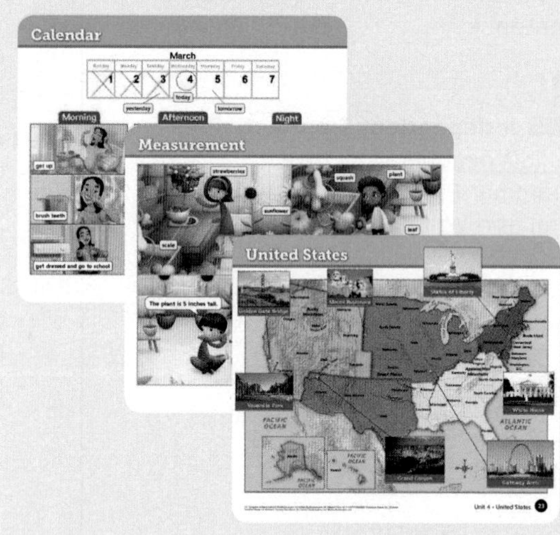

Newcomer Teacher's Guide

Provides three lessons for each Newcomer Card topic and student worksheets with reading and writing activities to help students transition into the English-speaking classroom.

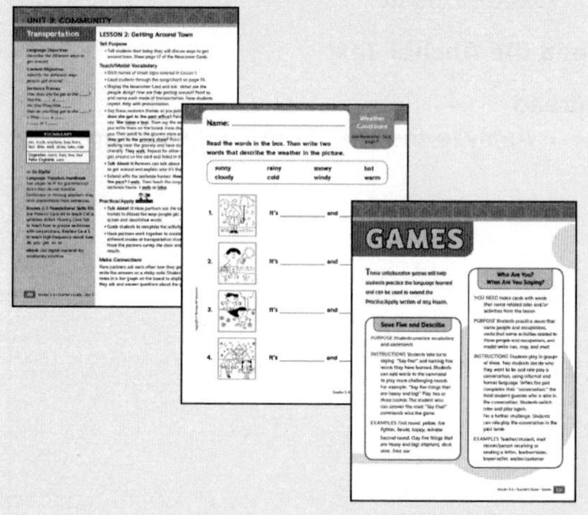

Suggested Planning: 4-Week Learning Blocks

Because newcomers can enter your classroom at any time during the year, the program is designed for flexibility with multiple entry-points for instruction:

- Use the Start Smart materials with new arrivals.
- The four units of instruction can be completed in any order, so new arrivals can join those who are already well underway.
- The Newcomer Teacher's Guide also provides songs and chants, reproducible manipulatives, conversation starters, and games.
- At the end of Start Smart and each unit, use the Progress Monitoring materials to measure students' progress.

UNIT 1: 4 WEEKS

Start Smart for new arrivals
- What's Your Name?
- Greetings
- Geometric Shapes
- Numbers

Unit 1: Life at School
- In the Classroom
- Computers
- A Day at School
- Calendar
- Weather

Materials
Newcomer Cards Start Smart, Unit 1
Newcomer Teacher's Guide
- Start Smart pp. 1–25
- Unit 1 pp. 26–57
- Optional Materials 154–T38
- Progress Monitoring T39–T45

Newcomer Visuals Start Smart, Unit 1
Newcomer Interactive Games

UNIT 2: 4 WEEKS

Start Smart for new arrivals
Unit 2: My Family and Me
- My Body
- Clothing
- Feelings
- My Family
- My Home

Materials
Newcomer Cards Start Smart, Unit 2
Newcomer Teacher's Guide
- Start Smart pp. 1–25
- Unit 2 pp. 58–89
- Optional Materials 154–T38
- Progress Monitoring T39–T45

Newcomer Visuals Start Smart, Unit 2
Newcomer Interactive Games

Newcomer Visuals

Additional opportunities for vocabulary building and oral language development for each topic through prompts and words and phrases students can use.

Newcomer Interactive Games

Online Interactive Games provide independent practice to build vocabulary.

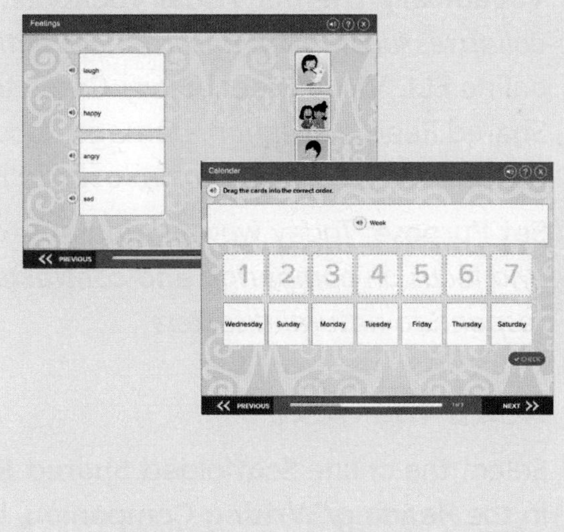

UNIT 3: 4 WEEKS

Start Smart for new arrivals
Unit 3: Community

- My Community
- Technology
- Transportation
- Food and Meals
- Shopping

Materials
Newcomer Cards Start Smart, Unit 3
Newcomer Teacher's Guide

- Start Smart pp. 1–25
- Unit 3 pp. 90–121
- Optional Materials 154–T38
- Progress Monitoring T39–T45

Newcomer Visuals Start Smart, Unit 3
Newcomer Interactive Games

UNIT 4: 4 WEEKS

Start Smart for new arrivals
Unit 4: The World

- Measurement
- Animals
- Growth and Change
- United States
- My World

Materials
Newcomer Cards Start Smart, Unit 4
Newcomer Teacher's Guide

- Start Smart pp. 1–25
- Unit 4 pp. 122–153
- Optional Materials 154–T38
- Progress Monitoring T39–T45

Newcomer Visuals Start Smart, Unit 4
Newcomer Interactive Games

LEARNING GOALS

We can read and understand an expository text.

OBJECTIVES

Describe the overall structure of events, ideas, concepts, or information in a text or part of a text.

Review the key ideas expressed and explain their own ideas and understanding in light of the discussion.

Use context as a clue to the meaning of a word or phrase.

Observe and identify slow changes to Earth's surface caused by weathering, erosion, and deposition from water, wind, and ice. **Science**

LANGUAGE OBJECTIVES

Students will inquire by comparing and contrasting using signal words.

ELA ACADEMIC LANGUAGE

- *compare, contrast, diagrams, headings, multiple*
- Cognates: *comparar, diagrama, contrastar*

MATERIALS

Reading/Writing Companion, pp. 12-15

Online Scaffolded Shared Read, "A World of Change"

Visual Vocabulary Cards

Online ELL Visual Vocabulary Cards

DIGITAL TOOLS

MULTIMODAL

Have students read along with the audio of the selection to develop comprehension and practice fluency and pronunciation.

"A World of Change"

Prepare to Read

Build Background Discuss with students changes that happen to Earth. Have students share what they know, such as volcanic eruptions or earthquakes, erosion on a beach, or landslides. Have them describe using: I know/learned about ___. Explain that changes are happening all the time to Earth's surface.

Vocabulary Use the **Visual Vocabulary Cards** to preteach the vocabulary: *alter, collapse, substantial, hazard, destruction, crisis, severe,* and *unpredictable.* Use the online **ELL Visual Vocabulary Cards** to teach additional Vocabulary from the Shared Read: *collection, damage, location, occurs, surface,* and *warn.* (Cognates: *destrucción, crisis, colección, ocurrir;* False Cognate: *alterar*)

Set Purpose *Today we will read an expository text called "A World of Change" and focus on* ***comparing and contrasting****. As we read, think about how people respond to natural disasters.*

Read the Text

Select the online **Scaffolded Shared Read** or the Shared Read in the **Reading/Writing Companion**, based on students' language proficiency.

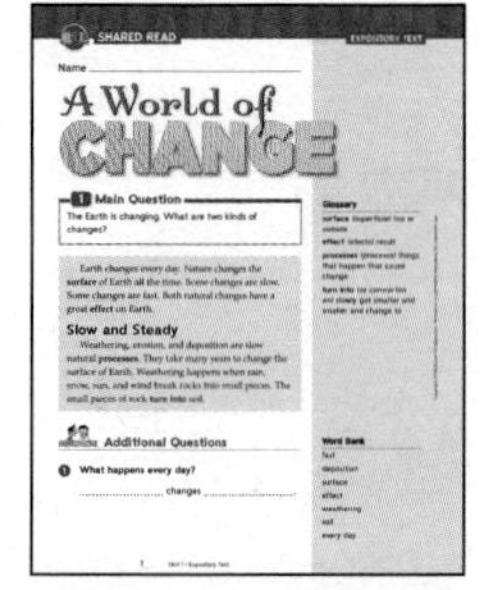

Scaffolded Shared Read, Lexile 580L

Beginning/ Early-Intermediate Use the online Scaffolded Shared Read to help partners work together to read and understand an expository text. Remind them to use the Glossary to help them read and the Word Bank to help them answer the Main and Additional Questions.

Intermediate/ Advanced Advanced High Read the text with students and use the Interactive Question-Response Routine to help them understand an expository text.

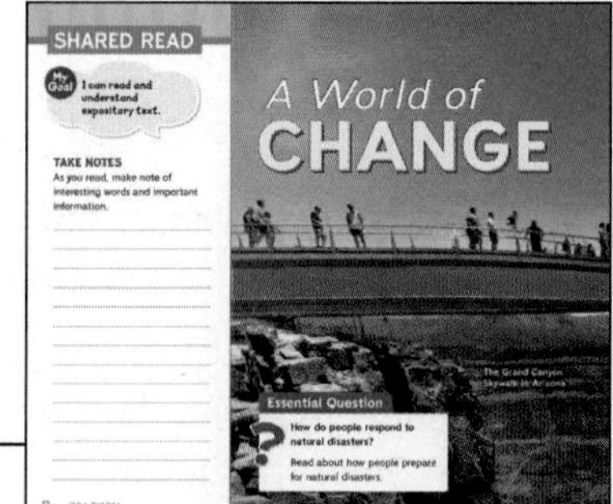

Reading/Writing Companion, Lexile 790L

Page 13

Paragraph 1 Read the text with students and review Vocabulary words *alter* and *surface. When do natural changes happen?* (every day) *What do fast and slow natural changes do?* (Both change Earth's surface.) Point to the word *whether* and explain that it tells that there are choices or possibilities. Have students read the last sentence. Ask: *What are the choices?* (Earth's changes are slow or fast.) Explain that *whether* sounds the same as *weather* but is spelled differently.

Intermediate Have partners use the words *whether* and *weather* to generate their own sentences and indicate the spelling of the word for each sentence: The weather is rainy. We will go to the movie whether it rains or snows.

COLLABORATE **Advanced/Advanced High** Point to the phrase "take place" in the third and fifth sentences and explain that this phrase has **multiple meanings**. It can mean "to happen" or "substitute for." Have students identify context clues to figure out the meaning of "take place." (happen)

Paragraphs 2–5 Read the text with students and review Vocabulary words *collapse, collection, substantial, location* and *occurs. What are the three processes that change Earth's surface slowly?* (weathering, erosion, deposition) *What happens during weathering?* (Rain, snow, sun, wind break down rocks into small pieces of rock.) *What happens during erosion?* (Rivers and natural forces carry away pieces of rock.) *What happens during deposition?* (Soil and rock from erosion get dropped at a new location.)

COLLABORATE Have partners **compare and contrast** erosion and deposition using signal words, such as *both* and *in contrast*. (Possible answer: Both erosion and deposition are processes that change Earth's surface. During erosion the small pieces of rock get carried away. In contrast, during deposition the small pieces of rock get dropped in a new location.)

Page 14

Paragraphs 1–3 Read the text with students. Review Vocabulary word *hazard. How do people prevent beach erosion?* (build structures to block waves from the shore, use heavy rocks, grow plants to hold soil)

Intermediate *Does* hazard *mean something good or bad?* (bad) *How do you know?* (text tells that some types of erosion are dangerous) *Which word has a meaning similar to* hazard*?* (dangerous)

Paragraphs 4–5 Read the text with students and review Vocabulary words *destruction* and *crisis*. Read the heading. Ask: *How is this heading different from the previous heading?* (fast is the opposite of slow, powerful means "with a lot of force") *What will the section be about?* (changes that happen quickly)

What natural processes are fast and powerful? (volcanic eruptions, landslides) *What causes a volcanic eruption?* (Pressure builds up under Earth's surface.)

Page 15

Paragraphs 1–3 Read the text with students and review Vocabulary words *severe, unpredictable, damage,* and *warn. What happens during a landslide?* (Dirt and rocks are loosened by rain and slide down the hill or mountain.) *Why is it important to have an emergency plan?* (People need to get to safe places quickly.)

Intermediate *Which words are signal words for compare and contrast?* ("Like volcanic eruptions," "In contrast") *What is the comparison in the first paragraph?* Both volcanic eruptions and landslides can happen without warning, or suddenly.

COLLABORATE **Advanced/Advanced High** Have partners contrast what people can do with slow- and fast-moving processes and why predicting natural disasters is important. (Unlike erosion, people cannot prevent landslides or volcanic eruptions. By predicting them, people will have time to move to safe places.)

COLLABORATE Reread the last section on page 15 with them and have students discuss why the author used the **heading** "Be Prepared."

COLLABORATE Review with students that a **diagram** text feature shows the parts of something or how a process works. Have partners retell what happens during a volcanic eruption using the diagram. (Possible answer: A volcano erupts when pressure builds under Earth's surface. Magma flows up the pipe and comes out through the vent of the crater.)

FORMATIVE ASSESSMENT

STUDENT CHECK-IN

Have partners retell the important ideas in the text. Ask them to reflect using the Check-in routine.

LEARNING GOALS

- **We can read and understand expository text by identifying the compare and contrast text structure.**
- **We can identify and use sentence types.**

OBJECTIVES

Paraphrase portions of a text read aloud or information presented in diverse media and formats, including visually, quantitatively, and orally.

Demonstrate command of the conventions of standard English capitalization, punctuation, and spelling when writing.

LANGUAGE OBJECTIVES

Students will explain compare and contrast text structure using key vocabulary.

ELA ACADEMIC LANGUAGE

- *capital letter, punctuation, period, statement, exclamation mark*
- Cognates: *identificar, puntuación*

MATERIALS

Reading/Writing Companion, pp. 12-15, 16-17

Online Scaffolded Shared Read, "A World of Change"

Online Shared Read Writing Frames, p. 1

Online Language Development Cards, 1A, 2A, 2B

Online Language Development Practice, pp. 1-3, 7-12

Online Language Transfers Handbook, pp. 15-19

"A World of Change"

Text Reconstruction

Focus on a single chunk of text to support comprehension and language development across the four domains.

1. Read aloud Paragraph 1 on page 15 while students listen.
2. Write the following on the board, providing definitions as needed: *occur, warning, loosened,* and *damage*. Instruct students to listen for them as you read the paragraph a second time. (Cognate: *ocurrir*)
3. Read the paragraph a third time. Tell students to listen and take notes.
4.  COLLABORATE Have students work with a partner to reconstruct the text from their notes. Help them write complete sentences as needed.
5. Have partners look at the original text. Ask them what the paragraph is mostly about. (landslides) Tell students they are going to see how the author uses a compare and contrast text structure to show how things are alike or different.
6. With students, read the first sentence and discuss the purpose. (possible answer: compares landslides to volcanic eruptions) Ask partners to explain the purpose of the rest of the paragraph. (second sentence describes what happens during a landslide: heavy rains loosen rocks and soil and cause them to slide down a hill or mountain; rest of the paragraph compares sizes of landslides and tells that large landslides can cause a lot of damage)
7. Have partners compare their text reconstructions to the original text. Have them check whether they also used signal words to describe the comparison between volcanic eruptions and landslides.

Beginning Have students follow along in the **Reading/Writing Companion** as you read the text aloud. Have them circle the words from Step 2 as they hear them.

Grammar in Context: Sentences

Notice the Form Display and read aloud the sentences from the text.

> *These processes can be gradual or swift. They help to make Earth the amazing planet that it is!*

Point to the circled letters and ask: *What do the capital letters tell you?* (beginning of a sentence) *Every sentence ends with a punctuation mark.* Point to the end punctuations and explain: *The period tells the sentence is a statement.* Point to the capital letter *E* and ask: *Is this the beginning of a sentence?* Elicit that it is not because there is no end punctuation before the word. *What does an exclamation tell?* (strong feeling) *When do we use an exclamation?* Have students describe examples, such as being surprised or excited. Discuss other types of sentences—questions and commands—and when to use them. (ask something; tell someone to do something) Have students give examples for each type of sentence and write them on the board.

Apply and Extend Delete the end punctuation from the example sentences. Have partners copy the sentences, add end punctuation, and identify the type. For additional practice, see **Language Development Cards,** Lessons 1A, 2A, and 2B, and **Language Development Practice,** pages 1-3 and 7-12.

Independent Time

Vocabulary Building Have students build glossaries.

Beginning/Early Intermediate Have students complete the Glossary Activities in the **Scaffolded Shared Read**.

Intermediate/Advanced/Advanced High Have students add the vocabulary from **Reading/Writing Companion** pages 16-17 and self-selected words or phrases they would like to learn to the chart.

Mixed Levels Pair students together: Beginning and Early-Intermediate students can teach words from Scaffolded Shared Read glossaries. Intermediate and Advanced/Advanced High students can teach self-selected words.

WORD/PHRASE	DEFINE	Use the Word/Phrase in a Sentence
Earth's crust	the outermost part of the planet	The Earth's crust splits during an earthquake.

COLLABORATE **Shared Read Writing Frames** Use the online leveled Shared Read Writing Frames for "A World of Change" to provide students with additional oral and written practice.

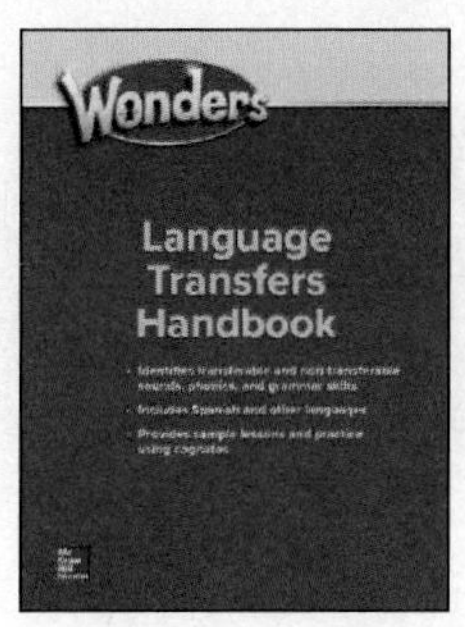

Language Transfers Handbook, Grammar Transfers, pp. 15-19

DIGITAL TOOLS

For additional support, use the online activities.

Grammar Video

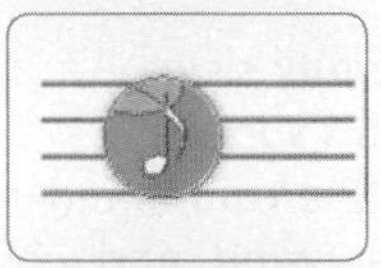

Grammar Song

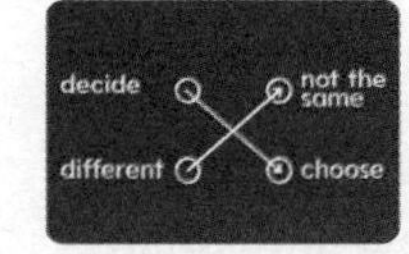

Vocabulary Activity

FORMATIVE ASSESSMENT

STUDENT CHECK-IN

Text Reconstruction Ask partners to share their notes. Have students reflect on their work using the Check-In routine.

Grammar in Context Ask partners to share the sentences they wrote. Have students reflect on their work using the Check-In routine.

LEARNING GOALS

Read We can read and understand an expository text.

Reread We can reread and analyze text, craft, and structure.

OBJECTIVES

Explain events, procedures, ideas, or concepts in a historical, scientific, or technical text, including what happened and why, based on specific information in the text.

Review the key ideas expressed and explain their own ideas and understanding in light of the discussion.

Observe and identify slow changes to Earth's surface caused by weathering, erosion, and deposition from water, wind, and ice. **Science**

LANGUAGE OBJECTIVES:

Students will inquire by answering questions about the text using content area vocabulary.

ELA ACADEMIC LANGUAGE

- *informational, article*
- Cognate: *informativo*

MATERIALS

Literature Anthology, pp. 10-19

Reading/Writing Companion, pp. 24-27

Online ELL Anchor Text Support BLMS pp. 1-3

DIGITAL TOOLS

MULTIMODAL

Have students read along with the audio of the selection to develop comprehension and practice fluency and pronunciation.

Earthquakes

Prepare to Read

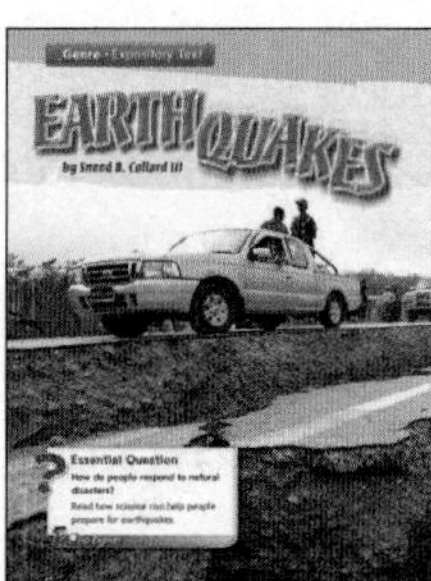

Literature Anthology, Lexile 870L

Build Background Discuss with students what they know about earthquakes. Use the photographs in the text to discuss with them what happens during an earthquake and the changes it creates on Earth. During an earthquake, the ground ____.

Vocabulary Use the **Visual Vocabulary Cards** to review the vocabulary: *alter, collapse, substantial, hazard, destruction, crisis, severe,* and *unpredictable.*

Set Purpose *Today we will read an expository text about an earthquake. As we read, think about how people respond to natural disasters.*

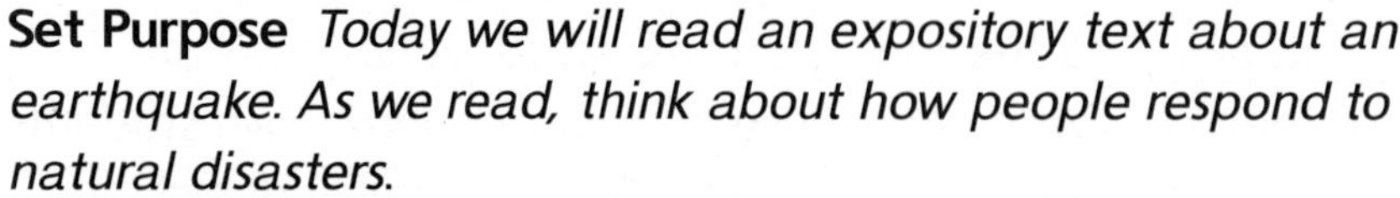

 Have students listen to the audio summary of the text, which is available in multiple languages.

Read

Literature Anthology, pp. 10–19

Use the **Interactive Question-Response Routine** to help students read and discuss ***Earthquakes.***

Beginning Help students discuss in complete sentences. Provide sentence frames: During an earthquake the ground shakes.

Intermediate Ask students to respond in complete sentences and add details. Provide sentence starters as needed: During an earthquake, the ground shakes and splits apart.

Advanced/Advanced High Have students respond in complete sentences and add details.

Independent Reading Practice Have mixed level pairs complete Online Anchor Text Support and share their responses with the group.

Reread

Use with **Reading/Writing Companion,** pages 24–27

Literature Anthology, pages 10-11

COLLABORATE **Text Features: Photographs** Read the text and restate them with students. Have them ask about words or phrases that are unfamiliar and define them for clarification, such as *jigsaw puzzle, sphere,* and *gel.* Remind them that photographs often give additional information and have students describe it using the caption. *What happens during an earthquake?* (The ground shakes.) *What are plates?* (pieces of Earth's crust) *What does the photograph show?* (large cracks on a road after an earthquake) *Where was the photograph taken?* (Myanmar) Use a map to point out Myanmar.

Beginning Read the first paragraph and restate sentences with students. *What do people feel during an earthquake?* People feel the ground shake. Help partners describe the photograph: Earthquakes make cracks on the road. Read the caption. *Where did the earthquake happen?* The earthquake happened in Myanmar.

Intermediate *What does the author compare Earth's crust to?* (jigsaw puzzle) How is Earth's crust like a jigsaw puzzle? Earth's crust is divided into pieces that fit together. *What damage did the earthquake cause?* (It damaged roads and buildings.)

Advanced/Advanced High Have partners describe what the heat inside Earth does. (It causes Earth's plates to slowly move.) *What does the photograph show?* (Possible answer: It shows damage to the road and that probably affects a lot of people.)

Literature Anthology, page 13

COLLABORATE **Genre: Informational Article** Read the text and restate it with students. Explain that a seismologist studies earthquakes. Have them ask about words or phrases that are unfamiliar and define them for clarification, such as *tsunami* and *magnitude. Who experienced an earthquake?* (Dr. Cifuentes) *When did the earthquake happen?* (May 21, 1960) *How is her experience different from the rest of the selection?* (She experienced the earthquake,so she can give details about each part of the experience)

Beginning Read sentences 1-5 and restate them with students. *Where did the earthquake happen?* The earthquake happened in Santiago, Chile. *What year was it?* It was the year 1960. *Who experienced the earthquake?* Dr. Cifuentes experienced the earthquake.

Intermediate Have partners discuss what Dr. Cifuentes experienced during the earthquake: She experienced the earthquake and later a tsunami.

Advanced/Advanced High *What did she experience during the earthquakes?* (woke up from the ground shaking.; felt the earthquake and tusnami) *What happened a year later?* (She visited and saw that the land had been raised up)

Literature Anthology, pages 16-17

COLLABORATE **Author's Craft: Word Choice** Read the text and restate them with students. Have them ask about words or phrases that are unfamiliar and define them for clarification, such as *tower* and *engulfed. What do underwater earthquakes cause?* (tsunamis) *What's the height of the tsunami waves at sea?* (a few feet high) *How does the author refer to the tsunami as it reaches shore?* (a towering monster) *Why is* "Tsunami Terror" *a good heading for this section?* (This section is about the destruction that tsunamis bring.)

Beginning Read paragraph 2 and restate sentences with students. Guide them to connect what they read about fast changes. *What makes a tsunami terrifying, or scary?* A tsunami can destroy shorelines.

Intermediate Have partners describe a tsunami: A tsunami is a wave that moves very fast. The wave can tower into a monster. *What does the heading tell you about this section?* This section is about the destruction that happens during a tsunami.

Advanced/Advanced High Have partners discuss why the author describes the wave as towering into a monster. Check understanding of "towering." (This metaphor shows how much bigger and scarier the waves become as they reach shore.)

FORMATIVE ASSESSMENT

STUDENT CHECK-IN

Read Have partners share their responses to the Anchor Text questions. Then have them reflect using the Check-In routine.

Reread Have partners share responses and text evidence on Reading/Writing Companion pages 24-26. Then have them reflect using the Check-In routine to fill in the bars.

LEARNING GOALS

- **We can read and understand expository text by identifying the compare and contrast text structure.**
- **We can identify subjects and predicates.**

OBJECTIVES

Paraphrase portions of a text read aloud or information presented in diverse media and formats, including visually, quantitatively, and orally.

Demonstrate command of the conventions of standard English grammar and usage when writing or speaking.

LANGUAGE OBJECTIVES

Students will inquire about the compare and contrast text structure using key vocabulary.

ELA ACADEMIC LANGUAGE

- *contrast, compound predicate, subject, predicate, conjunction*
- Cognates: *contrastar, sujeto, predicado, conjunción*

MATERIALS

Literature Anthology, pp. 10-19

Online Language Development Cards, 3A-3B

Online Language Development Practice pp. 13-18

Online Language Transfers Handbook, pp. 15-19

Earthquakes

Text Reconstruction

Focus on a single chunk of text to support comprehension and language development across the four domains:

1. Read aloud Paragraph 2 on page 11 in the **Literature Anthology** while students listen.
2. Write the following on the board, providing definitions as needed: *Earth's crust, jigsaw puzzle, resembles, sphere, plates, upper mantle, gel,* and *swirl.* Instruct students to listen for them as you read the paragraph a second time. (Cognate: *esfera*)
3. Read the paragraph a third time while students listen and take notes.
4. COLLABORATE Have students work with a partner to reconstruct the text from their notes. Help them write complete sentences as needed.
5. Have students look at the original text. Ask them what the paragraph is mostly about. (the Earth's crust) Tell students they are going to examine the compare and contrast text structure.
6. *In the first sentence, what does the author compare the Earth's crust to?* (a jigsaw puzzle.) *What words does the author use to show how the two are alike?* (resembles, like) *Ask students to find another comparison* (penultimate sentence). *What is the upper mantle compared to?* (thick gel)
7. Have students compare their text reconstructions to the original text. Have them check whether they also included words that compare and contrast.

Beginning Allow students to follow along in their **Literature Anthologies** as you read the text aloud. Have them point to the words from Step 2 as they hear them.

Apply Text Features: Photograph

Help students write a caption. Review: *Captions describe what is happening in a photograph and often include facts and information from the text.* Discuss with students the photograph on pages 10-11. Then have them rewrite the caption for the photograph. (Possible answer: People drive by a large crack in the road after an earthquake.)

Grammar in Context: Deconstruct a Sentence

Display this sentence from page 11: *Heat from deep inside the earth moves through the rock and causes it to slowly swirl and flow.* Deconstruct the sentence with students to help them understand subjects and predicates:

- Read the sentence with students and explain that it has a compound predicate. Help students find the subject and predicate. *Which words are the subject?* (heat from deep inside the earth) *What words are the predicates?* (moves through the rock, causes it to slowly swirl and flow)
- Circle the subject and underline the predicates. Point out that there are two predicates, and the conjunction *and* joins them. Rewrite the sentences into two, each with a simple predicate to demonstrate. *What does the conjunction* and *tell you?* (There is more than one action.) *What two things does heat do?* (moves through rock and causes rock to swirl and flow) Discuss what the sentence describes. (Possible answer: what causes rock to move)
- Write on the board: *As the mantle boils, it pushes the plates. As the mantle boils, it pulls the plates.* Have partners combine the sentences using *and.*

For more practice, see **Language Development Cards,** Lessons 3A-3B, and **Language Development Practice** pages 13-18.

Independent Time

Vocabulary Building Have students create vocabulary cards for new vocabulary they learned from the selection. Have partners copy four words onto index cards. On the back of each card, have them write a definition. Then have them take turns selecting a card, word face up, using the word in a sentence.

Beginning Allow students to write words or phrases or draw pictures.

Intermediate/Advanced/Advanced High Have students include some of the self-selected words they added to their glossaries.

COLLABORATE **Compound Subjects and Predicates** Pair students of mixed levels and have them use conjunctions and connecting words to write compound and complex sentences. Copy the chart on the board and use the first set of sentences to model combining sentences. Then have partners rewrite the sentences using conjunctions *and, but,* and *or* to describe events in *Earthquakes.* Have them copy the chart to use to rewrite their sentences:

SENTENCE	CONJUNCTION	COMPOUND SUBJECTS/ COMPOUND PREDICATES
Earth's plates crash. Earth's plates spread apart. Earth's plates slide against each other.	and	Earth's plates crash, spread apart, and slide against each other.
Earthquakes destroy buildings. Earthquakes create mountains.	but	

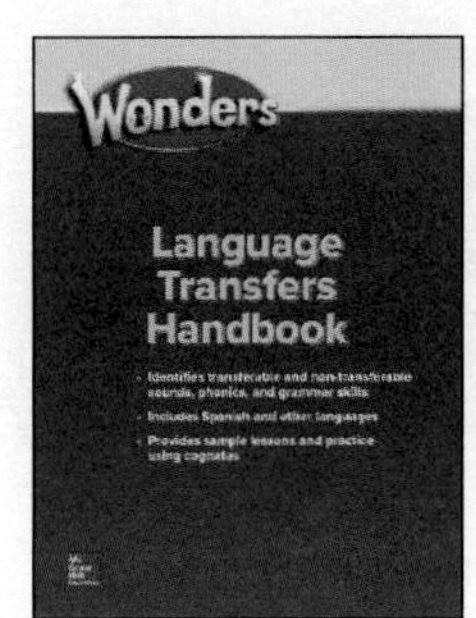

Language Transfers Handbook, Grammar Transfers, pp. 15-19

FORMATIVE ASSESSMENT

STUDENT CHECK-IN

Text Reconstruction Ask partners to share their notes. Have them reflect using the Check-In routine.

Grammar in Context Have students reflect on their deconstructions using the Check-In routine.

LEARNING GOALS

We can apply strategies and skills to read an expository text.

OBJECTIVES

Refer to details and examples in a text when explaining what the text says explicitly and when drawing inferences from the text.

Review the key ideas expressed and explain their own ideas and understanding in light of the discussion.

Use context as a clue to the meaning of a word or phrase.

LANGUAGE OBJECTIVES

Students will inquire about the topic by comparing and contrasting using key vocabulary.

ELA ACADEMIC LANGUAGE

- *compare, contrast*
- Cognates: *comparar, contrastar*

MATERIALS

Online ELL Genre Passage, "Rising Waters"

"Rising Waters"

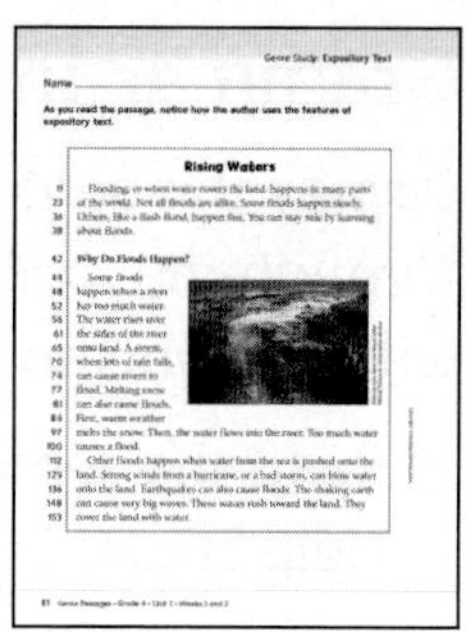

Genre Passage
Lexile 630L

Prepare to Read

Build Background Discuss with students what they know about floods, including what happens and what people need to do to stay safe. Have them describe, using: I know that floods cause ___. To stay safe people need to ___.

Read the title and explain that "rising waters" refers to the level of water in the river and floods often happen when water flows over onto land.

Vocabulary Use the Define/Example/Ask routine to preteach difficult words or unfamiliar concepts, such as *rise/rising/rose, flood, flash flood, sewer, levees, sponge*. Invite students to add new vocabulary to their glossaries.

Set Purpose *Today we will read "Rising Waters" and focus on comparing and contrasting. As we read, think about how people respond to natural disasters.*

Read the Text

Page E1, Introduction and "Why Do Floods Happen?"

COLLABORATE **Beginning** Read the first two paragraphs. Restate the sentences as needed. *What happens to land during a flood?* (water covers land) *Are all floods the same?* (no) *Which words tell you?* Help students find the text "Not all floods are alike." *How are they different?* Some floods happen fast. Some floods happen slowly. Help partners describe elements, such as water or wind, that move fast and slowly: Water can flow fast. Water can flow slowly.

COLLABORATE **Intermediate** *How do floods happen in rivers?* (river has too much water and water flows over to land) *What type of weather causes floods?* (storms, warm weather, hurricanes, earthquakes) Have partners discuss how floods happen in warm weather, using: First, the snow melts. Next, the water flows into the river. Then, the water rises and flows on land.

Advanced/Advanced High *How can hurricanes cause floods?* (Strong winds can blow water over land.) *How can earthquakes cause floods?* (The earth shakes during an earthquake and creates big waves that cover land with water.)

Page E2, "What Happens Next?"

Beginning Read the heading and explain that it refers to what happens after a flood. Read the paragraph with students. Restate as needed. *What do floods do to plants?* Floods can kill plants. *What can happen next?* People will have less food. *What do floods do?* Floods can damage buildings and bridges.

Intermediate Read the heading with students. *What does the heading refer to?* (what happens after a flood) *How do floods make it difficult for rescue workers?*

Rescue workers need bridges and roads to get to people. *What does it mean that people may be trapped by the water?* (They can't travel.)

Advanced/Advanced High Have partners describe the effects of floods: At farms, plants can die and there will be less food to eat. If bridges and roads get damaged, then rescue workers can't travel. Then people who need help get trapped.

Multiple-Meaning Words Have partners discuss the meanings of the multiple-meaning word *hard* and determine the meaning in sentences 6 and 7 using context clues. (difficult; do a lot of work)

Page E2, "How Do People Avoid Floods?"

Beginning Read the heading and explain that the word *avoid* means "to keep something away or stay away from something." Read the first paragraph with them. Restate as needed. Then help partners describe what a levee is: A levee is a wall. A levee keeps away water from the land.

Intermediate Have students find clues for levee. (walls) *What is a levee?* A levee is a wall made of soil. *How does a levee protect the land?* It blocks water. *What does the author compare a wetland to? Why?* A wetland is compared to a sponge because both soak up water. Which word tells you about a comparison? (like)

Advanced/Advanced High *How do levees prevent flooding?* (Levees are walls that are made up of soil. The soil blocks and absorbs water.) *How do wetlands prevent flooding?* (Wetlands absorb water from floods.) *Why is it important to know about floods?* (to keep people safe)

COLLABORATE

Text Structure: Compare and Contrast Have partners compare and contrast levees and wetlands: Levees and wetlands are similar because they both stop flooding. A levee is different from wetlands because levees are walls and wetlands are wet places.

Respond to Reading

Use the following instruction to help students answer the questions on page E3.

1. **Headings** *Read each heading. What is the topic of the heading?* (floods)
2. **Diagram** *What does the levee do?* (blocks or absorbs water) *Where is the levee?* (between water and land)
3. *What are effects of floods?* (Floods can kill plants that people need for food and damage buildings and roads. Floods can also make water unsafe to drink.)

Fluency Have partners take turns reading the passage.

Build Knowledge: Make Connections

Talk About the Text Have partners discuss how people respond to natural disasters.

Write About the Text Have students add their ideas to their Build Knowledge pages of their reader's notebooks.

FORMATIVE ASSESSMENT

STUDENT CHECK-IN

Have partners share their responses on page E3 and reflect using the Check-In routine.

LEVEL UP

IF students read the **ELL Level** of the **Genre Passage** fluently and answered the questions,

THEN pair them with students who have proficiently read the **On Level**. Have them:

- partner read the **On Level** passage.
- summarize how floods happen and how to prepare for them.

LEARNING GOALS

We can apply strategies and skills to read an expository text.

OBJECTIVES

Refer to details and examples in a text when explaining what the text says explicitly and when drawing inferences from the text.

Review the key ideas expressed and explain their own ideas and understanding in light of the discussion.

Read grade-level prose and poetry orally with accuracy, appropriate rate, and expression on successive readings.

LANGUAGE OBJECTIVES

Students will inquire by asking and answering questions about the topic.

ELA ACADEMIC LANGUAGE

- *diagram*
- Cognates: *diagrama*

MATERIALS

ELL Leveled Reader, *Changing Landscapes*

Online Differentiated Texts, "Alert! Floods and Landslides"

Visual Vocabulary Cards

DIGITAL TOOLS

MULTIMODAL

Have students read along with the audio of the selections to develop comprehension and practice fluency and pronunciation.

Changing Landscapes

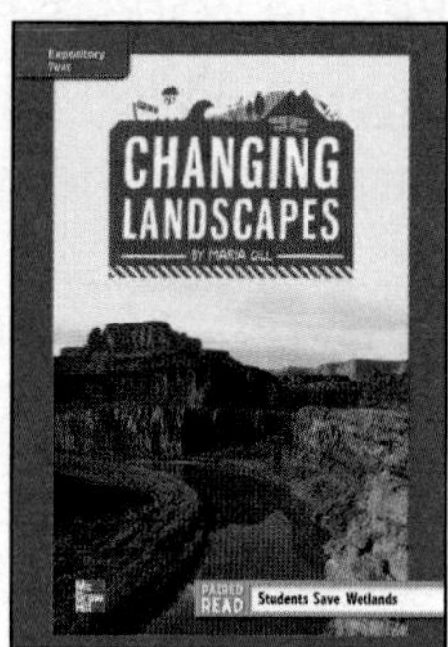

Leveled Reader
Lexile 740L

Prepare to Read

Build Background Have students share their experiences to discuss different types of landscapes that are near their community or other places they have been. Read the title aloud and discuss the image on the cover. Explain that the image is the Grand Canyon, and have students discuss what they know about it. Preview *Changing Landscapes* and "Students Save Wetlands" using the photographs in the text.

Vocabulary Use the routine on the **Visual Vocabulary Cards** to pre-teach ELL Vocabulary *damage* and *force* and glossary definitions on page 19. Have students add new vocabulary to their glossaries.

Set Purpose *Today we are going to read an expository text called* Changing Landscapes. *As we read, think about different changes to Earth's surface and how people respond to natural disasters.*

Read the Text

Pages 2–7, Introduction and Chapter 1

Beginning Read the text and the diagram on page 4 with students. *What words tell you what sediment is made of?* (sand, small rocks) *What other words do you know for sediment?* (dirt, ground, soil).

Intermediate *Look at the Wetlands diagram on page 7. What things do you see that absorb water and nutrients?* (plants) *What happens to the soil in the wetlands?* (The roots of the plants hold down the soil in place.)

Advanced *How are sand dunes like wetlands?* (They protect against erosion.) *How do they differ?* (Dunes are on beaches. Wetlands are marshes or swamps.)

Pages 8–11, Chapter 2

Beginning Help partners look for words in the text related to *damage.* (collapse, severe damage, dangerous, destruction, smash)

Intermediate *Is a landslide more likely to happen on a hill that has no trees or a hill with many trees?* (a hill with no trees) *Why?* A hill with no trees cannot slow down the soil or rocks that are going down. A landslide can damage buildings, roads, and bridges.

Advanced/Advanced High Have partners discuss what the waves of a hurricane can do. (break through storm barriers, carry away sand from beaches) Have students discuss how coastal wetlands help to protect against hurricanes. (Coastal wetlands can absorb water from rain and flooding. Also, a hurricane gets weaker when it hits land, so coastal wetlands can lessen damage from hurricanes.)

Pages 12–14, Chapter 3 and Conclusion

Reread Have partners reread page 12 and discuss what people can do to fix damage caused by erosion.

Beginning Read page 12 with students. *How can we slow down erosion?* We can plant trees.

Intermediate *What happens when sand dunes and wetlands are lost?* Losing sand dunes and wetlands can cause erosion or landslides.

Advanced/Advanced High Have students compare the hills on page 12, discussing how stable land can prevent landslides.

Respond to Reading Have partners discuss the questions on page 15 and answer them, using the new vocabulary.

Fluency: Intonation, Expression, Rate

Model Read page 9 with appropriate intonation, expression, and rate. Then read it aloud with students. For more practice, have students record their voices while they read a few times. Have them play their recordings and choose the best one.

Paired Read: "Students Save Wetlands"

Make Connections: Write About It

Before students write, discuss the questions on page 18. Review the word *restoration*. Reread *the first two paragraphs on page 16. What details tell you the importance of wetlands?* Erosion is a slow change caused by wind and water. To slow down erosion, we must protect sand dunes and replant wetlands. Sand dunes trap sand brought by waves and wind. Wetlands help prevent flooding.

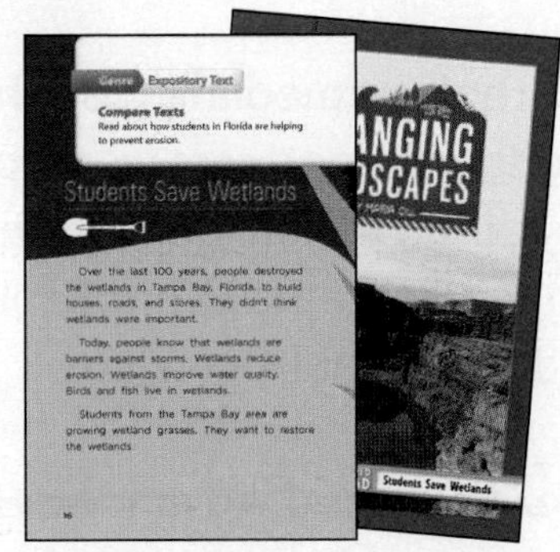

ELL Leveled Reader

Build Knowledge: Make Connections

Talk About the Text Have partners discuss different changes to Earth's surface and how people respond to natural disasters.

Write About the Text Have students add their ideas to their Build Knowledge pages of their reader's notebooks.

Self-Selected Reading

Have students choose another expository text from the online **Leveled Reader Library** or read the **Differentiated Text,** "Alert! Floods and Landslides."

FOCUS ON SCIENCE

Have students complete the activity on page 20 to research how to prepare for a natural disaster.

LITERATURE CIRCLES

Ask students to conduct a literature circle using the Thinkmark questions to guide the discussion.

FORMATIVE ASSESSMENT

STUDENT CHECK-IN

Have partners share their answers to Respond to Reading. Ask students to reflect on their learning using the Check-In routine.

LEVEL UP

IF students read the **ELL Level** fluently and answered the questions,

THEN pair them with students who have proficiently read the **On Level** and have students

- read the **On Level** main selection aloud with their partner.
- list words they find difficult.
- discuss these words with their partners.

ACT Access Complex Text

The **On Level** challenges students by including more **domain-specific words** and **complex sentence structures**.

LEARNING GOALS

We can read and understand a realistic fiction.

OBJECTIVES

Describe in depth a character, setting, or event in a story or drama, drawing on specific details in the text.

Review the key ideas expressed and explain their own ideas and understanding in light of the discussion.

Recognize and explain the meaning of common idioms, adages, and proverbs.

LANGUAGE OBJECTIVES

Students will narrate what happens to the conflict in the plot using key vocabulary.

ELA ACADEMIC LANGUAGE

- *conflict, resolve, solution, plot, idiom*
- Cognates: *conflicto, resolver, solución*

MATERIALS

Reading/Writing Companion, pp. 38-41

Online Scaffolded Shared Read, "The Talent Show"

Visual Vocabulary Cards

Online ELL Visual Vocabulary Cards

DIGITAL TOOLS

MULTIMODAL

Have students read along with the audio of the selection to develop comprehension and practice fluency and pronunciation.

"The Talent Show"

Prepare to Read

Build Background Have students share their experiences of solving a problem. Ask: *What did you do to solve a problem? How did you help others solve a problem?* Have students describe using: I solved the problem by ___. I helped other people solve a problem by ___. Then discuss with students actions that can have a positive or negative affect on others.

Vocabulary Use the **Visual Vocabulary Cards** to preteach the vocabulary: *uncomfortably, hesitated, desperately, inspiration, humiliated, accountable, advise,* and *self-esteem.* Use the online **ELL Visual Vocabulary Cards** to teach additional Vocabulary from the Shared Read: *considered, continuing, grip, interrupted, juggling, and resentful.* (Cognates: *consideró, interrumpió*)

Set Purpose *Today we will read "The Talent Show" and focus on understanding how a character solves her problem. As we read, think about how your actions affect others.*

Read the Text

Select the **Scaffolded Shared Read** or the Shared Read in the **Reading/Writing Companion**, based on students' language proficiency.

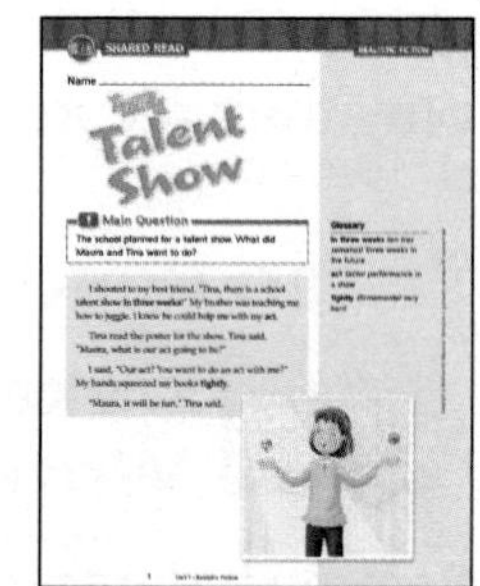

Scaffolded Shared Read, Lexile 400L

Beginning/Early-Intermediate Use the online **Scaffolded Shared Read** to help partners work together to read and understand realistic fiction. Remind them to use the Glossary to help them read and the Word Bank to help them answer the Main and Additional Questions.

Intermediate/Advanced Advanced High Read the text with students and use the Interactive Question-Response Routine to help them understand realistic fiction.

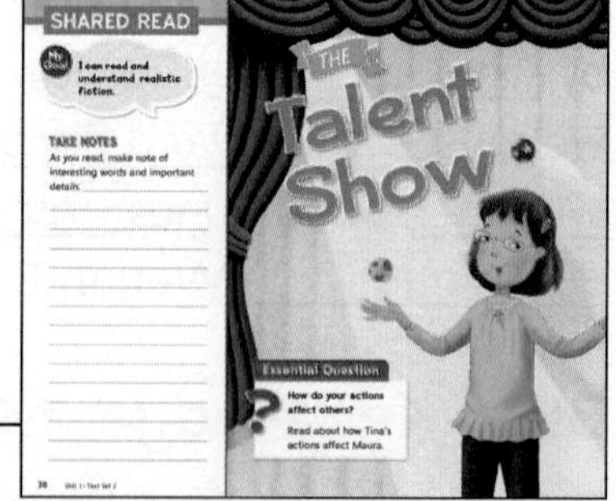

Reading/Writing Companion, Lexile 620L

Pages 38–39

Paragraphs 1–7 Read the text with students and review Vocabulary words *uncomfortably, hesitated, continuing, grip, interrupted,* and *juggling. What does Maura plan to do for the school talent show?* (juggle) *What did Maura's brother do?* (teach Maura to juggle) *What does Tina want to do for the talent show?* (She wants to perform at the talent show with Maura.) Point to the ellipses and explain that it shows that a character does not finish the sentence or thought.

Intermediate *Did Maura plan to do the talent show with Tina? How do you know?* (no; Maura says that her brother has been helping her with her act) Point to the ellipses. *Why doesn't Maura finish her sentence?* Maura doesn't finish her sentence because Tina interrupts Maura.

COLLABORATE **Advanced/Advanced High** *Why did Maura hesitate?* (She did not know how to tell Tina about her juggling act.) Have partners make predictions about whether or not Maura will tell Tina about her juggling act. (Possible answer: I predict that Maura will not tell Tina because she grips her book and hesitates to tell Tina that she's learning to juggle.)

Paragraphs 8–10 Read the text with students and review Vocabulary words *desperately* and *resentful.* Explain that the **idiom** "see eye to eye" means to have the same feeling, or attitude. Discuss the **conflict** in the plot with them. *What problem, or conflict, does Maura have?* (She wants to be in the talent show by herself, but Tina wants to be in it together.)

COLLABORATE **Intermediate** Discuss with a partner why Maura feels resentful at Tina: Maura feels resentful because Tina always takes charge and Maura. Maura does not speak up to say what she thinks. She ends up feeling resentful.

Page 40

Paragraphs 1–4 Read the text with students and review Vocabulary words *inspiration, humiliated* and *considered* (cognates: *inspiración* and *humillado.*) *What happened during lunch?* (Tina told Maura she wants to sing and dance.) *How did Tina react when Maura told her about juggling?* (Tina doesn't want to do it) Explain that the idiom "let off steam" means to get rid of strong feelings, such as anger.

COLLABORATE **Intermediate** Have partners describe why Tina doesn't want to juggle at the talent show: Tina doesn't want to juggle because it will be difficult to learn to juggle and she'll make mistakes.

Paragraphs 5–8 Read the text with students and review Vocabulary word *accountable. The idiom* "cat got your tongue" *means "you're being quiet." What does Maura's grandmother tell her?* (she tells Maura to speak up) Have students make predictions about what Maura will do. (Possible answer: I predict Maura will tell Tina because Maura wants to solve her problem.)

Intermediate *Why does the grandmother ask "Cat got your tongue?" to Maura?* Grandmother asks because Maura is not talking and is quiet.

COLLABORATE **Advanced** Have partners discuss why Maura's grandmother says that Maura is "not being respectful of her ideas." (Possible answer: Maura should believe in her own ideas by telling how she really feels to Tina.)

Advanced High *What does grandmother mean when she tells Maura she is accountable for her actions?* (Possible answer: Maura needs to work to solve her problem by telling Tina the truth.)

Page 41

Paragraphs 1–5 Read the text with students and review Vocabulary words *advise* and *self-esteem. What does Grandmother advise Maura to do?* (tell Tina the truth) *What does Maura do?* (calls Tina and tells her she wants to do her juggling act) *How does Tina react?* (she accepts Maura's feelings and next day they play a game that Maura chooses) Explain that the idiom "stand up for myself" and "pays off".

COLLABORATE **Intermediate** Have partners discuss Maura's solution to her problem. Maura solved her problem by telling Tina the truth. Tina responded by playing a game Maura chose.

Advanced/Advanced High *How did Maura and Tina change?* (Possible answer: Maura learned to stand up for herself and Tina learned to respect Maura.)

STUDENT CHECK-IN

Have partners orally narrate the events from the story. Ask them to reflect using the Check-In routine.

LEARNING GOALS

- **We can read and understand a realistic fiction by identifying the conflict in the plot.**
- **We can identify and write compound sentences.**

OBJECTIVES

Paraphrase portions of a text read aloud or information presented in diverse media and formats, including visually, quantitatively, and orally.

Use a comma before a coordinating conjunction in a compound sentence.

LANGUAGE OBJECTIVES

Students will discuss the conflict in the plot using key vocabulary.

Students will discuss compound sentences using academic language.

ELA ACADEMIC LANGUAGE

- *conflict, solution*
- Cognates: *conflicto, solución*

MATERIALS

Reading/Writing Companion, pp. 38-41, 42-43

Online Scaffolded Shared Read, "The Talent Show"

Online Shared Read Writing Frames, p. 2

Online Language Development Cards, Lesson 5B

Online Language Development Practice, pp. 28-30

Online Language Transfers Handbook, pp. 15-19

"The Talent Show"

Text Reconstruction

Focus on a single chunk of text to support comprehension and language development across the four domains.

1. Read aloud Paragraphs 2-4 on page 41 in the **Reading/Writing Companion** while students listen.
2. Write the following on the board, providing definitions as needed: *advise, truth, self-esteem* and *curt.* Instruct students to listen for them as you read the paragraph a second time.
3. Read the paragraphs a third time. Tell students to listen and take notes.
4.  COLLABORATE Have students work with a partner to reconstruct the text from their notes. Help them write complete sentences as needed.
5. Have students look at the original text. Ask them to tell what the paragraphs are mostly about. (how Maura solved her problem) Tell students they are going to examine the conflict, or problem, in the plot.
6. With students, locate the sentences that describe what Maura does to solve the problem. Read the first sentence and discuss its purpose. (to express that it is important to tell the truth) Ask students to explain the purpose of the rest of the text. (to show what the characters do to solve the problem and the results of finding the solution)
7. Have students compare their text reconstructions to the original text. Have them check whether they expressed a solution to the problem.

Beginning Have students follow along in the Reading/Writing Companion as you read the text aloud. Have them circle the words from Step 2 as they hear them.

Grammar in Context: Compound Sentences

Notice the Form Display the sentence, and circle the conjunction *and.*

> "We can sing along to a song and do a dance routine, and my mother can make us costumes."

What kind of sentence is this? (compound sentence) Review that compound sentences have two or more independent clauses that can stand alone as a sentence. Help students identify the independent clauses. Then rewrite them as simple sentences: *We can sing along to a song. We can do a dance routine. My mother can make us costumes.* Discuss: *Which words are subjects?* (we, mother) *Which words are verbs?* (sing, do; can make) Point to the compound sentence and explain that the word *and* is a conjunction. *What does the conjunction* and *do?* (combines the sentences) Point out that a comma appears before the conjunction *and.*

Apply and Extend Have partners copy the simple sentences and rewrite them as a compound sentence and label the conjunction.

For additional practice, see Language Development Card, Lesson 5B, and Language Development Practice, pages 28-30.

Independent Time

Vocabulary Building Have students build glossaries.

Beginning/Early Intermediate Have students complete the Glossary Activities in the **Scaffolded Shared Read**.

Intermediate/Advanced/Advanced High Have students add the vocabulary from **Reading/Writing Companion** pages 42–43 and self-selected words or phrases they would like to learn to a chart.

Mixed Levels Pair students together: Beginning and Early-Intermediate students can teach words from their **Scaffolded Shared Read** glossaries. Intermediate and Advanced/High students can teach their self-selected words.

WORD/PHRASE	DEFINITION	USE THE WORD/PHRASE IN A SENTENCE
act	performance in a show	Many people clapped for our act in the talent show.

COLLABORATE **Write a Summary** Have students use the online leveled **Shared Read Writing Frames** for "The Talent Show" to discuss the selection. Ask students to tell the main idea and some supporting details. Then have them write their own summaries.

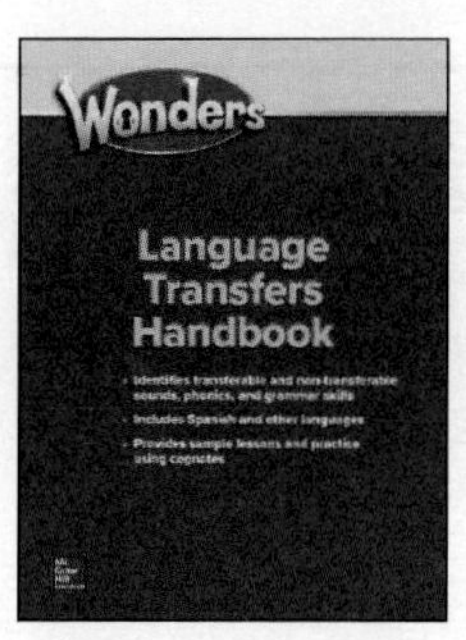

Language Transfers Handbook, Grammar Transfers pp. 15–19

DIGITAL TOOLS

Use the additional grammar and vocabulary resources.

Grammar Video

Grammar Song

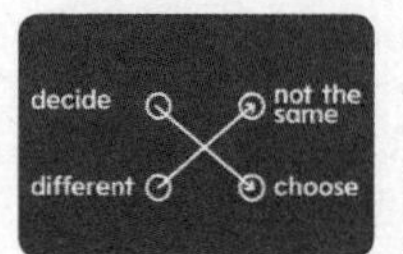

Vocabulary Activity

FORMATIVE ASSESSMENT

STUDENT CHECK-IN

Text Reconstruction Have partners share their notes. Have students reflect on their work using the Check-In routine.

Grammar in Context Have partners share their sentences. Have students reflect on their work using the Check-In routine.

LEARNING GOALS

Read We can read and understand a realistic fiction story.

Reread We can reread to analyze text, craft, and structure.

OBJECTIVES

Describe in depth a character, setting, or event in a story or drama, drawing on specific details in the text.

Engage effectively in a range of collaborative discussions with diverse partners on grade 4 topics and texts, building on others' ideas and expressing their own clearly.

LANGUAGE OBJECTIVES

Students will narrate by answering questions about the text using content area vocabulary

Students will explain author's word choice and dialogue using academic vocabulary.

ELA ACADEMIC LANGUAGE

- *realistic fiction, dialogue*
- Cognates: *ficción realista, diálogo*

MATERIALS

Literature Anthology, pp. 24-33

Reading/Writing Companion, pp. 50-53

Online ELL Anchor Text Support BLMS, pp. 4-6

DIGITAL TOOLS

MULTIMODAL

Have students read along with the audio of the selection to develop comprehension and practice fluency and pronunciation.

Experts, Incorporated

Prepare to Read

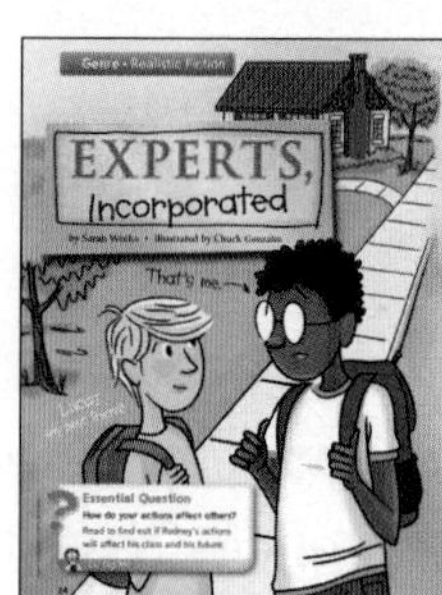

Literature Anthology, Lexile 730L

Build Background *We are going to read about a boy named Rodney and how his actions will affect his class and his future.* Invite students to share if their actions have affected their classmates.

Vocabulary Use the **Visual Vocabulary Cards** to review the vocabulary: *uncomfortably, hesitated, desperately, inspiration, humiliated, accountable, advise,* and *self-esteem.*

Set Purpose *Today we will read a realistic fiction about a boy named Rodney. As we read, think about how your actions affect others.*

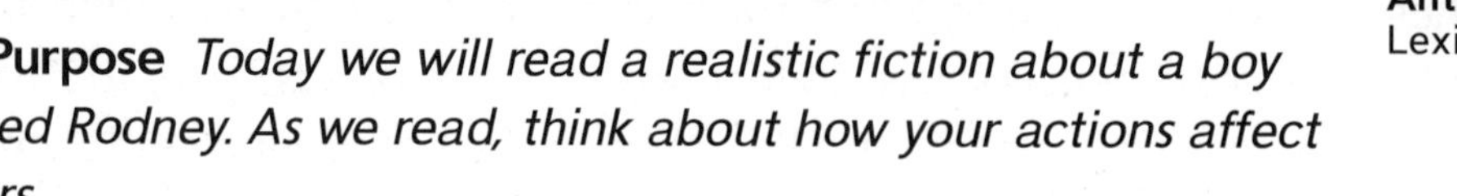

 Have students listen to the audio summary of the text, which is available in multiple languages.

Read

Literature Anthology, pp. 24-33

Use the **Interactive Questions-Response Routine** to help students read and discuss ***Experts, Incorporated.***

Beginning Help students discuss in complete sentences. Provide sentence frames: Rodney can't stand creative writing. He did not complete his writing assignment.

Intermediate Ask students to respond in complete sentences and add details. Provide sentence starters as needed: Rodney can't stand cucumber salad, wool sweaters, and creative writing. Rodney did not complete his writing assignment.

Advanced/Advanced High Have students respond in complete sentences and add details.

COLLABORATE

Independent Reading Practice Have mixed level pairs complete Online Anchor Text Support and share their responses with the group.

Reread

Use with **Reading/Writing Companion,** pages 50-53

Literature Anthology, page 27

COLLABORATE

Genre: Realistic Fiction Read the text and restate them with students. Have them ask about words or phrases that are unfamiliar and define them for clarification. *Who is speaking in the dialogue?* (Lucas, Jeremy, Russell, and Rodney) *What are some abbreviations and nicknames that Rodney and his* *friends use in their dialogue?* ("Rodd-o" and "'cause") *How does the author make the characters seem like people you might know in real life?* (The author uses words and phrases that kids use in real life.)

Beginning Read Paragraphs 1-2 with students. Restate sentences as needed. *Who is speaking?* (Lucas and Jeremy) Clarify to students that *'cause* is an abbreviation or shortened word for *because. Do people use the word* 'cause *in real life when they speak?* (yes)

Intermediate *What does "Rodd-o" mean?* (It is a nickname for Rodney.) *What does the word 'cause mean?* (It is an abbreivation for the word because.) *Is the author's use of dialogue realistic?* (yes)

Advanced/Advanced Have partners read the dialogue between Rodney and his friends to discuss how the author's use of dialogue is realistic. (Possible answer: Rodney and his friends use words and phrases that kids use in real life, such as yeah)

Literature Anthology, page 29

COLLABORATE **Author's Craft: Sentence Structure** Read the text and restate them with students. Review the Vocabulary words *desperately* and *inspiration. Why does Rod need an idea quickly?* (He has to turn in an essay.) *What does he need to write about?* (what he wants to be when he grows up) *How do you know Rodney got a good idea?* (He says "It hit me. I knew what I wanted to be.") Authors can show how a character feels by using sentence structure, or types of sentences. *When Rodney doesn't know what to do, are his sentences short or long?* (short)

Beginning Read Paragraph 3 with students. Restate the sentences as needed. *What does Rod ask himself?* He asks about what he wants to be. *Does he find an answer at first?* (no) *How do you know?* He says "No, no, no." *Does he find an answer in the end?* (yes) *How do you know?* He says "I knew what I wanted to be." Have students point to the text.

Intermediate *When Rod is talking to himself, what kinds of sentences does he use?* (short questions) *How do you think he feels?* (Worried) *When things shift into slow motion, what is happening?* (Rod is getting an idea.) *How do you know? Look for clues in the next sentences.* (He says "I knew what I wanted to be.")

Advanced/Advanced High Have partners discuss how the sentences change when everything changed to slow motion. (Sentences change from being very short sentences to being one long sentence.) What does this show? (Rodney goes from being worried to knowing what to do.)

Literature Anthology, page 32

COLLABORATE **Author's Craft: Dialogue** Read the text and restate them with students. Have them ask about words or phrases that are unfamiliar and define them for clarification, such as *hyphenated* and *expert*. Tell students to think about what information is in the dialogue as you read the text with them. *What does Rod want to be?* (a name expert) *What name does Rod use as an example?* (Jessica Pepper-Mintz)

Beginning Read Paragraphs 6-9 with students. Restate the sentences as needed. Explain that peppermint is a flavor and that Jessica has a last name Pepper-Mintz which sounds like peppermint. *What is Jessica's last name?* Jessica's last name is Pepper-Mintz.

Intermediate *What do you learn from the dialogue?* We learn how Rod got the idea to become a name expert. We also learn that Lucas changes his mind about Rod's idea.

Advanced/Advanced High What important information about Rod is told through dialogue? (How he got his idea to be a name expert) How do you know that Lucas has changed his mind about Rod's idea? (He says he wants to be Rod's partner)

FORMATIVE ASSESSMENT

STUDENT CHECK-IN

Read Have partners share their responses to the Anchor Text questions. Then have them reflect using the Check-In routine.

Reread Have partners share responses and text evidence on Reading/Writing Companion pages 50-53. Then have them reflect using the Check-In routine to fill in the bars.

LEARNING GOALS

- We can read and understand realistic fiction by identifying conflict in the plot.
- We can identify simple and compound sentences and conjunctions.

OBJECTIVES

Paraphrase portions of a text read aloud or information presented in diverse media and formats, including visually, quantitatively, and orally.

Demonstrate command of the conventions of standard English grammar and usage when writing or speaking.

LANGUAGE OBJECTIVES

Students will inquire about conflict in a story using key vocabulary.

Students will discuss clauses using academic vocabulary.

ELA ACADEMIC LANGUAGE

- *dialogue, conflict, resolve, solution*
- Cognates: *diálogo, conflicto, resolver, solución*

MATERIALS

Literature Anthology, pp. 24-33

Online Language Development Cards, 6A-6B

Online Language Development Practice, pp. 31-36

Online Language Transfers Handbook, pp. 15-19

Experts, Incorporated

Text Reconstruction

Focus on a single chunk of text to support comprehension and language development across the four domains.

1. Read aloud Paragraph 3 on page 29 in the **Literature Anthology** while students listen.
2. Write the following on the board, interpreting expressions as needed: *shifted into slow motion, came to rest, it hit me.* Instruct students to listen for them as you read the paragraph a second time.
3. Read the paragraph a third time while students listen and take notes.
4. COLLABORATE Have students work with a partner to reconstruct the text from their notes. Help them write complete sentences as needed.
5. Have students look at the original text. Ask them to tell what the paragraph is mostly about. (Rod's thoughts as he tries to find an idea for his paper) Tell students they are going to look at how the author uses conflict to show a character's feelings and how they will solve a problem.
6. *What is Rodney's problem?* (He needs to come up with an idea for his essay) *How does the author use conflict to show Rodney's feelings about this problem?* (uses short sentences to show he is panicking) *At the end, does Rodney have a solution?* (yes) *How does the author show Rodney's feelings about this solution?* (uses a long sentence to show he thinks he has found a good idea)
7. Have students compare their text reconstructions to the original text. Have them check whether they used conflict to show Rodney's feelings about the problem and solution.

Beginning Allow students to follow along in their Literature Anthologies as you read the text aloud. Have them point to the words from Step 2 as they hear them.

Apply Text Features: Dialogue

Review what dialogues tell about: *A dialogue shows a conversation, or words characters say aloud. Authors use dialogue to show what characters are thinking and feeling. Model first: On page 30, Rodney is talking with his friend Lucas. What are they talking about?* (Possible answer: Lucas asks Rodney what profession he wants to do; Rodney wants to be a name expert) Have students write their own version of the dialogue between Rodney and Lucas.

Grammar in Context: Deconstruct a Sentence

Write the sentence from page 29 on the board: *When the bell for lunch rang, I didn't join the others in the cafeteria.* Deconstruct the sentence with students:

- Read the sentence with students and restate what it describes. Discuss what makes up a clause and identify them in the sentence. (words with a subject and a verb) Then help students identify the subject and verb in each clause. (bell rang; I didn't join) Point to the parts of the sentence and label them as you explain: *This is a complex sentence. It has an independent clause and a dependent clause.*
- *What do the underlined words tell?* (tells the bell rang for lunch) *What kind of clause is this?* (dependent clause) *Can the clause be a separate sentence?* (no)
- *What does the rest of the sentence tell?* (tells the person did not go to the cafeteria) *What kind of clause is this?* (independent clause) *Can the clause be a separate sentence?* (yes)
- Circle *"didn't"* and remind students that this contraction is the two words "did" and "not" put together. Point to the comma after *rang* and explain that it separates the two clauses.

For additional practice, see Language Development Cards, Lessons 6A-6B, and Language Development Practice pages 31-36.

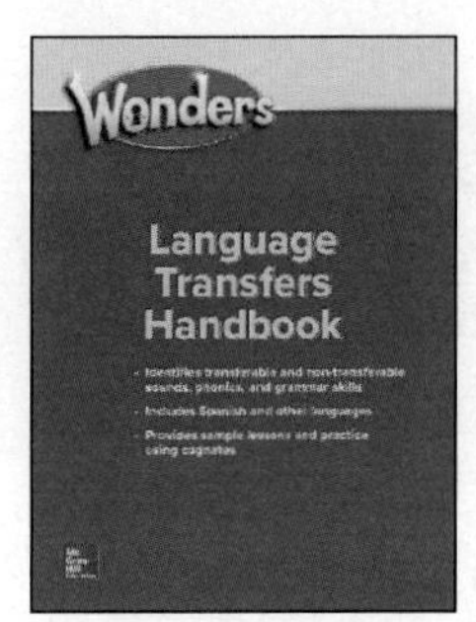

Language Transfers Handbook
See pp. 15-19

Independent Time

Vocabulary Building Have students create a display of idioms and expressions and present them. Assign each pair one or two pages of *Experts, Incorporated.* Have them find idioms or expressions. Write each on the front of an index card and the original sentence and the meaning on the back. Have them display their cards and take turns explaining the meaning to the group.

Beginning Allow students to draw pictures to tell the meaning.

Intermediate/Advanced/Advanced High Have students look up and include self-selected idioms or expressions commonly used by students.

COLLABORATE **Use Connecting Words** Pair students of mixed levels and have them use connecting words to combine clauses to write complex sentences. Display the chart and use the first complex sentence as a model to discuss. Then have partners combine the rest of the clauses using the connecting words *when, before,* and *after* to describe characters and events in *Experts, Incorporated.*

CLAUSES	CONNECTING WORD	COMPLEX SENTENCE
Lucas finished the assignment; Rod finished	before	Lucas finished the assignment before Rod finished.
Lucas blushed and hung his head; I felt sorry	when	

FORMATIVE ASSESSMENT

STUDENT CHECK-IN

Text Reconstruction Ask partners to share their notes. Have them reflect using the Check-In routine.

Grammar in Context Ask students to reflect on their deconstructions using the Check-In routine.

LEARNING GOALS

We can apply strategies and skills to read realistic fiction.

OBJECTIVES

Describe in depth a character, setting, or event in a story or drama, drawing on specific details in the text.

Engage effectively in a range of collaborative discussions with diverse partners on grade 4 topics and texts, building on others' ideas and expressing their own clearly.

Recognize and explain the meaning of common idioms, adages, and proverbs.

LANGUAGE OBJECTIVES

Students will discuss the conflict in the plot using key vocabulary.

ELA ACADEMIC LANGUAGE

- *idiom, problem, solve*
- Cognates: *problema*

MATERIALS

Online ELL Genre Passage, "Stormy Weather"

"Stormy Weather"

Prepare to Read

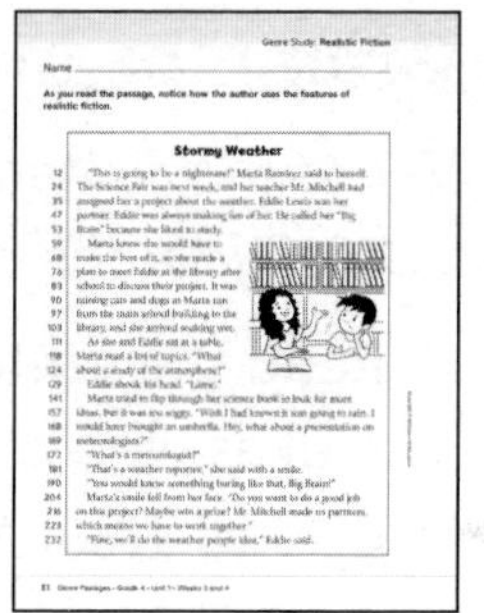

Genre Passage
Lexile 600L

Build Background Discuss with students experiences of when they worked on a school project with other people. Have them describe ways that they solved a problem, such as asking for help or doing research and discuss good ways to find a solution.

Choral read the title and ask: *What is stormy weather like?* Then have students **predict** what the story might be about. *As we read the story, think about why the author chose this title.*

Vocabulary Use the Define/Example/Ask routine to pre-teach difficult words or unfamiliar concepts, such as *atmosphere, diorama, soggy,* and *meteorologist.* Invite students to add new vocabulary to their glossaries.

Set Purpose *Today we will read "Stormy Weather" and focus on dialogue. As we read, think about how people respond to natural disasters.*

Read the Text

Page E1, Paragraphs 1–2

Idioms Read the second paragraph and discuss the meaning of the **idiom** "raining cats and dogs" in the second sentence. *Are cats and dogs falling from the sky?* (no) *What's happening?* (It is raining hard.) *What context clues support your answer?* (Marta gets soaking wet.) *What does the idiom "raining cats and dogs" describe?* (raining very hard).

Beginning Read the first paragraph with students. Restate as needed. *Who is talking in the first sentence?* (Marta) Point to the word *This* and ask: *What is Marta talking about by the word* This*?* Help students identify "Science Fair" in the next sentence and describe: Marta is talking about the Science Fair. *Who is Marta's partner?* Marta's partner is Eddie. *Does Eddie think Marta is smart?* (yes) *How do you know?* Eddie calls Marta Big Brain.

Intermediate Have partners describe why Marta is not excited to work with Eddie: Eddie makes fun of her and calls her Big Brain and now they are partners.

Advanced/Advanced High Discuss the meaning of the phrase "make the best of it." Have partners discuss what Marta decided to do and why she uses the phrase. (Possible answer: Marta decides to work with Eddie although she is not excited about it. She uses the phrase to say that she will do her best.)

Page E1, Paragraphs 3–10

Beginning Read paragraphs 5–7 with students and define the word *soggy.* Restate sentences as needed. Help students identify text that answers the questions: *What is soggy?* The book is soggy. *Did Marta know it was going to rain?* (no) *How do you know?* Marta doesn't have an umbrella. *What is a meteorologist?* A meteorologist is a weather reporter.

Intermediate *What ideas does Marta suggest?* (atmosphere, meteorologists) *How does Eddie respond?* (he doesn't like the ideas and makes fun of Marta)

COLLABORATE **Advanced/Advanced High** Have partners retell Marta and Eddie's dialogue. (Possible answer: Marta makes suggestions but Eddie doesn't like any of the ideas. He makes fun of her and makes her angry and Eddie finally decides on an idea.)

Advanced High Have students describe Marta and Eddie's attitude based on the dialogue.

Page E2

Beginning Read the first two paragraph with students. Restate sentences as needed. *What did Marta and Eddie learn?* They learned about meteorologists. *How does Eddie change?* Eddie was bored. Then he was more interested. Ask: *Are the words* bored *and* interested *synonyms or antonyms?* (antonyms)

Intermediate *What problem did Marta and Eddie have?* (they don't know how meteorologists use maps and charts) *How did they solve it?* (Marta asked a meteorologist)

Advanced/Advanced High *How can we tell that Eddie's attitude toward Marta has changed?* (Possible answer: He does not call her Big Brain and says that she's smart in a nice way.)

COLLABORATE **Advanced High** Discuss the meaning of the **idiom** "as busy as bees" and have partners use it to describe a person they know.

Respond to Reading

Use the following instruction to help students answer the questions on page E3.

1. **Dialogue** Review that authors use dialogue to show how a character thinks or behaves. *How does Eddie respond to Marta's suggestions?* (he doesn't like any of them and teases her)
2. **Plot: Conflict** Have students reread page E2. *What problem did Marta and Eddie have?* (They didn't know how meteorologists use their tools.) *What did Marta do to solve the problem?* (She emailed a meteorologist and visited the studio and took notes)
3. Have students look for words and phrases that tell how Eddie treated Marta at the beginning and end of the story. *What did Eddie realize?* (He realized that learning can be fun.)

Fluency Have partners take turns reading the passage.

Build Knowledge: Make Connections

Talk About the Text Have partners discuss how people respond to natural disasters.

Write About the Text Have students add their ideas to their Build Knowledge pages of their reader's notebooks.

FORMATIVE ASSESSMENT

STUDENT CHECK-IN

Have partners share their responses on page E3 and reflect using the Check-In routine.

LEVEL UP

IF students read the **ELL Level** of the **Genre Passage** fluently and answered the questions,

THEN pair them with students who have proficiently read the **On Level**. Have them

- partner read the **On Level** passage.
- summarize a problem described in the text and identify its solution.

LEARNING GOALS

We can apply strategies and skills to read realistic fiction.

OBJECTIVES

Describe in depth a character, setting, or event in a story or drama, drawing on specific details in the text.

Engage effectively in a range of collaborative discussions with diverse partners on grade 4 topics and texts, building on others' ideas and expressing their own clearly.

Read grade-level text with purpose and understanding.

LANGUAGE OBJECTIVES

Students will discuss the plot using key vocabulary.

ELA ACADEMIC LANGUAGE

- *prediction*
- Cognates: *predicción*

MATERIALS

ELL Leveled Reader, *Rosa's Garden*

Online Differentiated Texts, "It's Showtime!"

Visual Vocabulary Cards

DIGITAL TOOLS

Have students read along with the audio of the selections to develop comprehension and practice fluency and pronunciation.

Rosa's Garden

Leveled Reader
Lexile 540L

Prepare to Read

Build Background Discuss with students things people do to help the community. Have them share what they know or their experiences of helping out in the community or other people using: People help the community by ___. Then discuss what a community garden is and how it can help a neighborhood.

Vocabulary Use the routine on the **Visual Vocabulary Cards** to pre-teach *community, gardening, neighborhood (cognates: comunidad, jardinería).* Have students add these words to their glossaries.

Set purpose Today we are going to read a realistic fiction story called *Rosa's Garden.* As we read, think about how your actions affect others.

Read the Text

Pages 2–5, Chapter 1

Beginning Read page 2 with students. Restate the sentences as needed. Explain that the phrase "a lot" means a piece of land and use the illustration on page 2. Explain that with the verb *have,* it means "much or many". *What is a lot?* A lot is land. *What does it mean when I say I have a lot of pens?* You have many pens.

COLLABORATE **Intermediate** *What words help you picture the lot when it's raining on page 4?* ("trash soup") Have partners describe why Rosa describes the lot as a trash soup. (Possible answer: The lot is full of trash.)

COLLABORATE **Advanced/Advanced High** Have partners discuss why Rosa's mom uses the word *humiliated* on page 3. (Possible answer: The lot is dirty.)

Pages 6–8, Chapter 2

COLLABORATE **Make Predictions** Discuss the meaning of "cleared away" and "pull your weight." Have partners use the phrases in their own sentences: The lot looks better after trash is cleared away. If you do not work, you are not pulling your weight. Then have them make predictions about what will happen to the lot.

Intermediate Review the sequence words *first, then,* and *finally.* Have students retell the steps to clean up the lot using the pictures: First, the community asked permission to build the garden. Then, the city council approved the plan. Finally, the city council removed the trash.

COLLABORATE **Advanced High** On page 6, Rosa's dad says, "Hard work builds character and self-esteem." Have partners discuss it. (Possible answer: Working hard makes me feel good about myself.)

Pages 9–15, Chapters 3–4

Discuss the picture. *How does the community solve the raccoon problem?* (They put up a fence and build a gate.)

Beginning Read pages 13–14 with students. Restate the sentences as needed. Discuss how Rosa feels and help students describe: Rosa feels excited. Rosa smiles at friends and family. She is happy.

Intermediate Have students describe how Rosa and others solved the problem: Rosa tells her teacher. The teacher says it could be animals, so Rosa goes to the library to get a book on animal tracks.

Advanced/Advanced High Have partners compare their prediction in Chapter 2 with what happens in the story.

Respond to Reading Have partners discuss the questions on page 16 and answer them using the new vocabulary.

Fluency: Accuracy

Model reading pages 11–12 aloud with accuracy. Then read with students. For more practice, have students record their voices while they read a few times. Have them play their best recording.

Paired Read: "Fresh from the City"

Make Connections: Write About It

Before students write, discuss the questions on page 19 and help them respond using: A garden brings the community together. Help students find text evidence. Reread the title and paragraphs 1 and 2 on page 18, and the last paragraph on page 14.

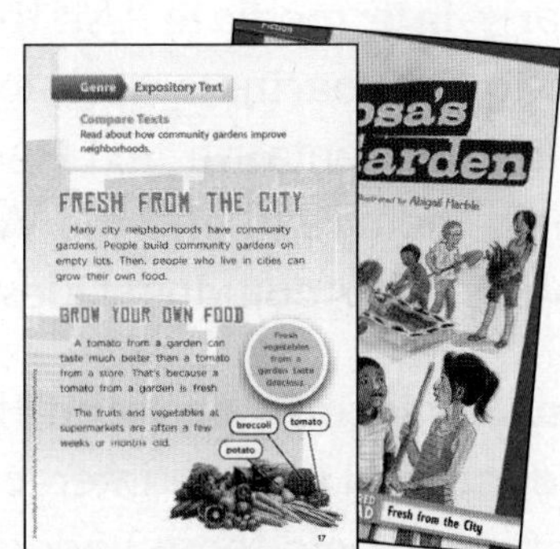

ELL Leveled Reader

Build Knowledge: Make Connections

Talk About the Text Have partners discuss how their actions affect others.

Write About the Text Have students add their ideas to their Build Knowledge pages of their reader's notebooks.

Self-Selected Reading

Have students choose another realistic fiction story from the online **Leveled Reader Library** or read the online **Differentiated Text,** "It's Showtime!".

FOCUS ON LITERARY ELEMENTS

Have students complete the activity on page 20 to research and use idioms.

LITERATURE CIRCLES

Ask students to conduct a literature circle using the Thinkmark questions to guide the discussion.

FORMATIVE ASSESSMENT

STUDENT CHECK-IN

Have partners share their answers to Respond to Reading. Ask students to reflect on their learning using the Check-In routine.

LEVEL UP

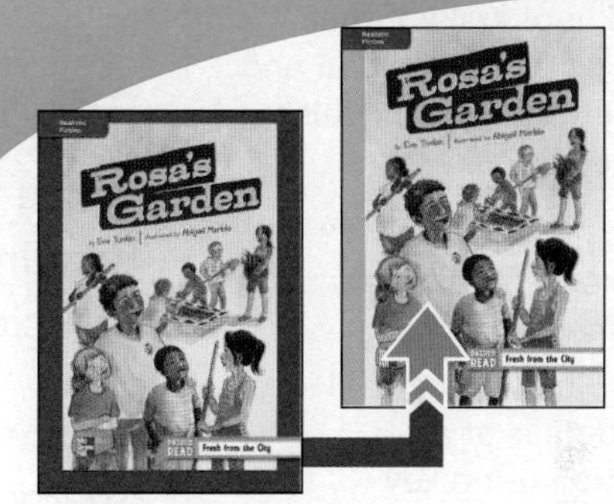

IF students read the **ELL Level** fluently and answered the questions,

THEN pair them with students who have proficiently read the On Level and have students

- echo-read the On Level main selection with their partner.
- list words they find difficult.
- discuss these words with their partners.

Access Complex Text

The On Level challenges students by including more **domain-specific words** and **complex sentence structures.**

LEARNING GOALS

We can read and understand argumentative text.

OBJECTIVES

Determine the central, or main, idea of a text and explain how it is supported by relevant, or key, details; summarize the text.

Determine the meaning of general academic and domain-specific words or phrases in a text relevant to a grade 4 topic or subject area.

Review the key ideas expressed and explain their own ideas and understanding in light of the discussion.

Entrepreneurs are people who start new businesses. Entrepreneurs do not know if their new businesses will be successful and earn a profit. Identify ways in which starting a business is risky for entrepreneurs.

LANGUAGE OBJECTIVES

Students will explain the central idea and important details of an argumentative text using key vocabulary.

ELA ACADEMIC LANGUAGE

- *details*
- Cognate: *detalle*

MATERIALS

Reading/Writing Companion, pp. 64-67

Online Scaffolded Shared Read, "Dollars and Sense"

Visual Vocabulary Cards

Online ELL Visual Vocabulary Cards

DIGITAL TOOLS

MULTIMODAL

Have students read along to the audio of the selection to develop comprehension and practice fluency and pronunciation.

"Dollars and Sense"

Prepare to Read

Build Background Discuss with students types of businesses that are in their community. Have students discuss what the businesses do, such as the kinds of things they sell or services they provide, using: *In my community, businesses ____.* Read the title "Dollars and Sense" and the heading and discuss that the meaning of the word *sense* in the title is "being reasonable" and elicit that the subtitle tells that some businesses want to also help people.

Vocabulary Use the **Visual Vocabulary Cards** to pre-teach the vocabulary: *compassionate, routine, undertaking, innovative, enterprise, funds, process,* and *exceptional.* Use the online **ELL Visual Vocabulary Cards** to teach additional words from the Shared Read: *desire, donated, encouraged, expanded, immediately,* and *purchased.* (Cognates: *deseo, donó, inmediatamente*)

Set Purpose *Today we will read "Dollars and Sense" and focus on the central idea and relevant details. As we read, think about how starting a business can help others.*

Read the Text

Select the **Scaffolded Shared Read** or the Shared Read in the **Reading/Writing Companion**, based on students' language proficiency.

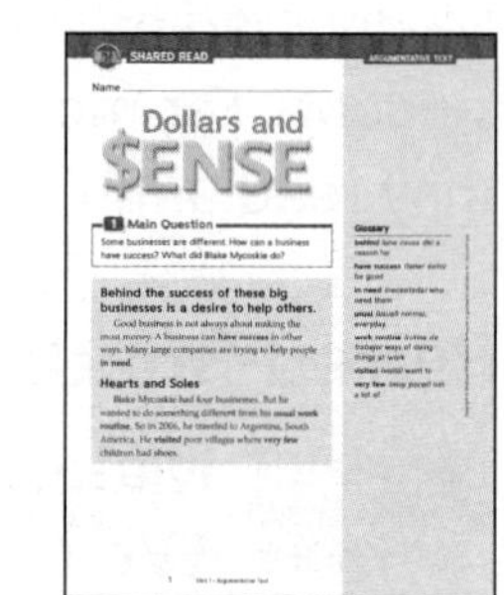

Scaffolded Shared Read, Lexile 610L

Beginning/Early-Intermediate Use the online **Scaffolded Shared Read** to help partners work together to read and understand an argumentative text. Remind them to use the Glossary to help them read and the Word Bank to help them answer the Main and Additional Questions.

Intermediate/Advanced Advanced High Read the text with students and use the Interactive Question-Response Routine to help them understand an argumentative text.

Reading/Writing Companion, Lexile 800L

Page 65

Paragraph 1 Read the text with students and review Vocabulary words *desire* and *compassionate*. Explain that the phrase "bottom line" refers to making money or profit. Ask: *What does the paragraph tell that compassionate businesses do?* (make money and help others) *Which sentence tells a detail about what compassionate companies do?* (last sentence)

Have partners describe the **central idea** and add **relevant details** of the paragraph: The central idea is that some companies make money and help others. One detail is that compassionate companies look for unusual ways to help people.

Paragraphs 2–5 Read the text with students and review Vocabulary words *routine, undertaking, innovative, immediately,* and *purchased. What did Blake Mycoskie do after his trip to Argentina?* (start a shoe company and give shoes to kids in need) *What does the one-for-one program do?* (For every pair of shoes the company sells, it gives a pair away.)

Intermediate *What details tell how Mycoskie began his business?* He used his own money to start the company. The shoes look like shoes that workers in Argentina traditionally wear and the shoes slip on.

COLLABORATE **Advanced/Advanced High** Have partners discuss the meaning of *innovative* and explain why the author uses the word to describe the one-for-one program. (Possible answer: *Innovative* means "new and creative." The one-for-one program is innovative because companies usually do not give away the same number of products they sell.)

Page 66

Paragraphs 1–2 Read the text with students and review the Vocabulary words *donated* and *expanded.* Ask: *What clues tell that the business expanded?* (The company is also selling eyeglasses.)

Paragraphs 3–5 Read aloud the heading and discuss "giving back." Elicit that it means to give something in return for help people received from the community. Discuss examples of giving back, such as volunteering. Read the text and review Vocabulary words *enterprise, funds,* and *process. What enterprise did the Hard Rock Cafe start?* (donating to charity) Explain that a motto is a short sentence or phrase that expresses a belief or goal of a person or group. *What does the motto "Love All, Serve All" mean?* (The company wants to help everyone.) *Does the company have one way to raise money?* (No, it encourages workers to raise money for their community.)

COLLABORATE **Intermediate** Have partners retell one way the Hard Rock Cafe raises money, using sequence words: First, stars design shirts. Next, the company sells shirts on the Internet. Finally, the company donates some of the money to charity.

COLLABORATE **Advanced/Advanced High** Have partners discuss whether they think it is a good idea for a company to have one idea or different ways to raise money for charity. (Answers will vary.)

Page 67

Paragraphs 1–2 Read the text with students and review Vocabulary word *exceptional.* Discuss with students the meaning of the phrase *put on,* meaning "to produce," and discuss other meanings of the phrase, such as "to dress" or "to increase."

Intermediate *What does* put on *mean in the second sentence?* The phrase *put on* in the second sentence means to produce. *How is the first paragraph related to the one before it?* (It tells an example of how workers in one Hard Rock Café helped raise money for charity.)

COLLABORATE Have partners discuss the author's opinion about business. Then have them express their opinion about whether they agree or disagree with the author. (Possible answers: Helping others is good business; I agree with the author's opinion because it is always good to help others.)

COLLABORATE Read the **heading** and caption for the **bar graph**. *How are the charities listed?* (by amount of money raised) Have partners describe the information in the bar graph, such as the charity that raised the most money.

FORMATIVE ASSESSMENT

STUDENT CHECK-IN

Have partners retell the important ideas in the text. Ask them to reflect using the Check-In routine.

LEARNING GOALS

- **We can read and understand argumentative text by identifying the central idea and relevant details.**
- **We can identify run-on sentences.**

OBJECTIVES

Paraphrase portions of a text read aloud or information presented in diverse media and formats, including visually, quantitatively, and orally.

Produce complete sentences, recognizing and correcting inappropriate fragments and run-ons.

LANGUAGE OBJECTIVES

Students will discuss the central idea and relevant details using key vocabulary.

ELA ACADEMIC LANGUAGE

- *central idea, details, support*
- Cognates: *idea central, detalles, soportar*

MATERIALS

Reading/Writing Companion, pp. 64-67, 68-69

Online Scaffolded Shared Read, p. 3

Online Shared Read Writing Frames, p. 3

Online Language Development Cards, 1B

Online Language Development Practice, pp. 4-6

Online Language Transfers Handbook, pp. 15-19

"Dollars and Sense"

Text Reconstruction

Focus on a single chunk of text to support comprehension and language development across the four domains:

1. Read aloud "The Bottom Line" on page 67 in the **Reading/Writing Companion** while students listen.
2. Write the following on the board, providing definitions as needed: *innovative, give back, own, profit,* and *good business.* Instruct students to listen for them as you read the paragraph a second time.
3. Read the paragraph a third time. Tell students to listen and take notes.
4.  COLLABORATE Have students work with a partner to reconstruct the text from their notes. Help them write complete sentences as needed.
5. Have students look at the original text. Ask them to tell what the paragraph is mostly about. (It is important for companies to help others.) Tell students that this is the central, or the most important, idea and that they are going to examine the relevant details.
6. *What do we learn from the first sentence?* (Companies are thinking of ways to help their community.) Point out and read the penultimate sentence. *How does this detail support the central idea?* (tells that helping others is important) Read the last sentence. *Does this sentence support the central idea?* (Yes) *How?* (tells that helping others is good business)
7. Have students compare their text reconstructions to the original text. Have them check whether they also included relevant details.

Beginning Have students follow along in the Reading/Writing Companion as you read the text aloud. Have them circle the words from Step 2 as they hear them.

Grammar in Context: Run-On Sentences

Notice the Form Display this sentence from the text, as shown.

> *In 2006, he traveled to Argentina, in South America, and while he was there he learned to sail and to dance.*

Cover the word *and,* and then read the sentence aloud. Discuss with students that the sentence is a run-on sentence because it is missing a connecting word. Explain what makes a run-on sentence: it has two or more independent clauses that have not been combined correctly. Ask: *What are the two independent clauses?* ("In 2006, he traveled to Argentina, in South America"; "he learned to sail and to dance") *What do they describe?* (The man went to Argentina and learned to sail and dance there.) *How can we correct the run-on sentence?* (add *and* before *while*) Uncover the word *and,* then read the sentence aloud. *What kind of word is* and*?* (conjunction) *What does the word* and *do?* (connects the independent clauses) Have students copy and label the sentence parts in their notebooks.

Apply and Extend Have partners rewrite the run-on sentence as two independent clauses. Check their work and provide corrective feedback.

For additional practice, see Language Development Cards, Lesson 1B, and Language Development Practice, pages 4-6.

Independent Time

Vocabulary Building Have students build glossaries.

Beginning/Early Intermediate Have students complete the Glossary Activities in the **Scaffolded Shared Read**.

Intermediate/Advanced/Advanced High After students add the vocabulary from **Reading/Writing Companion** pages 68-69 to the chart, have them scan the text for words or phrases they would like to learn and add to the chart.

Mixed Levels Pair students together: Beginning and Early-Intermediate students can teach words from their **Scaffolded Shared Read** glossaries. Intermediate and Advanced/Advanced High students can teach self-selected words or phrases.

WORD/PHRASE	DEFINE	EXAMPLE	ASK
charity	group or organization that helps people	The students gave books to a charity.	What can people give to a charity?

COLLABORATE **Shared Read Writing Frames** Use the online leveled **Shared Read Writing Frames** for "Dollars and Sense" to provide students with additional oral and written practice.

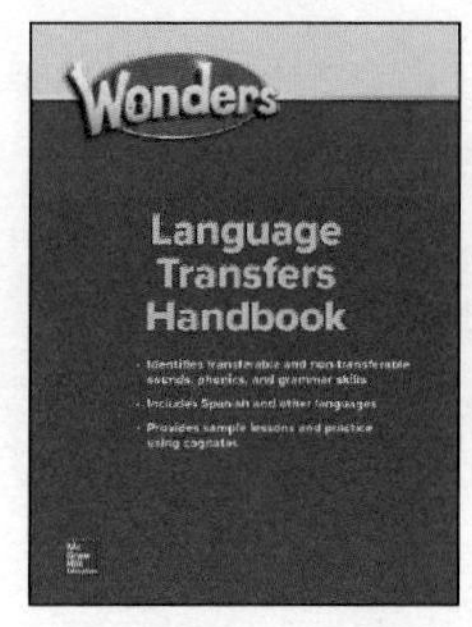

Language Transfers Handbook, Grammar Transfers pp. 15-19

DIGITAL TOOLS

For additional support, use the online activities.

Grammar Video

Grammar Song

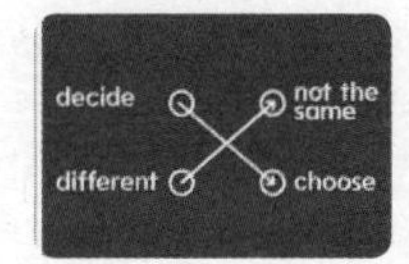

Vocabulary Activity

STUDENT CHECK-IN

Text reconstruction Have partners share their notes. Have students reflect on their work using the Check-In routine.

Grammar in Context Have partners share their corrected sentences. Have students reflect on their work using the Check-In routine.

LEARNING GOALS

Read We can read and understand an argumentative text.

Reread We can reread to analyze text, craft, and structure.

OBJECTIVES

Refer to details and examples in a text when explaining what the text says explicitly and when drawing inferences from the text.

Interpret information presented visually, orally, or quantitatively and explain how the information contributes to an understanding of the text in which it appears.

Review the key ideas expressed and explain their own ideas and understanding in light of the discussion.

Entrepreneurs are people who start new businesses. Entrepreneurs do not know if their new businesses will be successful and earn a profit. Identify ways in which starting a business is risky for entrepreneurs.

LANGUAGE OBJECTIVES

Students will narrate by answering questions using content area vocabulary.

Students will explain author's purpose using academic vocabulary.

ELA ACADEMIC LANGUAGE

- *author's purpose*
- Cognate: *propósito del autor/de la autora*

MATERIALS

Literature Anthology, pp. 40-43

Visual Vocabulary Cards

Online ELL Anchor Text Support BLMS, pp. 7-8

DIGITAL TOOLS

MULTIMODAL

Have students read along with the audio of the selection to develop comprehension and practice fluency and pronunciation.

Kids in Business

Prepare to Read

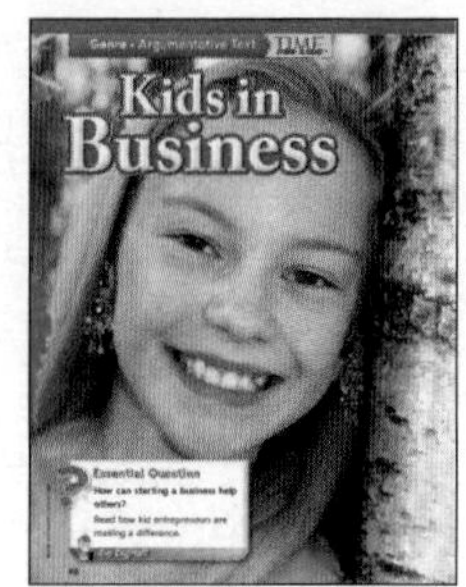

Literature Anthology, Lexile 790L

Build Background Explain that entrepreneurs are people who start a new business. Invite students to share what they know about starting a business. Then discuss with students if they think starting a business is easy or difficult, and explain why. *I think starting a business is easy/difficult because ____.*

Vocabulary Use the **Visual Vocabulary Cards** to review the vocabulary: *compassionate, routine, undertaking, innovative, enterprise, funds, process,* and *exceptional.*

Set Purpose *Today we will read an argumentative text about kid entrepreneurs. As we read, think about how starting a business can help others.*

Have students listen to the audio summary of the text, which is available in multiple languages.

Read

Literature Anthology, pp. 40-43

Use the **Interactive Question-Response Routine** to help students read and discuss ***Kids in Business***.

Beginning Help students discuss in complete sentences. Provide sentence frames: Hayleigh wears hearing aids. She started to make charms for hearing aids.

Intermediate Ask students to respond in complete sentences and add details. Provide sentence starters as needed: Since she was 18 months old, Hayleigh has been wearing hearing aids. She had an idea to make charms for hearing aids.

Advanced/Advanced High Have students respond in complete sentences and add details.

Independent Reading Practice Have mixed level pairs complete Online Anchor Text Support and share their responses with the group.

Reread

Use with **Reading/Writing Companion,** pages 76–78.

Literature Anthology, page 41

COLLABORATE **Author's Purpose** Read the text and restate it with students. Have them ask about words or phrases that are unfamiliar and define them for clarification, such as *entrepreneurs, charm, make a difference, foundation,* and *stamp out. What does the text tell you about entrepreneurs?* (It takes a lot of work to start a business and kids who do it are amazing.) *What did Hayleigh Scott do?* (started a business that makes hearing aids look like earrings) Have partners discuss why they think the author includes Hayleigh and Joshua. (Possible answer: They were both young entrepreneurs, and it takes a lot of work to start a business and run an organization. The author thinks the kids are amazing.)

Beginning Read the first two paragraphs with students. Discuss with them why some people use a hearing aid and describe a charm using the photographs to provide visual support. Help partners describe them: Some people cannot hear well. They need a hearing aid. The charm hangs from the hearing aid. *What does Hayleigh sell?* Hayleigh sells charms for the hearing aids. *Who helps Hayleigh?* Hayleigh's family helps her. Have partners identify the sentence that gives the information.

Intermediate Discuss with students the meaning of the phrase *stand out* and elicit that it means "to be seen easily." Then ask: *What did Hayleigh want to stand out?* (She wanted the hearing aid to stand out.) Have partners discuss the reason Hayleigh wanted the hearing aid to stand out. (Possible answer: She was proud of wearing the hearing aid.) *What did Joshua Williams do?* (started a foundation that gives food to people who need it) *Which words describe Joshua Williams and his foundation?* (youngest, compassionate) *What do the local businesses do?* (donate food and give help)

Advanced/Advanced High Discuss with students the meaning of the phrase *bring to life* and read the last sentence in the first paragraph with students. Have partners restate the sentence. (Possible answer: Her mother created a charm from Hayleigh's drawings of charms.) Discuss the meaning of *patent* in the last sentence. *Why do you think the author includes this information?* (Possible answer: The author thinks that Hayleigh is amazing.)

Literature Anthology, page 43

COLLABORATE

Author's Purpose Read the text on page 43 with students. Discuss with them the meaning of the word *literacy*—"the ability to read and write"—and what the phrase *global literacy* refers to. Help them describe: *Global literacy* refers to helping everybody in the world learn to read and write. *What is Better World Books?* (an organization that helps global literacy) *What does it do?* (collects and sells unwanted books at a discount or donates books to people who need them) *What happens to the money it makes?* (supports global literacy) Read the title of the bar graph and explain that the word *cumulative* means "adding together everything from before." Read the bar graph with students to discuss the information.

Beginning Read the bar graph with students. *How much money did the group raise in the year 2010?* In 2010 the group raised eight million dollars. *Do the amounts increase or decrease each year?* The amount increases each year. Review the meaning of the word cumulative and ask: *Does the amount for 2006 also include the amount from 2005?* (yes)

Intermediate *What does the amount for the year 2008 show?* The amount at 2008 shows the total amount from years 2005 to 2008. *How do you know?* I know that the word *cumulative* means adding together everything from before.

Advanced/Advanced High Have partners retell the information on the bar graph. *Do you think the bar graph shows that it is good to donate things to charity? Why or why not?* (Possible answer: I think the bar graph shows that it is good to donate things to charity because the group made a lot of money from selling the books people donated.)

FORMATIVE ASSESSMENT

STUDENT CHECK-IN

Read Have partners share their responses to the Anchor Text questions. Then have them reflect using the Check-In routine.

Reread Have partners share responses and text evidence on Reading/Writing Companion pages 76–78. Then have them reflect using the Check-In routine to fill in the bars.

LEARNING GOALS

- **We can read and understand argumentative text by identifying the central idea and relevant details.**
- **We can identify run-on sentences.**

OBJECTIVES

Paraphrase portions of a text read aloud or information presented in diverse media and formats, including visually, quantitatively, and orally.

Produce complete sentences, recognizing and correcting inappropriate fragments and run-ons.

LANGUAGE OBJECTIVES

Students will discuss the central idea and relevant details using key vocabulary.

ELA ACADEMIC LANGUAGE

- *central idea, details, identify, support*
- Cognates: *idea central, detalles, identificar, soportar*

MATERIALS

Literature Anthology, pp. 40-43

Online Language Development Cards, 5A-5B

Online Language Development Practice, pp. 25-30

Online Language Transfers Handbook, pp. 15-19

Kids in Business

Text Reconstruction

Focus on a single chunk of text to support comprehension and language development across the four domains.

1. Read aloud the "For the Love of a Good Book" section on page 43 in the **Literature Anthology** while students listen.
2. Write the following on the board, providing definitions as needed: *make a difference, donate, charity, discount, literacy, total, amount.* Instruct students to listen for them as you read the paragraph a second time.
3. Read the paragraph a third time while students listen and take notes.
4. COLLABORATE Have students work with a partner to reconstruct the text from their notes. Help them write complete sentences as needed.
5. Have students look at the original text. *What is the paragraph about?* (how Better World Books makes money for global literacy) Tell students they are going to describe the central idea and relevant details.
6. *What details does the section tell about how Better World Books helps global literacy?* (The group raises money by selling donated books and gives books away to people who need them.) *What is the central idea?* (People can donate goods instead of money to help others.) *What does Better World Books donate?* (The organization donates money it makes selling books and gives away books.)
7. Have students compare their reconstructions to the original text and check whether they also included words that tell details of how the group helps communities.

Beginning Allow students to follow along in their Literature Anthologies as you read the text aloud. Have them point to the words from Step 2 as they hear them.

Apply Author's Craft: Graphs

Review with students that authors use graphs to visualize data, or information in a text. Have students discuss the graph. Model first: *On page 43, the graph shows how much money Better World Books made. What does the graph show about the business?* (Possible answer: the business is successful) Have students write a sentence using information from the graph. Provide a sentence frame. The bar graph shows that in _____ Better World Banks made_____. Its funds increased from _____ to _____.

Grammar in Context: Deconstruct a Sentence

Write this sentence from page 42 on the board: *Cecilia took two sewing lessons. Then, she says, she just started sewing, ___ she hasn't stopped since.* Facilitate deconstructing this sentence for better comprehension:

- *The second sentence is a run-on sentence. It is missing a conjunction. What words are conjunctions?* (and, but, or) *What types of sentences have conjunctions?* (compound sentences)
- Then discuss what makes a run-on sentence: it has two or more independent clauses that have not been combined correctly.
- Ask questions to discuss: *What are the two independent clauses in the second sentence?* (she just started sewing; she hasn't stopped since) *What do they describe?* (the girl started sewing, she has continued to sew from then on)
- *How can we combine the two independent clauses?* (Add *and* before "she hasn't stopped since.")
- Read the original sentences on page 42 and have students check their work. Then discuss what the sentence is about. Note that the word *since* refers to the time Cecilia took sewing lessons. Then restate sentences. (Possible answer: Cecilia started sewing after she took two lessons and she is still sewing today.)

For more practice, see Language Development Cards, Lessons 5A-5B, and Language Development Practice, pages 25-30.

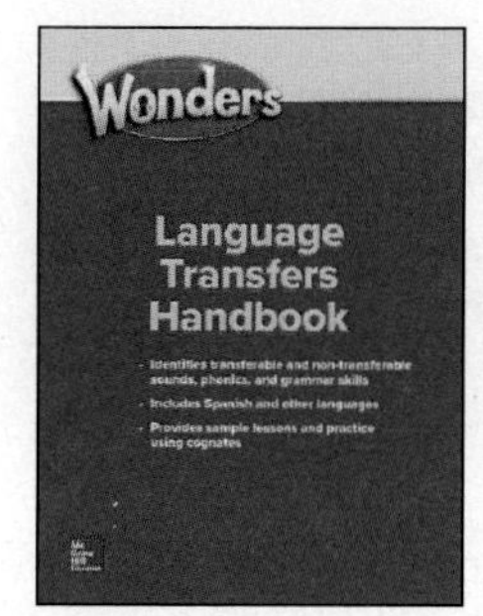

Language Transfers Handbook, Grammar Transfers pp. 15-19

Independent Time

Vocabulary Building Have students identify economic terms from the selection: *business, charities, donate* and *donations, entrepreneurs, foundation, fund, organizations, patent, program, sell.* Have them write each term on an index card and define the word on the back. They can take turns grouping related terms and explaining them.

Beginning Allow students to write clues or draw a picture for each word.

Intermediate/Advanced/Advanced High Have students include some of the self-selected words and content-area words they added to their glossaries.

COLLABORATE **Connecting Words** Help partners use connecting words to combine phrases and clauses in sentences. Have them select one kid they read about in *Kids in Business* and write sentences to describe him or her. Then have them rewrite the sentences using connecting words, such as *and, so, but,* or other conjunctions or connecting words they know. Provide an example and have them use a chart to rewrite the sentences:

SENTENCES	CONNECTING WORD	COMBINED SENTENCE
Joshua wanted to help people. He started a foundation.	so	Joshua wanted to help people, so he stared a foundation.

FORMATIVE ASSESSMENT

STUDENT CHECK-IN

Text Reconstruction Ask partners to share their notes. Have them reflect using the Check-In routine.

Grammar in Context Have students reflect on their deconstructions using the Check-In routine.

LEARNING GOALS

We can apply strategies and skills to read argumentative text.

OBJECTIVES

Determine the central, or main, idea of a text and explain how it is supported by key details; summarize the text.

Review the key ideas expressed and explain their own ideas and understanding in light of the discussion.

Use common, grade-appropriate Greek and Latin affixes and roots as clues to the meaning of a word.

LANGUAGE OBJECTIVES

Students will explain the central idea and key details using academic language.

ELA ACADEMIC LANGUAGE

- *suffix, main idea, key details*
- Cognates: *sufijo, detalles*

MATERIALS

Online ELL Genre Passage, "A Helping Hand"

"A Helping Hand"

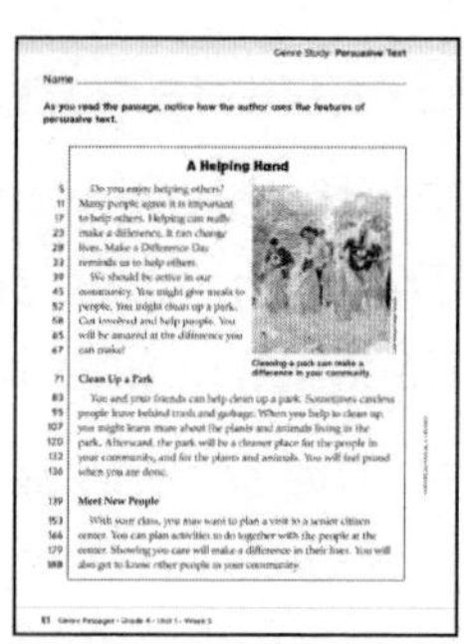

Genre Passage
Lexile 600L

Prepare to Read

Build Background Read the title and discuss the meaning of "a helping hand." Then discuss with students different ways they can make a difference or help the community.

Encourage students to share their own experiences of helping a group or participating in activities, such as recycling or cleaning up a park.

Vocabulary Use the Define/Example/Ask routine to preteach difficult words or unfamiliar concepts, such as *active, senior citizen center, appreciate, healthful, food bank, donations, grateful, creativity,* and *clinic* (cognates: *activo, apreciar, creatividad, clínica*). Invite students to add new vocabulary to their glossaries.

Set Purpose *Today we are going to read "A Helping Hand" and focus on the central idea and relevant details. As we read, think about how starting a business can help others.*

Read the Text

Page E1, Introduction

COLLABORATE **Beginning** Read the first paragraph with students. Restate sentences as needed. Discuss the meaning of the phrase "helping hand." *Which words tell you about what "helping hand" means?* (help others, helping out) Help partners describe the phrase using: A helping hand means helping others.

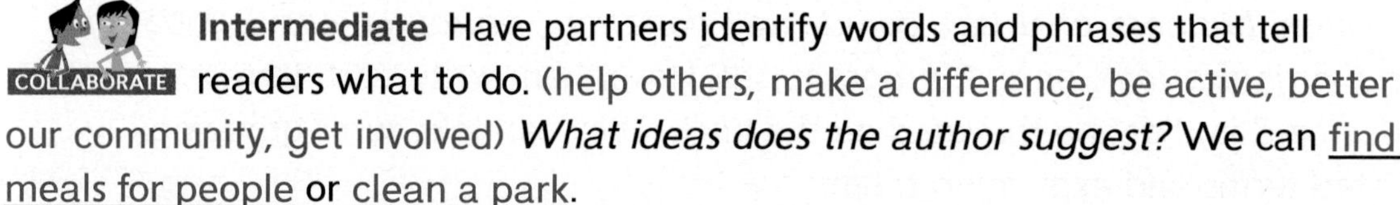

COLLABORATE **Intermediate** Have partners identify words and phrases that tell readers what to do. (help others, make a difference, be active, better our community, get involved) *What ideas does the author suggest?* We can find meals for people or clean a park.

Advanced/Advanced High *Which verb shows the author's strong belief in helping out?* (*should*) *When do you use the word* should? (Possible answer: to describe something that a person thinks needs to be done)

Page E1, "Clean Up a Park"

Suffixes Explain that the *suffix -less* means "without" and use it to discuss the meaning of the word *careless* with students. *What is the suffix?* (-less) *What does the suffix* -less *mean?* (without) *What does the word* careless *mean?* (without caring)

Beginning Read the paragraph with students. Restate sentences as needed. *How does cleaning a park help you?* We can learn about plants and animals.

Intermediate *What do careless people do?* Careless people leave trash and garbage behind in the parks.

Advanced/Advanced High Have partners describe the effects of cleaning up parks. (Possible answer: By cleaning up parks, we can learn about plants and animals that are in the park.)

Page E1, "Meet New People"

Beginning Read the paragraph with students. Restate sentences as needed. Discuss what happens at a senior citizen center and who uses it. *Who are senior citizens?* (elderly people) *How can you help at a senior citizen center?* I can visit and do activities.

Intermediate *How can you help at a senior citizen center?* My classmates and I can do activities with the senior citizens.

Advanced/Advanced High *Why is the heading of the section "Meet New People"?* (You can meet new people at a senior citizen center.)

Page E2, "Feed Someone in Need"

Beginning Read the paragraph with students. Restate sentences as needed. Discuss what happens at a food bank and who uses it. *What foods can you collect?* We can collect cans, fruit, and vegetables. *What is a food bank?* A food bank collects food.

Intermediate Have partners describe what they can do at a food bank: I can collect canned goods and fruits and vegetables.

Advanced/Advanced High *How can working at a food bank teach you about teamwork?* (Possible answer: You can learn teamwork because people work in groups to collect food.)

Page E2, "Be Creative"

Beginning Read the paragraph with students. Restate sentences as needed. Help partners describe ideas for things they can do: We can [make] an activity book.

Intermediate Read the caption with students and have them describe the **bar graph**. Discuss the meanings of *corporation, foundation,* and *individual. What does this bar measure?* The percentage of donations groups give. *Which group gave the most?* (individuals) *What does the **graph** show about what people can do?* The graph shows that people can make a big difference.

Respond to Reading

Use the following instruction to help students answer the questions on page E3.

1. **Central Idea and Relevant Details** Have students identify details the author gives. *What words express a benefit of cleaning up the park?* (good way to learn, helping to clean, useful)
2. **Text Features: Headings and Graphs** Read the labels on the bar graph with students. *What information is at the bottom?* (source of donations) *What information is along the side?* (percentage of donations from each source)
3. Have students describe the central idea. *What is the author's opinion?* (It is important to help others.)

Fluency Have partners take turns reading the passage.

Build Knowledge: Make Connections

Talk About the Text Have partners discuss how starting a business can help others.

Write About the Text Have students add their ideas to their Build Knowledge pages of their reader's notebooks.

FORMATIVE ASSESSMENT

STUDENT CHECK-IN

Have partners share their responses on page E3 and reflect using the Check-In routine.

IF students read the **ELL Level** of the **Genre Passage** fluently and answered the questions,

THEN pair them with students who have proficiently read the **On Level**. Have them

- partner read the **On Level** passage;
- summarize main idea and details.

LEARNING GOALS

We can apply strategies and skills to read an opinion text.

OBJECTIVES

Determine the central, or main, idea of a text and explain how it is supported by relevant, or key, details; summarize the text.

Review the key ideas expressed and explain their own ideas and understanding in light of the discussion.

Use context to confirm or self-correct word recognition and understanding, rereading as necessary.

LANGUAGE OBJECTIVES

Students will inform about how starting a business can help others using key vocabulary.

ELA ACADEMIC LANGUAGE

- *detail*
- Cognate: *detalle*

MATERIALS

Leveled Reader *Start Small, Think Big*

Online Differentiated Texts, "Helping People"

Visual Vocabulary Cards

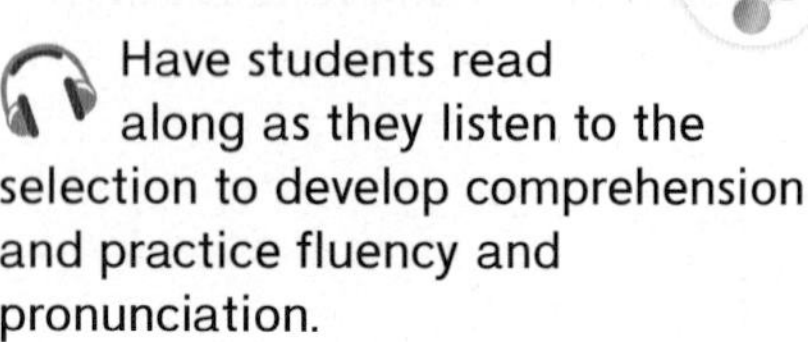

DIGITAL TOOLS

Have students read along as they listen to the selection to develop comprehension and practice fluency and pronunciation.

Start Small, Think Big

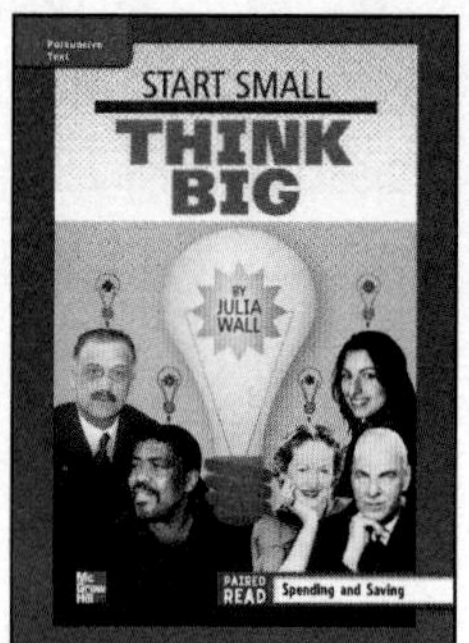

Leveled Reader
Lexile 710L

Prepare to Read

Build Background Review the Essential Question, *How can starting a business help others?* Have students share what they know about businesses that help their community.

Choral Read the title and discuss its meaning, eliciting examples from students. Read the headings in the selections with them. Then have students predict what they will read about.

Vocabulary Use the routine on the **Visual Vocabulary Cards** to preteach ELL Vocabulary *borrowed, donated, loaned,* and *operate*. Use the glossary on page 19. Have students add words to their glossaries.

Set Purpose Today we are going to read an opinion text called *Start Small, Think Big*. As we read, think about how starting a business can help others.

Read the Text

Pages 2–5, Chapter 1

COLLABORATE **Beginning** Read page 2 with students. Restate sentences as needed. What do entrepreneurs do? They start businesses. Have partners describe what people need to start a business: People need ideas/money.

Intermediate *What is someone who starts a business?* (an entrepreneur) *What do they need to start a business?* Entrepreneurs need good ideas and money to start their business.

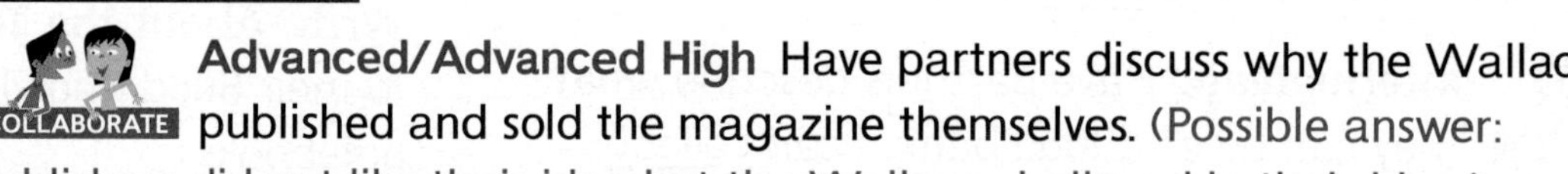

COLLABORATE **Advanced/Advanced High** Have partners discuss why the Wallaces published and sold the magazine themselves. (Possible answer: Publishers did not like their idea but the Wallaces believed in their idea.)

Pages 6–8, Chapter 2

Beginning Read pages 6–7 with students. Restate sentences as needed. *Who was Alvin Ailey?* He was a dancer. *What did he start?* (a dance company)

COLLABORATE **Intermediate** *How did Alvin Ailey become a dancer?* (He trained with a teacher.) Discuss the meaning of *trained*. *What is a similar word on page 7?* (*studied*) Have partners discuss an activity they or someone they know train for and describe what they do: When I train for the [race] I ____.

Advanced/Advanced High *How did Alvin Ailey give back to his community?* (He created programs to teach kids to dance and shared his experiences.)

Pages 9–11, Chapter 3

COLLABORATE **Beginning** Read page 9 with students. Restate sentences as needed. Define the word loan to help students describe Giannini. *How did*

Giannini help San Franciscans? He loaned money to people. *What did he start?* He started a bank.

Intermediate *What happened in 1906 in San Francisco?* (An earthquake destroyed many parts of the city.) *How did Giannini help?* (His bank loaned money to people to help businesses rebuild.)

Advanced/Advanced High *The author says Giannini is "compassionate." Which details support it?* (Possible answer: He helped by starting a bank that loaned money to ordinary people.)

Chapter 4, Pages 12–14

Reread Have partners reread the chapter and describe the central idea and details. (Possible answer: Entrepreneurs work hard to make their ideas succeed. They often help their communities.)

Respond to Reading Have partners discuss the questions on page 15 and use new vocabulary to answer them.

Fluency: Phrasing, Speed

Read pages 2–3 with appropriate phrasing and speed. Then read the passage with students. Have students record their voices while they read a few times. Have them play their recordings and choose the best one.

Paired Read: "Spending and Saving"

Make Connections: Write About It

Analytical Writing

Before students write, use frames to discuss the questions on page 18: A budget is a set amount of money to save and spend. Help students understand entrepreneurs who give back to their communities.

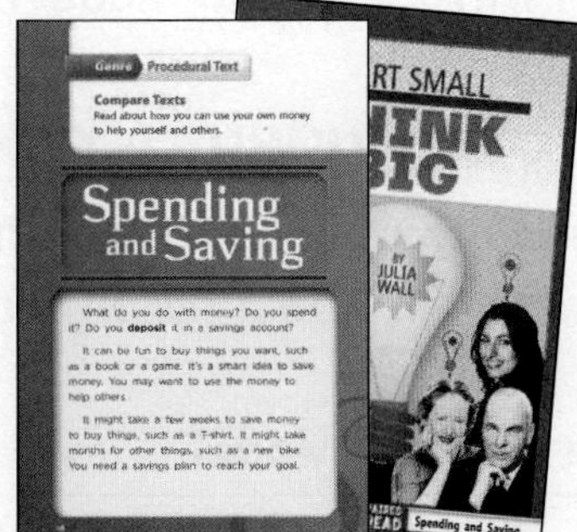

ELL Leveled Reader

Build Knowledge: Make Connections

Talk About the Text Have partners discuss how starting a business can help others.

Write About the Text Have students add their ideas to their Build Knowledge pages of their reader's notebooks.

Self-Selected Reading

Have students choose another opinion text from the online **Leveled Reader Library** or read the online **Differentiated Text,** "Helping People."

FOCUS ON SOCIAL STUDIES

Have students complete the activity on page 20 to practice making a plan to raise money.

LITERATURE CIRCLES

Ask students to conduct a literature circle using the Thinkmark questions to guide the discussion.

FORMATIVE ASSESSMENT

STUDENT CHECK-IN

Have partners share their answers to Respond to Reading. Ask students to reflect on their learning using the Check-In routine.

IF students read the **ELL Level** fluently and answered the questions,

THEN pair them with students who have proficiently read the On Level and have students

- echo-read the On Level main selection with their partners;
- list words they find difficult;
- discuss these words with their partners.

Access Complex Text

The On Level challenges students by including more **domain-specific words** and **complex sentence structures.**

LEARNING GOALS

- **We can identify a claim and relevant evidence.**
- **We can analyze a student model and student model sources.**

OBJECTIVES

Explain how an author uses reasons and evidence to support particular points of view.

Integrate information from two texts on the same topic in order to write or speak about the subject knowledgeably.

Draw evidence from literary or informational texts to support analysis, reflection, and research.

LANGUAGE OBJECTIVES

Students will discuss features of an argumentative writing using academic language.

ELA ACADEMIC LANGUAGE

- *paragraph, claim, source, relevant, evidence*
- Cognates: *párrafo, relevante, evidencia*

MATERIALS

Online ELL Extended Writing Resources BLMs:

- Maria's Model, pp. 1-3
- Analyze Maria's Model, pp. 4-5

Online Student Model Sources

Reading/Writing Companion, pp. 87-89

DIGITAL TOOLS

MULTIMODAL

Have students read along with Maria's Model to develop comprehension and build fluency.

Argumentative Writing

Make a Claim

Reread the paragraph on page 87 of **Reading/Writing Companion** with the students. Review with them that a claim clearly states the writer's opinion, or what the writer thinks or believes, about the topic and that the other sentences give details to support the claim. Have students describe using: The claim tells that everyone should evacuate during a natural disaster. The sentences explain what happens if people don't evacuate.

Compare Claims Write on the board: **Strong:** *If there is a natural disaster, such as a wildfire or hurricane, everyone should evacuate.* **Weak:** *People should evacuate.* Have students compare to elicit that the strong model gives specific information about when people need to evacuate.

Have partners describe what a claim tells about and compare the two claims.

Beginning Help partners describe using: The claim tells about what the writer thinks or feels about the topic. The weak model does not tell when people need to evacuate.

Intermediate Have partners describe: The claim tells about what the writer thinks or feels about a topic. The strong model is better because it tells when people should evacuate. The strong model gives specific information.

Advanced/Advanced High Have partners describe what a claim tells about and explain why the strong model is better than the weak model.

Analyze the Student Model and Sources

Analyze the Prompt Read the prompt on **Maria's Model** with students. Explain that the writer tells about his or her opinion in an argumentative essay.

Discuss the Student Model

Mixed Levels Use Maria's Model to read with students. Before reading, discuss *hurricane* and *evacuate* with students using the Glossary. After each paragraph, have mixed pairs of language proficiency levels ask and answer the questions with each other and share responses with the group.

Paragraph 1 *Where have hurricanes in the United States hit?* (all states on the Gulf and Atlantic coasts) *What is a category 5 hurricane?* (a storm with winds over 157 mph and strong storm surges) *When do people get an evacuation order?* (when there is a category 4 or 5 hurricane)

Paragraph 2 *What can happen after a storm?* (People can be left without power and drinking water, or houses can get flooded.) *What are some reasons people stay through a storm?* (They may don't have someone to help them leave or they don't want to leave their pets.) *How does Maria use the reasons?* (as evidence)

Paragraph 3 *What happened during Hurricane Rita?* (2.5 million people tried to evacuate and there was a 100-mile traffic jam. Some people ran out of gas or left their cars.) *How many people did the Department of Emergency Management try to evacuate for Hurricane Irma?* (6.3 million) *Why was this a problem?* (not enough police officers, dangerous roads)

Paragraph 4 *What happened to the writer's grandmother during Hurricane Harvey?* (She evacuated, and her house was destroyed.) *What is an evacuation plan?* (a plan to evacuate safely during an emergency) *Why are evacuation plans necessary?* (so people can get out safely, so they are prepared for an emergency) *Which sentence retells the claim?* (first sentence) *What does it tell?* (Maria doesn't think you can force people to evacuate.)

Analyze the Student Model: Organization

Analyze Organization Use **Analyze Maria's Model** to analyze the organization as you fill in the information with students.

- Point to the first column and discuss how the essay is organized. Elicit that the claim is in the first paragraph. Explain that a claim is one sentence that clearly answers the prompt and relevant evidence supports the claim. Point out that the conclusion retells the writer's claim, or opinion.
- Review that the claim tells the focus and purpose and the relevant evidence provides support to the writer's claims.
- Discuss with them the relevant evidence in the second paragraph. *What did Maria use for relevant evidence?* (The elderly and disabled may have no one to help them leave.) *What does the relevant evidence tell us about the claim?* (tells us reasons why people won't evacuate)

Mixed Levels Have partners complete columns 1 and 2 in Analyze Maria's Model.

Beginning Help partners identify the claim and relevant evidence using: The claim tells what the writer thinks about the topic. It is in the first paragraph. The relevant evidence gives information about the claim. Relevant evidence is in all the paragraphs.

Intermediate Have partners describe the claim and relevant evidence using: The relevant evidence tells about why it's hard to get people to evacuate. It explains the claim.

Advanced/Advanced High Have partners describe the claim and the relevant evidence.

Analyze the Student Model: Sources

Read the **Online Student Model Sources** with students. Have them underline the information Maria used.

Have partners complete the third column in Analyze Maria's Model. Discuss the following questions with students:

Paragraph 1 Point to paragraph 3 in Source 1 and paragraph 1 in Source 3. *What information did Maria use?* (that not everyone obeys evacuation orders and some evacuations put people in danger) Discuss with students that Maria used the information from Source 2 to explain the reasons for an evacuation order.

Paragraph 2 Discuss the information from Source 2. *What information did Maria use?* (different reasons why people stay during an evacuation) *How does she use this information?* (as support for her claim)

Paragraph 3 Discuss the information from Source 3. *What information did Maria use?* (information about the evacuation in Texas during Hurricane Rita) Elicit that Maria uses this relevant evidence to help her readers understand her claim better.

Paragraph 4 Discuss that Maria used Source 1 to remind them of her claim and identify it with them.

FORMATIVE ASSESSMENT

STUDENT CHECK-IN

Have partners share responses to Analyze Maria's Model. Ask students to reflect using the Check-in routine.

LEARNING GOALS

- **We can synthesize information from three sources to plan and organize an argumentative essay.**
- **We can draft and revise an argumentative essay.**

OBJECTIVES

Determine the central, or main, idea of a text and explain how it is supported by relevant, or key, details.

Introduce a topic or text clearly, state an opinion, and create an organizational structure in which related ideas are grouped to support the writer's purpose.

With guidance and support from peers and adults, develop and strengthen writing as needed by planning, revising, and editing.

LANGUAGE OBJECTIVES

Students will argue a claim by describing facts.

ELA ACADEMIC LANGUAGE

- *prompt, claim, evidence*
- Cognate: *evidencia*

MATERIALS

Reading/Writing Companion, pp. 90-97

Online ELL Extended Writing Resources BLMs:

- Glossary, p. 6
- My Writing Outline, pp. 7-8
- Draft: Relevant Evidence, p. 9

Online Language Development Practice, pp. 31-36

Online Language Development Cards, 6A-6B

DIGITAL TOOLS

MULTIMODAL

Have students read along with the student sources to develop comprehension and build fluency and pronunciation.

Argumentative Writing

Analyze the Sources

Review the Writing Prompt Display the prompt: *Write an argumentative essay to present to your class about whether people should build in flood zones.* Use the underlined words to discuss with students the information they will look for as they read.

Read the Sources/Take Notes Distribute the **Glossary** and read the sources on pages 91-93 in the **Reading/Writing Companion** with students. Help them identify and underline the relevant information in the text as they read.

Beginning Discuss the meaning of the words in the Glossary. Use visuals to discuss key concepts. Paraphrase challenging sentences for students. After each paragraph, help them describe: I learned about ___.

Intermediate Discuss the key concepts using the Glossary and visuals with students. Paraphrase challenging sentences with them. After each paragraph, help them retell the information.

Advanced/Advanced High Discuss the key concepts using the Glossary and visuals with students. Help them paraphrase challenging sentences. Have them retell the information after every two paragraphs.

Mixed Levels Have pairs read **Sources 1-3** and take notes. Use the questions to discuss each source with the group.

SOURCE 1 **"How to Build in Flood Zones"** *What is the claim?* (We can't stop people from building in flood zones.) *What problem can using fill dirt cause?* (greater flooding in nearby areas and costly damage) *What is more expensive than raising a building?* (rebuilding after a flood) *Why does the author say that houses need to be built up high?* (to protect them from flooding)

SOURCE 2 **"More Wetlands Needed"** *What is the claim?* (People should not build houses in flood zones.) *What is a storm surge?* (when ocean water rises very high and winds push the water onto land) *How do natural floodplains help during a flood?* (They create a barrier from the storm.)

SOURCE 3 **"Debate on Flood Zones"** *What do developers think about building in Louisiana flood zones?* (People need more buildings for the growing population.) *What do environmentalists think about building in Louisiana flood zones?* (We need to preserve and protect wetlands.) *What does the author think?* (Developers and environmentalists need to work together.) Point out that the claim appears at the end of the essay.

Plan/Organize Ideas

Synthesize Information Guide students on how to complete the graphic organizer on pages 94-95 of the Reading/Writing Companion. Model how students can transfer their information from their graphic organizer to **My Writing Outline**. Help students figure out their claims.

Beginning Help pairs write the claim and reasons using: People should/should not build in flood zones. People need more houses for the growing population/ wetlands to protect against floods.

Intermediate Have partners describe the claim and reasons: Building in flood zones is a good/bad idea because the population is growing/people need wetlands to protect against floods.

Advanced/Advanced-High Have partners describe their claims, reasons, and relevant evidence.

Draft

Review the Writing Plan. Have partners review the writing plan on their My Writing Outline.

- **Organization/My Draft** Check that the claim answers the writing prompt and appears in the first paragraph and the reasons and evidence appear in the next paragraphs. Help them paraphrase the claim for the conclusion.
- **Evidence and Sources** Check that the claim has supporting evidence and that the evidence comes from the three sources.
- **Relevant Evidence** Encourage students to choose their evidence carefully. Help them identify facts and details that support and do not support their claims.

Have students use My Writing Outline as they write their draft.

Beginning Help partners write complete sentences for their claims and reasons. Help them review that the claim answers the prompt.

Intermediate Have partners write the claim and check that it answers the prompt. Have them write the reasons and check that they support the claim. Help them check that they use relevant evidence from the sources.

Advanced/Advanced High Have partners review that their claim answers the prompt and that the reasons support the claim. Have them check for relevant evidence from the sources.

TEACHER CONFERENCES

To help students write their draft meet with each student to provide support and guidance. Discuss with students the relevant evidence in their writing and how it supports their claim.

Revise

Revising Checklist Review the Revising Checklist on page 97 of the Reading/Writing Companion.

Partner feedback Have partners use the checklist to give feedback on each other's work. Help all students provide feedback. For example:

Beginning Help them identify sentences that describe facts and claims. Then help students use signal words in their sentences.

Intermediate Have them identify sentences that describe facts and claims. Remind them to correct for conventions.

Advanced/Advanced High Have pairs identify signal words they can use to write about facts and claims. Have them check that they only chose relevant evidence and remind them to correct for conventions.

Before they revise, have partners discuss the revisions with each other.

For additional practice see Language Development Cards, Lessons 6A-6B, and Language Development Practice, pages 31-36.

TEACHER CONFERENCES

To help students revise, meet with each student and discuss the details of the revisions students will make.

FORMATIVE ASSESSMENT

STUDENT CHECK-IN

Plan Have partners share their My Writing Outline.

Draft Have partners share an example of relevant evidence.

Revise Have partners point out two revisions in their essays.

Ask students to reflect using the Check-in routine.

LEARNING GOALS

- **We can identify an argumentative statement and elaboration.**
- **We can analyze a student model and student model sources.**

OBJECTIVES

Refer to details and examples in a text when explaining what the text says explicitly and when drawing inferences from the text.

Integrate information from two texts on the same topic in order to write or speak about the subject knowledgeably.

Draw evidence from literary or informational texts to support analysis, reflection, and research.

LANGUAGE OBJECTIVES

Students will discuss features and organization of an argumentative essay using academic language.

ELA ACADEMIC LANGUAGE

- *elaboration, example, analyze, identify, prompt, introduction*
- Cognates: *ejemplo, analizar, identificar, introducción*

MATERIALS

Online ELL Extended Writing Resources BLMs:

- Greg's Model, pp. 10-12
- Analyze Greg's Model, pp. 13-14

Student Model Sources

Reading/Writing Companion, pp. 98-101

Literature Anthology, pp. 44-45

DIGITAL TOOLS

MULTIMODAL

Have students read along with Greg's Model to develop comprehension and build fluency

Argumentative Writing

Elaboration

Reread the paragraph on page 99 of **Reading/Writing Companion** with students. Review with them that elaboration adds details to clarify information and one way is to use examples. Describe the sentences in the paragraph using: Elaboration about jobs in tourism includes facts and examples. The sentences explain details about jobs in Colorado and examples from the writer's family.

Compare Elaboration Write on the board: **Strong:** *For example, my cousin works at a ski resort near Breckenridge. My uncle is a wilderness guide based in Boulder. Without the tourism industry, they would both be out of a job.* **Weak:** *Tourism gives my cousin and uncle jobs.* Have students compare to elicit that the weak model does not give specific information about why Greg's cousin and uncle have jobs from tourism.

Elaboration Read page 44 and the headline for each step on page 45 of the **Literature Anthology** with students. Restate challenging sentences. Discuss that writers use elaboration to help readers better understand their claim.

- Ask: *What is the author's claim?* (It's hard to become an entrepreneur, but it can be rewarding.) Point out that sometimes the claim can be more than one sentence. Then point to the headlines on page 45. Discuss with them why the steps are another way to elaborate. *How do these sentences support the claim?* (They tell the steps to become a successful entrepreneur.) *How are they an example of elaboration?* (They help explain the topic and add details about the claim.)

Have partners describe the claim and elaboration the author used.

Beginning Help partners describe using: The first two sentences are the claim. It tells that it is difficult to be an entrepreneur, but it is good. The steps are an example of elaboration.

Intermediate Have partners describe: The claim says that becoming an entrepreneur is hard, but rewarding. The steps are an example of elaboration. They describe how to become a good entrepreneur.

Advanced/Advanced High Have partners describe the claim and how elaboration helps support and build information for it.

Analyze the Student Model and Sources

Analyze the Prompt Read the prompt on **Greg's Model**. Explain that *economy* is the way people make and spend money.

Discuss the Student Model

Mixed Levels Use **Greg's Model** to read with students. Before reading, discuss *tourism* and *employees* using the **Glossary**. After each paragraph, have mixed pairs of language proficiency levels ask and answer the questions with each other and share responses with the group.

Paragraph 1 *What are some things people enjoy doing in Colorado?* (hiking in the mountains, shopping in Denver's outdoor malls, observing wild animals) *Why is it good that many people visit Colorado?* (It supports tourism and helps the economy.) *What does Greg say is an important part of Colorado's economy?* (tourism)

Paragraph 2 *What happens when tourists come to Colorado?* (They spend money.) *Who depends on money from tourists?* (business owners, state of Colorado) *Why does Greg talk about his grandparents?* (to give an example of how tourists help Colorado's economy)

Paragraph 3 *What else does tourism do for Colorado?* (It provides jobs.) *How many jobs in Colorado does the travel industry support?* (180,000) *Why does Greg talk about his cousin and uncle?* (to give an example of how tourism provides jobs)

Paragraph 4 *What makes up the biggest part of economy?* (tourism) *How many people visited Colorado in 2019?* (86.9 million) *Why is this good for everyone?* (Possible answer: People have fun visiting Colorado, and it keeps the economy strong.)

Analyze the Student Model: Organization

Use **Analyze Greg's Model** to analyze the organization as you fill in the information with students.

- Point to the first column and discuss with them how the essay is organized. Elicit where the claim and reasons appear. Help them identify where relevant evidence for the claims appear.
- Review with them that the claim tells what the writer thinks about the topic and the relevant evidence gives details to support the claims.
- Discuss ways Greg uses elaboration in the introduction and in the second and third paragraphs. *What did Greg use to elaborate on his claim?* (the example of his grandparents' restaurant) *What does this example tell about the claim?* (a reason why tourism is important.)

Mixed Levels Have partners complete columns 1 and 2 in Analyze Greg's Model.

Beginning Help partners identify the claim and elaboration: The claim is that tourism is most important to Colorado's economy. Greg uses examples of his relatives to elaborate.

Intermediate Have partners describe the claim and elaboration using: Greg uses examples of his relatives for elaboration. This helps readers understand why tourism is important to the economy in Colorado. It explains the claim.

Advanced/Advanced High Have partners describe the claim and how Greg uses elaboration.

Analyze the Student Model: Sources

Read the **Online Student Model Sources** with students. Have them underline the information Greg used.

COLLABORATE

Have partners complete the third column in Analyze Greg's Model. Discuss the following questions with students:

Paragraph 1 Point to paragraph 1 in Source 1 and paragraph 4 in Source 3. *What information did Greg use for evidence?* (Many tourists visit the capital city Denver and Rocky Mountain National Park.)

Paragraph 2 Discuss how Greg used Source 2 with students. *What information did Greg use?* (number of tourists to Colorado, infographic). *How does he use the information?* (as evidence to support his claim)

Paragraph 3 Discuss how Greg used Source 3. *What information did Greg use?* (how tourism helps the economy) *How does he use it?* (to support his claim)

Paragraph 4 Discuss that Greg used Source 1 to remind them of his claim.

FORMATIVE ASSESSMENT

STUDENT CHECK-IN

Have partners share responses to Analyze Greg's Model. Ask students to reflect using the Check-in routine.

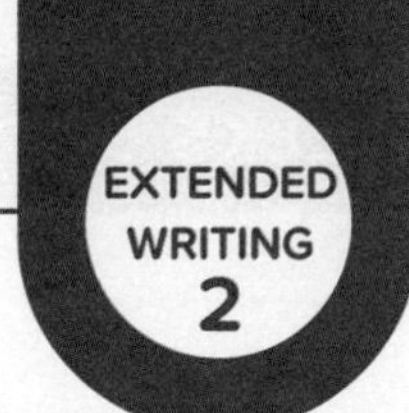

LEARNING GOALS

- We can synthesize information from three sources to plan and organize an argumentative essay.
- We can draft and revise an argumentative essay.

OBJECTIVES

Determine the central, or main, idea of a text and explain how it is supported by relevant, or key, details.

Introduce a topic or text clearly, state an opinion, and create an organizational structure in which related ideas are grouped to support the writer's purpose.

With guidance and support from peers and adults, develop and strengthen writing as needed by planning, revising, and editing.

LANGUAGE OBJECTIVES

Students will argue by writing an argumentative essay using a variety of sentences.

ELA ACADEMIC LANGUAGE

- *prompt, elaboration, source, relevant, introduction*
- Cognates: *elaboración, relevante, introducción*

MATERIALS

Reading/Writing Companion, pp. 102-109

Online ELL Extended Writing Resources BLMs:

- Glossary, p. 15
- My Writing Outline, pp. 16-17
- Draft: Strong Introduction , p. 18

Language Development Cards, 5A-5B

Language Development Practice, pp. 25-30

DIGITAL TOOLS

MULTIMODAL

Have students read along with the student sources to develop comprehension and build fluency and pronunciation.

Argumentative Writing

Analyze the Sources

Review the Writing Prompt Display the prompt: *Write an argumentative essay for the school newspaper about the skills students should be learning to prepare them for jobs in the future.* Use the underlined words to discuss with students the type of information they will look for as they read.

Read the Sources/Take Notes Distribute the **Glossary** and read the sources on pages 103-105 in the **Reading/Writing Companion** with students. Help them identify and underline the relevant information in the text as they read.

Beginning Discuss the meaning of the words in the Glossary. Use visuals to discuss key concepts. Paraphrase challenging sentences for students. After each paragraph, help them describe: I learned about ___.

Intermediate Discuss the key concepts using the Glossary and visuals with students. Paraphrase challenging sentences with them. After each paragraph, help them retell the information.

Advanced/Advanced High Discuss the key concepts using the Glossary and visuals with students. Help them paraphrase the author's claim. Have them retell the information after every two paragraphs.

Mixed Levels Take Notes Have pairs read **Sources 1-3** and take notes. Use the questions to discuss each source with the group.

SOURCE 1 **"Help Wanted"** *What is the claim?* (We need to prepare students for the future in order to have a strong economy.) *How does the space industry help people?* (makes jobs) *What does the example tell?* (NASA employs thousands of people in the United States.) *What skills do workers in the space industry need?* (science, math, and technology)

SOURCE 2 **"Skills for the Future"** *What is the claim? (Students are already learning the skills they need.) Why do people want to learn new skills?* (to keep their jobs) *Where are these skills being taught?* (in school and in the communities) Read the infographic "Skills for the Future" with students. Discuss examples to help them understand information in the visual.

SOURCE 3 **"Look to the Future"** Discuss with students what social entrepreneurs do and help them identify the claim. (people will need social entrepreneurs) *What is a social entrepreneur?* (someone who starts a new business to help improve the lives of others) *What example does the author use?* (a company that creates environmentally friendly cleaning products) *What skills will social entrepreneurs need?* (creativity, initiative, desire to help others)

Plan/Organize Ideas

Synthesize Information Guide students to complete the graphic organizer on **Reading/Writing Companion** pages 106-107. Model how students can transfer the information from their graphic organizer to **My Writing Outline**. Help students figure out their claim.

Beginning Help partners write the claim and reasons using: Students should be learning skills to prepare for jobs in the future. The kinds of skills students need are math and science skills/critical thinking and problem-solving skills.

Intermediate Have partners describe the claims and reasons using: Students should be learning skills to prepare for jobs in the future. The kinds of skills students need are math and science skills/critical thinking and problem-solving skills.

Advanced/Advanced High Have partners describe their claims, reasons, and evidence.

Draft

Have partners review the writing plan on My Writing Outline.

- **Organization** Check that the claim answers the writing prompt and appears in the first paragraph. Check for reasons and relevant evidence. Help them paraphrase the claim for the conclusion.
- **Evidence** Check that they use elaboration, such as examples, to explain their claim and that the evidence comes from the three sources.
- **Strong Introduction** Encourage students to use questions or exclamations in the introduction to make the readers want to read more.

 Have students use the completed My Writing Outline as they write their draft.

Beginning Help partners write complete sentences for their claim and organize relevant evidence. Help them write an example for elaboration.

Intermediate Have partners check that the claim answers the prompt and that the reasons support the claim. Have them include an example for elaboration and a question or exclamation in the introduction.

Advanced/Advanced High Have partners review their claim answers the prompt and evidence supports the claim. Have them include an example for elaboration and a question or exclamation in the introduction.

TEACHER CONFERENCES

To help students write their draft, meet with each student to provide support and guidance. Discuss their strong introduction and how it states their claim.

Revise

Revising Checklist Review the Revising Checklist on page 109 of the Reading/Writing Companion.

Partner feedback Have partners use the checklist to give feedback on each other's work. Help all students provide feedback. For example:

Beginning Help pairs write a question or exclamation to add or to revise their introduction.

Intermediate Have partners describe ways to write a strong introduction. Help them correct for conventions.

Advanced/Advanced High Have partners review their essays and describe how they can create a strong introduction. Remind them to check for conventions.

For additional practice see **Language Development Cards**, Lessons 5A-5B, and **Language Development Practice**, pages 31-36.

 Before they revise, have partners discuss the revisions with each other.

TEACHER CONFERENCES

To help students revise, meet with each student and discuss the details of the revisions students will make.

FORMATIVE ASSESSMENT

STUDENT CHECK-IN

Plan Have partners share their My Writing Outline.

Draft Have partners share an example of a strong introduction.

Revise Have partners point out two revisions in their essays.

Ask students to reflect using the Check-in routine.

Summative Assessment

Get Ready for Unit Assessment

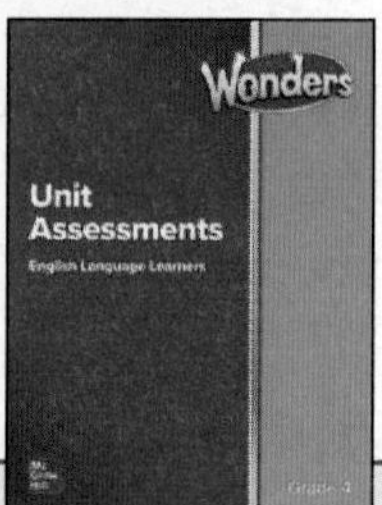

Unit 1 Tested Skills

LISTENING AND READING COMPREHENSION	VOCABULARY	GRAMMAR	SPEAKING AND WRITING
• Listening Actively • Comprehension • Text Structure • Cohesion	• Unit Vocabulary Words	• Sentences and Sentence Fragments • Simple and Compound Sentences • Combining Sentences	• Presenting • Writing • Supporting Opinions • Retelling/Summarizing • Text Structure

Create a Student Profile

Record data from the following resources in the Student Profile charts on pages 320–321 of the Assessment book.

COLLABORATIVE	INTERPRETIVE	PRODUCTIVE

• Collaborative Conversations Rubrics
  • Listening
  • Speaking
	• Leveled Unit Assessment:
	  • Listening Comprehension
	  • Reading Comprehension
	  • Vocabulary
	  • Grammar
	• Presentation Rubric
	  • Listening
	• *Wonders* Unit Assessment
		• Weekly Progress Monitoring
		• Leveled Unit Assessment
		  • Speaking
		  • Writing
		• Presentation Rubric
		  • Speaking
		• Write to Sources Rubric
		• *Wonders* Unit Assessment

The Foundational Skills Kit, Language Development Kit, and Adaptive Learning provide additional student data for progress monitoring.

Level Up

Use the following chart, along with your Student Profiles, to guide your Level Up decisions.

LEVEL UP	If **BEGINNING** level students are able to do the following, they may be ready to move to the **INTERMEDIATE** level:	If **INTERMEDIATE** level students are able to do the following, they may be ready to move to the **ADVANCED** level:	If **ADVANCED** level students are able to do the following, they may be ready to move to on-level:
COLLABORATIVE	• participate in collaborative conversations using basic vocabulary and grammar and simple phrases or sentences • discuss simple pictorial or text prompts	• participate in collaborative conversations using appropriate words and phrases and complete sentences • use limited academic vocabulary across and within disciplines	• participate in collaborative conversations using more sophisticated vocabulary and correct grammar • communicate effectively across a wide range of language demands in social and academic contexts
INTERPRETIVE	• identify details in simple read alouds • understand common vocabulary and idioms and interpret language related to familiar social, school, and academic topics • make simple inferences and make simple comparisons • exhibit an emerging receptive control of lexical, syntactic, phonological, and discourse features	• identify main ideas and/or make some inferences from simple read alouds • use context clues to identify word meanings and interpret basic vocabulary and idioms • compare, contrast, summarize, and relate text to graphic organizers • exhibit a limited range of receptive control of lexical, syntactic, phonological, and discourse features when addressing new or familiar topics	• determine main ideas in read alouds that have advanced vocabulary • use context clues to determine meaning, understand multiple-meaning words, and recognize synonyms of social and academic vocabulary • analyze information, make sophisticated inferences, and explain their reasoning • command a high degree of receptive control of lexical, syntactic, phonological, and discourse features
PRODUCTIVE	• express ideas and opinions with basic vocabulary and grammar and simple phrases or sentences • restate information or retell a story using basic vocabulary • exhibit an emerging productive control of lexical, syntactic, phonological, and discourse features	• produce coherent language with limited elaboration or detail • restate information or retell a story using mostly accurate, although limited, vocabulary • exhibit a limited range of productive control of lexical, syntactic, phonological, and discourse features when addressing new or familiar topics	• produce sentences with more sophisticated vocabulary and correct grammar • restate information or retell a story using extensive and accurate vocabulary and grammar • tailor language to a particular purpose and audience • command a high degree of productive control of lexical, syntactic, phonological, and discourse features

LEARNING GOALS

We can read and understand an expository text.

OBJECTIVES

Determine the central, or main, idea of a text and explain how it is supported by relevant, or key, details; summarize the text.

Explain events, procedures, ideas, or concepts in a historical, scientific, or technical text, including what happened and why, based on specific information in the text.

Review the key ideas expressed and explain their own ideas and understanding in light of the discussion.

Explore how structures and functions enable organisms to survive in their environment. **Science**

LANGUAGE OBJECTIVES

Students will explain the central idea and relevant details using content vocabulary.

ELA ACADEMIC LANGUAGE

- *headings, relevant details, central idea, photograph, caption*
- Cognates: *detalles relevantes, idea central, fotografía*

MATERIALS

Reading/Writing Companion, pp. 126-129

Online Scaffolded Shared Read, "Animal Adaptations"

Visual Vocabulary Cards

Online ELL Visual Vocabulary Cards

DIGITAL TOOLS

MULTIMODAL

Have students read along as they listen to the selection to develop comprehension and practice fluency and pronunciation.

"Animal Adaptations"

Prepare to Read

Build Background Discuss examples of adaptation to introduce the concept, such as things people do to keep warm or cool: *We wear coats, gloves, and hats to keep warm in the winter.* Discuss with students ways animals keep warm. Have students share examples they know, using: *I know that bears sleep during winter.*

Vocabulary Use the **Visual Vocabulary Cards** to preteach the vocabulary: *camouflaged, dribbles, extraordinary, poisonous, pounce, predator, prey,* and *vibrations.* Use the online **ELL Visual Vocabulary Cards** to teach additional Vocabulary from the Shared Read: *avoid, benefit, blends in, compact, decline,* and *harsh.*

Set Purpose *Today we will read an expository text called "Animal Adaptations" and focus on understanding the central idea and relevant details. As we read, think about what helps an animal survive.*

Read the Text

Select the **Scaffolded Shared Read** or the Shared Read in the **Reading/Writing Companion,** based on students' language proficiency.

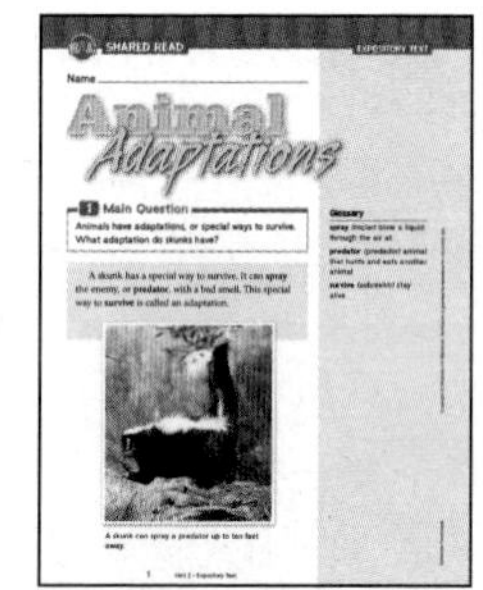

Scaffolded Shared Read, Lexile 610L

Beginning/Early-Intermediate Use the online **Scaffolded Shared Read** to help partners work together to read and understand an expository text. Remind them to use the Glossary to help them read and the Word Bank to help them answer the Main and Additional Questions.

Intermediate/Advanced Advanced High Read the text with students and use the Interactive Question-Response Routine to help them understand an expository text.

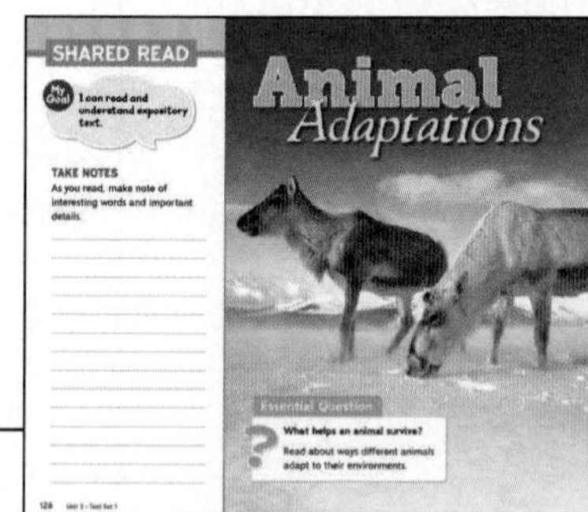

Reading/Writing Companion, Lexile 850L

Page 127, Introduction and "Staying Warm"

Paragraphs 1–4 Read the text with students and review Vocabulary words *predator, poisonous, vibrations, extraordinary, avoid, compact, and harsh.* *What can a skunk do?* (spray with a terrible smell) *What are two kinds of adaptations?* (physical traits and behavioral traits) *What are examples of physical traits?* (skunks' spray, bright colors and markings, sense vibrations) *What are examples of behavioral traits?* (birds migrate south in winter) *Where do caribou live?* (Arctic tundra) *How do caribou stay warm?* (have two layers of fur and thick layer of fat) *Why are the tips of the nose and mouth covered in short hair?* (warm the air in the lungs and keep the caribou warm when they look for food)

COLLABORATE Have partners take turns describing adaptations that help caribou survive in the tundra: Caribou stay warm because they have two layers of fur and thick fat. They also have hair on the nose to warm the air and protect the nose from the snow. Have students monitor as they listen to their partner's description and ask for clarification. For example: Can you repeat ___? Does the word/phrase ___ mean similar to ___?

Intermediate *What does the **heading** "Staying Warm" tell you about the section?* (The section will be about a cold place.) *What context clues help you figure out that the Arctic tundra is a very cold place?* ("annual temperature is an extraordinary 10° to 20° F," "Alaska, Canada, Greenland, and Russia")

Advanced/Advanced High *How are physical traits different from behavioral traits?* (Possible answer: Physical traits are ways animals use their body, behavioral traits are the way animals act.)

Page 128, "Finding Food" and "Insects in Disguise"

Paragraphs 1–2 Read the text with students and review Vocabulary words *dribble, camouflaged, blend in,* and *decline. Why do caribou have unusual stomachs?* (to digest lichen) *Why do they eat so much lichen?* (It is the only food they can eat during winter.) *What does the phrase "in disguise" mean?* (to hide or pretend to be something else) *What do the phasmids look like?* (leaves or twigs) *What do nocturnal animals do?* (They are active at night.)

COLLABORATE **Intermediate** Have partners describe what happens when phasmids camouflage their body: Phasmids camouflage their body to look like leaves or twigs. When they are camouflaged, predators cannot see them because they look like leaves or twigs. Phasmids are safe because the predators can't catch them.

Advanced/Advanced High *When do caribou travel to forests in the north?* (when they can't find lichen on the tundra) *Is this a physical or behavioral trait? Why or why not?* (Possible answer: behavioral trait because adaptation shows a way animals act)

Advanced High *How do the caribou know when to return to the tundra?* (When the snow melts, they know the season is changing.)

Page 129, "Water, Please!"

Paragraphs 1–2 Read the text with students and review Vocabulary words *prey* and *pounce.* Have students identify **relevant details**. *What do alligators do during dry season in the Everglades?* (Alligators clear dirt from holes and they fill up with water.) *What happens at the water holes?* (Plants grow and other animals get water.) *What do these important or **relevant details** have in common?* (They tell what some animals do to get water.) *What is the **central idea** of the section?* (Possible answer: Alligators adapt to get water during dry season.)

COLLABORATE Have partners ***summarize** how alligators' adaptations affect other animals.* (Possible answer: Alligators make water holes and other animals get water from there. Alligators can catch and eat the animals while they are in the watering holes.)

COLLABORATE **Intermediate** Have partners describe the alligator's environment: The Florida Everglades has a dry season that makes it difficult for animals and plants to get water. During the dry season, alligators use feet and snout to clean off dirt from water holes. When the ground is dry, alligators can drink water from the water holes.

Advanced/Advanced High *Why is it dangerous for animals to go to the water holes?* (Alligators can attack them.) *Why do they go back?* (to get water and the alligators do not hunt often)

Have partners describe the information **photographs** and **captions** tell in the text.

FORMATIVE ASSESSMENT

STUDENT CHECK-IN

Have partners retell the most important ideas in the text. Ask students to reflect using the Check-In routine.

LEARNING GOALS

- **We can read and understand an expository text by identifying the central idea and relevant details.**
- **We can identify and use common and proper nouns.**

OBJECTIVES

Paraphrase portions of a text read aloud or information presented in diverse media and formats, including visually, quantitatively, and orally.

Demonstrate command of the conventions of standard English capitalization, punctuation, and spelling when writing.

LANGUAGE OBJECTIVES

Students will explain the central idea and relevant details using words from the text.

Students will write complete sentences using common and proper nouns.

ELA ACADEMIC LANGUAGE

- *central idea, relevant details, common nouns*
- Cognates: *idea central, detalles relevantes*

MATERIALS

Reading/Writing Companion, pp. 126-129, 130-131

Online Scaffolded Shared Read, "Animal Adaptations"

Online Shared Read Writing Frames, p. 4

Online Language Development Cards, 8A

Online Language Development Practice, pp. 43-45

Online Language Transfers Handbook, pp. 15-19

"Animal Adaptations"

Text Reconstruction

Focus on a single chunk of text to support comprehension and language development across the four domains.

1. Read aloud "Insects in Disguise" on page 128 of the **Reading/Writing Companion** while students listen.
2. Write the following words on the board, providing definitions as needed: *disguise, blend, disappear, nocturnal,* and *avoid.* Instruct students to listen for the words as you read the paragraph a second time.
3. Read the paragraph a third time. Tell students to listen and take notes.
4.  COLLABORATE Have students work with a partner to reconstruct the text from their notes. Help them write complete sentences as needed.
5. Have students look at the original text. Ask them to tell what the paragraph is mostly about. (how phasmids use camouflage) Elicit that the central idea is that plasmids have adaptations that protect them from predators. Tell students they are going to look at details that support the central idea.
6. *What is the first relevant detail that supports the central idea?* (Phasmids look like leaves or twigs.) With students, list the rest of the relevant details as notes, for example: "change colors to blend in with surroundings." Point out that the purpose of the first four sentences is to introduce the phasmid. The rest of the sentences support the central idea.
7. Have students compare their text reconstructions to the original text. Have them check if they also included relevant details that support the central idea.

Beginning Have students follow along in the Reading/Writing Companion as you read the text aloud. Have them point to the words from Step 2 as they hear them.

Grammar in Context: Common and Proper Nouns

Notice the Form Display a sentence from the text, and underline the nouns.

> Welcome to the Arctic tundra of Alaska, Canada, Greenland, and Russia, home of the caribou.

What do the underlined words have in common? (They are nouns.) *Which words begin with a capital letter?* (Arctic, Alaska, Canada, Greenland, Russia) *What kinds of nouns are they?* (proper nouns) *Which words do not begin with a capital letter?* (tundra, home, caribou) *What kinds of nouns are they?* (common nouns) Have students describe each type using: Common nouns are ___. Proper nouns are ___. Discuss the rule for writing proper nouns: capitalize the first letter.

Apply and Extend Have partners write complete sentences using common and proper nouns to describe the Arctic tundra. Check their answers and provide corrective feedback.

For additional practice, see **Language Development Card**, Lesson 8A, and **Language Development Practice**, pages 43-45.

Independent Time

Vocabulary Building Have students build their glossaries.

Beginning/Early Intermediate Have students complete the Glossary Activities in the **Scaffolded Shared Read**.

Intermediate/Advanced/Advanced High Have students add the vocabulary from **Reading/Writing Companion** pages 130–131 and self-selected words or phrases they would like to learn to the chart.

Mixed Levels Pair students together: Beginning and Early-Intermediate students can teach words from Scaffolded Shared Read glossaries. Intermediate and Advanced/Advanced High students can teach self-selected words.

WORD/PHRASE	DEFINE	EXAMPLE	ASK
Bedrock	solid rock under the surface of the ground	An alligator is strong enough to dig through bedrock.	What makes bedrock different from other kinds of rock?

COLLABORATE **Common and Proper Nouns** Have partners identify common and proper nouns in one page of "Animal Adaptations." Have them write the words in a 2-column chart. Have partners present their chart to the group, describing each type of noun and the spelling rules for writing them.

Shared Read Writing Frames Use the online leveled Shared Read Writing Frames for "Animal Adaptations" to provide students with additional oral and written practice. Differentiated frames are available for all levels.

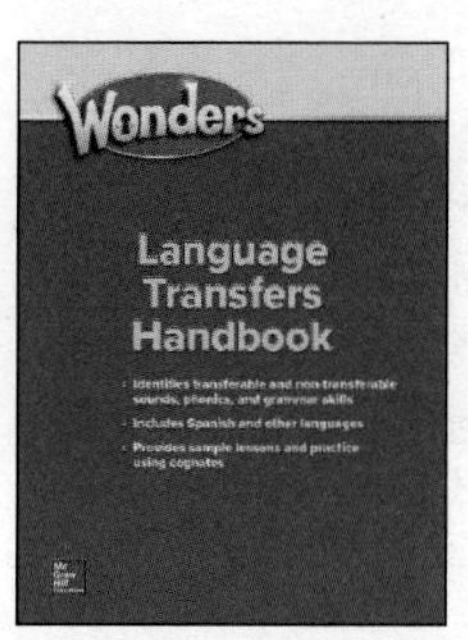

Language Transfers Handbook, Grammar Transfers pp. 15–19

DIGITAL TOOLS

For additional support, use the online activities.

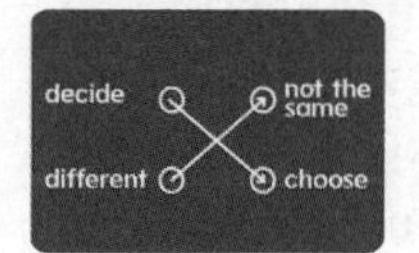

Vocabulary Activity

FORMATIVE ASSESSMENT

STUDENT CHECK IN

Text Reconstruction Have partners share their notes. Have students reflect on their work using the Check-In routine.

Grammar in Context Have partners share their sentences. Have students reflect on their work using the Check-In routine.

LEARNING GOALS

- **Read** We can read and understand an expository text.
- **Reread** We can reread and analyze text, craft, and structure.

OBJECTIVES

Refer to details and examples in a text when explaining what the text says explicitly and when drawing inferences from the text.

Review the key ideas expressed and explain their own ideas and understanding in light of the discussion.

 Explore how structures and functions enable organisms to survive in their environment. **Science**

LANGUAGE OBJECTIVES

Students will narrate by answering questions about the text using content area vocabulary.

Students will explain author's use of text features and word choice using academic vocabulary.

ELA ACADEMIC LANGUAGE

- *caption, perspective*
- Cognate: *perspectiva*

MATERIALS

Literature Anthology, pp. 90-105

Reading/Writing Companion, pp. 138-140

Visual Vocabulary Cards

Online ELL Anchor Text Support BLMs, pp. 9-11

DIGITAL TOOLS

MULTIMODAL

Have students read along as they listen to the selection to develop comprehension and practice fluency and pronunciation.

Spiders

Prepare to Read

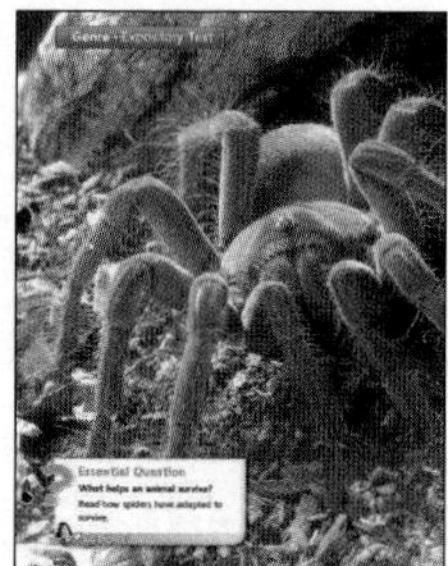

Literature Anthology, Lexile 820L

Build Background Invite students to discuss what they know about spiders. Use the photograph in the text to help them describe the features of a spider. A spider has ____.

Vocabulary Use the **Visual Vocabulary Cards** to review the vocabulary: *camouflaged, dribbles, extraordinary, poisonous, pounce, predator, prey,* and *vibrations.*

Set Purpose Today we will read an expository text about spiders. As we read, think about what helps an animal survive.

Have students listen to the audio summary of the text, which is available in multiple languages.

Read

Literature Anthology, pp. 90-105

Use the **Interactive Question-Response Routine** to help students read and discuss *Spiders.*

Beginning Help students discuss in complete sentences. Provide sentence frames: All spiders have eight legs, fangs, spin silk, and eat other animals. Spiders do not have wings.

Intermediate Ask students to respond in complete sentences and add details. Provide sentence starters as needed: All spiders have eight legs, fangs, spin silk, and eat other animals. Spiders do not have wings.

Advanced/Advanced High Have students respond in complete sentences and add details.

COLLABORATE **Independent Reading Practice** Have mixed level pairs complete pages 9-11 of ELL Anchor Text Support BLMs and share with the group.

Reread

Use with **Reading/Writing Companion,** pages 138-140

Literature Anthology, page 94

COLLABORATE **Author's Craft: Word Choice** Read the text with students and review Vocabulary word *prey.* Demonstrate the words *stab, dribbles,* and *slurp* to help them visualize how a spider eats its prey. *What does the spider do first?* (stabs its prey with its fangs) *Why does the spider dribble digestive juices on the prey, or animal?* (It turns the animal's insides into soup, so the spider can slurp it out.) *How do the words* stab, dribble, *and* slurp *help you visualize how a spider eats its prey?* (The words create an image of the spider eating its meal.)

Beginning Read the text and restate them with students. Clarify the meaning of the words *stab, dribbles,* and *slurp. What does the spider stab its prey with?* (fangs) *What does the spider dribble on the prey?* (digestive juices) *What does the spider do when the animal's insides turn into soup?* The spider slurps them out.

Intermediate Have students read the text and point to words *stab, dribbles,* and *slurp. How does the spider stab its prey?* The spider stabs its prey with its fangs. *What does the spider do to turn the animal's insides into soup?* The spider dribbles digestive juices on the animal. *Why does the spider do this?* So the spider can slurp out the animal's insides.

Advanced/Advanced High *What does the spider do with its fangs?* (The spider stabs its prey with its fangs.) *What does the spider do to turn the animal's insides into soup, so they can slurp them out?* (The spider dribbles digestive juices on the animal.)

Literature Anthology, page 98

COLLABORATE **Author's Perspective** Review the meaning of the Vocabulary words *extraordinary* and *vibrations* in the first paragraph on page 98. Explain that the word *senses* is used as a noun and verb in the text and help them distinguish the meanings. *What senses do we have?* (vision, hearing, touch, smell, taste) *What can the hairs on the spider's body sense?* (the sounds of a flying insect) *How do spiders smell things?* (Spiders smell things by walking on them.) *How does the author describe the spider's senses?* (The author thinks a spider's senses are extraordinary.)

Beginning Read the first paragraph with students and restate as needed. *What does the spider use to sense?* The spider uses hairs. *What do the spiders sense with their hair?* The spiders sense touch, vibrations, and sound with their hairs.

Intermediate *How do the spiders use the hairs all over its body?* Spiders use hairs to sense touch, vibrations, and sounds. *How do spiders use its feet to sense?* Spiders use the organs on its feet to smell and taste. *What other things can spiders sense?* Spiders can sense the taste of its silk.

Advanced/Advanced High *Why are spiders covered with hairs?* (They use the hairs to sense touch, vibrations, and sounds.) *How do spiders smell and taste?* (They use organs on their feet to smell and taste.) Have students discuss how the spiders' senses are extraordinary.

Literature Anthology

COLLABORATE **Text Features: Photographs and Captions** Read page 105 with students. Have students ask questions about the text or words or phrases they don't understand, such as "draped on hedges." *How does the spider walk if the web is sticky? What are "messy tangles"? Does thread mean the same as silk?* Restate sections with them to help clarify meaning.

Beginning Read the first paragraph with students and restate as needed. *What are spiderwebs made of?* (silk) *Is the shape of the spiderweb in the photograph round?* (yes) Explain that orb means something round. Read the caption with students. *What kind of spider is in the photograph?* It is an orb web spider. *What is the shape of the spiderweb?* The shape of the spiderweb is an orb, or round.

Intermediate Have students read the caption and discuss that the words "orb web" also appear in the text to elicit that the photograph shows an orb web. *What does the word* orb *mean?* (something that has a round shape) *What new information did you learn?* I learned from the caption that orb web spiders have claws and non-stick feet so they can walk on their web.

Advanced/Advanced High Have students identify the description of the spiderwebs and tell whether the photograph shows the descriptions. (Possible answer: I can see in the photograph and descriptions "old tissue paper," "messy tangles," and "orb web.") Have them read the caption and discuss what they learned about orb web spiders.

FORMATIVE ASSESSMENT

STUDENT CHECK IN

Read Have partners share their responses to the Anchor Text questions. Then have them reflect using the Check-In routine.

Reread Have partners share responses and text evidence on Reading/Writing Companion pages 138-140. Then have them reflect using the Check-In routine to fill in the bars.

LEARNING GOALS

- **We can read and understand expository text by identifying the central idea and relevant details.**
- **We can identify and use singular and plural nouns in sentences.**

OBJECTIVES

Paraphrase portions of a text read aloud or information presented in diverse media and formats, including visually, quantitatively, and orally.

Demonstrate command of the conventions of standard English grammar and usage when writing or speaking.

LANGUAGE OBJECTIVES

Students will use signal words from a text to explain the central idea and relevant details.

Students will inquire about the parts of a sentence using academic vocabulary.

ELA ACADEMIC LANGUAGE

- *identify, plural noun, singular noun*
- Cognate: *identificar*

MATERIALS

Literature Anthology, pp. 90-105

Online Language Development Cards, 10A-10B

Online Language Development Practice, pp. 55-60

Online Language Transfers Handbook, pp. 15-19

Spiders

Text Reconstruction

Focus on a single chunk of text to support comprehension and language development across the four domains.

1. Read aloud the first paragraph in *Spiders* on page 98 of the **Literature Anthology** while students listen.
2. Write the following on the board, providing definitions as needed: *senses, vibrations*. Instruct students to listen for them as you read the paragraph a second time.
3. Read the paragraph a third time while students listen and take notes.
4. COLLABORATE Have students work with a partner to reconstruct the text from their notes. Help them write complete sentences as needed.
5. Have students look at the original text. Ask them to tell what the paragraph is mostly about. (Spiders have senses all over their bodies.) Tell students they are going to examine the structure of a paragraph to identify the central idea and relevant details.
6. *Which sentence tells the central idea?* (2nd sentence: Even so, it has extraordinary senses all over its body) *What are the relevant details?* (Spiders have hairs that can sense touch, vibrations, and sounds.) *What other relevant details tell about extraordinary senses?* (hairs can sense the sound of an insect, organs on the feet can smell and taste)
7. Have students compare their text reconstructions to the original text. Have them check whether they also included the central idea and relevant details.

Beginning Allow students to follow along in their Literature Anthologies as you read the text aloud. Have them point to the words from Step 2 as they hear them. Have students describe the photograph on page 93.

Apply Author's Craft: Author's Perspective

Review that author's perspective shows how an author feels about a subject. Have students describe an animal they are familiar with using language that shows their perspective. Model first: *On page 98, what word does the author use to describe the spiders' sense?* (extraordinary) *What is the author's perspective about spiders?* (they are impressive) Have students write a short paragraph that shows their perspective about an animal. Provide an example. "Many dogs have an amazing sense of smell."

Grammar in Context: Deconstruct a Sentence

Write the sentences from page 92 on the board: *A spider's body has two main parts. The back part is called the abdomen.* Facilitate deconstructing the sentences for better comprehension.

- *What are the singular nouns?* (body, part) *What are the plural nouns?* (parts, spinnerets) *How are singular and plural nouns different?* (singular tells about one person, place, or thing and plural tells about more than one person, place, or thing)
- *How can you tell a singular noun from a plural noun?* (plural nouns end with letter *s*) Review the spelling rules for plural nouns with students. *How do you change a singular noun that ends in* s *or* ss *to a plural noun?* (add *es* at the end of the word) Point out adding *es* for nouns that end in *sh, ch, x,* or *z.*
- Review the spelling rules for nouns that end in *y*. *How do you change the singular noun 'body' into a plural noun?* (change *y* into *i* and add *es*)
- Read the sentences with students and point out the subject-verb agreement in each sentence and review the rules, as needed.

For additional practice, see **Language Development Cards,** Lessons 10A and 10B, and **Language Development Practice** pages 55-60.

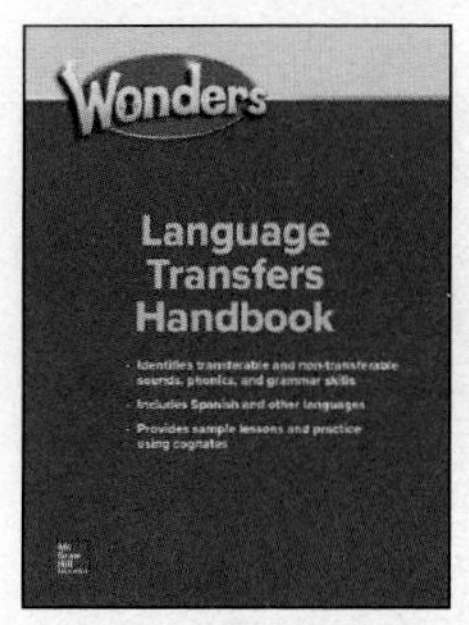

Language Transfers Handbook, Grammar Transfers, pp. 15-19

Independent Time

Vocabulary Building Have students create an interactive word wall with vocabulary from the selection. Hang an outline of a spider's body on the wall. Then have them select from the text words that identify spider body parts and behaviors and write them on the front of separate index cards. On the back of each card, have students write a detail about the body part or behavior. Have students hang the cards on the appropriate part of the diagram. Encourage students to learn a new fact about spiders and add it to the wall.

Beginning Have students work with a partner to write clues.

Intermediate/Advanced/Advanced High Have students include the self-selected words and content-area words to their glossaries.

Singular and Plural Nouns Have partners create a 3-column chart and select singular and plural nouns from one page of *Spiders*. Then have partners select verbs and identify the subject-verb agreement for each. Have students write a sentence using the nouns and verbs. Provide an example: *A spider uses hairs to feel touch.*

SUBJECT	VERB	SUBJECT-VERB AGREEMENT
a spider	use	a spider uses

FORMATIVE ASSESSMENT

STUDENT CHECK-IN

Text Reconstruction Ask partners to share their notes. Have them reflect using the Check-In routine.

Grammar in Context Ask partners to reflect on their deconstructions using the Check-In routine.

LEARNING GOALS

We can apply strategies and skills to read expository text.

OBJECTIVES

Determine the central, or main, idea of a text and explain how it is supported by relevant, or key, details; summarize the text.

Use common, grade-appropriate Greek and Latin affixes and roots as clues to the meaning of a word.

Review the key ideas expressed and explain their own ideas and understanding in light of the discussion.

LANGUAGE OBJECTIVES

Students will discuss the central idea and relevant details using content vocabulary.

Students will use academic vocabulary to discuss the meaning of new words in a text.

ELA ACADEMIC LANGUAGE

- *pronoun, prefix, antonym, synonym, central idea, relevant details*
- Cognates: *pronombre, prefijo, antónimo, sinónimo, idea central, detalles relevantes*

MATERIALS

Online ELL Genre Passage, "The Birds"

"The Birds"

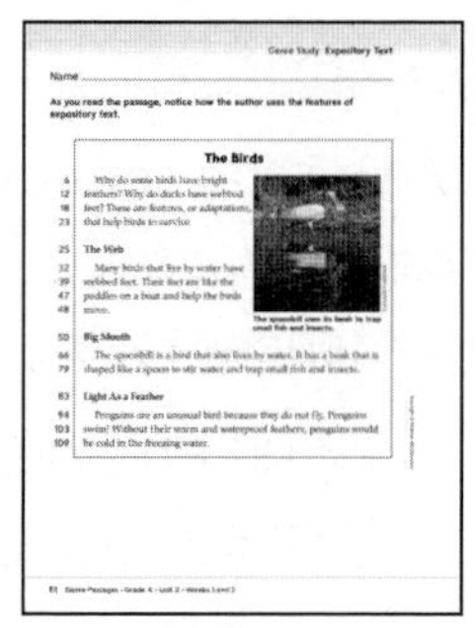

Genre Passage
Lexile 620L

Prepare to Read

Purpose for Reading Remind students that an expository text informs the reader and discuss with them the features it has, such as headings, photographs, and captions.

Discuss the birds in the photographs and have students share their knowledge or experience using: I know that birds have/can ___. To survive, they use their ___.

Vocabulary Use the **Define, Example, Ask** routine to pre-teach difficult words or unfamiliar concepts, such as *features, paddles, beak,* and *waterproof.* (Cognate: sobrevivir) Invite students to add new vocabulary to their glossaries.

Set Purpose *Today we will read an expository text called "The Birds" and focus on understanding the central idea and important details. As we read, think about what helps animals survive.*

Read the Text

Page E1, Introduction, "The Web," and "Big Mouth"

Beginning Read paragraph 1 with students. *Find the pronoun.* (these) *What does it refer to?* (bright feathers, webbed feet) Help students point to the pronoun *these* and the words it refers to in the first paragraph.

Intermediate *Discuss with a partner how birds use webbed feet and how the spoonbill uses its beak.* Birds use webbed feet to move in water. The spoonbill uses its beak to stir water and trap fish and insects.

Advanced/Advanced High *Why does the spoonbill have a beak shaped like a spoon?* (It is shaped like a spoon to stir water and catch fish and insects.)

Pages E1-E2, "Light As a Feather" and "True Colors"

Prefixes *What does the prefix* un- *tell about the meaning of unusual?* The prefix *un-* means it is the opposite of usual. *Why are penguins unusual?* They are unusual because they are birds, but they do not fly. *How do they keep warm in cold water?* They keep warm because they have waterproof feathers.

Beginning Read "Light as a Feather" with students. *What makes a penguin different from other birds?* Penguins are birds but they do not fly. *What word tells you that penguins are different?* (unusual) What do penguins do? Penguins swim.

Advanced/Advanced High *Discuss with a partner why some birds are colorful and some birds have dull colors.* (Possible answer: Colorful birds attract attention. Other birds are not colorful because they do not want attention.)

Page E2, "Voices Carry"

Beginning Read the first paragraph of the section with students. Help partners answer: *What do birds do when they make calls?* Birds talk to each other. *Where does the killdeer build a nest?* The killdeer builds a nest on the ground. *Is this safe?* No, it is not safe. *Which animals are predators and hunt the killdeer?* The predators are coyotes or raccoons.

Intermediate *What does* common *mean?* (usual) *What word is an antonym of* common*?* (unusual) *What word is a synonym?* (normal) *When does the killdeer give a loud call?* It gives a loud call when a predator is near the nest. *When does the killdeer return to the nest?* It returns when the predator is far away from the nest.

Advanced/Advanced High *How do birds talk to each other?* (Birds make calls, sing, and make noise.) *Why does the killdeer have a special call to protect the nest?* (The killdeer builds its nest on the ground. This makes it easy for predators to find the eggs.)

Advanced High *Why is the way the manakin makes noise unusual?* (Possible answer: It is unusual because it moves its feathers back and forth to make calls. Birds usually do not use feathers to make calls.)

Central Idea and Relevant Details *Discuss with a partner the central idea and relevant details of the section "Voices Carry."* Provide sentence frames as needed: The central idea is that birds make calls to survive, talk to each other, and keep safe from predators. The relevant details are that they make noise to talk to each other. The killdeer make loud calls when predators are near.

Respond to Reading

Use the following instruction to help students answer the questions on page E3.

1. *Read the second paragraph on page E2. What colors do the potoo have?* (dull colors) *Why do the potoo have dull colors?* (to look like tree bark) *How does this help the potoo to survive?* (The dull colors help the potoo blend in so predators cannot see it.)
2. **Text Features: Headings, Photographs, and Captions** *What text features does the text have?* (heading, photographs, and captions) *What information do the text features give you?* (The headings tell what each section is about and the photograph and captions show and tell additional information.)
3. *What did the sections tell?* (Sections give details about features that birds have to survive.) *What is the author's purpose for the text?* (The author's purpose is to explain the feature birds have to survive.)

Fluency Have partners take turns reading the passage.

Build Knowledge: Make Connections

Talk About the Text Have partners discuss what helps animals survive.

Write About the Text Have students add their ideas to their Build Knowledge pages of their reader's notebooks.

FORMATIVE ASSESSMENT

STUDENT CHECK IN

Have partners share their responses on page E3 and reflect using the Check-In routine.

LEVEL UP

IF students read the **ELL Level** of the **Genre Passage** fluently and answered the questions

THEN pair them with students who have proficiently read the On Level Have them

- partner read the On Level passage.
- discuss the main idea and details.

LEARNING GOALS

We can apply strategies and skills to read expository text.

OBJECTIVES

Determine the central, or main, idea of a text and explain how it is supported by relevant, or key, details; summarize the text.

Review the key ideas expressed and explain their own ideas and understanding in light of the discussion.

Read grade-level text with purpose and understanding.

LANGUAGE OBJECTIVES

Students will narrate by summarizing how animals survive using content vocabulary

ELA ACADEMIC LANGUAGE

- *summarize*

MATERIALS

ELL Leveled Reader, *Extreme Animals*

Online Differentiated Texts, "How Animals Survive"

Online ELL Visual Vocabulary Cards

DIGITAL TOOLS

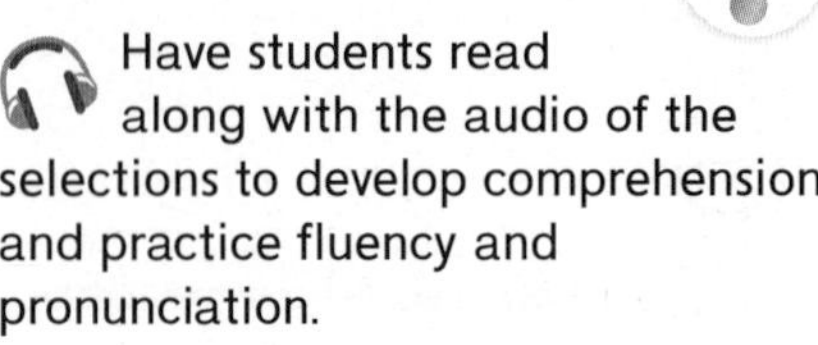

Have students read along with the audio of the selections to develop comprehension and practice fluency and pronunciation.

Extreme Animals

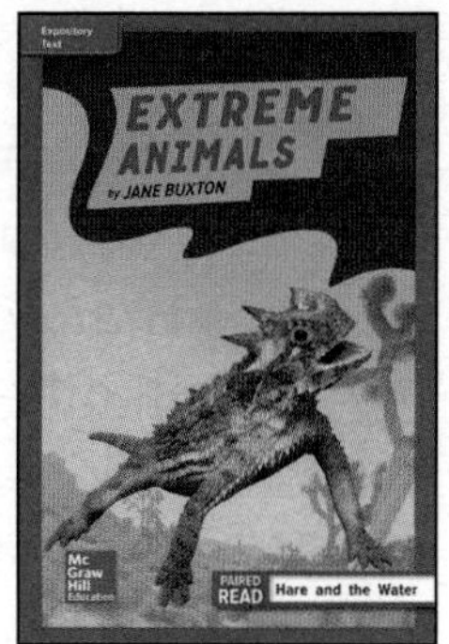

Leveled Reader
Lexile 680L

Prepare to Read

Build Background Discuss the things people need to live, such as food, water, shelter, and clothing. Have students describe using: People need ___ to live. People need food and water because ___. Discuss with students what animals need to live. Have them share what they know: I know that animals need ___ to live. I know from ___. Read aloud the title and discuss the meaning of *extreme*. Explain the title refers to animals that have unusual ways of surviving in their environment.

Vocabulary Use the routine on the **ELL Visual Vocabulary Cards** to preteach ELL Vocabulary: *habitat, pressure,* and *survive*. Use the glossary definitions on page 19 to define vocabulary in context. Have students add these words to their glossaries.

Set Purpose *Today we are going to read an expository text called "Extreme Animals". As we read, think about what helps animals survive.*

Read the Text

Introduction

COLLABORATE Have partners discuss the meaning of *survive*. Then have them discuss examples of how animals use adaptations. Students can respond using: Animals use adaptations to help them survive.

Beginning Choral read page 2. Help students identify types of environments and describe them using: A(n) desert/ocean/rain forest is one type of environment. A desert has sand. It is hot and dry. (Cognates: *desierto, océan*)

Chapter 1: Surviving in the Desert and the Rain Forest

Beginning *Where do the Texas horned lizard and javelina live?* They live in the desert. *What does the horned lizard have on its body?* The horned lizard has sharp spines. *How does the sloth move?* The sloth moves very slowly.

COLLABORATE **Intermediate** *How is the horned lizard unusual?* It is unusual because it squirts blood from the eyes. *Why is this unusual?* (Most animals do not squirt blood.) *What similar adaptation do the javelina and horned lizard have?* They have the similar adaptation of making their bodies look bigger.

Chapter 2: Watery Environments

Beginning Read the sentence about blubber on page 8. *What is another word for* blubber*?* (fat) *How do you know?* (commas and "or fat") Choral read the first paragraph on page 10. *Where do amphibians live?* They live on land and water. *Which sentence tells examples of amphibians?* (last sentence)

Advanced/Advanced High *Discuss with a partner what makes a duck-billed platypus unusual.* (Possible answer: It has webbed feet and a bill. It looks like a duck but it is a mammal.)

Chapter 3: Weird Creatures of the Deep

Intermediate *What happens when the cutter shark's body glows?* (The other fish can't see the shark above it.)

Advanced/Advanced High *How does the blobfish float?* (The pressure inside the body is similar to the pressure of the water.)

Summarize Have students identify important details about the cutter shark. Then have them summarize the information in their own words. (Possible answer: The bottom part of the cutter shark glows and helps to camouflage, or hide, from fish.)

Respond to Reading Have partners summarize the text and discuss the questions on page 15. Have them answer using new vocabulary.

Fluency: Expression and Intonation

Read aloud pages 10–11 with appropriate expression and intonation. Have students record themselves reading aloud to provide feedback.

Paired Read: "Hare and the Water"

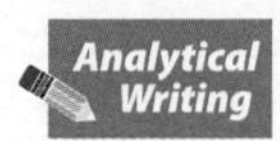

Make Connections: Write About It

Use the questions on page 18 before students write. Animals find water by digging in the ground. Animals need to find food and water and stay safe from predators to survive. The javelina makes noise to keep predators away. The animals in Africa worked together to find water.

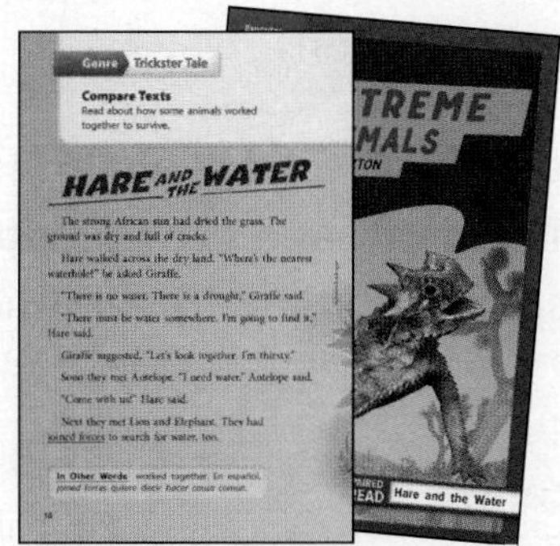

ELL Leveled Reader

Build Knowledge: Make Connections

Talk About the Text Have partners discuss how animals survive.

Write About the Text Have students add their ideas to their Build Knowledge pages of their reader's notebooks.

Self-Selected Reading

Have students choose another expository text from the online **Leveled Reader Library** or read the **Differentiated Text:** "How Animals Survive."

FOCUS ON SCIENCE

Have students complete the activity on page 20 to summarize an example of how an animal survives.

LITERATURE CIRCLES

Ask students to conduct a literature circle using the Thinkmark questions to guide the discussion.

FORMATIVE ASSESSMENT

STUDENT CHECK IN

Have partners share their answers to Respond to Reading. Ask students to reflect on their learning using the Check-In routine.

LEVEL UP

IF students read the **ELL Level** fluently and answered the questions

THEN pair them with students who have proficiently read the **On Level** and have students

- echo-read the **On Level** main selection with their partner;
- list words they find difficult;
- discuss these words with their partners.

Access Complex Text

The **On Level** challenges students by including more **academic language**, and **complex sentence structures**.

LEARNING GOALS

We can read and understand a drama.

OBJECTIVES

Determine a theme of a story, drama, or poem from details in the text; summarize the text.

Demonstrate understanding of words by relating them to their opposites and to words with similar but not identical meanings.

Engage effectively in a range of collaborative discussions with diverse partners on grade 4 topics and texts, building on others' ideas and expressing their own clearly.

LANGUAGE OBJECTIVES

Students will inquire about the characters, setting, and plot by asking and answering questions.

Students will discuss the theme of the drama using key vocabulary.

ELA ACADEMIC LANGUAGE

- *dialogue, antonyms*
- Cognates: *diálogo, antónimos*

MATERIALS

Reading/Writing Companion, pp. 152-155

Online Scaffolded Shared Read, "The Ant and the Grasshopper"

Visual Vocabulary Cards

Online ELL Visual Vocabulary Cards

DIGITAL TOOLS

MULTIMODAL

Have students read along with the audio of the selection to develop comprehension and practice fluency and pronunciation.

"The Ant and the Grasshopper"

Prepare to Read

Build Background Have students discuss stories they know about animals. Discuss whether they teach any lessons and elicit that they teach life lessons. Discuss the types of animal characters, such as foxes, who are clever and trick others.

Vocabulary Use the **Visual Vocabulary Cards** to preteach the vocabulary: *annoyed, attitude, commotion, cranky, familiar, frustrated, selfish,* and *specialty.* Use the online **ELL Visual Vocabulary Cards** to teach additional Vocabulary for the Shared Read: *advice, approach, attention, halt, nervously,* and *pause.*

Set Purpose *Today we will read a drama called "The Ant and the Grasshopper" and focus on understanding the theme. As we read, think about how animal characters change familiar stories.*

Read the Text

Select the **Scaffolded Shared Read** or the Shared Read in the **Reading/Writing Companion**, based on students' language proficiency.

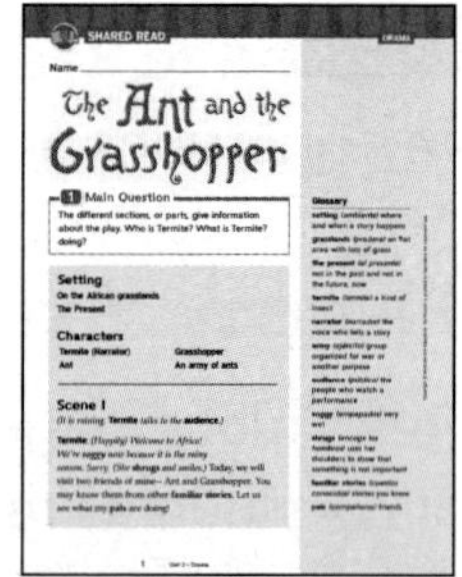
Scaffolded Shared Read, Lexile NP

Beginning/Early-Intermediate Use the online **Scaffolded Shared Read** to help partners work together to read and understand a drama. Remind them to use the Glossary to help them read and the Word Bank to help them answer the Main and Additional Questions.

Intermediate/Advanced Advanced High Read the text with students and use the Interactive Question-Response Routine to help them understand a drama.

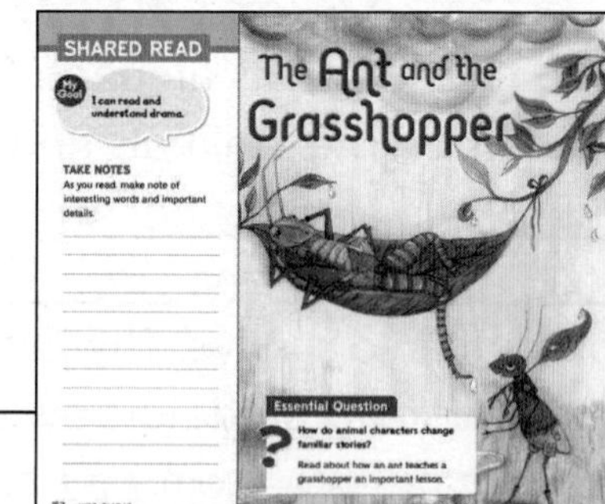

Reading/Writing Companion, Lexile NP

Page 153, Scene I

Read the text with students and review Vocabulary words *familiar, commotion, approach,* and *halt.* *What is the setting?* (African grasslands at present) *Who does Termite talk to?* (the audience) *Why does Termite talk to the audience?* Termite talks to the audience because Termite is the narrator. *Which season is it?* (rainy season) *What is Grasshopper doing?* (resting under a plant) *What is Ant doing?* (leading an army of ants carrying leaves filled with water)

Intermediate *How does Termite describe Grasshopper and Ant?* (They are very different from each other.) *How are Grasshopper and Ant different?* Grasshopper is resting but Ant is carrying leaves filled with water.

Advanced *Why do you think the ants are carrying water?* (Possible answer: The ants are collecting water so they can use it later.)

Advanced High *How is the setting important for understanding why the ants are working?* (African grasslands are dry. The ants will need water after it stops raining.)

COLLABORATE Have partners discuss the meaning of *commotion. What does* commotion *mean?* (*making lots of noise*) *What context clues help you understand the word* commotion*?* (*march in, feet pounding*)

Page 154, Scene I

Read the text with students and review Vocabulary words *annoyed, specialty, frustrated, attitude,* and *attention. What does Ant tell Grasshopper?* (There is work to do when it rains.) *Why does Ant work when it rains?* (to collect water and prepare for the future) *What does Grasshopper tell Ant?* (there is plenty of water now so no need to work so hard) *What does Ant tell Grasshopper that he will regret?* (being lazy and not being energetic during the rainy season)

COLLABORATE **Intermediate** *What kind of character is Ant?* (Possible answer: He works hard and thinks about the future.) *What word is an* ***antonym*** *for serious?* (carefree) *What word in the dialogue is a synonym for hard work?* (toil) *What word in the dialogue is an* ***antonym*** *for lazy?* (energetic)

Advanced/Advanced High *What words describe Grasshopper's "carefree attitude?"* (sleepily rises, scratching his head, laughing, continues to laugh) *What does Grasshopper say to show his attitude?* ("You need to relax. You're much too tense." "Stop working so hard all the time!")

COLLABORATE Review with students the meaning of the words *annoyed* and *frustrated.* Have partners discuss why Ant is annoyed and frustrated. (He thinks Grasshopper should collect rain.)

Page 154-155, Scene II

Read the text with students and review Vocabulary words *selfish, cranky, nervously, advice,* and *pause. What is the setting in Scene II?* (A few months have passed and the plains are dry and brown.) *How is Grasshopper?* (weak and sickly) *What is an* ***antonym*** *for sickly?* (healthy) *Why is Grasshopper at Ant's door?* (He needs water but can't find it anywhere.) *What does Ant tell Grasshopper?* (Ant can share only a few drops of water.) *Who does Termite talk to?* (the audience) *What lesson did Grasshopper learn?* (Grasshopper learned to prepare for the future.)

COLLABORATE **Intermediate** Have students retell how Ant responded to Grasshopper: First, Ant tries to shut the door. Then he pauses to think. Finally, Ant showed kindness by giving Grasshopper water. Why does Ant ask Grasshopper to not think them selfish? (He wants to help Grasshopper, but the ants need the water they collected.)

COLLABORATE **Advanced/Advanced High** *Discuss with your partner why Ant gives Grasshopper only a few drops of water. What reason does he give Grasshopper?* (Possible answer: The ants worked hard by collecting water during the rainy season. They need water for themselves during the dry season.)

COLLABORATE Have partners compare and contrast Ant and Grasshopper. Then discuss the **theme** with students. *How are they the same?* (Possible answers: They both live in the African grasslands.) *How are their actions different?* (Possible answers: Ant makes plans and prepares for the future, but Grasshopper thinks only about the present and doesn't plan for the future.) *Who do you think is wise, Ant or Grasshopper? Why or why not?* (Possible answer: Ant is wise because he plans for the future.) What is the **theme**, or the lessons the characters learned? (Possible answer: Grasshopper learned it is important to plan for the future.)

FORMATIVE ASSESSMENT

STUDENT CHECK-IN

Have partners retell the most important events in the story. Ask students to reflect using the Check-In routine.

LEARNING GOALS

- **We can read and understand a drama by identifying the theme.**
- **We can identify plural nouns and write complete sentences.**

OBJECTIVES

Paraphrase portions of a text read aloud or information presented in diverse media and formats, including visually, quantitatively, and orally.

Demonstrate command of the conventions of standard English capitalization, punctuation, and spelling when writing.

LANGUAGE OBJECTIVES

Students will discuss the setting and theme of a drama using words from the text.

Students will write sentences using plural nouns.

ELA ACADEMIC LANGUAGE

- *theme, singular, plural*
- Cognates: *tema, singular, plural*

MATERIALS

Reading/Writing Companion, pp. 152-155, 156-157

Online Scaffolded Shared Read, "The Ant and the Grasshopper"

Online Shared Read Writing Frames, p. 5

Online Language Development Cards, 11A-11B

Online Language Development Practice, pp. 61-66

Online Language Transfers Handbook, pp. 15-19

"The Ant and the Grasshopper"

Text Reconstruction

Focus on a single chunk of text to support comprehension and language development across the four domains.

1. Read aloud Scene II on pages 154-155 in the **Reading/Writing Companion** while students listen.
2. Write the following on the board, providing definitions as needed: *dusty, appearing, sickly, seeming.* Instruct students to listen for them as you read the scene a second time.
3. Read the scene a third time. Tell students to listen and take notes.
4.  COLLABORATE Have students work with a partner to reconstruct the text from their notes. Help them write complete sentences as needed.
5. Have students look at the original text. Ask them to tell the lesson Grasshopper learned from Ant. (Grasshopper learned that it is important to be prepared) Tell students they are going to discuss the theme, or the message or lesson, that the author wants the reader to learn. Remind them to look at the character's words and actions to help them figure out the theme.
6. *What does Grasshopper ask Ant?* (Grasshopper asks for some water) *Why?* (It is dry everywhere.) *What does Ant do?* (Ant will not let Grasshopper suffer, so gives him a few drops of water) *What did Ant tell Grasshopper?* (Grasshopper should be prepared.) *What is the theme?* (It is good to be prepared.)
7. Have students compare their text reconstructions to the original text. Have them check whether they also included information about the character's words and actions that describes the theme.

Beginning Have students follow along in the Reading/Writing Companion as you read the text aloud. Have them circle the words from Step 2 as they hear them.

Grammar in Context: Irregular Plural Nouns

Notice the Form Display two sentences from the text, and underline the nouns.

> *Termite: . . . Let's see what my buddies are up to!*
> *(An army of ants march in, carrying leaves filled with water . . .)*

What do the underlined words have in common? (They are all nouns.) *Which nouns are singular?* (army, water) *Which nouns are plural?* (buddies, ants, leaves) With students, review spelling rules for plural nouns and words that end in -y, -f, and -fe. Discuss examples, such as *shelf/shelves. What is the singular form of leaves?* (leaf) Have students copy and label the nouns in their notebooks.

Apply and Extend Have partners rewrite the text in their own words. Check their new sentences and spelling of plural nouns and provide feedback as needed.

For additional practice in identifying plural nouns and writing sentences, see **Language Development Cards**, Lessons 11A-11B and **Language Development Practice**, pages 61-66.

Independent Time

Vocabulary Building Have students build their glossaries.

Beginning/Early Intermediate Have students complete the Glossary Activities in the **Scaffolded Shared Read**.

Intermediate/Advanced/Advanced High Have students add the vocabulary from **Reading/Writing Companion** pages 156-157 and self-selected words or phrases they would like to learn to the chart.

WORD/PHRASE	DEFINE	EXAMPLE	ASK
suffer	to feel hurt or face hardship	He did not want to suffer from a sunburn.	What is an antonym for *suffer*?

COLLABORATE **Mixed Levels** Have partners complete the online leveled **Shared Read Writing Frames** to summarize the selection. Check their sentences and provide corrective feedback as needed. When students summarize the play, have them include what Grasshopper learns.

COLLABORATE **Subject-Verb Agreement** Have partners use a 2-column chart to write singular and plural nouns. Then have them generate verbs and write the correct verb forms. Provide an example: *The leaf blows in the wind. The leaves blow in the wind.* Check their work and provide corrective feedback.

Shared Read Writing Frames Use the online leveled Shared Read Writing Frames for "The Ant and the Grasshopper" to provide students with additional oral and written practice. Differentiated frames are available to provide support for all levels.

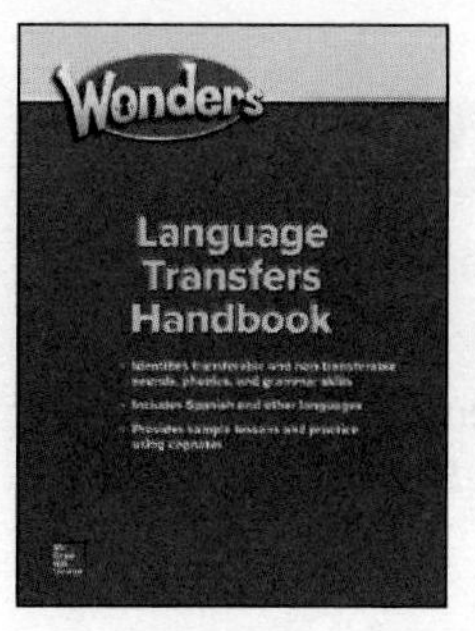

Language Transfers Handbook, Grammar Transfers pp. 15–19

DIGITAL TOOLS

For additional support, use the online activities.

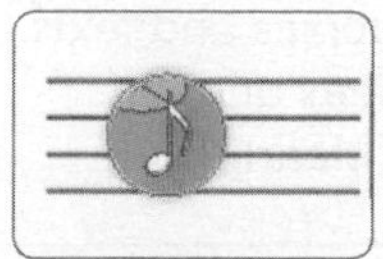

Grammar Song

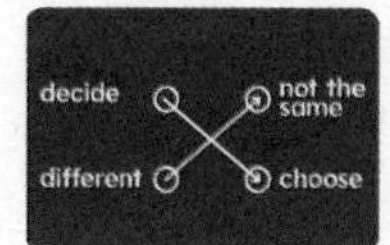

Vocabulary Activity

FORMATIVE ASSESSMENT

STUDENT CHECK IN

Text Reconstruction Have partners share their notes. Have students reflect on their work using the Check-In routine.

Grammar in Context Have partners share their sentences with plural nouns. Have students reflect on their work using the Check-In routine.

LEARNING GOALS

- **Read** We can read and understand a drama.
- **Reread** We can reread and analyze text, craft, and structure.

OBJECTIVES

Describe in depth a character, setting, or event in a story or drama, drawing on specific details in the text.

Engage effectively in a range of collaborative discussions with diverse partners on grade 4 topics and texts, building on others' ideas and expressing their own clearly.

LANGUAGE OBJECTIVES

Students will inquire by answering questions about the text using key vocabulary.

Students will explain author's use of word choice using academic vocabulary.

ELA ACADEMIC LANGUAGE

- *dialogue, stage directions, setting*
- Cognates: *diálogo*

MATERIALS

Literature Anthology, pp. 110-125

Reading/Writing Companion, pp. 164-166

Visual Vocabulary Cards

Online ELL Anchor Text Support BLMs, pp. 12-14

DIGITAL TOOLS

MULTIMODAL

Have students read along with the audio of the selection to develop comprehension and practice fluency and pronunciation.

Ranita, The Frog Princess

Prepare to Read

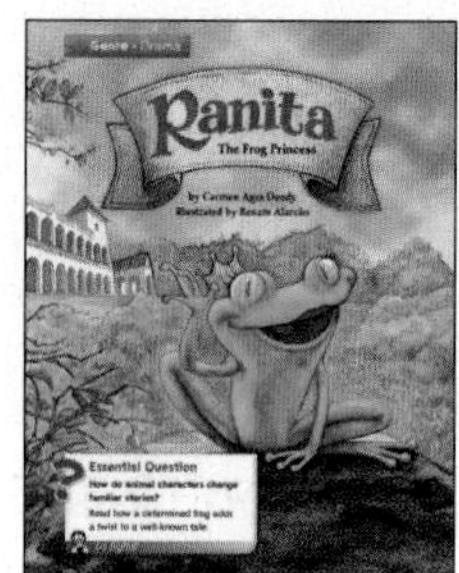

Literature Anthology

Build Background Explain that a drama, or play is a story that is acted out for an audience. Remind students that animals are often characters in a story. Invite students to talk about a story or play they have read or seen that has animal characters.

Vocabulary Use the **Visual Vocabulary Cards** to review the vocabulary: *annoyed, attitude, commotion, cranky, familiar, frustrated, selfish,* and *specialty*.

Set Purpose Today we will read a drama about Ranita, the frog princess. As we read, think about how animal characters change familiar stories

Have students listen to the audio summary of the text, which is available in multiple languages.

Read

Literature Anthology, pp. 110-125

Use the **Interactive Question-Response Routine** to help students read and discuss *Ranita, The Frog Princess.*

Beginning Help students discuss in complete sentences. Provide sentence frames: Ranita finds Felipe's golden arrow. Felipe is surprised to see a talking frog.

Intermediate Ask students to respond in complete sentences and add details. Provide sentence starters as needed: Ranita finds Felipe's golden arrow in the forest. Felipe was not expecting to meet a talking frog.

Advanced/Advanced High Have students respond in complete sentences and add details.

COLLABORATE **Independent Reading Practice** Have mixed level pairs complete pages 12-14 of ELL Anchor Text Support BLMs and share responses with others.

Reread

Use with **Reading/Writing Companion,** pages 164-166.

Literature Anthology, page 114

COLLABORATE **Author's Craft: Word Choice** Read the text with students and point to the Spanish words on the page. *What three things does Ranita want to do?* Ranita wants to eat from Felipe's *plato*. She wants to sleep in Felipe's *cama*. Ranita wants Felipe to give her a *beso*. Point out that the English translations of the Spanish words appear in the following sentences.

Beginning Read page 114 with students and restate the sentences as needed. Point to Ranita's first dialogue and ask a question for partners to discuss and answer: *What are the italicized words?* (Spanish words) Point to Felipe's first dialogue and ask: *What is the English word for* plato*?* (plate) *What is the English word for* cama*?* (bed) *What is the English word for* beso*?* (kiss)

Intermediate *What does Ranita want Felipe to promise to do?* Ranita wants Felipe to promise to let her eat from his *plato*, sleep in his *cama*, and give her a *beso*. *What do the Spanish words* plato, cama, *and* beso *mean*? (plate, bed, and kiss) *How do you know from the dialogues?* I know because Felipe repeats the Spanish words in English.

Advanced *How does the author let you know the meaning of the Spanish words?* (The author repeats the words in English in the following sentences.) *Is Felipe happy about making a promise to Ranita? How do you know?* (No, he says the promises Ranita asks are "disgusting.")

Literature Anthology, page 116

COLLABORATE **Author's Craft: Dialogue** Read the text with students. Point to the stage directions and discuss the meaning of the words that describe how the characters feel and react. Remind students that the stage directions tell the actors how to say their dialogue. Discuss what the descriptions tell about how the characters feel about Felipe.

Beginning Read paragraphs 3-6 with students and restate as needed. Discuss what Viceroy, his wife, and the servants think and feel about Felipe. *What does Viceroy's wife and Servant Two think Felipe is doing?* They think Felipe is giving birds to the cat. *What does Servant One do?* He smiles quietly.

Intermediate Have partners discuss the words that describe how the other characters feel about Felipe. Have them use details from the text: The other characters think Felipe is mean and do not like him because they describe that Felipe is feeding birds to the cat and Felipe's servant, Pepe, smiles and lets Ranita go.

Advanced/Advanced High Have partners discuss what the stage directions and words *exasperated, wistfully, muffles laugh,* and Pepe's actions, tell about their feeling about Felipe. (Possible answer: The words in the stage directions tell that the characters make a joke about Felipe being mean. Pepe does not like Felipe because he lets Ranita go.)

Literature Anthology, page 121-122

COLLABORATE **Plot: Setting** Guide students to identify the setting and characters of the play on page 112 and clarify the terms *Viceroy, mistreated,* and *servant.* Read scene 3 on pages 121-122 with students and point out the stage directions. Have them ask about words or phrases that are unfamiliar and define them for clarification. *Who is Pepe?* (Pepe is Felipe's servant.) *Why do the servants have to listen to Felipe?* (Felipe is a nobleman. He has a lot of power over his servants.)

Beginning Read page 121 with students and restate as needed. *Who is Felipe's servant?* (Pepe) *Look at the stage directions, do you think Felipe treats Pepe badly?* (yes) *Do you think life was easy or difficult for servants during that time in Mexico?* (difficult)

Intermediate Have partners read the text and discuss how Felipe treats Pepe. *How does Felipe treat Pepe?* Felipe treats Pepe badly. *Why does Pepe have to listen to Felipe?* Pepe has to listen to Felipe because he is Felipe's servant.

Advanced/Advanced High Have partner discuss why the setting is important to the plot. *How does the setting help you understand how Felipe treats his servants?* (The setting helps me understand that Felipe has a lot of power over his servants.)

FORMATIVE ASSESSMENT

STUDENT CHECK IN

Read Have partners share their responses to the Anchor Text questions. Then have them reflect using the Check-In routine.

Reread Have partners share responses and text evidence on Reading/Writing Companion pages 164-166. Then have them reflect using the Check-In routine to fill in the bars.

LEARNING GOALS

- We can read and understand drama by identifying the theme.
- We can identify and use possessive nouns.

OBJECTIVES

Paraphrase portions of a text read aloud or information presented in diverse media and formats, including visually, quantitatively, and orally.

Demonstrate command of the conventions of standard English grammar and usage when writing or speaking.

LANGUAGE OBJECTIVES

Students will inform about the theme of a text using signal words.

Students will inquire about the parts of a sentence using academic language.

ELA ACADEMIC LANGUAGE

- *theme, apostrophe, possessive noun*
- cognates: *tema*

MATERIALS

Literature Anthology, pp. 110-125

Online Language Development Cards, 12A-12B

Online Language Development Practice, pp. 67-72

Online Language Transfers Handbook, pp. 15-19

Ranita, The Frog Princess

Text Reconstruction

Focus on a single chunk of text to support comprehension and language development across the four domains.

1. Read aloud page 122 of the **Literature Anthology** while students listen.
2. Write the following on the board, providing definitions as needed: *smug, dazzles, enchanted, spoiled, brat.* Instruct students to listen for them as you read the page a second time.
3. Read the page a third time while students listen and take notes.
4. COLLABORATE Have students work with a partner to reconstruct the text from their notes. Help them write complete sentences as needed.
5. Have students look at the original text. Ask them to tell the theme, or the overall message or lesson. (It is not good to break a promise) Tell students they are going to examine the character's actions and dialogue to figure out the theme of the story.
6. *Did Felipe keep his promise to Ranita?* (no) *Why not?* (He made Pepe kiss Ranita instead) *What happened after Pepe kissed Ranita?* (Ranita was no longer a frog.) *Who is Ranita?* (a princess) *Who will she marry?* (Pepe) *What is the theme?* (Possible answer: It is important to keep a promise.)
7. Have students compare their text reconstructions to the original text. Have them check if they also included descriptions of the characters' actions and dialogue that tell about the theme.

Beginning Allow students to follow along in their **Literature Anthologies** as you read the text aloud. Have them point to the words from Step 2 as they hear them.

Apply Author's Craft: Word Choice

Remind students that authors use descriptive words that describe how a character thinks, feels, and acts. *On page 120, the text says Felipe is snappish. What other words describe Felipe?* (desperate, whining) Discuss the meaning of the words desperate and whining and have partners write sentences using the words to describe Felipe.

Grammar in Context: Deconstruct a Sentence

Write this line of dialogue on the board:

Ranita: *—the Spanish Viceroy's Rotten Son. And I am . . . the Mayan Emperor's Lucky Daughter.*

Facilitate deconstructing this sentence for better comprehension:

- *What are the words that have an apostrophe and an -s?* (Viceroy's, Emperor's) *What do these words do?* (describe what or to whom something belongs) *What part of speech are these words?* (nouns) *What kind of nouns are they? (possessive nouns)*
- *How do you form the possessive for singular nouns?* (add an apostrophe and an *-s*) *How does adding an apostrophe and an -s change the word?* (It makes the noun into a possessive noun.)
- *Where do you use possessive nouns?* (use it before another noun) Have students point to the possessive nouns and the nouns after them. (Viceroy's hunting lodge, Emperor's Lucky Daughter) *Who owns the hunting lodge? (the Viceroy) Who is related to the Viceroy? (the Rotten Son) Who is related to the Emperor? (the Lucky Daughter)* Point out that the possessive nouns tell about the person who owns things, and that with people they show relationships.
- Have partners work together to write sentences to describe friends using possessive nouns. Provide samples: Juan's father is a pilot.

For additional practice, see **Language Development Cards**, Lessons 12A-12B, and **Language Development Practice**, pages 67-72.

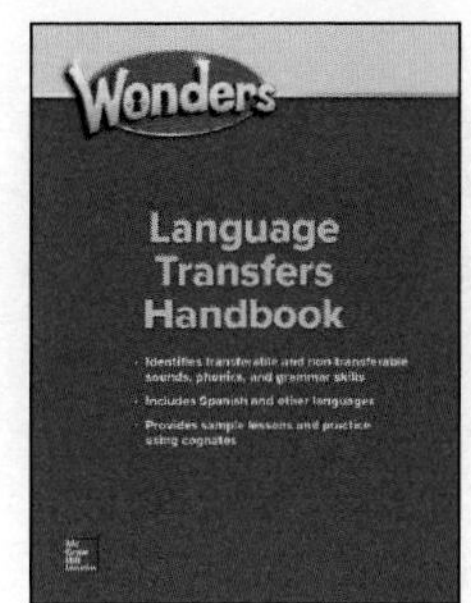

Language Transfers Handbook Grammar Transfers, pp. 15-19

Independent Time

Vocabulary Building Have students create an interactive word game with vocabulary from the selection. First, have students select five adjectives from the text and copy them onto index cards. Have them generate synonyms and antonyms for each word.

Beginning Have students group the words as synonyms and antonyms.

Intermediate/Advanced/Advanced High Have students write sentences using the words from the text and rewrite using synonyms or antonyms.

Dialogue Have partners work together to write a brief dialogue of the Vieja Sabia telling a friend why she turned Felipe into a frog.

Beginning Provide sentence frames. **Vieja Sabia:** I turned Felipe into a frog because he was rude. He would not give me water.

Intermediate Provide sentence frames. **Vieja Sabia:** Today I turned Felipe into a frog. I did it because he was rude. He wouldn't get me water. He needs to learn manners.

Advanced/Advanced High Have partners include both Vieja Sabia telling about why she turned Felipe into a frog and what that friend might say back.

FORMATIVE ASSESSMENT

STUDENT CHECK-IN

Text Reconstruction Ask partners to share their notes. Have them reflect using the Check-In routine.

Grammar in Context Ask partners to reflect on their deconstructions using the Check-In routine.

LEARNING GOALS

We can apply strategies and skills to read drama.

OBJECTIVES

Determine a theme of a story, drama, or poem from details in the text; summarize the text.

Demonstrate understanding of words by relating them to their opposites and to words with similar but not identical meanings.

Engage effectively in a range of collaborative discussions with diverse partners on grade 4 topics and texts, building on others' ideas and expressing their own clearly.

LANGUAGE OBJECTIVES

Students will discuss the theme using key vocabulary.

Students will identify antonyms using context clues.

ELA ACADEMIC LANGUAGE

- *evidence, theme, antonyms*
- Cognates: *evidencia, tema, antónimos*

MATERIALS

Online ELL Genre Passage, *The Dragon Problem*

The Dragon Problem

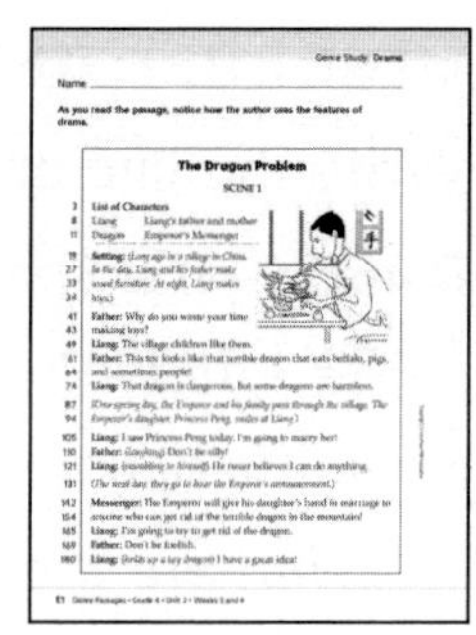

Genre Passage
Lexile NP

Prepare to Read

Build Background Discuss with students drama **structure,** such as the setting, a list of characters, and stage directions. Review the types of important information they learn about what characters do and feel and how they react. Have them discuss using: I can use the setting/stage directions to learn about ____. Review the other features of a drama, such as scenes, dialogue, and how to identify character tags.

Vocabulary Use the Define/Example/Ask routine to preteach difficult words or unfamiliar concepts, such as *Emperor, messenger, dangerous.* (Cognates: emperador, mensajero) Invite students to add new vocabulary to their glossaries.

Set Purpose *Today we will read a drama called "The Dragon Problem" and focus on understanding the* ***theme****. As we read, think about how animal characters change familiar stories.*

Read the Text

Page E1, Scene 1, Paragraphs 1–5

Beginning Read the List of Characters and Setting with students. *Who are the characters?* The characters are Liang, Dragon, Liang's father and mother, and Emperor's Messenger. *What is the setting?* The setting is a village in China long ago. *What does Liang make?* Liang makes toys.

Intermediate *Discuss with a partner Father's attitude about Liang making toys.* Liang's father thinks Liang is wasting his time.

Advanced/Advanced High *What does Liang's reply to Father's comment about the dragon tell you about Liang?* (Possible answer: Liang knows a lot more about dragons because he replies that some dragons are harmless.)

COLLABORATE **Antonyms** Talk About the Text *Read Paragraphs 5 and 6 and discuss with a partner the antonym for* dangerous. *Look for clues in the text:* The antonym for *dangerous* is harmless. I know because *harmless* means without danger.

Page E1, Scene 1, Paragraphs 6–14

COLLABORATE **Beginning** *Who is the Emperor's daughter?* (Princess Peng) *What does Liang tell his father after Liang sees Princess Peng?* Liang says he is going to marry Princess Peng. Read the last four paragraphs on page E1 with students and describe the meaning of *get rid of. Discuss with a partner what Liang plans to do with the dragon and how Father responds:* Liang is going to get rid of the dragon. Father thinks Liang is foolish.

Intermediate *What announcement does the Emperor give?* The Emperor's Messenger explains that the person who gets rid of the dragon will marry Princess Peng. *What does Liang plan to do?* Liang decides to get rid of the dragon. *What does his father think about the plan?* He thinks Liang is foolish.

COLLABORATE **Advanced/Advanced High** *Discuss with a partner why you think the Emperor wants to get rid of the dragon. Use text evidence to support your response.* (Possible answer: I think he wants to get rid of the dragon because it is dangerous. Liang's father said that it eats buffalo, pigs, and people.)

COLLABORATE **Advanced High** *How does Liang feel about his father's attitude toward him?* (Possible answer: Liang is not happy about it. He mumbles that his father thinks he can't do anything.)

Page E2, Scene 2, Paragraphs 1–14

Beginning *What is the setting in Scene 2?* The setting is one week later and at the dragon's cave. *What words tell you the dragon is inside the cave?* (the words "a ball of fire shoots out from the cave") *What does Liang put against a rock?* (statue of a dragon)

Intermediate *What does Father say is dangerous?* Father thinks it is dangerous to be near the dragon's cave. *What word describes how the dragon felt? (nervously) What is the root word? (nervous)*

COLLABORATE **Advanced/Advanced High** *Discuss with a partner: How is Mother's attitude different from Liang's father's attitude?* (Possible answer: Mother believes in Liang. However, Father thinks Liang is doing something dangerous.) *How does Liang use his skills to get rid of the dragon?* (He makes a wooden statue of a dragon to scare it away.)

Respond to Reading

Use the following instruction to help students answer the questions on page E3.

1. *Read page E1 and look for Father's responses to Liang when he says that he will marry Princess Ping. What does Father tell Liang?* (Don't be silly.) *Why might Father think this?* (Possible answer: He doesn't believe in his son.)
2. **Story Elements: Drama** *What is a setting?* (It is the time and place where the action occurs.) *Where do dramas describe the setting?* (at the beginning of each scene) Find the setting on page E1.
3. **Theme** *How did Father's attitude toward Liang change?* (In the beginning, Father thought Liang was silly. At the end of the story, Father said that he believed in Liang.)

Fluency Have partners take turns reading the passage.

Build Knowledge: Make Connections

Talk About the Text Have partners discuss how animal characters change familiar stories.

Write About the Text Have students add their ideas to their Build Knowledge pages of their reader's notebooks.

FORMATIVE ASSESSMENT

STUDENT CHECK IN

Have partners share their responses on page E3 and reflect using the Check-In routine.

LEVEL UP

IF students read the **ELL** of the **Genre Passage** fluently and answered the questions,

THEN pair them with students who have proficiently read the **On Level** Have them

- partner read the **On Level** passage.
- retell the theme of the story.

LEARNING GOALS

We can apply strategies and skills to read drama.

OBJECTIVES

Describe in depth a character, setting, or event in a story or drama, drawing on specific details in the text.

Engage effectively in a range of collaborative discussions with diverse partners on grade 4 topics and texts, building on others' ideas and expressing their own clearly.

Read grade-level prose and poetry orally with accuracy, appropriate rate, and expression on successive readings.

LANGUAGE OBJECTIVES

Students will inquire about the theme of a drama by asking and answering questions.

ELA ACADEMIC LANGUAGE

- *evidence, theme*
- cognates: *evidencia, tema*

MATERIALS

ELL Leveled Reader, *The Prince Who Could Fly*

Online Differentiated Texts, "Grasshopper's Search for Water"

Online ELL Visual Vocabulary Cards

DIGITAL TOOLS

MULTIMODAL

Have students read along with the audio of the selections to develop comprehension and practice fluency and pronunciation.

The Prince Who Could Fly

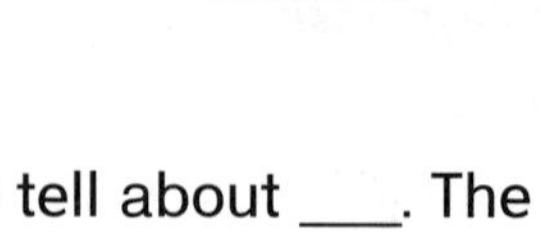

Leveled Reader Lexile NP

Prepare to Read

Build Background Review the Essential Question, *How do animal characters change familiar stories?* Have students describe stories they know that have animal characters. Ask: *Did the animal character learn a lesson or help to teach a lesson to another character?* Have students discuss using: I know a story about ___. The story has an animal character who learns/teaches a lesson about ___. Have students review the text features of a play, such as setting, characters, and stage directions. Have them discuss using: The setting/characters tell about ___. The stage directions tell about ___.

Based on the title, have students predict the animals they might read about. For example: The word *fly* is in the title, so I predict that a bird is a character.

Vocabulary Use the routine on the **ELL Visual Vocabulary Cards** to preteach ELL Vocabulary *comfortable, deserve, lonely*. Have students add these words to their glossaries.

Set Purpose *Today we are going to read a drama called "The Prince Who Could Fly." As we read, think about how animal characters change familiar stories.*

Read the Text

Scene 1, Pages 2–6

Beginning Read page 3 with students and have them describe the meaning of *lonely. Is Princess lonely? Why?* Yes, Princess is lonely. She sits by the window and looks at the trees. Have students locate the text that tells them.

COLLABORATE **Intermediate** *Discuss with a partner what King and Queen disagree on about the princess:* King wants Princess to live with him and Queen, but Queen wants Princess to stay alone in the castle.

Advanced/Advanced High *How do you know the queen treats the princess badly?* (The maid says the queen's specialty is being mean.)

Scene 2, Pages 7–10

COLLABORATE **Beginning** Read the stage directions and Princess's dialogue on page 9 with students. Demonstrate "turning the pages forward." *What happens when Princess turns the page forward?* A canary flies inside. *How do you know?* (the stage directions say "A yellow canary flies in through the window.")

Intermediate *How does the wise woman help the Princess?* (gives her a book that turns the prince into a bird so he can visit her. When he is inside, the book turns him back into a prince.)

Scene 3, Pages 11–15

Beginning *How does Queen hurt Prince?* Queen puts a pin on the cushion. *Who helps Prince?* The maid and Princess help Prince.

Advanced/Advanced High *What kind of person is the maid? Use examples to support your response.* (Possible answers: She is kind and cares about Princess. She helps Princess rescue Prince.)

Ask and Answer Questions Have partners *ask and answer questions about the theme.* (Possible answer: Why is it important to be kind? If you are kind, other people will help you.)

Respond to Reading Have partners summarize and answer the questions on page 16 using the new vocabulary.

Fluency: Accuracy

Read pages 3–4 with appropriate accuracy. Read the passage aloud again and have students read along with you. For practice, have students record their voices while they read. Have them play their recordings to you and choose the best one.

Paired Read: "The Mystery of the Spotted Dog"

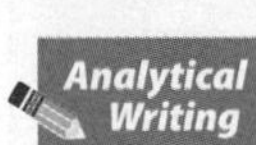

Make Connections: Write About It

Help students discuss the questions on page 19 using: Detective Dog helps Mrs. Marjoram find the real Dalmatian puppies. The Wise Woman helps Princess and Prince spend time together. Help them find text evidence on pages 8–9 and respond using: The Wise Woman gives Princess a book and tells Maid to turn pages forward and back to change Prince into a canary.

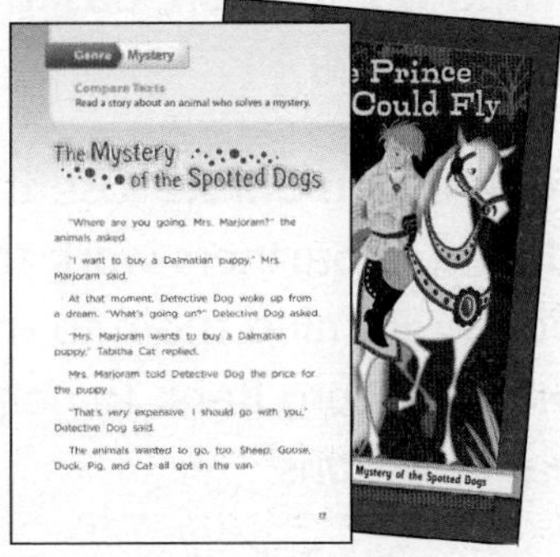

ELL Leveled Reader

Build Knowledge: Make Connections

Talk About the Text Have partners discuss how animal characters change familiar stories.

Write About the Text Have students add their ideas to their Build Knowledge pages of their reader's notebooks.

Self-Selected Reading

Have students choose another drama from the online **Leveled Reader Library** or read the **Differentiated Text:** "Grasshopper's Search for Water."

FOCUS ON SOCIAL STUDIES

Have students complete the activity on page 20 to practice finding and using text features of a drama.

LITERATURE CIRCLES

Ask students to conduct a literature circle using the Thinkmark questions to guide the discussion.

FORMATIVE ASSESSMENT

STUDENT CHECK IN

Have partners share their answers to Respond to Reading. Ask students to reflect on their learning using the Check-In routine.

LEVEL UP

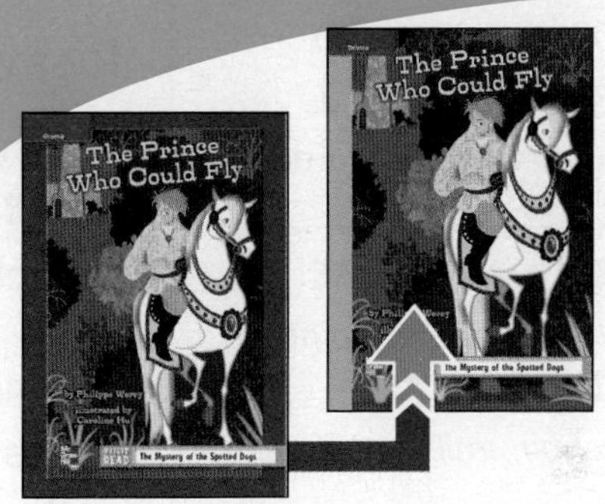

IF students read the **ELL Level** fluently and answered the questions

THEN pair them with students who have proficiently read the **On Level** and have students

- echo-read the **On Level** main selection with their partner
- list words they find difficult.
- discuss these words with their partners

Access Complex Text

The **On Level** challenges students by including more **dialogue** and **complex sentence structures**.

LEARNING GOALS

We can read and understand poetry.

OBJECTIVES

Explain major differences between poems, drama, and prose, and refer to the structural elements of poems and drama when writing or speaking about a text.

Explain the meaning of simple similes and metaphors in context.

Engage effectively in a range of collaborative discussions with diverse partners on grade 4 topics and texts, building on others' ideas and expressing their own clearly.

LANGUAGE OBJECTIVES

Students will discuss the character perspective using key vocabulary.

Students will discuss similes and metaphors using descriptive words

ELA ACADEMIC LANGUAGE

- *describe, simile, metaphor, point of view, perspective*
- Cognates: *describir, imil, metáfora, perspectiva*

MATERIALS

Reading/Writing Companion, pp. 178-181

Online Scaffolded Shared Read, "Dog," "The Eagle," "Chimpanzee," and "Rat"

Visual Vocabulary Cards

Online ELL Visual Vocabulary Cards

DIGITAL TOOLS

MULTIMODAL

Have students read along with the audio of the selection to develop comprehension and practice fluency and pronunciation.

"Dog," "The Eagle," "Chimpanzee," and "Rat"

Prepare to Read

Build Background Discuss with students characteristics of poems, including form. Say: *Lyric poetry expresses thoughts and feelings about something. It often* ***rhymes*** *and has* ***meter***. Clap "Twinkle, Twinkle Little Star" to demonstrate rhythm and **meter**. *A haiku has three lines. The first and last lines have 5 syllables each, and the middle line has 7 syllables. Haikus do not usually* ***rhyme***.

Vocabulary Use the **Visual Vocabulary Cards** to preteach the vocabulary: *creative, descriptive, brittle,* and *outstretched.* Use the online **ELL Visual Vocabulary Cards** to teach additional Vocabulary from the Shared Read: *wrinkled* and *patiently.*

Set Purpose *Today, we will read the poems "Dog," "The Eagle," "Chimpanzee," and "Rat" and focus on the point of view or* ***perspective*** *in each poem. As we read, think about how writers are inspired by animals.*

Read the Text

Select the **Scaffolded Shared Read** or the Shared Read in the **Reading/Writing Companion,** based on students' language proficiency.

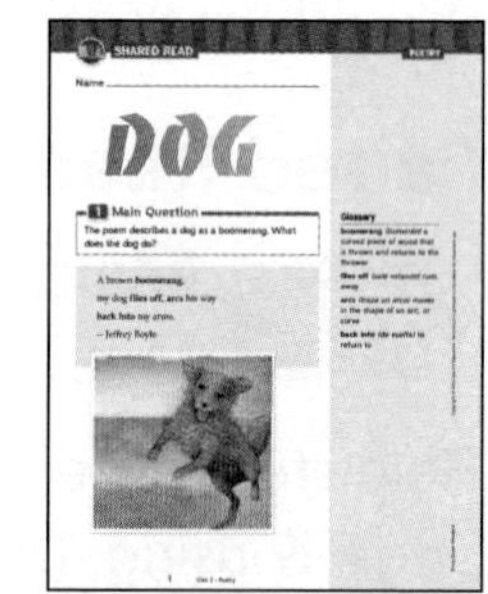

Scaffolded Shared Read, Lexile NP

Beginning/Early-Intermediate Use the online **Scaffolded Shared Read** to help partners work together to read and understand poetry. Remind them to use the Glossary to help them read and the Word Bank to help them answer the Main and Additional Questions.

Intermediate/Advanced Advanced High Read the text with students and use the Interactive Question-Response Routine to help them understand poetry.

Reading/Writing Companion, Lexile NP

Page 178, "Dog"

Lines 1–3 Read the poem with students. Discuss what the poem tells about the dog. *What words describe the dog?* (brown boomerang, flies off, arcs his way) Define the words *boomerang* and *arcs* using visuals and gestures. Point to the phrase "A brown boomerang, my dog flies off" and explain that it is a ***metaphor***. *A* ***metaphor*** *compares two different things. What two things are being compared?* (a dog and a boomerang) *What does the dog do?* (goes away and returns) *What does a boomerang do?* Elicit that they both do the same thing.

Intermediate *What does "flies off" mean?* (go away) *What does "arcs" mean?* (curves) *What shape is the dog when it flies off?* (curves like a boomerang)

Advanced/Advanced High *What does a boomerang do?* (It comes back after it is thrown.) *Do you think the dog knows the speaker?* (Possible answer: Yes. The speaker says "my dog" and he comes back.)

COLLABORATE Have partners discuss why the speaker compares the dog to a boomerang. (Possible answer: The dog returns, just like a boomerang.)

Page 179, "The Eagle"

Stanza 1 Read the stanza with students. Define the words *crag* and *azure*. Point out that "crooked hands" refers to the talon, or claws. Have students choose other words or phrases and define them. Have students circle the pronouns to identify the point of view or **perspective**. (He, he) *Who is the speaker talking about by using the pronoun* he? (the eagle) *What does the eagle do?* (The eagle stands on a cliff.)

Intermediate Read line 1 and have students restate what the eagle is doing: The eagle is holding onto a cliff with his claws.

Stanza 2 Read the stanza with students and review Vocabulary word *wrinkled. What makes the sea seem wrinkled?* (the moving waves, seen from the eagle's position) Explain that "And like a thunderbolt he falls" is a ***simile***. *A **simile** compares two different things. A **simile** uses the words* like *or* as. *What two things are being compared?* (a thunderbolt and an eagle)

Advanced/Advanced High *What does the **simile** tell about the eagle?* (It is fast and powerful.)

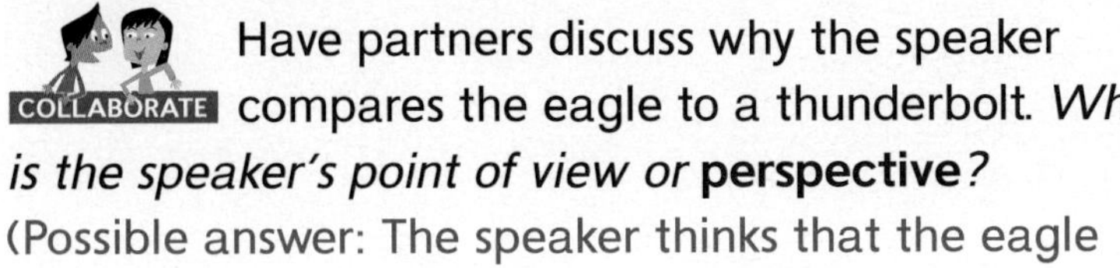
COLLABORATE Have partners discuss why the speaker compares the eagle to a thunderbolt. *What is the speaker's point of view or* **perspective**? (Possible answer: The speaker thinks that the eagle can fly down quickly like a thunderbolt.)

Page 180, "Chimpanzee"

Stanzas 1–3 Read the stanzas with students and review the meaning of *outstretched, patiently,* and *brittle*. Clarify that *bare* means "not having a cover" and that it sounds like *bear* but has a different spelling and meaning. Have students circle the pronouns to identify the character. (I) *Who is the speaker of the poem?* (the chimpanzee) *Is the speaker a character in the poem?* (yes) *How do you know?* (Possible answer: The title is "Chimpanzee" and the speaker uses the pronoun *I*.) *What does the chimpanzee call the skinny branch?* (a bridge) *Is this a **metaphor** or **simile**?* (a metaphor) *How do you know?* (makes a comparison without using *like* or *as*) *What does this tell about the chimpanzee's point of view, or **perspective**?* (Possible answer: The chimpanzee probably thinks that he will get bugs easily.)

Intermediate Read line 1 and have students restate what the chimpanzee is doing: The chimpanzee is swinging from branch to branch with his arms. *What does the chimpanzee want to do?* (eat bugs)

Advanced/Advanced High *What does the chimpanzee do with the stick?* (Possible answer: Uses the stick to get bugs out of the hole.)

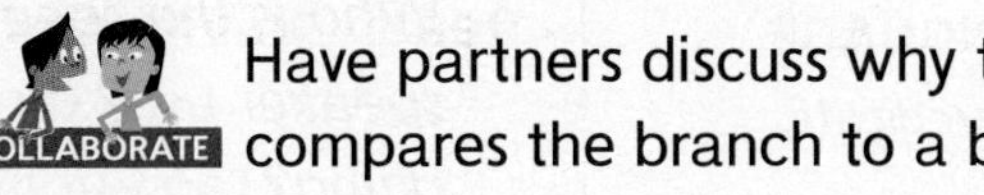
COLLABORATE Have partners discuss why the speaker compares the branch to a bridge. (Possible answer: The bugs walk on the branch like a bridge.)

Page 181, "Rat"

Lines 1–3 Read the poem with students. Define the words *jackhammer* and *concrete* using visuals and gestures. *Who is the speaker?* (the rat) *How do you know?* (pronoun *I*) *What does the speaker compare in lines 1 and 2?* The speaker compares the rat's teeth to a jackhammer. *What does the rat do with its teeth?* (chews through concrete)

COLLABORATE Have partners discuss why the rat compares its teeth to a jackhammer. (Possible answer: The rat has strong teeth that can chew concrete and a jackhammer cuts through concrete.)

FORMATIVE ASSESSMENT

STUDENT CHECK-IN

Have partners retell the important ideas in the text. Ask students to reflect using the Check-In routine.

LEARNING GOALS

- **We can read and understand poetry by identifying character perspective.**
- **We can combine sentences.**

OBJECTIVES

Paraphrase portions of a text read aloud or information presented in diverse media and formats, including visually, quantitatively, and orally.

Demonstrate command of the conventions of standard English grammar and usage when writing or speaking.

LANGUAGE OBJECTIVES

Students will inform by identifying character perspective using context clues in poetry.

Students will write using a conjunction to combine sentences.

ELA ACADEMIC LANGUAGE

- *perspective, subject, predicate, conjunction*
- Cognates: *perspectiva, sujeto, predicado, conjunción*

MATERIALS

Reading/Writing Companion, pp. 178-181, 182-183

Online Scaffolded Shared Read, "Dog," "The Eagle," "Chimpanzee," and "Rat"

Online Shared Read Writing Frames, p. 6

Online Language Development Practice Cards 70A, 70B

Online Language Development Practice, pp. 415-420

Online Language Transfers Handbook, pp. 15-19

"Dog," "The Eagle," "Chimpanzee," and "Rat"

Text Reconstruction

Focus on a single chunk of text to support comprehension and language development across the four domains.

1. Read aloud "The Eagle" on page 179 of the **Reading/Writing Companion** while students listen.
2. Write the following on the board, providing definitions as needed: *clasps, crag, crooked,* and *azure*. Instruct students to listen for them as you read the poem a second time.
3. Read the poem a third time. Tell students to listen and take notes of descriptive words in the poem.
4.  COLLABORATE Have students work with a partner to reconstruct the text from their notes.
5. Have students look at the original text. Ask them to tell what the poem is mostly about. (the eagle looking down from a high cliff) Tell students they are going to examine the perspective, or how the character feels about something.
6. *Who is the speaker?* (someone who sees the eagle) *What pronoun does the speaker use?* (he) *What does the speaker tell you about what the eagle is doing?* (an eagle is up on a cliff looking down at the sea, then falls like a thunderbolt) *What does this tell you about the speaker's perspective?* (Possible: he is amazed, impressed by the eagle)
7. Have students compare their text reconstructions to the original text. Have them check if they also included the author's perspective about the eagle.

Beginning Have students follow along in the Reading/Writing Companion as you read the text aloud. Have them circle the words from Step 2 as they hear them.

Grammar in Context: Combining Sentences

Notice the Form Display the sentences and underline the conjunction *and.*

> The eagle watches from his mountain walls. The eagle falls like a thunderbolt.
>
> The eagle watches from his mountain walls and falls like a thunderbolt.

What is the subject in the first two sentences? (The eagle) Circle *The eagle* in both sentences. *What is the predicate of each sentence?* (watches from his mountain wall, falls like a thunderbolt) Then read the last sentence. *What is the underlined word?* (and) Explain that *and* combines what the eagle does in the first two sentences. Have students copy and label the sentences in their notebooks.

Apply and Extend Have partners practice combining sentences using the word *and* by writing sentences to describe the location of their classmates in the classroom. Provide a model: *Diego sits by the window. Sue sits by the window. Diego and Sue sit by the window.* Check their answers and provide feedback.

For additional practice, see **Language Development Cards,** Lessons 70A-70B and **Language Development Practice,** pages 415–420.

Independent Time

Vocabulary Building Have students build their glossaries.

Beginning/Early Intermediate Have students complete the Glossary Activities in the **Scaffolded Shared Read.**

Intermediate/Advanced/Advanced High Have students add to the chart the vocabulary from **Reading/Writing Companion** pages 182-183 and self-selected words or phrases they would like to learn.

WORD/PHRASE	DEFINE	EXAMPLE	ASK
arc	to curve or bend	The light arced through the window.	Is this where the word *arch* comes from?

COLLABORATE **Make Comparisons** Have partners choose an animal from the poems in the Reading/Writing Companion or another animal and write their own simile or metaphor. Have them discuss what the animals look like and what they do to generate words and ideas. Then have each pair share their comparison and tell whether the comparison is a metaphor or a simile.

Shared Read Writing Frames Use the online leveled Shared Read Writing Frames for "Dog," "The Eagle," "Chimpanzee," and "Rat" to provide students with additional oral and written practice. Differentiated frames are available to provide support for all levels.

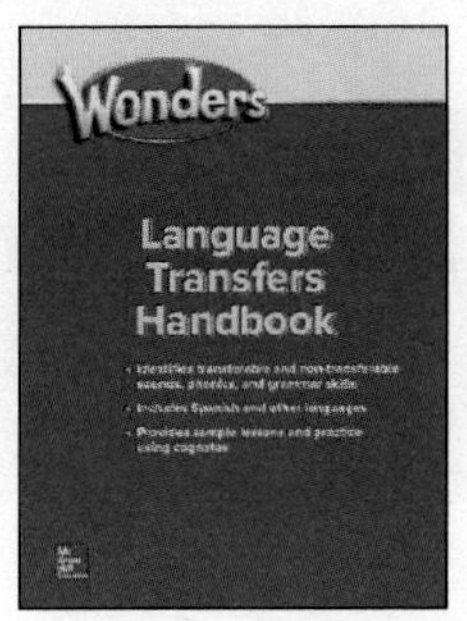

Language Transfers Handbook, Grammar Transfers pp. 15-19

DIGITAL TOOLS

For additional support, use the online activities.

Grammar Video

Grammar Song

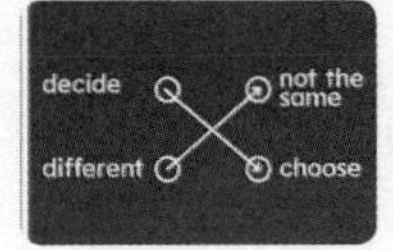

Vocabulary Activity

FORMATIVE ASSESSMENT

STUDENT CHECK IN

Text Reconstruction Have partners share their notes. Have students reflect on their work using the Check-In routine.

Grammar in Context Have students share the sentences they wrote. Have them reflect on their work using the Check-In routine.

LEARNING GOALS

- **Read** We can read and understand poetry.
- **Reread** We can reread and analyze text, craft, and structure.

OBJECTIVES

Explain major differences between poems, drama, and prose, and refer to the structural elements of poems and drama when writing or speaking about a text.

Engage effectively in a range of collaborative discussions with diverse partners on grade 4 topics and texts, building on others' ideas and expressing their own clearly.

LANGUAGE OBJECTIVES

Students will inquire by answering questions about the text using key vocabulary.

Students will explain author's use of figurative language using academic vocabulary.

ELA ACADEMIC LANGUAGE

- *figurative language, mood*
- cognate: *lenguaje figurado*

MATERIALS

Literature Anthology, pp. 132-134

Reading/Writing Companion, pp. 190-191

Visual Vocabulary Cards

Online ELL Anchor Text Support BLMs, p. 15

DIGITAL TOOLS

MULTIMODAL

Have students read along as they listen to the selection to develop comprehension and practice fluency and pronunciation.

"The Sandpiper," "Bat," "The Grasshopper Springs," "Fireflies at Dusk"

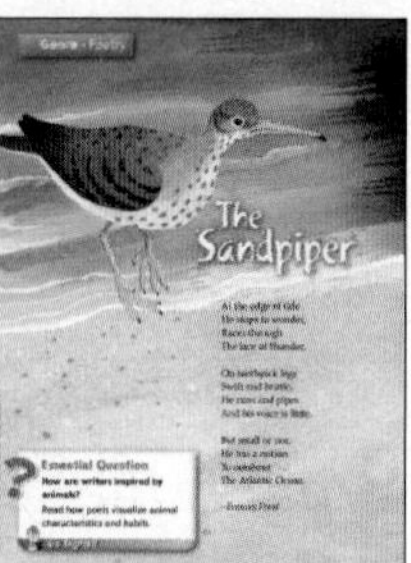
Literature Anthology

Prepare to Read

Build Background Use visuals to describe the characteristics of a sandpiper, bat, grasshopper, and firefly. Explain that they will read how poets visualize animal characteristics and habitats. Invite students to talk about a poem they have read in the past.

Vocabulary Use the **Visual Vocabulary Cards** to review the vocabulary: *creative, descriptive, brittle,* and *outstretched.*

Set Purpose Today we will read poems that help us visualize animal characteristics and habitats. As we read, think about how writer are inspired by animals.

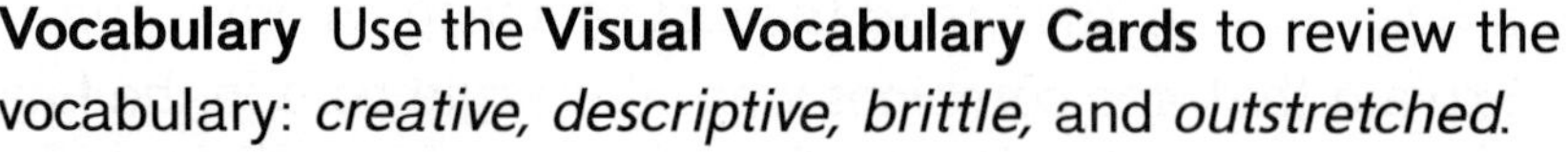

Have students listen to the audio summary of the text, which is available in multiple languages.

Read

Literature Anthology, pp.132-134

Use the **Interactive Question-Response Routine** to help students read and discuss "The Sandpiper," "Bat," "The Grasshopper Springs," "Fireflies at Dusk"

Beginning Help students discuss in complete sentences. Provide sentence frame: The poet uses the word toothpick to describe the sandpiper's legs.

Intermediate Ask students to respond in complete sentences and add details. Provide sentence starters as needed: The poet uses the words toothpick, swift, and brittle to describe the sandpiper's legs.

Advanced/Advanced High Have students respond in complete sentences and add details.

COLLABORATE

Independent Reading Practice Have mixed level pairs complete page 15 of ELL Anchor Text Support BLMs and share responses with the group.

Reread

Use with **Reading/Writing Companion,** pages 190-191.

Literature Anthology, page 133

COLLABORATE

Author's Craft: Figurative Language Read the first stanza with students. Define the words *eaves* and *forage*. Have students describe what happens to leaves in the fall. (colors change and get dark) *What do the bats look like while they drowse, or sleep?* (collapsed tents) *What looks like a tent?* (the bat's wings) Point to the phrases "Like tents collapsed for storage" and "like fall leaves" and explain that they are ***similes***. *A simile compares two different things. What two things are being compared in the similes?* (bats and tents, dusk and fall leaves)

Beginning Read line 1 with students and define the meaning of *drowse*. *What do the bats do all day?* (drowse) *What is another word for drowse?* (sleep) Read line 2 with students and define the meaning of *collapsed* and *storage*. *What do bats look like when they drowse, or sleep?* The bats look like tents. *Do the words "tents collapsed for storage" tell you that the bat's wings are open or closed?* (closed)

Intermediate *What do the bats do at night?* (Bats forage, or look for food.) *How does the poet help you visualize the bats when they are sleeping?* (compares them to collapsed tents) *How does the poet help you visualize the bats starting to move at dusk?* (compares them to fall leaves)

Advanced/Advanced High Have partners discuss why the speaker compares bats to collapsed tents and to fall leaves. (Possible answer: The bats sleep with their wings folded like collapsed tents. When they start to fly, their wings look like falling leaves.)

Literature Anthology, page 134

COLLABORATE **Author's Craft: Figurative Language** *Read "The Grasshopper Springs" with students and review the meaning of the Vocabulary word outstretched. What does the grasshopper do?* (The grasshopper springs in the air with his outstretched wings.) *What mood does the poet create when he uses the words spring, catches, and overstretched to describe the grasshopper?* (The poet creates an energetic mood.)

Beginning Read the poem with students and point to the picture of the grasshopper to explain the meaning of the words *spring* and *outstretched*. *What does the poet describe in the poem?* (a grasshopper) *Do the words* spring *and* outstretched *match the energy of the grasshopper?* (yes)

Intermediate *What does the poet tell about?* The poet tells about a grasshopper that springs with outstretched wings. *What words does the poet use to create an energetic mood?* (springs, catches, outstretched)

Advanced/Advanced High *How does the poet use words to create a different mood?* (Possible answers: The use of "springs" and "outstretched" in the first poem gives it an energetic mood.)

Literature Anthology, page 134

COLLABORATE **Author's Craft: Figurative Language** *Read "Fireflies at Dusk" with students. What does the poet describe in the poem* (fireflies) *What words or phrases does the poet use to describe the fireflies?* (dance, tiny lanterns, lighting) *What mood does the poet create?* (The poet creates a calm mood.)

Beginning Read the poem with students. Define the words *dusk* and *lanterns*. *What dances at dusk?* (fireflies) *When can you see fireflies?* I can see fireflies at night. *What does the speaker do with fireflies?* The speaker uses fireflies to see.

Intermediate Have students find a comparison in the poem. *What does the speaker compare fireflies to?* (tiny lanterns in the dark) *Is this comparison a simile or metaphor? How do you know?* (It is a metaphor; it does not use *like* or *as*.)

Advanced/Advanced High *How does the poet use words to create a different mood?* (Possible answers: The words "dusk," "tiny lanterns," and "home" in the second poem create a calm mood.)

FORMATIVE ASSESSMENT

STUDENT CHECK IN

Read Have partners share their responses to the Anchor Text questions. Then have them reflect using the Check-In routine.

Reread Have partners share responses and text evidence on Reading/Writing Companion pages 190-191. Then have them reflect using the Check-In routine to fill in the bars.

LEARNING GOALS

- **We can read and understand poetry by identifying character perspective.**
- **We can combine sentences.**

OBJECTIVES

Paraphrase portions of a text read aloud or information presented in diverse media and formats, including visually, quantitatively, and orally.

Demonstrate command of the conventions of standard English grammar and usage when writing or speaking.

LANGUAGE OBJECTIVES

Students will discuss character perspective in poetry using key vocabulary.

Students will inquire by analyzing the parts of a sentence using academic language.

ELA ACADEMIC LANGUAGE

- *perspective, pronouns, verbs*
- Cognate: *perspectiva, pronombres, verbos*

MATERIALS

Literature Anthology, pp. 132-134

Online Language Development Cards, 70A-70B

Online Language Development Practice, pp. 415-420

Online Language Transfers Handbook, pp. 15-19

"The Sandpiper," "Bat," "The Grasshopper Springs," "Fireflies at Dusk"

Text Reconstruction

Focus on a single chunk of text to support comprehension and language development across the four domains.

1. Read aloud the poem "Bat" on page 133 in the **Literature Anthology** while students listen.
2. Write the following on the board, providing definitions as needed: *drowse, eaves, tents, collapsed, dusk, forage, to clear the air.* Instruct students to listen for them as you read the poem a second time.
3. Read the paragraph a third time while students listen and take notes.
4. COLLABORATE Have students work with a partner to reconstruct the text from their notes.
5. Have students look at the original text. Ask them to tell what the poem describes. (what bats do all day and at dusk) Tell students they are going to examine character's perspective.
6. *What do bats do?* (They sleep during the day and hunt bugs at night.) *What pronoun is in the poem?* (they) *Who are they?* (the bats) *Is the speaker a character in the poem?* (no) *Who is the speaker?* (the speaker is someone who is describing the bats)
7. Have students compare their text reconstructions to the original text. Have them check whether they also included words that describe the bats sleeping, falling, and foraging.

Beginning Allow students to follow along in their Literature Anthologies as you read the text aloud. Have them point to the words from Step 2 as they listen.

Apply Author's Craft: Figurative Language

Review with students that authors use figurative language to help readers visualize. Discuss the figurative language on page 133: During the day, bats sleep and look like collapsed tents. At dusk, they look like falling leaves. Have partners write sentences to describe what bats do using their own words.

Grammar in Context: Deconstruct a Sentence

Write this text on the board: *The grasshopper springs. The grasshopper catches the summer wind with his outstretched wings.* Facilitate deconstructing this text for better comprehension:

- *What are the verbs in the sentences?* (springs, catches) *What springs and catches the summer wind?* (the grasshopper) *What does the pronoun "his" refer to?* (the grasshopper)
- *What is another word for "springs?"* (jumps, hops) *What does "catches the summer wind with his outstretched wings" describe?* For support, help them think about what a grasshopper does with its wings and how they move. (how the grasshopper uses its wings)
- *What word can you use to combine the sentences?* (and) Review with students how to combine the sentences by using the word *and*. Have students rewrite the sentence using *and*. Check their sentences and provide corrective feedback.

For additional practice, see **Language Development Cards**, Lessons 70A-70B, and **Language Development Practice**, pages 415-420.

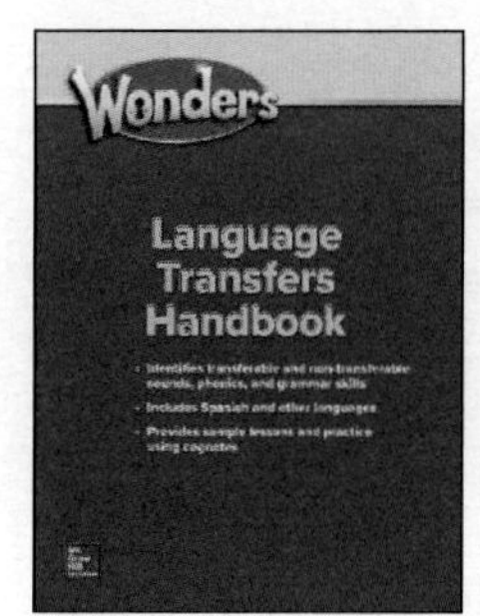

Language Transfers Handbook, Grammar Transfers, pp. 15-19

Independent Time

INDEPENDENT TIME

Vocabulary Building Create an interactive display with new vocabulary. Randomly assign one Vocabulary word to each student. Then have partners write the words and draw a picture showing the meaning. Then have partners take turns explaining what they have drawn. Post the drawings.

Beginning Allow students to add labels to the drawings.

Intermediate/Advanced/Advanced High Have students include some of the self-selected words and content-area words they added to their glossaries.

COLLABORATE **Make Connections** Have partners connect the Essential Question to their own experiences. Have them use figurative language to express how they feel about an animal. Provide sentence frames as needed:

Beginning [Animals] are like ___. (simile) I like/don't like ___.

Intermediate [Animals] are like ___. (simile) I like/don't like them because they are ___. (opinion/point of view)

Advanced/Advanced High Have partners use both a metaphor and a simile to describe an animal.

COLLABORATE **Connecting Words** Have partners generate connecting words they can use to combine sentences and ideas and list them on a 3-column chart. Have them write sentences using the connecting words.

CONNECTING WORDS	SENTENCE	COMBINED SENTENCE
but	I sit in front of Diego. I sit behind Sue.	I sit in front Diego, but behind Sue.

FORMATIVE ASSESSMENT

STUDENT CHECK-IN

Text Reconstruction Ask partners to share their notes. Have them reflect using the Check-In routine.

Grammar in Context Have partners reflect on their deconstructions using the Check-In routine.

LEARNING GOALS

We can apply strategies and skills to read poetry.

OBJECTIVES

Explain major differences between poems, drama, and prose, and refer to the structural elements of poems and drama when writing or speaking about a text.

Explain the meaning of simple similes and metaphors in context.

Engage effectively in a range of collaborative discussions with diverse partners on grade 4 topics and texts, building on others' ideas and expressing their own clearly.

LANGUAGE OBJECTIVES

Students will discuss characteristics of poetry using academic language.

ELA ACADEMIC LANGUAGE

- *describe, simile, illustration, rhyme, perspective, lyric poetry*
- Cognates: *describir, símil, ilustración, rima, perspectiva*

MATERIALS

Online ELL Genre Passage, "Deer" and "The Nautilus"

"Deer" and "The Nautilus"

Genre Passage
Lexile NP

Prepare to Read

Build Background Discuss with students what they know about deer. Have them describe what they look like, where they live, and how they move. Then describe the illustration on page E1. *The expression "deer in the headlights" describes someone who is surprised or shocked.* Have students use the expression to describe a time when they were surprised or shocked using: I/We looked like deer in the headlights when ___.

Vocabulary Use the **Define, Example, Ask** routine to preteach difficult words or unfamiliar concepts, such as *dart, spears, pride, ponds, creature, baffling, spiral, puzzling.* Invite students to add new vocabulary to their glossaries.

Set Purpose *Today we will read two poems called "Deer" and "The Nautilus" and focus on understanding character perspective. As we read, think about how writers are inspired by animals.*

Read the Text

Page E1, "Deer," Stanzas 1–2

Beginning Ask students to point to stanzas as they answer questions about the deer: *What are the deer doing in stanza 1?* The deer are sitting under the trees. *What are the deer doing in stanza 2?* The deer dart away.

Intermediate *Is the speaker alone or with someone?* (with someone) *How do you know?* I see the word we. Point out that the pronouns *we* and *my* show that the speaker is also a character in the poem.

Advanced *What does the speaker compare the deer to?* (a family in a photo) Have partners talk about the **simile**. How is a family photo similar to the group of deer? (In a photo, parents and children stand still, together.)

Metaphor *Talk with a partner about the metaphor in stanza 2. What does the poet compare the deer tail to?* (The poet calls the tails six white arrows.)

Page E1, Stanzas 3–4

Beginning Point to *disappear* and have students circle the prefix *dis-*. Explain that it is the opposite of appear. *In stanza 3, what disappears into the night?* (deer)

Intermediate *Where do the deer go at night?* (into the night) *How does the speaker describe the place where the deer hide?* (as their point of pride) Explain that "point of pride" means something that one feels satisfied about.

Advanced/Advanced High *How fast do the deer move?* (as quick as spears) *What words tell you about a comparison?* ("as ... as")

Page E1, Stanzas 5–6

COLLABORATE **Beginning** *A calm place is a quiet place.* Display visuals of a pond. *How is a pond calm?* The water does not move. Have students talk about other things that are calm. A ___ is calm.

COLLABORATE **Intermediate** *What do the deer do when the "sky gets bright"?* (stand and leave) Have partners restate the speaker's questions and discuss possible answers. Where do deer go when it is morning? The deer go to find food. *Where do deer go in the afternoon*? The deer go to rest.

Respond to Reading

Use the following instruction to help students answer the questions on page E2.

1. **Simile** *Read the first stanza. What does the speaker compare?* (deer to a photograph of a family) *What kind of comparison is it?* (a simile) *What word tells what kind of comparison it is?* (the word *like*)
2. **Poetry: Rhyme and Structure** *How many stanzas does the poem have?* (6) *Read the second stanza. Which words rhyme?* (high, sky, goodbye)
3. **Character Perspective** *Read the last two stanzas. What words does the speaker use to describe where the deer go?* ("they stand and leave"; "where do they go when it gets light?") *What does the speaker think about the deer?* (They are mysterious.)

Fluency Have partners take turns reading the poem.

Page E3, "The Nautilus"

COLLABORATE *What does spiral mean, based on the illustration?* A spiral shell has a rounded shape. *Why is the nautilus on a backward trip?* The nautilus is moving backward. *Tell a partner what you feel when you're moving backward:* When I move backward, I feel ___.

Respond to Reading

Use the following instruction to help students answer the questions on page E3.

1. **Text Structure: Lyric Poetry** *Read the poem. Do the words in the poem rhyme?* (yes) *What does the poem tell about?* (tells how the poet feels about the nautilus)
2. **Poetry: Rhyme and Structure** *Which lines have rhyming words?* (lines 1, 3, 5, 7; lines 2, 4, 6, and 8)
3. **Character Perspective** *Read lines 3–4 and 7–8. What does the speaker say about the nautilus?* (it is baffling, it moves backwards, it doesn't seem to know how to steer) *What does the speaker think about the nautilus?* (the nautilus is strange)

Build Knowledge: Make Connections

Talk About the Text Have partners discuss how writers are inspired by animals.

Write About the Text Have students add their ideas to their Build Knowledge pages of their reader's notebooks.

FORMATIVE ASSESSMENT

STUDENT CHECK IN

Have partners share their responses on page E3 and reflect using the Check-In routine.

LEVEL UP

IF students read the **ELL Level** of the **Genre Passage** fluently and answered the questions,

THEN pair them with students who have proficiently read the **On Level**. Have them

- partner read the **On Level** passage
- identify figurative language and use complex sentence structures

LEARNING GOALS

We can apply strategies and skills to read realistic fiction.

OBJECTIVES

Describe in depth a character, setting, or event in a story or drama, drawing on specific details in the text.

Engage effectively in a range of collaborative discussions with diverse partners on grade 4 topics and texts, building on others' ideas and expressing their own clearly.

Read grade-level text with purpose and understanding.

LANGUAGE OBJECTIVES

Students will inquire about the characters in the story by asking and answering questions.

ELA ACADEMIC LANGUAGE

- *pronoun, illustration, simile*
- Cognates: *pronombre, ilustración, símil*

MATERIALS

ELL Leveled Reader, *The Big One*

Online Differentiated Texts, "An Animal Friend"

Online ELL Visual Vocabulary Cards

DIGITAL TOOLS

Have students read along with the audio of the selections to develop comprehension and practice fluency and pronunciation.

The Big One

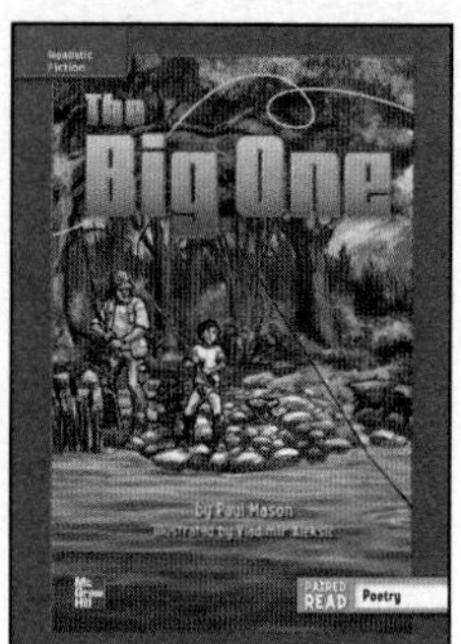

Leveled Reader
Lexile: 530L

Prepare to Read

Build Background Have students share their ideas about animals that they admire or wonder about. Have them describe using: I like/admire ___ because they can ___. Have students choral read the title. Remind students that *one* is a pronoun. Elicit the meaning of the title and invite students to predict, noting the illustration on the cover. *What are the two people holding?* Preview *The Big One* and "Peacock," "Grass Snake," and "Robin": *Let's read and think about how animals inspired these writers.*

Vocabulary Use the routine on the **ELL Visual Vocabulary Cards** to preteach ELL Vocabulary *manage* and *surface*. Have students add new words to their glossaries.

Set Purpose *Today we are going to read a realistic fiction text called "The Big One." As we read, think about how writers are inspired by animals.*

Read the Text

Pages 2–6, Chapters 1–2

Beginning *Who is going to the family cabin?* (Sal and Uncle Mikey) *What does Sal want to do?* Sal wants to catch a catfish. Read the last paragraph on page 2. *What does "no technology" mean?* Ricky can't watch TV or play video games.

Intermediate Have partners compare what Sal and Ricky like to do. Sal is very excited about fishing but Ricky likes to play computer games.

Advanced/Advanced High *Why does Sal want to catch the Big One?* (No one has caught him.) *How does he plan to do it?* (use smelly bait)

Pages 7–12, Chapters 2–3

COLLABORATE **Ask and Answer Questions** Have partners ask and answer questions about what happens with Sal and the fish. Read paragraph 4 on page 7. Find words that describe the actions of Sal and the fish. (pull, slack, disappear) Have partners retell what happened. (Possible answer: Sal is fighting the fish.)

Beginning *What size is the fish?* (big) Discuss the meaning of the word *enormous*. Have partners describe the fish. *The fish is* enormous.

Intermediate Have students read the **simile** on page 9: "The water was as smooth as glass." The author compares water and glass. *How are water and glass alike?* They are smooth and reflect objects.

COLLABORATE **Advanced/Advanced High** Have partners compare Sal and the Big One. (Possible answer: Sal pulled his fishing rod and the fish tugged on the line to escape.)

Pages 13–15, Chapter 4

Have students read the last paragraph on page 15. *What does "follow in my great-grandfather's footsteps" mean?* (to do what he did, a family tradition)

Beginning Have students look at the illustration on page 14. *Uncle Mikey helps Sal show the Big One. How does he do that?* He takes pictures. *What does Uncle Mikey use?* (a camera)

Intermediate *What do you think Sal says about the Big One?* Invite partners to write ideas in complete sentences.

Respond to Reading Have partners discuss the questions on page 16 and answer them using the new vocabulary.

Fluency: Expression and Phrasing

Read pages 12–13 with appropriate expression and phrasing. Have students read along and record themselves for feedback.

Paired Read: "Peacock," "Grass Snake," and "Robin"

Make Connections: Write About It

Have students read the last two paragraphs on page 13. *What is Sal's perspective?* Sal thought that he should not keep the fish. Why? The catfish was old *and* had lived in the lake for many years. Read the second line of "Peacock" on page 17. *The poet describes the tail as a* cloak of blue. Read the second line of "Robin" on page 19. *The poet compares the robin to a* dancer.

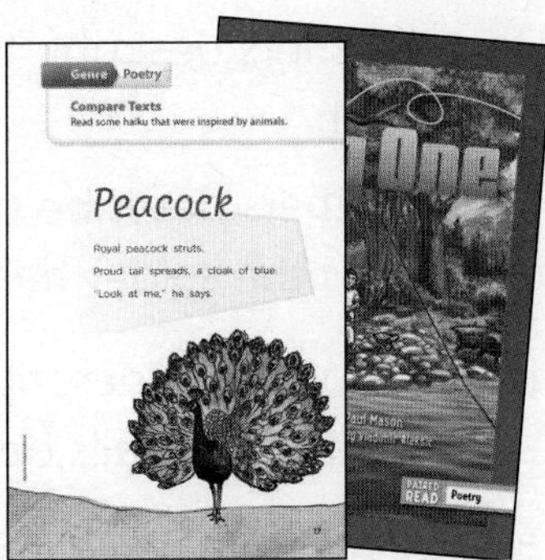

ELL Leveled Reader

Build Knowledge: Make Connections

Talk About the Text Have partners discuss how writers are inspired by animals.

Write About the Text Have students add their ideas to their Build Knowledge pages of their reader's notebooks.

Self-Selected Reading

Have students choose another realistic fiction text from the online **Leveled Reader Library** or read the **Differentiated Text:** "An Animal Friend."

FOCUS ON LITERARY ELEMENT

Have students complete the activity on page 20 to practice writing a haiku.

LITERATURE CIRCLES

Ask students to conduct a literature circle, using the Thinkmark questions to guide the discussion.

FORMATIVE ASSESSMENT

STUDENT CHECK IN

Have partners share their answers to Respond to Reading. Ask students to reflect on their learning using the Check-In routine.

LEVEL UP

IF students read the **ELL Level** fluently and answered the questions,

THEN pair them with students who have proficiently read the **On Level** and have students

- echo-read the **On Level** main selection with their partner
- list words they find difficult
- discuss these words with their partners

Access Complex Text

The **On Level** challenges students by including more **academic language** and **complex sentence structures.**

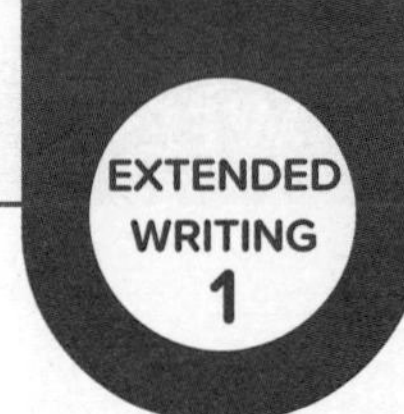

LEARNING GOALS

- **We can identify a central idea and supporting details.**
- **We can analyze a student model and student model sources.**

OBJECTIVES

Determine the central, or main, idea of a text and explain how it is supported by relevant, or key, details; summarize the text.

Explain how an author uses reasons and evidence to support particular points in a text.

Draw evidence from literary or informational texts to support analysis, reflection, and research.

LANGUAGE OBJECTIVES

Students will discuss features and organization of an expository essay using academic language.

ELA ACADEMIC LANGUAGE

- *evidence, relevant details, central idea*
- Cognates: *evidencia, detalles relevantes, idea central*

MATERIALS

Online ELL Extended Writing Resources BLMs:

- Sonya's Model, pp. 19-21
- Analyze Sonya's Model, pp. 22-23

Online Student Model Sources

Reading/Writing Companion, pp. 200-211

DIGITAL TOOLS

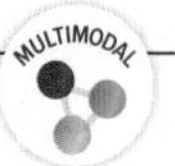

Have students read along with Sonya's Model to develop comprehension and build fluency.

Expository Writing

Central Idea

Reread the example paragraph on page 201 of **Reading/Writing Companion** with students. Review with them that the central idea tells the main idea. Discuss what the other sentences tell about it: The central idea tells that invasive species harm the environment and human activities. The sentences explain how invasive species affect the Great Lakes.

Compare Central Ideas Write on the board: **Strong:** *Invasive species harm the environment and human activities.* **Weak:** *Invasive species are bad.* Have students compare to elicit that the weak model does not give specific information about why invasive species are bad.

Supporting Details Read page 92 in the **Literature Anthology** with students. Discuss with them that relevant, or supporting, details describe or explain the central idea to help readers understand it better.

Identify the central idea with students. Then discuss the second and fourth sentences. *What do the sentences tell about?* (the back and front part of a spider) *How do the sentences support the central idea?* (The sentences give more infomration about the two parts of the spider.)

Have partners describe the central idea and relevant details in the paragraph.

Beginning Help partners describe using: This sentence is the central idea/relevant detail. It tells the spider has two main parts/the back and front part.

Intermediate Have partners describe: The central idea tells how many parts spiders have. The relevant details describe what the parts are and where.

Advanced/Advanced High Have partners describe the central idea and relevant details in the paragraph and describe what they tell about.

Analyze the Student Model and Sources

Analyze the Prompt Read the prompt on **Sonya's Model** with students. Explain that invasive species are animals and plants that live and grow in a new place. They spread in a way that damages people or the environment.

Discuss the Student Model

Mixed Levels Read Sonya's Model with students. Before reading, discuss *ecosystem* and *populations* using the Glossary. After each paragraph, have mixed pairs of language proficiency levels ask and answer the questions.

Paragraph 1 *What happened in the Great Lakes in November 2019?* (A scientific study told about mercury levels in the Great Lakes' big game fish.) *What is a zebra mussel an example of?* (an invasive species) *What can invasive species do?*

(hurt the environment and change human activities)

Paragraph 2 Explain that people brought invasive species into the Great Lakes. *How did zebra mussels get to the Great Lakes?* (They were in wastewater that was dumped there in the 1980s.) *How did the zebra mussels affect the ecosystem?* (They ate the tiny plants that native animals needed.)

Paragraph 3 *What is another example of an invasive species?* (purple loosestrife) *Why are they bad for the Great Lakes' wetlands?* (It takes space away from native plants. Also, native birds and moths do not like to live near it.) *What are nearby states doing to fight the purple loosestrife?* (They are using beetles. They are also warning visitors to clean seeds from their clothing, boats, and footwear.)

Paragraph 4 *What is an example of a new invasive species?* (Asian carp) *What did government groups do in 2020?* (agreed to pay for protections to keep Asian carp out of the Great Lakes) *Why is it important to know about invasive species?* (to protect the ecosystems)

Analyze the Student Model: Organization

Use **Analyze Sonya's Model** to analyze organization with students.

- Point to the first column of Analyze Sonya's Model and discuss how the essay is organized: the central idea is in the first paragraph, followed by relevant evidence. Point out that the conclusion retells the central idea.
- Review that the central idea tells the focus and purpose of the essay and the relevant evidence support and develop the central idea.
- Discuss the second paragraph. *What is Sonya's relevant evidence about?* (zebra mussels in the Great Lakes) *How does it support the central idea?* (tells about the problems invasive species cause)

Mixed Levels Have partners complete columns 1 and 2 in Analyze Sonya's Model.

Beginning Help partners identify the central idea and relevant evidence using: The central idea tells about the main idea. It appears in the first paragraph. The relevant evidence support the central idea. They are in the second and third paragraphs.

Intermediate Have partners describe the central idea and relevant evidence using: The relevant evidence tells about purple loosestrife and problems they cause. They support the central idea.

Advanced/Advanced High Have partners describe the central idea and relevant evidence.

Analyze the Student Model: Sources

Read the **Online Student Model Sources** with students. Have them underline the information Sonya used.

Have partners complete the third column in Analyze Sonya's Model. Discuss the following questions with students:

Paragraph 1 Point to the example of the study released about the Great Lakes' big game fish in Source 2 and the definition of invasive species in Source 1. *What information did Sonya use?* (example of zebra mussels and definition of invasive species) Discuss with students that a definition helps readers understand the topic better.

Paragraph 2 Discuss with students information from Source 2. *What information did Sonya use?* (how zebra mussels got to the Great Lakes and the problems they caused) *How does she use the information?* (as an example of a problem to the ecosystem)

Paragraph 3 Discuss information from Source 3. *What information did Sonya use?* (how purple loosestrife affect the ecosystem of the Great Lakes) *How does she use the information?* (as an example of a problem)

Paragraph 4 Discuss the information from Source 1. *What does Sonya use as an example of new invasive species?* (Asian carp) *What did government groups agree to do?* (pay for protections to keep Asian carp invaders out of the Great Lakes) Elicit that Sonya uses this information to support the central idea.

FORMATIVE ASSESSMENT

STUDENT CHECK-IN

Have partners share responses to Analyze Sonya's Model. Ask students to reflect using the Check-In routine.

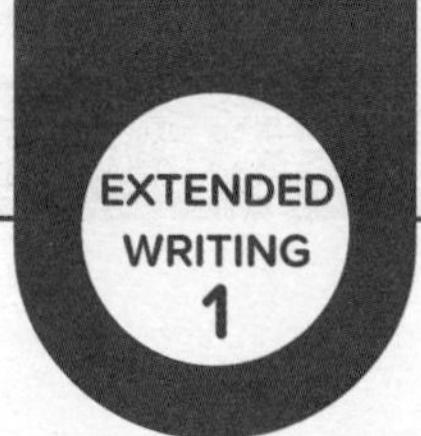

LEARNING GOALS

- **We can synthesize information from three sources to plan and organize an expository essay.**
- **We can draft and revise an expository essay.**

OBJECTIVES

Recall relevant information from experiences or gather relevant information from print and digital sources; take notes and categorize information.

Link ideas within categories of information using words and phrases.

With guidance and support from peers and adults, develop and strengthen writing as needed by planning, revising, and editing.

LANGUAGE OBJECTIVES

Students will explain using linking words to connect ideas.

ELA ACADEMIC LANGUAGE

- *central idea, supporting ideas, source, relevant evidence, transitional strategies, connect*
- Cognates: *idea central, evidencia relevante, conectar*

MATERIALS

Reading/Writing Companion, pp. 204-211

Online ELL Extended Writing Resources:

- Glossary, p. 24
- My Writing Outline, pp. 25-26
- Draft: Transitional Strategies, p. 27
- Take Notes: Expository Writing, p. 75

Language Development Practice, pp. 31-36

Language Development Cards, pp. 6A-6B

DIGITAL TOOLS

MULTIMODAL

Have students read along with the student sources to develop comprehension and build fluency and pronunciation.

Expository Writing

Analyze the Sources

Review the Writing Prompt Display the prompt: *Write an expository essay to present to your class about* how plants, animals, and humans depend on each other *to survive in their environment.* Use the underlined words to discuss with students the type of information they will look for as they read.

Read the Sources/Take Notes Read the sources on pages 205-207 in the **Reading/Writing Companion** with students. Use the definitions in the **Glossary** and help them identify and underline relevant information as they read.

Beginning Discuss the meaning of the words in the Glossary. Use visuals to discuss key concepts. Paraphrase challenging sentences for students. After each paragraph, help them describe: I learned about ___.

Intermediate Discuss the key concepts using the Glossary and visuals with students. Paraphrase challenging sentences with them. After each paragraph, help them retell the information.

Advanced/Advanced High Discuss the key concepts using the Glossary and visuals with students. Help them paraphrase challenging sentences. Have them retell the information after every two paragraphs.

Mixed Levels Take Notes Have pairs read **Sources 1-3** and take notes. Use the questions to discuss each source with the group.

SOURCE 1 **"Life in Coral Reefs"** *How do coral reefs and animals help each other?* (Coral and zooxanthellae build a reef; zooxanthellae live in the coral and give coral oxygen and nutrients.) *How do people depend on coral reefs?* (They need fish and other animals for food.) *Why are reefs protected?* (to keep them healthy and help stop their decline)

SOURCE 2 **"Where Are the Bees?"** *What happened when bee hives disappeared?* (Production of honey decreased.) *How do honeybees help people and plants?* (They make honey and help pollinate plants so fruits and vegetables can grow.) *Why do farmers rent colonies of bees?* (to pollinate crops so they will produce fruit and seeds)

SOURCE 3 **"Energy in the Everglades Ecosystem"** *What are in the Everglades ecosystem?* (animals and plants) *What are producers and consumers in a food web?* (Producers make their own food using sunlight; consumers eat living things for food.) *How do the animals and plants in the Everglades ecosystem depend on each other?* (Energy passes from one living thing to another.) Discuss with students the role of producers, consumers, and the food web.

Plan/Organize Ideas

Synthesize Information Guide students on how to complete the graphic organizer on pages 208-209 of the **Reading/Writing Companion.** Model how students can transfer their information from their graphic organizer to **My Writing Outline**.

Beginning Help partners write the supporting idea and relevant evidence using: People have problems with coral reefs and bees. Coral reefs are decreasing. Bees are disappearing.

Intermediate Have partners describe the supporting idea and relevant evidence using: People have problems when coral reefs and bees decrease.

Advanced/Advanced High Have partners identify and describe the supporting idea and relevant evidence.

Draft

Have partners review the plan on My Writing Outline.

- **Organization/My Draft** Check that the central idea answers the writing prompt and check the supporting ideas are relevant. Help them paraphrase the central idea for the conclusion.
- **Evidence and Sources** Check that the central idea has supporting ideas and that the relevant evidence comes from the three sources.
- **Transitional Strategies** Encourage students to use transition words to connect ideas. Review words for cause and effect, such as *because, since, as a result.*

 Have students use the completed My Writing Outline to help them write their draft.

Beginning Help partners write the central idea and supporting ideas using linking words to connect ideas.

Intermediate Have partners check that the central idea answers the prompt and the supporting ideas are relevant. Help them to connect ideas using linking words and write a concluding sentence.

Advanced/Advanced High Have pairs check that the central idea answers the prompt and the supporting ideas are relevant. Have them use linking words to connect ideas and add evidence to the conclusion.

 TEACHER CONFERENCES

To help students write their draft meet with each student to provide support and guidance. Discuss with students transitional strategies in their writing.

Revise

Revising Checklist Review the Revising Checklist on page 211 of the Reading/Writing Companion.

Partner feedback Have partners use the checklist to give feedback on each other's work. Help all students provide feedback.

Beginning Help pairs use linking words *so* or *because* and identify the position. Then model using the linking words and help them to add to their sentences.

Intermediate Have partners describe the position of linking words and revise using linking words in their sentences. Remind them to correct for conventions.

Advanced/Advanced High Have partners describe how they used the linking words. Have them look for places to add the revised sentence to their writing. Remind them to correct for conventions.

 Before they revise, have partners discuss the revisions with each other.

For additional practice see **Language Development Cards,** Lessons 6A-6B, and **Language Development Practice,** pages 31-36.

 TEACHER CONFERENCES

To help students revise, meet with each student to provide support and guidance.

FORMATIVE ASSESSMENT

STUDENT CHECK-IN

Plan Have partners share their writing outline.

Draft Have partners share an example of transitional strategies in their essays.

Revise Have partners describe revisions in their essays.

Ask students to reflect using the Check-In routine.

LEARNING GOALS

- **We can identify important ideas to write a strong conclusion for an expository essay.**
- **We can analyze a student model and student model sources.**

OBJECTIVES

Determine the central, or main, idea of a text and explain how it is supported by relevant, or key, details; summarize the text.

Explain how an author uses reasons and evidence to support particular points in a text.

Draw evidence from literary or informational texts to support analysis, reflection, and research.

LANGUAGE OBJECTIVES

Students will discuss features and organization of an expository essay using academic language.

ELA ACADEMIC LANGUAGE

- *conclusion, analyze, prompt, introduction, evidence, central idea*
- Cognates: *conclusíon, analizar, introducción, evidencia, idea central*

MATERIALS

Online ELL Extended Writing Resources:

- Jackie's Model, pp. 28-30
- Analyze Jackie's Model, pp. 31-32

Online Student Model Sources

Literature Anthology, p. 39

Reading/Writing Companion, pp. 212-215

DIGITAL TOOLS

MULTIMODAL

Have students read along with Jackie's Model.

Expository Writing

Strong Conclusion

Reread the paragraph on page 213 of **Reading/Writing Companion** with the students. Review with them that a strong conclusion restates the central idea and offers a satisfying ending to an essay. The conclusion tells that North Atlantic right whales face many issues.

Compare Conclusions Write on the board: **Strong:** *Finally, to keep our economy strong, we must protect our beaches because they are a big tourist attraction.* **Weak:** *Finally, we should protect our beaches.* Have students compare and elicit that the weak model does not give specific information about why we should protect our beaches. The strong concluding sentence explains beaches attract tourists and keep the economy strong.

Satisfying Endings Read page 39 in the **Literature Anthology** with students. Point out that the last paragraph is the conclusion. Discuss with students that a strong conclusion restates the central idea, summarizes the main points, and includes a final observation or thought.

- Identify the central idea in the introduction on page 37 with students. (One of the toughest issues facing students today is bullying.) Ask: *How does the author offer a solution to bullying in the conclusion on page 39?* (as a final thought) *Why is this a satisfying conclusion to this informational text about bullying?* (It gives a way to fight back by speaking up against bullying.)

Have partners describe the conclusion on page 39 in the Literature Anthology and another way to present the central idea.

Beginning Help partners describe using: *This conclusion restates the* central idea *as a* final thought. *It tells people to stand up to* bullying.

Intermediate Have partners describe using: *This conclusion restates* the central idea as a final thought. *It tells* people to stand up to bullying by speaking up.

Advanced/Advanced High Have partners describe the conclusion and tell how the writer gives a final thought about the central idea of bullying.

Analyze the Student Model and Sources

Analyze the Prompt Read the prompt on **Jackie's Model** with students. Discuss examples of the types of issues faced by some animals, such as changes to their environments that affect their food or health.

Discuss the Student Model

Mixed Levels Read Jackie's Model with students. Before reading, discuss *gentle* and *migrate* using the Glossary. After each paragraph, have mixed pairs of language proficiency levels ask and answer questions.

Paragraph 1 *Where did large numbers of North Atlantic right whales once live?* (in the Atlantic Ocean) *What happened to them by 1970?* (They became endangered.) *Why does the writer use "however"?* (to show that the status of North Atlantic right whales changed)

Paragraph 2 *Why did people like to hunt North Atlantic right whales?* (The whales are slow and easy to hunt; they provided food and oil for lamps.) *How many of the whales were left by 1930?* (only 100) *How do these details support the central idea?* (They explain why North Atlantic right whales are endangered.)

Paragraph 3 *What are three dangers to North Atlantic right whales?* (Boats can hit and kill them; they can get tangled in fishing gear; underwater noise makes it hard for them to communicate.) *Why do North Atlantic right whales cross shipping and fishing lanes?* (They migrate to look for food.) *How does warming ocean water add to the danger?* (It forces them to change patterns of migration.) Discuss how Jackie provides evidence about the dangers for North Atlantic right whales. This supports his central idea.

Paragraph 4 *What final thought is in the conclusion?* (We should save North Atlantic right whales.)

Analyze the Student Model: Organization

Use **Analyze Jackie's Model** to review the organization with students.

- Point to the first column and discuss how the essay is organized. The central idea is in the first paragraph followed by supporting ideas.
- Review that the central idea tells the purpose and the evidence supports the central idea.
- Discuss with them the logical progression of the essay from the introduction to the conclusion and ask: *How does Jackie restate the central idea in his conclusion?* (as a final thought)

Mixed Levels Have partners complete columns 1 and 2 in Analyze Jackie's Model.

Beginning Help partners describe using: The conclusion restates the central idea. The writer may tell it as a final thought in the conclusion.

Intermediate Have partners describe using: The conclusion may restate the central idea as a final thought at the end of the essay.

Advanced/Advanced High Have partners describe the conclusion and what makes it strong.

Analyze the Student Model Sources

Read the **Online Student Model Sources** with students. Have them underline the information Jackie used.

Have partners complete the third column in Analyze Jackie's Model. Discuss the following questions with students:

Paragraph 1 Point to "Fact #3" in Source 2. *What information did Jackie use?* (North Atlantic right whales have been on the endangered species list since 1970.)

Paragraph 2 Discuss with students the information from Sources 1 and 2. Ask: *Which source describes how North Atlantic right whales got their name?* (Source 1) *Why were right whales easy to hunt?* (They are slow swimmers; they stay close to shorelines.) *How many right whales are there now?* (100) *What did Jackie use from Source 2?* (the size/weight of the whales)

Paragraph 3 Point to "Fact #3" in Source 2. *What did Jackie use from this section?* (human-made reasons right whales are in danger; we must protect them) *How does he use the information?* (as evidence for the central idea)

Paragraph 4 Discuss that Jackie used Source 3 to support the central idea in the conclusion. Ask: *What group started a campaign to save right whales?* (Oceana) *How do they protect the whales?* (They ask for new rules about fishing and boat speeds.) *What final thought is in the conclusion?* (We need to solve the issues right whales face.)

FORMATIVE ASSESSMENT

STUDENT CHECK IN

Have partners share responses to Analyze Jackie's Model. Ask students to reflect on their learning using the Check-in routine.

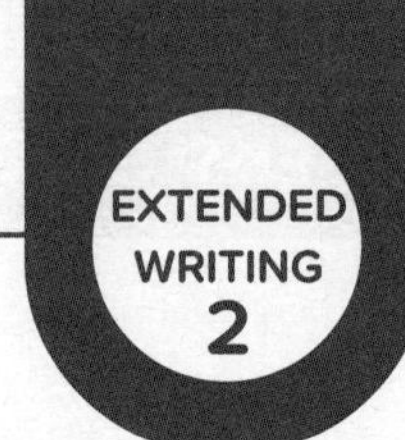

LEARNING GOALS

- We can synthesize information from three sources to plan and organize an expository essay.
- We can draft and revise an expository essay.

OBJECTIVES

Recall relevant information from experiences or gather relevant information from print and digital sources; take notes and categorize information.

Develop the topic with facts, definitions, concrete details, quotations, or other information and examples related to the topic.

With guidance and support from peers and adults, develop and strengthen writing as needed by planning, revising, and editing.

LANGUAGE OBJECTIVES

Students will argue a central idea using information from sources.

ELA ACADEMIC LANGUAGE

- *central idea, supporting details, relevant evidence, conclusion*
- Cognates: *idea central, evidencia relevante, conclusión*

MATERIALS

Reading/Writing Companion, pp. 217-223

Online ELL Extended Writing Resources:

- Glossary, p. 33
- My Writing Outline, pp. 34-35
- Draft: Relevant Evidence, p. 36

Language Development Cards, 70A-70B

Language Development Practice, pp. 415-420

DIGITAL TOOLS

MULTIMODAL

Have students read along with the student sources to develop comprehension and build fluency and pronunciation.

Expository Writing

Analyze the Sources

Review the Writing Prompt Display the prompt: *Write an expository essay for a school magazine about how writers were inspired by special places.* Use the underlined words to discuss with students the type of information they will look for as they read.

Read the Sources/Take Notes Distribute the **Glossary** and read the sources on pages 217-219 in the **Reading/Writing Companion** with students. Help them identify and underline the relevant information in the text as they read.

Beginning Discuss the meaning of the words in the Glossary. Use visuals to discuss key concepts. Paraphrase challenging sentences for students. After each paragraph, help them describe: I learned about ___.

Intermediate Discuss the key concepts using the Glossary and visuals with students. Paraphrase challenging sentences with them. After each paragraph, help them retell the information.

Advanced/Advanced High Discuss the key concepts using the Glossary and visuals with students. Help them paraphrase challenging sentences. Have them retell the information after every two paragraphs.

Mixed Levels Take Notes Have pairs read **Sources 1-3** and take notes. Use the questions to discuss each source with the group.

SOURCE 1 **"A Fight to Truly Be Heard"** *Where did Mourning Dove grow up?* (on the Colville Reservation in what is now Washington State) *What inspired Mourning Dove to write a novel?* (She saw the last roundup of free ranging bison.) *What book did she write about the Pacific Northwest?* (*Coyote Stories*)

SOURCE 2 **"Inspiration on a Farm"** *Why did E. B. White move to a farm in Maine?* (He wasn't happy living in the city; the farm made him think of his childhood.) *What inspired White to write* Charlotte's Web*?* (He became curious about a spider.) *Why did White feel comfortable with the animals on his farm?* (He felt shy in public.)

SOURCE 3 **"A Writer to Celebrate"** *What inspired Hurston's writing?* (the place she lived, Eatonville, Florida, and the wilderness) *Why did Hurston leave Eatonville as a young woman?* (for her education) *What language did Hurston use to write about nature in Florida?* (birds sang, curtain of trees, miles of purple flowers) *Why do people in Eatonville continue to honor her?* (She celebrated their community.)

Plan/Organize Ideas

Synthesize Information Guide students to complete the graphic organizer on pages 220-221 in the Reading/Writing Companion. Model how students can transfer their information from their graphic organizer to **My Writing Outline**.

Beginning Help partners write about the writers being inspired by living in special places. Use: Mourning Dove followed traditions on a reservation. White observed animals on a farm. Both writers were inspired by living in special places.

Intermediate Have partners describe how the writers were inspired by living in special places. Use: White and Hurston both enjoyed observing animals. However, Mourning Dove observed traditions. The three writers were inspired by things they saw and experienced in special places.

Advanced/Advanced High Have partners identify and describe the relevant evidence about the writers living in special places that relates to their central idea.

Draft

Have partners review the plan in My Writing Outline.

- **Organization** Check that the central idea answers the writing prompt and that relevant evidence supports the central idea. Help them paraphrase the central idea for the conclusion.
- **Supporting Ideas** Check that the supporting ideas are related to the central idea.
- **Relevant Evidence** Encourage students to use evidence from all three sources and check that it relates to the central idea of their essay.

Have students use their completed My Writing Outline to help them write their drafts.

Beginning Help partners write the central idea and relevant evidence in complete sentences.

Intermediate Have partners review that their central idea answers the prompt about how writers were inspired by living in special places and that the relevant evidence supports the central idea.

Advanced/Advanced High Have partners review that the central idea answers the prompt and that the relevant evidence supports it. Then have them write a strong conclusion.

TEACHER CONFERENCES

To help students write their draft meet with each student to provide support and guidance. Discuss their relevant evidence and how it supports the central idea of their essay.

Revise

Revising Checklist Review the items in the Revising Checklist on page 223 in the Reading/Writing Companion.

Partner feedback Have partners use the checklist to give feedback on each other's work. Help all students provide feedback. For example:

Beginning Help partners identify the central idea. Then read the rest of the paragraph, stopping to ask if the information supports the central idea and identify the relevant evidence.

Intermediate Have partners identify relevant evidence. Have them explain how it supports the central idea. Remind them to check their spelling and punctuation.

Advanced/Advanced High Have partners look for and discuss information that is relevant, and check their spelling, punctuation, and grammar.

Before they revise, have partners discuss the revisions with each other.

For additional practice, see **Language Development Cards,** Lessons 70A-70B, and **Language Development Practice,** pages 415-420.

TEACHER CONFERENCES

To help students revise, meet with each student to provide support and guidance.

FORMATIVE ASSESSMENT

STUDENT CHECK IN

Plan Have partners share their Writing Outline.

Draft Have partners share the relevant evidence they used.

Revise Have partners describe revisions in their essays.

Ask students to reflect using the check in routine.

Summative Assessment

Get Ready for Unit Assessment

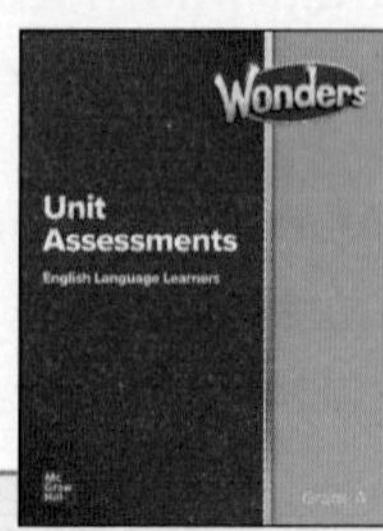

Unit 2 Tested Skills

LISTENING AND READING COMPREHENSION	VOCABULARY	GRAMMAR	SPEAKING AND WRITING
• Listening Actively • Comprehension • Text Structure • Cohesion	• Unit Vocabulary Words	• Nouns and Noun Phrases • Combining Sentences	• Presenting • Supporting Opinions • Retelling/Summarizing • Text Structure

Create a Student Profile

Record data from the following resources in the Student Profile charts on pages 320–321 of the Assessment book.

COLLABORATIVE	INTERPRETIVE	PRODUCTIVE

• Collaborative Conversations Rubrics
  • Listening
  • Speaking
	• Leveled Unit Assessment:
	  • Listening Comprehension
	  • Reading Comprehension
	  • Vocabulary
	  • Grammar
	• Presentation Rubric
	  • Listening
	• *Wonders* Unit Assessment
		• Weekly Progress Monitoring
		• Leveled Unit Assessment
		  • Speaking
		  • Writing
		• Presentation Rubric
		  • Speaking
		• Write to Sources Rubric
		• *Wonders* Unit Assessment

The Foundational Skills Kit, Language Development Kit, and Adaptive Learning provide additional student data for progress monitoring.

Level Up

Use the following chart, along with your Student Profiles, to guide your Level Up decisions.

LEVEL UP	If **BEGINNING** level students are able to do the following, they may be ready to move to the **INTERMEDIATE** level:	If **INTERMEDIATE** level students are able to do the following, they may be ready to move to the **ADVANCED** level:	If **ADVANCED** level students are able to do the following, they may be ready to move to on-level:
COLLABORATIVE	• participate in collaborative conversations using basic vocabulary and grammar and simple phrases or sentences • discuss simple pictorial or text prompts	• participate in collaborative conversations using appropriate words and phrases and complete sentences • use limited academic vocabulary across and within disciplines	• participate in collaborative conversations using more sophisticated vocabulary and correct grammar • communicate effectively across a wide range of language demands in social and academic contexts
INTERPRETIVE	• identify details in simple read alouds • understand common vocabulary and idioms and interpret language related to familiar social, school, and academic topics • make simple inferences and make simple comparisons • exhibit an emerging receptive control of lexical, syntactic, phonological, and discourse features	• identify main ideas and/or make some inferences from simple read alouds • use context clues to identify word meanings and interpret basic vocabulary and idioms • compare, contrast, summarize, and relate text to graphic organizers • exhibit a limited range of receptive control of lexical, syntactic, phonological, and discourse features when addressing new or familiar topics	• determine main ideas in read alouds that have advanced vocabulary • use context clues to determine meaning, understand multiple-meaning words, and recognize synonyms of social and academic vocabulary • analyze information, make sophisticated inferences, and explain their reasoning • command a high degree of receptive control of lexical, syntactic, phonological, and discourse features
PRODUCTIVE	• express ideas and opinions with basic vocabulary and grammar and simple phrases or sentences • restate information or retell a story using basic vocabulary • exhibit an emerging productive control of lexical, syntactic, phonological, and discourse features	• produce coherent language with limited elaboration or detail • restate information or retell a story using mostly accurate, although limited, vocabulary • exhibit a limited range of productive control of lexical, syntactic, phonological, and discourse features when addressing new or familiar topics	• produce sentences with more sophisticated vocabulary and correct grammar • restate information or retell a story using extensive and accurate vocabulary and grammar • tailor language to a particular purpose and audience • command a high degree of productive control of lexical, syntactic, phonological, and discourse features

LEARNING GOALS

We can read and understand realistic fiction.

OBJECTIVES

Describe in depth a character, setting, or event in a story or drama, drawing on specific details in the text.

Engage effectively in a range of collaborative discussions with diverse partners on grade 4 topics and texts, building on others' ideas and expressing their own clearly.

Explain how individuals can participate voluntarily in civic affairs at state and local levels through activities such as holding public officials to their word, writing letters, and participating in historic preservation and service projects. **Social Studies**

LANGUAGE OBJECTIVES

Students will discuss flashback and other events using key vocabulary.

ELA ACADEMIC LANGUAGE

- *first-person, narrator, point of view, perspective*
- Cognates: *narrador, perspectiva*

MATERIALS

Reading/Writing Companion, pp. 12-15

Online Scaffolded Shared Read, "Remembering Hurricane Katrina"

Visual Vocabulary Cards

Online ELL Visual Vocabulary Cards

DIGITAL TOOLS

MULTIMODAL

Have students read along with the audio of the selection to develop comprehension and practice fluency and pronunciation.

"Remembering Hurricane Katrina"

Prepare to Read

Build Background Have students share what they know about hurricanes. Use a map, photographs, and online resources to share background about Hurricane Katrina. *Hurricane Katrina was a huge storm that hit Gulf Coast cities. Many places were destroyed or damaged. Hundreds of thousands of people lost their homes and had to go to other cities. Many people went to Houston.*

Vocabulary Use the **Visual Vocabulary Cards** to preteach the vocabulary: *scattered, residents, selective, assigned, organization, generosity, mature, gingerly.* Use the online **ELL Visual Vocabulary Cards** to teach additional words from the Shared Read: *anxious, delayed, effort, ferocious, improved, possessions.*

Set Purpose *Today we will read a realistic fiction text called "Remembering Hurricane Katrina". As we read, think about ways you can help your community.*

Read the Text

Select the **Scaffolded Shared Read** or the Shared Read in the **Reading/Writing Companion**, based on students' language proficiency.

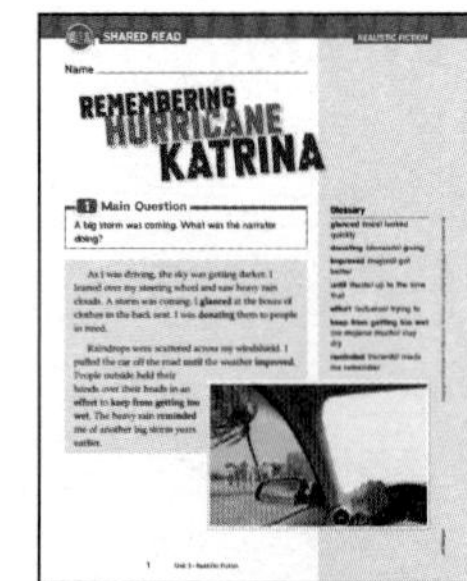

Scaffolded Shared Read, Lexile 610L

Beginning/Early-Intermediate Use the online Scaffolded Shared Read to help partners work together to read and understand realistic fiction. Remind them to use the Glossary to help them read and the Word Bank to help them answer the Main and Additional Questions.

Intermediate/Advanced Advanced High Read the text with students and use the Interactive Question-Response Routine to help them understand the story.

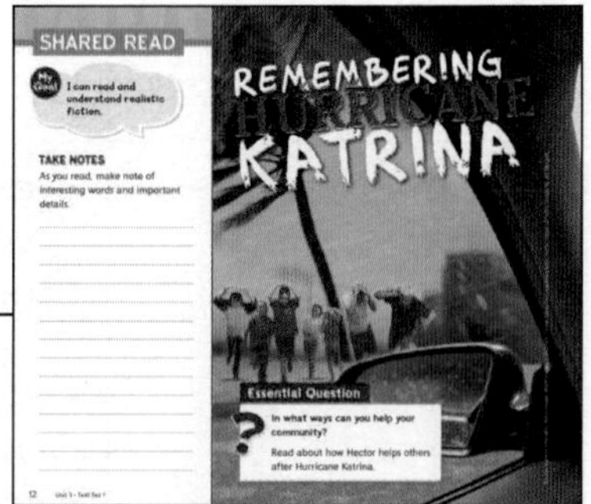

Reading/Writing Companion, Lexile 800L

Page 13

Paragraphs 1–4 Read the text with students and review Vocabulary words *scattered, effort, ferocious,* and *improved. What is the narrator doing in the first paragraph?* (driving) *Describe the weather.* (The sky is dark and it is raining.) *What is inside the car?* (boxes of clothes) *What does the narrator see from the car?* (people putting bags over their heads, children playing in the rain) *What does the narrator remember?* (a storm from ten years ago) *The narrator tells a* ***flashback****, or an event in the past. What event does he tell about?* (Hurricane Katrina) *How old is the narrator in the flashback?* (nine)

Intermediate *What action words tell you what the narrator is doing?* (Possible answers: leaning, watched, glancing, smiled) *What action words tell you what* *people are doing?* (Possible answers: held, screamed, danced) *What words or phrases tell that the narrator is describing an event in the past?* (Possible answers: reminded me, I was)

COLLABORATE Have partners describe the details that help them ***visualize*** the people at the Astrodome. To **visualize**, I can use the details Possible answer: "torn and dirty clothes," "no shoes on their feet"

Advanced *Why do you think people went to the Astrodome?* (Possible answer: People needed a safe place during the hurricane.)

Advanced High *Why do you think the narrator describes the Astrodome as "one of my strongest memories from that time"?* (Possible answer: He was surprised to see so many people needing help.)

Page 14

Paragraphs 1–3 Read the text with students and review Vocabulary words *possessions, residents, selective, anxious, and assigned. Do these paragraphs describe something that is happening now, or is it a flashback?* (It is a flashback.) *How can you tell?* (He is talking to his aunt; phrase "Just a few days ago, Hurricane Katrina...") *How do you know the narrator's name?* (Aunt Lucia calls him "Hector.")

COLLABORATE **Intermediate** Have partners discuss what they learned about the people at the Astrodome. (They are from New Orleans. Hurricane Katrina destroyed their homes.)

Advanced/Advanced High *What does* temporary residents *mean?* (people who stay at a place for a short time) *What clues help you understand what* temporary residents *means?* ("a place for them to stay until it's safe to go home")

Paragraphs 4–6 *Where is the TV news reporter?* (at the Astrodome) *What does Hector decide to do?* (collect toys for the children at the Astrodome) *Who did Hector work with?* (the Houston Helpers)

Intermediate *Why did Hector and the Houston Helpers make a list?* They made a list because they had a lot of tasks to do.

Advanced/Advanced High *What do you think is the goal of Houston Helpers?* (Possible answer: I think they want to help people because they worked to collect toys for kids.)

Page 15

Paragraphs 1–2 Read the text with students and review Vocabulary words *organizations, generosity, mature, gingerly* and *delayed. How did the Houston Helpers collect toys?* (They asked people at their schools and organizations to help.) *How did the families at the Astrodome react?* (The toys made the families happy.)

COLLABORATE **Intermediate** Have partners find at least three other action verbs in paragraph 2. (Possible answers: forget, entered, lit up, pulled, thanked, complimented).

Advanced/Advanced High *Why does Hector say that he'll "never forget" giving toys to the children? Support your answer with text evidence.* (Possible answer: The children were happy and the parents were thankful. He probably felt good about helping.)

Paragraphs 3–7 *How do you know the flashback ends?* (phone rings, "back to the present") *What is he going to do?* (make a donation for victims of a tornado)

Intermediate *What makes the* BZZZZ *sound?* (Hector's phone) *Why does Hector have clothes in his car?* (He is taking donations to people who survived a tornado.)

COLLABORATE Review that the narrator uses the pronouns *I, me, my, we, our,* and *us,* so the story has a first-person **point of view**. Discuss the narrator's **perspective** with students. *Who is the narrator?* (Hector) *How does Hector feel about helping others?* (Possible answer: He feels he can make a difference.)

FORMATIVE ASSESSMENT

STUDENT CHECK-IN

Have partners retell the important events in the text. Ask them to reflect using the Check-In routine.

LEARNING GOALS

- **We can read and understand realistic fiction by identifying the narrator's point of view and character perspective in a text.**
- **We can identify action verbs.**

OBJECTIVES

Paraphrase portions of a text read aloud or information presented in diverse media and formats, including visually, quantitatively, and orally.

Demonstrate command of the conventions of standard English grammar and usage when writing or speaking.

LANGUAGE OBJECTIVES

Students will discuss the point of view using pronouns in the story.

Students will inquire by identifying action verbs in sentences.

ELA ACADEMIC LANGUAGE

- first-person, narrator, point of view
- Cognates: *narrador*

MATERIALS

Reading/Writing Companion, pp. 12–15, 16–17

Online Scaffolded Shared Read, "Remembering Hurricane Katrina"

Online Shared Read Writing Frames, p. 7

Online Language Development Cards, 16A–16B

Online Language Development Practice, pp. 91–96

Online Language Transfers Handbook, pp. 15–19

"Remembering Hurricane Katrina"

Text Reconstruction

Focus on a single chunk of text to support comprehension and language development across the four domains.

1. Read aloud paragraph 5 on page 14 in the **Reading/Writing Companion** while students listen.
2. Write the following on the board, providing definitions as needed: *volunteer, devised, plan, collect, donating, happiness.* Instruct students to listen for them as you read the paragraph a second time.
3. Read the paragraph a third time. Tell students to listen and take notes.
4. COLLABORATE Have students work with a partner to reconstruct the text from their notes. Help them write complete sentences as needed.
5. Have students look at the original text. Ask them to tell what the paragraph is mostly about. (Hector and his friends planning to give toys to children in the Astrodome) Tell students they are going to examine the author's use of narrator's point of view and character perspective.
6. *What pronouns show you that a story is told in the first-person point of view?* (I, me, my, we, our, and us) *What pronouns does the narrator use in the story?* (The narrator uses pronouns *my, me, and we*) *What is the point of view?* (first-person; Hector's point of view) *What clues show you Hector's perspective, or what he thinks and feels?* (Possible: Hector and his friends wanted to help; they wanted to bring happiness to people)
7. Have students compare their text reconstructions to the original text. Have them check if they also included words that identify the narrator and the point of view.

Beginning Have students follow along in the Reading/Writing Companion as you read the text aloud. Have them circle the words from Step 2 as they hear them.

Grammar in Context: Action Verbs

Notice the Form Display the following sentences from the text, and underline the action verbs. Circle the *be* verbs.

> Are they here because of the hurricane?" I asked softly. Aunt Lucia nodded. "Sí, Hector. These people are from New Orleans, Louisiana. Just a few days ago, Hurricane Katrina destroyed their homes . . ."

What are the subjects in the sentences? (they, I, Aunt Lucia, These people, Hurricane Katrina) *What are the action verbs?* (asked, nodded, destroyed) *What do the action verbs tell you?* (what the subject is doing) Have students identify the verb *are. What does the verb* are *help to tell you about?* (1st sentence: where the people are; 4th sentence: where the people came from.)

Apply and Extend Have partners write sentences to describe what happened a few days ago. Check for action verbs and provide corrective feedback.

For additional practice, see **Language Development Cards**, Lesson 16A–16B, and **Language Development Practice,** pages 91–96.

Independent Time

Vocabulary Building Have students build glossaries.

Beginning/Early Intermediate Have students complete the Glossary Activities in the **Scaffolded Shared Read**.

Intermediate/Advanced/Advanced High Have students add to the chart the vocabulary from **Reading/Writing Companion** pages 16–17 and self-selected words or phrases they would like to learn.

Mixed Levels Pair students together: Beginning and Early-Intermediate students can teach words from their Scaffolded Shared Read glossaries. Intermediate and Advanced/Advanced High students can teach self-selected words.

WORD/PHRASE	DEFINE	EXAMPLE	ASK
flickered	flashed or blinked	The flame flickered and danced.	What does it look like when light flickers?

Shared Read Writing Frames Use the online leveled Shared Read Writing Frames for "Remembering Hurricane Katrina" to provide additional practice. Differentiated frames are available to provide support for all levels.

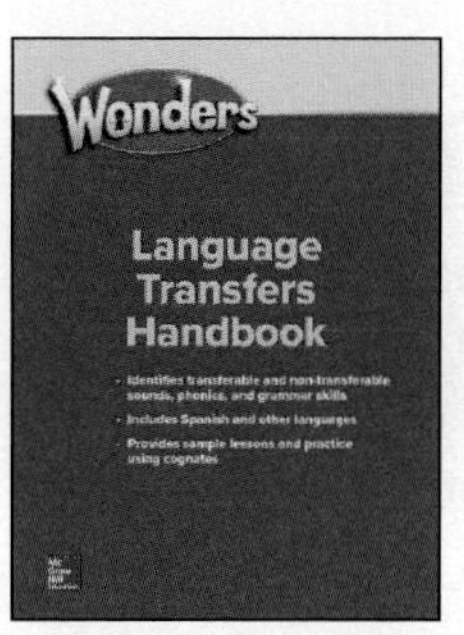

Language Transfers Handbook, Grammar Transfers, pp. 15–19

DIGITAL TOOLS

For additional support, use the online activities.

Grammar Song

Grammar Video

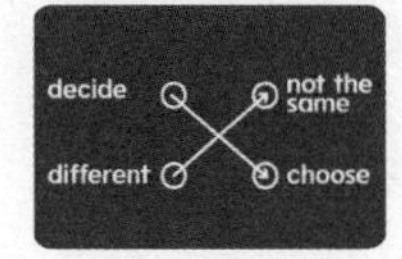

Vocabulary Activity

FORMATIVE ASSESSMENT

STUDENT CHECK IN

Text Reconstruction Have partners share their notes. Have students reflect on their work using the Check-In routine.

Grammar in Context Have partners share their sentences with action verbs. Have students reflect on their work using the Check-In routine.

LEARNING GOALS

- **Read** We can read and understand a realistic fiction story.
- **Reread** We can reread to analyze text, craft, and structure.

OBJECTIVES

Describe in depth a character, setting, or event in a story or drama, drawing on specific details in the text.

Refer to details and examples in a text when explaining what the text says explicitly and when drawing inferences from the text.

Engage effectively in a range of collaborative discussions with diverse partners on grade 4 topics and texts, building on others' ideas and expressing their own clearly.

LANGUAGE OBJECTIVES

Students will inquire by answering questions about the story using key vocabulary.

Students will explain character development and dialogue using academic vocabulary.

ELA ACADEMIC LANGUAGE

- *author, character, dialogue*
- Cognates: *autor, diálogo*

MATERIALS

Literature Anthology, pp. 178-189

Reading/Writing Companion, pp. 24-26

Visual Vocabulary Cards

Online ELL Anchor Text Support BLMs, pp. 16-18

DIGITAL TOOLS

MULTIMODAL

Have students read along with the audio of the selection to develop comprehension and practice fluency and pronunciation.

Aguinaldo

Prepare to Read

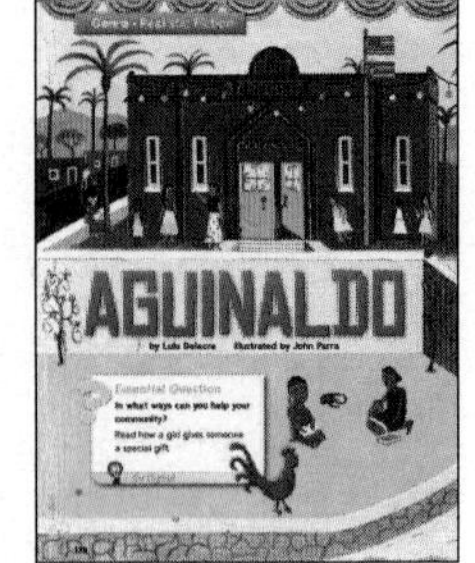

Literature Anthology, Lexile 650L

Build Background Explain to students that the story takes place in Puerto Rico and the characters in the story will use both English and Spanish words. Invite students to share what they know about Puerto Rico.

Vocabulary Use the **Visual Vocabulary Cards** to review the vocabulary: *scattered, residents, selective, assigned, organization, generosity, mature, gingerly.*

Set Purpose *Today we will read about how a girl named Marilia gives someone in her community a special gift. As we read, think about in what ways you can help your community.*

Have students listen to the summary in their first language before they read.

Read

Literature Anthology, pp. 178–189

Use the **Interactive Question-Response Routine** to help students read and discuss ***Aguinaldo.***

Beginning Help students discuss in complete sentences. Provide sentence frames: Marilia lives in Puerto Rico. Her fifth grade class decides to visit the nursing home.

Intermediate Ask students to respond in complete sentences and add details. Provide sentence starters as needed: Marilia lives in Puerto Rico. Her fifth grade class decides to visit the nursing home.

Advanced/Advanced High Have students respond in complete sentences and add details.

Independent Reading Practice Have mixed level pairs complete pages 16–18 of **ELL Anchor Text Support BLMs** and share with the group.

Reread

Use the following prompts when working on **Reading/Writing Companion,** pages 24–26

Literature Anthology, pages 182–183

COLLABORATE **Author's Craft: Character Development** Read the text with students and review Vocabulary word *residents.* Have them ask about words or phrases that are unfamiliar, such as *concern* and *indigestion,* and define them. Help them identify texts that describe a character's feeling or thinking through his or her words or actions.

Beginning Read aloud the section of the dialogue between Marilia and her teacher in Paragraphs 1–2 on page 182. *What did Marilia ask Señorita Antonia?* Marilia wants to stay in school tomorrow. She wants to do an extra book report. *What did Señorita Antonia tell her?* Señorita Antonia said Marilia cannot do an extra book report. *Can Marilia stay in school tomorrow?* (no)

Intermediate Have partners discuss what Marilia tried to do to stay home: Marilia wants to avoid the field trip. She tries to do extra work, give herself indigestion, and pretend that she is sick. Marilia's actions show how badly she wants to avoid visiting the nursing home.

Advanced/Advanced High *What is Marilia thinking when Señorita Antonia tells her she can't stay at school?* (She still isn't going to the nursing home.) *What does Marilia do at dinner time?* (She eats a lot of food.) *What does this tell you about Marilia's feelings?* (She is so unwilling to go that she tries to make herself sick.)

Literature Anthology, page 187

COLLABORATE **Author's Craft: Dialogue** Read the text with students and review Vocabulary words and define words or phrases that are unfamiliar, such as *mischieviously, relished,* or *mischief.* Help students restate the dialogue between Marilia and Elenita. *When everyone was passing around the coconut sweets, who asked for two?* (Elenita) *Who can eat the sweets?* (the residents at the nursing home) *Why did Elenita ask for two sweets?* (She wanted to share them with Marilia.) *What details in the dialogue tell you?* (Elenita says "Nobody said I couldn't give you one of mine.") *What does the dialogue tell you about the relationship between Marilia and Elenita?* (Possible answer: The dialogue shows they are friends.)

Beginning Help students restate the dialogue between Marilia and Elenita. *How many sweets did Elenita ask for?* She asked for two sweets. *Why?* Elenita wanted to share the sweets with Marilia.

Intermediate Have partners restate the dialogue between Marilia and Elenita: Señorita Antonia told Marilia that the sweets are only for the residents at the nursing home. However, Elenita asked for two sweets because she wanted to give one to Marilia. Elenita knew that Marilia was not supposed to eat the sweets.

Advanced/Advanced High Have students rephrase the dialogue in their own words. *What is the relationship between Marilia and Elenita?* (Possible answer: They like each other and are friends.)

Literature Anthology, page 188

COLLABORATE **Author's Craft: Dialogue** Read the text with students. Clarify any unfamiliar words or phrases. *How does Marilia feel as she leaves the nursing home?* (light, warm, and peaceful.) *What sentence tells you that Marilia is looking forward to coming back to the nursing home next year?* ("I couldn't wait to come back next year when I was in sixth grade.") *What does Margarita ask Marilia?* ("Are you going to wait until next Christmas to give her your collage?") *What does Marilia's response tell you?* (She wants to visit Elenita before Christmas.)

Beginning Read Paragraphs 6–8 on page 188 with students. Restate sentences as needed. *What words tell you that Marilia feels happy when she leaves the nursing home?* (light, warm, and peaceful.) *What does Marilia want to make Elentia and bring to her before Christmas?* (a collage)

Intermediate *What words describe how Marilia feel as she leaves the nursing home?* (light, warm, and peaceful.) *What does Marilia's response to Margarita tell you about how she feels?* (Marilia can't wait to return next year. She wants to visit Elenita before Christmas.)

Advanced/Advanced High Have partners retell Marilia's conversation with Margarita. (Possible answers: Marilia tells Margarita that she can't wait to come back next year. She will bring Elenita a collage. Marilia says she can visit Elenita sooner if her Mami brings her.)

FORMATIVE ASSESSMENT

STUDENT CHECK-IN

Read Have partners share their responses to the Anchor Text questions. Then have them reflect using the Check-In routine.

Reread Have partners share responses and text evidence on Reading/Writing Companion pages 24–26. Then have them reflect using the Check-In routine to fill in the bars.

LEARNING GOALS

- **We can read and understand realistic fiction by identifying the narrator's point of view and character perspective in a text.**
- **We can identify and use action verbs and verb tenses.**

OBJECTIVES

Paraphrase portions of a text read aloud or information presented in diverse media and formats, including visually, quantitatively, and orally.

Demonstrate command of the conventions of standard English grammar and usage when writing or speaking.

LANGUAGE OBJECTIVES

Students will discuss the point of view and perspective using vocabulary from the text.

Students will inquire about verb tenses using academic language.

ELA ACADEMIC LANGUAGE

- *first-person, narrator, point of view, past tense, action verb, subject*
- Cognates: *narrador, verbo de accion, sujeto*

MATERIALS

Literature Anthology, pp. 178–189

Online Language Development Cards, 27B

Online Language Development Practice, pp. 160–162

Online Language Transfers Handbook, pp. 15–19

Aguinaldo

Text Reconstruction

Focus on a single chunk of text to support comprehension and language development across the four domains.

1. Read aloud page 189 of the **Literature Anthology** while students listen.
2. Write the following on the board, providing definitions as needed: *remembered, touch, visit, friendship.* Instruct students to listen for them as you read the paragraph a second time.
3. Read the paragraph a third time while students listen and take notes about Marilia's feelings.
4. COLLABORATE Have students work with a partner to reconstruct the text from their notes. Help them write complete sentences as needed.
5. Have students look at the original text. Ask them to tell what the paragraph is mostly about. (how Marilia feels about her visit to the nursing home) Tell students they are going to examine the narrator's point of view and character perspective that the author uses.
6. *What point of view is the story told from?* (first-person; Marilia's point of view) *What words show that the story is told in the first-person point of view?* (*I, my, we*) *What clues tell you about Marilia's thoughts and feelings, or perspective?* (Possible: Elenita's hand felt good to touch; she didn't want to go to the nursing home that morning; she couldn't wait to visit again; she thinks her new friend Elenita is special.)
7. Have students compare their text reconstructions to the original text. Have them check if they also included first-person pronouns like *I, my, we,* or *us.*

Beginning Allow students to follow along in their Literature Anthologies as you read the text aloud. Have them point to the words from Step 2 as they listen.

Apply Author's Craft: Dialogue

Review with students that authors use dialogue, or conversation between characters, to show relationships. Read the dialogue on page 187 of *Aguinaldo* with students and discuss what it shows about the relationship between Marilia and Elenita. *What does Elenita give Marilia?* (Coconut sweets) *What does this tell you about their relationship?* (They are friends because Elenita wants to share the sweets with Marilia) *Which words and phrases in the dialogue tell you?* (Elenita says "Nobody said I couldn't give you one of mine.") Have partners write the dialogue between Elenita and Marilia on page 187 in their own words.

Grammar in Context: Deconstruct a Sentence

Write this sentence from Page 186 on the board: *I knelt down beside her and, in as vivid detail as I could, described the three wise men I had drawn.* Facilitate deconstructing this sentence for better comprehension:

- *What are the three action verbs in this sentence?* (knelt, described, had drawn)
- *Which verbs are in the past tense?* (knelt, described, had drawn) *What do they express?* (the actions happened in the past)
- *What is the subject of each verb?* (I) Write on the board on separate lines: *I knelt and described; I knelt down beside her and described three wise men.* Explain that the first sentence shows the subject and the action verbs and the second sentence adds details about the action verbs.
- Point to the phrases that give more details about Marilia's actions. *What had Marilia drawn?* (three wise men) *How did Marilia describe the three wise men?* (in as vivid detail as I could)
- Help students paraphrase the sentence. (Possible answer: I sat next to her and told her all the details in my drawing of the three wise men.)

For additional practice, see **Language Development Cards**, Lesson 27B, and **Language Development Practice,** pages 160-162.

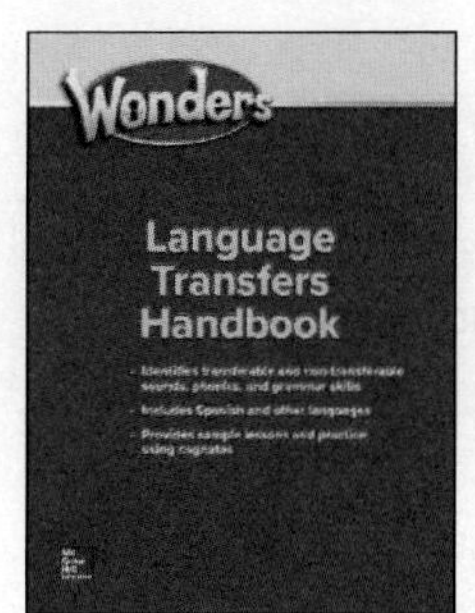

Language Transfers Handbook, Grammar Transfers, pp. 15-19

Independent Time

Vocabulary Building Have students create an interactive word wall with vocabulary from the selection. Have partners copy the words onto index cards. On the back of each card, have them write a clue to the meaning and tape the index cards to the wall with the clue-side facing out. Have other students look at a clue, guess the word, and turn the card over for the answer.

Beginning Allow students to draw clues or help them write clues in English.

Intermediate/Advanced/Advanced High Have students include some of the self-selected words and content-area words they added to their glossaries.

COLLABORATE **Types of Words** Have partners read pages 182–183 or 188–189. Have partners look for action verbs and words and phrases that tell about feelings and thoughts about each character in *Aguinaldo*. Have them copy the four-column chart below and add words to it. Have them write sentences using the words on the chart. Have them check that they used appropriate verb tenses. Encourage them to add details in their sentences. Provide examples: *Marilia tossed and turned all night. She felt unlucky because she had to go on a trip.*

CHARACTER	ACTION VERBS	THOUGHTS	FEELINGS
Marilia	tossed and turned	I wasn't going	unlucky

FORMATIVE ASSESSMENT

STUDENT CHECK-IN

Text Reconstruction Ask partners to share their notes. Have them reflect using the Check-In routine.

Grammar in Context Have students reflect on their deconstructions using the Check-In routine.

LEARNING GOALS

We can apply strategies and skills to read a realistic fiction text.

OBJECTIVES

Describe in depth a character, setting, or event in a story or drama, drawing on specific details in the text.

Use context as a clue to the meaning of a word or phrase.

Pose and respond to specific questions to clarify or follow up on information, and make comments that contribute to the discussion and link to the remarks of others.

LANGUAGE OBJECTIVES

Students will inquire about the meaning of unfamiliar words using clues in the text.

Students will discuss plot and flashbacks in a story using past tense verbs.

ELA ACADEMIC LANGUAGE

- *point of view, perspective, restate, context clues, flashback*
- Cognate: *perspectiva*

MATERIALS

Online ELL Genre Passage, "How Vera Helped"

"How Vera Helped"

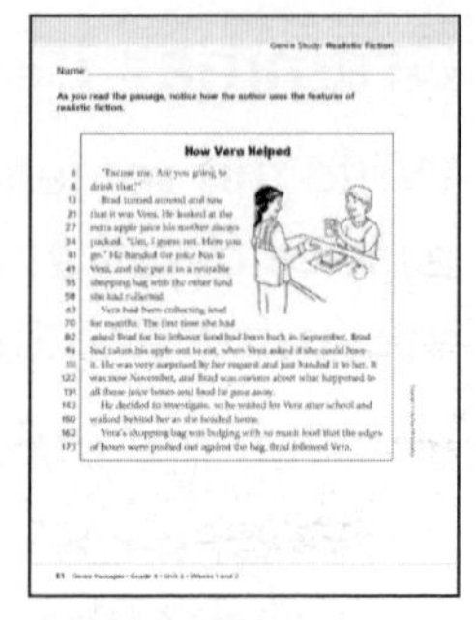

Genre Passage
Lexile 600L

Prepare to Read

Build Background Tell students that they will read a realistic fiction story about a girl who collects food from other kids. Have students discuss reasons why a person might collect food.

Review with students the elements of realistic fiction. Have students discuss the types of characters, setting, and events they expect to read about.

Vocabulary Use the Define/Example/Ask routine to pre-teach difficult words or unfamiliar concepts, such as *reusable, leftover, curious, investigate, bulging, puzzled.* (Cognates: *reutilizable, sobrante, curioso, investigar, abultado, perplejo*) Invite students to add new vocabulary to their glossaries.

Set Purpose *Today we will read a realistic fiction text called "How Vera Helped". As we read, think about ways you can help your community.*

Read the Text

Page E1, Paragraphs 1–3

COLLABORATE **Beginning** *Discuss with a partner: What does Vera ask Brad?* Vera asks Brad for the extra apple juice. *What words help you understand the meaning of extra?* (second apple juice) Discuss Brad's response with students and help partners restate his response using: Brad told Vera "You can have the second apple juice."

Intermediate *Discuss with a partner what happened in September. What did Vera ask Brad for?* (his leftover food) Explain that leftover means "that remains or is left." Have partners restate what Vera asked Brad for using: Vera asked Brad for the food that remains or was left.

Advanced/Advanced High *What words tell you that Brad has been giving Vera food for a long time?* ("back in September...It was now November") Have partners restate the information using the words *long time* and *since*.

Page E1, Paragraphs 4–5, and Page E2, Paragraphs 1–2

Beginning Explain to students that the word *bulging* means "full or stuffed with." *Which **context clues** help you figure out the meaning of the word* bulging*?* ("so much food that the edges of boxes were pushed out against the bag") *Have students restate the information using: Vera's bag was stuffed with* food.

COLLABORATE **Intermediate** *Discuss with a partner what happened when Brad investigated to find out what Vera did with the food she collected.* Brad followed Vera to her house. He saw Vera come out of the house with a box of food.

Advanced/Advanced High *Why did Brad think Vera collected food?* (He thought Vera's family needed the food.) *Why was Brad confused?* (He saw that she lived in a beautiful house and realized that she didn't need the food.)

Context Clues *What is the definition of the word* confused? (to not understand or think clearly) *What context clue helped you figure out the definition?* ("he did not understand")

Page E2, Paragraphs 3–7

Beginning *Who did Vera visit?* She visited an elderly man. *What did she do?* She gave the man a box of food. Help students ask questions to clarify meanings and define words and phrases in the section using: What does the word/phrase ___ mean? The word/phrase ___ means the same as/is different from ___.

Intermediate *What did Brad find out from his investigation?* He found out that Vera gave the food to an elderly man. Help students ask questions to clarify meanings and define words and phrases in the section using: Does the word/phrase ___ mean the same as/something different from ___?

Advanced/Advanced High *What does the phrase "at a house four doors down" mean?* (four houses away) *Why do you think the elderly man smiles at Vera?* (Possible answer: He knows that she is there to deliver food to him.) Help students ask questions to clarify meanings and define words and phrases in the section using: Can I use the word ___ to describe ___?

COLLABORATE Discuss with a partner why Vera gives food to the elderly man. Vera gives food to the elderly man because it is hard for him to leave his house when the weather gets cold. *How does Brad react?* Brad thinks Vera's idea is good because he asks her about helping her.

Respond to Reading

Use the following instruction to help students answer the questions on page E3.

1. **Point of View and Perspective** *Read the second paragraph. How does Brad respond to Vera's response?* (He gives Vera the apple juice.) *What does Brad's response tell you about the kind of person he is?* (Possible answer: He is kind.) *What does it tell you about what he thinks?* (Possible answer: He thinks sharing is good.)
2. **Plot: Flashback** *What does Brad remember?* (an event in September) *Is this from the past or in the present?* (past) *Which words tell you?* ("for months," "back in September") *What event in September did Brad tell about?* (the first time Vera asked him for food)
3. *What did Brad think was the reason that Vera collected food?* (She needed the food.) *What did he find out?* (She uses the food to help the elderly.) *How does Brad react?* (He wants to help Vera.)

Fluency Have partners take turns reading the passage.

Build Knowledge: Make Connections

Talk About the Text Have partners discuss ways they can help their community.

Write About the Text Have students add their ideas to their Build Knowledge pages of their reader's notebooks.

FORMATIVE ASSESSMENT

STUDENT CHECK-IN

Have partners share their responses on page E3 and reflect using the Check-In routine.

LEVEL UP

IF students read the **ELL Level** of the **Genre Passage** fluently and answered the questions,

THEN pair them with students who have proficiently read the **On Level**. Have them

- partner read the **On Level** passage.
- summarize how someone in the passage helps a community.

LEARNING GOALS

We can apply strategies and skills to read a realistic fiction text.

OBJECTIVES

Describe in depth a character, setting, or event in a story or drama, drawing on specific details in the text.

Read grade-level text with purpose and understanding.

Pose and respond to specific questions to clarify or follow up on information, and make comments that contribute to the discussion and link to the remarks of others.

LANGUAGE OBJECTIVES

Students will discuss the details they can visualize using descriptive words and phrases.

ELA ACADEMIC LANGUAGE

- *definitions, glossary, visualize*
- Cognates: *definiciones, glosario, visualizar*

MATERIALS

ELL Leveled Reader *Brick by Brick*

Online Differentiated Texts, "Clean-Up Day at the Park"

Online ELL Visual Vocabulary Cards

DIGITAL TOOLS

Have students read along with the audio of the selections to develop comprehension and practice fluency and pronunciation.

Brick by Brick

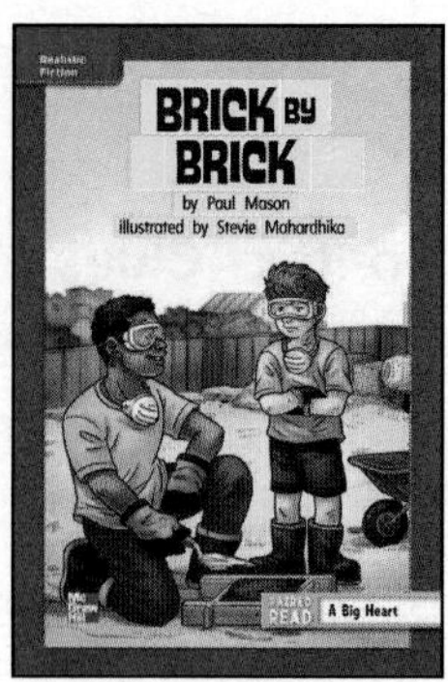

Leveled Reader
Lexile 500L

Prepare to Read

Build Background Review the Essential Question, *In what ways can you help your community?* Have students share their experiences using: I know people help by ____. Read the title and explain that the meaning of *brick by brick* refers to putting one brick on top of another, and it describes doing something a little at a time. Have students predict what they will read about, using the title.

Vocabulary Use the routine on the **ELL Visual Vocabulary Cards** to pre-teach ELL Vocabulary *focus* and *respect*. Have students add these words to their glossaries.

Set Purpose Today we are going to read a realistic fiction story called "Brick by Brick." As we read, think about ways you can help your community.

Read the Text

Chapter 1

Beginning Read aloud pages 2–3 with students. *What words describe graffiti?* ("writing on the wall") *Why did Alec write on the wall? He was* angry. *How did Mr. Burgess feel about Alec? He was* disappointed. *What other words describe feelings?* ("worried") *What words are similar to* angry?

Intermediate *Why was Alec's heart thumping?* (He was writing on the wall.) *How do you feel when your heart is thumping?* (nervous, scared)

COLLABORATE **Advanced/Advanced High** *Talk to a partner about Mr. Burgess's reaction. Why is he disappointed?* (Possible answers: He is unhappy that Alec is damaging property; he hoped Alec would behave better.)

Chapter 2

COLLABORATE **Visualize** *What details on page 6 help you visualize the community garden?* ("four areas with low walls;" "walls made from mud bricks")

Intermediate *What does the word* level *mean?* (to make something flat and even) *What **context clues** tell you?* ("flat and even")

Advanced/Advanced High *How does Alec feel about working in the garden?* (He doesn't like it; He "couldn't wait to leave," "dragging his feet and scowling.")

Chapter 3

Beginning *What did Seydou teach Alec?* (how to make bricks) *Where did Seydou come from?* (Africa) Explain the difference between the words *mixture* and *mixer* to students. Help students ask questions to clarify **definitions,** or meanings, of the two words using: What does the word ___ mean? Does the word ___ mean the same as ___?

COLLABORATE Review the meaning of *assigned* on page 8 with students. *Discuss with a partner the job Seydou assigned to Alec. Discuss details of Alec's job.* Seydou assigned Alec to make bricks. Alec needed to make a mixture with gravel, clay, cement, and water.

Chapter 4

COLLABORATE *How has Alec changed?* (He has learned to enjoy the garden.) *What has happened in the garden before Alec arrives?* (Vandals have pushed over the mixer and scattered tools.)

Intermediate *What does* seedlings *on page 13 mean?* (a young plant grown from seed) *How can you tell?* (It includes the root *seed.*)

COLLABORATE **Respond to Reading** Have students use the graphic organizer to summarize. Then have partners discuss the questions on page 22 and answer them using the new vocabulary.

Fluency: Expression

Read pages 11–12 with appropriate expression. Then read the passage aloud again and have students read with you. For more practice, have students record their reading.

Paired Read: "A Big Heart"

Make Connections: Write About It

Use the sentence frames to discuss the questions on page 19: Joshua helps his community by collecting food and backpacks for people who need them. Alec helps his community by helping to build a community garden. Then ask: *How does Alec start helping his community?* (by working at the community center.)

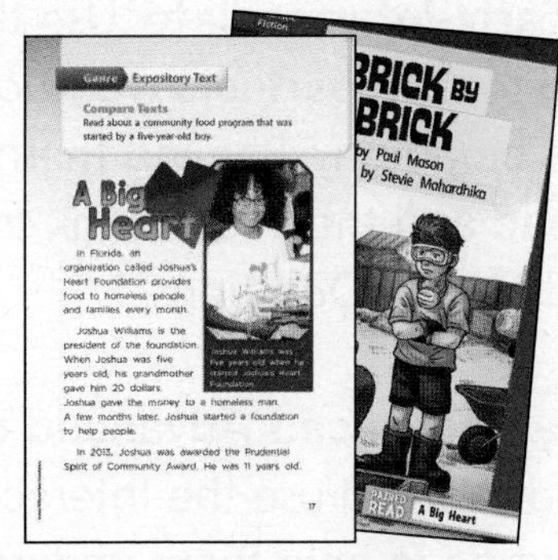

ELL Leveled Reader

Build Knowledge: Make Connections

Talk About the Text Have partners discuss ways they can help their community.

Write About the Text Have students add their ideas to their Build Knowledge pages of their reader's notebooks.

Self-Selected Reading

Have students choose another realistic fiction from the online **Leveled Reader Library** or read the **Differentiated Text,** "Clean-Up Day at the Park."

FOCUS ON LITERARY ELEMENTS

Have students complete the activity on page 20 to practice identifying who is speaking.

LITERATURE CIRCLES

Ask students to conduct a literature circle using the Thinkmark questions to guide the discussion.

FORMATIVE ASSESSMENT

STUDENT CHECK IN

Have partners share their answers to Respond to Reading. Ask students to reflect on their learning using the Check-In routine.

LEVEL UP

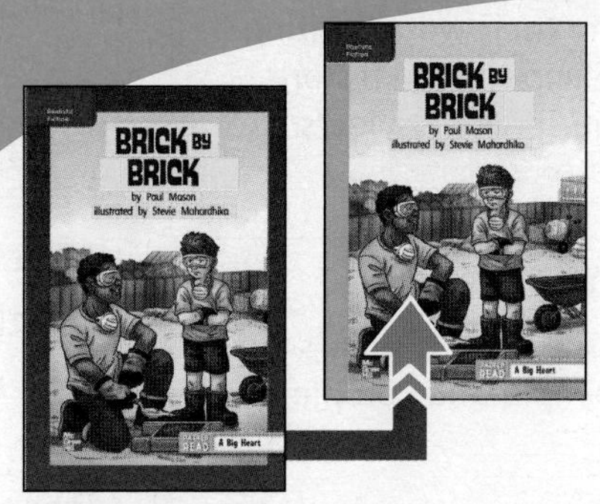

IF students read the **ELL Level** fluently and answered the questions

THEN pair them with students who have proficiently read the **On Level** and have students

- read aloud the **On Level** main selection with their partner.
- list words they find difficult.
- discuss words with their partners.

ACT Access Complex Text

The **On Level** challenges students by including more **domain-specific words** and **complex sentence structures**.

LEARNING GOALS

We can read and understand an expository text.

OBJECTIVES

Explain how an author uses reasons and evidence to support particular points in a text.

Demonstrate understanding of words by relating them to their opposites (antonyms) and to words with similar but not identical meanings (synonyms).

Engage effectively in a range of collaborative discussions with diverse partners on grade 4 topics and texts, building on others' ideas and expressing their own clearly.

Explain how individuals can participate voluntarily in civic affairs at state and local levels through activities such as holding public officials to their word, writing letters, and participating in historic preservation and service projects. **Social Studies**

LANGUAGE OBJECTIVES

Students will discuss the author's perspective in simple and complex sentences.

ELA ACADEMIC LANGUAGE

- *synonym, perspective*
- Cognates: *sinónimo, perspectiva*

MATERIALS

Reading/Writing Companion, pp. 38–41

Online Scaffolded Shared Read, "Judy's Appalachia"

Visual Vocabulary Cards

Online ELL Visual Vocabulary Cards

DIGITAL TOOLS

MULTIMODAL

Have students read along with the audio of the selection to develop comprehension and practice fluency and pronunciation.

"Judy's Appalachia"

Prepare to Read

Build Background Discuss with students ways people use coal as an energy source. *How do people use coal for energy? Where does coal come from?* Explain that much of the coal comes from mines in the Appalachia region. Point to it on a map and use photographs in the text to describe a coal mine. *Coal mining has been an important industry in Appalachia.*

Vocabulary Use the **Visual Vocabulary Cards** to review the vocabulary: *boycott, encouragement, fulfill, injustice, mistreated, protest, qualified, registered.* Use the online **ELL Visual Vocabulary Cards** to teach additional Vocabulary from the Shared Read: *afford, awarded, destroyed, generations, preserve, supported.*

Set Purpose *Today we will read an expository text called "Judy's Appalachia". As we read, think about how one person can make a difference.*

Read the Text

Select the **Scaffolded Shared Read** or the Shared Read in the **Reading/Writing Companion**, based on students' language proficiency.

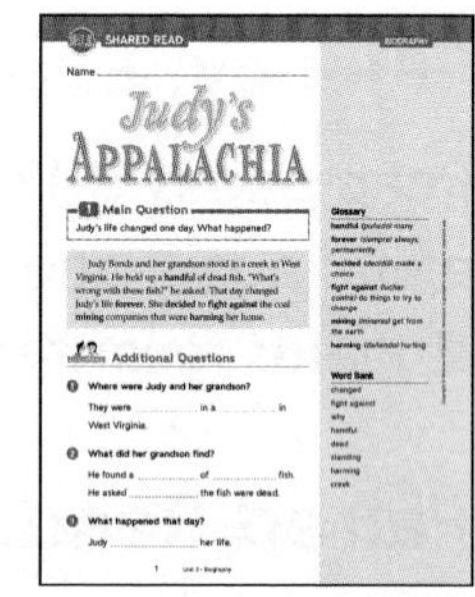
Scaffolded Shared Read, Lexile 640L

Beginning/ Early-Intermediate Use the online **Scaffolded Shared Read** to help partners work together to read and understand a biography. Remind them to use the Glossary to help them read and the Word Bank to help them answer the Main and Additional Questions.

Intermediate/ Advanced Advanced High Read the text with students and use the Interactive Question-Response Routine to help them understand a biography.

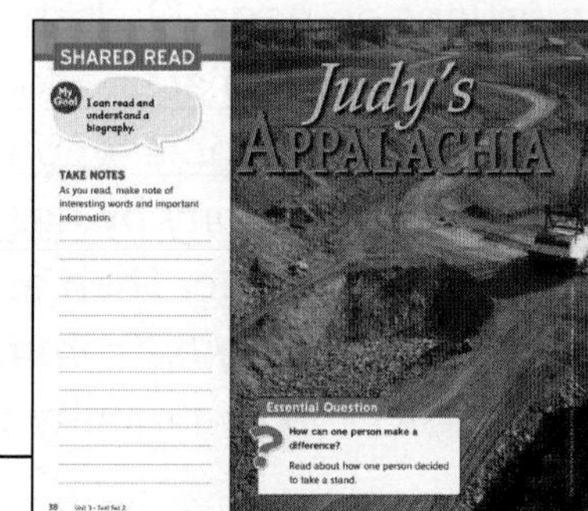

Reading/Writing Companion, Lexile 830L

Page 39, Introduction/Paragraph 1

Read the text with students. *What did Judy's grandson find in the creek?* Her grandson found many dead fish in a creek. *What did Judy Bonds decide to do?* Judy Bonds decided to fight the coal mining companies.

Page 39, "Marfork, West Virginia"

Paragraphs 1–2 Read the text with students and review Vocabulary word *generations. What do many people who live in Marfork do?* (work as coal miners) *What did you learn about Judy Bonds?* (Her father was a coal miner. She grew up and lived in Marfork.) *What surrounds Marfork?* (Appalachian Mountains)

Intermediate *Why is coal mining important in Marfork?* Coal mining is important because it provides many people with jobs. *How was coal used?* Coal was used to provide energy and light for homes.

Advanced/Advanced High *What is a* ***synonym*** *of* valley*?* (holler) *With a partner, describe the valley and the things people do there.*

Pages 39–40, "Mountaintop Removal Mining"

Paragraphs 1–3 Read the text with students and review the Vocabulary word *mistreated*. *Why did the company blow off the tops of mountains?* (to get large amounts of coal) *What is the process called?* (mountaintop removal mining) *What problems did it cause?* (It destroyed forests, polluted the area and made people sick.)

Intermediate *What is one advantage of mountaintop removal mining?* (quicker than digging underground) *How did it cause pollution? Which sentences tell you?* (dust from the explosion landed all over the town and in creeks and rivers; Paragraph 2)

Have partners discuss why people "packed up and left," or moved: People moved because pollution from mountaintop removal made them sick.

Pages 40–41, "Working for Change"

Paragraphs 1–2 Read the text with students. Review Vocabulary *protest, qualified, injustice, registered, boycott, supported,* and *awarded*. *What group did Judy join?* (Coal River Mountain Watch) *What did the group do?* (fought mountaintop removal mining) *Why did some miners support mountaintop removal mining?* (They needed jobs.) *What did Judy want to do?* (change the mining process) *What details show the* ***author's perspective*** *on the miners?* (The author explains that the miners needed mining jobs and could not afford to leave.)

Have partners retell the events in sequence: First, Judy joined Coal River Mountain Watch. Next, she joined in protests against mining companies. Then, Judy worked to change the mining process and protect mining communities. Finally, she received an award for her work.

Intermediate *What does the word* qualified *mean?* (able to do something) *What did Judy feel she was* qualified *to talk about?* (problems in the mining town: people having to move, mountains and forests getting destroyed) *Why did she feel* qualified *to do that?* She felt she was *qualified* because she grew up in a mining family.

Advanced *What does the word* boycott *mean?* (refusing to do something) *Why did the author say "Judy knew it would be impossible to* boycott *the mining companies"?* (The coal miners would lose their jobs.) *What did Judy decide to do instead?* (change the mining process)

Advanced High *Why did some miners support the mining companies?* (Companies gave them jobs.) *How is changing the mining process a solution?* (The coal miners can have work, and the mining town can be protected.)

Page 41, "Remembering Judy"

Read the text with students and review Vocabulary words *fulfill, encouragement,* and *preserve*. *How did Judy help her community?* (Her work will help to protect the Appalachian Mountains and people who live in the area.)

Have partners identify and describe words that are **synonyms** and **antonyms**. (synonyms: encouragement and supported, boycott and protest, injustice and mistreated; antonyms: destroyed and preserve)

FORMATIVE ASSESSMENT

STUDENT CHECK-IN

Have partners retell the important ideas in the text. Ask them to reflect using the Check-In routine.

LEARNING GOALS

- **We can read and understand a biography by identifying the author's perspective.**
- **We can identify and use main and helping verbs.**

OBJECTIVES

Paraphrase portions of a text read aloud or information presented in diverse media and formats, including visually, quantitatively, and orally.

Demonstrate command of the conventions of standard English grammar and usage when writing or speaking.

LANGUAGE OBJECTIVES

Students will discuss the author's perspective using key words from the text.

Students will inquire about main and helping verbs by analyzing verb tenses.

ELA ACADEMIC LANGUAGE

- *author's perspective, helping verb, main verb*
- cognate: *verbo*

MATERIALS

Reading/Writing Companion, pp. 38–41, 42–43

Online Scaffolded Shared Read, "Judy's Appalachia"

Online Shared Read Writing Frames, p. 8

Online Language Development Cards, 15A–15B

Online Language Development Practice, pp. 85–90

Online Language Transfers Handbook, pp. 15–19

"Judy's Appalachia"

Text Reconstruction

Focus on a single chunk of text to support comprehension and language development across the four domains.

1. Read aloud the paragraph under the subheading "Remembering Judy" on page 41 in the **Reading/Writing Companion** while students listen.
2. Write the following on the board, providing definitions as needed: *fulfill, diagnosed, success, encouragement, activists, preserve, remain.*

   Instruct students to listen for them as you read the paragraph a second time.
3. Read the paragraph a third time. Tell students to listen and take notes to identify events in order.
4. COLLABORATE Have students work with a partner to reconstruct the text from their notes. Help them write complete sentences as needed.
5. Have students look at the original text. Ask them to tell what the paragraph is mostly about. (why Judy's successes were important) Tell students they are going to examine how the author's perspective is presented.
6. *How does the first sentence help readers know the author's perspective, or how the author feels, about Judy and her goal?* (tells that the author is sad Judy couldn't fulfill her goals) *What clues show you that the author thinks that what Judy did was helpful?* (she was encouraging to other activists; last sentence tells how Judy helped protect the mountains and helped people keep their homes)
7. Have students compare their text reconstructions to the original text. Have them check whether they also included words that show the author's perspective.

Beginning Have students follow along in the Reading/Writing Companion as you read the text aloud. Have them circle the words from Step 2 as they hear them.

Grammar in Context: Main and Helping Verbs

Notice the Form Display the sentence from the text, and circle the main verb. Underline the helping verb.

> *But her success has provided encouragement to other activists.*

What kind of verb is has? (It is a helping verb.) *What does a helping verb show?* (shows present, past, and future tenses) *What tense does this helping verb* has *show?* (past tense) *What is the circled verb called?* (the main verb) *The main verb tells the action. Together, the helping verb and main verb make up a verb phrase.*

Apply and Extend Have partners rewrite the sentence in the present tense. Have them use a helping verb and a main verb. Check their answers.

For additional practice, see **Language Development Cards,** Lessons 15A–15B, and **Language Development Practice,** pages 85–90.

Independent Time

Vocabulary Building Have students build glossaries.

Beginning/Early Intermediate Have students complete the Glossary Activities in the **Scaffolded Shared Read**.

Intermediate/Advanced/Advanced High Have students add the vocabulary from **Reading/Writing Companion** pages 42–43 and self-selected words or phrases they would like to learn to the chart.

Mixed Levels Pair students together: Beginning and Early-Intermediate students can teach vocabulary from their Scaffolded Shared Read glossaries. Intermediate and Advanced/Advanced High students can teach self-selected words.

WORD/PHRASE	DEFINE	EXAMPLE	ASK
preserve	conserve, protect, maintain	We work to preserve our natural resources.	How can one person help preserve the environment?

COLLABORATE **Main and Helping Verbs** Have partners select one paragraph from "Judy's Appalachia" and find sentences that have helping and main verbs. Have partners write the information in a 3-column chart and present their sentences to the group using: The main verb is ___. The helping verb is ___. The helping verb ___ shows the past/present/future tense. Have partners rewrite the sentences using different helping verbs to change the verb tenses. Provide an example.

Shared Read Writing Frames Use the online leveled Shared Read Writing Frames for "Judy's Appalachia" to provide additional practice.

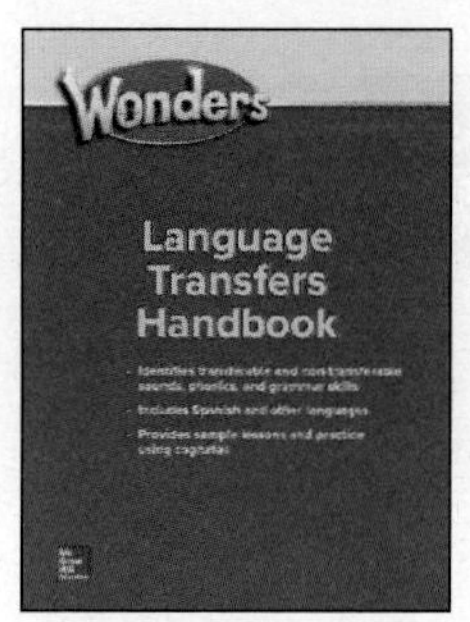

Language Transfers Handbook, Grammar Transfers, pp. 15-19

DIGITAL TOOLS

For additional support, use the online activities.

Grammar Song

Grammar Video

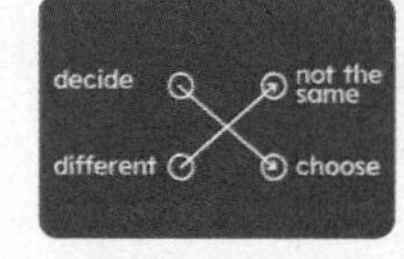

Vocabulary Activity

FORMATIVE ASSESSMENT

STUDENT CHECK IN

Text Reconstruction Have partners share their notes. Have students reflect on their work using the Check-In routine.

Grammar in Context Have partners share their sentences. Have students reflect on their work using the Check-In routine.

LESSONS 3-8

LEARNING GOALS

- **Read** We can read and understand a biography.
- **Reread** We can reread to analyze text, craft, and structure.

OBJECTIVES

Refer to details and examples in a text when explaining what the text says explicitly and when drawing inferences from the text.

Explain events, procedures, ideas, or concepts in a historical, scientific, or technical text, including what happened and why, based on specific information in the text.

Engage effectively in a range of collaborative discussions with diverse partners on grade 4 topics and texts, building on others' ideas and expressing their own clearly.

LANGUAGE OBJECTIVES

Students will inquire by answering questions about the text using key vocabulary.

Students will explain author's craft and purpose using academic vocabulary.

ELA ACADEMIC LANGUAGE

- author's purpose, character
- Cognate: *propósito del autor*

MATERIALS

Literature Anthology, pp. 196-213

Reading/Writing Companion, pp. 50-52

Visual Vocabulary Cards

Online ELL Anchor Text Support BLMs, pp. 19-21

DIGITAL TOOLS

Have students read along with the audio of the selection to develop comprehension and practice fluency and pronunciation.

Delivering Justice

Prepare to Read

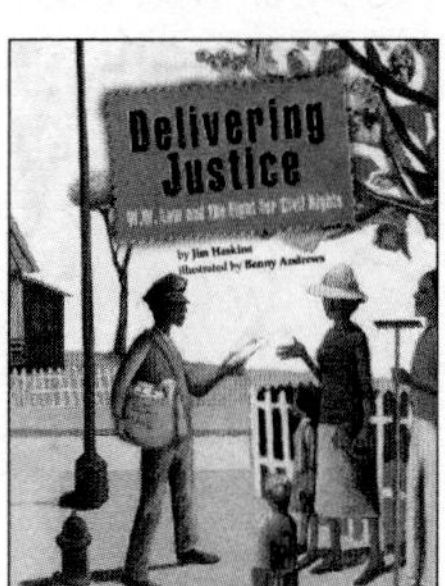

Literature Anthology, Lexile 830L

Build Background Explain that during Civil Rights Movement, which lasted from 1954–1968, people fought to establish more equality and change laws that treated African Americans unfairly. Invite students to talk about a person they know about who took a stand and fought against unfair laws.

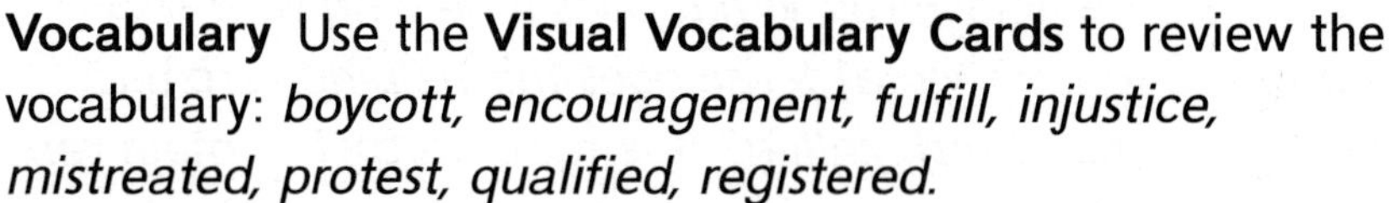

Vocabulary Use the **Visual Vocabulary Cards** to review the vocabulary: *boycott, encouragement, fulfill, injustice, mistreated, protest, qualified, registered.*

Set Purpose *Today we will read about how a man named Westley Law became a Civil Rights leader in his community. As we read, think about how one person can make a difference.*

Have students listen to the summary in their first language before they read.

Read

Literature Anthology, pp. 196–213

Use the **Interactive Question-Response Routine** to help students read and discuss ***Delivering Justice.***

Beginning Help students discuss in complete sentences. Provide sentence frames: Westley is excited to see his mother on her day off. She works for a white family the rest of the week.

Intermediate Ask students to respond in complete sentences and add details. Provide sentence starters as needed: Westley is excited it is Thursday because he gets to see his mother. The rest of the week, she works for a white family.

Advanced/Advanced High Have students respond in complete sentences and add details.

COLLABORATE **Independent Reading Practice** Have mixed level pairs complete pages 19–21 of **ELL Anchor Text Support BLMs** and share with the group.

Reread

Use the following prompts when working on **Reading/Writing Companion,** pages 50-52

Literature Anthology, page 199

COLLABORATE **Author's Purpose** Read the text with students. Clarify any unfamiliar words or phrases. Ask them to use the details about what the people do to picture what is happening. *Why are Westley and his grandmother at the department store?* (to buy an outfit) *Why did they have to wait for the* *saleswoman?* (The saleswoman did not serve them until she helped all the white customers.) *How did the saleswoman treat Westley's grandmother?* (like a kid) *What did Westley's grandmother do?* (left the store without buying anything)

Beginning Read the second and third paragraphs with students. Restate sentences as needed. Explain the meaning of *polite*. Is the saleswoman polite to the white women? (yes) The text says that the saleswoman politely called the white women "Miss" and "Mrs." Did the saleswoman treat the grandmother fairly? (no)

Intermediate Have partners compare how the saleswoman treated Westley's grandmother with how she treated the white customers: The saleswoman served all the white customers first. She called the white customers "Miss" and "Mrs" but she treated Grandma like a child.

Advanced/Advanced High *Which sentence tells about how Westley's grandma was treated? What does Grandma's reaction to the saleswoman tell you about her?* (first and second sentences in the second paragraph; she expects people to treat others politely and fairly. She does not like being treated unfairly.)

Literature Anthology, page 203

COLLABORATE **Author's Craft: Character** Read the text with students. Clarify any unfamiliar words or phrases, such as *register*. *Why didn't many black people vote?* (They had to pass a test to register to vote.) *Why was it difficult for black people to register to vote?* (The test was difficult to keep them from voting.) *How did Westley help other black people?* (He helped black people register to vote.)

Beginning Read the last paragraph with students and restate sentence as needed. *What did Westley talk to people about?* He talked to people about voting. *Who did Westley take to voter school?* (people who did not register to vote)

Intermediate *Which sentence tells you why the text was difficult?* (last sentence in first paragraph) *Why did the Youth Council start a voter school?* The Youth Council started a voter school to help black people prepare to take the test. *How did Westley help?* He took voters to voter school. He went with some of them to take the test.

Advanced/Advanced High Have partners discuss how Westley helped people become registered voters. (He took people to voter school. He took some of them to the courthouse to take the test.) Have partners discuss what Westley's actions show about him. (Answers will vary.)

Literature Anthology, pages 208–209

COLLABORATE **Author's Purpose** Read the text with students. Review Vocabulary word *boycott*. *What are Westley and his group doing?* (They are dumping baskets of charge cards on the ground.) *Where are they?* (on Broughton Street) *What does Westley announce will happen?* (Black people will not shop at any stores on Broughton Street.)

Beginning Read the first and second paragraphs on page 209 and restate sentences as needed. Help partners use the illustration on page 208 to describe Westley and his group: Westley and his group went downtown. They carried baskets. They stopped in front of the store. They dumped cards.

Intermediate *Why did Westley and the group dump charge cards?* They dumped charge cards because they wanted to show that they will not shop at the stores. *How do they want to be treated?* They want to be treated equally when they shop at the stores. *Does their action describe a boycott? What does boycott mean?* (yes; stop doing something because people think something is wrong or unfair)

Advanced/Advanced High *What words describe a boycott?* ("no black people would shop at any store") *What do Westley and his group do for the boycott?* (They dump charge cards in front of the store and announce that they will not shop there.)

FORMATIVE ASSESSMENT

STUDENT CHECK-IN

Read Have partners share their responses to the Anchor Text questions. Then have them reflect using the Check-In routine.

Reread Have partners share responses and text evidence on Reading/Writing Companion pages 50–52. Then have them reflect using the Check-In routine to fill in the bars.

LEARNING GOALS

- We can read and understand a biography by identifying the author's perspective.
- We can identify and use helping verbs and contractions.

OBJECTIVES

Paraphrase portions of a text read aloud or information presented in diverse media and formats, including visually, quantitatively, and orally.

Demonstrate command of the conventions of standard English grammar and usage when writing or speaking.

LANGUAGE OBJECTIVES

Students will discuss the author's perspective using vocabulary from the text.

ELA ACADEMIC LANGUAGE

- *author's perspective*

MATERIALS

Literature Anthology, pp. 196–213

Online Language Development Cards, 24A–24B

Online Language Development Practice, pp. 139–144

Online Language Transfers Handbook, pp. 15–19

Delivering Justice

Text Reconstruction

Focus on a single chunk of text to support comprehension and language development across the four domains.

1. Read aloud paragraphs 1 and 2 on page 205 of the **Literature Anthology** while students listen.
2. Write the following on the board, providing definitions as needed: *sit-in, served, department stores, violence, politely.* Instruct students to listen for them as you read the paragraphs a second time.
3. Read the paragraphs a third time while students listen and take notes.
4. COLLABORATE Have students work with a partner to reconstruct the text from their notes. Help them write complete sentences as needed.
5. Have students look at the original text. Ask them to tell what the paragraphs are mostly about. (how Westley came to lead sit-ins and other nonviolent protests) Tell students they are going to examine the author's perspective, or attitude, about Westley's actions.
6. *What are some characteristics that Westley has, and how do you know?* (he spent long evenings at the NAACP office; he helped students train for a sit-in he is a leader) What did Westley remember about his grandma? (she had been treated unfairly at Levy's) What did his memory about his grandma make him want to do? (to help the students protest) What did Westley teach the students about how they should protest? (without fighting back). *How does the writer feel about Westley and his actions?* (positive)
7. Have students compare their text reconstructions to the original text. Have them check if their reconstructions show Westley is a hard-working, helpful, smart leader.

Beginning Allow students to follow along in their **Literature Anthologies** as you read the text aloud. Have them point to the words from Step 2 as they hear them.

Apply Text Feature: Illustrations

Review with students that authors use illustrations to help visualize details in a story. *On pages 200–201, the illustration shows two separate water fountains. A little boy waits in line at the "Colored" water fountain, but no one is using the "White" water fountain. This helps me understand what segregation is and that it is unfair.* Have students choose an illustration and write about it. Provide sentence frames: The illustration on page ______ shows ______. This helps me understand ______.

Grammar in Context: Deconstruct a Sentence

Write this sentence from page 204 on the board: *If you don't know where you've been, how do you know where you're going?* Deconstruct the sentence with students to reinforce comprehension:

- *What verbs do you see?* Underline the entire phrase as students respond.
- *Three of the phrases have helping verbs in contractions. A contraction runs together two words by dropping letters. The apostrophe shows where letters have been dropped. What are the contractions?* (don't, you've, you're)
- On the board, rewrite each contraction in its full form: *do not know, you have been, you are going.*
- *Which words are the main verbs?* Circle them as students answer. (know, been, know, going) *Which words are the helping verbs?* Underline them as students answer. (do, have, do, are)
- Help students understand each clause and the relationship between the clauses. Help students restate the sentence to confirm their understanding: *What does the question ask you to figure out?* (what happened in the past) *Why do you need to know?* (helps to figure out what we need to do in the future)
- Discuss with students: *What does this sentence say about history?* (You have to understand the past to move forward.)

For additional practice, see **Language Development Cards** lessons 24A–24B, and **Language Development Practice,** pages 139–144.

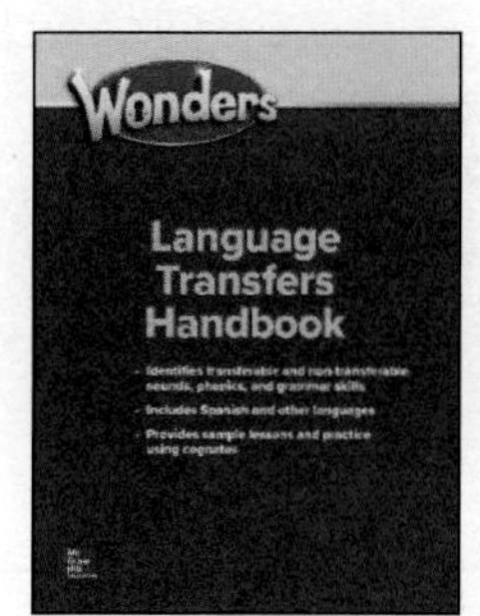

Language Transfers Handbook, Grammar Transfers, pp. 15–19

Independent Time

Vocabulary Building Have students use synonyms and antonyms to help them learn vocabulary words they added to their glossaries for this selection. For each word, students can use a dictionary or a thesaurus to choose synonyms or antonyms.

Beginning Pair students and have them identify synonyms and antonyms. Check their list of words and provide feedback.

Intermediate/Advanced/Advanced High Have students discuss the meaning of their self-selected and content-area words in their glossaries to identify synonyms and antonyms they might already know. Check their work and provide feedback.

COLLABORATE **Contractions** Have partners scan *Delivering Justice* and find sentences that have contractions. Have them discuss to identify the words that make up the contractions in a 2-column chart. Have them share their work with the group: The contraction ___ has the words ___ and ___.

WORDS IN THE CONTRACTION	CONTRACTION
do not	don't
you are	you're

FORMATIVE ASSESSMENT

STUDENT CHECK-IN

Text Reconstruction Ask partners to share their notes. Have them reflect using the Check-In routine.

Grammar in Context Have students reflect on their deconstructions using the Check-In routine.

LEARNING GOALS

We can apply strategies and skills to read a biography.

OBJECTIVES

Explain how an author uses reasons and evidence to support particular points in a text.

Demonstrate understanding of words by relating them to their opposites (antonyms) and to words with similar but not identical meanings (synonyms).

Engage effectively in a range of collaborative discussions with diverse partners on grade 4 topics and texts, building on others' ideas and expressing their own clearly.

LANGUAGE OBJECTIVES

Students will explain the author's perspective by identifying positive and negative words in the text.

Students will inquire about the meanings of words using synonyms and antonyms.

ELA ACADEMIC LANGUAGE

- *biography, synonym, context, author's perspective, timeline*
- Cognates: *biografía, sinónimo, contexto*

MATERIALS

Online ELL Genre Passage, "The Life of Barbara Jordan"

"The Life of Barbara Jordan"

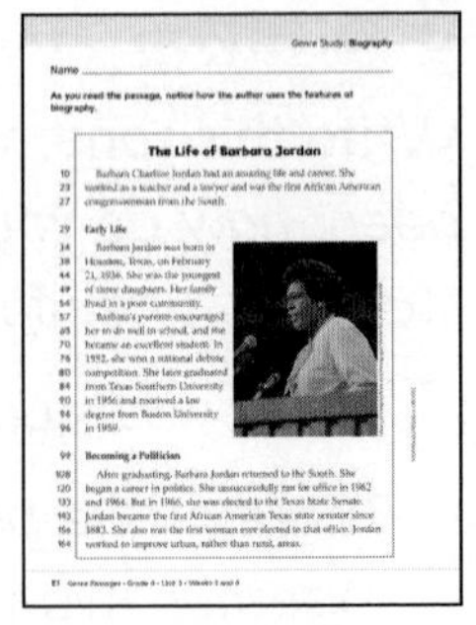

Genre Passage
Lexile 710L

Prepare to Read

Build Background Tell the class that they will be reading a biography about Barbara Jordan, who was a civil rights leader and politician. Review with students elements of a biography. *What kinds of information can you learn about in a biography?* Have students use their prior knowledge and experience to generate ideas.

Vocabulary Use the Define/Example/Ask routine to preteach difficult words or unfamiliar concepts, such as *congresswoman, debate, urban, rural, convention,* and *keynote.* (Cognates: *congresista, debate, urbano, rural, convención*) Invite students to add new vocabulary to their glossaries.

Set Purpose *Today we will read "The Life of Barbara Jordan". As we read, think about how one person can make a difference.*

Read the Text

Page E1, Introduction and "Early Life"

COLLABORATE **Beginning** Read the first paragraph and discuss the meaning of *career* with students. *What jobs did Barbara Jordan have?* (lawyer, teacher, congresswoman) *Do these words describe* career*? What is another word for* career*?* Another word for *career* is job/work.

Intermediate *What does the heading "Early Life" tell?* The heading tells me the section is about Barbara Jordan when she was young. *What does the first sentence tell you?* The first sentence tells where and when she was born.

Advanced/Advanced High *What does the word* encourage *mean?* (give help, inspire) *What context clues tell you?* ("and she became an excellent student.")

Page E1, "Becoming a Politician"

Beginning *What did Barbara Jordan do after she graduated?* She returned to the South. Discuss the meaning of the phrase "unsuccessfully ran for office" with students. *When did she run for office? When was she elected?* She ran for office in the years 1962, 1964, and 1966. She was elected in 1966.

COLLABORATE **Synonyms or Antonyms** *Discuss the meanings of* urban *and* rural*. Are these words synonyms or antonyms? What context clues tell you?* The words *urban* and *rural* are antonyms. The context clues ____ tell me the words have similar/opposite meaning(s). Review synonyms and antonyms as needed.

Intermediate *At which level of government did she work? How do you know?* (state; she was a state senator.) Point to the phrase "rather than" and discuss the meaning. *What other words can you use?* I can use the words instead of.

Page E2, "Becoming a Congresswoman"

Beginning *What happened in 1972?* Barbara Jordan was elected to the U.S. House of Representatives. *Did this make her a congresswoman?* (yes) *How do you know?* I know from the words "She was the first African American congresswoman."

Intermediate *Discuss with a partner the work Barbara Jordan did in Congress. What issues did she work on?* She worked for workers' wages and voting rights for Mexican Americans.

Advanced/Advanced High *What context clues help you understand the meaning of* address *as it is used in this section?* ("The keynote speech was one of the most important speeches . . .") *Which word in the section is a synonym for* address? (speech)

Page E2, "Life After Congress"

COLLABORATE **Beginning** *What did Jordan do after she retired?* She was a professor. *What is a synonym of professor?* (teacher) *What words help you figure out the meaning of* professor? ("teaching")

Intermediate Explain that the prefix *auto-* means "self." *What is the meaning of* autobiography? (story of a person's life written by the person)

Advanced *What word is a synonym of* autobiography? (self-portrait) *How is a biography different from an autobiography?* (A biography is about someone else.)

Advanced High *What does it mean to say that a speech was "well received"?* (The speech was admired and praised.)

Respond to Reading

Use the following instruction to help students answer the questions on page E3.

1. **Author's Perspective** *What positive or negative words does the author use to describe Barbara Jordan?* (Possible answers: "amazing life and career," "excellent student," "Her speech was praised," "earned her a great deal of respect") *What do these words tell you about the author's perspective?* (The author has a positive opinion of Barbara Jordan and her work.)
2. **Text Features: Timeline** *What information does the timeline show?* (It shows important dates in Barbara Jordan's life.) *How is a timeline useful in a biography?* (It helps readers learn about the person's life.)
3. *What are some of Jordan's achievements? What details show why each achievement was important?* (Possible answers: She was elected to the Texas State Senate and was "the first African American Texas Senator since 1883" and "the first woman ever elected to that office." She was on the committee that investigated President Richard Nixon and "it earned her a great deal of respect.")

Fluency Have partners take turns reading the passage.

Build Knowledge: Make Connections

Talk About the Text Have partners discuss how one person can make a difference.

Write About the Text Have students add their ideas to their Build Knowledge pages of their reader's notebooks.

FORMATIVE ASSESSMENT

STUDENT CHECK-IN

Have partners share their responses on page E3 and reflect using the Check-In routine.

LEVEL UP

IF students read the **ELL level** of the **Genre Passage** fluently and answered the questions,

THEN pair them with students who have proficiently read the **On Level**. Have them

- partner read the **On Level** passage.
- identify how someone in the passage makes a positive difference

LEARNING GOALS

We can apply strategies and skills to read a biography.

OBJECTIVES

Explain how an author uses reasons and evidence to support particular points in a text.

Use context to confirm or self-correct word recognition and understanding, rereading as necessary.

Engage effectively in a range of collaborative discussions with diverse partners on grade 4 topics and texts, building on others' ideas and expressing their own clearly.

LANGUAGE OBJECTIVES

Students will inquire about synonyms using story words.

ELA ACADEMIC LANGUAGE

- *biography, synonyms, context, reread*
- Cognates: *biografía, sinónimos, contexto*

MATERIALS

ELL Leveled Reader *Jacob Riis: Champion of the Poor*

Online Differentiated Texts, "Cesar Chavez Fights Injustice"

Online ELL Visual Vocabulary Cards

DIGITAL TOOLS

MULTIMODAL

Have students read along with the audio of the selections to develop comprehension and practice fluency and pronunciation.

Jacob Riis: Champion of the Poor

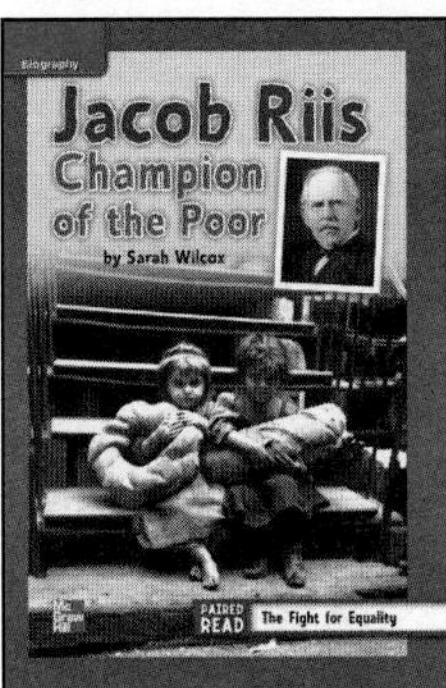

Leveled Reader
Lexile 650L

Prepare to Read

Build Background Describe Jacob Riis to help students develop background information. Explain that Jacob Riis's writing about the lives of the poor in the early twentieth century helped to change laws. Discuss the meaning of the word *champion*. Point out that in the title, the word means "a person who works for a cause." With students, discuss champions they know and what each did to help, such as Mother Teresa. Have students discuss using: I learned about ___. She/He helped ___. Have students use their knowledge to talk about ways people make a difference using: A person/groups can make a difference by ___.

Vocabulary Use the routine on the **ELL Visual Vocabulary Cards** to preteach ELL Vocabulary *conditions, investigate,* and *opportunities*. Use the definitions on page 19 to define vocabulary. Have students add these words to their glossaries.

Set Purpose *Today we are going to read a biography called* Jacob Riis: Champion of the Poor. *As we read, think about how one person can make a difference.*

Read the Text

Chapter 1: Beginnings and Early Days

Beginning Read aloud the first paragraph on page 2 with students. *Where is Jacob Riis from?* (Denmark) *Where did he immigrate to?* (New York) *What words describe* slums*?* ("The slums were dark, dirty, and overcrowded places.") What does *immigrated/immigrant mean?* Discuss the difference and have students use the words to describe Jacob Riis: He ___ to New York. He was an ___.

COLLABORATE **Intermediate** *Discuss with a partner: What were tenements? What was it like to live in tenements?* Tenements were <u>buildings</u> where immigrants <u>lived</u>. Tenements were ___. (Possible answers: dirty, crowded, without light or fresh air)

Advanced/Advanced High *Describe the Five Points neighborhood. What clues or information tell you that it was a slum?* (Possible answers: poor neighborhood, people lived in tenements and sheds.)

Chapter 2: A Journalist with a New Weapon

COLLABORATE **Reread** Have partners reread the last paragraph on page 10 and discuss why it was dangerous to use flash photography. It was dangerous to use flash photograph because ___.

Beginning *What was Riis's job?* (reporter) *What does a reporter do?* (A reporter tells the news and writes about people's lives.) *What did Riis write about in his book?* He wrote about <u>poverty</u>.

Intermediate *Why was working as a reporter important for Riis?* The job was important because he wrote about people living in poverty. *What is a* ***synonym*** *for* reporter*? What context clues tell you?* (journalist; answers will vary)

Advanced/Advanced High *Why did Riis use flash photography?* (Possible answer: to show what life is like living in slums)

Chapter 3: The Battle to Clean Up the Slums

Discuss with a partner about how people reacted to Riis's stories and photographs: His work shocked people, and people worked to improve living conditions for the poor.

Intermediate *What happened to Five Points?* (Possible answer: The city cleaned up Five Points and improved the neighborhood.)

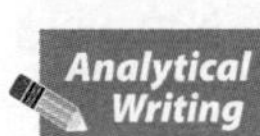

Respond to Reading Have partners complete their graphic organizers and discuss the questions on page 15.

Fluency: Accuracy, Expression

Read aloud pages 8–9 with accuracy and expression. Then read aloud again as students read along. For practice, have students record themselves while they read aloud and play their recordings to you.

Paired Read: "The Fight for Equality"

Analytical Writing — Make Connections: Write About It

Discuss the question on page 21. Have students use text evidence to support their answers. Have students write using: Sylvia Mendez/Jacob Riis made a difference by ___. They are alike/different because ___.

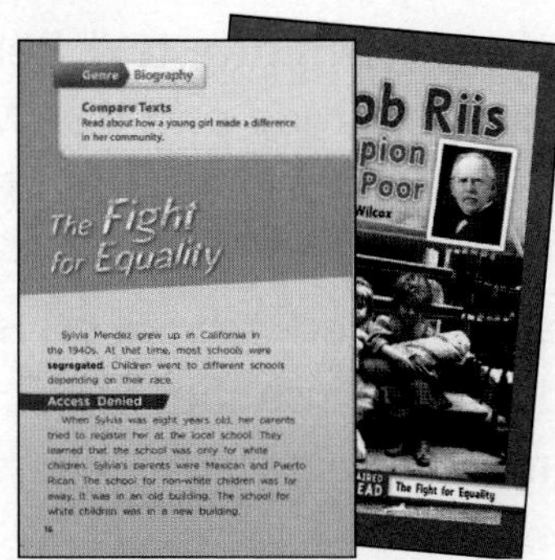

ELL Leveled Reader

Build Knowledge: Make Connections

Talk About the Text Have partners discuss how one person can make a difference.

Write About the Text Have students add their ideas to their Build Knowledge pages of their reader's notebooks.

Self-Selected Reading

Have students choose another biography from the online **Leveled Reader Library** or read the **Differentiated Text:** "Cesar Chavez Fights Injustice."

FOCUS ON SOCIAL STUDIES

Have students use the activity on page 20 to plan ways to make a difference.

LITERATURE CIRCLES

Ask students to conduct a literature circle using the Thinkmark questions to guide the discussion.

FORMATIVE ASSESSMENT

STUDENT CHECK IN

Have partners share their answers to Respond to Reading. Ask students to reflect on their learning using the Check-In routine.

LEVEL UP

IF students read the **ELL Level** fluently and answered the questions

THEN pair them with students who have proficiently read the **On Level** and have students

- echo-read the **On Level** main selection with their partner
- list words they find difficult.
- discuss these words with their partners

Access Complex Text

The **On Level** challenges students by including more **domain-specific words** and **complex sentence structures.**

LEARNING GOALS

We can read and understand an argumentative text.

OBJECTIVES

Explain how an author uses reasons and evidence to support particular points in a text.

Interpret information presented visually, orally, or quantitatively and explain how the information contributes to an understanding of the text in which it appears.

Engage effectively in a range of collaborative discussions with diverse partners on grade 4 topics and texts, building on others' ideas and expressing their own clearly.

Analyze, evaluate, and critique science explanations by using evidence, logical reasoning, and experimental and observational testing. **Science**

LANGUAGE OBJECTIVES

Students will discuss the author's claim using transition words.

ELA ACADEMIC LANGUAGE

- *author's claim*

MATERIALS

Reading/Writing Companion, pp. 64–67

Online Scaffolded Shared Read, "Food Fight"

Visual Vocabulary Cards

Online ELL Visual Vocabulary Cards

DIGITAL TOOLS

MULTIMODAL

Have students read along with the audio of the selection to develop comprehension and practice fluency and pronunciation.

"Food Fight"

Prepare to Read

Build Background Discuss with students what they know about foods that grow on a farm and problems farmers face, such as battling insects or bad weather. Explain that scientists have found ways to solve the problems by altering, or changing, the genes in crops, and that these are called GM foods.

Vocabulary Use the **Visual Vocabulary Cards** to pre-teach the vocabulary: *characteristics, inherit, advancements, agriculture, resistance, disagreed, prevalent,* and *concerns.* (Cognate: características) Use the online **ELL Visual Vocabulary Cards** to teach additional vocabulary from the Shared Read: *altering, contain, cycle, environment, interfere,* and *superior.* (Cognates: interferir, superior, ciclo)

Set Purpose *Today we will read "Food Fight". As we read, think about the ways advances in science can be helpful or harmful.*

Read the Text

Select the **Scaffolded Shared Read** or the Shared Read in the **Reading/Writing Companion**, based on students' language proficiency.

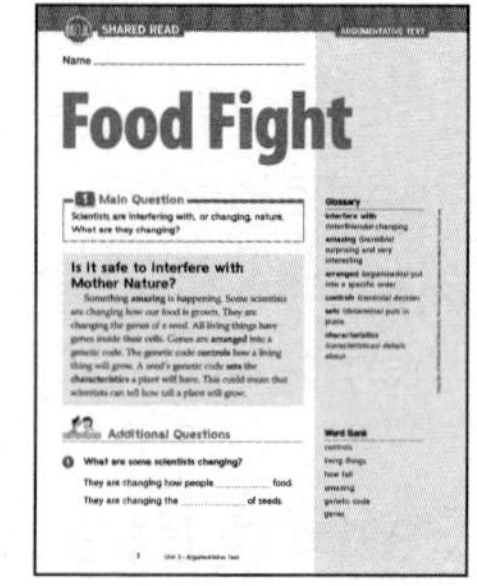

Scaffolded Shared Read, Lexile 660L

Beginning/Early-Intermediate Use the online **Scaffolded Shared Read** to help partners work together to read and understand an argumentative text. Remind them to use the Glossary to help them read and the Word Bank to help them answer the Main and Additional Questions.

Reading/Writing Companion, Lexile 870L

Intermediate/Advanced Advanced High Read the text with students and use the Interactive Question-Response Routine to help them understand an argumentative text.

Pages 65

Paragraphs 1–2 Read the paragraphs with students, including the title and subtitle. Review the Vocabulary words *interfere, characteristics, inherit, advancements, agriculture, altering, contain, cycle,* and *superior.* Explain that "Mother Nature" is a common name for nature. *What does the subtitle tell you about the section?* (Possible answer: It tells about changing nature.) *What is genetic modification?* (a way to change genes in seeds) Explain that the word modifications means "changes." *What other word has a similar meaning?* (altering) *What did the farmers do to crossbreed?* (mixed different plants to make a new plant) *What problems did the farmers have with crossbreeding?* (did not always work, took a long time to get good results)

Paragraphs 3–4 Read the paragraphs with students. Point to the phrase "living thing" in the last sentence of the third paragraph and explain that the next sentence gives examples. *What shortcuts did the scientists create?* (put a gene of one living thing into another) *What are examples of the living thing?* (plant, bacterium, virus, another animal)

Intermediate *What are examples of characteristics the seeds will inherit?* Examples of characteristics the seeds will inherit are how big the seed will grow and the nutrients it will have. *Why did scientists create GM foods?* (to create foods that survive insects, bad weather, or grow faster)

COLLABORATE **Advanced/Advanced High** Have partners discuss what makes GM foods different from other foods. (Possible answer: GM foods have genes from another living thing.)

COLLABORATE Review that the ***author's claim*** tells about the author's opinion on a topic. Have partners discuss whether the section gives facts or opinions and why it ends with a question: The section tells about facts/opinions because ___. I think the section ends with a question because ___.

Page 66

Read the paragraphs with students and review the Vocabulary word *resistance. What makes Bt corn a GM food?* (It has an insect-killing gene.) *What are benefits of Bt corn and other superfoods?* (Bt corn needs fewer chemicals, so it is good for the environment. Some superfoods are more nutritious.)

Discuss the **sidebar** with students. *What do the foods have in common?* (A new type of rice, salmon, and tomatoes have genetic modification.)

COLLABORATE **Intermediate** Have partners discuss the benefits of Bt corn and golden rice: The benefits of Bt corn are that they resist pests and disease and need fewer chemicals to grow. The benefit of golden rice is that it can prevent blindness.

Advanced/Advanced High *What genetic modification is in Bt corn and golden rice?* (Bt corn has an insect-killing gene from a bacterium. Golden rice has genes from a bacterium and daffodils.)

COLLABORATE Have partners summarize the author's perspective on GM foods: The author perspective is positive/negative because ___.

Page 67

Read the page with students and review the Vocabulary words *disagreed, prevalent,* and *concerns. What problems does the author tell about GM foods?* (People worry because they think that plants will crossbreed with weeds and make pesticide-resistant weeds and that GM foods will cause allergies.) Discuss what the signal phrase "As a result" tells about. *Why do companies avoid using GM foods?* (Some people will not buy them because of health concerns.)

Discuss with students how the key can help them read the **map**. Then have students take turns describing one piece of information from the map.

Intermediate Help students define *pesticide-resistant.* Read the third sentence in the second paragraph and restate it with them. *What evidence does the author give for health concerns?* One health concern is that GM foods can leave new or unfamiliar materials inside us and cause problems.

Advanced/Advanced High *What does the author believe is important to do?* (research GM foods because they can cause problems)

COLLABORATE Have partners summarize the author's perspective about GM foods: The author's perspective is positive/negative because ___.

FORMATIVE ASSESSMENT

STUDENT CHECK-IN

Have partners retell the most important ideas in the text. Ask them to reflect using the Check-In routine.

LEARNING GOALS

- **We can read and understand an argumentative text by identifying the author's claim.**
- **We can identify irregular verbs and write complete sentences.**

OBJECTIVES

Paraphrase portions of a text read aloud or information presented in diverse media and formats, including visually, quantitatively, and orally.

Demonstrate command of the conventions of standard English grammar and usage when writing or speaking.

LANGUAGE OBJECTIVES

Students will discuss the author's claim using vocabulary from the text.

Students will inquire about irregular verbs.

ELA ACADEMIC LANGUAGE

- *claim, past tense, irregular verb*
- Cognate: *verbo irregular*

MATERIALS

Reading/Writing Companion, pp. 64–67, 68–69

Online Scaffolded Shared Read, "Food Fight"

Online Shared Read Writing Frames, p. 9

Online Language Development Cards, 29A–29B

Online Language Development Practice, pp. 169–174

Online Language Transfers Handbook, pp. 15–19

"Food Fight"

Text Reconstruction

Focus on a single chunk of text to support comprehension and language development across the four domains.

1. Read aloud Paragraph 1 on page 67 in the **Reading/Writing Companion** while students listen.
2. Write the following on the board, providing definitions as needed: *concern, crossbreed, pesticide-resistant weeds, trigger allergies.* Instruct students to listen for them as you read the paragraph a second time.
3. Read the paragraph a third time. Tell students to listen and take notes.
4. COLLABORATE Have students work with a partner to reconstruct the text from their notes. Help them write complete sentences as needed.
5. Have students look at the original text. Ask them to tell what the paragraph is mostly about. (the reasons some people think genetically modified foods, or GM foods, can be unsafe.) Tell students they are going to examine how the author presents the claim that GM foods might be unsafe.
6. *What is the author's claim in the first sentence?* (many people think GM foods are not a good idea; the author is against GM foods) *What details support the author's claim?* (GM foods will hurt the environment and humans; GM plants will make pesticide resistant weeds; they may trigger allergies.) *What words and phrases tell you that the author is against GM foods? (hurt the environment; pesticide-resistant; trigger allergies)*
7. Have students compare their text reconstructions to the original text. Have them check whether they also included details that support the author's claim.

Beginning Have students follow along in the Reading/Writing Companion as you read the text aloud. Have them circle the words from Step 2 as they hear them.

Grammar in Context: Irregular Verbs

Notice the Form Display the sentences. Underline the past tense verbs.

For thousands of years, farmers made crops better. They would add pollen from the sweetest melon plants to the flowers of plants that produced the biggest melons.

Do the underlined verbs tell the present or past tense? (past tense) *What is the present tense of the verbs?* (*make* and *produce*) *How do you form the past tense of regular verbs?* (add *-ed* or *-d* at the end of the verb) *Which is the regular verb?* (*produce*) *What happened to the verb* made *in the past tense?* (The spelling changed.) Explain that verbs that do not end in *-ed* or *-d* in the past tense are irregular verbs. *What are irregular verbs?* (verbs that do not end in *-ed* or *-d* in the past tense) *What other verbs do you know that are irregular verbs?* (Possible answers: grow/grew, read/read, write/wrote, tell/told, say/said) Have students copy and label the irregular verbs in their notebooks.

Apply and Extend Have partners write their own sentences using the irregular verbs. Check their work and help them correct as needed.

For additional practice, see **Language Development Cards,** 29A–29B, and **Language Development Practice,** pages 169–174.

Independent Time

Vocabulary Building Have students build their glossaries.

Beginning/Early Intermediate Have students complete the Glossary Activities in the **Scaffolded Shared Read**.

Intermediate/Advanced/Advanced High Have students add the vocabulary from **Reading/Writing Companion** pages 68–69 and self-selected words or phrases they would like to learn to the chart.

Mixed Levels Pair students together. Beginning and Early-Intermediate students can teach vocabulary from their Scaffolded Shared Read glossaries. Intermediate and Advanced/Advanced High students can teach their self-selected words.

WORD/PHRASE	DEFINE	EXAMPLE	ASK
virus	a very small particle that causes disease	The illness is caused by a virus.	Can a virus spread to another person?

COLLABORATE **Shared Read Writing Frames** Use the online leveled Shared Read Writing Frames for "Food Fight" to provide students with additional oral and written practice. Differentiated frames are available for all levels.

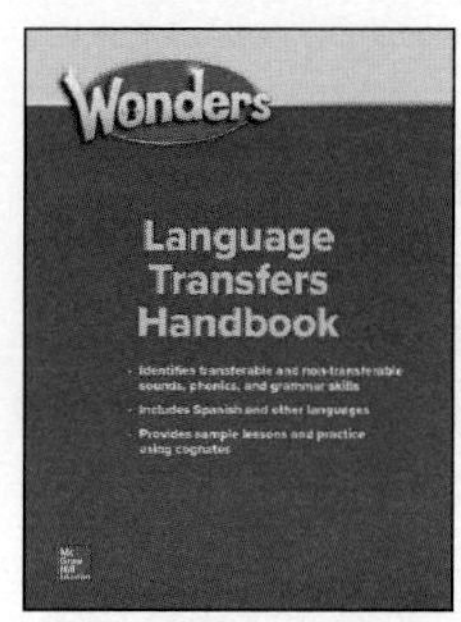

Language Transfers Handbook, Grammar Transfers, pp. 15–19

DIGITAL TOOLS

For additional support, use the online activities.

Grammar Video

Grammar Song

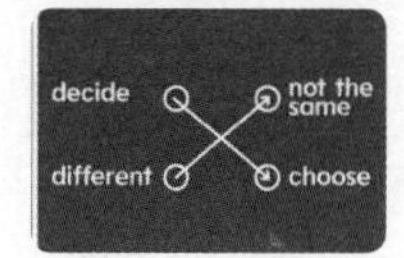

Vocabulary Activity

FORMATIVE ASSESSMENT

STUDENT CHECK IN

Text Reconstruction Have partners share their notes. Have students reflect on their work using the Check-In routine.

Grammar in Context Have partners share their sentences. Have students reflect on their work using the Check-In routine.

LEARNING GOALS

- **Read** We can read and understand an argumentative text.
- **Reread** We can reread to analyze text, craft, and structure.

OBJECTIVES

Explain how an author uses reasons and evidence to support particular points in a text.

Interpret information presented visually, orally, or quantitatively and explain how the information contributes to an understanding of the text in which it appears.

Pose and respond to specific questions to clarify or follow up on information, and make comments that contribute to the discussion and link to the remarks of others.

Analyze, evaluate, and critique science explanations by using evidence, logical reasoning, and experimental and observational testing. **Science**

LANGUAGE OBJECTIVES

Students will inquire by answering questions about the text using key vocabulary.

Students will explain author's craft and perspective using academic vocabulary.

ELA ACADEMIC LANGUAGE

- *pie chart, feature, perspective*
- Cognate: *perspectiva*

MATERIALS

Literature Anthology, pp. 220–223

Reading/Writing Companion, pp. 76–77

Visual Vocabulary Cards

Online ELL Anchor Text Support BLMs, pp. 21–23

DIGITAL TOOLS

Have students read along with the audio of the selection to develop comprehension and practice fluency and pronunciation.

A New Kind of Corn

Prepare to Read

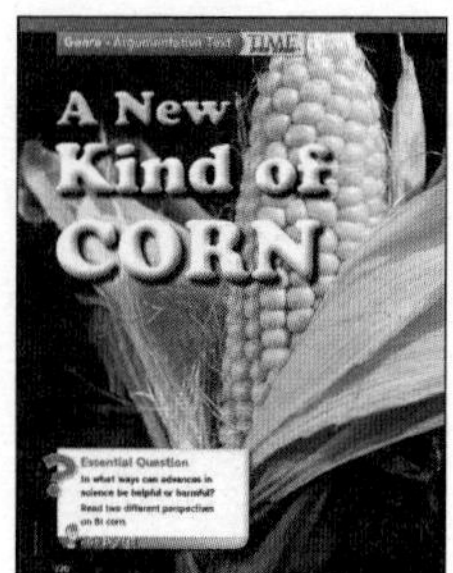

Literature Anthology, Lexile 910L

Build Background Explain to students that they will read two different perspectives on a new kind of corn, called Bt corn. Invite students to share what they know about corn and farming.

Vocabulary Use the **Visual Vocabulary Cards** to review the vocabulary: *characteristics, inherit, advancements, agriculture, resistance, disagreed, prevalent,* and *concerns.* (Cognates: *características, avances, agricultura, resistencia, prevalente*)

Set Purpose *As we read* A New Kind of Corn, *think about how advances in science can be helpful or harmful.*

Have students listen to the summary in their first language before they read.

Read

Literature Anthology, pp. 220–223

Use the **Interactive Question-Response Routine** to help students read and discuss ***A New Kind of Corn.***

Beginning Help students discuss in complete sentences. Provide sentence frames: Bt corn is used in many foods. Scientists change the genetic code of corn to make Bt corn.

Intermediate Ask students to respond in complete sentences and add details. Provide sentence starters as needed: Bt corn is used in many foods. Scientists change the genetic code of corn to make Bt corn.

Advanced/Advanced High Have students respond in complete sentences and add details.

COLLABORATE **Independent Reading Practice** Have mixed level pairs complete pages 21–23 of **ELL Anchor Text Support BLMs** and share with the group.

Reread

Use with **Reading/Writing Companion,** pages 76–77

Literature Anthology, page 221

COLLABORATE **Author's Craft: Text Features** Read the page with students. Review the Vocabulary words *advancements, prevalent, characteristics,* and *inherit.* Read the sidebar "Uses of Corn" with students. *What does the pie chart show?* (the uses of corn in the United States) *What is corn used for the most?* (animal feed) *What is corn used for the least?* (human consumption)

Beginning Read the sidebar with students. Restate sentences as needed. Explain that the word *consume* means "eat" and *animal feed* refers to the food animals eat. Point to the pie chart and read the labels with students. *What does the pie chart show?* The pie chart shows how people use corn. *How is corn used the most?* Corn is used the most for animal feed. *How is corn used the least?* Corn is used the least for human consumption.

Intermediate Have partners retell the information from the pie chart: The chart shows how people use corn in the United States. Corn is used the most to feed animals. *How does this text feature help you understand the text?* (Possible answer: The sidebar tells about how people use Bt corn.)

Advanced/Advanced High *What information does the sidebar provide?* (ways people use corn in the United States) *Why do you think the author included the sidebar?* (Possible answer: It helps people visualize how corn is used.)

Literature Anthology, page 222

COLLABORATE **Author's Perspective** Remind students that authors include information to help them explain their view about a topic. Read the text with students and review the Vocabulary word *concerns. Whose perspective, or point of view, are you going to read?* (a farmer) *What does the farmer think about Bt corn?* (The farmer thinks Bt corn is better.)

Beginning Read the headings and the first paragraph with students. Explain that the word *perspective* has a similar meaning to *point of view. What does the heading tell you?* The point of view is that Bt corn is good. *Who wrote the section?* (a farmer)

Intermediate *How does the farmer respond to the concern that Bt is poisonous?* (It is toxic only to rootworm beetles and corn borers.) *Retell what happens to other insects.* (Possible answer: Other insects are not harmed by Bt corn. Since farmers of Bt corn don't need to spray insecticides, other insects can live safely in and around these farms.)

Advanced/Advanced High *Discuss with a partner how the farmer has been affected by growing Bt corn.* (Possible answer: Growing Bt corn resulted in an increase of profit and productivity.) Have partners discuss the point of view of the farmer and describe the evidence the farmer uses. (Possible answer: Bt corn is good because it increases profit and productivity.)

Literature Anthology, page 223

COLLABORATE **Author's Perspective** Read the text with students and review Vocabulary words *agriculture, resistance,* and *disagrees. Whose perspective, or point of view, are you going to read?* (a consumer) *What concerns does the consumer have about Bt corn?* (There is not much research on its long-term effects.) *What happened to the lab rodents that were used to test GM foods?* (Lab rodents had damage in their stomachs and died during the tests.) *What resistance have rootworm beetles developed already?* (resistance to Bt corn) *Why is this important?* (Possible answer: The benefit of Bt corn being able to resist pests is no longer true.)

Beginning Read the headings and the first paragraph with students. Restate the sentence as needed. *Who wrote the section?* (a consumer) Have partners discuss the questions and help them respond: *Why is the consumer worried?* We know little about Bt corn.

Intermediate Have partners retell the consumer's concerns. *What worries the consumer?* The consumer is worried about the long-term effects of GM foods because there is little research about them.

Advanced/Advanced High *Why does the author include the information about the rodents?* (Possible answer: This example makes him question what Bt corn may do to people.) *Why does the author say that farmers need to make sure the crops do not harm the environment and inhabitants?* (Possible answer: People and animals eat the crops, so they need to be safe.)

FORMATIVE ASSESSMENT

STUDENT CHECK IN

Read Have partners share their responses to the Anchor Text questions. Then have them reflect using the Check-In routine.

Reread Have partners share responses and text evidence on Reading/Writing Companion pages 76–77. Then have them reflect using the Check-In routine to fill in the bars.

LEARNING GOALS

- **We can read and understand an argumentative text by identifying the author's claim.**
- **We can identify and use helping verbs and irregular verbs.**

OBJECTIVES

Paraphrase portions of a text read aloud or information presented in diverse media and formats, including visually, quantitatively, and orally.

Demonstrate command of the conventions of standard English grammar and usage when writing or speaking.

LANGUAGE OBJECTIVES

Students will discuss the author's claim using vocabulary from the text.

Students will inquire about the parts of a sentence by analyzing helping verbs and irregular verbs.

ELA ACADEMIC LANGUAGE

- *claim, details, text, past tense, irregular verb*
- Cognates: *detalles, texto, verbo irregular*

MATERIALS

Literature Anthology, pp. 220–223

Online Language Development Cards, 29A–29B

Online Language Development Practice, pp. 169–174

Online Language Transfers Handbook, pp. 15–19

A New Kind of Corn

Text Reconstruction

Focus on a single chunk of text to support comprehension and language development across the four domains.

1. Read aloud Paragraph 4 in "Bt Corn Is Better" in the **Literature Anthology** on page 222 while students listen.
2. Write the following on the board, providing definitions as needed: *profit, productivity, developing countries, staple*. Instruct students to listen for them as you read the paragraph a second time.
3. Read the paragraph a third time while students listen and take notes.
4. COLLABORATE Have students work with a partner to reconstruct the text from their notes. Help them write complete sentences as needed.
5. Have students look at the original text. Ask them to tell what the paragraph is mostly about. (how more Bt corn benefits more people and helps save money) Tell students that they are going to examine how the author supports his or her claim that Bt corn is better.
6. *What is the author's claim in the first sentence?* (Bt corn has helped on farms around the world) *Which details support the claim that corn helps farms around the world?* (It supports developing countries where corn is a staple; more food available benefits hungry nations) *Why does the author think that Bt corn is good for developing countries and hungry nations?* (more food is available to them)
7. Have students compare their text reconstructions to the original text. Have them check whether they also included details that support the claim that Bt corn is better.

Beginning Allow students to follow along in the Literature Anthology as you read the text aloud. Have them point to the words from Step 2 as they hear them.

Apply Text Features: Charts

Review with students that authors use charts to make it easier to visualize and compare information. *What does the chart on page 221 show?* (how corn is used). *How much corn is used for animal feed and industrial use?* (47%; 30%) *How much corn do humans consume?* (humans eat 10% of corn produced) *How does human consumption of corn compare to other ways corn is used?* (Possible: human consumption of corn is less than other uses of corn) Have partners use the chart to write sentences in their own words about the uses of corn.

Grammar in Context: Deconstruct a Sentence

Write these sentences from page 221 on the board:

Have you heard of Bt corn? Probably not. But you have probably eaten it.

Facilitate deconstructing these sentences for better comprehension. As needed, review run-on sentences and helping verbs:

- *Which of these word groups is not a complete sentence?* (*probably not*) *Does it contain a verb, or action word?* (no)
- *What are the verbs in the other sentences?* (*Have heard, have eaten*) *What word is used as a helping verb in each sentence?* (have)
- *What is the verb tense in these sentences?* (past)
- Circle *heard. What is the present tense of this verb?* (hear)
- Point to *heard. How do you know it is an irregular verb?* (It does not follow this rule for making a verb past tense: add *-ed* at the end of the word.)
- Have partners rewrite the sentences in their own words. Check their work and help students make corrections as needed.

For additional practice, see **Language Development Cards,** Lessons 29A-29B, and **Language Development Practice,** pages 169-174.

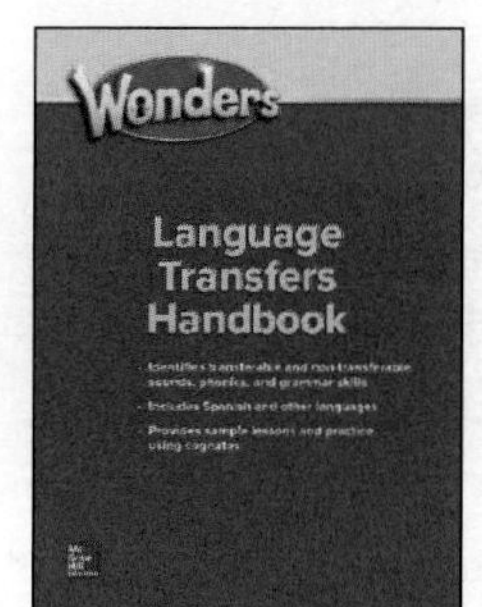

Language Transfers Handbook, Grammar Transfers, pp. 15-19

Independent Time

Vocabulary Building Have students create an interactive vocabulary activity. Have partners identify vocabulary and other words from "A New Kind of Corn" that have the Greek roots *gen, techn, agri,* and *chron*. Have partners write the Greek roots on index cards, writing the root on one side and the meaning on the back of each card. Then have them use the Greek roots to generate words.

Beginning Have students add sketches to the cards.

Intermediate/Advanced/Advanced High Have students include some of the self-selected words and content-area words they added to their glossaries.

COLLABORATE **Irregular Verbs** Help partners generate a list of irregular verbs using a 2-column chart. Have partners share irregular verbs they already know and use **Reading/Writing Companion** to look for other irregular verbs. Then have them write sentences using both present and past tenses. Encourage them to use time words that give clues to past or present tense. Provide a model:

I bought a notebook yesterday. I still need to buy a pencil today.

I bought a notebook yesterday, but I still need to buy a pencil.

PRESENT TENSE	PAST TENSE
buy	bought
catch	caught

FORMATIVE ASSESSMENT

STUDENT CHECK-IN

Text Reconstruction Have students share their notes. Have them reflect using the Check-In routine.

Grammar in Context Have students reflect on their deconstructions using the Check-In routine.

LEARNING GOALS

We can apply strategies and skills to read an argumentative text.

OBJECTIVES

Explain how an author uses reasons and evidence to support particular points in a text.

Use common, grade-appropriate Greek and Latin affixes and roots as clues to the meaning of a word.

Engage effectively in a range of collaborative discussions with diverse partners on grade 4 topics and texts, building on others' ideas and expressing their own clearly.

LANGUAGE OBJECTIVES

Students will explain the meaning of new words by identifying Greek roots and prefixes.

Students will discuss the author's claim in simple and complex sentences.

ELA ACADEMIC LANGUAGE

- *Greek roots, process, prefix, author's claim, headings, diagram, benefits*
- Cognates: *proceso, prefijo, diagrama, beneficios*

MATERIALS

Online ELL Genre Passage, "Food for Thought"

"Food for Thought"

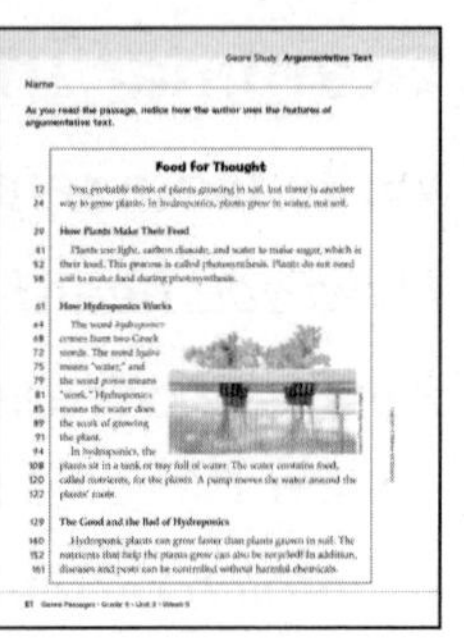

Genre Passage
Lexile 710L

Prepare to Read

Build Background Explain to students that people have been growing crops for over 10,000 years. Discuss with students what they know about ways farmers grow crops and whether it is possible to grow food without soil or chemicals.

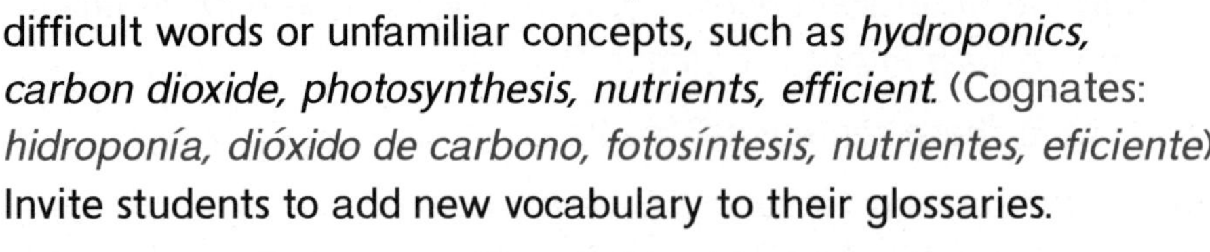

Vocabulary Use the Define/Example/Ask routine to pre-teach difficult words or unfamiliar concepts, such as *hydroponics, carbon dioxide, photosynthesis, nutrients, efficient.* (Cognates: *hidroponía, dióxido de carbono, fotosíntesis, nutrientes, eficiente*) Invite students to add new vocabulary to their glossaries.

Set Purpose *Today we will read "Food for Thought." As we read, think about the ways advances in science can be helpful or harmful.*

Read the Text

Page E1, Introduction and "How Plants Make Their Food"

Beginning *Where do many plants grow?* Many plants grow in soil. *In hydroponics, plants do not grow in soil. Where do the plants grow?* Plants grow in water. *What do plants use to make food?* Plants use light, carbon dioxide, and water.

Intermediate *How do plants make food?* Plants use light, carbon dioxide, and water to make sugar. *What happens in hydroponics?* Plants do not need soil.

COLLABORATE **Advanced/Advanced High** Have partners discuss the process of photosynthesis. (Possible answer: During photosynthesis, plants use light, carbon dioxide, and water to make sugar.)

Page E1, "How Hydroponics Works"

COLLABORATE **Greek roots** Have partners discuss how they know the meaning of *hydroponics*: The word *hydroponics* means water works to grow plants. I know the meaning from the Greek roots. The Greek root *hydro* means "water" and the Greek root *ponos* means "work."

Beginning *What are* nutrients*?* Nutrients are food for plants. *How does the plant get its food?* The plant's roots get nutrients from the water.

Intermediate How does the water pump help plants get nutrients? The water pump moves the water and the nutrients around the plants' roots.

Advanced/Advanced High Have partners discuss how plants get nutrients in the tank. (Water around the roots contains nutrients.)

Pages E1–E2, "The Good and Bad of Hydroponics"

Beginning Read the last paragraph on page E1 with students. *The word* recycle *means "use again."* Point to the prefix *re-* and discuss its meaning. *What is recycled in hydroponics? What is in the water?* The water has nutrients.

Intermediate *What can be recycled?* The nutrients in the water can be recycled. *How can plants grow in new places?* Plants can grow in new places because hydroponics can be in small places, like apartments, barns, or laboratories.

Advanced/Advanced High *Why can disease spread quickly in hydroponics?* (Possible answer: Disease can spread quickly because disease in the water is absorbed quickly through the roots.)

COLLABORATE Have partners discuss the benefits and problems with hydroponics. The benefits are that (Possible answer: Plants can grow faster than in soil and nutrients can be recycled.) The problems are that (Possible answer: It is more expensive than growing plants in soil. If disease gets in the water, it can spread quickly.)

Page E2, "The Bottom Line"

COLLABORATE **Beginning** Read the heading with students. *The term* bottom line *refers to the most important idea or fact. What words describe hydroponics?* (not perfect, efficient, important, new) Have partners describe the "bottom line": Hydroponics is not perfect. It is new and important.

COLLABORATE **Intermediate** Discuss the meaning of the word *efficient*. Have partners compare growing food on a farm to hydroponics. (Farming takes more labor than hydroponics.)

Advanced *What is the author's claim about hydroponics?* (Possible answer: People need skills to make hydroponics work, but it is efficient.)

Advanced High *Why does the author say hydroponics is not perfect?* (Possible answer: The author explains that there are problems with it.)

Respond to Reading

Use the following instruction to help students answer the questions on page E3.

1. **Text Features: Headings** *Read the third heading on page E1. Which word in the section means "good"?* (benefit) *Read the first sentence in paragraphs 2 and 3 of "The Good and Bad of Hydroponics." How is the section organized?* (benefits and problems)
2. *Look at the diagram. What is labeled?* (the direction the water flows and the water pump) *What does this tell you about the pump?* (It moves the water.) *What makes the pump work?* (electricity)
3. **Author's Claim** *Read paragraphs 1 and 2 of "The Good and Bad of Hydroponics." Find details that describe benefits of growing hydroponic plants.*

Fluency Have partners take turns reading the passage.

Build Knowledge: Make Connections

Talk About the Text Have partners discuss the ways advances in science can be helpful or harmful.

Write About the Text Have students add their ideas to their Build Knowledge pages of their reader's notebooks.

FORMATIVE ASSESSMENT

STUDENT CHECK IN

Have partners share their responses on page E3 and reflect using the Check-In routine.

LEVEL UP

IF students read the **ELL Level** of the **Genre Passage** fluently and answered the questions,

THEN pair them with students who have proficiently read the On Level. Have them

- partner read the On Level passage.
- summarize the author's point of view.

LEARNING GOALS

We can apply strategies and skills to read an argumentative text.

OBJECTIVES

Explain how an author uses reasons and evidence to support particular points in a text.

Read grade-level prose and poetry orally with accuracy, appropriate rate, and expression on successive readings.

Engage effectively in a range of collaborative discussions with diverse partners on grade 4 topics and texts, building on others' ideas and expressing their own clearly.

LANGUAGE OBJECTIVES

Students will inquire about people's perspectives about pesticides using key vocabulary.

ELA ACADEMIC LANGUAGE

- *context clues*

MATERIALS

ELL Leveled Reader, *The Battle Against Pests*

Online Differentiated Texts, "Are Pesticides Helpful or Harmful?"

Online ELL Visual Vocabulary Cards

DIGITAL TOOLS

MULTIMODAL

Have students read along with the audio of the selections to develop comprehension and practice fluency and pronunciation.

The Battle Against Pests

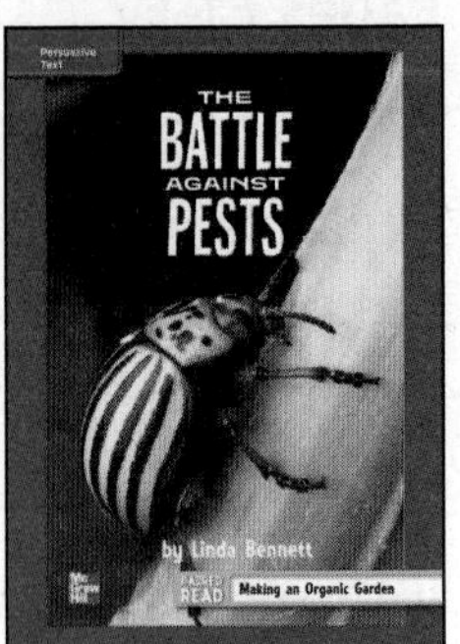

Leveled Reader
Lexile 770L

Prepare to Read

Build Background Review the Essential Question, *In what ways can advances in science be helpful or harmful?* Have students share their opinion and give examples. Have students choral read the title *The Battle Against Pests* and look at the cover of the reader. *The insect that you see is a pest. Pests are things that harm plants and crops. Do you think that this insect harms plants and crops?* Ask students if they know the name of the insect and the plant that it is on. Then preview "Making an Organic Garden." *We will also read about ways to grow better foods without the use of harmful chemicals.*

Vocabulary Use the routine on the **ELL Visual Vocabulary Cards** to pre-teach ELL Vocabulary *controlled* and *destructive.* (Cognate: *destructivo*) Discuss the appendices on page 19 of the Leveled Reader.

Set Purpose *Today we are going to read an argumentative text called "The Battle Against Pests." As we read, think about ways advances in science can be helpful or harmful.*

Read the Text

Pages 2–4, Chapter 1

Have students generate questions they have about the chapter and reread to find answers. Read the first paragraph on page 3. *Which word has a similar meaning to the word* destructive? (destroyed)

Beginning *What are pests?* Pests are insects, weeds, and disease. *Which plants attack crops?* (weeds) *What causes plants to rot?* (disease)

Intermediate Have partners discuss what happened in Ireland. Many people in Ireland died because a disease caused potato crops to rot.

Advanced/Advanced High Have partners discuss why farmers rotate crops. (Possible answers: It keeps pests away and prevents disease.)

Pages 5–10, Chapters 2–3

COLLABORATE **Beginning** Have partners read the label and caption on page 5. *What does the caption tell you about the photograph?* The caption tells the names of the pest and the plant. Have partners take turns asking and answering questions about pests. *What pest do you see?* I see a beetle. *What is the beetle eating?* It is eating the leaf.

Intermediate Have partners discuss what DDT does: DDT is a type of pesticide. DDT kills insects by paralyzing the nervous system.

COLLABORATE

Advanced/Advanced High *What context clues tell you about the meaning of* paralyze*?* ("the insect can't move or breathe")

Pages 12–14, Chapter 4

Intermediate *What are some reasons for using pesticides?* Some reasons are to kill pests, prevent crop damage, and prevent a famine.

COLLABORATE

Reread Have students reread the chapter. Then have partners discuss why some people are against pesticides. (Some pesticides harm the environment and people's health.)

Respond to Reading Have partners complete their graphic organizers and discuss the questions on page 15.

Fluency: Accuracy, Rate

Read pages 12–13 with accuracy and appropriate rate. Then read the passage aloud again and have students read along with you. For more practice, have students record their voices while they read a few times. Have them play their recordings and choose the best one.

Paired Read: "Making an Organic Garden"

Make Connections: Write About It

Before students write, use sentence frames: When I grow an organic garden, I don't use pesticides. I plant organic seeds and seedlings. I use natural sprays that repel pests. I pull out weeds when I see them.

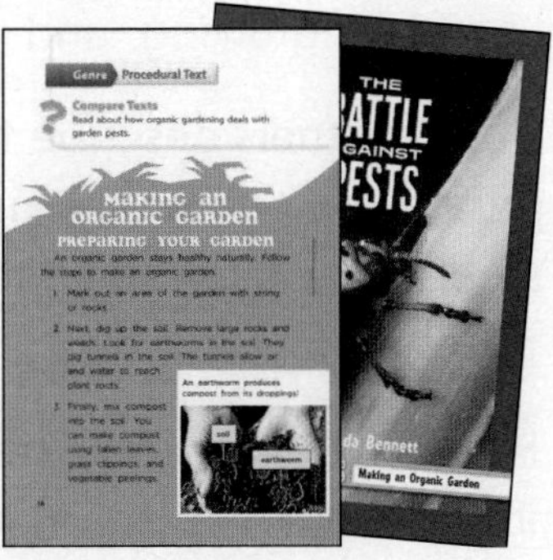

ELL Leveled Reader

Build Knowledge: Make Connections

Talk About the Text Have partners discuss the ways advances in science can be helpful or harmful.

Write About the Text Have students add their ideas to their Build Knowledge pages of their reader's notebooks.

Self-Selected Reading

Have students choose another argumentative text from the online **Leveled Reader Library** or read the **Differentiated Text:** "Are Pesticides Helpful or Harmful?"

FOCUS ON SCIENCE

Have students complete the activity on page 20 to make an argument for or against pesticides.

LITERATURE CIRCLES

Ask students to conduct a literature circle using the Thinkmark questions to guide the discussion.

FORMATIVE ASSESSMENT

STUDENT CHECK-IN

Have partners share their answers to Respond to Reading. Ask students to reflect on their learning using the Check-In routine.

LEVEL UP

IF students read the **ELL Level** fluently and answered the questions,

THEN pair them with students who have proficiently read the **On Level** and have students

- echo-read the **On Level** main selection with their partner.
- list words they find difficult.
- discuss these words with their partner.

Access Complex Text

The **On Level** challenges students by including more **domain-specific words** and **complex sentence structures.**

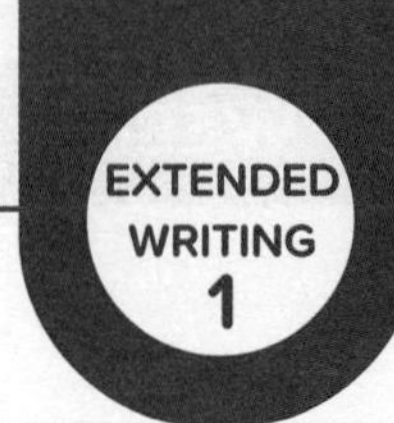

LEARNING GOALS

- **We can identify a claim and supporting details.**
- **We can analyze a student model and student model sources.**

OBJECTIVES

Describe the overall structure of events, ideas, concepts, or information in a text or part of a text.

Explain how an author uses reasons and evidence to support particular points in a text.

Draw evidence from literary or informational texts to support analysis, reflection, and research.

LANGUAGE OBJECTIVES

Students will discuss features and organization of an argumentative essay using academic language.

ELA ACADEMIC LANGUAGE

- *logical, evidence, prompt, source*
- Cognates: *lógico, evidencia*

MATERIALS

Online ELL Extended Writing BLMS:

- Michael's Model, pp. 37–39
- Analyze Michael's Model, pp. 40–41

Online Student Model Sources

Reading/Writing Companion, pp. 86–89

Literature Anthology, p. 222

DIGITAL TOOLS

Have students read along with Michael's Model to develop comprehension and build fluency.

Argumentative Writing

Logical Progression

Reread the paragraph on page 87 of **Reading/Writing Companion** with students. Review with them that *logical progression* means an essay goes in order from beginning to end. The introduction has a claim, and other sentences in the middle support the claim. The conclusion is at the end and retells the claim. Help students describe using: The claim tells that good things happen when kids volunteer. The sentences explain some ways kids can volunteer.

Compare Logical Progression Write on the board: **Strong:** *Did you know that some students plant flowers to attract butterflies and help the environment? Good things happen when kids volunteer. In Livingston, New Jersey, middle school students worked with community members to create a monarch-friendly butterfly garden.* **Weak:** *In New Jersey, community members worked with middle school students. Kids can volunteer. Planting flowers attracts butterflies.* Compare and discuss the ideas with students so they understand that the weak model does not present ideas in a logical order.

Organize Ideas Read "Bt Corn Is Better: A Farmer's Perspective" on **Literature Anthology** page 222 with students.

- Identify the claim with students. (The farmer is confident in growing Bt corn.) Then ask: *What does the second paragraph tell about?* (Bt corn needs less pesticides. This saves time and money.) *How does the author present a logical progression of ideas?* (The farmer first introduces his claim. He says that Bt corn is good for growing, and explains benefits in the next paragraph.)

Have partners describe the logical progression of ideas in the first paragraph on page 87 in the Reading/Writing Companion. Encourage students to read aloud the paragraph to one another and then read the second paragraph.

Beginning Help partners using: The questions give examples and lead logically into the claim. The claim tells that kids should volunteer. The next paragraph talks about the example in a middle school in New Jersey.

Intermediate Have partners describe: The questions are examples that support the claim. Then the claim says kids should volunteer. The next paragraph focuses on students in New Jersey creating a butterfly garden.

Advanced/Advanced High Have partners discuss the claim and the logical progression of ideas.

Analyze the Student Model and Sources

Analyze the Prompt Read the prompt on **Michael's Model** with students. Explain that the audience for the essay, an assembly, is a gathering of all the students in a school.

Discuss the Student Model

Mixed Levels Use **Michael's Model** to read with students using the **Glossary**. After each paragraph, have pairs of mixed language proficiency levels ask and answer the questions.

Paragraph 1 *What is something that helps the environment and kids?* (planting flowers to attract butterflies) *What should all kids do?* (volunteer) *What happens when kids volunteer?* (good things)

Paragraph 2 *What did community members in Livingston, New Jersey do?* (helped middle school students create a butterfly garden) *How do butterfly gardens help?* (They support native plant habitats. It is a fun way to be in nature and learn about plants.) *How can planting a vegetable garden help?* (can eat vegetables at school or donate them; kids learn)

Paragraphs 3–4 *How many Americans volunteer?* (27%) *How did Ryan raise money?* (He made and sold sea animal items.) *What does the Ocean Conservancy do?* (It elps to protect our oceans.) *What was the claim of the article about volunteering? Why did Micheal include this?* (kids shouldn't volunteer; a it is counterpoint. Michael argues aganist it)

Paragraph 5 *What claim does Michael restate in his conclusion?* (all kids should volunteer)

Analyze the Student Model: Organization

Use **Analyze Michael's Model** to analyze the organization with students.

- Discuss how the essay is organized. The claim is in the first paragraph followed by relevant evidence. There is a logical progression of ideas. The conclusion retells the writer's claim.
- The claim tells the focus and purpose, and the relevant evidence supports the claim.
- *What is the relevant evidence in the second paragraph?* (planting a garden benefits the kids and others; supports claim that kids should volunteer)

Mixed Levels Have partners complete columns 1 and 2 in Analyze Michael's Model.

Beginning Help partners using: The claim answers the prompt in the first paragraph. The relevant evidence supports the claim. The conclusion restates the claim.

Intermediate Have partners describe using: The relevant evidence tells about ways that kids can volunteer. It explains the claim.

Advanced/Advanced High Have partners describe the claim and the relevant evidence, focusing on the logical progression of ideas.

Analyze the Student Model: Sources

Read the **Online Student Model Sources** with students. Have them underline the information Michael used. Have partners complete the chart. Discuss the questions with students:

Paragraph 1 Discuss Source 1. *What information did Michael use and why?* (facts about the butterfly garden project; kids volunteering has good results) Discuss how questions lead into his claim.

Paragraph 2 Discuss Source 2. *What information did Michael use?* (benefits of planting vegetable gardens in schools) *How does he use it?* (supports his claim with examples of benefits to kids' health and learning)

Paragraphs 3–4 Discuss Source 4. *What information did Michael use?* (percentage of people volunteering) *What example did Michael give?* (Ryan's volunteering example) Elicit that Michael shows that kids make important positive changes in the world.

Paragraph 4 Discuss Source 3. *What information did Michael use?* (claim that kids should focus on school and fun, not volunteer) *Why did he give opposing information?* (as a counterpoint to his argument; as a chance to strongly state his claim again)

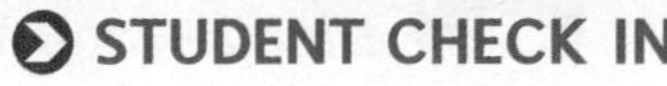

STUDENT CHECK IN

Have partners share responses to Michael's Model. Ask them to reflect on their learning using the Check-in routine.

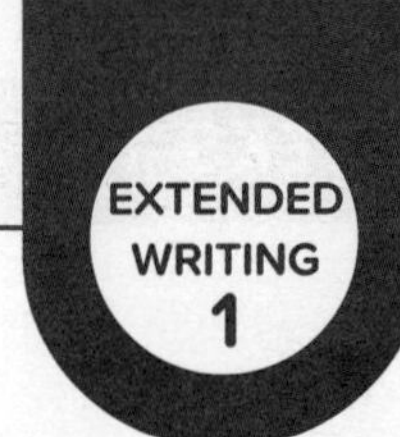

LEARNING GOALS

- We can synthesize information from four sources to plan and organize an argumentative essay.
- We can draft and revise an argumentative essay.

OBJECTIVES

Recall relevant information from experiences or gather relevant information from print and digital sources.

Produce clear and coherent writing in which the development and organization are appropriate to task, purpose, and audience.

With guidance and support from peers and adults, develop and strengthen writing as needed by planning, revising, and editing.

LANGUAGE OBJECTIVES

Students will argue their claim using transition words.

ELA ACADEMIC LANGUAGE

- *sentence fluency, transition words*

MATERIALS

Reading/Writing Companion, pp. 90–97

Literature Anthology, pp. 216–219

Online Language Development Cards, 62A–62B

Online Language Development Practice, pp. 367–372

Online ELL Extended Writing Resources BLMs:

- Glossary, pp. 42–43
- My Writing Outline, pp. 44–45
- Draft: Sentence Fluency, p. 46

DIGITAL TOOLS

Have students read along with the student sources to develop comprehension and build fluency and pronunciation.

Argumentative Writing

Analyze the Sources

Review the Writing Prompt Display the prompt: *Write an argumentative essay for a school bulletin board display about why the civil rights movement was needed.* Use the underlined words to discuss with students the kind of information they will look for as they read.

Read the Sources/Take Notes Read sources 1–3 on pages 91–93 in the **Reading/Writing Companion** and source 4, "Keeping Freedom in the Family" on pages 216–219 in the **Literature Anthology**.

Beginning Discuss the meaning of the words in the **Glossary**. Use visuals to discuss key concepts. Paraphrase challenging sentences for students. After each paragraph, help them describe: I learned about ____.

Intermediate Discuss the key concepts using the Glossary and visuals with students. Paraphrase challenging sentences with them. After each paragraph, help them retell the information.

Advanced/Advanced High Discuss the key concepts using the Glossary and visuals with students. Help them paraphrase challenging sentences. Have them retell the information after every two paragraphs.

Mixed Levels Take Notes Have pairs read **Sources 1–4** and take notes. Use the questions to discuss each source with the group.

SOURCE 1 **"Civil Rights Pioneers"** *Who were Harry and Harriet Moore?* (civil rights activists in Florida) *What did they fight for?* (equal rights: equal salaries, desegregated schools, voting rights) *What was the purpose of the Progressive Voters League?* (to help African Americans to vote)

SOURCE 2 **"The Montgomery Bus Boycott?"** *Why do people use boycotts?* (to protest peacefully) *Why did Rosa Parks refuse to give up her seat on the bus?* (She wanted to take a stand and make a change.) *What did Dr. King and others do after Parks was arrested?* (boycotted city buses) Discuss the impact of the Montgomery bus boycott with students.

SOURCE 3 **"Freedom Summer and the Civil Rights Movement"** *What did the SNCC want to do? (address the problems African Americans faced when they tried to vote) What did Freedom Summer want students to do? (continue to seek and stand up for their rights) What were the results of Freedom Summer? (led to the passage of Civil Rights Act of 1964 and Voting Rights Act of 1965; doubled percentage of African American registered voters)*

SOURCE 4 **"Keeping Freedom in the Family"** *What did the writer Nora Davis Day learn from her parents?* (Her family protested injustice.) *What injustices does the writer describe happening?* (Four black girls were killed in a church bombing and black actors and actresses had fewer rights than others.)

Plan/Organize Ideas

Synthesize Information Guide students on how to complete the graphic organizer on pages 94–95 of the **Reading/Writing Companion**. Model how students can transfer their information to **My Writing Outline**.

Beginning Help partners describe using: Civil rights are important because all people should have equal rights. Before there were civil rights for African Americans, people like the Moores had to fight for civil rights. There were peaceful protests for equal rights for African Americans.

Intermediate Help partners describe using: Civil rights are important because people of all races should have equal rights under the law. The Moores and others fought for civil rights for people with peaceful boycotts and protests, because it was important.

Advanced/Advanced High Have partners describe their claim, supporting reasons, and relevant evidence.

Draft

Have partners review the plan on My Writing Outline.

- **Organization/My Draft** Check that the claim answers the writing prompt. *Is the claim in the first paragraph? Are supporting reasons with relevant evidence in the body paragraphs?* Help them paraphrase their claim for the conclusion.
- **Evidence and Sources** Check that the supporting reasons are related to the claim and that the evidence comes from the four sources.
- **Sentence Fluency** Encourage students to combine short sentences using transition words.

 Have students use **My Writing Outline** as they write their draft.

Beginning Help partners write complete sentences for the claim and supporting reasons.

Intermediate Have partners review their claim and whether the supporting reasons and evidence support it. Help them read their essays for sentence fluency. Then have students write a concluding sentence.

Advanced/Advanced High Have partners review their claim and whether the supporting reasons have relevant evidence. Have them review for fluency and restate their claim in the conclusion.

 **TEACHER CONFERENCES**

To help students write their draft, meet with each student to provide support and guidance. Discuss with students transition words in their writing. For additional support, use **Draft: Sentence Fluency**.

Revise

Revising Checklist Review the Revising Checklist in the Reading/Writing Companion on page 97.

Partner feedback Help partners use the checklist to give feedback. For example:

Beginning Say: *I see the first sentence and the second sentence are short. How can we combine them?* Help partners create one sentence with a transition word.

Intermediate Have partners describe how they combined the first two sentences using a transition word. Then have them read it aloud to one another.

Advanced/Advanced High Have partners describe how they combined the first two sentences and then look for other sentences they can revise.

 Have students revise their essays.

For additional practice 62A and 62B, see **Language Development Cards**, Lessons and **Language Development Practice**, pages 367–372.

 **TEACHER CONFERENCES**

To help students revise, meet with each student to provide support and guidance.

STUDENT CHECK-IN

Plan Have partners share their Writing Outline.

Draft Have partners share examples of sentences with transition words.

Revise Have partners describe revisions in their essays.

Ask students to reflect using the Check-in routine.

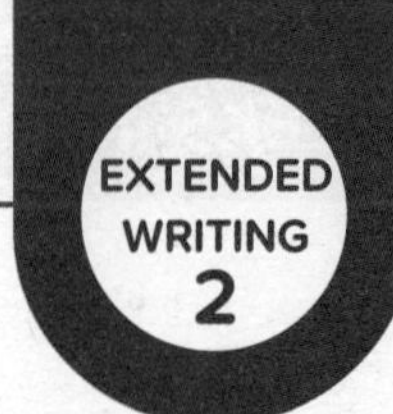

LEARNING GOALS

- We can identify transitional strategies.
- We can analyze a student model and student model sources.

OBJECTIVES

Link opinion and reasons using words and phrases

Explain how an author uses reasons and evidence to support particular points in a text.

Draw evidence from literary or informational texts to support analysis, reflection, and research.

LANGUAGE OBJECTIVES

Students will discuss features and organization of an argumentative essay using academic language.

ELA ACADEMIC LANGUAGE

- *transition, link, evidence*
- Cognates: *transición, evidencia*

MATERIALS

Online ELL Extended Writing Resources BLMs:

- Michelle's Model, pp. 47–49
- Analyze Michelle's Model, pp. 50–51

Online Student Model Sources

Literature Anthology, p. 199

Reading/Writing Companion, pp. 98–101

DIGITAL TOOLS

Have students read along with Michelle's Model to develop comprehension and build fluency.

Argumentative Writing

Transitional Strategies

Reread the paragraph on page 99 of **Reading/Writing Companion** with students. Review with them that using transitions helps to connect ideas. Guide students to connect these sentences with linking words: A waterwheel is a big wheel with paddles on the rim. Ancient Egyptians used river currents to turn wheels, and the ancient Greeks and Romans used hydropower.

Compare Linking Words Write on the board: **Strong:** *The force of the water turns the wheel, and then the wheel runs machinery that is linked to it.* **Weak:** *The water turns the wheel. The wheel runs machinery.* Have students compare to elicit that the strong model uses linking words to connect ideas.

Transition Words Read "Easter Shopping at Levy's" on **Literature Anthology** page 199 with students. Elicit that linking words improve the flow of writing in the first paragraph.

- Discuss the second paragraph. *What two ideas are in the first sentence?* (The saleswoman would not serve them; the white customers had to be helped.) *What linking word connects these ideas?* (until) Explain that word *until* shows sequence, because it explains the order of events.

Have partners add linking words to the paragraph on page 99, read it aloud to each other, and discuss how it improves the flow of ideas.

Beginning Help partners using: Linking words help to connect ideas. Some linking words I can use are *also, finally, but, for example, next*.

Intermediate Have partners describe using: Linking words are transitions that help to connect ideas. Some examples of linking words are *also, finally, but, for example, next*.

Advanced/Advanced High Have partners describe transitions and practice using them to connect ideas in sentences.

Analyze the Student Model and Sources

Analyze the Prompt Read the prompt on **Michelle's Model** with students. Explain that an *editorial* is a newspaper article that gives an opinion on an issue.

Discuss the Student Model

Mixed Levels Use Michelle's Model to read the model with students. Before reading, discuss *solar energy* with students using the Glossary. After each paragraph, have mixed pairs of language proficiency levels ask and answer the questions with each other and share responses.

Paragraph 1 *What is a free source of energy?* (solar energy) *What are some concerns about it?* (It costs a lot of money.) *How will solar energy help the elementary school and the library?* (It will save money and help the environment.)

Paragraphs 2–3 *What do solar panels do?* (change sunlight into electricity) *How did New Mexico make solar panels cheaper to install?* (It passed a solar tax credit.) *How many days of sun does Silver City have each year?* (295 days/year) *What is a negative effect of using oil or gas?* (air pollution)

Paragraph 4 *What are problems with solar energy?* (too expensive) *How many years can it take for the savings from using solar panels to cover the cost of the solar panels?* (about ten years) Discuss with students how Michelle includes evidence that goes against her claim in order to make her argument stronger.

Paragraph 5 *What is the writer's claim?* (Silver City should invest in solar energy.) *What is a benefit of solar energy?* (It is a renewable resource.) *Why will future residents be grateful for it?* (It is good for the environment; it will save money over time.)

Analyze the Student Model: Organization

Use **Analyze Michelle's Model** as you fill in the information with students.

- Point to the first column and discuss the essay organization. The claim is in the first paragraph followed by paragraphs with relevant evidence. The conclusion retells the writer's claim.
- Review that the claim tells the focus and the relevant evidence supports the claim.
- Discuss transitions with students. *How did Michelle connect the ideas in the second and third paragraphs?* (The word since transitions to an idea about the school and library.)

Mixed Levels Have partners complete columns 1 and 2 in Analyze Michelle's Model.

Beginning Help partners using: The claim answers the prompt. The claim argues that we should put solar panels on the library and the elementary school. The relevant evidence supports the claim. The conclusion restates the claim.

Intermediate Have partners describe using: The claim argues that we should put solar panels on the library and the elementary school. The relevant evidence supports the claim. The conclusion restates the claim.

Advanced/Advanced High Have partners describe the claim, relevant evidence, and transitional strategies that connect ideas.

Analyze the Student Model: Sources

Read the **Online Student Model Sources** with students. Have them underline the information Michelle used.

Have partners complete the third column in Analyze Michelle's Model.

Paragraph 1 Discuss Sources 1 and 2 with students. *What information did Michelle use?* (Solar power is free energy; New Mexico has plenty of sunshine.) This is evidence that supports her claim, which is in this introduction.

Paragraphs 2–3 Discuss Sources 1 and 2 with students. *What information did Michelle use?* (New Mexico passed a solar tax credit; Silver City averages many days of sun per year; solar energy doesn't produce air pollution.) *How does Michelle use the information?* (examples of how solar energy is a good idea) Discuss how statistics give evidence and strengthen Michelle's argument.

Paragraph 4 Discuss Source 3. *What information did Michelle use?* (problems with solar energy: expense of installation of solar panels) *Why does she include this information that opposes her claim?* (She responds with a counterpoint.) Point out that a writer shares opposing evidence to show he/she has considered all evidence. The writer makes a stronger argument.

Paragraph 5 Discuss the information from Source 1. *What information did Michelle use in the conclusion and why?* (that New Mexico ranks number one in peak sun hours; restates her claim in favor of solar energy)

FORMATIVE ASSESSMENT

STUDENT CHECK-IN

Have partners share responses to Michelle's Model. Ask them to reflect on their learning using the Check-In routine.

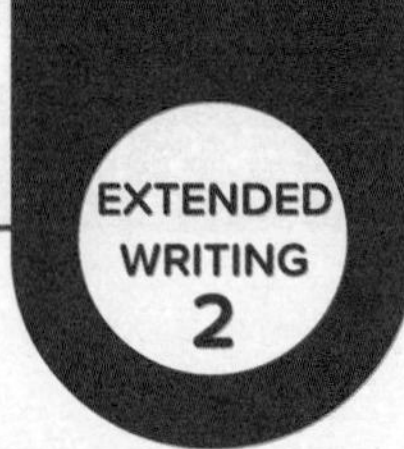

LEARNING GOALS

- **We can synthesize information from three sources.**
- **We can write an argumentative essay.**

OBJECTIVES

Recall relevant information from experiences or gather relevant information from print and digital sources.

Acquire and use accurately grade-appropriate general academic and domain-specific words and phrases, including those that signal precise actions, emotions, or states of being and that are basic to a particular topic.

With guidance and support from peers and adults, develop and strengthen writing as needed by planning, revising, and editing.

LANGUAGE OBJECTIVES

Students will argue using domain-specific vocabulary in an argumentative essay.

ELA ACADEMIC LANGUAGE

- *domain-specific, precise*
- Cognate: *preciso*

MATERIALS

Reading/Writing Companion, pp. 102–109

Online ELL Extended Writing Resources BLMs:

- Glossary, p. 52
- My Writing Outline, pp. 53-54
- Draft: Domain-Specific Vocabulary, p. 55
- Take Notes: Argumentative Writing, p. 74

Online Language Development Cards, 29A–29B

Online Language Development Practice, pp. 169–174

DIGITAL TOOLS

Have students read along with the student sources to develop comprehension and build fluency and pronunciation.

Argumentative Writing

Analyze the Sources

Review the Writing Prompt Display the prompt: *Write an argumentative essay for your class explaining why stricter protections are needed for Oregon's Willamette River basin.* Use the underlined words to discuss with students the type of information they will look for as they read.

Read the Sources/Take Notes Read the sources on pages 103–105 in the **Reading/Writing Companion** with students. Use the definitions in the **Glossary** and help them identify and underline relevant information as they read.

Beginning Discuss the meaning of the words in the Glossary. Use visuals to discuss key concepts. Paraphrase challenging sentences for students. After each paragraph, help them describe: I learned about ___.

Intermediate Discuss the key concepts using the Glossary and visuals with students. Paraphrase challenging sentences with them. After each paragraph, help them retell the information.

Advanced/Advanced High Discuss the key concepts using the Glossary and visuals with students. Help them paraphrase challenging sentences. Have them retell the information after every two paragraphs.

Mixed Levels Take Notes Have pairs read **Sources 1–3** and take notes. Use the questions to discuss each source with the group.

SOURCE 1 **"A River in Danger"** *What is a watershed?* (an area where water drains into one place) *What can harm the Willamette River?* (pollutants like fertilizer, trash and oil) *Why is the Willamette River an important source of water?* (the river gives life to crops; communities get their drinking water there)

SOURCE 2 **"Balancing Conservation and Energy Needs"** *What act did the EPA change?* (the Clean Water Act) *Why did they change the act?* (to grow infrastructure) *What are some examples of infrastructure?* (roads, energy pipelines, buildings)

SOURCE 3 **"A Winter Refuge for Geese"** *Where do migrating geese spend the winter?* (in the Willamette River Basin) *How did conservationists protect the geese?* (They created a wildlife refuge.) *What challenges do the wetlands still face?* (pollution; pressure to build infrastructure projects)

Plan/Organize Ideas

Synthesize Information Guide students on how to complete the graphic organizer on pages 106–107 of the Reading/Writing Companion. Model how students can transfer their information from their graphic organizer to **My Writing Outline**.

Beginning Oregon's Willamette River Basin needs stricter protections. This is important for the environment and all living things.

Intermediate Have partners write using: Stricter protections are needed for Oregon's Willamette River Basin.

Advanced/Advanced High Have partners describe the claim. Discuss how they synthesized information from the sources.

Draft

Have partners review the plan on **My Writing Outline**.

- **Organization/My Draft** Check that the claim answers the writing prompt and the body paragraphs include supporting reasons with relevant evidence. Help them paraphrase the claim for the conclusion.
- **Evidence and Sources** Check that the supporting reasons are related to the claim and that the evidence comes from the three sources.
- **Domain-Specific Vocabulary** Have students use precise, domain-specific words to discuss the topic.

Have students use their completed My Writing Outline to help them write their drafts.

Beginning Help partners write and organize complete sentences for the claim and supporting reasons. Make sure they check that the claim answers the prompt.

Intermediate Have partners review that the claim answers the prompt and whether the reasons support the claim. Help them use academic and domain-specific vocabulary. Then have students write a concluding sentence.

Advanced/Advanced High Have partners review that the claim answers the prompt and the evidence is relevant and provides support. Have them review how they used academic and domain-specific vocabulary. Then have them add evidence to the conclusion.

TEACHER CONFERENCES

To help students write their draft meet with each student to provide support and guidance. Discuss with them domain-specific vocabulary in their writing.

Revise

Revising Checklist Review the items in the Revising Checklist in the **Reading/Writing Companion** on page 109.

Partner feedback Have partners use the checklist to give feedback. For example:

Beginning Help pairs read the paragraph. Say: *I see this word* pesticide *and I'm not sure what it means. Where can I find its meaning?* Have partners use a dictionary, and then write a sentence that defines *pesticide.*

Intermediate Have partners describe how they identified the definition of *pesticide.* Remind them to check their spelling and punctuation.

Advanced/Advanced High Have partners describe how they found their information. Have them look for where they can use domain-specific vocabulary in their writing and remind them to check their spelling, punctuation, and grammar.

For additional practice, see **Language Development Cards**, Lessons 29A and **Language Development Practice**, pages 169–174.

Before they revise, have partners discuss the revisions with each other.

TEACHER CONFERENCES

To help students revise, meet with each student to provide support and guidance.

FORMATIVE ASSESSMENT

STUDENT CHECK-IN

Plan Have partners share My Writing Outline.

Draft Have partners share examples of domain-specific words.

Revise Have partners describe revisions in their essays.

Ask students to reflect using the Check-In routine.

Summative Assessment

Get Ready for Unit Assessment

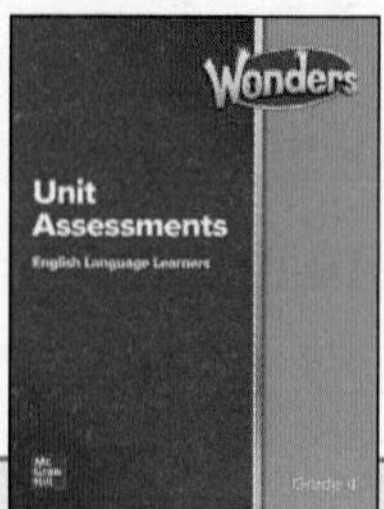

Unit 3 Tested Skills

LISTENING AND READING COMPREHENSION	VOCABULARY	GRAMMAR	SPEAKING AND WRITING
• Listening Actively • Comprehension • Text Structure • Cohesion	• Unit Vocabulary Words	• Verbs and Verb Phrases	• Presenting • Writing • Supporting Opinions • Retelling/Summarizing • Text Structure

Create a Student Profile

Record data from the following resources in the Student Profile charts on pages 320–321 of the Assessment book.

COLLABORATIVE	INTERPRETIVE	PRODUCTIVE

• Collaborative Conversations Rubrics
  • Listening
  • Speaking
	• Leveled Unit Assessment:
	  • Listening Comprehension
	  • Reading Comprehension
	  • Vocabulary
	  • Grammar
	• Presentation Rubric
	  • Listening
	• *Wonders* Unit Assessment
		• Weekly Progress Monitoring
		• Leveled Unit Assessment
		  • Speaking
		  • Writing
		• Presentation Rubric
		  • Speaking
		• Write to Sources Rubric
		• *Wonders* Unit Assessment

The Foundational Skills Kit, Language Development Kit, and Adaptive Learning provide additional student data for progress monitoring.

Level Up

Use the following chart, along with your Student Profiles, to guide your Level Up decisions.

LEVEL UP	If **BEGINNING** level students are able to do the following, they may be ready to move to the **INTERMEDIATE** level:	If **INTERMEDIATE** level students are able to do the following, they may be ready to move to the **ADVANCED** level:	If **ADVANCED** level students are able to do the following, they may be ready to move to on-level:
COLLABORATIVE	• participate in collaborative conversations using basic vocabulary and grammar and simple phrases or sentences • discuss simple pictorial or text prompts	• participate in collaborative conversations using appropriate words and phrases and complete sentences • use limited academic vocabulary across and within disciplines	• participate in collaborative conversations using more sophisticated vocabulary and correct grammar • communicate effectively across a wide range of language demands in social and academic contexts
INTERPRETIVE	• identify details in simple read alouds • understand common vocabulary and idioms and interpret language related to familiar social, school, and academic topics • make simple inferences and make simple comparisons • exhibit an emerging receptive control of lexical, syntactic, phonological, and discourse features	• identify main ideas and/or make some inferences from simple read alouds • use context clues to identify word meanings and interpret basic vocabulary and idioms • compare, contrast, summarize, and relate text to graphic organizers • exhibit a limited range of receptive control of lexical, syntactic, phonological, and discourse features when addressing new or familiar topics	• determine main ideas in read alouds that have advanced vocabulary • use context clues to determine meaning, understand multiple-meaning words, and recognize synonyms of social and academic vocabulary • analyze information, make sophisticated inferences, and explain their reasoning • command a high degree of receptive control of lexical, syntactic, phonological, and discourse features
PRODUCTIVE	• express ideas and opinions with basic vocabulary and grammar and simple phrases or sentences • restate information or retell a story using basic vocabulary • exhibit an emerging productive control of lexical, syntactic, phonological, and discourse features	• produce coherent language with limited elaboration or detail • restate information or retell a story using mostly accurate, although limited, vocabulary • exhibit a limited range of productive control of lexical, syntactic, phonological, and discourse features when addressing new or familiar topics	• produce sentences with more sophisticated vocabulary and correct grammar • restate information or retell a story using extensive and accurate vocabulary and grammar • tailor language to a particular purpose and audience • command a high degree of productive control of lexical, syntactic, phonological, and discourse features

LEARNING GOALS

We can read and understand narrative nonfiction.

OBJECTIVES

Describe the overall structure of events, ideas, concepts, or information in a text or part of a text.

Engage effectively in a range of collaborative discussions with diverse partners on grade 4 topics and texts, building on others' ideas and expressing their own clearly.

LANGUAGE OBJECTIVES

Students will explain the cause and effect of events using signal words.

ELA ACADEMIC LANGUAGE

- *cause and effect*
- Cognate: *causa y efecto*

MATERIALS

Reading/Writing Companion, pp. 126–129

Online Scaffolded Shared Read, "A World Without Rules"

Visual Vocabulary Cards

Online ELL Visual Vocabulary Cards

DIGITAL TOOLS

MULTIMODAL

Have students read along with the audio of the selection to develop comprehension and practice fluency and pronunciation.

"A World Without Rules"

Prepare to Read

Build Background Discuss with students the rules and laws they and other people follow in school, community, state, or country. Have them describe examples using: I follow rules/laws when I ___. Rules/Laws are important because ___. Discuss with students and elicit that they protect people and keep them safe. Then have them discuss what it would be like to live without rules.

Vocabulary Use the **Visual Vocabulary Cards** to preteach the vocabulary: *amendments, commitment, compromise, democracy, eventually, legislation, privilege,* and *version.* Use the online **ELL Visual Vocabulary Cards** to teach additional vocabulary from the Shared Read: *confusion, inspect, invaded, maintain, sensible,* and *services.*

Set Purpose *Today we will read a narrative nonfiction text called* "A World Without Rules". *As we read, think about why we need government.*

Read the Text

Select the **Scaffolded Shared Read** or the Shared Read in the **Reading/Writing Companion,** based on students' language proficiency.

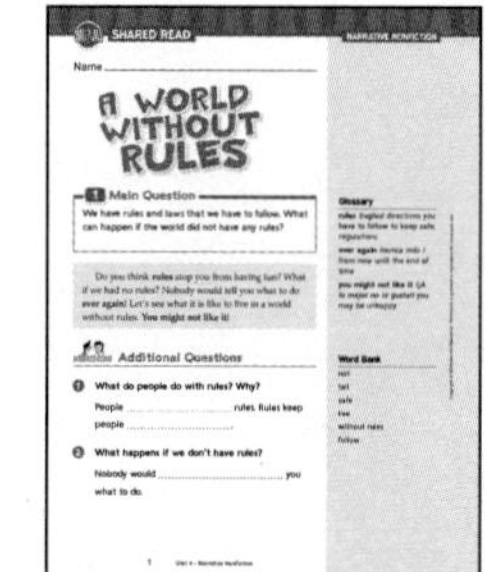

Scaffolded Shared Read, Lexile 580L

Beginning/Early-Intermediate Use the online **Scaffolded Shared Read** to help partners work together to read and understand narrative nonfiction. Remind them to use the Glossary to help them read and the Word Bank to help them answer the Main and Additional Questions.

Intermediate/Advanced/Advanced High Read the text with students and use the Interactive Question-Response Routine to help them understand narrative nonfiction.

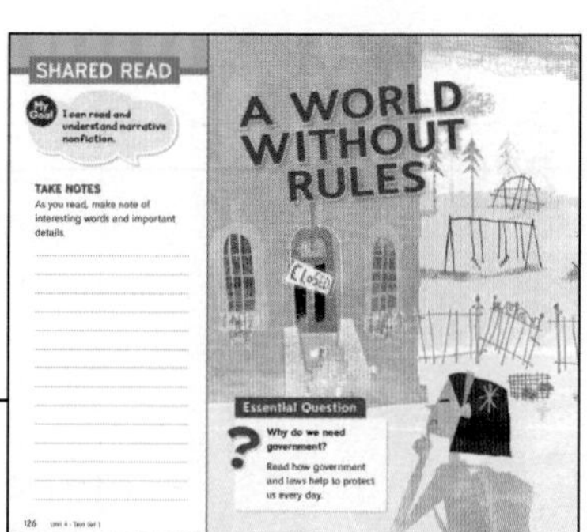

Reading/Writing Companion, Lexile 830L

Page 127, Introduction

Read the text with students. *What does the author ask?* ("But what if we had no rules at all?") *Why?* (to find out what it is like to live without rules) *Which words or phrase tell you?* ("Well, let's see what it's like to inhabit a world without rules.") *What does the word* inhabit *mean?* (live in)

Intermediate *What pronoun begins the passage?* (*You*) *Who is the author talking to?* (the reader) *What does the expression "Sounds great, right?" refer to?* (not having rules) *What might the reader "change their mind" about?* (living without rules)

COLLABORATE Have partners express their opinions about living without any rules: In my opinion, it would/would not be good because ___.

Page 127, "A Strange Morning"

Read the text with students and review Vocabulary *eventually, compromise,* and *sensible. What does the **heading** tell you about the section?* (This section will tell about a strange morning.) *What strange things happen?* (eats cookies for breakfast; don't need to brush teeth) *Are they normal or strange?* (strange)

COLLABORATE **Cause and Effect** Explain that a cause is an event that causes something to happen. An effect is the result, or what happens. Have partners discuss the relationship between not having rules and eating cookies for breakfast. *Which event is the cause?* (not having rules) *Which is the effect?* (eating cookies for breakfast)

Intermediate *Which sentence tells you what will happen if we don't brush our teeth?* (last sentence) *Have students state the relationship using: You may have a cavity because* you don't brush your teeth.

Advanced/Advanced High *What compromise did you read about?* (crumble cookies over cereal) *How is this a compromise?* (Possible answer: The author tells that eating cookies is one choice, but it is not sensible, so adding cookies to sensible cereal is a compromise.)

Page 127, "A Community in Confusion"

Read the text with students and review Vocabulary *confusion, services, maintain,* and *invaded. What is it like to cross the street?* (Cars zip by and honk at each other.) *Who takes care of the playground?* (nobody) *Will there be lifeguards?* (no) *In the real world, who takes care of the parks?* (state and local governments)

COLLABORATE **Intermediate** *Have partners describe the **effects** of not having a police officer:* Without a police officer, cars go by very fast and honk at each other. As a result, it is not safe to cross the street.

Advanced/Advanced High *What are some things the government takes care of?* (keeping people safe in traffic, taking care of playgrounds and parks, protecting the country)

Page 128, "Back to Reality"

Read the text with students and review Vocabulary *version, democracy, privilege, legislation, amendments, commitment,* and *inspect. What does the word* version *refer to?* (a world without rules) *In our real world, what is our, or people's, role in government?* (vote for people who run the country) *What do they do?* (pass laws, pass amendments to laws) *Who are some people who work for the government?* (crossing guards, police officers, lifeguards) *What do laws do?* (protect people and keep everyone safe)

Intermediate Review the meaning of *amendment* with students. *What happens when the government passes an amendment to a law?* The government makes a change to the law. Read the sentence with the word *outgrows* and define the word. *What do you think it means by "outgrows an old law"?* (Possible answer: The old law is no longer working.) *Does the phrase describe a **cause** or **effect**? Why?* The phrase describes a cause because it tells that the old law needs to change.

Advanced/Advanced High Have students read the fifth sentence in the third paragraph. *What is the sentence about?* (community workers and government agencies) *What does the phrase* such as *tell you?* (gives specific examples of a topic) *Which word connects the two topics in the sentence?* (while) *What do the two topics have in common?* (The topics describe what the government does.)

Advanced High *How can you restate the last sentence to describe **cause and effect**?* (Possible answer: Our country has a government and laws because they protect the people and keep us safe.)

FORMATIVE ASSESSMENT

STUDENT CHECK-IN

Have partners retell the important ideas in the text. Ask them to reflect using the Check-In routine.

LEARNING GOALS

- **We can read and understand narrative nonfiction by identifying the cause-and-effect text structure.**
- **We can identify and use pronouns.**

OBJECTIVES

Paraphrase portions of a text read aloud or information presented in diverse media and formats, including visually, quantitatively, and orally.

Demonstrate command of the conventions of standard English grammar and usage when writing or speaking.

LANGUAGE OBJECTIVES

Students will discuss cause and effect using signal words.

Students will inquire about pronouns using academic language.

ELA ACADEMIC LANGUAGE

- *cause, effect, identify, signal, pronoun*
- Cognates: *causa, efecto, identificar, pronombre*

MATERIALS

Reading/Writing Companion, pp. 126–129, 130–131

Online Scaffolded Shared Read, "A World Without Rules"

Online Shared Read Writing Frames, p. 10

Online Language Development Cards, 40A–40B

Online Language Development Practice, pp. 235–240

Online Language Transfers Handbook, pp. 15–19

"A World Without Rules"

Text Reconstruction

Focus on a single chunk of text to support comprehension and language development across the four domains.

1. Read aloud the first paragraph on page 128 in the **Reading/Writing Companion**, while students listen.
2. Write the following on the board, providing definitions as needed: *maintain, pollution, air quality, gas mask.* Instruct students to listen for them as you read the paragraph a second time.
3. Read the paragraph a third time. Tell students to listen and take notes.
4.  COLLABORATE Have students work with a partner to reconstruct the text from their notes. Help them write complete sentences as needed.
5. Have students look at the original text. Ask them to tell what the paragraph is mostly about. (what would happen if we had no laws or government) Tell students they are going to examine the cause-and-effect text structure.
6. *Let's identify the cause in the third sentence. What happens to parks without state and local governments?* (Parks won't be maintained.) Point out the signal word "so." *What is the effect?* (You can't play in the parks.) *What is another cause and effect?* (People have to wear a gas mask because of pollution.) *What is the signal word or phrase?* ("as a result") Have students tell the cause and the effect.
7. Have students compare their text reconstructions to the original text. Have them check to be sure they show cause-and-effect relationships.

Beginning Have students follow along in the **Reading/Writing Companion** as you read the text aloud. Have them point to the words from Step 2 as they hear them. Have students use their books.

Grammar in Context: Introduce Pronouns

Notice the Form Display these sentences from the text. Underline the pronouns.

> Broken swings dangle from rusty chains.
> They dangle from rusty chains.
> A huge tree branch lies across the sliding board.
> It lies across the sliding board.

Read the sentences aloud and explain that the second and fourth sentences replace the noun phrases with pronouns. *What are the pronouns?* (They, It) *What do the pronouns* They *and* It *refer to?* (swings; branch) Point out that plural nouns have plural pronouns and singular nouns have singular pronouns. *What do you notice about the nouns and pronouns?* (The pronouns are singular or plural to match the noun.) Circle the nouns and draw arrows from them to the pronouns.

Apply and Extend Have partners rewrite the first and third sentences to describe what the nouns look like in their own words, using pronouns. Check their answers.

For additional practice, see **Language Development Cards**, Lessons 40A and 40B, and **Language Development Practice,** pages 235–240.

Independent Time

Vocabulary Building Have students build their glossaries.

Beginning/Early Intermediate Have students complete the Glossary Activities in the **Scaffolded Shared Read**.

Intermediate/Advanced/Advanced High Have students add the vocabulary from **Reading/Writing Companion** pages 130–131 and self-selected words or phrases they would like to learn to the chart.

Mixed Levels Pair students together: Beginning and Early-Intermediate students can teach vocabulary from their **Scaffolded Shared Read** glossaries. Intermediate and Advanced/Advanced High students can teach their self-selected words.

WORD/PHRASE	DEFINE	EXAMPLE	ASK
wonder	to be curious about; to think about	I wonder how old the stars are.	When you wonder, are you using your imagination?

COLLABORATE **Shared Read Writing Frames** Use the online leveled **Shared Read Writing Frames** for "A World Without Rules" to provide students with additional oral and written practice. Have them identify the sentences that describe the cause-and-effect relationships in the text. Provide corrective feedback if needed. Differentiated frames are available to provide support for all levels.

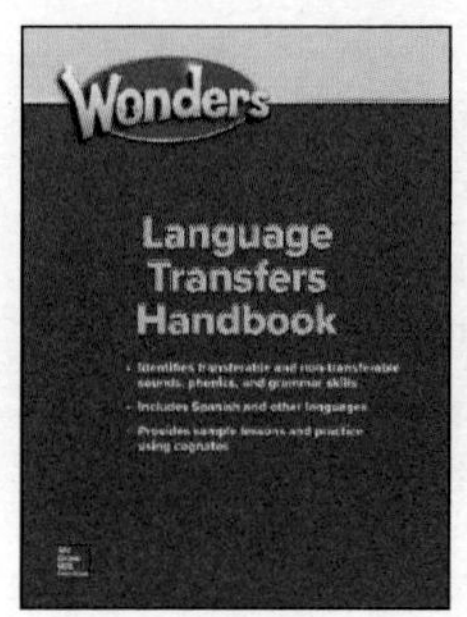

Language Transfers Handbook, Grammar Transfers, pp. 15–19

DIGITAL TOOLS

For additional support, use the online activities.

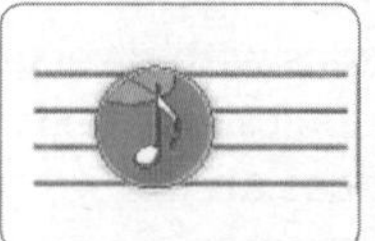

Grammar Song

FORMATIVE ASSESSMENT

STUDENT CHECK-IN

Text Reconstruction Have partners share their notes. Have students reflect on their work using the Check-In routine.

Grammar in Context Ask partners to share the sentences they wrote. Have them reflect on their work using the Check-In routine.

LEARNING GOALS

- **Read** We can read and understand narrative nonfiction.
- **Reread** We can reread to analyze text, craft, and structure.

OBJECTIVES

Refer to details and examples in a text when explaining what the text says explicitly and when drawing inferences from the text.

Engage effectively in a range of collaborative discussions with diverse partners on grade 4 topics and texts, building on others' ideas and expressing their own clearly.

Identify the intent, meaning, and importance of the Declaration of Independence, the U.S. Constitution, and the Bill of Rights. **Social Studies**

LANGUAGE OBJECTIVES

Students will inquire by answering questions about the text using key vocabulary.

Students will explain author's purpose using academic vocabulary.

ELA ACADEMIC LANGUAGE

- *author's purpose*
- Cognate: *propósito del autor*

MATERIALS

Literature Anthology, pp. 270-281

Visual Vocabulary Cards

Online ELL Anchor Text Support BLMs, pp. 24-26

DIGITAL TOOLS

Have students read along with the audio of the selection to develop comprehension and practice fluency and pronunciation.

See How They Run

Prepare to Read

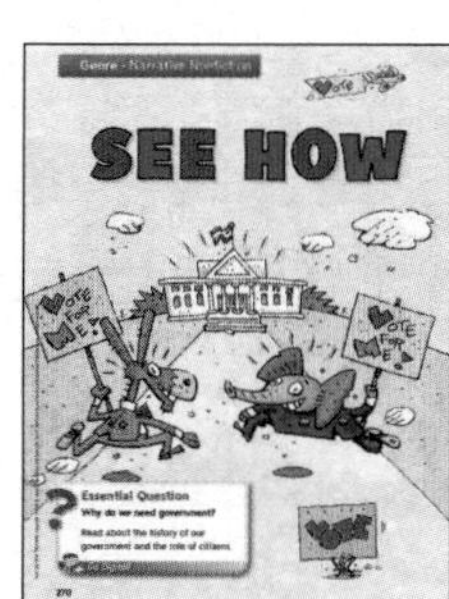

Literature Anthology, Lexile 870L

Build Background *We will learn about the history of the U.S. government and the role of citizens.* Invite students to share what they know about the U.S. government. I know that the U.S. government ____.

Vocabulary Use the **Visual Vocabulary Cards** to review the vocabulary: *amendments, commitment, compromise, democracy, eventually, legislation, privilege, version.*

Set Purpose *Today we will read about the history of the U.S. government and the role of citizens. As we read, think about why we need government.*

Play the audio summary of the text, available in multiple languages.

Read

Literature Anthology, pp. 270–281

Use the **Interactive Question Response Routine** to help students read and discuss *See How They Run.*

Beginning Help students discuss in complete sentences. Provide sentence frames: The ancient Greeks created democracy. Democracy means rule by the people.

Intermediate Ask students to respond in complete sentences and add details. Provide sentence starters as needed: The ancient Greeks invented democracy, which means rule by the people.

Advanced/Advanced High Have students respond in complete sentences and add details.

COLLABORATE **Independent Reading Practice** Have mixed level pairs work together to complete **ELL Anchor Text Support BLMs** pages 24–26. Then have them share their responses with the rest of the group.

Reread

Use the following prompts when working on **Reading/Writing Companion,** pages 138–140.

Literature Anthology, p. 273

COLLABORATE **Author's Purpose** Read the text with students. Have them ask about words or phrases that are unfamiliar, such as *legal,* and define them. *What did George Washington and the Founding Fathers borrow?* (ideas from past democracies) *Where did the name* Senate *come from?* (Roman Senate)

What did they borrow from the British? (ideas that the government must respect a citizen's legal rights) *What did the Founding Fathers want the people to have?* (a say in how to rule the country)

Beginning Read the first paragraph with students and restate the sentences as needed. Point to *Founding Fathers*. Say: *Founding Fathers are leaders who created the government in the United States.* Read the first sentence. *Is George Washington a Founding Father?* (yes)

Intermediate *With a partner, discuss how the author helps you understand what the Founding Fathers did.* The author tells that the Founding Fathers borrowed ideas from ancient Romans and Britain. They rejected the Greek way of citizens voting on laws.

Advanced/Advanced High *How does this help you understand about previous sections?* (Possible answer: It helps me to understand where they got their ideas and what they borrowed and rejected.)

Literature Anthology, p. 274

COLLABORATE **Author's Purpose** Read the sidebar on page 274 with students. Have them ask about words or phrases that are unfamiliar, such as *republic* and *in other words,* and define them. *What did the woman ask Benjamin Franklin?* (the type of government Franklin and the other Founding Fathers created) *What was Franklin's response?* (He and the Founding Fathers created a republic.) Discuss with students what people need to do in a republic and what Franklin meant by "if you can keep it." *What did he mean when he said "if you can keep it."?* (People have to vote to elect leaders in a republic, so they need to make sure they vote.) *What does the author want the readers to do?* (vote)

Beginning Restate sentences in the sidebar with students as needed. Explain that in a republic, people need to vote. *What do people need to do in a republic?* (vote) *How can you keep a republic?* (vote)

Intermediate *What do people need to do in a republic?* In a republic, people need to vote to elect leaders and make laws.

Advanced/Advanced High Have partners discuss why voting is a way to preserve a republic. (Possible answer: People have the power to choose and elect.)

Literature Anthology, pp. 278-279

COLLABORATE **Author's Purpose** Read the text with students. Have them ask about words or phrases that are unfamiliar, such as *bill* and define them. *What did the kids in Massachusetts do?* (helped make the ladybug the state insect) *What similar thing happened in New Hampshire?* (kids helped to make the pumpkin a state fruit) *What did Shadia and Kids Against Pollution do?* (made the Superfund bill a law to clean up toxic waste sites)

Beginning Read page 279 with students. Restate sentences as needed. *The phrase "pass this bill" means legislators vote to make a bill into a law. What bill did Shadia want lawmakers to pass?* (Superfund bill) *What did Shadia sell at the steps of the state capitol?* (drinks and toxic dump cake) *Who did the Shadia send the profits to?* (the governor)

Intermediate *What caused kids from Massachusetts to make the ladybug a state insect?* They learned that any state resident can give legislators ideas for new laws. *What did Shadia do with the profits from selling drinks and toxic dump cake?* She sent the profits to the governor to help pay for the Superfund bill.

Advanced/Advanced High Help partners discuss the real-life examples of kids as leaders. *What did the students in Massachusetts convince lawmakers to do?* (They convinced the lawmakers to make the ladybug the state insect.) *What did Shadia do to make the Superfund bill a law?* (Shadia had a lemonade stand on the steps of the capitol. She sent the profits to the governor to help pay for the Superfund.)

FORMATIVE ASSESSMENT

STUDENT CHECK-IN

Read Have partners share their responses to the Anchor Text questions. Then have them reflect using the Check-In routine.

Reread Ask partners to share their responses on **Reading/Writing Companion** pages 138-140. Have students reflect using the Check-In routine.

LEARNING GOALS

- We can read and understand narrative nonfiction by identifying the cause-and-effect text structure.
- We can understand and use pronouns and antecedents.

OBJECTIVES

Paraphrase portions of a text read aloud or information presented in diverse media and formats, including visually, quantitatively, and orally.

Demonstrate command of the conventions of standard English grammar and usage when writing or speaking.

LANGUAGE OBJECTIVES

Students will discuss the cause-and-effect text structure using academic vocabulary.

ELA ACADEMIC LANGUAGE

- *cause, effect, identify, signal*
- Cognates: *causa, efecto, identificar, pronombre*

MATERIALS

Literature Anthology, pp. 270–281

Online Language Development Cards, 40A–40B

Online Language Development Practice, pp. 235–240

Online Language Transfers Handbook, pp. 15–19

Online Oral Language Sentence Frames, p. 1

See How They Run

Text Reconstruction

Focus on a single chunk of text to support comprehension and language development across the four domains.

1. Read aloud the paragraph on page 279 in the **Literature Anthology** while students just listen.
2. Write the following on the board, providing definitions as needed: *toxic waste, convince, bill, lemonade stand, profits, shaming.* Instruct students to listen for them as you read the paragraph a second time.
3. Read the paragraph a third time while students listen and take notes.
4. COLLABORATE Have students work with a partner to reconstruct the text from their notes. Help them write complete sentences as needed.
5. Have students look at the original text and tell what the paragraph is mostly about. (how the Superfund bill became law) Tell students they are going to examine the use of the author's cause-and-effect text structure.
6. *What did Shadia and Kids Against Pollution do?* (Shadia sold drinks and "toxic dump" cake at a lemonade stand at the state capitol.) *Why did they do this?* (to make the lawmakers pass the Superfund bill) *What did Shadia do with the money?* (She sent the money to the governor to pay for the Superfund site.) *What happened next?* (TV and newspaper reporters noticed.) *What happened as a result?* (The Superfund bill became law.)
7. Have students compare their reconstructions to the original text. Have them check if they also use the cause-and-effect text structure.

Beginning Allow students to follow along in the **Literature Anthology** as you read the text aloud. Have them point to the words from Step 2 as they hear them.

Apply Author's Craft: Strong Conclusion

Review with students that a conclusion is the end of a piece of writing. *To make a strong conclusion, you can restate the central idea you want the reader to remember.* Read the conclusion on page 281. *How does the author retell the central idea?* (The author lists ways kids can help in government.) *What is the central idea?* (It's important for kids to be involved in politics.) Have partners rewrite the conclusion on page 281 in their own words.

Grammar in Context: Deconstruct a Sentence

Write these sentences from page 275 on the board: *Is the Constitution a perfect plan? Nope, but the people who wrote it were smart enough to know that. They improved it right away by writing the Bill of Rights.* Facilitate deconstructing these sentences for better comprehension:

- *Look at the pronouns* it, that, *and* They. *These pronouns refer to other words—their antecedents.*
- *What does the pronoun* it *refer to?* (Constitution) *What does the pronoun* that *refer to?* (the idea that the Constitution is not a perfect plan) *What does the pronoun* They *refer to?* (people)
- *The author says that the people who wrote the Constitution made it better. How did they do this?* (They added amendments, creating the Bill of Rights.)
- *If the Constitution is not perfect, why do we follow its rules? Use one or more pronouns in your answer.* Have students write their responses. Check their sentences for correct use of pronouns and pronoun-verb agreement and help them edit their sentences accordingly. (Possible answer: Although the Constitution is not perfect, it has amendments.)

For additional practice, see **Language Development Cards**, Lessons 40A and 40B, and **Language Development Practice,** pages 235–240.

Independent Time

Vocabulary Building Invite students to make flashcards of the vocabulary words and take turns testing each other on the words until they become familiar.

Beginning Allow students to define the words in their native languages before defining them in English.

Intermediate/Advanced/Advanced High Have students include some of the self-selected words and content-area words they added to their glossaries.

COLLABORATE **Asking and Answering Questions** Have partners use the sentence frames on page 1 of the online leveled **Oral Language Sentence Frames** to generate questions about the text and reread to find the answers. Have them share their questions and answers with the rest of the group.

COLLABORATE **Make Connections** Help students connect the Essential Question to their own lives. Have them discuss their prior knowledge or experiences to discuss ways that they can participate in helping their leaders make or change laws.

Beginning Students can use: We can ___ to make/change laws.

Intermediate Students can use: One way we can participate is to ___.

Advanced/Advanced High Encourage students to provide specific details in their description.

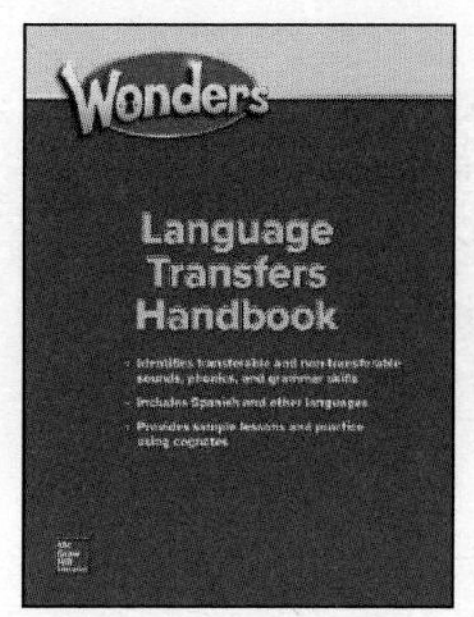

Language Transfers Handbook, Grammar Transfers, pp. 15–19

FORMATIVE ASSESSMENT

STUDENT CHECK-IN

Text Reconstruction Ask partners to share their notes. Have them reflect using the Check-In routine.

Grammar in Context Ask partners to reflect on their deconstructions using the Check-In routine.

LEARNING GOALS

We can apply strategies and skills to read narrative nonfiction.

OBJECTIVES

Describe the overall structure of events, ideas, concepts, or information in a text or part of a text.

Use common, grade-appropriate Greek and Latin affixes and roots as clues to the meaning of a word.

Engage effectively in a range of collaborative discussions with diverse partners on grade 4 topics and texts, building on others' ideas and expressing their own clearly.

LANGUAGE OBJECTIVES

Students will explain the meaning of new vocabulary using Latin roots.

ELA ACADEMIC LANGUAGE

- *cause and effect, heading*
- Cognate: *causa y efecto*

MATERIALS

Online ELL Genre Passage, "Get Involved!"

"Get Involved!"

Prepare to Read

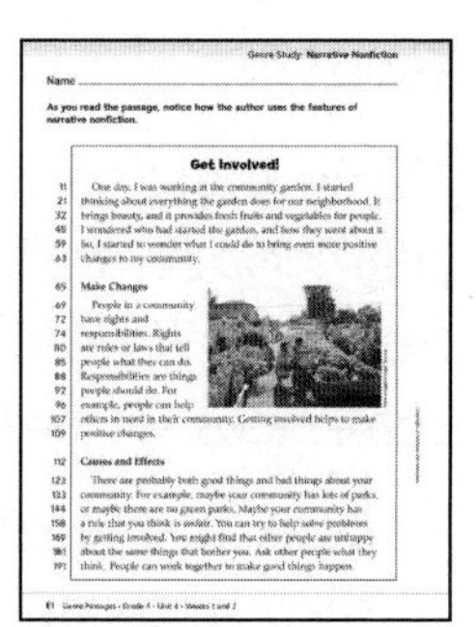

"Get Involved!"
Lexile 720L

Build Background Use the photograph on page E1 to discuss with students what people do at a community garden. Ask students to share their experiences or prior knowledge about ways people use a community garden.

Explain that working at a community garden is one way people can help their community. Then discuss with students other things they can do to help their community.

Vocabulary Use the Define/Example/Ask routine to pre-teach difficult words or unfamiliar concepts, such as *beauty, provide, responsibilities, involved, persuade, volunteer.* (Cognates: *belleza, proporcionar, responsabilidades, involucrado, persuadir, voluntario*) Invite students to add the new vocabulary to their glossaries.

Set Purpose *Today we will read "Get Involved!" As we read, think about why we need government.*

Read the Text

Page E1, Introduction and "Make Changes"

Beginning *What does a community garden have?* A community garden has fresh fruits and vegetables. *What are rights and responsibilities?* Rights are rules or laws. Responsibilities are things people should do. *Read the first two sentences. Which word has a meaning similar to* community? (*neighborhood*)

Intermediate *What does the word* wonder *mean?* (ask or think about something) *What clues help you figure out the meaning?* (*who had started, how they went*) *What are rights?* (things people can do) *What are responsibilities?* (things people should do) *Why do people have both rights and responsibilities?* (Possible answer: People can work to make positive changes.)

Advanced/Advanced High *What* **causes** *the author to wonder how to make positive changes in the community?* (enjoying the good that the garden brings)

COLLABORATE **Latin Roots** *The Latin root* communis *means "in common" or "shared by all."* Have partners explain the meanings of *community* and give examples using the Latin root *commun*: A community is a place where people have something in common. A school is a community because it is shared by all the students who go to the school.

Page E1–E2, "Causes and Effects" and "Education Is Important"

Beginning *How can people solve a problem?* People can work together to solve it. *What do you need to do before you try to solve a problem?* Make sure you understand a problem before you try to solve it.

Intermediate *Discuss with a partner what to do when you think a rule is unfair.* (Possible answer: One way is to get information about the rule.)

Advanced *Why should you study a problem before you try to solve it?* (Possible answer: You need to get as much information as you can to understand it.)

Advanced High *What does it mean to "listen to both sides of the story"?* (to get different points of view) *Why does the author tell the reader to "listen to both sides of the story" to form an opinion?* (Possible answer: It is important to learn about all the different points of view before forming an opinion.)

"Take Action!"

Remind students that asking and answering questions can help them understand a text. Model asking questions: What does "take action" mean? (do something, act) Have partners read and ask questions about word meanings and ideas in the section. Encourage students to reread to find the answers.

Beginning *Talk with a partner about ways you can take action.* We can take action in many ways. We can talk to others and write letters. We can also create a petition, and volunteer to help.

Intermediate *What is a petition?* A petition is a letter that asks for a change. *How is a petition a good way to ask for change?* (It shows that a lot of people feel the same way as you.)

Advanced/Advanced High *Why is it important to work for change?* (Possible answer: It is important to make changes to help improve the community.) *What do you think would be the* ***effect*** *if nobody worked to make their own communities better?* (Possible answer: Their communities would have lots of problems.)

Respond to Reading

Use the following instruction to help students answer the questions on page E3.

1. **Text Structure: Cause and Effect** *Read the "Make Changes" section. Why do people have responsibilities?* (Possible answer: People have responsibilities because we need to take care of our communities.)
2. **Text Features: Headings** *What do the headings tell you about the text?* (Possible answer: The headings tell what each section is mostly about.)
3. *What are the steps to making positive changes in your community?* (Possible answer: The author tells the reader to learn and get information about the problem before making decisions.)

Fluency Have partners take turns reading the passage.

Build Knowledge: Make Connections

Talk About the Text Have partners discuss why we need government.

Write About the Text Have students add their ideas to their Build Knowledge pages of their reader's notebooks.

FORMATIVE ASSESSMENT

STUDENT CHECK-IN

Have partners share their responses on page E3 and reflect using the Check-In routine.

LEVEL UP

IF students read the **ELL Level** of the **Genre Passage** fluently and answered the questions,

THEN pair them with students who have proficiently read the **On Level**. Have them

- partner read the **On Level** passage.
- identify how someone in the passage helps a community.

LEARNING GOALS

We can apply strategies and skills to read narrative nonfiction.

OBJECTIVES

Describe the overall structure of events, ideas, concepts, or information in a text or part of a text.

Use context to confirm or self-correct word recognition and understanding, rereading as necessary.

Pose and respond to specific questions to clarify or follow up on information, and make comments that contribute to the discussion and link to the remarks of others.

LANGUAGE OBJECTIVES

Students will inquire about government by asking and answering questions using key vocabulary.

ELA ACADEMIC LANGUAGE

- *phrasing, rate*
- Cognate: *fraseo*

MATERIALS

ELL Leveled Reader, *A Day in the Senate*

Online Differentiated Texts, "Protecting the Environment"

Online ELL Visual Vocabulary Cards

DIGITAL TOOLS

MULTIMODAL

Have students read along with the audio of the selections to develop comprehension and practice fluency and pronunciation.

A Day in the Senate

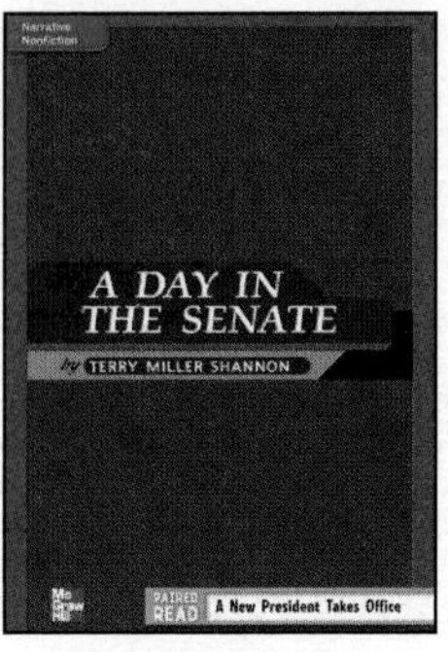

Leveled Reader
Lexile 800L

Prepare to Read

Build Background Review the Essential Question, *Why do we need government?* Have students share their ideas about why government is useful.

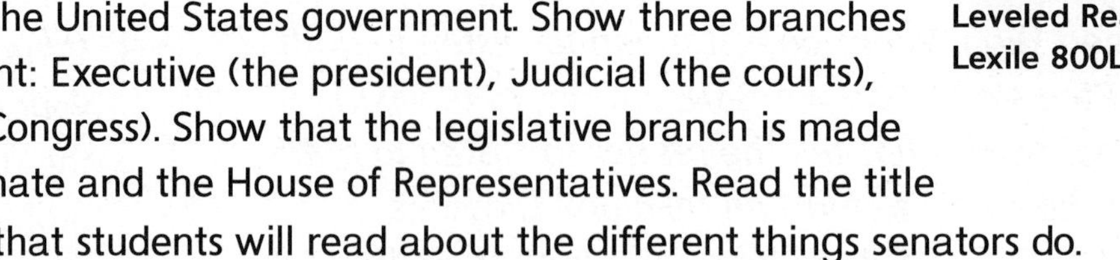

Draw a diagram on the board to help them understand the structure of the United States government. Show three branches of government: Executive (the president), Judicial (the courts), Legislative (Congress). Show that the legislative branch is made up of the Senate and the House of Representatives. Read the title and explain that students will read about the different things senators do.

Vocabulary Use the routine on the **ELL Visual Vocabulary Cards** to pre-teach ELL Vocabulary *debate* and *voters*. Discuss the appendices on page 19 of the Leveled Reader.

Set Purpose *Today we are going to read a narrative nonfiction text called "A Day in the Senate." As we read, think about why we need government.*

Read the Text

Chapter 1: "Meet a Senator"

Beginning *What do senators do?* Senators make laws for the country. *What makes up Congress?* Congress is made up of the Senate and the House of Representatives. *What is another word for* legislation? (laws) *What text clues tell you this?* (the comma and words *or laws* after the word *legislation*)

Intermediate *How does a person become a senator?* (People choose senators in an election.) *What do staffers do?* (help senators) *What do committees do?* (work on subjects like education or the budget)

COLLABORATE **Advanced/Advanced High** *Discuss with a partner the different jobs staffers do for the senators. Why do you think staffers are important to the senators?* (Possible answers: Staffers organize meetings and get information that senators need. They are important because they help plan the senator's day.)

Chapter 2: "Working Together"

COLLABORATE **Ask and Answer Questions** Encourage students to ask and answer questions as they read. Guide partners to reread to find the answers. For example: What happens at committee meetings? Senators study new bills. What is a bill? A bill is something that might become a law.

Beginning *What do senators do at a committee meeting?* The senators study new bills. *Is a bill the same as a law?* (no) *Which sentence tells you?* (fourth sentence on page 6)

Intermediate *Discuss with a partner an example of a bill. How is a bill different from a law?* (It becomes a law after Congress approves it.)

COLLABORATE **Advanced/Advanced High** *Why does the committee ask government agencies or experts for information?* (to make changes to the bill)

Chapter 3: "A Senate Vote"

COLLABORATE Have partners ask and answer questions about the Senate Chamber. For example: *What happens after the House of Representatives and the Senate approve a bill?* (After they discuss the bill, they vote on it. If approved, the bill is sent to the president.)

Intermediate *Review the meaning of* compromise. *Why do senators need to compromise? (people have different points of view)*

COLLABORATE **Respond to Reading** Have partners complete their graphic organizers and discuss the questions on page 15.

Fluency: Phrasing, Rate

Read pages 2-3 demonstrating phrasing and rate. Read the passage aloud again and have students read along. Have students record their voices while they read a few times, then choose their best recording.

Paired Read: "A New President Takes Office"

Analytical Writing — Make Connections: Write About It

Use the sentence starters and frames to discuss the questions on page 18: Senators' jobs mostly include studying issues and writing laws. The president is the leader of the United States. The president promises to preserve, protect, and defend the government and laws of the United States.

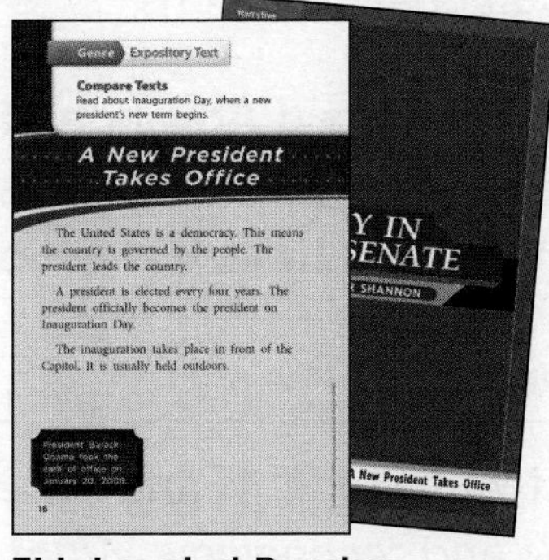

ELL Leveled Reader

Build Knowledge: Make Connections

Talk About the Text Have partners discuss why we need government.

Write About the Text Have students add their ideas to their Build Knowledge pages of their reader's notebooks.

Self-Selected Reading

Have students choose another narrative nonfiction from the online **Leveled Reader Library** or read the **Differentiated Text:** "Protecting the Environment."

FOCUS ON SOCIAL STUDIES

Have students complete the activity on page 20 to find out why people run for public office.

LITERATURE CIRCLES

Ask students to conduct a literature circle using the Thinkmark questions to guide the discussion.

FORMATIVE ASSESSMENT

STUDENT CHECK-IN

Have partners share their answers to Respond to Reading. Ask students to reflect on their learning using the Check-In routine.

LEVEL UP

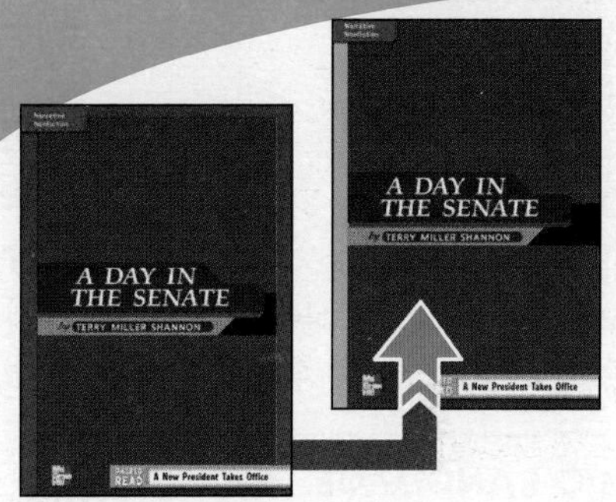

IF students read the **ELL Level** fluently and answered the questions

THEN pair them with students who have proficiently read the **On Level** and have students

- echo-read the **On Level** main selection with their partner.
- list words they find difficult.
- discuss these words with their partner.

ACT Access Complex Text

The **On Level** challenges students by including more **domain-specific words** and **complex sentence structures**.

LEARNING GOALS

We can read and understand historical fiction.

OBJECTIVES

Describe in depth a character, setting, or event in a story or drama, drawing on specific details in the text.

Compare and contrast the point of view from which different stories are narrated, including the difference between first- and third-person narrations.

Demonstrate understanding of words by relating them to their opposites and to words with similar but not identical meanings.

Engage effectively in a range of collaborative discussions with diverse partners on grade 4 topics and texts, building on others' ideas and expressing their own clearly.

LANGUAGE OBJECTIVES

Students will discuss details in a historical fiction text, using simple and complex sentences.

ELA ACADEMIC LANGUAGE

- *setting, predict, synonym, point of view, perspective*
- Cognates: *predecir, sinónimo, perspectiva*

MATERIALS

Reading/Writing Companion, pp. 152–155

Online Scaffolded Shared Read, "A Telephone Mix-Up"

Visual Vocabulary Cards

Online ELL Visual Vocabulary Cards

DIGITAL TOOLS

MULTIMODAL

Have students read along with the audio of the selection to develop comprehension and practice fluency and pronunciation.

"A Telephone Mix-Up"

Prepare to Read

Build Background Discuss background information about how telephones worked when it was a new technology. Say: *People made calls through a local telephone operator. The operator connected the callers so they could talk to each other. Callers could hear more than one person, so anyone could pick up their telephone and hear another conversation.* Discuss with students how people communicated with each other before the invention of the telephone.

Vocabulary Use the **Visual Vocabulary Cards** to preteach the vocabulary: *gleaming, scouted, decade, tinkering, squirmed, directing, engineering, technology.* Use the online **ELL Visual Vocabulary Cards** to teach additional words from the Shared Read: *gestured, installed, linked, marvel, miserable, progress.*

Set Purpose *Today we will read a historical fiction text called "A Telephone Mix-Up." As we read, think about how inventions and technology affect your life.*

Read the Text

Select the **Scaffolded Shared Read** or the Shared Read in the **Reading/Writing Companion,** based on students' language proficiency.

Beginning/Early-Intermediate Use the online **Scaffolded Shared Read** to help partners work together to read and understand historical fiction. Remind them to use the Glossary to help them read and the Word Bank to help them answer the Main and Additional Questions.

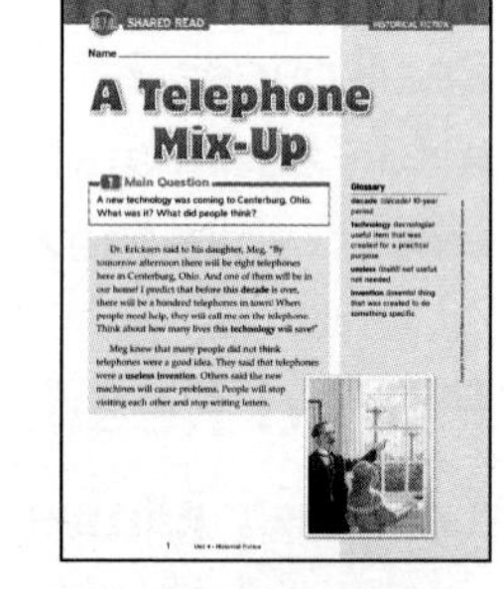

Scaffolded Shared Read, Lexile 720L

Intermediate/Advanced Advanced High Read the text with students and use the Interactive Question-Response Routine to help them understand historical fiction.

Reading/Writing Companion, Lexile 950L

Page 153, Paragraph 1

Read the text with students and review Vocabulary words *decade* and *technology. What details tell you that the **setting** is in the past?* (text: first sentence; illustration: the lamp, and clothing) Read the first sentence with students. *What does the pronoun "them" refer to when Dr. Ericksen says "one of them will be ours"?* (eight telephones) *What does the pronoun "ours" refer to?* (something that belongs to Dr. Ericksen and his family) *Why is Dr. Ericksen excited?* (telephone will arrive tomorrow) *How many years is a decade?* (10)

COLLABORATE **Intermediate** Have partners discuss what Dr. Ericksen predicted about the telephone: Dr. Ericksen predicted that Possible answer: people will call him on the telephone when they need help.

Advanced/Advanced High *Point to the word foresee in the third sentence. What is a* **synonym** *for* foresee*?* (predict) *What context clues help you find the* **synonym***?* ("I predict that before this decade is over," "That's how fast I foresee")

Page 153, Paragraphs 2–4

Read the text with students and review Vocabulary words. Point out the idiom "progress marched on." Explain that it means something continues and doesn't stop. *What does progress refer to in the story?* (the telephone's development) *Which detail tells the* **setting***?* (October 9, 1905)

COLLABORATE Explain that when the narrator is not a character in the story, the story is told from a third-person **point of view**. *Who is the main character?* (Meg) *Who is describing Meg?* (the narrator) *What pronouns does the narrator use to describe Meg?* (she, her)

Intermediate *Why did some people think the telephone would cause problems?* (Possible answer: It is easier to talk on the telephone than to visit others or write letters.)

Advanced/Advanced High *What opinions did other people have about telephones?* (they are useless, cause trouble, and cause people to stop visiting and writing letters.) *Did their opinions have an effect on Centerburg? Why?* (No, because more places in Centerburg installed the telephone.)

Advanced High *What is the main idea in paragraph 2?* (Some people are concerned about the telephone causing trouble.) *What do Meg's actions tell you about her?* (Possible answer: She is impatient and excited, and she knows the new technology will bring change.)

Page 154, Paragraphs 1–3

Read the text with students and review Vocabulary words. *What words give clues for the meaning of* scouted*?* (looking for) *What was Meg looking for?* (telephone poles) *What do the wires do?* (carry conversations from one telephone to another) *Why did Meg hurry into the house?* (to see the telephone)

COLLABORATE Remind students that **perspective** is an attitude, or how someone feels about something. Have partners discuss which characters in the story liked or disliked the telephone. (Possible answer: Dr. Ericksen and Meg thought the telephone would be good for the town. Other people did not like it because they thought it would change the way people communicated.)

Intermediate *What words tell you how Dr. Ericksen feels about the new telephone?* Dr. Ericksen uses the words <u>beauty *and* magnificence</u>.

COLLABORATE **Advanced/Advanced High** Have partners discuss context clues that tell what Meg thinks about the telephone. (Possible answer: She is excited because she imagines the wires carrying words and conversations of friends and neighbors.)

Page 154, Paragraphs 4–8

Who called the Ericksens? (Mrs. Kane) *Why did she call?* (to tell Dr. Ericksen to go to Turner farm)

COLLABORATE Read the dialogue between Dr. Ericksen and Mrs. Kane with students. Have partners discuss what Mrs. Kane probably told Dr. Ericksen. (Possible answer: someone at the Turner farm is sick.)

Page 155, Paragraphs 1–7

Read the dialogue with students and review Vocabulary word *miserable*. *What happened at the farm?* (Mr. Turner's goat needs a veterinarian.) *Look back on page 154. How did the telephone mix-up happen?* (The phone static made it hard to hear Mrs. Kane.) *Who is Dr. Kerrigan?* (the veterinarian)

COLLABORATE Have partners discuss why people in town called a missed communication "another sick goat." (Possible Answer: People remembered the mix-up of the telephone call at the Turner farm.)

FORMATIVE ASSESSMENT

STUDENT CHECK-IN

Have partners retell the important ideas in the text. Ask them to reflect using the Check-In routine.

LEARNING GOALS

- **We can read and understand a historical fiction text by identifying the character's perspective.**
- **We can identify and write pronoun-verb agreement.**

OBJECTIVES

Paraphrase portions of a text read aloud or information presented in diverse media and formats, including visually, quantitatively, and orally.

Demonstrate command of the conventions of standard English grammar and usage when writing or speaking.

LANGUAGE OBJECTIVES

Students will discuss the character's perspective using key vocabulary.

ELA ACADEMIC LANGUAGE

- *narrator, pronoun, noun, subject, verb*
- Cognates: *narrador, pronombre, verbo*

MATERIALS

Reading/Writing Companion, pp. 152-155, 156-157

Online Scaffolded Shared Read, "A Telephone Mix-Up"

Online Shared Read Writing Frames, p. 11

Online Language Development Cards, 41A-41B

Online Language Development Practice, pp. 241-246

Online Language Transfers Handbook, pp. 15-19

"A Telephone Mix-Up"

Text Reconstruction

Focus on a single chunk of text to support comprehension and language development across the four domains.

1. Read aloud the first paragraph on page 154 in "A Telephone Mix-Up" in the **Reading/Writing Companion** while students listen.
2. Write the following on the board, providing definitions as needed: *scouted, wooden poles, wire, linked, neighbors, zipping.* Instruct students to listen for them as you read a second time.
3. Read the paragraph again. Have students listen for details and take notes.
4.  COLLABORATE Have students work with a partner to reconstruct the text from their notes. Help them write complete sentences as needed.
5. Have partners look at the original text. *What is the paragraph mostly about?* (Meg is imagining how people will use the telephone.) Tell students they will examine the character's perspective.
6. *What did Meg see while walking home?* (tall wooden poles and thick wires that linked the poles together) *What did Meg imagine about the wires?* (that they would carry people's conversations) *What is Meg's perspective about the telephone?* (Possible: Meg is excited about it.)
7. Have partners compare their text reconstructions to the original text. Have them check whether they show the narrator's point of view and the character's perspective.
8. Beginning Have students follow along in the **Reading/Writing Companion** as you read the text aloud. Have them circle the words from Step 2 as they hear them.

Grammar in Context: Pronoun-Verb Agreement

Notice the Form Display these two sentences and underline the verbs as shown.

> "Jake, I got here as quick as I could," Dr. Ericksen said. "Is it Mrs. Turner? Little Emma?"

What part of speech are the underlined words? (verbs) *What is the pronoun in the first sentence?* (I) *What is the pronoun in the second sentence?* (it) *What do the pronouns have in common?* (The pronouns are subjects of the sentences.) Explain that when a pronoun is a subject of the sentence, the verbs follow the same rules for when nouns are subjects of a sentence. Write simple examples on the board: *Sue reads a book./She reads a book.* Elicit that the verbs in both sentences have the same form. Repeat for the sentences *Sam and Tali read books./They read books.* Review the rules for pronoun-verb agreement.

Apply and Extend Have partners write sentences about the text using subject pronouns and nouns. Then have pairs check for pronoun-verb agreements.

For additional practice, see **Language Development Cards**, Lessons 41A and 41B, and **Language Development Practice**, pages 241–246.

Independent Time

Vocabulary Building Have students build their glossaries.

Beginning/Early Intermediate Have students complete the Glossary Activities in the **Scaffolded Shared Read**.

Intermediate/Advanced/Advanced High Have students add the vocabulary from **Reading/Writing Companion** pages 156–157 and self-selected words or phrases they would like to learn to the chart.

Mixed Levels Beginning and Early-Intermediate students can work together to teach each other vocabulary from their **Scaffolded Shared Read** glossaries. Intermediate and Advanced/Advanced High students can teach each other their self-selected words.

WORD/PHRASE	DEFINE	EXAMPLE	ASK
switchboard	a system that connects telephone calls	The switchboard operator connected the caller to the doctor.	Are switchboards still used today?

Shared Read Writing Frames Use the online leveled **Shared Read Writing Frames** for "A Telephone Mix-Up" to provide students with additional oral and written practice. Differentiated frames are available to provide support for all levels.

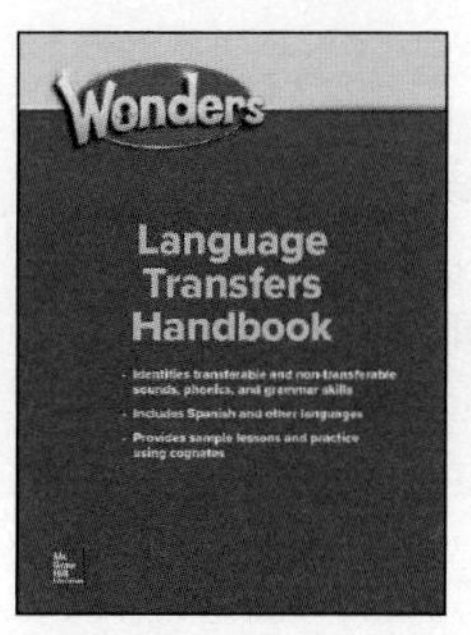

Language Transfers Handbook, Grammar Transfers, pp. 15–19

DIGITAL TOOLS

For additional support, use the online activities.

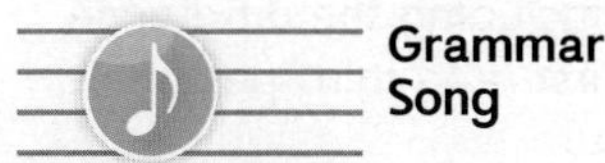

Grammar Song

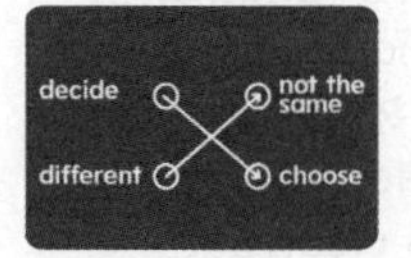

Vocabulary Activity

FORMATIVE ASSESSMENT

STUDENT CHECK-IN

Text Reconstruction Have partners share their notes. Have students reflect on their work using the Check-In routine.

Grammar in Context Have partners share their sentences. Have students reflect on their work using the Check-In routine.

LEARNING GOALS

- **Read** We can read and understand a historical fiction story.
- **Reread** We can reread to analyze text, craft, and structure.

OBJECTIVES

Describe in depth a character, setting, or event in a story or drama, drawing on specific details in the text.

Compare and contrast the point of view from which different stories are narrated, including the difference between first- and third-person narrations.

Engage effectively in a range of collaborative discussions with diverse partners on grade 4 topics and texts, building on others' ideas and expressing their own clearly.

LANGUAGE OBJECTIVES

Students will inquire by answering questions about the story using key vocabulary.

Students will explain the author's craft and use of figurative language using academic vocabulary.

ELA ACADEMIC LANGUAGE

- *figurative language*
- Cognate: *lenguaje figurado*

MATERIALS

Literature Anthology, pp. 288–303

Reading/Writing Companion, pp. 164–167

Visual Vocabulary Cards

Online ELL Anchor Text Support BLMs, pp. 27–29

DIGITAL TOOLS

MULTIMODAL

Have students read along with the audio of the selection to develop comprehension and practice fluency and pronunciation.

The Moon Over Star

Prepare to Read

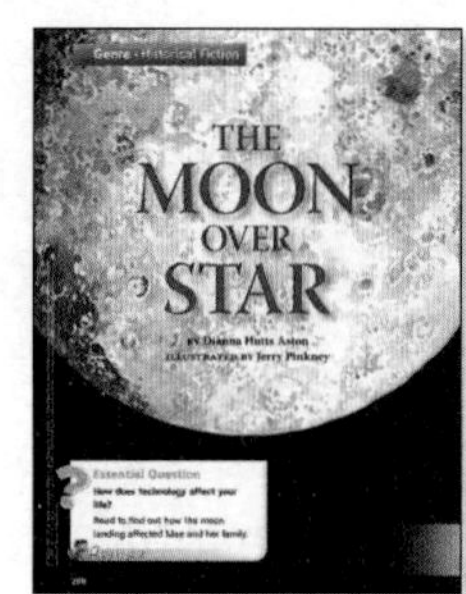

Literature Anthology, Lexile 860L

Build Background Explain that historical fiction is set in the past and is based on real events. *In this story, the real event takes place in 1969 when three U.S. astronauts land on the moon.* Invite students to share what they know about the first moon landing or astronauts.

Vocabulary Use the **Visual Vocabulary Cards** to review the vocabulary: *gleaming, scouted, decade, tinkering, squirmed, directing, engineering, technology.*

Set Purpose *Today we will read about how the moon landing affected a girl named Mae and her family. As we read, think about how technology affects your life.*

Play the audio summary of the text, available in multiple languages.

Read

Literature Anthology, pp. 288–303

Use the Interactive Question Response Routine on page R3 to help students read and discuss *The Moon Over Star.*

Beginning Help students discuss in complete sentences. Provide sentence frames: Mae and the people at her church pray for the astronauts. Mae dreams of going to the moon one day.

Intermediate Ask students to respond in complete sentences and add details. Provide sentence starters as needed: Mae and the people at her church pray for the astronauts. Mae dreams that one day she can go to the moon.

Advanced/Advanced High Have students respond in complete sentences and add details.

COLLABORATE **Independent Reading Practice** Have mixed level pairs work together to complete **ELL Anchor Text Support BLMs** pages 27–29. Then have them share their responses with the rest of the group.

Reread

Use the following prompts when working on **Reading/Writing Companion,** pages 164–167.

Literature Anthology, pp. 294–295

COLLABORATE **Author's Craft: Character** Review that Mae and her cousins were helping Gramps with his tractor when Gran yelled that the rocket was about to land on the moon. Then read paragraph 2, instructing students to focus on what Gramps does and what this tells about him. Have students ask questions about any words or phrases they don't understand.

Beginning Read paragraph 2 with students. Restate any sentences they don't understand to clarify meaning. *What does Gramps do when he hears the rocket is landing?* He continues to tinker with the engine. *What do the children do?* They run into the house. *What does this tell you about Gramps?* That he is not very excited about the rocket landing.

Intermediate Have partners discuss how the family feels about the moon landing and whether Gramps is excited about it. The family is excited because they ran to the front of the television. Gramps is not excited because he is busy working on the engine.

Advanced/Advanced High *How does the author show you that Gramps is not excited about the moon landing?* (The sentence "Gramps kept right on tinkering with the engine" tells me that he is not interested in the moon landing.)

Literature Anthology, pp. 298–299

COLLABORATE **Author's Craft: Figurative Language** Read the paragraph with students, stopping after the second sentence. Define unfamiliar or difficult words. Ask if the cornstalks are really whispering. (no) *What does it mean that cornstalks "whisper"?* (They rub together in the breeze and make a soft, whispering sound.) Note the use of figurative language. Review that with figurative language, words are used in ways that are different from their usual meanings. Authors use figurative language to create interesting images in the reader's mind.

Beginning Reread the second sentence. Restate the descriptions of the night sky. Then ask, *How do these images help you visualize, or see, the sky?* The images help me see the what the stars and moon look like.

Intermediate *What words does the author use to describe the night sky?* ("pearly slice of moon","stars gleaming like spilled sugar") *What does a pearly slice of moon look like?* (Possible answer: The moon is glowing.)

Advanced/Advanced High *What does the author compare the moon and the stars to?* (The author compares the moon to pearls and the stars to sugar that sparkles.) *How do you think Mae and her family are feeling, based on the description of the night?* (Possible answer: They are feeling relaxed and happy.)

COLLABORATE **Author's Craft: Character** Read page 300 with students. Discuss with students that the moon landing was the first time a man walked on the moon. *What is the date of the event?* (July 20, 1969) *Who is Commander Armstrong?* (the astronaut on the moon) *How did Gramps react to watching the astronaut walk on the moon?* (He says it's an event he'll remember.)

Beginning Reread the second sentence. Who is Mr. Cronkite talking about? (Neil Armstrong) Where is Neil Amstrong standing? (on the surface of the Moon) When does this happen? (July 20, 1969)

Intermediate *Why does Mae mention places around the world?* She mentions them because 600 million people around the world watched the event.

Advanced/Advanced High Have partners discuss how the author shows that Gramps changed his mind about the moon landing. (Gramps puts his hand on Mae's shoulder; he says, "I reckon that's something to remember.")

COLLABORATE Have partners describe how Gramps's attitude about the moon landing changed. Have them use evidence from the text to support their response. (Possible answer: Gramps was not interested before, but he realized that it was an important event.)

FORMATIVE ASSESSMENT

STUDENT CHECK-IN

Read Have partners share their responses to the Anchor Text questions. Then have them reflect using the Check-In routine.

Reread Ask partners to share their responses on **Reading/Writing Companion** pages 164–167. Have students reflect using the Check-In routine.

LEARNING GOALS

- **We can read and understand a historical fiction text by identifying a character's perspective.**
- **We can identify and use possessive pronouns.**

OBJECTIVES

Paraphrase portions of a text read aloud or information presented in diverse media and formats, including visually, quantitatively, and orally.

Demonstrate command of the conventions of standard English grammar and usage when writing or speaking.

LANGUAGE OBJECTIVES

Students will discuss the character's perspective using key vocabulary.

ELA ACADEMIC LANGUAGE

- *perspective, possessive pronoun*
- Cognate: *perspectiva*

MATERIALS

Literature Anthology, pp. 288–303

Online Language Development Card, 39B

Online Language Development Practice, pp. 232–234

Online Language Transfers Handbook, pp. 15–19

The Moon Over Star

Text Reconstruction

Focus on a single chunk of text to support comprehension and language development across the four domains.

1. Read aloud paragraphs 3–6 on page 294 and page 296 in *The Moon Over Star* in the **Literature Anthology** while students listen.
2. Write the following on the board, providing definitions as needed: *commander, forward, newsman, split, Eagle.* Instruct students to listen for these words as you read the paragraphs a second time.
3. Read the paragraphs a third time while students listen and take notes.
4. COLLABORATE Have students work with a partner to reconstruct the text from their notes. Help them write complete sentences as needed.
5. Have students look at the original text. Ask them to tell what the paragraphs are mostly about. (the time astronauts first landed on the moon) Tell students they are going to examine the character's perspective.
6. *What happened after the newsman announced that the spaceship landed?* (Possible: Everyone was silent.) *Why were they silent?* (They wanted to hear the astronauts speak.) *How did they feel about the moon landing?* (They were excited.) *Everyone was excited about the mission to the moon. Who had a different perspective?* (Gramps) *How did Gramps feel about the mission?* (He thought people should solve problems on Earth instead of going to the moon.)
7. Have students compare their text reconstructions to the original text. Have them check whether they also included words that describe character's perspective.

Beginning Allow students to follow along in the **Literature Anthology** as you read the text aloud. Have them circle the words from Step 2 as they hear them.

Apply Author's Craft: Figurative Language

Review with students that authors use figurative language to help readers visualize details and to create a feeling or mood. *On page 298, what word does the author use to describe the cornstalks?* (whispered) *How does a whisper feel and sound?* (soft) *What simile does the author use to describe the stars?* ("gleaming like spilled sugar") *What feeling do these images create?* (it is magical; better than any picture show) Help students rewrite sentences in their own words, using figurative language.

Grammar in Context: Deconstruct a Sentence

Write these sentences from page 302 on the board: *A sigh in Gramps's voice made my heart squeeze. "Keep on dreaming, Mae," he said. "Just remember, we're here now together on the prettiest star in the heavens."* Facilitate deconstructing this sentence for better comprehension:

- *What tells you someone is speaking?* (the quotation marks and he said)
- *What are the three pronouns in these sentences?* (*my, he, we're*) *Which are singular?* (*my, he*) *plural?* (*we*) *What does each refer to?* (*my:* Mae, *he:* Gramps, *we:* all people) *Write the verb for each.* (*he said, we are*) Explain that *my* is a possessive pronoun that tells whose heart.
- Point to the first sentence. *What is the simple subject?* (sigh) *What does Mae say about the sigh?* (The sigh squeezed my heart)
- Circle *prettiest star* and remind students that authors often use synonyms or rephrase something to keep from repeating the same words or to describe it visually. *What is the author talking about?* (Earth)
- Circle the phrase "we're here now together" and ask how it gives Gramps's point of view. *What is the simple subject and verb?* (We are) *What advice is he giving Mae?* (Be grateful for this moment together.)

For additional practice, see **Language Development Cards**, Lesson 39B, and **Language Development Practice**, pages 232–234.

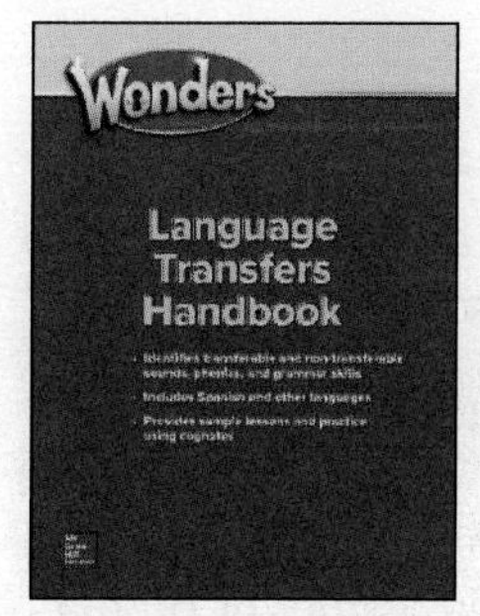

Language Transfers Handbook, Grammar Transfers, pp. 15-19

Independent Time

Vocabulary Building Invite students to create an interactive word wall with vocabulary from the selection. First, have students copy the words onto index cards. On the back of each card they should write a clue to elicit the word. Students should tape the index cards to the wall with the clue-side facing out. Other students then look at the card, guess the word, and turn the card over to confirm their answer.

Beginning Allow students to draw or write clues in words and phrases.

Intermediate/Advanced/Advanced High Have students include some of their self-selected words and content-area words they added to their glossaries.

COLLABORATE **Possessive Pronouns** Have partners practice using possessive pronouns. Have them use a 2-column chart to list possessive pronouns—*my, your, his, her, its, our,* and *their*—in one column and corresponding nouns that show possession in the other column. Have partners write sentences using both. Provide examples: Juan rides his bike every day. Juan's bike has red lights. Check their work and provide feedback as needed.

POSSESSIVE PRONOUNS	NOUNS
his	Juan's bike

FORMATIVE ASSESSMENT

STUDENT CHECK-IN

Text Reconstruction Ask partners to share their notes. Have them reflect using the Check-In routine.

Grammar in Context Have students reflect on their deconstructions using the Check-In routine.

LEARNING GOALS

We can apply strategies and skills to read historical fiction.

OBJECTIVES

Describe in depth a character, setting, or event in a story or drama, drawing on specific details in the text.

Compare and contrast the point of view from which different stories are narrated, including the difference between first- and third-person narrations.

Demonstrate understanding of words by relating them to their opposites and to words with similar but not identical meanings.

Engage effectively in a range of collaborative discussions with diverse partners on grade 4 topics and texts, building on others' ideas and expressing their own clearly.

LANGUAGE OBJECTIVES

Students will discuss the narrator's point of view, using simple and complex sentences.

ELA ACADEMIC LANGUAGE

- *character, narrator, point of view, perspective, synonym*
- Cognates: *narrador, perspectiva, sinónimo*

MATERIALS

Online ELL Genre Passage, "Leonardo's Mechanical Knight"

"Leonardo's Mechanical Knight"

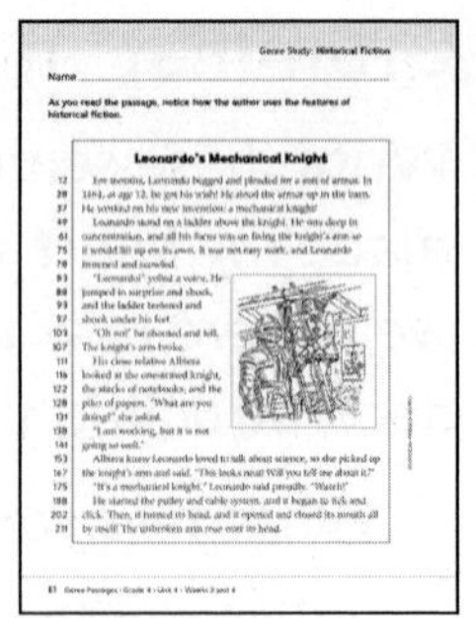

"Leonardo's Mechanical Knight"
Lexile 610L

Prepare to Read

Build Background Discuss with students what life might have been like during the fifteenth century. Have students think about whether people had machines or technology to use in their daily lives and the different ways of doing things, such as traveling, communicating, cooking, reading, or getting information.

Explain that they will read about a boy who lived in the fifteenth century and that the boy want to invent a mechanical knight. Ask students to share what they know about knights. Then have students share prior experience about inventing something new.

Vocabulary Use the Define/Example/Ask routine to pre-teach difficult words or unfamiliar concepts, such as *suit* of *armor, mechanical, concentration, pulley,* and *modest.* (Cognates: *mecánico, concentrar, modesto*) Invite students to add new vocabulary to their glossaries.

Set Purpose *Today we will read "Leonardo's Mechanical Knight." As we read, think about how inventions and technology affect your life.*

Read the Text

Page E1, Paragraphs 1–2

Point of View and Perspective *Who is the passage about?* (Leonardo) Discuss *narrator* and *character* with students: A narrator tells a story. A character is a person in a story. *In sentence 2, what detail shows Leonardo's perspective, or feelings?* ("he got his wish!") *How do we know Leonardo is not the narrator?* (the pronoun *he*) Help students identify the narrator's point of view: I know the passage has a third-person point of view because the narrator is not a character.

Beginning Read the first paragraph. Help students restate sentences they have difficulty understanding to clarify the meaning. *What did Leonardo do?* He used a suit of armor to make a mechanical knight.

COLLABORATE **Intermediate** Have partners identify **synonyms** in sentence 1 that mean "asked for." (*begged, pleaded*) *How does the narrator show Leonardo's perspective?* The narrator explains that Leonardo wanted the suit of armor for a long time. The exclamation points show that Leonardo feels excited.

COLLABORATE **Advanced/Advanced High** Have partners identify context clues that help explain *concentration.* (focus) Have them discuss whether concentration and focus are **synonyms**. *What do readers know about Leonardo's perspective?* (He likes working on inventions. He doesn't mind hard work.)

Page E1, Paragraphs 3-9

Beginning Read paragraphs 3, 4, and 5 with students. *Who surprised Leonardo?* (Albiera) *What did Leonardo do?* (*He jumped.*) Point out that Leonardo jumped in surprise *and* shock. *What is a* ***synonym*** *of surprise?* (*shock*)

Intermediate *What causes Leonardo to fall?* (Albiera yells and surprises him.) *What happened to the mechanical arm?* (It is broken.)

Advanced/Advanced High *Discuss with a partner what Leonardo is referring to when he says "it is not going so well."* (Possible answer: Leonardo is not happy because he can't get the mechanical arm to work.)

Page E2, Paragraphs 1–12

COLLABORATE **Beginning** Read Paragraph 4. Point to the pronoun *it* and discuss what *it* refers to. Elicit that the pronoun *it* refers to the mechanical knight. *Discuss with a partner what the mechanical knight will do when it is finished:* The mechanical knight will sit up and walk.

Intermediate *Why did Albiera ask Leonardo to tell her about the mechanical knight?* (Albiera knows that Leonardo is happy when he talks about his inventions.)

Advanced/Advanced High *What does Leonardo use to get the mechanical knight to move?* (He uses the pulley and cable system.)

Advanced High *Why does Albiera say that Leonardo is modest? Contrast Leonardo and Albiera's perspective on the invention.* (Possible answer: Leonardo says the invention is simple, but Albiera thinks the invention is incredible. Leonardo knows more about science and machines.)

Respond to Reading

Use the following instruction to help students answer the questions on page E3.

1. **Character Perspective** *Read the first paragraph on page E2. What words does Albiera use to describe the mechanical knight?* (*bravo, great*) *Read paragraph 3. What does Albiera tell Leonardo?* (She's never seen anything like the mechanical knight.)
2. **Plot: Setting** *Read the first paragraph on page E1. What information do you look for to figure out the setting?* (place and time the story takes place) *What information tells you about the setting?* (the year 1464)
3. *Read the second paragraph on page E2. Does Leonardo like to brag?* (no) *What word does the author use to describe how Leonardo talks?* (humble) *What does humble mean?* (not bragging)

Fluency Have partners take turns reading the passage.

Build Knowledge: Make Connections

Talk About the Text Have partners discuss how inventions and technology affect their lives.

Write About the Text Have students add their ideas to their Build Knowledge pages of their reader's notebooks.

FORMATIVE ASSESSMENT

STUDENT CHECK-IN

Have partners share their responses on page E3 and reflect using the Check-In routine.

LEVEL UP

IF students read the **ELL Level** of the **Genre Passage** fluently and answered the questions,

THEN pair them with students who have proficiently read the **On Level**. Have them

- partner read the **On Level** passage.
- describe the narrative point of view.

LEARNING GOALS

We can apply strategies and skills to read historical fiction.

OBJECTIVES

Describe in depth a character, setting, or event in a story or drama, drawing on specific details in the text.

Read grade-level prose and poetry orally with accuracy, appropriate rate, and expression on successive readings.

Engage effectively in a range of collaborative discussions with diverse partners on grade 4 topics and texts, building on others' ideas and expressing their own clearly.

LANGUAGE OBJECTIVES

Students will inquire about their predictions about the story in complete sentences.

ELA ACADEMIC LANGUAGE

- *predict*
- Cognate: *predecir*

MATERIALS

ELL Leveled Reader, *The Freedom Machine*

Online Differentiated Texts, "A Great Adventure"

Online ELL Visual Vocabulary Cards

DIGITAL TOOLS

MULTIMODAL

Have students read along with the audio of the selections to develop comprehension and practice fluency and pronunciation.

The Freedom Machine

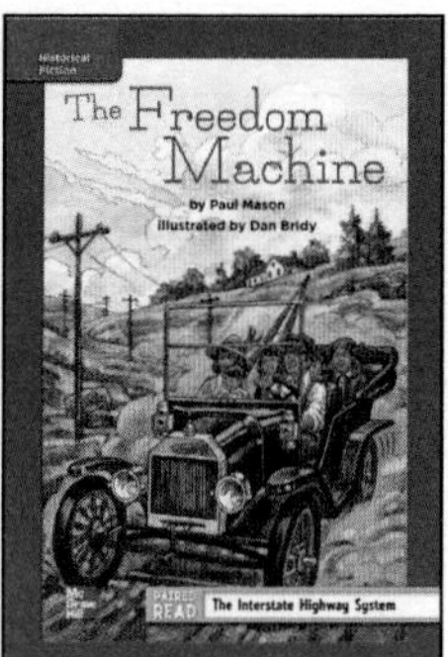

Leveled Reader
Lexile 540L

Build Background

Build Background With students, choral read the title. Elicit the meaning of the word *freedom*. Ask: *What kind of machines have given you freedom?* Point out that in *The Freedom Machine,* the main characters have different points of view about cars.

Vocabulary Use the routine on the **ELL Visual Vocabulary Cards** to pre-teach ELL Vocabulary *afford* and *bothered*. Discuss the appendices on page 19 of the Leveled Reader.

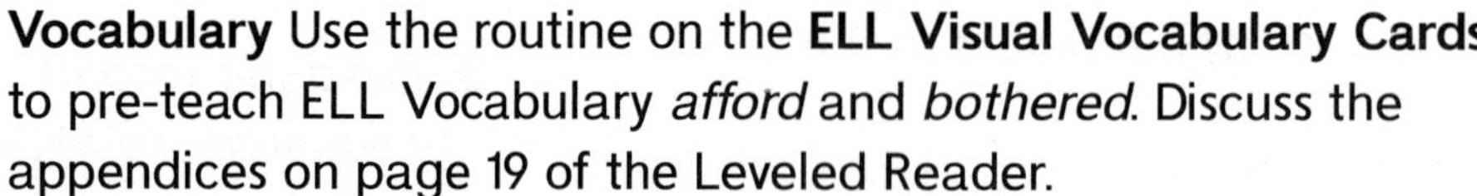

Set Purpose *Today we are going to read a historical fiction text called* The Freedom Machine. *As we read, think about how inventions and technology affect your life.*

Read the Text

Chapter 1

Beginning Read the first paragraph. *Who is Mrs. Williams?* (Dad works for her.) *What words tell you about her?* ("Dad works for," "her large house and garden," "generous") *What are Dad and the narrator doing?* (walking home with bags of apples) Ask questions to help student comprehension. Provide examples: *Is a sack similar to a bag? Can I say "take care of" to mean "help with"?*

Make Predictions Have pairs use clues from the story to make predictions about what will happen next: On page 2, I noticed that Alice smiles at the car. This makes me think Alice likes the car. I predict that Alice will go for a car ride. Guide students to continue reading and find other clues that can help them confirm or revise the predictions.

Chapter 2

Intermediate *Why does Alice's dad learn how to drive?* (Mrs. Williams buys a car.) *How does Alice's dad feel about driving?* (He is worried.)

Advanced/Advanced High *With a partner, discuss why Mr. Dawson says the car is not a toy.* (He thinks cars are wasteful and a lot of work.)

Chapter 3

COLLABORATE **Intermediate** *Talk with a partner about Mr. Dawson's problem:* The problem was that the engine overheated and needed water.

Advanced/Advanced High *What do Mr. Dawson's actions tell you about him?* (Mr. Dawson knew how to fix the car because he read the instructions. This tells me that he is responsible.)

Chapter 4

Beginning Read page 14 with students. *What did Mom and Baby John do?* They played in the water. *What did Alice find on the beach?* She found seaweed, shells, starfish, and tiny fish.

Intermediate *What did Alice and her family do at the beach?* They played in the water and explored the beach.

Advanced/Advanced High *Did Mr. Dawson's perspective change? Explain.* (Before Mr. Dawson had a negative perspective toward cars. Now he agrees with Alice that cars can be a good thing.)

Respond to Reading Have partners complete their graphic organizers and discuss the questions on page 16.

Fluency: Expression, Accuracy

Read page 10 with accuracy and appropriate expression. Then read the passage again and have students read along with you. For more practice, have students record their voices while they read.

Paired Read: "The Interstate Highway System"

Make Connections: Write About It

Before students write, use the following sentence frames to discuss the questions on page 19. Interstate highways made it easier to travel and move goods. It became easier for people to get from one place to another.

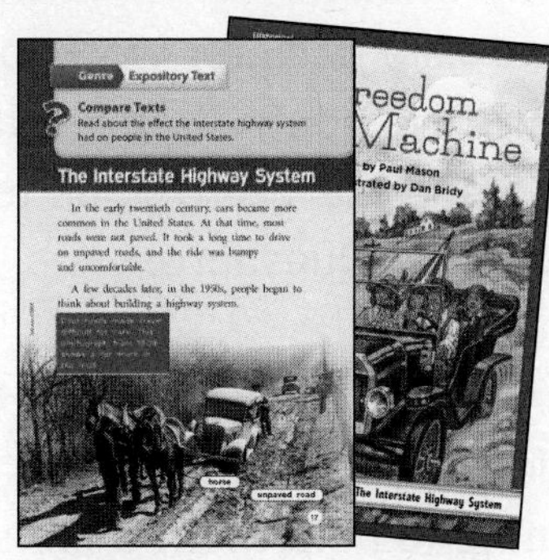

ELL Leveled Reader

Build Knowledge: Make Connections

Talk About the Text Have partners discuss how inventions and technology affect their lives.

Write About the Text Have students add their ideas to their Build Knowledge pages of their reader's notebooks.

Self-Selected Reading

Have students choose another historical fiction text from the online **Leveled Reader Library** or read the **Differentiated Text:** "A Great Adventure."

FOCUS ON GENRE

Have students complete the activity on page 20 to practice writing vivid details describing life in the past.

LITERATURE CIRCLES

Ask students to conduct a literature circle using the Thinkmark questions to guide the discussion.

FORMATIVE ASSESSMENT

STUDENT CHECK-IN

Have partners share their answers to Respond to Reading. Ask students to reflect on their learning using the Check-In routine.

LEVEL UP

IF students read the **ELL Level** fluently and answered the questions,

THEN pair them with students who have proficiently read the **On Level** and have students

- echo-read the **On Level** main selection with their partner.
- list words they find difficult.
- discuss these words with their partners.

ACT Access Complex Text

The **On Level** challenges students by including more **dialogue** and **complex sentence structures.**

LEARNING GOALS

We can read and understand narrative poetry.

OBJECTIVES

Determine a theme of a story, drama, or poem from details in the text; summarize the text.

Explain major differences between poems, drama, and prose, and refer to the structural elements of poems when writing or speaking about a text.

Engage effectively in a range of collaborative discussions with diverse partners on grade 4 topics and texts, building on others' ideas and expressing their own clearly.

LANGUAGE OBJECTIVES

Students will discuss the theme of the poem using key vocabulary.

ELA ACADEMIC LANGUAGE

- *narrative poetry, character, stanza, figurative language, theme*
- Cognates: *poesía narrativa, lenguaje figurado, tema*

MATERIALS

Reading/Writing Companion, pp. 178–181

Online Scaffolded Shared Read, "Sing to Me" and "The Climb"

Visual Vocabulary Cards

Online ELL Visual Vocabulary Cards

DIGITAL TOOLS

MULTIMODAL

Have students read along with the audio of the selection to develop comprehension and practice fluency and pronunciation.

"Sing to Me" and "The Climb"

Prepare to Read

Build Background Share information about narrative poetry and its characteristics. Explain to students that a narrative poem has characters and a plot and reads like a story. Have students discuss poems that they know with characters and a plot and talk about the story in the poem.

Vocabulary Use the **ELL Visual Vocabulary Cards** to review the vocabulary: *dangling, hovering, attain,* and *triumph.* Use the online **ELL Visual Vocabulary Cards** to teach additional vocabulary from the Shared Read: *awkward, fading, repetitive,* and *slippery.* (Cognates: *triunfo, repetitivo*)

Set Purpose *Today we will read two narrative poems called "Sing to Me" and "The Climb". As we read, think about how writers look at success in different ways.*

Read the Text

Select the **Scaffolded Shared Read** or the Shared Read in the **Reading/Writing Companion,** based on students' language proficiency.

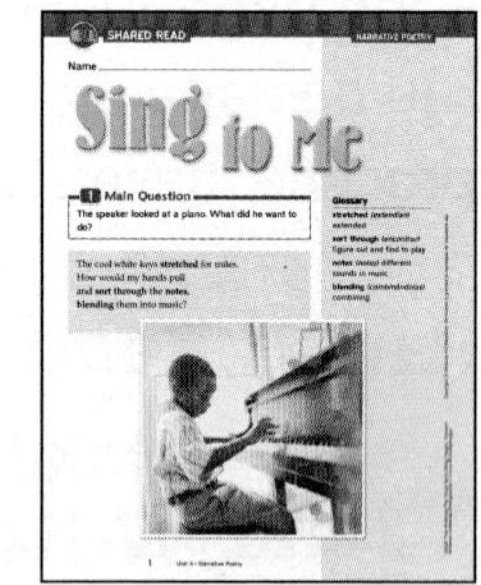

Scaffolded Shared Read, Lexile NP

Beginning/Early-Intermediate Use the online **Scaffolded Shared Read** to help partners work together to read and understand narrative poetry. Remind them to use the Glossary to help them read and the Word Bank to help them answer the Main and Additional Questions.

Intermediate/Advanced Advanced High Read the text with students and use the Interactive Question-Response Routine to help them understand narrative poetry.

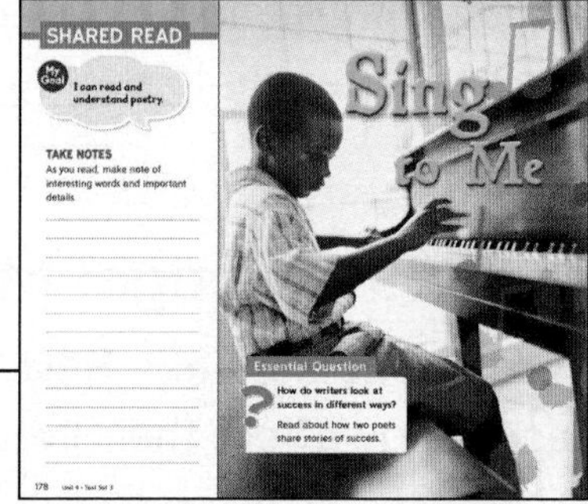

Reading/Writing Companion, Lexile NP

Page 179, "Sing to Me"

Stanzas 1–3 Read the stanzas. Review the Vocabulary word *dangling.* Have students ask about words or phrases they don't know and find their meanings. Have them restate the words and phrases for clarification. *Who is the speaker?* (a child who wants to learn to play the piano) Point out examples of repetition. *What do the repeated lines do?* (tell the speaker's emotions) Have students identify stanzas. *What does each stanza tell?* (tells about an idea)

Intermediate Read the first stanza. *What does "stretched for miles" mean?* There are many keys on the piano. *What does the speaker wonder?* The speaker wonders if he can learn to play the piano. *What does "out of reach" mean?* (not able to grab, do, or finish)

COLLABORATE Review similes and metaphors with students. Have partners identify the simile in Stanza 2 that tells what the melody does. (compares the melody to an apple dangling out of reach) *Restate the simile using your own words.* (Possible answer: The speaker can almost play the melody, but it does not quite sound right.)

COLLABORATE **Stanzas 4–7** Read the stanzas with students. Review the Vocabulary and ELL Vocabulary words *hovering, awkward,* and *fading.* Remind students that the theme of a poem is the overall idea or message that the speaker wants to communicate. Review the repeated word *practiced* in Stanza 2. Then have partners find the repeated sentence in Stanza 6. *How does repetition help you learn the* message? (Possible answer: The poet repeats the word *practice* to show how hard he works. Later he repeats "I can do it" to show that he can play the piano.) *What is the* ***theme*** *of the poem?* (Practice leads to success.)

Intermediate *Who helps the speaker?* The speaker's mother helps the speaker practice. *What does the speaker do to learn to play?* (The speaker practices.) *What lines are repeated at the end?* ("I can do this.") *What lesson does the speaker learn?* The speaker learns that he needs to practice to learn.

COLLABORATE **Advanced/Advanced High** Have partners reread Stanza 4. *What words describe the notes?* (leaping, hovering briefly, crash, awkward jangle, a tangle of noise, fading away) Have partners discuss and retell what Stanza 4 tells about the notes. (Possible answer: The notes turn into noise because the speaker cannot play the piano.)

Page 180 "The Climb"

COLLABORATE **Stanzas 1–5** Read the stanzas with students. Review the ELL Vocabulary words *repetitive* and *slippery. Is the speaker describing something that is happening now or in the past?* (now) *How can you tell?* (present tense verbs *are waiting, reach*) *What is the speaker's problem?* (can't climb a tree) Have partners discuss how they think the speaker feels. *What clues tell how the speaker feels?* I think the speaker feels ___. The clues in ___ tell me that ___. *What is important about the word* Again? (It shows the speaker tried to climb a tree before and failed.)

Intermediate *What length of time is the setting?* (one day) *What is special about this day?* (It is the speaker's birthday.) *What kind of day does the speaker have at school?* (a bad day)

Advanced/Advanced High *What does* mocking *mean?* ("making fun of") *What is the brother's voice compared to?* (a jaybird's screech) Is the **connotation** of *screeching* positive or negative? (negative) *Why does the poet say the tree wasn't "any smaller or bigger"?* (This shows that the tree hasn't changed, but the speaker has changed.)

Page 181

Stanzas 6–7 Read the stanzas with students. Point out that the exclamation marks express strong feeling.

COLLABORATE **Intermediate** Have students demonstrate *push and pull* as it relates to climbing. Have partners summarize the stanzas: The speaker lost a dare and had a bad day at school. Then the speaker succeeds at climbing the tree after school.

Advanced/Advanced High *What does the phrase "rooted on the ground" tell about the brother?* (The brother is on the ground like a tree, far below the speaker.) *How does the brother react to the speaker climbing the tree?* (Possible answer: He is probably surprised because he stares and doesn't move.)

Advanced High *What figurative language does the speaker use to describe what would happen if the speaker continued to climb?* (The speaker uses a metaphor about becoming a cloud to describe that the speaker is as high as it is possible to go.)

FORMATIVE ASSESSMENT

STUDENT CHECK-IN

Have partners retell the important ideas in the text. Ask them to reflect using the Check-In routine.

LEARNING GOALS

- **We can read and understand narrative poetry by identifying the theme.**
- **We can identify and write homophones including pronouns.**

OBJECTIVES

Paraphrase portions of a text read aloud or information presented in diverse media and formats, including visually, quantitatively, and orally.

Correctly use frequently confused words.

LANGUAGE OBJECTIVES

Students will discuss the theme of a poem using key vocabulary.

ELA ACADEMIC LANGUAGE

- *theme, stanza, homophone*
- Cognates: *tema, homófono*

MATERIALS

Reading/Writing Companion, pp. 178–181, 182

Online Scaffolded Shared Read, "Sing to Me" and "The Climb"

Online Shared Read Writing Frames, p. 12

Online Language Development Cards, 42B

Online Language Development Practice, pp. 250–252

Online Language Transfers Handbook, pp. 15–19

Oral Language Sentence Frames, p. 6

"Sing to Me" and "The Climb"

Text Reconstruction

Focus on a single chunk of text to support comprehension and language development across the four domains.

1. Read aloud Stanzas 4–7 of "Sing to Me" on page 179 in the **Reading/Writing Companion** as students listen.
2. Write the following on the board, providing definitions as needed: *crash, awkward, jangle, tangle, forehead, slender, plucking.* Instruct students to listen for them as you read the stanzas a second time.
3. Read the stanzas a third time. Tell students to listen and take notes of how the speaker solves a problem.
4.  COLLABORATE Have students work with a partner to reconstruct the text from their notes.
5. Have students look at the original text. Ask them to tell what these stanzas are mostly about. (The speaker struggles playing piano and his mother helps.) Tell students they are going to examine the theme in the poem.
6. *What instrument did the speaker learn to play?* (the piano) *How did the speaker feel about playing the piano?* (He felt like quitting.) *What did the speaker's mother do?* (She helped the speaker learn to play the piano.) *How does the speaker feel when he gets help?* (He says he can do this.) *What is the theme of the poem?* (Possible answer: Keep trying and never give up.)
7. Have students compare their text reconstructions to the original text. Have them check whether they also included words that describe the theme.

Beginning Have students follow along in the **Reading/Writing Companion** as you read the text aloud. Have them circle the words from Step 2 as they hear them.

Grammar in Context: Homophones

Notice the Form Display these sentences. Circle the homophones. *What do the circled words have in common?* (They sound the same.)

> *The girl looks up at the top of the tree. She sees the oak tree's branches and their outstretched leaves hanging up there.*

Point to the words *their* and *there*. *How are the words different?* (*Their* means "belonging to them"; *there* means "in that place." The words are spelled differently.) *Words that sound the same but have different spellings and meanings are homophones.* Provide other examples, such as *ate/eight* and *hear/here*. Have students copy and label the homophones in their notebooks.

Apply and Extend Retell with students what the girl is doing and what she sees. Then have partners rewrite their own sentences about the poem using *there* and *their*. Check their work and offer corrective feedback.

For additional practice, see **Language Development Cards**, Lesson 42B, and **Language Development Practice,** pp. 250–252.

Independent Time

Vocabulary Building Have students build their glossaries.

Beginning/Early Intermediate Have students complete the Glossary Activities in the **Scaffolded Shared Read**.

Intermediate/Advanced/Advanced High Have students add the vocabulary from **Reading/Writing Companion** page 182 and self-selected words or phrases they would like to learn to the chart.

Mixed Levels Pair students together. Beginning and Early-Intermediate students can teach vocabulary from their **Scaffolded Shared Read** glossaries. Intermediate and Advanced/Advanced High students can teach their self-selected words.

WORD/PHRASE	DEFINE	EXAMPLE	ASK
immense	extremely large	An immense portrait of her dog covered the wall.	What are some antonyms and synonyms of *immense*?

COLLABORATE **Evaluating Language Choices** Have partners use the sentence frames on page 6 of the online **Oral Language Sentence Frames** to discuss the use of description in "Sing to Me."

Shared Read Writing Frames Use the online leveled **Shared Read Writing Frames** for "Sing to Me" to provide students with additional oral and written practice. Differentiated frames are available to provide support for all levels.

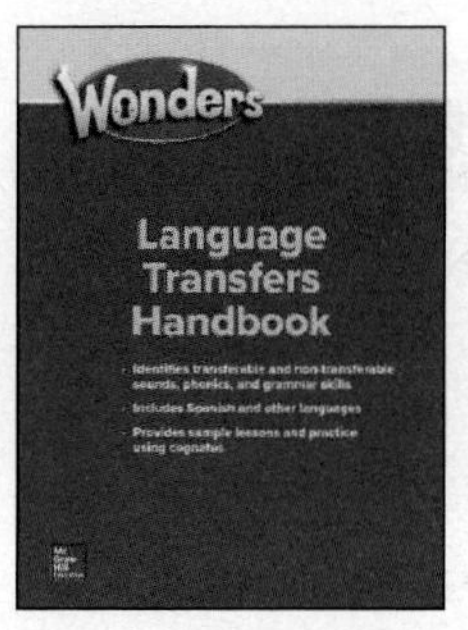

Language Transfers Handbook, Grammar Transfers, pp. 15–19

DIGITAL TOOLS

For additional support, use the online activities.

Grammar Video

Grammar Song

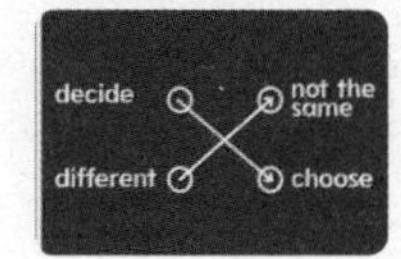

Vocabulary Activity

STUDENT CHECK-IN

Text Reconstruction Have partners share their notes. Have students reflect on their work using the Check-In routine.

Grammar in Context Have partners share their sentences. Have students reflect on their work using the Check-In routine.

LEARNING GOALS

- **Read** We can read and understand poetry.
- **Reread** We can reread to analyze text, craft, and structure.

OBJECTIVES

Determine a theme of a story, drama, or poem from details in the text; summarize the text.

Explain major differences between poems, drama, and prose, and refer to the structural elements of poems when writing or speaking about a text.

Engage effectively in a range of collaborative discussions with diverse partners on grade 4 topics and texts, building on others' ideas and expressing their own clearly.

LANGUAGE OBJECTIVES

Students will inquire by answering questions about poems using key vocabulary.

Students will explain author's use of sensory language using academic vocabulary.

ELA ACADEMIC LANGUAGE

- *mood, sensory language, feeling*
- Cognate: *lenguaje sensorial*

MATERIALS

Literature Anthology, pp. 310-312

Reading/Writing Companion, pp. 190-191

Visual Vocabulary Cards

Online ELL Anchor Text Support BLMs, p. 30

DIGITAL TOOLS

MULTIMODAL

Have students read along with the audio of the selection to develop comprehension and practice fluency and pronunciation.

"Swimming to the Rock" and "The Moondust Footprint"

Prepare to Read

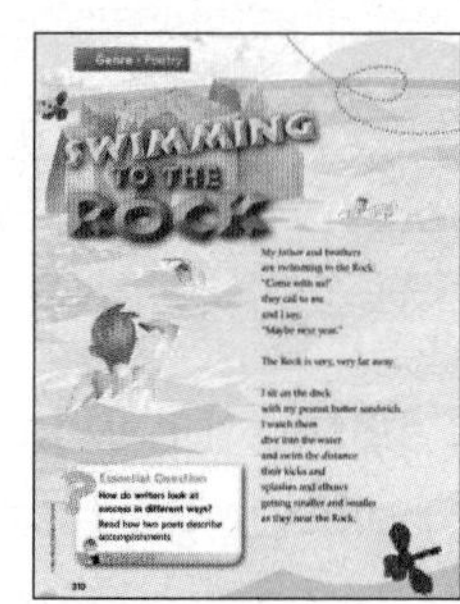

Literature Anthology
Lexile NP

Build Background Explain that a narrative poem tells a story and has characters. *Today we will read about how two poets describe accomplishments.* Invite students to talk about an accomplishment.

Vocabulary Use the **Visual Vocabulary Cards** to review the vocabulary: *dangling, hovering, attain,* and *triumph.*

Set Purpose *As we read, think about how writers look at success in different ways.*

Play the audio summary of the text, available in multiple languages.

Read

Literature Anthology, pp. 310–312

Use the **Interactive Question-Response Routine** to help students read and discuss "Swimming to the Rock" and "The Moondust Footprint."

Beginning Help students discuss in complete sentences. Provide sentence frames: In the poem, the family is swimming.

Intermediate Ask students to respond in complete sentences and add details. Provide sentence starters as needed: The poem tells about astronauts landing on the moon.

Advanced/Advanced High Have students respond in complete sentences and add details.

Independent Reading Practice Have mixed level pairs work together to complete **ELL Anchor Text Support BLMs** page 30. Then have them share their responses with the rest of the group.

Reread

Use with **Reading/Writing Companion,** pages 190-191.
Literature Anthology, Pages 310–311

COLLABORATE **Author's Craft: Sensory Language** Review that sensory language helps readers see, hear, feel, smell, or taste what is being described. *Who is the speaker?* (the girl sitting on the dock) *What is she doing?* (watching her brother and father swimming) Stop after each stanza to check for comprehension.

Beginning Help partners retell what the swimmers do after getting to the Rock in Stanza 5 using: The swimmers wave their arms. They make fists and cheer. Use miming to demonstrate. *Why do they do this?* (to celebrate)

Intermediate *What does she think her family is doing at the rock?* She thinks they are cheering. *What does she say the loons are doing?* (celebrating their arrival) *What words are used to describe what the speaker sees when her family swims back?* She sees their faces with wild, wet smiles. *What effect does this have on the speaker?* She thinks she will swim this year.

Advanced/Advanced High *How does the speaker describe her family at the rock?* (fists in the air, cheering) *How does she describe them swimming back?* (wild, wet smiles) *How does this help you understand why the speaker says "next year"?* (She sees her family having fun. She wants to join in.)

Literature Anthology, Page 312

COLLABORATE **Author's Craft: Sensory Language** Read page 312 with students. Clarify any unfamiliar words or phrases. *Why do you think the poet repeats the word "watching"?* (To show how long the speaker was waiting to see the astronauts land and how excited he or she was.) *What words or phrases create a mood of excitement?* ("I was holding my breath") *How does the poet express the mood and feeling of the speaker?* (By repeating words and telling what she sees and feels)

Beginning Read the stanzas. Have students ask about words or phrases they do not know or understand and define and restate them for clarification. Choral read the first line in the poem. *What word does the poet repeat?* (watching) *What do you think the poet wants to show with that word?* (how long the speaker was waiting to see the astronauts land; how excited he or she was)

Intermediate *What event does the speaker refer to by "A new chapter of history"?* (the moon landing) *How does the poet help you visualize what the speaker is seeing?* The speaker describes how Apollo approaches, or gets closer to, the moon. *In stanza 3, how does the poet show how excited the speaker is?* The poet uses the phrase "I was holding my breath" to show excitement.

Advanced/Advanced High Have partners discuss what the last two lines of the first stanza tell about the speaker's mood. (Possible answer: The speaker is excited and paying close attention to what is happening.) *How does the poet help you visualize the speaker's feelings?* (Possible answer: The poet describes Aunt Mary and the speaker both holding their breath. An exclamation point shows the speaker's emotion.)

FORMATIVE ASSESSMENT

STUDENT CHECK-IN

Read Have partners share their responses to the Anchor Text questions. Then have them reflect using the Check-In routine.

Reread Ask partners to share their responses on **Reading/Writing Companion** pages 190–191. Have students reflect using the Check-In routine.

LEARNING GOALS

- **We can read and understand narrative poetry by identifying the theme.**
- **We can identify and write homophones including pronouns.**

OBJECTIVES

Paraphrase portions of a text read aloud or information presented in diverse media and formats, including visually, quantitatively, and orally.

Correctly use frequently confused words.

LANGUAGE OBJECTIVES

Students will discuss the theme of a poem using key vocabulary.

ELA ACADEMIC LANGUAGE

- *theme, stanza, homophones, pronouns*
- Cognates: *tema, homófono*

MATERIALS

Literature Anthology, pp. 310-312

Online Language Development Card, 42B

Online Language Development Practice, pp. 250-252

Online Language Transfers Handbook, pp. 15-19

"Swimming to the Rock" and "The Moondust Footprint"

Text Reconstruction

Focus on a single chunk of text to support comprehension and language development across the four domains.

1. Read aloud Stanzas 3-5 in "The Moondust Footprint" on page 312 of the Literature Anthology while students listen.
2. Write the following on the board, providing definitions as needed: *ribbed, awesome.* Instruct students to listen for them as you read the stanzas a second time.
3. Read the stanzas a third time while students listen and take notes.
4. COLLABORATE Have students work with a partner to reconstruct the text from their notes. Help them write complete sentences as needed.
5. Have students look at the original text. Ask them to tell what the stanzas are mostly about. (the first landing on the moon) Tell students they are going to examine the theme of the poem.
6. *What did Aunt Mary and the speaker do after the others went to bed?* (watched the Apollo mission on TV) *What words describe what they saw on TV?* (slow stage, hovering, moving oh so carefully) *What words tell you how Aunt Mary and the speaker felt while they watched TV?* (repetition of *watching, holding my breath;* anticipation) *What is the theme of the poem?* (it is an important experience from the speaker's childhood.)
7. Have students compare their text reconstructions to the original text. Have them check whether they also included words that describe the theme.

Beginning Allow students to follow along in the **Literature Anthology** as you read the text aloud. Have them point to the words from Step 2 as they hear them.

Apply Author's Craft: Sensory Language

Review that authors use sensory language to express the mood and feeling of the narrator. *On page 312, the poet repeats the word* watching *and uses the phrase "I was holding my breath." What does this show about how the narrator feels?* (anticipation) *What mood do the words "The Apollo slowed . . . then quickened" express?* (excitement, amazement) Have partners rewrite sentences in their own words using sensory language.

Grammar in Context: Deconstruct a Sentence

Write these lines from page 311 on the board: *My father and brothers come closer and from the water lift their faces with wild wet smiles.* Facilitate deconstructing these lines for better comprehension:

- *The pronouns in these lines are* my, their, *and* I. *Which are singular?* (*my, I*) *plural?* (*their*) *possessive?* (*my, their*) *Which pronoun is a homophone?* (*their*)
- *Which nouns are the subject of the first sentence?* (father and brothers)
- Point to *their. Who does this pronoun refer to?* (the father and brothers) *What is a homophone of* their*?* (there)
- Circle *lift their faces* and *wild wet smiles* and discuss with students. *What is another way to say this?* (They came out of the water grinning.)
- Circle *wild. What two meanings does "wild" have?* (plants or animals growing naturally; excited) Ask students which meaning is used here. (excited)

For additional practice, see **Language Development Cards,** Lesson 42B, and **Language Development Practice**, pages 250–252.

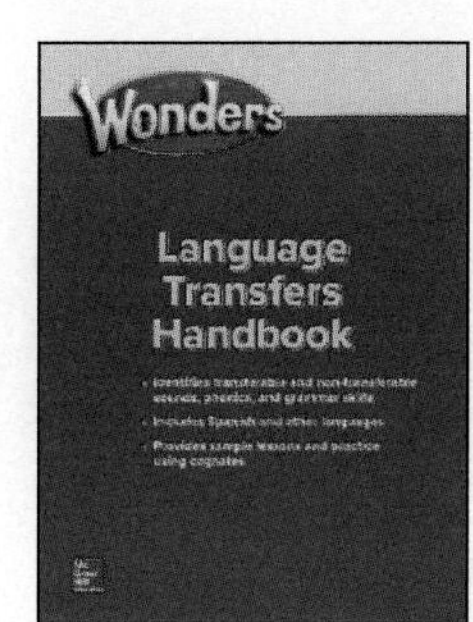

Language Transfers Handbook, Grammar Transfers, pp. 15-19

Independent Time

Vocabulary Building Have students create a word game with vocabulary from the selection. Help students identify words with multiple meanings in the poems. (*call, dock, watch, stand, wave, wild, stage,* etc.) Then, on each index card, have partners copy a sentence with one of the words and label the word's part of speech. Next, have them find another meaning and write a sample sentence onto the back of the index card and label the word's part of speech. Then have partners read aloud their sentences and have the rest of the group identify the part of speech.

Beginning/Intermediate Allow students to draw clues or describe with words.

Advanced/Advanced High Have students include some of the self-selected words and content-area words they added to their glossaries.

COLLABORATE **Express Opinion** Help students connect the Essential Question to express their opinions. Have partners choose a character from one of the poems and describe their opinion on whether or not the character was successful. Then, have them take turns agreeing and disagreeing about the opinion. Provide sentence frames:

Beginning The character learns to ____. I think he/she was successful. I disagree. The character did not learn to____. I think he/she was not successful.

Intermediate/Advanced/Advanced High The character was successful by ____. In my opinion, he/she succeeded, because ____. I disagree. I think the character was not successful, because ____. I think success happens when ____.

FORMATIVE ASSESSMENT

STUDENT CHECK-IN

Text Reconstruction Ask partners to share their notes. Have them reflect on their work using the Check-In routine.

Grammar in Context Have partners reflect on their deconstructions using the Check-In routine.

LEARNING GOALS

We can apply strategies and skills to read poetry.

OBJECTIVES

Determine a theme of a story, drama, or poem from details in the text; summarize the text.

Explain major differences between poems, drama, and prose, and refer to the structural elements of poems when writing or speaking about a text.

Use context as a clue to the meaning of a word or phrase.

Engage effectively in a range of collaborative discussions with diverse partners on grade 4 topics and texts, building on others' ideas and expressing their own clearly.

LANGUAGE OBJECTIVES

Students will discuss the themes of poems in simple and complex sentences.

ELA ACADEMIC LANGUAGE

- *stanza, speaker, theme, denotation, connotation*
- Cognates: *tema, denotación, connotación*

MATERIALS

Online ELL Genre Passage, "Spelling Bee" and "The Principal's Office"

"Spelling Bee" and "The Principal's Office"

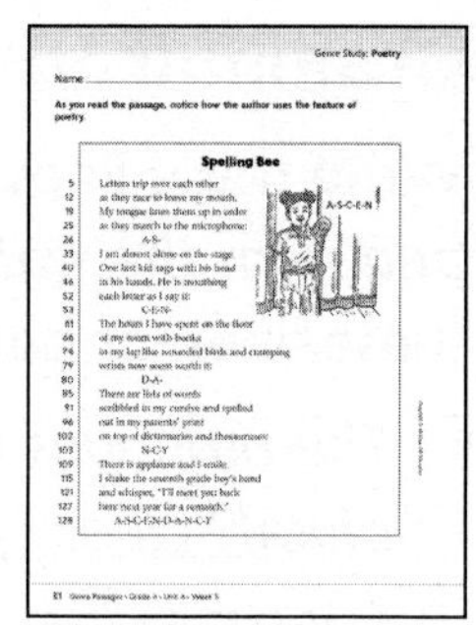

"Spelling Bee" and "The Principal's Office"
Lexile NP

Prepare to Read

Build Background Remind students that narrative poetry is sometimes told from a first-person point of view. This means that the speaker is telling his or her own story.

Tell students they will read two poems with themes about success. Remind them to listen for rhyme, rhythm, and rising action.

Vocabulary Use the Define/Example/Ask routine to pre-teach difficult words or unfamiliar concepts, such as *sags, wounded, cramping, scribbled, cursive,* and *rematch.* Invite students to add new vocabulary to their glossaries.

Set Purpose *Today we will read "Spelling Bee" and "The Principal's Office." As we read, think about how writers look at success in different ways.*

Read the Text

Page E1, "Spelling Bee," Stanzas 1–2

Beginning Read the title and explain that the word *bee* in the title refers to a competition. Point out the picture and describe it with students. *What does the "bee" in the title mean?* (competition) Read Stanza 1 with students. *What is the speaker doing?* The speaker is spelling a word.

Intermediate Have partners describe what the speaker in the poem is doing: The speaker is spelling a word at a spelling bee. The speaker spells one letter at a time.

Advanced *What do the letters tell you about what the speaker is doing?* (The girl is spelling only a few letters at a time.)

Advanced High Have students read lines 1–2. *In real life, do letters trip or race?* (no) *What can trip or race?* (people, animals) *Why is the poet using this image?* (Possible answer: to show that the girl is nervous)

Page, E1, "Spelling Bee," Stanzas 3–5

Display examples of cursive and print writing. *Who wrote words in cursive?* (the speaker of the poem) *Where do the words come from?* (dictionaries, thesauruses)

Beginning *What word tells you that people are proud of the girl?* (*applause*) *What words tell you that the girl is happy at the end?* (*I smile*)

Intermediate *What does the girl do to prepare for the spelling bee?* She studies books and makes lists of words. *What does she mean that it was "worth it"?* She means that studying helped her do her best.

COLLABORATE **Advanced/Advanced High** *What is the setting for stanzas 3 and 4?* (in the past, in the narrator's room) *In stanza 5?* (the present) Have partners discuss why birds are being compared to the room with books. (Possible answer: They are compared to wounded birds because pages look like bird wings.)

Respond to Reading

Use the following instruction to help students answer the questions on page E2.

1. **Theme** Have students read Stanza 3. *What word shows she worked for a long time?* (*hours*)
2. Have students read the last stanza. *Which words have a long* a *sound?* (*shake, grade*)
3. *Is this a feeling of being in control or out of control?* (out of control)

Page E3, "The Principal's Office"

Denotation and Connotation Read the title with students and discuss the denotation and connotation of going to the principal's office with them. Read the dialogue, noting the punctuation. Discuss the meaning of the words *district* and *robotics*. *What is the speaker's name*? (Daniel Birnbaum) *What is the speaker interested in*? (robotics) *How do you know*? (He made the district youth robotics team.)

COLLABORATE **Beginning** *Who is Ms. Lee?* She is the principal. *What is the setting?* The setting is the principal's office. Point to the phrase "my heart was pounding in my chest" and demonstrate the meaning. *How do you feel when your heart is pounding?* I feel nervous.

COLLABORATE **Intermediate** Have partners discuss: *What does the speaker mean by "I've really done it" in line 2?* I'm in trouble. *What does this expression mean at the end?* I've done something good.

Advanced/Advanced High *Was the speaker surprised? How do you know?* (Possible answer: The speaker thought he was in trouble. Instead, he was awarded by being picked for a district team.)

COLLABORATE **Theme** Have partners discuss the theme, or the message of the poem. (When we expect bad things to happen, we might get upset for no reason. Wait to find out the truth.)

Respond to Reading

Use the following instruction to help students answer the questions on page E3.

1. **Narrative Poetry** *Read the dialogue and look for text that tells the speaker's name.* (Ms. Lee says "Daniel Birnbaum.")
2. *Where is the sentence that repeats?* (at the beginning and end of the poem)
3. *How would you feel if you were called to the principal's office?* (nervous)

Fluency Have partners take turns reading the passages.

Build Knowledge: Make Connections

Talk About the Text Have partners discuss how writers look at success in different ways.

Write About the Text Have students add their ideas to their Build Knowledge pages of their reader's notebooks.

FORMATIVE ASSESSMENT

STUDENT CHECK-IN

Have partners share their responses on page E3 and reflect using the Check-In routine.

IF students read the **ELL Level** of the **Genre Passage** fluently and answered the questions,

THEN pair them with students who have proficiently read the **On Level**. Have them

- partner read the **On Level** passage.
- identify figurative language and theme(s).

LEARNING GOALS

We can apply strategies and skills to read realistic fiction.

OBJECTIVES

Determine a theme of a story, drama, or poem from details in the text; summarize the text.

Describe in depth a character, setting, or event in a story or drama, drawing on specific details in the text.

Read grade-level prose and poetry orally with accuracy, appropriate rate, and expression on successive readings.

Engage effectively in a range of collaborative discussions with diverse partners on grade 4 topics and texts, building on others' ideas and expressing their own clearly.

LANGUAGE OBJECTIVES

Students will discuss the theme of a realistic fiction text in simple and complex sentences.

ELA ACADEMIC LANGUAGE

- *theme, connotation*
- Cognates: *tema, connotación*

MATERIALS

ELL Leveled Reader, *The Math-lete*

Online Differentiated Texts, "A Personal Triumph"

Online ELL Visual Vocabulary Cards

DIGITAL TOOLS

Have students read along with the audio of the selections to develop comprehension and practice fluency and pronunciation.

The Math-lete

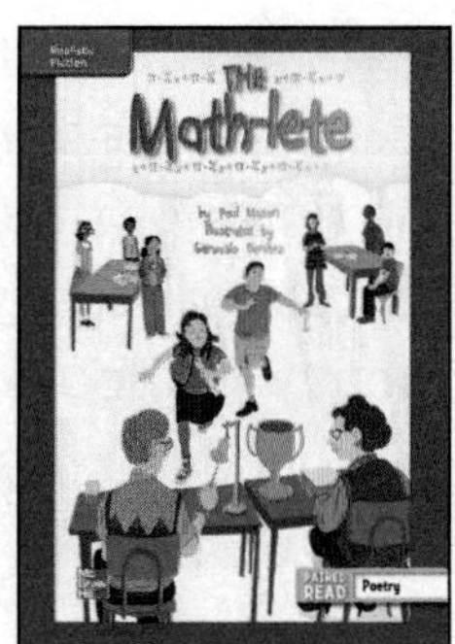

Leveled Reader
Lexile 510L

Prepare to Read

Build Background Have students share their experiences with achieving success. Write the title on the board. Point out that the title combines two words. *What two words are joined in the title?* (math and athlete) Display the word *athlete. Athletes train and practice. What do you think this story will be about?*

Preview *The Math-lete* and "Running the Race." Read aloud the title of each chapter. *Let's read about a student who gets over her fear of math. She practices and becomes a math-lete.*

Vocabulary Use the routine on the **ELL Visual Vocabulary Cards** to pre-teach ELL Vocabulary *district* and *struggling.* Have students add the words to their glossaries.

Set Purpose *Today we are going to read a realistic fiction text called* The Math-lete. *As we read, think about how writers look at success in different ways.*

Read the Text

Pages 2–5, Chapter 1

Beginning *What doesn't Abby want to do anymore?* Abby doesn't want to be on the math team. *Why?* She says math is difficult for her.

Intermediate *Why does Keisha think Abby is good at math?* Abby got an A on an assignment. *How did Abby get that grade?* Abby worked every night for a week.

COLLABORATE **Theme** Clarify the meaning of *give up* on page 4. *What does Mr. Nelson think Abby should do?* (stay on the math team; get help) Help partners discuss the theme of Mr. Nelson's story: Mr. Nelson describes a time he gave up on a math test because he thought a math problem was too difficult. *What phrase does he repeat?* (give/gave up) *What lesson did he learn?* (He just needed to look at the problem differently. He gave up too easily.)

Pages 6–12, Chapters 2–3

Beginning *What happens during practice?* The team did well. Abby did not do well. *What does Keisha do to help?* Keisha helps Abby work on math problems.

COLLABORATE **Intermediate** Have partners discuss what happens after practice: Abby knows she needs more practice, so she asks Keisha to help her practice. This makes me think Abby doesn't want to give up.

Advanced/Advanced High *What do you feel when your head spins?* (dizzy) *What is the **connotation**? Explain.* (negative; it describes confusion)

Have students describe how Abby changed after Keisha helped her. (Possible answer: Abby did not want to be on the math team. Then she became excited to be in the competition.)

Chapter 4, Pages 13–15

Beginning Read page 13 with students. *What did Abby remember?* Abby remembered the problem she worked on with Keisha.

Intermediate Have partners discuss how Abby solved the final problem: Abby remembered that she worked on a similar problem and knew what to do.

Advanced/Advanced High Have partners discuss why Mr. Nelson says "I told you so." (Possible answer: Mr. Nelson knew that Abby would figure out a way to solve her problem.)

Respond to Reading Have partners complete their graphic organizers and answer the questions on page 16.

Fluency: Expression, Rate

Read pages 4–5 with appropriate expression and rate. Then reread the passage aloud and have students read along. Have students record their voices while they read and choose their best recording.

Paired Read: "Running the Race"

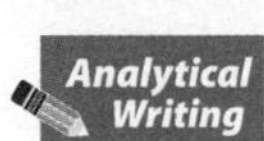

Make Connections: Write About It

Discuss the questions on page 19. Have students find lines that repeat and describe how the words change. Have students tell why Ben repeats the lines, and what that tells them about him. Then have students describe how Abby improves in math.

ELL Leveled Reader

Build Knowledge: Make Connections

Talk About the Text Have partners discuss how writers look at success in different ways.

Write About the Text Have students add their ideas to their Build Knowledge pages of their reader's notebooks.

Self-Selected Reading

Have students choose another realistic fiction text from the online **Leveled Reader Library** or read the **Differentiated Text**: "A Personal Triumph."

FOCUS ON LITERARY ELEMENTS

Have students complete the activity on page 20 to identify repetition and rhythm.

LITERATURE CIRCLES

Ask students to conduct a literature circle using the Thinkmark questions to guide the discussion.

FORMATIVE ASSESSMENT

STUDENT CHECK-IN

Have partners share their answers to Respond to Reading. Ask students to reflect on their learning using the Check-In routine.

LEVEL UP

IF students read the **ELL Level** fluently and answered the questions,

THEN pair them with students who have proficiently read the On Level and have students

- echo-read the On Level main selection with their partner.
- list words they find difficult.
- discuss these words with their partner.

Access Complex Text

The On Level challenges students by including more **figurative language** and **complex sentence structures**.

LEARNING GOALS

- **We can identify a logical text structure in an expository essay.**
- **We can analyze a student model and student model sources.**

OBJECTIVES

Describe the overall structure of events, ideas, concepts, or information in a text or part of a text.

Explain how an author uses reasons and evidence to support particular points in a text.

Draw evidence from literary or informational texts to support analysis, reflection, and research.

LANGUAGE OBJECTIVES

Students will discuss features and organization of an expository essay using academic language.

ELA ACADEMIC LANGUAGE

- *evidence, logical, analyze,*
- Cognates: *evidencia, lógico, analizar*

MATERIALS

Online ELL Extended Writing Resources BLMs:

- Mia's Model, pp. 56–58
- Analyze Mia's Model, pp. 59–60

Online Student Model Sources

Reading/Writing Companion, pp. 200–203

Literature Anthology, p. 194

DIGITAL TOOLS

Have students read along with Mia's Model to develop comprehension and build fluency.

Expository Writing

Logical Text Structure

Reread the paragraph on page 201 of **Reading/Writing Companion** with students. Review that logical progression means an essay goes in order from beginning to end. The compare-and-contrast text structure is one way to organize ideas. Help students identify the central idea: *Cats and dogs make good pets*. The following sentences explain ways that cats and dogs are similar and different.

Compare-and-Contrast Text Structure Write on the board: **Strong:** *Both cats and dogs make good pets.* **Weak:** *Cats are good pets. Dogs are good pets.* Discuss the examples and show that the weak model does not use the compare-and-contrast text structure.

Organize Information Read page 194 in the **Literature Anthology** with students. Discuss how the writer uses the compare-and-contrast text structure to create a logical progression of ideas. Ask: *What is the author comparing on this page?* (the volunteer projects of Alex Lin and Erica Fernandez) *How does the compare-and-contrast text structure help you understand the text?* (Comparing the two projects helps organize the ideas.) Point out that the signal word *also* in paragraph 5 helps show the logical progression of ideas.

Have partners describe the text structure in the paragraph.

Beginning Help partners describe using: The author compares the volunteer projects of two students. The signal word *also* helps me know the author is using the compare-and-contrast text structure.

Intermediate Have partners describe using: The author compares the volunteer projects of Alex Lin and Erica Fernandez. The signal word *also* helps me identify that the author uses the compare-and-contrast text structure.

Advanced/Advanced High Have partners describe the compare-and-contrast text structure and the logical progression of ideas.

Analyze the Student Model and Sources

Analyze the Prompt Read the prompt on **Mia's Model** with students. Explain that *to vote* means to choose between two or more candidates in an election. An *election* is when people vote for someone to hold a public position.

Discuss the Student Model

COLLABORATE **Mixed Levels** Use **Mia's Model** to read the model with students. Discuss the meaning of the word *elections* using the Glossary. After each paragraph, have mixed pairs of language proficiency levels share responses with the group.

Paragraphs 1-2 *Why do people vote?* (to elect people who will represent them in government) *What are some elected positions people vote for?* (local officials, a city mayor, county commissioner, governor of a state)

Paragraph 3 *Who is least likely to vote in an election?* (young people aged 18 to 29) *Why is this group the least likely to vote?* (They believe their vote won't matter.) *What does the writer say about this?* (Young people need to vote for changes they want.)

Paragraphs 4 *What happens when people cannot vote?* (They cannot choose the people who will change laws.) *When did women get the right to vote?* (1920) *What other groups had to wait for the right to vote?* (Native Americans and African Americans) *Why is this history important?* (All people have not always had this right.)

Paragraph 5 *Who does the writer think it is important to vote for?* (representatives who will make good decisions) *What does the program Kids Voting USA do for students?* (gets students involved in elections)

Analyze the Student Model: Organization

Use **Analyze Mia's Model** to analyze the organization with students.

- Point to the first column and discuss how the essay is organized. The central idea is followed by supporting ideas. There is a logical order of ideas.
- Review that the central idea tells the purpose and the supporting ideas support the central idea.
- Discuss with them the supporting ideas in the fourth paragraph. *What relevant evidence does Mia include?* (Women, Native Americans, and African Americans have struggled to get voting rights.) *How does the relevant evidence support the central idea?* (It shows how it is important for people to have the right to vote and to vote.)

Mixed Levels Have partners complete columns 1 and 2 in Analyze Mia's Model.

Beginning Have partners use: The central idea tells the main idea. It is in the first paragraph. The relevant evidence provides information that supports the central idea.

Intermediate Have partners describe using: The relevant evidence tells about how groups of people fought for the right to vote. It explains the central idea about why voting is important.

Advanced/Advanced High Have partners describe the central idea and the relevant evidence.

Analyze the Student Model: Sources

Read the **Online Student Model: Sources** with students. Have them underline the information Mia used.

Have partners complete the third column in Analyze Mia's Model. Discuss with students:

Paragraphs 1–2 Point out that a question and a situation create interest in Paragraph 1.

Paragraph 2 Discuss the information from Source 2. *What information did Mia use?* (various elected positions in state and local government) *Why does she tell this information?* (to tell about positions to vote for on a local level) Discuss how Mia uses relevant evidence to tell about more voting opportunities and how it strengthens her central idea.

Paragraph 3 Discuss the information from Source 3. *What information did Mia use?* (why young people do not vote in elections) *How does she use the information?* (to support her central idea and to explain why young people should vote)

Paragraph 4 Discuss the information from Source 1. *What information did Mia use?* (Women, Native Americans, and African Americans could not vote for a long time.) *How does she use it?* (shows unfair treatment and the importance of their gaining the right to vote)

Paragraph 5 Discuss the information from Source 4. What information did Mia use? (the Kids Voting USA program) Ask: *Is this is a strong conclusion?* (Possible response: Yes, because it is inspiring to hear about young kids voting. They inspire their parents to vote!)

FORMATIVE ASSESSMENT

STUDENT CHECK-IN

Have partners share responses to Analyze Mia's Model. Ask students to reflect using the Check-In routine.

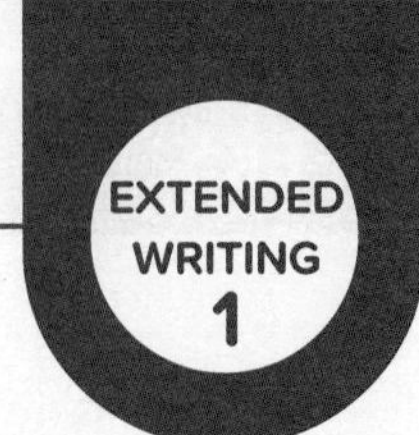

LEARNING GOALS

- We can synthesize information from four sources to plan and organize an expository essay.
- We can draft and revise an expository essay.

OBJECTIVES

Recall relevant information from experiences or gather relevant information from print and digital sources

Develop the topic with facts, definitions, concrete details, quotations, or other information and examples related to the topic.

With guidance and support from peers and adults, develop and strengthen writing as needed by planning, revising, and editing.

LANGUAGE OBJECTIVES

Students will inform by writing an essay using quotations, definitions, and examples.

ELA ACADEMIC LANGUAGE

- *elaborate, support, conclusion*
- Cognates: *elaborar, conclusión*

MATERIALS

Reading/Writing Companion, pp. 204–211

Literature Anthology, pp. 284–287

Online ELL Extended Writing Resources BLMs:

- Glossary, p. 61
- My Writing Outline, pp. 62–63
- Draft: Elaboration, p. 64
- Take Notes: Expository Writing, p. 75

Online Language Development Cards, 7A–7B

Online Language Development Practice, 37–42

DIGITAL TOOLS

Have students read along with the student sources to develop comprehension and build fluency and pronunciation.

Expository Writing

Analyze the Sources

Review the Writing Prompt Display the prompt: *Write an expository essay for your class comparing the three branches of the federal government to the three branches of state governments.* Use the underlined words to discuss with students that they will look at the branches, or parts, of the government.

Read the Sources/Take Notes Read the sources on pages 205–207 in the **Reading/Writing Companion** and pages 284–287 in the **Literature Anthology** with students. Help them identify relevant information and underline the text.

Beginning Discuss the meaning of the words in the **Glossary**. Use visuals to discuss key concepts. Paraphrase challenging sentences for students. After each paragraph, help them describe: I learned about ___.

Intermediate Discuss the key concepts using the Glossary and visuals with students. Paraphrase challenging sentences with them. After each paragraph, help them retell the information.

Advanced/Advanced High Discuss the key concepts using the Glossary and visuals with students. Help them paraphrase challenging sentences. Have them retell the information after every two paragraphs.

Mixed Levels Take Notes Have pairs read **Sources 1–4** and take notes. Use the questions to discuss each source.

SOURCE 1 **"State Government: The Executive Branch"** *What divides a state's government into three branches?* (the state constitution) *Who is the head of a state's executive branch?* (the governor) *Who helps the governor run the state government?* (the people in the cabinet)

SOURCE 2 **"State Government: The Legislative Branch"** *What does the legislative branch of a state's government do?* (make laws for the state) *What can the governor do to a bill once it is passed by the Senate and House of Representatives?* (sign the bill into law or veto/reject it)

SOURCE 3 **"State Government: The Judicial Branch"** *What is a state's judicial branch?* (the court system) *Who makes decisions in cases that are brought to the court?* (judges and justices) *Which is the highest court?* (Supreme Court)

SOURCE 4 **"The Birth of American Democracy" (Literature Anthology pp. 284–287)** *What are the three branches of federal or US government, and who leads them?* (Legislative Branch: Congress; Executive Branch: President, Vice President, Cabinet Members; Judicial Branch: Supreme Court) *What do the branches do?* (Legislative Branch makes laws. Executive Branch carries out laws. Judicial Branch makes decisions about conflicts with laws.)

Plan/Organize Ideas

Synthesize Information Guide students on how to complete the graphic organizer on pages 208–209 of the Reading/Writing Companion. Model how to transfer the information to **My Writing Outline**.

Beginning Have partners discuss supporting ideas as they compare evidence about federal and state government structures. Partners can write the central idea using: Both the federal government and the state government have three branches.

Intermediate Have partners discuss supporting ideas and relevant evidence using: The legislative branch makes laws. Senators and representatives propose bills and vote on them. For the central idea use: Both the federal government and the state government have three separate branches with similar roles.

Advanced/Advanced High Have partners study the sources, discuss, and synthesize the supporting ideas and evidence. Have partners write their central idea.

Draft

Have partners review the plan on My Writing Outline.

- **Organization/My Draft** Check that the central idea answers the writing prompt and the supporting ideas appear in the next paragraphs. Help them paraphrase the central idea for the conclusion.
- **Evidence and Sources** Check that the relevant evidence come from the four sources.
- **Elaboration** Encourage students to elaborate using quotations, definitions, and examples.

Have students use the completed My Writing Outline to help them write their draft.

Beginning Have students check their central idea answers the prompt. Help partners check that the supporting ideas are relevant and in logical order.

Intermediate Have partners review that the central idea answers the prompt and that the supporting ideas are relevant. Help them elaborate and check that they have a strong conclusion.

Advanced/Advanced High Have partners review the relevant supporting ideas for the central idea and elaborate on key ideas. Have them check that their ideas are in logical order with a strong conclusion.

TEACHER CONFERENCES

Meet to provide support and guidance with student drafts. Discuss elaboration in their writing.

Revise

Revising Checklist Review the Revising Checklist on page 211 in the Reading/Writing Companion.

Partner feedback Have partners use the checklist to give feedback. For example:

Beginning Help pairs see how the final sentence in the paragraph uses an example to give more information about the sentence before it.

Intermediate Have pairs underline the elaborative sentences and explain the technique. Have them correct for conventions.

Advanced/Advanced High Have pairs describe how they determined which sentence was an example of elaboration. Have them correct for conventions.

Have students revise their essays.

For additional practice, see **Language Development Cards**, Lessons 7A and 7B, and **Language Development Practice**, pages 37–42.

TEACHER CONFERENCES

To help students revise, meet with each student to provide support and guidance.

FORMATIVE ASSESSMENT

STUDENT CHECK-IN

Plan Have partners share My Writing Outline.

Draft Have partners share examples of elaboration.

Revise Have partners describe revisions in their essays.

Ask students to reflect using the Check-In routine.

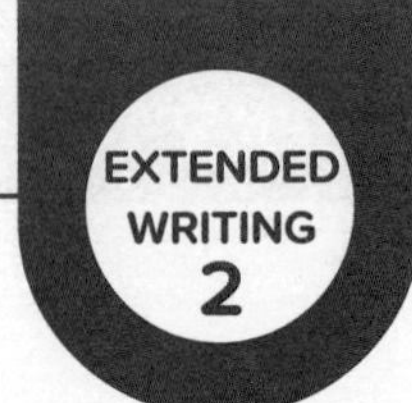

LEARNING GOALS

- **We can identify a central idea.**
- **We can analyze a student model and student model sources.**

OBJECTIVES

Determine the central, or main, idea of a text and explain how it is supported by relevant, or key, details; summarize the text.

Explain how an author uses reasons and evidence to support particular points in a text.

Draw evidence from literary or informational texts to support analysis, reflection, and research.

LANGUAGE OBJECTIVES

Students will discuss features and organization of an expository essay using academic language.

ELA ACADEMIC LANGUAGE

- *evidence, support, paragraph, source*
- Cognates: *evidencia, párrafo*

MATERIALS

Online ELL Extended Writing Resources BLMs:

- John's Model, pp. 65–67
- Analyze John's Model, pp. 68–69

Online Student Model Sources

Reading/Writing Companion, pp. 212–215

Literature Anthology, p. 318

DIGITAL TOOLS

Have students read along with John's Model to develop comprehension and build fluency.

Expository Writing

Central Idea

Reread the paragraph on **Reading/Writing Companion** page 213 with students. Review that all the details and facts connect back to and support the central idea. Help students describe the main idea in the paragraph using: The central idea tells that people have used coins as currency for many years. The other sentences explain details about metal coins.

Compare Central Ideas Write on the board: **Strong:** *People have used coins as currency for a long time.* **Weak:** *China, Europe, and the Middle East have used coins as currency.* Have students compare to elicit that the weak model does not give specific information: how long people have used the coins.

Stating the Central Idea Read **Literature Anthology** page 318 with students. Discuss with them that the supporting details explain the central idea.

Read the paragraph together and help students identify the central idea. Ask: *What is the central, or main idea?* (the Moon is the most mysterious nighttime object.) *How do the other sentences describe the central idea?* (The supporting sentences and the pictures tell how the Moon's appearance changes.) *Why are they important?* (They give details about the central idea.)

COLLABORATE Have partners describe the central idea and supporting details in the paragraph about the Moon.

Beginning Help partners describe using: This sentence is the central idea/supporting detail. It tells that the Moon is mysterious./about the Moon's appearance.

Intermediate Have partners describe: The central idea tells that the Moon is the most mysterious nighttime object. The supporting details describe how the Moon changes appearance over time.

Advanced/Advanced High Have partners describe the central idea and supporting details in the paragraph.

Analyze the Student Model and Sources

Analyze the Prompt Read the prompt on **John's Model** with students. Remind students that an *invention* is something that people create for the first time. Invite students to give examples of *inventions* they think are important. Encourage them to discuss how the *inventions* have helped people.

Discuss the Student Model

COLLABORATE **Mixed Levels** Use **John's Model** to read the Student Model. Before reading, discuss *visual impairments* using the Glossary. After reading, have mixed pairs ask and answer the questions with each other.

Paragraph 1 *Who did Patricia Bath help?* (people with visual impairments) *What did she invent?* (the Laserphaco Probe) *How else did she help people?* (She helped people get eye care.)

Paragraph 2 *Why did Bath face obstacles?* (She was African American.) *What inspired her to dream about becoming a scientist?* (Her mother gave her a chemistry set when she was little.) *What did Bath discover when she was 16?* (an equation related to cancer cells)

Paragraph 3 *What was Bath concerned about?* (African Americans were more likely to have visual impairments than White Americans.) *What idea did she come up with to solve the problem?* (community opthalmology)

Paragraphs 4–5 *What was Bath's most important invention?* (the Laserphaco Probe) *What did the invention do?* (It helped remove cataracts.) *What does the writer think Bath inspires people to do?* (never give up on their dreams)

Analyze the Student Model: Organization

Use **Analyze John's Model** to analyze the organization with students.

- Discuss how the essay is organized: the central idea appears first, followed by supporting ideas with relevant details. The conclusion appears at the end and retells the central idea.
- Review that the central idea tells the focus and purpose and the supporting ideas give evidence that supports the central idea.
- Discuss with them the second paragraph. *What relevant evidence did John include?* (details about Bath's early life) *How does it support the central idea?* (provides facts and details about how Bath became interested in science)

Mixed Levels Have partners complete columns 1 and 2 in the chart.

Beginning Help partners describe using: The central idea tells the main idea about the life of Patricia Bath. It appears in the first paragraph. The supporting ideas tell examples.

Intermediate Have partners describe using: The supporting ideas tell about how Patricia Bath became a scientist and helped people. They support and explain the central idea with examples.

Advanced/Advanced High Have partners describe the central idea and the supporting ideas.

Analyze the Student Model: Sources

Read the **Online Student Model Sources** with students. Have them underline the information John used.

Have partners complete the third column in **Analyze John's Model**. Discuss the following questions with students:

Paragraph 1 Discuss how this summary of Patricia Bath's life is based on information from Source 3. *What is in this introduction?* (an overview of how Bath helped people with visual impairments)

Paragraph 2 Discuss the information from Sources 1 and 3. *What facts did John use?* (the obstacles Bath faced as an African American; how she became inspired to be a scientist at an early age) *How does he use the information?* (examples of Bath's early interest and success support the central idea)

Paragraph 3 Discuss the information from Source 3. *What information did John use?* (the way Bath helped African Americans have easier access to eye care) *How does he use the information?* (to show how Bath helped people with visual impairments) Elicit that John uses these examples from Bath's life to support his central idea.

Paragraphs 4–5 Discuss the information from Source 2. *What facts did John use?* (Bath's invention of the Laserphaco Probe, a more effective and painless way to remove cataracts) *Why does John use this information from Source 3 in his conclusion?* (to show how Bath's interest in science and inventions helped people with visual impairments)

FORMATIVE ASSESSMENT

STUDENT CHECK-IN

Have partners share responses to Analyze John's model. Ask them to reflect on their learning using the Check-In routine.

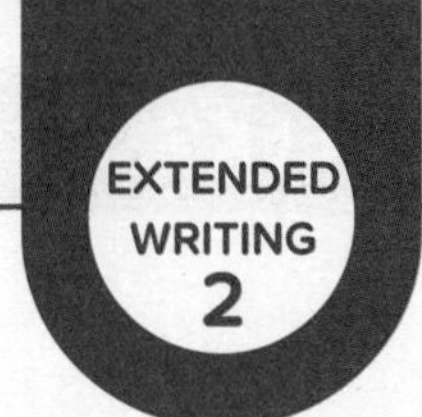

LEARNING GOALS

- **We can synthesize information from three sources to plan and organize an expository essay.**
- **We can draft and revise an expository essay.**

OBJECTIVES

Recall relevant information from experiences or gather relevant information from print and digital sources; take notes and categorize information, and provide a list of sources.

Use precise language and domain-specific vocabulary to inform about or explain the topic.

With guidance and support from peers and adults, develop and strengthen writing as needed by planning, revising, and editing.

LANGUAGE OBJECTIVES

Students will inform by using precise language to describe ideas.

ELA ACADEMIC LANGUAGE

- *supporting ideas, source, precise*
- Cognate: *preciso*

MATERIALS

Reading/Writing Companion, pp. 216-223

Online ELL Extended Writing Resources:

- Glossary, p. 70
- My Writing Outline, pp. 71-72
- Draft: Precise Language, p. 73
- Take Notes: Expository Writing, p. 75

Online Language Development Cards, 20A-20B

Online Language Development Practice, pp. 115-120

DIGITAL TOOLS

MULTIMODAL

Have students read along with the student model sources to develop comprehension and build fluency.

Expository Writing

Analyze the Sources

Review the Writing Prompt Display the prompt: *Write an expository essay on the positive impacts of technology.* Use the underlined words to discuss with students the type of information they will look for as they read.

Read the Sources/Take Notes Read the sources on pages 217-219 in the **Reading/Writing Companion** with students. Help them identify relevant information and underline the text as they read.

Beginning Discuss the meaning of the words in the Glossary. Use visuals to discuss key concepts. Paraphrase challenging sentences for students. After each paragraph, help them describe: I learned about ___.

Intermediate Discuss the key concepts using the Glossary and visuals with students. Paraphrase challenging sentences with them. After each paragraph, help them retell the information.

Advanced/Advanced High Discuss the key concepts using the Glossary and visuals with students. Help them paraphrase challenging sentences. Have them retell the information after every two paragraphs.

Mixed Levels Have pairs read **Sources 1-3** on pages 217-219 and take notes. Use the questions to discuss each source with the group.

SOURCE 1 **"How Technology Is Aiding Senior Citizens"** *What is one issue older adults face?* (loneliness) *How are technology companies helping to address this issue?* (They create robot companions.) *What did they create to help senior citizens with brain injuries?* (a virtual reality headset) *How does the technology help them?* (It makes therapy like a game; it records how the patients are doing.)

SOURCE 2 **"The New Science of Animal Prosthetics"** *What does the science of animal prosthetics do?* (It replaces a body part with an artificial part.) *What are some animals that have received prosthetics?* (dogs, bald eagles, goats, sheep, turtles) *What do scientists use to create prosthetic limbs?* (a 3D computer printer)

SOURCE 3 **"Healthcare and Drones"** *What is a drone?* (an aircraft with no pilot) *How did drones help Puerto Rico after Hurricane Maria?* (They flew over destroyed roads and dropped off supplies.) *Why are drones important in the field of medical care?* (They deliver tests to laboratories and vaccines to clinics in remote areas.)

Plan/Organize Ideas

Synthesize Information Guide students on how to complete the graphic organizer on Reading/Writing Companion pages 220–221. Model how students can transfer their information from their graphic organizer to **My Writing Outline**.

Beginning Have partners discuss supporting ideas as they compare evidence in the three sources. Then have them write a central idea using: Modern technology helps people and animals.

Intermediate Have partners discuss supporting ideas and elaborative details they synthesize using: Technology can help people and animals recover from injuries. Devices such as virtual reality headsets and robot companions can help senior citizens. Animal prosthetics help animals with disabilities to have better lives.

Advanced/Advanced High Have partners study the information in the sources, then synthesize the supporting ideas that support a central idea. Have partners write their central idea.

Draft

Have partners review the plan on My Writing Outline.

- **Organization/My Draft** Check that the central idea answers the writing prompt. Check for supporting ideas and elaborative details. Help students paraphrase the central idea for the conclusion.
- **Evidence and Sources** Check that the evidence comes from all three sources.
- **Precise Language** Remind students to use precise language that clearly communicates their ideas.

Have students use the completed My Writing Outline as they write their draft.

Beginning Help partners write complete sentences for the central idea using precise language.

Intermediate Have partners review that the central idea answers the prompt and the elaborative details support the central idea. Help partners include precise language.

Advanced/Advanced High Have partners review that the central idea answers the prompt and that the elaborative details provide relevant evidence. Help partners check for precise language.

TEACHER CONFERENCES

Meet to provide support and guidance as students write their drafts. Discuss with students precise language in their writing.

Revise

Revising Checklist Review the items in the checklist on page 223 in the Reading/Writing Companion.

Partner feedback Have partners use the checklist to give feedback. For example:

Beginning Model using precise language, combining sentences, and deleting unnecessary words. Help students use precise language in their essay.

Intermediate Have partners identify the revisions they made. Remind them to correct for conventions.

Advanced/Advanced High Have partners explain their revisions. Remind them to correct for conventions.

Before they revise, have partners discuss the revisions with each other.

For additional practice, see **Language Development Cards**, Lessons 20A and 20B. and **Language Development Practice**, pages 115–120.

TEACHER CONFERENCES

To help students revise, meet with each student to provide support and guidance.

FORMATIVE ASSESSMENT

STUDENT CHECK-IN

Plan Have partners share My Writing Outline.

Draft Have partners share examples of precise language.

Revise Have partners describe revisions in their essays.

Ask students to reflect using the Check-In routine.

Summative Assessment

Get Ready for Unit Assessment

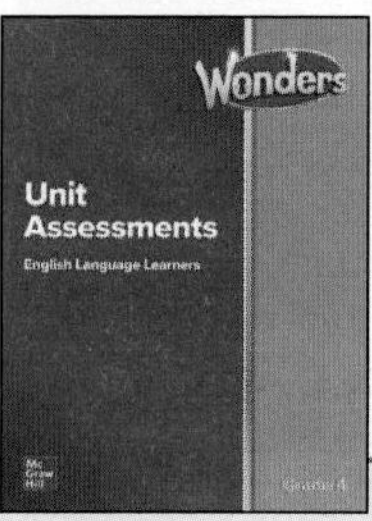

Unit 4 Tested Skills

LISTENING AND READING COMPREHENSION	VOCABULARY	GRAMMAR	SPEAKING AND WRITING
• Listening Actively • Comprehension • Text Structure • Cohesion	• Unit Vocabulary Words	• Pronouns • Connecting Ideas	• Presenting • Supporting Opinions • Retelling/Summarizing • Text Structure

Create a Student Profile

Record data from the following resources in the Student Profile charts on pages 320–321 of the Assessment book.

COLLABORATIVE	INTERPRETIVE	PRODUCTIVE

• Collaborative Conversations Rubrics
  • Listening
  • Speaking
	• Leveled Unit Assessment:
	  • Listening Comprehension
	  • Reading Comprehension
	  • Vocabulary
	  • Grammar
	• Presentation Rubric
	  • Listening
	• *Wonders* Unit Assessment
		• Weekly Progress Monitoring
		• Leveled Unit Assessment
		  • Speaking
		  • Writing
		• Presentation Rubric
		  • Speaking
		• Write to Sources Rubric
		• *Wonders* Unit Assessment

The Foundational Skills Kit, Language Development Kit, and Adaptive Learning provide additional student data for progress monitoring.

Level Up

Use the following chart, along with your Student Profiles, to guide your Level Up decisions.

LEVEL UP	If **BEGINNING** level students are able to do the following, they may be ready to move to the **INTERMEDIATE** level:	If **INTERMEDIATE** level students are able to do the following, they may be ready to move to the **ADVANCED** level:	If **ADVANCED** level students are able to do the following, they may be ready to move to on-level:
COLLABORATIVE	• participate in collaborative conversations using basic vocabulary and grammar and simple phrases or sentences • discuss simple pictorial or text prompts	• participate in collaborative conversations using appropriate words and phrases and complete sentences • use limited academic vocabulary across and within disciplines	• participate in collaborative conversations using more sophisticated vocabulary and correct grammar • communicate effectively across a wide range of language demands in social and academic contexts
INTERPRETIVE	• identify details in simple read alouds • understand common vocabulary and idioms and interpret language related to familiar social, school, and academic topics • make simple inferences and make simple comparisons • exhibit an emerging receptive control of lexical, syntactic, phonological, and discourse features	• identify main ideas and/or make some inferences from simple read alouds • use context clues to identify word meanings and interpret basic vocabulary and idioms • compare, contrast, summarize, and relate text to graphic organizers • exhibit a limited range of receptive control of lexical, syntactic, phonological, and discourse features when addressing new or familiar topics	• determine main ideas in read alouds that have advanced vocabulary • use context clues to determine meaning, understand multiple-meaning words, and recognize synonyms of social and academic vocabulary • analyze information, make sophisticated inferences, and explain their reasoning • command a high degree of receptive control of lexical, syntactic, phonological, and discourse features
PRODUCTIVE	• express ideas and opinions with basic vocabulary and grammar and simple phrases or sentences • restate information or retell a story using basic vocabulary • exhibit an emerging productive control of lexical, syntactic, phonological, and discourse features	• produce coherent language with limited elaboration or detail • restate information or retell a story using mostly accurate, although limited, vocabulary • exhibit a limited range of productive control of lexical, syntactic, phonological, and discourse features when addressing new or familiar topics	• produce sentences with more sophisticated vocabulary and correct grammar • restate information or retell a story using extensive and accurate vocabulary and grammar • tailor language to a particular purpose and audience • command a high degree of productive control of lexical, syntactic, phonological, and discourse features

LEARNING GOALS

We can read and understand an expository text.

OBJECTIVES

Describe the overall structure of events, ideas, concepts, or information in a text or part of a text.

Review the key ideas expressed and explain their own ideas and understanding in light of the discussion.

Observe and identify slow changes to Earth's surface caused by weathering, erosion, and deposition from water, wind, and ice. **Science**

LANGUAGE OBJECTIVES

Students will explain how fruit decays using time-order words.

ELA ACADEMIC LANGUAGE

- *prefix, antonym, photograph, caption, chronology, signal*
- Cognates: *prefijo, antónimo, fotografía, cronología*

MATERIALS

Reading/Writing Companion, pp. 12–15

Online Scaffolded Shared Read, "Your World Up Close"

Visual Vocabulary Cards

Online ELL Visual Vocabulary Cards

DIGITAL TOOLS

MULTIMODAL

Have students listen to the selection to develop comprehension and practice fluency and pronunciation.

"Your World Up Close"

Prepare to Read

Build Background Show a magnifying glass or microscope. Ask: *Have you ever looked through a microscope or telescope? What did you see?* Have students discuss their experiences of using a microscope and things they discovered using: I used a microscope to ____. I saw/observed up close _____.

Vocabulary Use the **Visual Vocabulary Cards** to preteach the vocabulary: *cling, dissolves, gritty, humid, magnify, microscope, mingle,* and *typical.* (Cognate: *microscopio*) Use the online **ELL Visual Vocabulary Cards** to teach additional vocabulary from the Shared Read: *allows, capture, decays, extreme, fresh,* and *images.*

Set Purpose *Today we will read "Your World Up Close." As we read, think about what you can discover when you look closely at something.*

Read the Text

Select the **Scaffolded Shared Read** or the Shared Read in the **Reading/Writing Companion,** based on students' language proficiency.

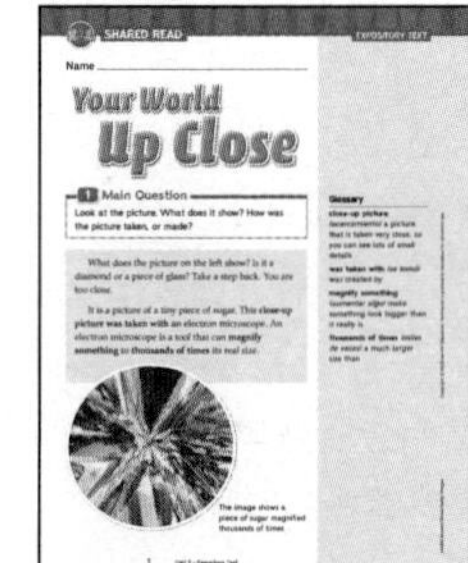

Scaffolded Shared Read, Lexile 660L

Beginning/Early-Intermediate Use the online Scaffolded Shared Read to help partners work together to read and understand an expository text. Remind them to use the Glossary to help them read and the Word Bank to help them answer the Main and Additional Questions.

Intermediate/Advanced/Advanced High Read the text with students and use the Interactive Question-Response Routine to help them understand an expository text.

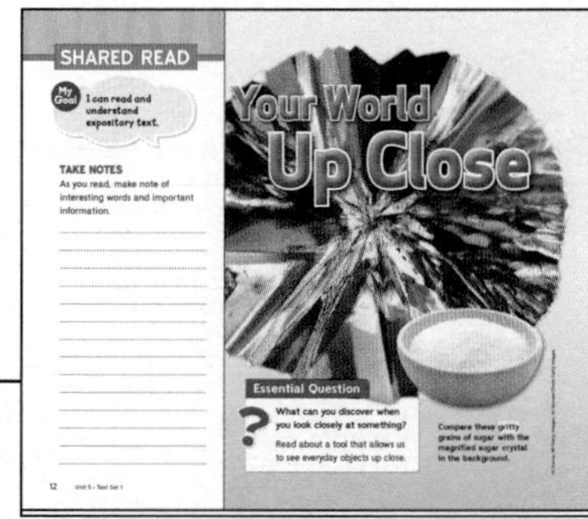

Reading/Writing Companion, Lexile: 860L

Page 13

Paragraphs 1–3 Read text with students and review Vocabulary words *magnify* and *extreme* with students. *What does an electron microscope do?* (takes pictures of things up close) *What are pictures taken by an electron microscope called?* (photomicrographs) *What does the prefix micro- mean?* (small)

COLLABORATE *What word in paragraph 2 tells what a microscope does?* (magnify) *Does magnify mean to make bigger or smaller?* (make bigger) *What text clue supports your answer?* (thousands of times its actual size)

Paragraph 4 Read the text with students and review Vocabulary words *microscope, typical,* and *images. Who invented photomicrography?* (Alfred Donné)

Why does Wilson Bentley have "Snowflake" in his name? (He took the first photograph of a snowflake with a microscope.) Have students look at the photo and read the caption. Explain that the word part *-gon* means "corner" or "angle" and *hex-* means "six." Have students trace the angles of the snowflakes in the photos. *How many angles do snowflakes have?* (six) *How does the author describe snowflakes?* (each is unique) *What word in the paragraph is an antonym, or opposite, of* unique? (typical)

Intermediate Have students describe the photographs and read the caption. *What shape are snowflakes?* Snowflakes are hexagons.

Advanced/Advanced High *What did Bentley's photographs show?* (each snowflake is unique)

COLLABORATE Have partners describe things that are *unique* and things that are *typical.* Have them present their ideas to the class.

Page 14

Paragraphs 1–3 Read the text with students and review the Vocabulary *dissolves, allows,* and *capture. How is a light microscope different from an electron microscope?* (A light microscope is weak and an electron microscope is powerful.) *What happens when an image is magnified?* (We can see more details in the image.) *What is the most magnification for an electron microscope?* (2 million times the original size) *How do scientists use electron microscopes?* (Scientists use them to study what causes diseases.)

COLLABORATE **Intermediate** *Which words in the text compare light and electron microscopes?* (weak, powerful) Have partners compare the two types of microscopes: A light microscope is weak and does not show a lot of details. An electron microscope is powerful and shows many more details.

Advanced/Advanced High *Why do you think the author shows a photograph of a fingerprint?* (Possible answer: The author wants us to compare what we can see with our eyes to what we can see with an electron microscope.) *Which words help you understand what* dissolves *means?* ("into a drop of water")

Page 15

Paragraphs 1–2 Read the text with students and review the Vocabulary words *cling, mingle, humid, decays,* and *fresh. What is another reason that scientists use electron microscopes?* (to observe how things change over time) Have students describe the photographs and read the caption on the page. *What kind of change over time do these photos show?* (a strawberry getting moldy) Invite students to point to the mold in the photo. *Read the caption at the top of the page. What looks like grapes in the photo?* (mold) Review that **chronology** is the order in which things happen, and that time-order words and phrases signal a chronological text structure. Ask: *What are some examples of time-order words?* (first, next, then, last)

Beginning Explain that *decay* means to change for the worse. *How does the fruit look first?* First, the fruit looks fresh. *What happens after a few days?* After a few days, the fruit softens.

Intermediate *What word does the author use to describe change in fruit?* (decay) *Does the word mean a change for the better or for the worse?* (a change for the worse) *What words and phrases tell how a fruit changes in paragraph 1? Look for words that signal time order.* (First, After a few days, Then, Days pass, and eventually)

COLLABORATE **Advanced/Advanced High** Have partners use time-order words to retell what happens to fruit as it decays. (Possible answer: First, the fruit is fresh. After a few days, the fruit softens. Then, there's some mold on the fruit. Eventually, the fruit is covered in mold.) *Why does the author use time-order words to describe how a fruit decays?* (Possible answer: To help readers understand how fruit changes over time.)

FORMATIVE ASSESSMENT

STUDENT CHECK-IN

Have partners retell the important ideas in the text. Ask them to reflect using the Check-In routine.

LEARNING GOALS

- **We can read and understand expository text by identifying the chronology in the text structure.**
- **We can identify and use common and proper adjectives.**

OBJECTIVES

Paraphrase portions of a text read aloud or information presented in diverse media and formats, including visually, quantitatively, and orally.

Demonstrate command of the conventions of standard English grammar and usage when writing or speaking.

LANGUAGE OBJECTIVES

Students will discuss chronology using signal words.

Students will inquire about adjectives using academic language.

ELA ACADEMIC LANGUAGE

- *signal, identify, chronology*
- Cognates: *identificar, cronología*

MATERIALS

Reading/Writing Companion, pp. 12–15, 16–17

Online Scaffolded Shared Read, "Your World Up Close"

Online Shared Read Writing Frames, p. 13

Online Language Development Cards, Lesson 48A

Online Language Development Practice, pp. 283–285

Online Language Transfers Handbook, pp. 15–19

"Your World Up Close"

Text Reconstruction

Focus on a single chunk of text to support comprehension and language development across the four domains.

1. Read aloud paragraph 1 on page 15 in the **Reading/Writing Companion** while students listen.
2. Write the following on the board, providing definitions as needed: *fresh, over time, decays, mold, days pass, microscope.* Instruct students to listen for them as you read the paragraph a second time.
3. Read the paragraph a third time. Tell students to listen and take notes.
4.  COLLABORATE Have students work with a partner to reconstruct the text from their notes. Help them write complete sentences as needed.
5. Have students look at the original text. Ask them to tell what the paragraph is mostly about. (how a microscope can help us observe fruit decay) Tell students they are going to look at how the author uses a chronology in the text structure to tell how fruit decays.
6. *First, what does the fruit look like?* (It looks fresh.) *What is the next thing that happens to the fruit?* (It softens) *Which words tell you how much time it takes for fruit to soften?* ("After a few days") *What happens next?* (Specks of mold appear.) *What words tell you that the mold continues to grow on the fruit?* ("Days pass") *What does the fruit look like in the end?* (It is covered in mold.)
7. Have students compare their text reconstructions to the original text. Have them check whether they also included time-order words that show the chronology in the text structure.

Beginning Have students follow along in the Reading/Writing Companion as you read the text aloud. Have them circle the words from Step 2 as they hear them.

Grammar in Context: Adjectives

Notice the Form Display these sentences from the text, and circle the adjectives *typical* and *unique*.

> *There is no such thing as a typical snowflake. Each is unique.*

What do the circled words have in common? (They are adjectives.) *What do adjectives do?* (describe a noun or pronoun) Point to the adjective *typical* and the noun *snowflake*. *Where do adjectives usually appear?* (before the noun) *What does* typical *describe?* (snowflake) Point to the linking verb *is* and the adjective *unique*. *Adjectives can also follow a linking verb. What does* unique *describe?* (Each) Read the sentences and compare what each tells about snowflakes.

Apply and Extend Have partners rewrite the sentences using different adjectives. Check their answers to provide corrective feedback.

For additional practice, see **Language Development Cards**, Lesson 48A, and **Language Development Practice**, pages 283–285.

Independent Time

Vocabulary Building Have students build glossaries.

Beginning/Early Intermediate Have students complete the Glossary Activities in the **Scaffolded Shared Read**.

Intermediate/Advanced/Advanced High Have students add the vocabulary from **Reading/Writing Companion** pages 16–17 and self-selected words or phrases they would like to learn to the chart.

Mixed Levels Have students with different proficiency levels work together to learn vocabulary: Beginning and Early-Intermediate students can teach each other vocabulary from their Scaffolded Shared Read glossaries. Intermediate and Advanced/Advanced High students can teach their self-selected words.

WORD/PHRASE IN ENGLISH	DEFINITION IN ENGLISH	PART OF SPEECH	USE THE WORD/PHRASE IN A SENTENCE
capture	to record like a photograph	verb	A photograph captures a moment.

COLLABORATE **Shared Read Writing Frames** Have students use the online leveled **Shared Read Writing Frames** for "Your World Up Close" to provide students with additional oral and written practice. Differentiated frames are available to provide support for all levels.

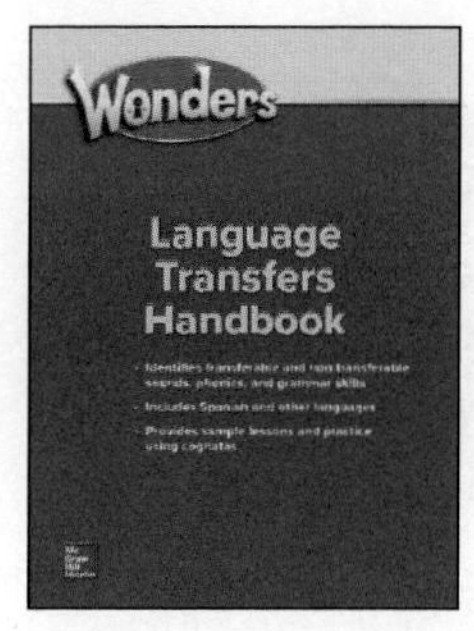

Language Transfers Handbook, Grammar Transfers, pp. 15–19

DIGITAL TOOLS

For additional support, use the online activities.

Grammar Song

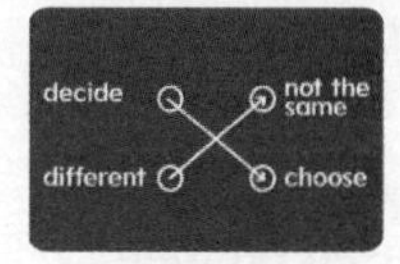

Vocabulary Activity

FORMATIVE ASSESSMENT

STUDENT CHECK-IN

Text Reconstruction Ask partners to share their notes. Have students reflect using the Check-In routine.

Grammar in Context Ask partners to share the sentences they wrote. Have them reflect using the Check-In routine.

LEARNING GOALS

- **Read** We can read and understand an expository text.
- **Reread** We can reread to analyze text, craft, and structure.

OBJECTIVES

By the end of year, read and comprehend informational texts, including history/social studies, science, and technical texts, in the grades 4–5 text complexity band proficiently, with scaffolding as needed at the high end of the range.

Review the key ideas expressed and explain their own ideas and understanding in light of the discussion.

Measure and compare objects and materials based on their physical properties including: mass, shape, volume, color, hardness, texture, odor, taste, attraction to magnets. **Science**

LANGUAGE OBJECTIVES

Students will inquire by answering questions using key vocabulary.

Students will explain the use of photographs and repetition using academic language.

ELA ACADEMIC LANGUAGE

- *photograph, repetition, perspective*
- Cognates: *fotografía, repetición, perspectiva*

MATERIALS

Literature Anthology, pp. 362–379

Reading/Writing Companion, pp. 24–26

Visual Vocabulary Cards

Online ELL Anchor Text Support BLMs, pp. 31–33

DIGITAL TOOLS

Have students read along as they listen to the selection to develop comprehension and practice fluency and pronunciation.

A Drop of Water

Prepare to Read

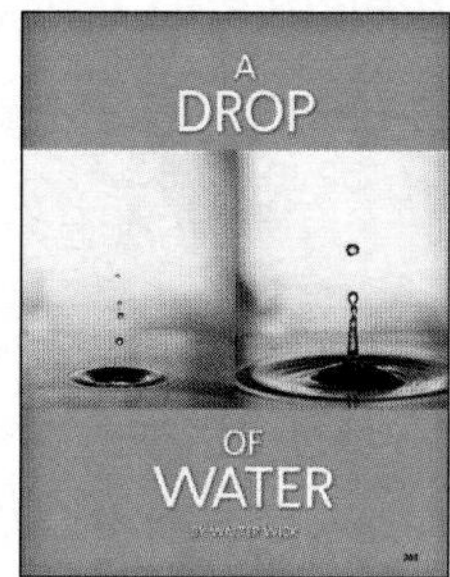

Literature Anthology, Lexile: 870L

Build Background Have students brainstorm different forms of water they know. Select some examples and ask students if they know how they form.

Vocabulary Use the **Visual Vocabulary Cards** to review *mingle, humid, dissolves, gritty, cling, typical.*

Set Purpose *Today we will read about how water molecules change. As we read, think about what we can learn by looking closely at a drop of water.*

Have students listen to the audio summary of the text, which is available in multiple languages.

Read

Literature Anthology, pages 362–379

Use the **Interactive Question-Response Routine** to help students read and discuss *A Drop of Water.*

Beginning Help students respond in complete sentences. Provide sentence frames: Water changes forms. Water molecules move with heat.

Intermediate Ask students to respond in complete sentences and add details. Provide sentence starters as needed: Water changes forms. Water molecules move with heat.

Advanced/Advanced High Have students respond in complete sentences and add details.

Independent Reading Practice Have mixed level pairs complete pages 31–33 of ELL Anchor Text Support BLMs and share with the group.

Reread

Use with the **Reading/Writing Companion,** pages 24–26.

Literature Anthology, pages 364–365

COLLABORATE **Text Features: Photographs** Read the text with students. Have students ask about words or phrases they don't know or understand. Then have them look at the photograph. *What does the photograph show?* (what happens to a drop of blue water in a jar of clear water)

Beginning Read the second paragraph with students. Restate the sentences as needed. *What does the photograph show?* The photograph shows a drop of blue water. *Where is the drop?* The drop is in a jar. *What does the jar have?* The jar has clear water. *How does the water look at the end?* The water looks blue.

Intermediate Have partners look at the photograph and describe what happens to the drop of blue water: The drop of blue water splits up. Parts of the drop sink. They swirl or move in different directions. The drop breaks. After that, the drop is part of the whole jar of water.

Advanced/Advanced High Have partners compare and contrast the pictures. (Possible answer: First the drop looks blue and the water in the jar is clear. Next the drop splits and swirls. At the end, the water in the jar looks blue.)

Literature Anthology, page 366

COLLABORATE **Author's Craft: Repetition** Read the text with students. Discuss the meaning of *rigid* and explain that it means "hard." Have students ask about words or phrases they don't know or understand. Remind students how the author described what happens to a drop of water in a jar. *What does the author repeat to explain how water becomes ice?* (The author continues talking about a drop of blue water and shows photos of blue ice cubes.) Have partners discuss why the author uses a blue drop of water to explain how water becomes ice. (It helps readers remember the description and photos of the blue drop of water in the jar and to see how that drop stops moving.)

Beginning Read the first paragraph with students. Restate the sentences as needed. *What does the author talk about?* The author talks about a drop of blue water. Have partners look at the photos and discuss what happens when water cools. *What happens to the drop of blue water when the water cools?* The drop doesn't move.

Intermediate Have partners describe what happens to the drop of blue water when water cools: The drop of blue water stops moving.

Advanced/Advanced High *What happens to the drop of blue water when water cools?* (The drop no longer moves.) *Why?* (Water turns solid. It changes to solid.)

Literature Anthology, page 379

COLLABORATE **Author's Perspective** Read the text with students. Have students ask about words or phrases they don't know or understand. Reread the first sentence in paragraph 2. *How does this help you understand the author's perspective, or feelings, about water?* (He says it is precious, which means he understands how important it is.)

Beginning Read paragraph 2 with students, restating information as needed. *How does the author feel about water?* Water is precious. No living thing can survive without water.

Intermediate Why does the author say that "water is precious"? Water is precious because every living thing needs water to survive.

Advanced *Why do you think the author tells about the water cycle?* (possible answer: to show that water is everywhere)

Advanced High *How does the author show that water is precious?* (The author gives details telling that not a single thing could survive without water.)

FORMATIVE ASSESSMENT

STUDENT CHECK-IN

Read Have partners share their responses to the Anchor Text questions. Then have them reflect using the Check-In routine.

Reread Have partners share responses and text evidence on Reading/Writing Companion pages 24–26. Then have them reflect using the Check-In routine to fill in the bars.

LEARNING GOALS

- We can read and understand expository text by identifying chronology in the text structure.
- We can understand and use articles.

OBJECTIVES

Paraphrase portions of a text read aloud or information presented in diverse media and formats, including visually, quantitatively, and orally.

Demonstrate command of the conventions of standard English grammar and usage when writing or speaking.

LANGUAGE OBJECTIVES

Students will explain events in a text using signal words.

Students will inquire about adjectives and articles using academic language.

ELA ACADEMIC LANGUAGE

- *identify, organize, chronology, signal*
- Cognates: *identificar, organizar, cronología*

MATERIALS

Literature Anthology, pp. 362-379

Online Language Development Cards, 44B

Online Language Development Practice, pp. 262-264

Online Language Transfers Handbook, pp. 15-19

A Drop of Water

Text Reconstruction

Focus on a single chunk of text to support comprehension and language development across the four domains.

1. Read aloud Paragraph 3 in the section "Water Vapor" on page 367 in the **Literature Anthology** while students listen.
2. Write the following on the board, providing definitions as needed: *kettle, evaporation, stove, steam, spout, invisible, molecules.* Instruct students to listen for them as you read the paragraph a second time.
3. Read the paragraph a third time while students listen and take notes.
4. COLLABORATE Have students work with a partner to reconstruct the text from their notes. Help them write complete sentences as needed.
5. Have students look at the original text. Ask them to tell what the paragraph is mostly about. (how heated water evaporates and turns into vapor) Tell students they are going to identify how the information is organized using chronology in the text structure.
6. *What is described first?* (Heat from the stove makes water in a kettle turn to steam.) *What do you see after the steam hits the cooler air?* (a cloud of tiny droplets.) *What words tell how long it takes for the tiny droplets to change into invisible vapor?* (Almost immediately) *What signal word tells you what happens next?* (then) *Then what happens?* (water molecules mingle with other molecules that make up air.)
7. Have students compare their text reconstructions to the original text. Have them check whether they also included time order words.

Beginning Allow students to follow along in the Literature Anthology as you read the text aloud. Have them point to the words from Step 2 as they hear them.

Apply Text Features: Photographs

Review with students that authors use photographs to help explain complex ideas. Have students write sentences about the photographs. Model first: *On page 375, the last paragraph describes how a snowflake can change directly from ice to vapor. How does the photograph show how that happens?* (The snowflake gets smaller as it disappears.) Have students choose a photograph from the selection and write sentences about the photograph.

Grammar in Context: Deconstruct a Sentence

Write this sentence from page 370 on the board: *Clouds are made of tiny water droplets, too small to be seen without a microscope.* Facilitate deconstructing these sentences for better comprehension:

- Point to the words *tiny* and *water.* Ask: *What information do the words tell about droplets?* (size, type) *What kind of word are they?* (adjectives) Discuss that *water* describes the type of droplets.
- *What noun does the adjective* small *describe?* (*droplets*) Point to the comma and *small.* Explain that the comma indicates that the words that follow describe droplets. Explain that the phrase after the comma can be rewritten as a sentence. Write on the board: *Clouds are made of tiny water droplets. The droplets are too small to be seen with a microscope.*
- Point to the article *a* in the sentence. *What kind of word is* a*?* (an article) Explain that we use the article *a* to refer to a general person, place, or thing. Then provide an example: A droplet of water is tiny. Diego is a student. Have students write examples using the article *a.*

For additional practice, see **Language Development Cards**, Lesson 44B, and **Language Development Practice**, pages 262–264.

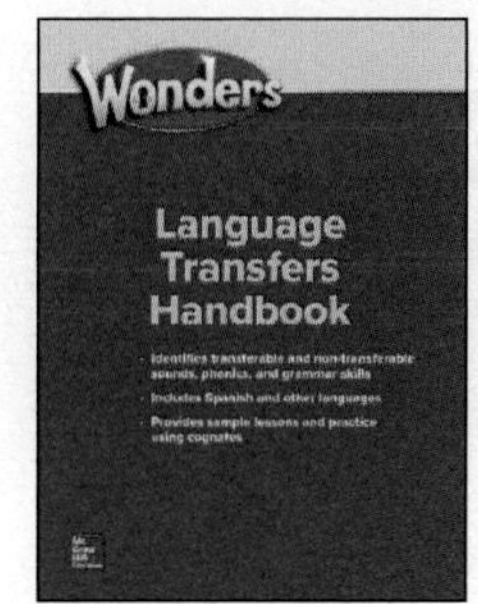

Language Transfers Handbook, Grammar Transfers, pp. 15–19

Independent Time

Vocabulary Building Have partners create a diagram to show a process that happens with water that they read about in the selection, such as evaporation or condensation. Have partners discuss the steps and write each step on an index card. On the back of each card, have them number the step. Then have partners draw a picture of the process and tape the drawing to the wall. Have other students place the index cards in the appropriate sequence.

Beginning Allow students to use words, phrases, or pictures.

Intermediate/Advanced/Advanced High Have students include some of the self-selected words and content-area words they added to their glossaries.

COLLABORATE **Use Adjectives** Have partners use the photographs on pages 366, 368–369, 371, 374, or 377 to describe using adjectives. Have them list adjectives to describe opinion, size, and color and write a sentence for each adjective. Then have them rewrite the sentences by combining the adjectives. Have them review the order of adjectives before they combine and write their sentences on a chart to share them with the group.

ADJECTIVES	SENTENCE WITH ADJECTIVES	SENTENCE WITH ADJECTIVES COMBINED
beautiful, large, blue	The ice cubes are beautiful. I see large ice cubes. The ice cubes are blue.	I see beautiful, large, blue ice cubes.

FORMATIVE ASSESSMENT

STUDENT CHECK-IN

Text Reconstruction Ask partners to share their notes. Have them reflect using the Check-In routine.

Grammar in Context Have students reflect on their deconstructions using the Check-In routine.

LEARNING GOALS

We can apply strategies and skills to read an expository text.

OBJECTIVES

Describe the overall structure of events, ideas, concepts, or information in a text or part of a text.

Review the key ideas expressed and explain their own ideas and understanding in light of the discussion.

Demonstrate understanding of words by relating them to their opposites and to words with similar but not identical meanings.

LANGUAGE OBJECTIVES

Students will discuss an expository text using key vocabulary.

ELA ACADEMIC LANGUAGE

- *antonym, context clues, chronology, sequence, event, photograph, caption*
- cognates: *antónimo, cronología, secuencia, fotografía*

MATERIALS

Online ELL Genre Passage, "At Your Fingertips"

"At Your Fingertips"

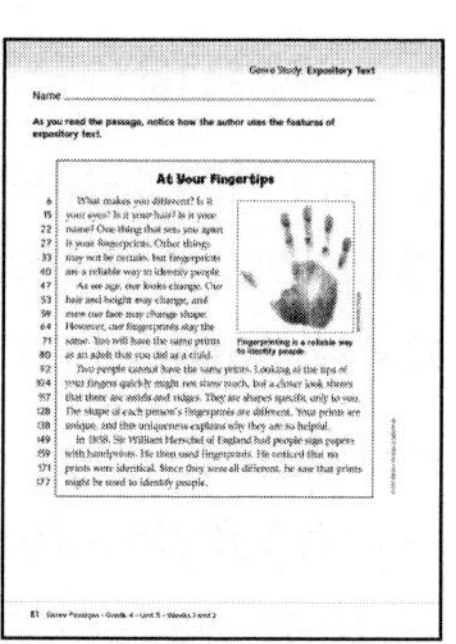

Genre Passage
Lexile: 660L

Prepare to Read

Build Background Explain to students that they will read about how people use fingerprints. Ask students to share what they know about different ways people use fingertips.

Read the title and discuss meaning. Point out that the phrase "at your fingertips" is an idiom and means something that can be reached and used easily. Discuss examples of things that are at their fingertips: *An encyclopedia has all the information I need at my fingertips.* Have students describe other examples.

Vocabulary Use the Define, Example, Ask routine to pre-teach difficult words or unfamiliar concepts, such as *methods, identity, reliable, specific,* and *arrest* (Cognates: *identidad, específico, arrestar*). Invite students to add new vocabulary to their glossaries.

Set Purpose *Today we will read an expository text called "At Your Fingertips." As we read, think about what you can discover when you look closely at something.*

Read the Text

Page E1, Paragraphs 1–3

COLLABORATE **Antonyms** Read the first sentence of paragraph 3 with students. *What is an antonym for the word* same? (different) *With a partner, read paragraph 3. What context clues can help you identify the meaning of* different? (Sample context clues: "specific only to you," "your prints are unique")

Beginning Read paragraph 2 with students and restate sentences as needed. *Which parts of our body change as we grow older?* Our <u>hair, height,</u> and <u>face</u> change. *Which parts do not change?* Our fingerprints <u>do not</u> change.

Intermediate *Something that "sets you apart" makes you different. What is one thing that sets you apart from others?* (fingerprints) *What context clues tell you?* ("Two people cannot have the same prints.") *Does the phrase "specific only to you" mean the same as* unique? *What clues tell you?* ("Your prints are unique.")

COLLABORATE **Summarize** Help student read the caption on page E1 and discuss how it shows the central idea. Guide students to reread each paragraph and highlight relevant details. Have partners arrange the details in a logical order and summarize the ideas in their own words. Provide sentence frames, if needed: Fingerprinting is a reliable way to identify <u>someone</u>. Everyone's fingerprints are <u>unique</u> and <u>stay the same for life</u>. Fingerprints can be used to <u>identify people</u>.

E2, Paragraphs 1–2

Text Structure: Chronology *What happened in 1892?* (A scientist wrote a book about fingerprints.) *What are the dates in paragraph 2?* (1901, 1903) *What do you notice about the dates?* (arranged in time order) Review chonology with students: The author uses chronology to tell readers the sequence of events.

Beginning Read paragraph 1 with students and restate sentences as needed. Write the number for one billion on the board to help students understand the word. *What did Sir Francis Galton do?* Sir Francis Galton wrote a book about fingerprints. He proved that a person's fingerprints do not change.

Intermediate Help students understand the phrase "1 in 64 billion" in the last sentence of paragraph 5. *Is the chance high or low for 1 person in 64 billion people?* The chance is _____ because _____.

Advanced/Advanced High Have partners discuss why using fingerprints is a good way to identify people. (Possible answer: Although our features change, fingerprints stay the same, so it is a good way to identify people.)

Page E2, Paragraphs 3–4

Beginning Read the last paragraph with students and restate as needed. Help partners identify one way people use fingerprints: People use fingerprints to identify people.

Intermediate Have partners describe the reasons the text provides about why fingerprints are important: I read that fingerprints are important because ____. (They help to identify people.)

Advanced Have partners describe how fingerprints can be used to keep things safe. (Pictures of fingerprints can be used to unlock doors or open files on a computer.)

Advanced High Have students discuss why the author uses the word *key* in quotations. (Possible answer: Fingerprints can be used to unlock doors or open files, like a key.)

Respond to Reading

Use the following instruction to help students answer the questions on page E3.

1. *Read the third sentence in the second paragraph. What does the word* however *signal?* (It tells about something that contrasts.)
2. **Text Features: Photographs and Captions** *Look at the photograph and read the caption. What is the purpose for the photograph?* (to give information about fingerprints)
3. *Read the first paragraph on page E2. What did Sir Francis Galton discover?* (Fingerprints do not change.)

Fluency Have partners take turns reading the passage.

Build Knowledge: Make Connections

Talk About the Text Have partners discuss what you can discover when you look closely at something.

Write About the Text Have students add their ideas to their Build Knowledge pages of their reader's notebooks.

FORMATIVE ASSESSMENT

STUDENT CHECK-IN

Have partners share their responses on page E3. Ask students to reflect using the Check-In routine.

LEVEL UP

IF students read the **ELL** of the **Genre Passage** fluently and answered the questions,

THEN pair them with students who have proficiently read the **On Level**. Have them

- partner read the **On Level** passage
- summarize the main idea and details

LEARNING GOALS

We can apply strategies and skills to read an expository text.

OBJECTIVES

Determine the central, or main, idea of a text and explain how it is supported by relevant, or key, details; summarize the text.

Review the key ideas expressed and explain their own ideas and understanding in light of the discussion.

Read grade-level text with purpose and understanding.

LANGUAGE OBJECTIVES

Students will inform about the water cycle by summarizing in complete sentences.

ELA ACADEMIC LANGUAGE

- *summarize, diagram*
- Cognates: *diagrama*

MATERIALS

ELL Leveled Reader: *Secrets of the Ice*

Online Differentiated Texts: "A Close-Up of Our Universe"

Visual Vocabulary Cards

DIGITAL TOOLS

Have students read along with the audio of the selections to develop comprehension and practice fluency and pronunciation.

Secrets of the Ice

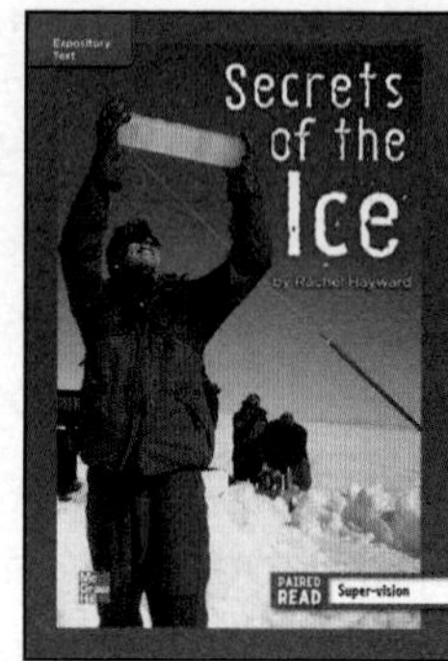

Leveled Reader
Lexile 780L

Prepare to Read

Build Background Read the title aloud and help students discuss the cover image. *These people are scientists in Antarctica.* Point to Antarctica on a map or globe. Ask students to discuss what they know about Antarctica and what they think the climate is like. Explain: *The ice in Antarctica built up in layers over hundreds of thousands of years. What do you think scientists might learn from studying the ice?*

Vocabulary Use the routine on the **Visual Vocabulary Cards** to pre-teach ELL vocabulary *captures, extract,* and *substance*. Discuss the appendices on page 19 of the Leveled Reader.

Set Purpose *Today we will read an expository text called "Secrets of the Ice." As we read, think about what you can discover when you look closely at something.*

Read the Text

Pages 2–3

Use details from the text and photographs to support understanding of *properties* and *states*. Discuss with students the properties of water: *How can water change?* (freeze, melt, boil) What happens to other substances in water? (They dissolve.)

Beginning Read with students the caption on page 3. *How did the water change?* The water froze to make ice. The bottle broke because water expands, or gets bigger, when it freezes.

Pages 4–5

COLLABORATE **Summarize** Review with students that readers can use visuals to understand key information. Have partners match each step in the diagram to details in the text. Help students summarize the water cycle: In the water cycle, water is always moving and changing. When water heats up, it changes to vapor. When vapor cools down, it can change to liquid and solid ice.

COLLABORATE **Intermediate** *What word is similar to the word* circle*?* (cycle) Have partners discuss the diagram: The events in a cycle happen over and over. The diagram shows that the water moves over and over in a cycle.

Pages 6–9

Beginning Read with students paragraph 1 on page 6. Help partners describe snowflakes: Snowflakes are made of groups of ice crystals.

COLLABORATE **Intermediate** Have partners describe the shape of ice crystals at very cold and warmer temperatures. (They have a simple shape when it is cold and complicated shapes when warmer.)

Advanced/Advanced High *How do layers of snow build up in polar regions?* (A new layer of snow presses down on an older layer of snow. Snow, dust, and air bubbles get compacted and build up into ice.)

Pages 10–12, Chapter 3

Have partners describe what scientists do to extract ice. (use a drill to cut through the ice; remove the sections)

Beginning Read the first paragraph on page 11 with students. Restate the sentences as needed. *What is an ice core?* (a column of ice)

Intermediate *How are the last two sentences on page 12 similar?* (begin with "If"; have the words "it might") *What do the words tell you?* (They tell what events are possible.)

Respond to Reading Have partners complete their graphic organizers and discuss the questions on page 15.

Fluency: Expression, Intonation, Phrasing

Read pages 11–12 with appropriate expression, intonation, and phrasing. Have students read along with you. For practice, have them record their voices and play their recordings for your feedback.

Paired Read: "Super-Vision"

Make Connections: Write About It

Have students discuss the questions on page 18: Before Mia's vision changed, things looked ordinary, which means normal. After her vision changed, things looked extraordinary because she had microscopic vision. Have students reread page 12. The scientists studied very small things with microscopes.

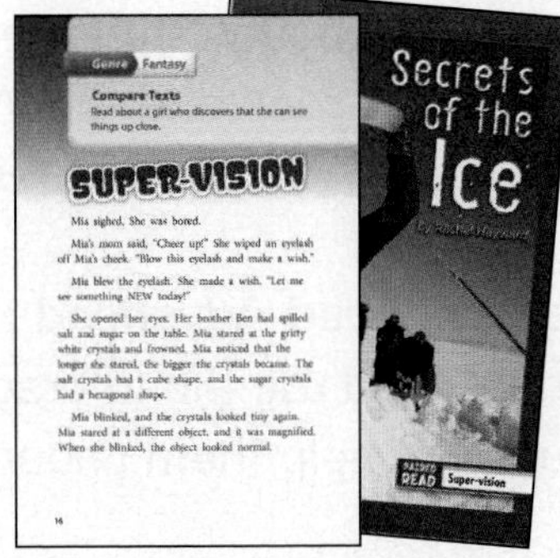

ELL Leveled Reader

Build Knowledge: Make Connections

Talk About the Text Have partners discuss what you can discover when you look closely at something.

Write About the Text Have students add their ideas to their Build Knowledge pages of their reader's notebooks.

Self-Selected Reading

Have students choose an expository text from the **Leveled Reader Library** or read the **Differentiated Text**: "A Close-Up of Our Universe."

FOCUS ON SCIENCE

Have students complete the activity on page 20 to observe a mini water cycle.

LITERATURE CIRCLES

Ask students to conduct a literature circle using the Thinkmark questions to guide the discussion.

FORMATIVE ASSESSMENT

STUDENT CHECK-IN

Have partners share their answers to Respond to Reading. Ask students to reflect on their learning using the Check-In routine.

LEVEL UP

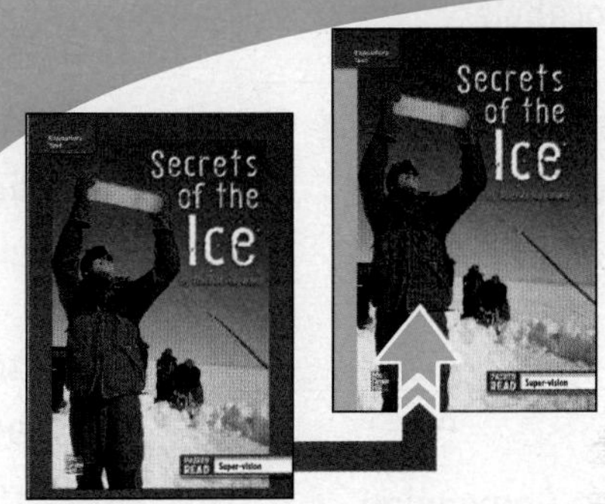

IF students read the **ELL Level** fluently and answered the questions,

THEN pair them with students who have proficiently read the **On Level** and have students:

- read the **On Level** main selection with their partner aloud.
- list words they find difficult.
- discuss these words with their partners.

Access Complex Text

The **On Level** challenges students by including more **domain-specific words** and **complex sentence structures**.

LEARNING GOALS

We can read and understand realistic fiction.

OBJECTIVES

Describe in depth a character, setting, or event in a story or drama, drawing on specific details in the text.

Engage effectively in a range of collaborative discussions with diverse partners on grade 4 topics and texts, building on others' ideas and expressing their own clearly.

Use context as a clue to the meaning of a word or phrase.

LANGUAGE OBJECTIVES

Students will discuss conflict in the plot using key vocabulary.

ELA ACADEMIC LANGUAGE

- *conflict, solution, foreshadow*
- Cognates: *conflicto, solución*

MATERIALS

Reading/Writing Companion, pp. 38–41

Online Scaffolded Shared Read, "Sadie's Game"

Visual Vocabulary Cards

Online ELL Visual Vocabulary Cards

DIGITAL TOOLS

MULTIMODAL

Have students read along with the audio of the selection to develop comprehension and practice fluency and pronunciation.

"Sadie's Game"

Prepare to Read

Build Background Discuss with students examples of things people do to show they care about each other. Ask: *How do you show your family and friends that you care for them?* Have them use their prior experiences to respond using: I show I care by ___. Then discuss some things people do when they argue or fight. *What can you do to apologize or solve the problem?* Discuss with students what they and others do that helped them to resolve the situation using: We can ___ to resolve the problem.

Vocabulary Use the **Visual Vocabulary Cards** to preteach the vocabulary: *express, whirl, emotions, fussy, encircle, bouquet, sparkled,* and *portraits.* Use the online **ELL Visual Vocabulary Cards** to teach additional vocabulary from the Shared Read: *signaling, collided, substitution, preferred, gaze,* and *bowed.*

Set Purpose *Today we will read an historical fiction called "Sadie's Game." As we read, think about the* ways people show they care about each other.

Read the Text

Select the **Scaffolded Shared Read** or the Shared Read in the **Reading/Writing Companion**, based on students' language proficiency.

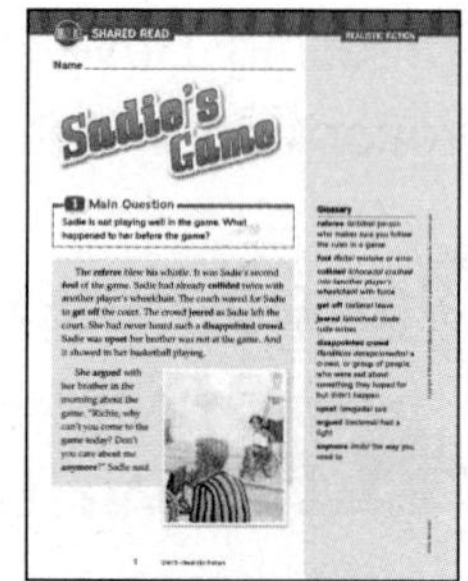

Scaffolded Shared Read, Lexile 660L

Beginning/Early-Intermediate Use the online **Scaffolded Shared Read** to help partners work together to read and understand a realistic fiction story. Remind them to use the Glossary to help them read and the Word Bank to help them answer the Main and Additional Questions.

Intermediate/Advanced Advanced High Read the text with students and use the Interactive Question-Response Routine to help them understand a realistic fiction story.

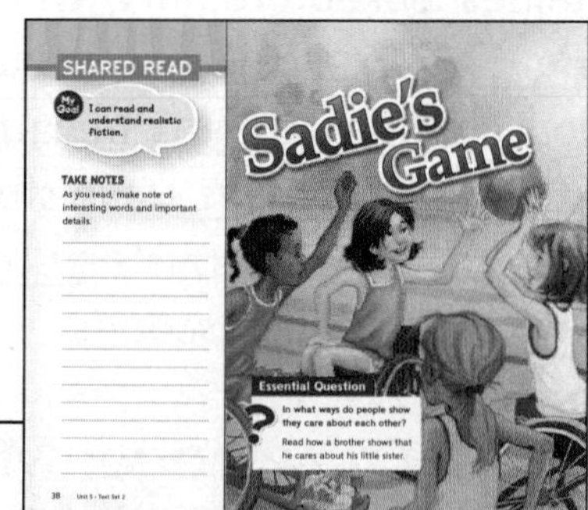

Reading/Writing Companion, Lexile 850L

Page 39

Paragraphs 1–2 Read the text with students and review Vocabulary words *express, whirl, emotions, signaling, collided,* and *substitution. Where is Sadie and what is she doing at the beginning of the story?* (She is at a basketball game and playing in the game.) *Is Sadie playing well in the game? How do you know?* (No. She had two fouls in the game and collided with another player.) *What did the coach do?* (He substituted Sadie with another player.) Explain *catcalls* and *jeered. Imagine you are playing. How do you feel when a crowd shouts catcalls and jeers? I feel ___. How did Sadie feel while she* *watched her teammates play?* (confused) *What happened to Sadie in the morning?* (She argued with her brother.)

COLLABORATE **Intermediate** Have partners identify the words that describe the sound of the whistle and whether or not the sound is pleasant. The whistle sounds like a shrieking bird. The sound of the whistle is/is not pleasant because ___. (Possible answer: the sound of shrieking is not nice.)

Advanced *Which context clue helps you understand the word* foul? ("had already collided twice with another player's wheelchair") *Why did the crowd shout catcalls and jeer?* The crowd is shouting because they are disappointed in Sadie. *Which sentence describes how the crowd felt?* ("She had never seen a crowd express such disappointment before.")

COLLABORATE **Advanced/Advanced High** Have partners restate the sentence "Her emotions were all over the place, and it showed in her basketball playing." (Possible answer: She is feeling confused and she cannot focus on playing the game, so she collided with other players.)

Page 40

Paragraphs 1–4 Plot: Read the text with students and review the Vocabulary words *fussy, encircle, portraits, bouquet, sparkled, preferred, gaze,* and *bowed. Did Sadie and Richie get along in the past? How do you know?* (Yes; Richie taught Sadie to play basketball after her accident.) *How has their relationship changed?* (Richie spends time with his new friends from high school and on his new car.) *What did Sadie do when Richie left, and why?* (She cried because she felt lonely.) *What is the problem, or* ***conflict,*** *now?* (Sadie thinks she is not important to Richie anymore.) *Who does Sadie see in the crowd?* (her mother and brother) *What does Richie do?* (He jogs toward her with a bouquet of flowers.)

COLLABORATE **Intermediate** Have partners describe what Sadie's mother's tells Sadie: Sadie's mother tells Sadie that Richie loves her and still cares for her.

COLLABORATE **Advanced/Advanced High** Have partners discuss the emotions conveyed by the phrases "Sadie's whole world" and "did not want to get out of bed." *What does Richie do after Sadie's accident?* (Richie teaches her to play sports in a wheelchair. He gets Sadie out of bed because he wants her to be happy again.)

Page 41

Paragraphs 1–3 Read the text with students. Discuss the **solution** to Sadie's **conflict**: *What does Richie tell Sadie?* (He tells Sadie that she is his best friend.) *How does this affect Sadie?* (She starts scoring in the game.)

COLLABORATE **Intermediate** Have partners discuss how Sadie feels after Richie gives her the flowers using evidence from the text using: Sadie puts the flowers on her lap while she plays because ___. She starts to score in the game because ___. (Possible answer: She feels happy about being her brother's best friend; she wants to make her bother proud of her.)

Advanced/Advanced High *What does the author tell earlier in the story to* **foreshadow**, *or hint, about how Richie feels about Sadie?* (Possible answer: The author tells that Richie helped Sadie after her accident, when she needed him. This hints that Richie is caring.)

FORMATIVE ASSESSMENT

STUDENT CHECK-IN

Have partners retell the events in the story. Ask them to reflect using the Check-In routine.

LEARNING GOALS

- **We can read and understand realistic fiction by identifying the resolution to the conlict in the plot.**
- **We can identify and use adjectives that compare.**

OBJECTIVES

Paraphrase portions of a text read aloud or information presented in diverse media and formats, including visually, quantitatively, and orally.

Demonstrate command of the conventions of standard English grammar and usage when writing or speaking.

LANGUAGE OBJECTIVES

Students will explain the resolution to the conflict in the plot using academic language.

Students will inform using comparative adjectives in complete sentences.

ELA ACADEMIC LANGUAGE

- *conflict, resolution, adjectives, compare*
- Cognates: *conflicto, resolución, adjetivos, comparar*

MATERIALS

Reading/Writing Companion, pp. 38–41, 42–43

Online Scaffolded Shared Read, "Sadie's Game"

Online Shared Read Writing Frames, p. 14

Online Language Development Cards, 47A–47B

Online Language Development Practice, pp. 277–282

Online Language Transfers Handbook, pp. 15–19

"Sadie's Game"

Text Reconstruction

Focus on a single chunk of text to support comprehension and language development across the four domains.

1. Read aloud paragraph 3 on page 41 in the **Reading/Writing Companion** while students listen.
2. Write the following on the board, providing definitions as needed: *rested, lap, court, bouquet, sidelines, opponent, dribbled, shots.* Instruct students to listen for them as you read the paragraph a second time.
3. Read the paragraph a third time. Tell students to listen and take notes.
4.  COLLABORATE Have students work with a partner to reconstruct the text from their notes. Help them write complete sentences as needed.
5. Have students look at the original text. Ask: *What is the paragraph mostly about?* (Sadie's brother gave her flowers and she played the rest of the game with them on her lap.) Discuss that a conflict is a problem in the story and that it has a resolution. Sadie's conflict is that she doesn't feel important to her brother Richie anymore. Students will identify how the conflict was resolved.
6. *What did Sadie think Richie should say to her?* ("I'm sorry.") *What did Richie do instead?* (He came to her basketball game and gave her flowers.) *How did the flowers make Sadie feel?* (happy) *What did Sadie do with the flowers?* (She played the rest of the game with them on her lap.) *How did Richie show Sadie's game was important to him?* (he stayed and watched from the sidelines) *What details show you that the conflict was resolved?* (Possible answer: Sadie started to play better when her brother came to her game.)
7. Have students compare their text reconstructions to the original text. Have them check whether they also included words that describe conflict in the plot and resolution.

Beginning Have students follow along in the Reading/Writing Companion as you read the text aloud. Have them circle the words from Step 2 as they hear them.

Grammar in Context: Adjectives That Compare

Notice the Form Display this sentence from the text, and underline the adjectives.

> *"It's great to have a lot of new friends, but I realized that you're my best friend."*

What kinds of words are the underlined words? (adjectives) *What do adjectives do?* (describe nouns and pronouns) Review that we also use adjectives to compare two or more things. Point to the word *best* and discuss that it is the superlative form of the adjective *good.* Write on the board: *good, better,* and *best.* Provide a model, such as: Apples are *good,* but bananas are *better* than apples. Grapes are *best.* Point out that we can use *good* to describe one thing; *better* to compare two things; and *best* to compare more than two things. Read the sentence again with students. *What does the adjective* best *describe?* (friends) *Who does Richie compare?* (his new friends and his sister) *Who is his best friend?* (his sister) Then have students copy the sentence and label the adjectives in their notebooks.

Apply and Extend Have partners write a sentence using adjectives that compare to describe an object. Check their answers and provide corrective feedback.

For additional practice, see **Language Development Cards**, Lessons 47A–47B, and **Language Development Practice**, pages 277–282.

Independent Time

Vocabulary Building Have students build glossaries.

Beginning/Early Intermediate Have students complete the Glossary Activities in the **Scaffolded Shared Read**.

Intermediate/Advanced/Advanced High Have students add the vocabulary from **Reading/Writing Companion** pages 42–43 and self-selected words or phrases they would like to learn to the chart.

WORD	DEFINITION	SENTENCE FROM THE TEXT
nook	a hidden corner or place	Richie polished every little nook of his new car.

Mixed Levels Have students at different proficiency levels work together to learn vocabulary: Beginning and Early-Intermediate students can teach each other vocabulary from their Scaffolded Shared Read glossaries. Intermediate and Advanced/Advanced High students can teach each other their self-selected words.

COLLABORATE **Shared Read Writing Frames** Use the online leveled **Shared Read Writing Frames** for "Sadie's Game" to provide students with additional oral and written practice. Differentiated frames are available to provide support for all levels.

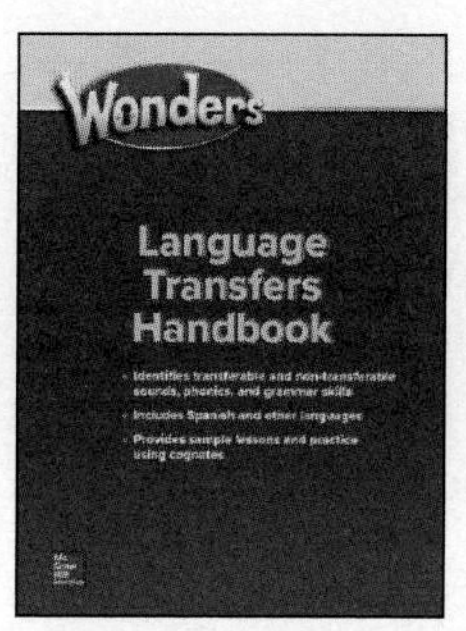

Language Transfers Handbook, Grammar Transfers, pp. 15–19

DIGITAL TOOLS

For additional support, use the online activities.

Grammar Video

Grammar Song

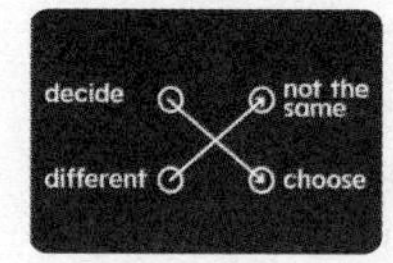

Vocabulary Activity

FORMATIVE ASSESSMENT

STUDENT CHECK-IN

Text Reconstruction Ask partners to share their notes. Have students reflect using the Check-In routine.

Grammar in Context Ask partners to share their sentences. Have students reflect using the Check-In routine.

LEARNING GOALS

- **Read** We can apply strategies and skills to read realistic fiction.
- **Reread** We can analyze text, craft, and structure and compare texts.

OBJECTIVES

Describe in depth a character, setting, or event in a story or drama, drawing on specific details in the text.

Demonstrate understanding of figurative language, word relationships, and nuances in word meanings.

Engage effectively in a range of collaborative discussions with diverse partners on grade 4 topics and texts, building on others' ideas and expressing their own clearly.

LANGUAGE OBJECTIVES

Students will inquire about the story by answering questions using key vocabulary.

ELA ACADEMIC LANGUAGE

- *simile, figurative language, visualize, inferences, illustration*
- Cognates: *símil, inferencia, ilustración*

MATERIALS

Literature Anthology, pp. 386-401

Reading/Writing Companion, pp. 50-52

Visual Vocabulary Cards

Online ELL Anchor Text Support BLMs, pp. 34-36

DIGITAL TOOLS

MULTIMODAL

Have students read along as they listen to the audio of the selection to develop comprehension and practice fluency and pronunciation.

Mama, I'll Give You the World

Prepare to Read

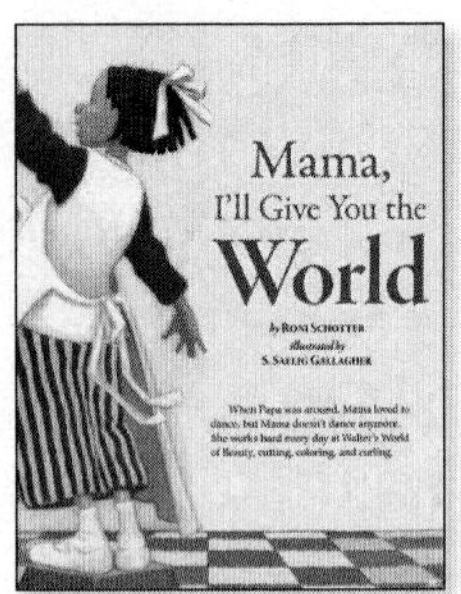

Literature Anthology, Lexile 970L

Build Background Tell students they will read a story that takes place at a beauty salon. Have them talk about what happens at beauty salons or barber shops.

Vocabulary Use the **Visual Vocabulary Cards** to review *bouquet, emotion, encircle, express, fussy, portraits, sparkles, whirl.*

Set Purpose *Today we will read about a girl named Luisa and how she plans a special surprise for her mother. As we read, think about how people show they care for others.*

 Have students listen to the audio summary of the text, which is available in multiple languages.

Read

Literature Anthology, pp. 386–401

Use the **Interactive Question-Response Routine** to help students read and discuss *Mama, I'll Give You the World.*

Beginning Help students discuss in complete sentences. Provide sentence frames: Luisa plans a surprise party for her mother's birthday.

Intermediate Ask students to respond in complete sentences and add details. Provide sentence starters as needed: Luisa shows she cares for her mother by planning a surprise party.

Advanced/Advanced High Have students respond in complete sentences and add details.

Independent Reading Practice Have mixed level pairs complete pages 34-36 of **ELL Anchor Text Support BLMs** and share with the group.

Reread

Use with the **Reading/Writing Companion**, pages 50–52.

Literature Anthology, page 389

COLLABORATE **Author's Craft: Figurative Language** Elicit that authors use figurative language to help their readers visualize and understand ideas. Review that authors often use figurative language to compare something to something else. Say, *One way authors do this is by using a **simile**. A simile compares two things using the words* like *or* as. Discuss what has happened so far in the story. Then, reread the text with students, and have them ask about words or phrases they don't understand. Reread the first sentence. Elicit that the reader knows that something is being compared because of the word *like*.

Beginning Read the first sentence with students and discuss what magicians do. Elicit from students that they change things. Have students describe the simile. *What does Mama do?* Mama changes the color of Mrs. Koo's hair. *How is Mama like a magician?* Mama changes the color of hair like a magician.

Intermediate Have partners describe what the simile compares in the second paragraph: The author compares Mama's work to the work of a magician. *How do you know this is a simile?* The comparison has the word like. *Why does the author use the simile?* The simile describes how Mama changes Mrs. Koo's hair color. *What does Luisa write about?* A girl with a magic brush. *What does that tell about Mama and Luisa's relationship?* (possible answer: Luisa is proud of her Mama.)

Advanced/Advanced High *What does Luisa write about?* (a girl with a magic brush that takes away people's worries) *What does Luisa's story tell you about how she feels about Mama's work?* Have partners discuss who they think the girl with a magic brush might be about. (Possible answer: I think the story is about Mama because Mama is like a magician and the girl has a magic brush.)

Literature Anthology, pp. 394–395

COLLABORATE **Author's Craft: Make Inferences** Read the text with students. Discuss with them the meaning of the expression "I will give the world to you." *Who uses the expression?* (Mama and Luisa) *What does the expression mean?* (give someone everything the person wants) Have partners describe what the expression tells about how Luisa and Mama feel about each other. (Possible answer: They love each other and want to give the best of everything.)

Page 395 *What does Luisa ask Mama to do?* (put on a dress) *Why does Luisa say she needs to go back to the World?* (Luisa left her book at the World.)

Beginning Read Paragraphs 4–7 with students. Restate the sentences as needed. Discuss the meaning of the word *pretend* and elicit that it means to act as if something is true. *What does Luisa pretend to do?* Luisa pretends to look for a book. *Did she really leave her book at the World?* (no)

Intermediate *Does Mama want to put on a dress? What clues tell you?* (No. At first, Mama tells her no and that she is tired.) *Does Mama want to go back to the World? What clues tell you?* (No. At first, Mama tells Luisa to wait until tomorrow.)

Literature Anthology, page 399

COLLABORATE **Illustrator's Craft** Have students look at the illustration. *How do you think Luisa and Mama feel? How do you know?* (Possible answers: happy; They are smiling.) *What does Mama ask Luisa?* (She asks Luisa to dance with her.) *How is this different from before?* (It is different because now Mama wants to dance.)

Beginning Have student's look at Mama's face and describe how she feels. *What does Mama do? Mama* smiles. Repeat for Luisa. *What does Luisa do? Luisa* smiles *too. Are they happy?* (yes) *What does Mama ask Luisa?* Mama asks Luisa to dance with her.

Intermediate *How does the illustration show how Mama feels now?* The illustration shows that Mama is happy. She is smiling and wants to dance.

Advanced/Advanced High Have students discuss how the illustration shows how Mama's feelings have changed. (Possible answer: In the beginning, Mama did not smile often, but now she is happy and asks Luisa to dance.)

FORMATIVE ASSESSMENT

STUDENT CHECK-IN

Read Have partners share their responses to the Anchor Text questions. Then have them reflect using the Check-In routine.

Reread Have partners share responses and text evidence on Reading/Writing Companion pages 50–52. Then have them reflect using the Check-In routine to fill in the bars.

LEARNING GOALS

- **We can read and understand realistic fiction by identifying the resolution to the conflict in the plot.**
- **We can identify and use adjectives that compare.**

OBJECTIVES

Paraphrase portions of a text read aloud or information presented in diverse media and formats, including visually, quantitatively, and orally.

Demonstrate command of the conventions of standard English grammar and usage when writing or speaking.

LANGUAGE OBJECTIVES

Students will discuss the resolution to conflict using academic language.

Students will inquire about adjectives that compare by analyzing the parts of a sentence.

ELA ACADEMIC LANGUAGE

- *conflict, resolution, adjective, comparative, superlative*
- Cognates: *conflicto, resolución, adjetivo, comparativo, superlativo*

MATERIALS

Literature Anthology, pp. 386–401

Online Language Development Cards, 46B

Online Language Development Practice, pp. 274–276

Online Language Transfers Handbook, pp. 15–19

Mama, I'll Give You the World

Text Reconstruction

Focus on a single chunk of text to support comprehension and language development across the four domains.

1. Read aloud pages 396 and 397 in the **Literature Anthology** while students listen.
2. Write the following on the board, providing definitions as needed: *dark, portraits dance along the walls, mirrors, lights, wink.* Instruct students to listen for them as you read the paragraphs a second time.
3. Read the paragraphs a third time while students listen and take notes.
4. COLLABORATE Have students work with a partner to reconstruct the text from their notes. Help them write complete sentences as needed.
5. Have students look at the original text. Ask students what is being described. (Mama's surprise party at the World.) Discuss with students Luisa's conflict that she wanted to plan a surprise birthday party for her mother, who was tired and sad. Tell students they are going to identify details that show how Luisa resolved the conflict.
6. *What words show how Luisa feels when Mama opens the door?* ("Luisa holds her breath"; she feels anticipation) *What happens when Mama turns on the lights?* (Music turns on; she sees the surprise party) *What do the phrases "portraits dance along the walls" and "tiny lights that wink like eyes" tell you?* (Possible answers: the party is exciting and special.) *Who is at the party?* (Mama's favorite customers.) *What shows that Luisa resolved the conflict in the story?* (Mama is smiling and happy.)
7. Have students compare their text reconstructions to the original text. Have them check whether they also included words that describe conflict in the plot and resolution.

Beginning Allow students to follow along in the Literature Anthology as you read the text aloud. Have them point to the words from Step 2 as they hear them.

Apply Author's Craft: Figurative Language

Review with students that a simile is a comparison using *like* or *as.* Have students write their own descriptions using a simile. Model first: *On page 393, what is Mrs. Fogelman's fluffy hair compared to?* (a great, gray cloud) Have students select a character and write a description of the character's hair using a simile. Provide sentence frames: Mrs. Fogelman's hair is as high as a cloud. Mrs. Rodriguez's hair is smooth like satin.

Grammar in Context: Deconstruct a Sentence

Write this sentence from page 395: *At home that evening Luisa asks Mama to try on her prettiest dress.* Facilitate deconstructing this sentence for better comprehension.

- *What kind of word is* prettiest*?* (adjective) *What does this word do?* (It describes the word *dress,* telling us *what kind* or *which one.*) *Does the word* prettiest *make a comparison with other dresses?* (yes)
- Discuss with students that we can use adjectives to make comparisons. Write on the board: *pretty, prettier,* and *prettiest. Which adjective do we use to describe one dress?* (pretty) *two dresses?* (prettier) *three or more dresses?* (prettiest) Write comparisons on the board: *The red dress is pretty, but the blue dress is prettier. The yellow dress is the prettiest.* Discuss that prettier compares the red and blue dresses and prettiest compares all the dresses. *What are the adjectives* prettier *and* prettiest *called?* (comparative, superlative)
- Review with students how to form comparative and superlative adjectives: adding *-er* or the word *more/less* for comparative and adding *-est* or the word *most/least*. Review the comparative forms for *good* and *bad*.

For additional practice, see **Language Development Cards**, Lesson 46B, and **Language Development Practice**, pages 274–276.

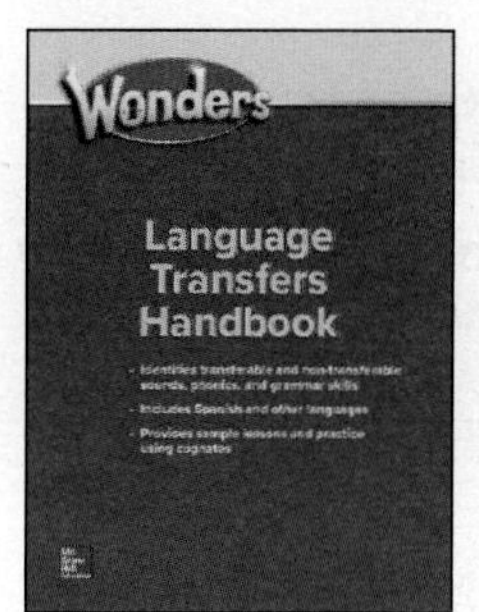

Language Transfers Handbook, Grammar Transfers, pp. 15–19

Independent Time

Vocabulary Building Have partners copy words that describe feelings from the selection onto index cards. On the back, have them write antonyms and synonyms. Have partners take turns selecting a card and using the word in a sentence while others confirm proper use of the word.

Beginning Allow students to add visual clues.

Intermediate/Advanced/Advanced High Have students include some of the self-selected words and content-area words they added to their glossaries.

Compare with Adjectives Have partners generate adjectives they know to add to the chart. Have them write comparative and superlative forms of the adjectives. Have students include comparative forms for *good* and *bad*. Have them write sentences using the adjectives to compare. Check their work and provide corrective feedback.

ADJECTIVES	COMPARATIVE ADJECTIVES	SUPERLATIVE ADJECTIVES
quick	quicker	quickest
beautiful	more/less beautiful	most/least beautiful

FORMATIVE ASSESSMENT

STUDENT CHECK-IN

Text Reconstruction Have partners share their notes. Have students reflect on their work using the Check-In routine.

Grammar in Context Have partners reflect on their deconstructions using the Check-In routine.

LEARNING GOALS

We can apply strategies and skills to read realistic fiction.

OBJECTIVES

Describe in depth a character, setting, or event in a story or drama, drawing on specific details in the text.

Demonstrate understanding of figurative language, word relationships, and nuances in word meanings.

Engage effectively in a range of collaborative discussions with diverse partners on grade 4 topics and texts, building on others' ideas and expressing their own clearly.

LANGUAGE OBJECTIVES

Students will discuss figurative language in the story using key vocabulary.

ELA ACADEMIC LANGUAGE

- *simile, metaphor, foreshadowing, predict, plot, conflict*
- Cognates: *símil, metáfora, predecir, conflicto*

MATERIALS

Online ELL Genre Passage, "The Stray Dog"

"The Stray Dog"

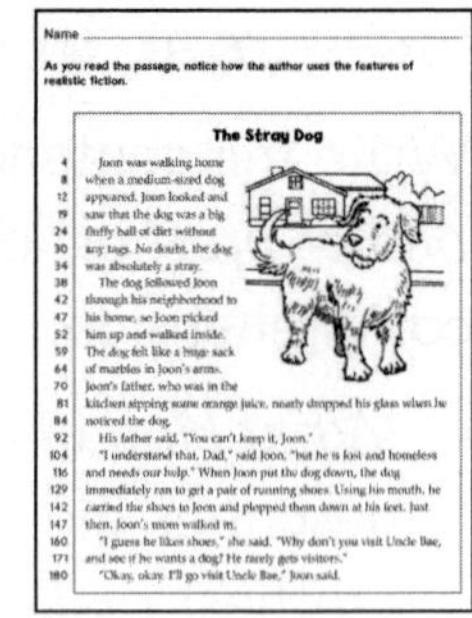

Genre Passage
Lexile 820L

Prepare to Read

Build Background Read the title with students. Explain that a stray animal is an animal without a home. Discuss reasons why the animal may be a stray, such as being lost. Explain to students that they will read about a boy who sees a stray dog.

Vocabulary Use the Define, Example, Ask routine to pre-teach difficult words or unfamiliar concepts, such as *tags, marbles, hint, leash,* and *relative* (Cognates: *mármol, relativo*). Invite students to add new vocabulary to their glossaries.

Set Purpose *Today we will read a realistic fiction story called "The Stray Dog." As we read, think about the ways people show they care about each other.*

Read the Text

Page E1, Paragraphs 1–2

COLLABORATE **Figurative Language** Review figurative language with students. *Two types of figurative language are simile and metaphor. Simile and metaphor compare two things that are not the same.* Have partners identify examples of figurative language that describe the dog: The dog was a big fluffy ball of dirt. The dog felt like a huge sack of marbles.

Beginning Read the first paragraph with students and restate sentences as needed. *What does Joon find?* (a dog) *What does the dog look like?* The dog looks like a fluffy ball of dirt. This means the dog's fur was covered with dirt.

Intermediate *A simile uses the words* like *or* as. *What is the simile?* (The dog felt like a huge sack of marbles.) *What does the simile show about the dog?* It shows that the dog feels very heavy and is hard to carry.

Advanced/Advanced High *Why do you think the author compares the dog to a big fluffy ball of dirt?* (The dog's eyes or legs may not be visible behind the dirty fur.)

Page E1, Paragraphs 3–6

Plot: Conflict *What is the dog's problem?* (The dog doesn't have a home.) Review with students that the conflict is something a main character wants to do. *What is the conflict?* Joon wants to help the dog find a home.

COLLABORATE **Beginning** Read the paragraphs with students and restate the sentences as needed. Help partners describe how Joon's parents reacted to the dog: *What does Joon's father tell him?* Joon cannot keep the dog. *What advice does Joon's mom have?* Joon can ask if Uncle Bae wants a dog.

Intermediate *What does Joon say is the problem?* Joon says the dog is "lost and homeless and needs our help."

Advanced/Advanced High *Have partners describe the family's reaction to the dog.* (Joon's father says Joon cannot keep the dog. Joon's mom suggests that Joon go and ask his uncle if he wants the dog.)

Page E2, Paragraphs 1–3

Beginning Read the first paragraph with students and restate sentences as needed. *What kind of person is Uncle Bae?* He is not friendly. He is angry.

Intermediate Have partners identify and explain the figurative language: A simile compares Uncle Bae to a block of ice. This means Joon thinks Uncle Bae is not very friendly. *What other words do you think might describe Uncle Bae?* (Possible answers: not warm or caring, grumpy)

Advanced/Advanced High Have students read the last sentence. *What can you predict about what happens next?* (Possible answer: Uncle Bae looks unhappy, so he probably doesn't want the dog.)

Page E2, Paragraphs 4–6

Beginning Read the last paragraph with students and restate the sentences as needed. *What does the dog do?* The dog gets the shoes. *What does uncle Bae do?* He smiles at the dog. *What does the Uncle decide to do?* Uncle Bae decides to keep the dog.

Intermediate Have partners describe how Uncle Bae reacts: *How does Uncle Bae react to the dog at first?* (He is not happy.) *What changes his mind?* He sees the dog bring him his shoes.

Advanced/Advanced High Read the last sentence. *What does the text tell you about what will happen next?* (Uncle Bae will keep the dog because he asks Joon about a name to call the dog.)

Respond to Reading

Use the following instruction to help students answer the questions on page E3.

1. **Figurative Language** *Read the first paragraph. What does "big fluffy ball of dirt" refer to?* (the dog's fur) *What kind of dogs have tags?* (dogs with homes, not stray dogs)
2. **Literary Elements: Foreshadowing** *Reread paragraph 4 on page E1. What does the dog do?* (The dog carried shoes to Joon.) *What is Uncle Bae's challenge?* (He cannot see well.) *How do you think the dog could help Uncle Bae?* I think Uncle Bae can't see where he left his shoes. This means the dog could help Uncle Bae find things.
3. *What words compare Uncle Bae to something else?* (*as warm as a block of ice*) *What does that tell you about Uncle Bae?* (He is not warm or kind.)

Fluency Have partners take turns reading the passage.

Build Knowledge: Make Connections

Talk About the Text Have partners discuss the ways people show they care about each other.

Write About the Text Have students add their ideas to their Build Knowledge pages of their reader's notebooks.

FORMATIVE ASSESSMENT

STUDENT CHECK-IN

Have partners share their responses on page E3. Ask students to reflect using the Check-In routine.

LEVEL UP

IF students read the **ELL Level** of the **Genre Passage** fluently and answered the questions,

THEN pair them with students who have proficiently read the **On Level**. Have them

- partner read the **On Level** passage.
- summarize a **problem** described in the text and identify its **solution**.

LEARNING GOALS

We can apply strategies and skills to read realistic fiction.

OBJECTIVES

Describe in depth a character, setting, or event in a story or drama, drawing on specific details in the text.

Engage effectively in a range of collaborative discussions with diverse partners on grade 4 topics and texts, building on others' ideas and expressing their own clearly.

Read grade-level text with purpose and understanding.

LANGUAGE OBJECTIVES

Students will discuss conflict in the plot using complete sentences.

ELA ACADEMIC LANGUAGE

- *conflict, resolution, character, visualize*
- Cognates: *conflicto, resolución, visualizar*

MATERIALS

ELL Leveled Reader: *The Perfect Present*

Online Differentiated Texts: "The Contest"

Visual Vocabulary Cards

DIGITAL TOOLS

MULTIMODAL

Have students read along with the audio of the selections to develop comprehension and practice fluency and pronunciation.

The Perfect Present

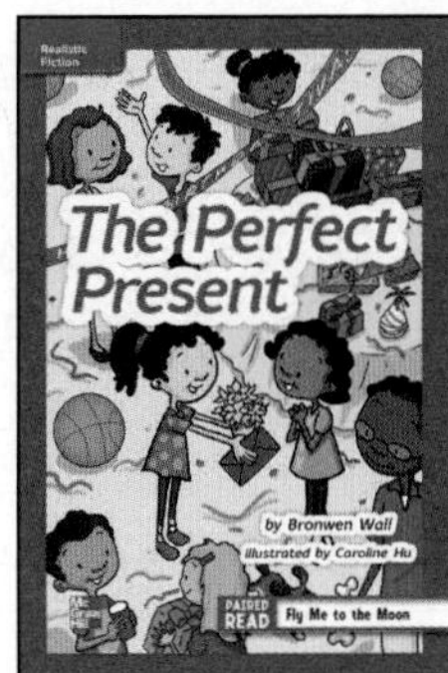

Leveled Reader
Lexile 560L

Build Background

Build Background Read the title aloud. Talk with students about the multiple meanings and pronunciations of *present*. Have students talk about the presents in the cover illustration. Clarify that *gift* is another word for *present*. Talk with students about reasons people give or receive presents and gifts. Invite students to talk about the favorite things to give and receive, and to share other ways people can show they care about each other. Then ask: *What do you think this text will be about?*

Vocabulary Use the routine on the **Visual Vocabulary Cards** to pre-teach ELL vocabulary *appreciated* and *coordination*. Discuss the vocabulary in context. Invite students to add new vocabulary to their glossaries.

Set Purpose *Today we will read a realistic fiction text called "The Perfect Present". As we read, think about the ways people show they care about each other.*

Read the Text

Pages 3–4

Conflict Review that a story's conflict is something a main character wants to change or do. *How does the ballet teacher want Tiva to dance?* (like swans) *How does Tiva want to dance?* (She wants to leap around.) *Describe Tiva's problem.* Tiva does not want to take ballet lessons. Instead, she wants to try Irish dancing.

Beginning *What sports does Tiva play?* She usually plays baseball or basketball. *Did Tiva like her ballet lesson?* (no) *Does Tiva want to try Irish dancing?* (yes)

Intermediate *Why does Tiva's mom want her to take ballet?* Tiva's mom thinks ballet will improve her balance and coordination to become a better athlete.

Pages 8–10

Beginning Read page 8 with students and restate sentences as needed. *What does Maggie make?* Maggie makes a birthday card. *What is another word for portraits?* (photos)

COLLABORATE **Advanced/Advanced High** Have partners describe the compliment Maggie received and discuss the meaning of *appreciated.* (Possible answer: Maggie's brother tells Maggie that she did a great job on the card. Maggie feels glad and thankful about the compliment.)

Pages 14–15

Visualize *Describe the illustration*: Maggie is giving Tiva flowers and an envelope. *What sentence helps you visualize what happens next?* (*Maggie held her breath when Tiva opened the envelope.*) *What does this show?* Maggie feels nervous.

Intermediate Help students visualize Tiva's reaction: Tiva's arms encircle Maggie. In other words, Tiva hugs Maggie. Tiva says a dance lesson is so cool and is a perfect present. It shows Tiva feels happy.

Advanced/Advanced High *What details show how Tiva feels about the present?* (*so cool; perfect present*)

COLLABORATE **Plot: Conflict** Help partners talk about the plot: *What is Tiva's conflict?* (Tiva wants to try Irish dancing instead of ballet.) *What is Maggie's conflict?* (Maggie wants to give Tiva the perfect present.) Help students describe what leads to a resolution for both girls. (Maggie gives Tiva a free Irish dance lesson as a gift.)

COLLABORATE **Respond to Reading** Have partners complete their graphic organizers and answer the questions on page 16.

Fluency: Expression, Intonation, Phrasing

Read pages 4–5 with appropriate expression, intonation, and phrasing. Read it again and have students read it with you. For practice, have students record their voices a few times and then choose the best one.

Paired Read: "Fly Me to the Moon"

Make Connections: Write About It

Use the sentence frames to discuss the questions on page 19: *What problem do Toby and Poppa have?* Toby feels angry. Poppa feels grumpy. *What tells you Toby cares?* Toby thinks about the next visit. *Reread paragraphs 1–3 on page 15. What does each character do to show that he or she cares?* Maggie gives Tiva a thoughtful gift. Tiva hugs and thanks Maggie.

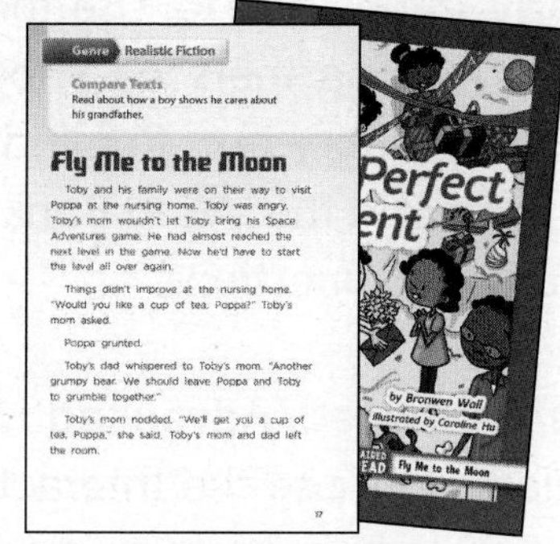

ELL Leveled Reader

Build Knowledge: Make Connections

Talk About the Text Have partners discuss the ways people show they care about each other.

Write About the Text Have students add their ideas to their Build Knowledge pages of their reader's notebooks.

Self-Selected Reading

Have students choose another realistic fiction text from the online **Leveled Reader Library** or the **Differentiated Text:** "The Contest."

FOCUS ON GENRE

Have students complete the activity on page 20 to discuss the story elements of realistic fiction.

LITERATURE CIRCLES

Ask students to conduct a literature circle using the Thinkmark questions to guide the discussion.

FORMATIVE ASSESSMENT

STUDENT CHECK-IN

Have partners share their answers to Respond to Reading. Ask students to reflect on their learning using the Check-In routine.

LEVEL UP

IF students read the **ELL Level** fluently and answered the questions,

THEN pair them with students who have proficiently read the **On Level** and have students

- read the **On Level** main selection aloud with their partner.
- list words they find difficult.
- discuss the words with their partners.

Access Complex Text

The **On Level** challenges students by including more **domain-specific words** and **complex sentence structures.**

LEARNING GOALS

We can read and understand an expository text.

OBJECTIVES

Determine the central, or main, idea of a text and explain how it is supported by key details; summarize the text.

Describe the overall structure of events, ideas, concepts, or information in a text or part of a text.

Engage effectively in a range of collaborative discussions with diverse partners on grade 4 topics and texts, building on others' ideas and expressing their own clearly.

LANGUAGE OBJECTIVES

Students will inform about the events in Jamestown using chronology words.

ELA ACADEMIC LANGUAGE

- *chronology, proverb, sidebar, summarize*
- Cognates: *cronología, proverbio*

MATERIALS

Reading/Writing Companion, pp. 64–67

Online Scaffolded Shared Read, "The Founding of Jamestown"

Visual Vocabulary Cards

Online ELL Visual Vocabulary Cards

DIGITAL TOOLS

MULTIMODAL

Have students read along with the audio of the selection to develop comprehension and practice fluency and pronunciation.

"The Founding of Jamestown"

Prepare to Read

Build Background Discuss with students what they know about the first English settlements in the United States. Have students discuss what they know about what life was like in the first settlements, including Jamestown.

Vocabulary Use the **ELL Visual Vocabulary Cards** to review the vocabulary: *expedition, permanent, tremendous, era, evidence, archaeology, document,* and *uncover* (cognates: expedición, permanente, tremendo, era, evidencia, documento). Use the online **Visual Vocabulary Cards** to teach additional vocabulary from the Shared Read: *artifacts, challenges, endanger, experienced, expert,* and *scarce.* (Cognates: *artefactos, experto*)

Set Purpose *Today we will read an expository text called "The Founding of Jamestown." As we read, think about how learning about the past can help you understand the present.*

Read the Text

Select the **Scaffolded Shared Read** or the Shared Read in the **Reading/Writing Companion**, based on students' language proficiency.

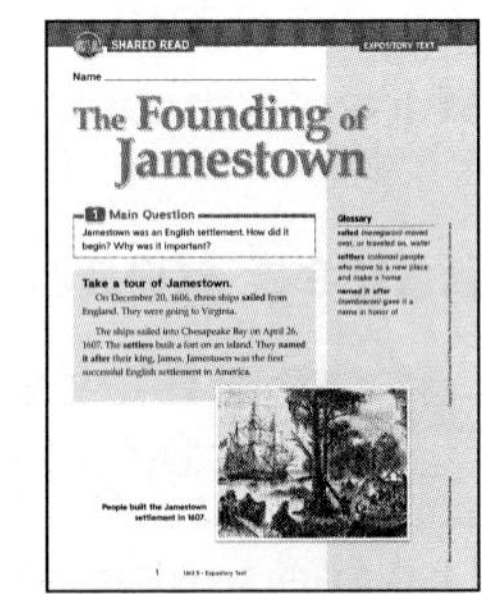

Scaffolded Shared Read, Lexile 740L

Beginning/Early-Intermediate Use the online **Scaffolded Shared Read** to help partners work together to read and understand an expository text. Remind them to use the Glossary to help them read and the Word Bank to help them answer the Main and Additional Questions.

Intermediate/Advanced/Advanced High Read the text with students and use the Interactive Question-Response Routine to help them understand an expository text.

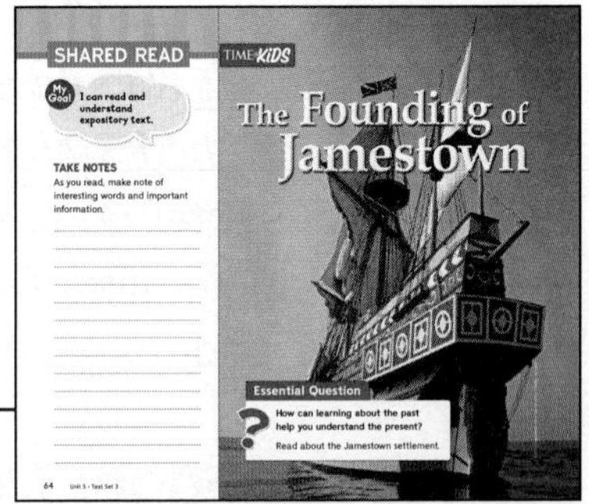

Reading/Writing Companion, Lexile 930L

Page 65

Paragraphs 1–2 Read the text with students and review the Vocabulary words *expedition, permanent* and *scarce. What are the* Susan Constant, Godspeed, *and* Discovery? (names of ships in the expedition) *Where did the people come from?* (London, England) *Where are they going?* (Virginia) *Where did they arrive?* (Chesapeake Bay) *What kind of place is the settlement?* (an island in a river) *What did the people do first?* (They built a fort.) *Why did the people call the place Jamestown?* (They named it after King James.)

Have partners describe the events of the expedition in a sequence or **chronology:** *The expedition began on* December 20, 1606, from

London, England. They traveled for four months. For a while, they thought they were lost. Then on April 26, 1607, they reached Chesapeake Bay.

Advanced/Advanced High *What does the word* permanent *tell you about what people planned to do?* (Possible answer: They planned to make a home.)

Paragraph 3 Review the Vocabulary words *tremendous* and *challenges*. Help students understand the meaning of the **proverb** "ignorance is bliss." *What problems did the settlers have?* (Water was not safe to drink. Native Americans did not like the settlers taking their land.) *What is another word for* challenges*?* (Possible answer: problems, difficulties)

Intermediate *What was scarce?* (food) *If the settlers had known more about where they were going, what could they have done differently?* (Possible answer: Some people may not have gone there, or they could have prepared differently.)

COLLABORATE **Advanced/Advanced High** Have partners discuss the meaning of the proverb "ignorance is bliss" and why the author uses it to describe the settlers. (Possible answer: The settlers did not know how hard it would be to survive. If they had known, they may not have decided to leave England.)

Page 66

Paragraphs 1–2 Read the text with students and review Vocabulary words *experienced* and *endanger*. *What words does the author use to describe John Smith?* (leader of the colony, experienced military man, tough) *What rule did he tell the colonists to follow?* ("He that will not work, shall not eat.") *Who is Chief Powhatan and Pocahontas?* (Native American leader of the western Chesapeake area and his daughter) *What is an* ally*?* (a friend)

COLLABORATE **Intermediate** Have partners discuss whether the expression "He that will not work, shall not eat" is a good rule to follow for the colonists: I think the expression is/is not a good rule because _____.

Sidebar Read the text with students and review the Vocabulary word *era*. Define *bound* as needed. *Who did Pocahontas save?* (John Smith) *Why was the marriage between John Rolfe and Pocahontas unusual?* (It was the first marriage in that time between an Englishman and a Native American.)

Page 67

Paragraphs 1–3 Read the text with students and review Vocabulary words *evidence, archaeology, document, uncover, artifacts,* and *expert*. *What does the heading "Taking a Closer Look" mean?* (studying or observing) *What time period does the text describe?* (present) *What did the archaeologists find?* (artifacts, remains of a fort, burial grounds, records) *What kind of government got started there?* (representative government)

Intermediate Review the meaning of *archaeology*. Then ask students the meaning of *archaeologist*. *What words give details about what archaeologists do in Jamestown?* (digging, discovered, worked, document, uncover, mapped out)

Advanced/Advanced High Have students distinguish the meanings of the words *colony, colonists,* and *colonial*. Have them reread sentences that have these words on pages 66 and 67 to find and use context clues.

COLLABORATE Have students **summarize** what archaeologists learned about Jamestown: The archaeologists discovered artifacts and evidence in the fort. These objects are evidence that the settlers and the Native Americans had a close relationship. They also found records that showed that the first representative government started in Jamestown.

FORMATIVE ASSESSMENT

STUDENT CHECK-IN

Have partners retell the events of the text. Ask them to reflect using the Check-In routine.

LEARNING GOALS

- **We can use read and understand expository text by identifying the chronological text structure.**
- **We can compare using *Good*.**

OBJECTIVES

Paraphrase portions of a text read aloud or information presented in diverse media and formats, including visually, quantitatively, and orally.

Demonstrate command of the conventions of standard English grammar and usage when writing or speaking.

LANGUAGE OBJECTIVES

Students will discuss chronology in the text using signal words.

Students will inquire about using the adjectives good and bad.

ELA ACADEMIC LANGUAGE

- *signal, chronology, adjectives, compare*
- Cognates: *señal, cronología, adjetivos, comparar*

MATERIALS

Reading/Writing Companion, pp. 64-67, 68-69

Online Shared Read Writing Frames, "The Founding of Jamestown"

Online Shared Read Writing Frames, p. 15

Online Language Development Cards, 47B

Online Language Development Practice, pp. 280-282

Online Language Transfers Handbook, pp. 15-19

"The Founding of Jamestown"

Text Reconstruction

Focus on a single chunk of text to support comprehension and language development across the four domains.

1. Read aloud paragraphs 1 and 2 on page 65 in the **Reading/Writing Companion** while students listen.
2. Write the following words on the board, providing definitions as needed: *sailed, expedition, bound, voyager, fort, permanent,* and *settlement.* Instruct students to listen for them as you read the paragraphs a second time.
3. Read the paragraphs a third time. Tell students to listen and take notes.
4.  COLLABORATE Have students work with a partner to reconstruct the text from their notes. Help them write complete sentences as needed.
5. Have students look at the original text. Ask them to tell what the paragraphs are mostly about. (Voyagers sailed from London, England and made the first English settlement in Chesapeake Bay.) Tell students they are going to identify signal words that show chronology in the text.
6. *When did The Susan Constant, the Godspeed, and the Discovery sail to Virginia?* (on December 20, 1606) *When did they land?* (on *April 26, 1607)* *What word tells you that the trip took a long time?* (finally) *What does the word "later" tell you?* (Some time passed after the people landed.) *What happened later?* (The people built a permanent settlement in Jamestown.) *Why is Jamestown important?* (It was the first successful permanent English settlement in the New World.)
7. Have students compare their text reconstructions to the original text. Have them check whether they included words that signal chronology and tell the correct order of events.

Beginning Have students follow along in the Reading/Writing Companion as you read the text aloud. Have them circle the words from Step 2 as they hear them.

Grammar in Context: Comparing with *Good* and *Bad*

Notice the Form Display this sentence from the text, and circle the adjectives.

> *In the words of one voyager, they found "fair meadows and goodly tall trees."*

What do the circled words have in common? (They are adjectives.) *What do adjectives do?* (They describe nouns.) *What does the word* one *tell about* voyager*?* (how many, which voyager) *What does* fair *tell about* meadows*?* (how the meadow looks) *What does* tall *tell about* trees*?* (size) Underline the word *goodly* and explain that it is an adverb that is no longer used much, but it means "of good size." Explain that we use *good* as an adjective and *better* and *best* to compare two or more things. With students, write sample sentences using *good, better,* and *best.* Have students copy and label the adjectives in their notebooks.

Apply and Extend Have partners write their own sentences using *good, better,* and *best.* Then have them list and label the adjectives in their notebooks.

For additional practice, see **Language Development Cards**, Lesson 47B, and **Language Development Practice**, pages 280–282.

Independent Time

Vocabulary Building Have students build their glossaries.

Beginning/Early Intermediate Have students continue the Glossary Activities in the **Scaffolded Shared Read**.

Intermediate/Advanced/Advanced High After students add the vocabulary from **Reading/Writing Companion** pages 68–69 to the chart, have them scan for self-selected words or phrases they would like to learn, and add them to the chart.

WORD/PHRASE IN ENGLISH	DEFINITION IN ENGLISH	MEANING IN YOUR HOME LANGUAGE	USE THE WORD/PHRASE IN A SENTENCE
survive	continue to live during hardship	sobrevivir	Jamestown settlers survived the voyage.

Mixed Levels Pair students together. Beginning and Early-Intermediate students will teach vocabulary from their Scaffolded Shared Read glossaries. Intermediate and Advanced/High students will teach each other their self-selected words.

COLLABORATE **Shared Read Writing Frames** Use the online leveled **Shared Read Writing Frames** for "The Founding of Jamestown" to provide students with additional oral and written practice. Differentiated frames are available to provide support for all levels.

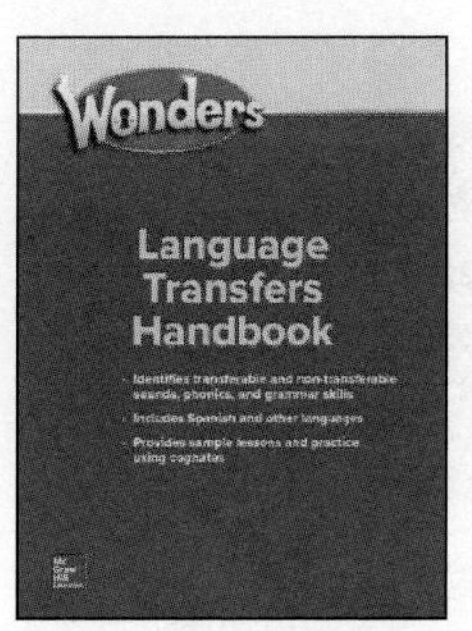

Language Transfers Handbook, Grammar Transfers, pp. 15–19

DIGITAL TOOLS

For additional support, use the online activities.

Grammar Video

Grammar Song

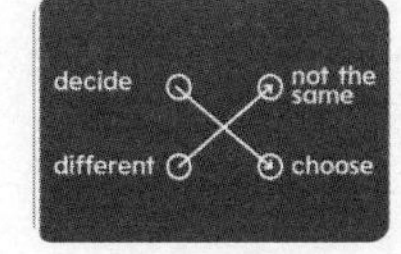

Vocabulary Activity

FORMATIVE ASSESSMENT

STUDENT CHECK-IN

Text Reconstruction Have partners share their notes. Have students reflect on their work using the Check-In routine.

Grammar in Context Have partners share their sentences. Have students reflect on their work using the Check-In routine.

LEARNING GOALS

- **Read** We can read and understand an expository text.
- **Reread** We can reread to analyze text, craft, and structure.

OBJECTIVES

By the end of year, read and comprehend informational texts, including history/social studies, science, and technical texts, in the grades 4-5 text complexity band proficiently, with scaffolding as needed at the high end of the range.

Engage effectively in a range of collaborative discussions with diverse partners on grade 4 topics and texts, building on others' ideas and expressing their own clearly.

LANGUAGE OBJECTIVES

Students will inquire about the text by answering questions using key vocabulary.

Students will explain photographs and sidebars using academic language.

ELA ACADEMIC LANGUAGE

- *photograph, caption, sidebar, chronology, summarize*
- Cognates: *fotografía, cronología*

MATERIALS

Literature Anthology, pp. 408-411

Reading/Writing Companion, pp. 76-77

Visual Vocabulary Cards

Online ELL Anchor Text Support BLMs, pp. 37-38

DIGITAL TOOLS

Have students listen to the selection to develop comprehension and practice fluency and pronunciation.

Rediscovering Our Spanish Beginnings

Prepare to Read

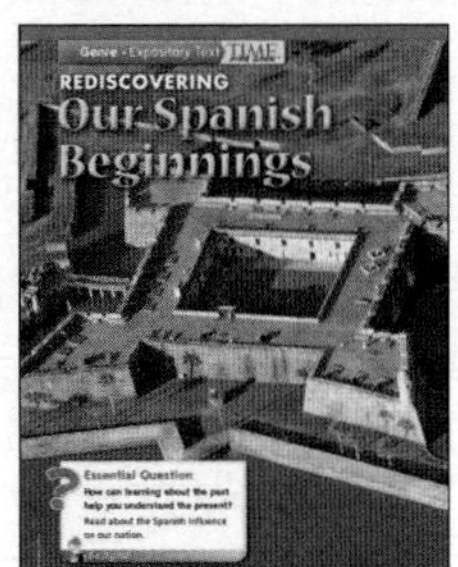

Literature Anthology, Lexile 940L

Build Background Review that an expository text gives facts and information about a topic. It usually includes features such as maps, sidebars, and captions. Point out Florida and Spain on a map. Have students share what they know about these places.

Vocabulary Use the **Visual Vocabulary Cards** to review *archaeology, document, era, evidence, expedition, permanent, tremendous, uncover.*

Set Purpose *Today we will read an expository text about the Spanish explorers who settled in Florida. As we read, think about what people can learn about the present from the past.*

Have students listen to the audio summary of the text, which is available in multiple languages.

Read

Literature Anthology, pp. 408–411

Use the **Interactive Question-Response Routine** to help students read and discuss *Rediscovering Our Spanish Beginnings.*

Beginning Help students respond in complete sentences. Provide sentence frames: Ponce de León looked for the Fountain of Youth. Ponce de León founded Florida.

Intermediate Ask students to respond in complete sentences and add details. Provide sentence starters as needed: Ponce de León looked for the Fountain of Youth. Ponce de León got lost on his expedition. He founded Florida.

Advanced/Advanced High Have students respond in complete sentences and add details.

COLLABORATE **Independent Reading Practice** Have mixed level pairs complete page 37-38 of the **ELL Anchor Text Support BLMs** and share their responses with the group.

Reread

Use with the **Reading/Writing Companion,** pages 76-77.

Literature Anthology, page 409

COLLABORATE **Author's Craft: Photographs** Read the text with students and review the Vocabulary word *expedition.* Have students ask about words or phrases that are unfamiliar and define or clarify the meaning. *What happened in 1493?* (Ponce de León joined Columbus's expedition.) Have students point to the picture of Ponce de León. *When did Ponce de León find Florida?* (1513) *What had* *he been looking for?* (Fountain of Youth) Explain the Fountain of Youth for students. *Where did the name* Florida *come from?* (Spanish word) *What problems did the Spanish explorers have when they attempted to settle in Florida?* (European crops did not grow, it was hot and humid, dangerous animals, did not get along with native tribes) *Why did the Spanish king send Pedro Menéndez de Avilés to Florida?* (to colonize and rule Florida) Have students discuss in pairs how the photographs and captions support the text using: The topic of the text is Spanish explorers in Florida. The captions and photographs tell me about who founded Florida and St. Augustine.

Beginning Read aloud the caption about St. Augustine, Florida, and Ponce de León on page 409 with students. Point to the word *founded* and explain that it means "created or started." Discuss the photograph and caption with students. Help partners describe using: The picture shows Ponce de León. The caption tells about who founded Florida.

Intermediate Have partners retell the events in chronological order: In 1493, Ponce de León sailed with Christopher Columbus. Later, Ponce de León sailed on his own to look for the Fountain of Youth. In 1513, his expedition found Florida. Read the last sentence in the second paragraph with students. Discuss the meanings of *risk* and *ignored* with them. *Why was Florida a risk and ignored?* (the explorers had a lot of problems when they tried to settle there)

Advanced/Advanced High Have partners **summarize** Ponce de León's life. (In 1493, Ponce de León sailed with Christopher Columbus. Later, he set out on his own expedition to seek the Fountain of Youth. They got lost. In 1513, they found Florida.) Have partners find the photo of Pedro Menéndez de Avilés. Why did he destroy the French colony? (The king wanted Spain to rule Florida and did not want France to have a colony near them.)

Literature Anthology, pp. 410–411

COLLABORATE **Author's Purpose: Sidebars** Read the sidebar on page 410 with students. Have students ask about words or phrases that are unfamiliar and define or clarify the meaning. *Why did the Spanish build the Castillo de San Marcos?* (to protect St. Augustine) *How was the Castillo de San Marcos different from the other forts?* (It was made with stone and had tall, thick towers so enemies could not tear them down.) Read the sidebar on page 411 with students and discuss the meaning of *entered*. *What does the sidebar tell about the English language?* (shows how the Spanish language influenced American culture) Have partners discuss how the information in the sidebars on pages 410 and 411 tell about the present and the past.

Beginning Read the sidebar on page 410 with students. Restate the sentences as needed. Point to the illustration and photograph. Explain what the workers did to build it and what the fort looks like today. *Why did the Spanish build the fort?* The Spanish built the fort to protect St. Augustine.

Intermediate Have partners discuss why the Castillo de San Marcos was better than previous forts: The castle was built with shell stone or coquina. Its walls were tremendous. They were very tall and thick.

Advanced/Advanced High Read the sidebar with students. Why is "A Fearsome Fort" a good title for this sidebar? (The text in the sidebar compares the fort to other castles. It tells why the Castillo de San Marcos is stronger.)

FORMATIVE ASSESSMENT

STUDENT CHECK-IN

Read Have partners share their responses to the Anchor Text questions. Then have them reflect using the Check-In routine.

Reread Have partners share responses and text evidence on Reading/Writing Companion pages 76–77. Then have them reflect using the Check-In routine to fill in the bars.

LEARNING GOALS

- **We can read and understand expository text by identifying the chronological text structure.**
- **We can compare using *Good* and *Bad*.**

OBJECTIVES

Paraphrase portions of a text read aloud or information presented in diverse media and formats, including visually, quantitatively, and orally.

Demonstrate command of the conventions of standard English grammar and usage when writing or speaking.

LANGUAGE OBJECTIVES

Students will discuss chronological structure in the text using key vocabulary.

Students will inquire about comparatives and superlatives of the adjectives good and bad.

ELA ACADEMIC LANGUAGE

- *signal, chronological, comparative, superlative*
- Cognates: *señal, cronología, comparativo, superlativo*

MATERIALS

Literature Anthology, pp. 408–411

Online Language Development Cards, 47A–47B

Online Language Development Practice, pp. 277-282

Online Language Transfers Handbook, pp. 15–19

Rediscovering Our Spanish Beginnings

Text Reconstruction

Focus on a single chunk of text to support comprehension and language development across the four domains.

1. Read aloud paragraph 2 on page 410 in the **Literature Anthology** while students listen.
2. Write the following on the board, providing definitions as needed: *before long, threat, settled, colonize, constant, fort, fortress, remains.* Instruct students to listen for them as you read the paragraph a second time.
3. Read the paragraph a third time while students listen and take notes.
4. COLLABORATE Have students work with a partner to reconstruct the text from their notes. Help them write complete sentences as needed.
5. Have students look at the original text. Ask them to tell what the paragraph is mostly about. (how Spanish settlers were threatened by others) Tell students they are going to identify signal words that show a chronological text structure.
6. *When did the English colonize the east coast?* (After they settled in Jamestown in 1607) *What does the word "continued" tell you?* (The English did not stop building colonies.) *What was happening to the Spanish settlers during that time?* (pirates and enemy ships attacked them.) *How did Spain help?* (Spain sent money in order to build a fortress) *What word tells you that building a fortress happened last?* (the word "finally")
7. Have students compare their text reconstructions to the original text. Have them check whether they also included words and phrases that signal time.

Beginning Allow students to follow along in the Literature Anthology as you read the text aloud. Have them point to the words from Step 2 as they hear them.

Apply Text Features: Photograph

Review with students that captions describe what is happening in a photograph and often include facts and information from the text. Discuss with students the photographs on pages 408 and 409. Then have students use the information from the text to write the new caption. Model first: *For the illustration of Ponce de León on page 409, the caption could be: Ponce de Leon claimed Florida for Spain in 1513.* Have students rewrite the captions in their own words.

Grammar in Context: Deconstruct a Sentence

Write the sentence from page 409 on the board: *St. Augustine, Florida, is the oldest city founded by Europeans in the United States.* Facilitate deconstructing this sentence for better comprehension:

- *What is the adjective in this sentence?* (oldest) *What does it modify?* (city) *Where is the position of the adjective?* (The adjective is before the noun.)
- *What question does* oldest *answer?* ("which one?")
- *Adjectives that are used to compare are called comparative adjectives.* Oldest *is the superlative form. What are the other forms?* (old, older) Review how to form the comparative and superlative forms: by adding *-er* or *-est*. Remind them that generally for long adjectives, the word *more* and *most* is added and discuss examples: beautiful, more beautiful, most beautiful.
- Discuss with students the comparative forms of other adjectives they know. Then review the different forms of *good* and *bad*. (good, better, best; bad, worse, worst)

For additional practice, see **Language Development Cards**, Lessons 47A–47B, and **Language Development Practice**, pages 277–282.

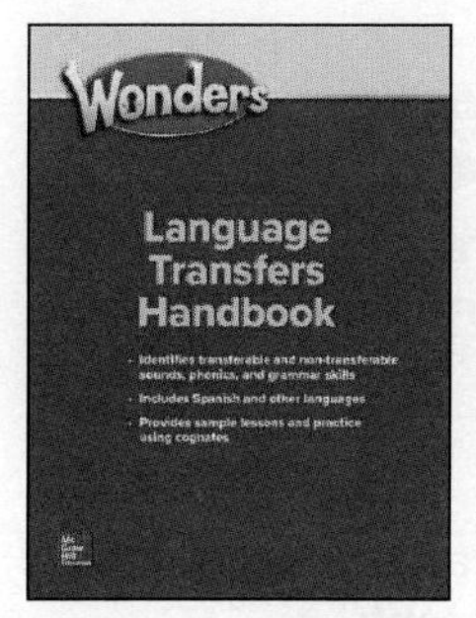

Language Transfers Handbook, Grammar Transfers, pp. 15–19

Independent Time

INDEPENDENT TIME

Vocabulary Building Have students create an interactive word wall with vocabulary from the selection. Have partners copy the words onto index cards. On the back of each card, have them write a clue to the word's meaning and tape the index cards to the wall with the clue-side facing out. Have other students look at a clue, guess the word, and turn the card over to confirm their answer.

Beginning/Intermediate Allow students to draw clues.

Intermediate/Advanced/Advanced High Have students include some of the self-selected words and content-area words they added to their glossaries.

COLLABORATE **Make Connections** Help students connect the Essential Question by sharing what they have learned about the past from museums, books, or watching a program.

Beginning Have partners share information about a historical figure or event they learned about: I learned about ___. He/She/It was a ___.

Intermediate Have partners share a historical event or figure: I learned about ___. It helped me understand that ___.

Advanced/Advanced High Have partners make the connection from the past to the present.

COLLABORATE **Comparing with *Good* and *Bad*** Have partners write sentences comparing the past and present using comparative forms of *good* and *bad*. Check students' work and provide feedback as needed.

FORMATIVE ASSESSMENT

STUDENT CHECK-IN

Text Reconstruction Have partners share their notes. Have students reflect on their work using the Check-In routine.

Grammar in Context Have partners reflect on their deconstructions using the Check-In routine.

LEARNING GOALS

We can apply strategies and skills to read an expository text.

OBJECTIVES

Describe the overall structure of events, ideas, concepts, or information in a text or part of a text.

Engage effectively in a range of collaborative discussions with diverse partners on grade 4 topics and texts, building on others' ideas and expressing their own clearly.

Use context as a clue to the meaning of a word or phrase.

LANGUAGE OBJECTIVES

Students will summarize by discussing relevant details in the text.

ELA ACADEMIC LANGUAGE

- *text structure, proverb, chronology, sequence, summarize, map*
- Cognates: *estructura de texto, cronología, secuencia, mapa*

MATERIALS

Online ELL Genre Passage,
"Eastern Influence"

"Eastern Influence"

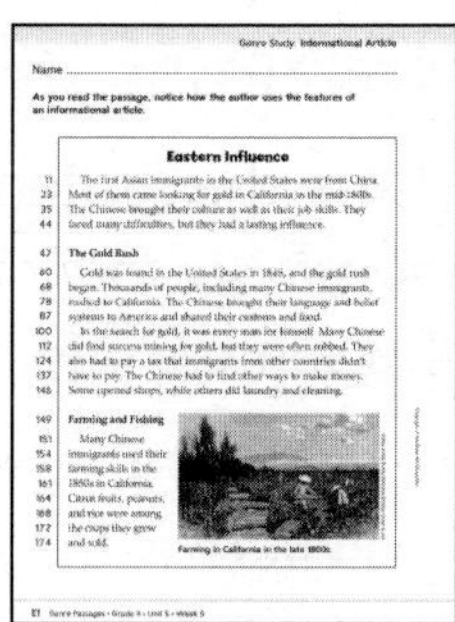

Genre Passage
Lexile 810L

Prepare to Read

Build Background Use a globe or a map to discuss with students the different immigrant groups that came to the United States. Explain that many of the things we have today, such as foods and words that we use, come from other cultures that the immigrants brought to the United States. Invite students to share examples they know or have learned about.

Explain that the gold rush was a period of time in the mid-1850s when people from all over the world went to California to look for gold. Point out that very few people found enough gold to get rich. Explain that in the 1860s the United States built a railroad across the United States and that many Chinese immgrants worked to build the railroad.

Vocabulary Use the Define, Example, Ask routine to pre-teach difficult words or unfamiliar concepts, such as *culture, custom, tax, role,* and *discriminated* (cognates: *cultura, costumbre, rol, discriminar*). Invite students to add new vocabulary to their glossaries.

Set Purpose *Today we will read an expository text called "Eastern Influence." As we read, think about how learning about the past can help you understand the present.*

Read the Text

Page E1, Introduction and "The Gold Rush"

Beginning Read the first paragraph with students. Use a number line to explain that *mid-1800s* refers to the middle of the 1800s, or in the 1850s. *In what years did Chinese immigrants first come to the United States?* The Chinese immigrants first came in the 1850s. *Why did they come?* They came to look for gold.

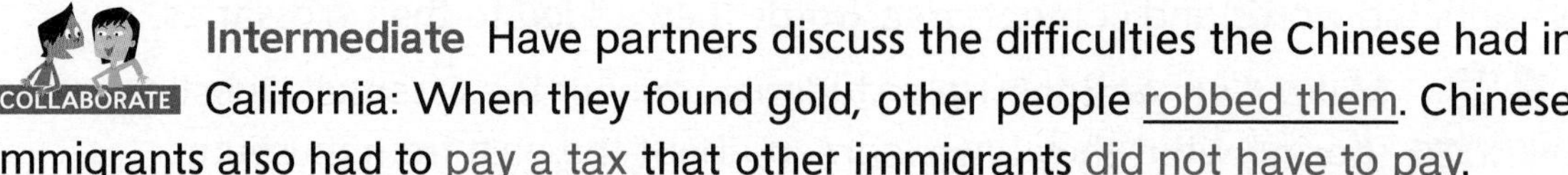

COLLABORATE **Intermediate** Have partners discuss the difficulties the Chinese had in California: When they found gold, other people robbed them. Chinese immigrants also had to pay a tax that other immigrants did not have to pay.

Advanced/Advanced High *How were the Chinese immigrants treated differently?* (They had to pay a tax that other immigrants did not have to pay.) *What does the phrase "every man for himself" mean?* (Possible answer: don't ask others for help)

COLLABORATE Discuss the meaning of the **proverb** "every man for himself." Then have partners express their opinions about whether or not it is a good way to look for gold. (Possible answer: I think it is not a good way because it is better to work together and help each other than working only for oneself. When there are problems, it is easier to have other people help you solve problems.)

Pages E1–E2, "Farming and Fishing"

COLLABORATE **Beginning** Read the text with students. *What did the Chinese farmers grow?* They grew fruits, peanuts, and rice. *Where did they fish?* They fished in California. *Does the word* local *mean near or distant?* Help partners discuss the meaning of *local* using clues in the sentence: *Shipped* means to send away to distant places. So, *local* means near.

COLLABORATE **Intermediate** Have partners **summarize** how the Chinese immigrants used their skills: The Chinese used their farming skills to grow crops and caught many types of fish. They sold them in markets or shipped them. *What context clues tell you what* local *means?* ("or shipped to other areas")

Advanced/Advanced High *What does the word* expert *mean?* (good at doing something) *What clues tell you?* ("they fished cod, flounder, and shark" tells they caught different types and were good at fishing)

Page E2, "The Transcontinental Railroad"

Beginning Guide students to circle relevant details and **summarize** the section. Read with students the first two paragraphs of the section and use the map to support comprehension. Guide students to circle relevant details and summarize: Chinese immigrants helped build the first transcontinental railroad. It was not easy work. Chinese immigrants worked very hard.

Intermediate *What was the Transcontinental Railroad?* (the first railroad that connected east and west) *What did the Chinese do?* (laid tracks, built tunnels) *How were they treated unfairly?* (They were paid less.)

COLLABORATE **Advanced/Advanced High** Have partners summarize what working on the railroad was like for the Chinese immigrants. (Possible answer: They cleared land and mountains and made tunnels. They worked long hours and even worked during bad weather. However, they were not paid the same as the other immigrants.)

Respond to Reading

Use the following instruction to help students answer the questions on page E3.

1. **Text Structure: Chronology** Have students find signal words that tell about the time period in the first paragraph. (mid-1800s) Then have them find dates and elicit that the article tells the events in sequence.
2. **Map** Have students describe the map. Then discuss how it relates to the "The Transcontinental Railroad" section. *What is the purpose of the map?* (shows where the railroad was built and places it connects)
3. *What difficulties did the Chinese immigrants have during the gold rush?* (They got robbed and paid a tax that other immigrants did not.)

Fluency Have partners take turns reading the passage.

Build Knowledge: Make Connections

Talk About the Text Have partners discuss how learning about the past can help you understand the present.

Write About the Text Have students add their ideas to their Build Knowledge pages of their reader's notebooks.

FORMATIVE ASSESSMENT

STUDENT CHECK-IN

Have partners share their responses on page E3. Ask students to reflect using the Check-In routine.

LEVEL UP

IF students read the **ELL Level** of the Genre Passage fluently and answered the questions,

THEN pair them with students who have proficiently read the **On Level**. Have them

- partner read the **On Level** passage.
- summarize the main idea and details.

LEARNING GOALS

We can apply strategies and skills to read an expository text.

OBJECTIVES

Describe the overall structure of events, ideas, concepts, or information in a text or part of a text.

Engage effectively in a range of collaborative discussions with diverse partners on grade 4 topics and texts, building on others' ideas and expressing their own clearly.

Read grade-level prose and poetry orally with accuracy, appropriate rate, and expression on successive readings.

LANGUAGE OBJECTIVES

Students will inform about chronology of events using time-order words.

ELA ACADEMIC LANGUAGE

- *summarize, sequence, signal words, verb tense, time order, antonym*
- Cognates*: secuencia, antónimo*

MATERIALS

ELL Leveled Reader: *Treks Through Time*

Online Differentiated Texts: "Rediscovering Egypt's Past"

Visual Vocabulary Cards

DIGITAL TOOLS

MULTIMODAL

Have students read along with the audio of the selections to develop comprehension and practice fluency and pronunciation.

Treks Through Time

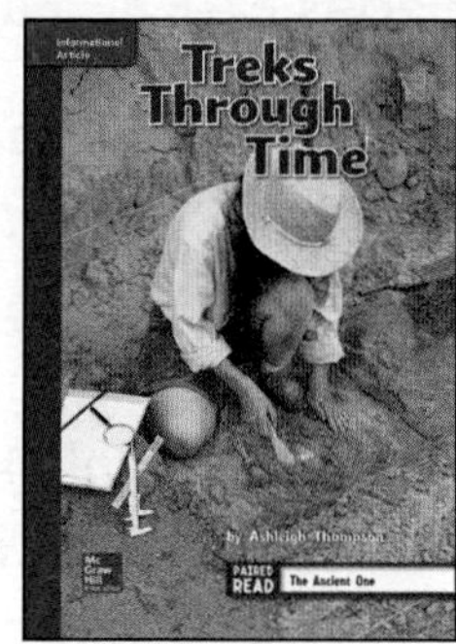

Leveled Reader
Lexile: 730L

Prepare to Read

Build Background Review with students that archaeologists study the past. Have students share what they know or learned about archaeologists. Display the photographs in the Leveled Reader. Discuss with students what they see. *Archaeologists study the things people have made or used in the past, and the places people used to live. With a partner, talk about things archaeologists do:* Archaeologists look for and study ____.

Vocabulary Use the routine on the **Visual Vocabulary Cards** to pre-teach ELL vocabulary *abandoned, excavate,* and *recent*. Discuss the appendices on page 19 of the Leveled Reader.

Set Purpose *Today we are going to read an expository text called "Treks Through Time". As we read, think about how learning about the past can help you understand the present.*

Read the Text

Page 2, Paragraph 2

Beginning Read aloud the second paragraph on page 2 with students. Review the meaning of *excavate* and restate the sentences as needed. *What words describe* excavate*?* ("to dig") *What do archaeologists do?* Archaeologists excavate, or dig up, artifacts. Artifacts are things from the past.

Page 4

COLLABORATE **Text Structure: Chronology** Review how words and verb tenses can signal time. *With a partner, describe how Dr. Smith learns about Cahokia.* First, Dr. Smith reads and learns about Mississipian culture. Next, she will study artifacts at museums. Then, she can talk to descendent communities and excavate the site.

Advanced/Advanced High *What clues help you figure out the meaning of* descendent*?* (The author tells that descendent communities may have ancestors who built Cahokia and have oral traditions and records, so *descendent* means people who come after or inherit.) *What is an antonym of* descendent*?* (ancestor)

Page 8

COLLABORATE **Beginning** Read with students the first paragraph and caption. Help partners describe the photograph: The student is recording information. Another word for *record* is write.

Intermediate *What words are similar to the verb* document*?* (write down, record) Have students describe what archaeology teams document: They document artifacts by recording the location of artifacts and other useful information.

Summarize Have partners summarize the relationship between the age of the artifact and where it is found under the ground: When teams dig for artifacts, they usually find newer artifacts near the surface and older artifacts deeper underground.

Pages 10–11

Intermediate *What information did the team learn from studying hide scrapers?* The team learned where the hide scrapers are from. If they come from far away, then the culture traded with others.

Advanced/Advanced High *How do archaeologists use carbon to tell the age of artifacts?* (Carbon ages, or decays, over time, so when it is left on the artifacts, it can tell how old the artifacts are.)

Respond to Reading Have partners complete their graphic organizers and discuss the questions on page 15.

Fluency: Rate, Expression

Read pages 7–8 with appropriate rate and expression. Read it again and have students read it with you. For more practice, have students record their voices a few times and choose the best one.

Paired Read: "The Ancient One"

Make Connections: Write About It

Analytical Writing

Before students write, discuss the questions on page 18: *Reread page 17 and the first paragraph on page 18. What did the Umatilla want to do with the Ancient One?* The Umatilla wanted to rebury the Ancient One, but the courts said the Ancient One was not Native American. *Reread pages 10 and 11.* I think the scientists probably documented the remains and used radiocarbon dating.

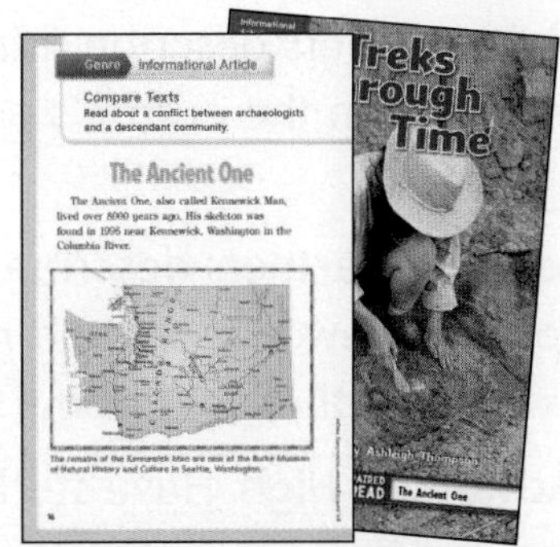

ELL Leveled Reader

Build Knowledge: Make Connections

Talk About the Text Have partners discuss how learning about the past can help you understand the present.

Write About the Text Have students add their ideas to their Build Knowledge pages of their reader's notebooks.

Self-Selected Reading

Have students choose another expository text from the online **Leveled Reader Library** or the **Differentiated Text,** "Rediscovering Egypt's Past."

FOCUS ON SOCIAL STUDIES

Have students complete the activity on page 20 to think about how an object changes over time.

LITERATURE CIRCLES

Ask students to conduct a literature circle using the Thinkmark questions to guide the discussion.

FORMATIVE ASSESSMENT

STUDENT CHECK-IN

Have partners share their answers to Respond to Reading. Ask students to reflect on their learning using the Check-In routine.

LEVEL UP

IF students read the **ELL Level** fluently and answered the questions,

THEN pair them with students who have proficiently read the **On Level** and have students

- read aloud the **On Level** main selection with their partner.
- list words they find difficult.
- discuss these words with their partners.

Access Complex Text

The **On Level** challenges students by including more **domain-specific words** and **complex sentence structures.**

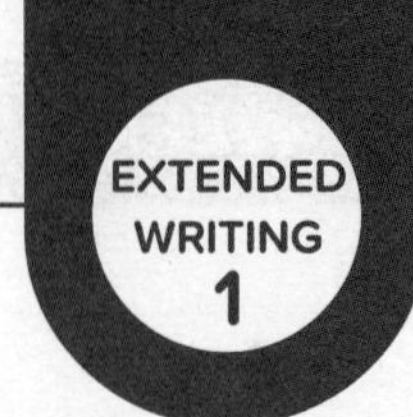

LEARNING GOALS

- **We can identify features of a personal narrative.**
- **We can plan a personal narrative.**
- **We can draft a personal narrative.**

OBJECTIVES

Orient the reader by establishing a situation and introducing a narrator and/or characters; organize an event sequence that unfolds naturally.

Use a variety of transitional words and phrases to manage the sequence of events.

Use concrete words and phrases and sensory details to convey experiences and events precisely.

LANGUAGE OBJECTIVES

Students will narrate by writing a personal narrative using sequence words.

ELA ACADEMIC LANGUAGE

- *point of view, sequence, transitional, sensory*
- Cognates: *sequencia, sensorio/sensorial*

MATERIALS

Online ELL Extended Writing Resources BLMs, pp. 76–77

- My Writing Outline
- Draft: Sensory Details

Online Graphic Organizer 17

Online Language Development Cards, 13B, 83A–83B

Online Language Development Practice, pp. 76–78, 493–498

Reading/Writing Companion, pp. 86–89

Literature Anthology, p. 22

Personal Narrative

Expert Model

Features of a Personal Narrative

Review the features of a Personal Narrative. Read the story "Weathering the Storm" on page 22 of the **Literature Anthology** with students. Use it to discuss the features and identify examples together.

- *What is a personal narrative?* (a true story about the writer's life) *What does the author tell about?* (a Girl Scout camping trip during a storm)
- *A personal narrative tells the story from the author's point of view, so the writer uses first-person pronouns. What are words that show the author's point of view? (I, me, my, mine)*
- *The writer describes the events in a narrative in a logical order from an introduction to a conclusion. What words does the author use to tell the sequence of events? (same weekend, on Friday afternoon, after, that night)*
- *A personal narrative uses sensory, concrete, and figurative language to share the writer's experience. What are examples the author uses?* (She uses a metaphor; she describes "our island" because it is so flooded.)

Have partners describe features of a personal narrative and tell examples to each other.

Beginning Help partners describe using: A personal narrative is a story. It tells about true events from the author's point of view. The author tells about when she was in a flood.

Intermediate Have partners describe features. For example: Writers use words to show their point of view like *me* and *my*. The writer also uses sequence words like *then* and *next*. The author tells about her experiences in a flood.

Advanced/Advanced High Have students describe features of a personal narrative using examples from the story on page 22.

Help students learn first-person pronouns. Have partners list the first-person pronouns at the beginning of "Weathering the Storm." (me, we, us) *What do these words tell us?* They show the author's point of view. *You will use first-person pronouns in your narrative, as well.*

Plan: Choose Your Topic

Writing Prompt

Confirm students understand the prompt: Write a personal narrative. Write about a time you tried your hardest to do something.

Ask partners to discuss: *What does "try your hardest" mean? When did you try your hardest?* Use the discussion to help students select their writing topic.

Plan: Sequence of Events

Signal Words for Sequence

Help students plan. Review that transitional, or signal, words such as *first, earlier, then,* and *finally* tell when events happen. Have students retell events in "Weathering the Storm" in time order. Then help students order events in their narratives using: First, my sister climbed a tree. Then, I stretched. Next, I climbed the tree and slipped. Finally, I tried my hardest and climbed the tree. Give students time to write the main events of their personal narratives in the online Sequence of Events **Graphic Organizer 17**.

Mixed Levels Have mixed-proficiency pairs create a word wall of temporal words they can use.

Have partners use **My Writing Outline** to plan their writing.

Draft

Sensory Details

COLLABORATE **Add Sensory Details** Display page 89 of the **Reading/Writing Companion**. Discuss how sensory words for sight, sound, touch, taste, and feeling help readers get more engaged in the story. Ask: *What sensory words does Anna use?* (see flash floods, play in puddles, a tiny taste) Have partners use sensory words to write sentences about Anna's experience and discuss the placement of the words in each sentence.

Mixed Levels Have partners use **Draft: Sensory Details** to practice adding sensory details to sentences in their narratives.

COLLABORATE **Use Similes and Metaphors** *Writers use figurative language to help readers picture moments.* Review that a simile compares two things using *like* or *as: The leaf felt as soft as silk.* Review that a metaphor describes something as if it were something else: *Sam has a heart of gold.*

Language Development Practice For practice using noun phrases, see Language Development Cards, lesson 13B. For practice using figurative language, see Language Development lessons 83A–83B.

Write a Draft

Have students orally share their narrative with a partner. Students should refer to My Writing Outline as they share.

Beginning My personal narrative is about the time I tried to ______. In the beginning ______. Then ______. In the end ______.

Intermediate My personal narrative is about ______. In the beginning ______. I felt ______. Then ______. In the end ______. I felt ______.

Advanced/Advanced High Have partners summarize their personal narrative and discuss how they felt.

Have students work independently to write their personal narratives.

TEACHER CONFERENCES

To help students write their drafts, meet with each student to provide support and guidance.

Beginning Help students write about the events in sequence using signal words. Discuss ways they can add sensory details throughout.

Intermediate Have students describe and read the sentences they like and sentences that are challenging. Provide suggestions to help them use signal words for sequence and add sensory details.

Advanced/Advanced High Have students discuss what they like about their draft and focus on the sequence of events and sensory details in their drafts.

FORMATIVE ASSESSMENT

STUDENT CHECK-IN

Features of a Personal Narrative Have partners name three features of a personal narrative.

Plan Have partners share My Writing Outline.

Draft Have partners point out two examples of sensory details in their drafts.

Ask students to reflect using the Check-In routine.

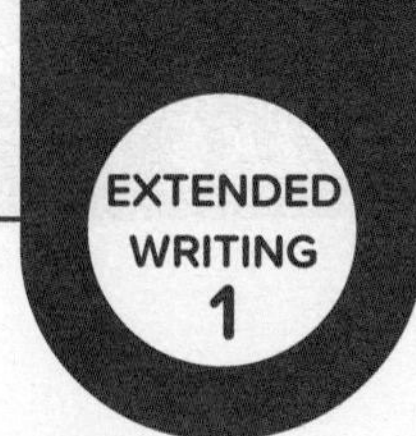

LEARNING GOALS

- **We can revise a personal narrative.**
- **We can edit and proofread a personal narrative.**
- **We can publish, present, and evaluate a personal narrative.**

OBJECTIVES

Provide a conclusion that follows from the narrated experiences or events.

With guidance and support from peers and adults, develop and strengthen writing as needed by planning, revising, and editing.

Follow agreed-upon rules for discussions and carry out assigned roles.

LANGUAGE OBJECTIVES

Students will inquire about strong conclusions by revising sentences.

ELA ACADEMIC LANGUAGE

- *conclusion, purpose, peer, publish, rubric*
- Cognates: *conclusion, propósito, publicar*

MATERIALS

Literature Anthology, pp. 23

Reading/Writing Companion, pp. 90–93

Online ELL Extended Writing Resources BLMs, p. 78

- Revise: Strong Conclusions

Online Language Development Cards, 1A–3B, 62A–62B

Online Language Development Practice, 1–18, 367–372

Personal Narrative

Revise

Strong Conclusions

Remind students that good personal narratives have strong conclusions that are satisfying and support the purpose of the narrative. Discuss with students some strategies for writing strong conclusions: summing up the purpose for writing and ending with a memory or thought. Have students use these strategies as they revise their personal narratives.

Sum Up the Purpose for Writing Review with students that a conclusion supports the purpose for writing a narrative essay. *A conclusion reminds readers why the writer wrote the narrative.* Have partners read the paragraph on **Reading/Writing Companion** page 90. Discuss with students how the author summed up the experience in the conclusion by reflecting back on events. *What was the author's purpose for writing?* (to tell about the experience of practicing every day to make the basketball team) Discuss the clear purpose of the writer explaining how he/she made the basketball team.

Have partners sum up for each other the purpose for writing their personal narratives.

Beginning Help students complete sentence frames to share their purpose for writing: I wrote about this because ____. I want my audience to know ____.

Intermediate Ask questions to help students explain their purpose for writing: *What did you want to tell your audience?* Help students describe using: My purpose in writing the narrative was____.

Advanced/Advanced High Have partners ask and answer questions about their personal narratives. Then have them explain their purpose for writing them.

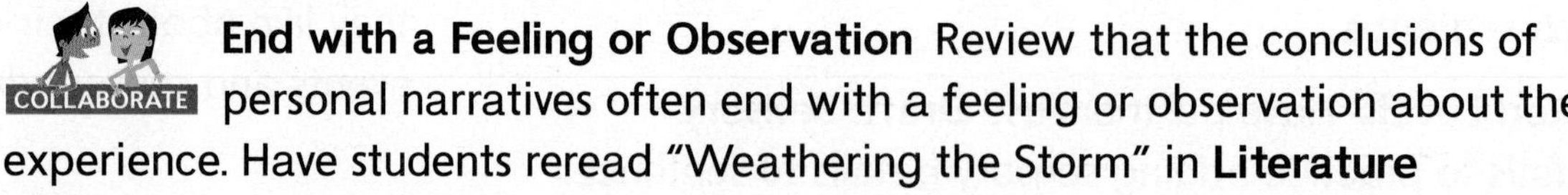

End with a Feeling or Observation Review that the conclusions of personal narratives often end with a feeling or observation about the experience. Have students reread "Weathering the Storm" in **Literature Anthology** page 23. *Discuss the last line with a partner.* (Next time I go camping, though, I am going to cancel at the slightest hint of rain!) *How does the writer end this personal narrative?* (She says she hopes to go camping again, but not in the rain.) *How is this conclusion strong?* (The writer sums up the events and shares that she feels both positive and negative about her experience.) Point out the use of connecting words "Even though" in the first sentence of the conclusion. Discuss how these words help bring various experiences and feelings of the writer together as she sums them up in the conclusion.

Mixed Levels Have partners complete **Revise: Strong Conclusions** for support in improving strong conclusions.

Language Development Practice For additional practice with coordinating conjunctions, see Language Development lessons 62A and 62B.

Revise

Prepare students to revise their drafts. First have them work with partners, and then independently.

Discuss features of the genre, such as using first-person pronouns and sharing their feelings about an event.

Remind students that as they revise, they should make sure the events in their narratives are in order.

Review using sensory details and figurative language in their writing.

Review with students the strategies they learned to revise for a strong conclusion. Help them apply these strategies to their own writing. Have partners describe their revisions to each other.

Beginning Have partners describe their revisions. For example: I will change this sentence into a question. I will add an exclamation to show how I felt.

Intermediate Have partners describe their revisions. For example: I will change this sentence to a question. I will add an exclamation to show how I felt.

Advanced/Advanced High Invite partners to describe their revisions to each other.

Peer Conferencing

Partner Feedback

Review the Revising Checklist on page 91 of the **Reading/Writing Companion** with students. Have partners use the checklist to give feedback on each other's work. Help all students provide feedback. For example:

Beginning There is/is not a logical sequence of events in your narrative. I can/cannot tell there is a beginning, middle, and end. I like how you used the word ____ to describe ____.

Intermediate When I read your narrative, there is a logical sequence of events. I like this part because _____. You can add another detail to describe _____.

Advanced/ Advanced High After using the Revising Checklist with their partners, have students reflect on which suggestions were most helpful.

TEACHER CONFERENCES

To help students revise, meet with each student to provide support and guidance.

Beginning Help students describe the events in sequence and their revision to the conclusion.

Intermediate Have students describe and read the sentences they like and sentences that are challenging. Provide suggestions to help them.

Advanced/Advanced High Discuss with students what they like about their draft and what they want to improve. Help them find suggestions.

Edit and Proofread

Using the Editing Checklist

Discuss the items in the Editing Checklist on Reading/Writing Companion page 92 to make sure students understand what each one means.

Have partners edit and proofread each other's drafts using the Editing Checklist.

If students need more support with editing and proofreading, use **Language Development** lessons: Sentences and Fragments (1A and 1B), Punctuation (2A and 2B), Subjects and Predicates (3A and 3B). You may also wish to revisit the Language Development lessons from Draft and Revise.

Publish, Present, Evaluate

Evaluate

Have students use the rubric on Reading/Writing Companion page 93 to evaluate their own writing. Explain the language in the rubric to make sure students understand what the terms describe. Have them apply the rubric to their own writing, and then describe their thinking to a partner.

FORMATIVE ASSESSMENT

STUDENT CHECK-IN

Revise Ask partners to share ways they improved their conclusion.

Edit and Proofread Ask students to share the partner feedback they gave.

Publish, Present, Evaluate Ask partners to share the scores they gave themselves using their rubrics.

Have students reflect using the Check-In routine.

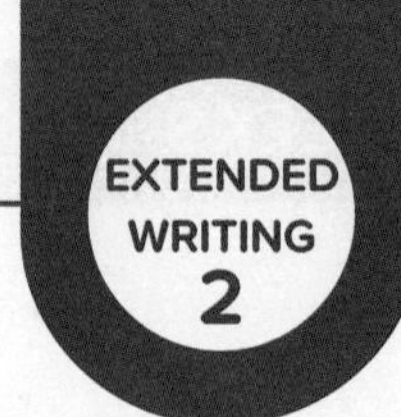

LEARNING GOALS

- **We can identify features of an expository essay.**
- **We can plan an expository essay.**
- **We can draft an expository essay.**

OBJECTIVES

Introduce a topic clearly and group related information in paragraphs and sections.

Develop the topic with facts, definitions, concrete details, quotations, or other information and examples related to the topic.

Write routinely over extended time frames and shorter time frames for a range of discipline-specific tasks, purposes, and audiences.

LANGUAGE OBJECTIVES

Students will explain by writing an expository essay using facts and details.

ELA ACADEMIC LANGUAGE

- *logical, organize, outline, draft, facts, definitions, quotations*
- Cognates: *lógico, organizar, definiciónes*

MATERIALS

Online ELL Extended Writing Resources BLMs, pp. 79–80

- My Writing Outline
- Draft: Relevant Evidence

Online Graphic Organizer 18

Online Language Development Cards, 8A

Online Language Development Practice, 43–45

Reading/Writing Companion, pp. 96–97

Literature Anthology, p. 409

Expository Essay

Expert Model

Features of an Expository Essay

Review the features of an expository essay. Read page 409 of *Rediscovering Our Spanish Beginning* in the **Literature Anthology** to discuss features and examples.

- *An expository essay is a text that includes facts, details, and text features on a topic. What topic does the author write about?* (how the Spanish claimed and settled in Florida) Have students identify and share some facts in the essay.
- *The facts and details are in a logical order. What are some words in this essay that show a logical order?* (after, then, later)
- *Expository essays use tex*
- *t features to present information. What text features does the author use to present facts?* (photos, illustrations, captions, sidebars)Discuss with students how these different visuals add more information.
- *The essay ends with a strong conclusion connected to the topic. How does this essay end?* (how the Spanish founded St. Augustine)

Have partners describe examples to identify features of an expository essay.

Beginning Confirm understanding of what an expository essay is. An expository essay gives information on a topic. It has facts and details about a topic.

Intermediate Have partners describe other features of an expository essay. For example: The writer uses text features to present information. The writer also uses order words like *after* and *then*.

Advanced/Advanced High Have students describe features of an expository essay using examples from "Rediscovering Our Spanish Beginnings."

Plan: Choose Your Topic

Writing Prompt

Confirm students understand the prompt: Write an expository essay about a Native American group that lived in your state before European exploration. Ask partners to discuss: *What does the word* exploration *mean? What are some Native American groups?* Use the discussion to help students select their topic.

Plan: Write an Outline

Get Organized

Help students plan. Model how to create an outline using **Reading/Writing Companion** page 96. Then guide them by asking questions such as: *What is the topic and central idea? Where do you put this information on the outline?* Provide time for students to discuss and write facts and details by creating an outline to plan for their expository essays.

Have partners use **My Writing Outline** to plan their writing.

Draft

Relevant Evidence

Add Facts, Definitions, Quotations, and Examples Discuss how supporting details can be facts, definitions, quotations, or examples about the topic. Display page 97 in the **Reading/Writing Companion**. Ask: *What is the main idea of the paragraph?* (John Smith, an experienced military man, became head of the colony in 1608.) Ask: *What is a supporting detail?* (John found local tribes to trade food for English copper and beads.) Have students discuss other supporting details. Point out that the quotation by Smith, "He that will not work, shall not eat," is a supporting detail.

Beginning Have partners describe the central idea and supporting details in the paragraph using: John Smith was the head of the colony. He traded with the Native Americans.

Intermediate Have partners complete the sentence frame: As head of the colony, John Smith was tough with both the Native Americans and the Englishmen.

Advanced/Advanced High Have partners identify details in the paragraph and describe to one another how they support the central idea.

Mixed Levels Have students use **Draft: Relevant Evidence** to practice using relevant evidence.

Use Proper Nouns Display page 97. Explain that a proper noun is the name of a person, place, or thing and each proper noun begins with a capital letter. Help students identify proper nouns in the paragraph: *John Smith, English. Ask: What are two other proper nouns in the first paragraph?* (Indians, Englishmen)

Language Development Practice For additional practice with proper nouns, see Language Development lesson 8A.

Write a Draft

Have students prepare for writing a draft by orally sharing their expository essay with a partner. Students can refer to **My Writing Outline** as they share.

Beginning My expository essay is about the topic ______. The central idea is ______. A supporting idea is ______.

Intermediate My expository essay is about ______. The central idea is ______. The supporting ideas are ______.

Advanced/Advanced High Have partners summarize their expository essay.

Have students work independently on their expository essays.

TEACHER CONFERENCES

To help students write their draft, meet with each student to provide support and guidance.

Beginning Help students write about the central idea. Discuss the relevant evidence they can use for supporting ideas.

Intermediate Have students identify the sentences they like and sentences they are struggling with. Provide suggestions to help them write an outline and add relevant evidence to use for supporting ideas.

Advanced/Advanced High Discuss with students the central idea and relevant evidence they can use for supporting ideas. Discuss with them how they can use facts, definitions, quotations, and examples.

FORMATIVE ASSESSMENT

STUDENT CHECK-IN

Features of an Expository Essay Have partners name three features of an expository essay.

Plan Have partners share My Writing Outline.

Draft Have partners point out two examples of relevant evidence in their drafts.

Ask students to reflect using the Check-In routine.

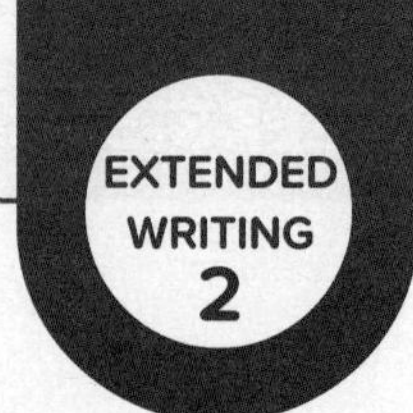

LEARNING GOALS

- We can revise an expository essay.
- We can edit and proofread an expository essay.
- We can publish, present, and evaluate an expository essay.

OBJECTIVES

Link ideas within categories of information using words and phrases.

With guidance and support from peers and adults, develop and strengthen writing as needed by planning, revising, and editing.

Pose and respond to specific questions to clarify or follow up on information, and make comments that contribute to the discussion and link to the remarks of others.

LANGUAGE OBJECTIVES

Students will inquire about revising by using a variety of sentences.

ELA ACADEMIC LANGUAGE

- *sentence fluency, transition, connect, simple sentence, compound sentence*
- Cognates: *sentencia, transición, conectar, simple*

MATERIALS

Online ELL Extended Writing BLMs, p. 81

- Revise

Online Language Development Cards, 1A–3B, 70A–70B

Online Language Development Practice, pp. 1–18, 415–420

Reading/Writing Companion, pp. 98–101

Expository Essay

Revise

Sentence Fluency

Remind students that sentence fluency refers to how words sound together within a sentence, and how sentences sound when read one after the other. Focus on specific strategies for improving sentence fluency: using transition words to connect sentences, simple and compound sentences, and varying sentences.

COLLABORATE **Use Transition Words** Review that transition words connect ideas in sentences and make writing easier to understand. *Transition words show things like cause and effect, the order in which things happen, and other ways ideas relate to one another.* Have partners find examples of transition words in the paragraph comparing bears on page 98 of the **Reading/Writing Companion** (*too, that*) Have partners discuss how these transition words connect ideas in the sentences. (*Too* connects that both brown and polar bears have claws; *that* connects the bears' fur colors with the environments in which they hide.)

Ask students to think of places in their essay where they can use transition words to connect ideas in sentences.

Beginning Help students use transition words. For example: A long time ago, many Native Americans lived in _____, but today the population is much smaller.

Intermediate Provide more models for using transition words. For example: This group lived in _____, so many places there have Native American names. Today they live in _____ and still practice their traditions. Have partners explain how each transition word connects ideas.

Advanced/Advanced High Invite students to find sentences in their draft that includes transition words. Have partners discuss more transitions they could add.

COLLABORATE **Use Simple and Compound Sentences** Discuss with students that a simple sentence shows a complete thought and a compound sentence has two complete thoughts.

Beginning Help partners form a compound sentence using *and.*

Intermediate Have students identify conjunctions, such as *so* or *because,* that they can use to combine sentences. Then have them write compound sentences.

Advanced/Advanced High Have partners discuss the differences between simple and compound sentences, and conjunctions they can use.

Mixed Levels Have partners complete **Revise: Sentence Fluency** for support in improving sentence fluency.

Language Development Practice For additional practice using compound sentences, see Language Development lessons 70A and 70B.

Revise

Prepare students to revise their drafts. First have them work with partners, and then independently.

Discuss features of the genre, such as using a variety of details, such as facts, definitions, and examples.

Remind students that as they revise, they should refer to the outline they used to plan their writing.

Review using transition words and a variety of sentences for sentence fluency.

COLLABORATE Review with students the strategies they learned to revise for sentence fluency. Help them apply these strategies to their own writing. Then have partners describe their revisions to each other.

Beginning Have partners describe their revisions. For example: I will combine these sentences using and.

Intermediate Have partners describe their revisions. For example: I will combine these two sentences.

Advanced/Advanced High Invite partners to describe their revisions to each other.

Peer Conferencing

Partner Feedback

Review the Revising Checklist on page 99 of the **Reading/Writing Companion** with students. Have partners use the checklist to give feedback. Help students provide feedback. For example:

Beginning The information is/is not in a logical order. I can/cannot see that you used signal words. I like how you used the word ____ to describe ____.

Intermediate When I read your essay, there is a logical sequence of events. I like this part because _____. You can add another detail to describe _____.

Advanced/ Advanced High After using the Revising Checklist with their partners, have students reflect on which suggestions were most helpful.

TEACHER CONFERENCES

To help students revise, meet with each student to provide support and guidance.

Beginning Help students use the word *and* to improve sentence fluency. Discuss ways they can add relevant evidence and use a variety of sentences.

Intermediate Have students describe ways they can add relevant evidence and use a variety of sentences. Provide suggestions to help them use transition words.

Advanced/Advanced High Have students discuss the relevant evidence they used and ways to add a variety of sentence types in their writing.

Edit and Proofread

Using the Editing Checklist

Discuss the items in the Editing Checklist on page 100 in the Reading/Writing Companion to make sure students understand what each one means.

Have partners edit and proofread each other's drafts using the Editing Checklist.

If students need more support with editing and proofreading, use **Language Development** lessons: Sentences and Fragments (1A and 1B), Punctuation (2A and 2B), Subjects and Predicates (3A and 3B). You may also wish to revisit the Language Development lessons from Draft and Revise.

Publish, Present, Evaluate

Evaluate

Have students use the rubric on Reading/Writing Companion page 101 to evaluate their own writing. Explain the language in the rubric to make sure students understand what the terms describe. Have them apply the rubric to their own writing, and then describe their thinking to a partner.

FORMATIVE ASSESSMENT

STUDENT CHECK-IN

Revise Ask partners to share ways they included sentence fluency.

Edit and Proofread Ask students to share the partner feedback they gave.

Publish, Present, Evaluate Ask partners to share the scores they gave themselves using their rubrics.

Have students reflect using the Check-In routine.

Summative Assessment

Get Ready for Unit Assessment

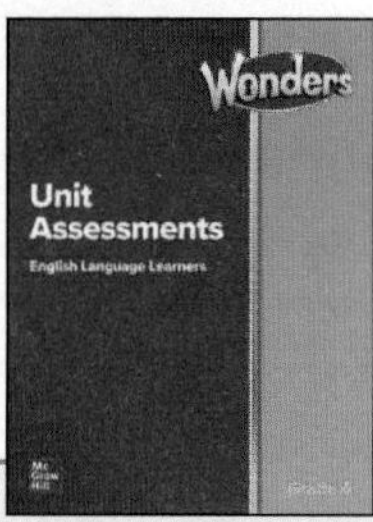

Unit 5 Tested Skills

LISTENING AND READING COMPREHENSION	VOCABULARY	GRAMMAR	SPEAKING AND WRITING
• Listening Actively • Comprehension • Text Structure • Cohesion	• Unit Vocabulary Words	• Nouns and Noun Phrases • Adjectives • Prepositional Phrases	• Writing • Supporting Opinions • Retelling/Summarizing • Text Structure

Create a Student Profile

Record data from the following resources in the Student Profile charts on pages 320–321 of the Assessment book.

COLLABORATIVE	INTERPRETIVE	PRODUCTIVE

• Collaborative Conversations Rubrics
  • Listening
  • Speaking
	• Leveled Unit Assessment:
	  • Listening Comprehension
	  • Reading Comprehension
	  • Vocabulary
	  • Grammar
	• Presentation Rubric
	  • Listening
	• *Wonders* Unit Assessment
		• Weekly Progress Monitoring
		• Leveled Unit Assessment
		  • Speaking
		  • Writing
		• Presentation Rubric
		  • Speaking
		• Write to Sources Rubric
		• *Wonders* Unit Assessment

The Foundational Skills Kit, Language Development Kit, and Adaptive Learning provide additional student data for progress monitoring.

Level Up

Use the following chart, along with your Student Profiles, to guide your Level Up decisions.

LEVEL UP	If **BEGINNING** level students are able to do the following, they may be ready to move to the **INTERMEDIATE** level:	If **INTERMEDIATE** level students are able to do the following, they may be ready to move to the **ADVANCED** level:	If **ADVANCED** level students are able to do the following, they may be ready to move to on-level:
COLLABORATIVE	• participate in collaborative conversations using basic vocabulary and grammar and simple phrases or sentences • discuss simple pictorial or text prompts	• participate in collaborative conversations using appropriate words and phrases and complete sentences • use limited academic vocabulary across and within disciplines	• participate in collaborative conversations using more sophisticated vocabulary and correct grammar • communicate effectively across a wide range of language demands in social and academic contexts
INTERPRETIVE	• identify details in simple read alouds • understand common vocabulary and idioms and interpret language related to familiar social, school, and academic topics • make simple inferences and make simple comparisons • exhibit an emerging receptive control of lexical, syntactic, phonological, and discourse features	• identify main ideas and/or make some inferences from simple read alouds • use context clues to identify word meanings and interpret basic vocabulary and idioms • compare, contrast, summarize, and relate text to graphic organizers • exhibit a limited range of receptive control of lexical, syntactic, phonological, and discourse features when addressing new or familiar topics	• determine main ideas in read alouds that have advanced vocabulary • use context clues to determine meaning, understand multiple-meaning words, and recognize synonyms of social and academic vocabulary • analyze information, make sophisticated inferences, and explain their reasoning • command a high degree of receptive control of lexical, syntactic, phonological, and discourse features
PRODUCTIVE	• express ideas and opinions with basic vocabulary and grammar and simple phrases or sentences • restate information or retell a story using basic vocabulary • exhibit an emerging productive control of lexical, syntactic, phonological, and discourse features	• produce coherent language with limited elaboration or detail • restate information or retell a story using mostly accurate, although limited, vocabulary • exhibit a limited range of productive control of lexical, syntactic, phonological, and discourse features when addressing new or familiar topics	• produce sentences with more sophisticated vocabulary and correct grammar • restate information or retell a story using extensive and accurate vocabulary and grammar • tailor language to a particular purpose and audience • command a high degree of productive control of lexical, syntactic, phonological, and discourse features

LEARNING GOALS

I can read and understand narrative nonfiction.

OBJECTIVES

Determine the central, or main, idea of a text and explain how it is supported by key details; summarize the text.

Pose and respond to specific questions to clarify or follow up on information, and make comments that contribute to the discussion and link to the remarks of others.

Identify and classify Earth's renewable resources, including air, plants, water, and animals; and nonrenewable resources, including coal, oil, and natural gas; and the importance of conservation. **Science**

LANGUAGE OBJECTIVES

Students will inquire about the central idea of the text using key vocabulary.

ELA ACADEMIC LANGUAGE

- *central idea, relevant details, sidebar, evidence*
- Cognates: *idea central, detalles relevantes, evidencia*

MATERIALS

Reading/Writing Companion, pp. 118–121

Online Scaffolded Shared Read, "The Great Energy Debate"

Visual Vocabulary Cards

Online ELL Visual Vocabulary Cards

DIGITAL TOOLS

MULTIMODAL

Have students read along as they listen to the selection to develop comprehension and practice fluency and pronunciation.

"The Great Energy Debate"

Prepare to Read

Build Background Guide students in a discussion of types of energy, such as wind, solar, coal, and oil, and how people use these resources. Explain that people have different opinions and attitudes about the types of energy we should use. Have them share their opinions about what they think is a good source of energy. Have students describe using: I think a good source of energy is ___ because ___.

Vocabulary Use the **Visual Vocabulary Cards** to review the vocabulary: *incredible, consequences, renewable, converted, efficient, installed, consume,* and *coincidence.* Use the online **ELL Visual Vocabulary Cards** to teach additional vocabulary: *ability, ancient, entire, percent, population,* and *related.*

Set Purpose *Today we will read "The Great Energy Debate" and focus on learning about the benefits and drawbacks, or problems, of using different energy sources. As we read, think about the Essential Question: How have our energy resources changed over the years?*

Read the Text

Select the **Scaffolded Shared Read** or the Shared Read in the **Reading/Writing Companion,** based on students' language proficiency.

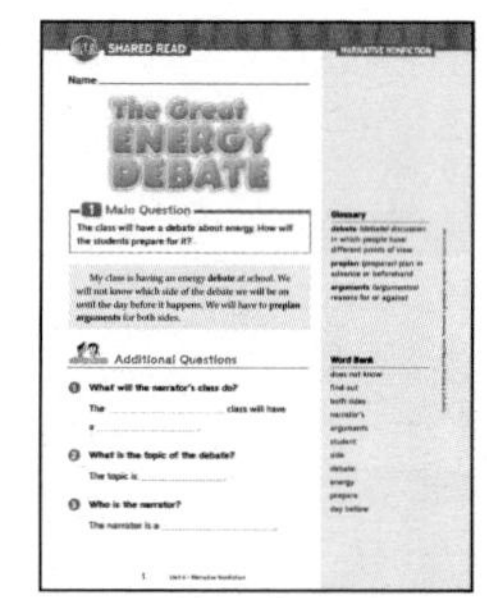

Scaffolded Shared Read, Lexile 720L

Beginning/Early-Intermediate Use the online Scaffolded Shared Read to help partners work together to read and understand narrative nonfiction. Remind them to use the Glossary to help them read and the Word Bank to help them answer the Main and Additional Questions.

Intermediate/Advanced Advanced High Read the text with students and use the Interactive Question-Response Routine to help them understand narrative nonfiction.

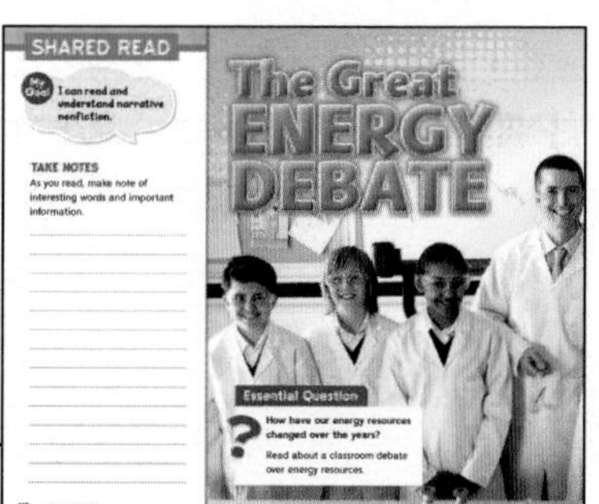

Reading/Writing Companion, Lexile: 910L

Pages 118–119

Paragraphs 1–2 Read the text with students and review the Vocabulary words *incredible, related,* and *consequences.* Discuss the meaning of *debate* and what happens when students debate. *What words provide clues about the meaning of debate?* (which side; preplan arguments for both sides) *When there is a debate, people express opposing opinions. We call each opinion a side.* Clarify the meaning of *side* using an example: My sister and I argued. This time, my mother thought I was right. She was on my side. *What is the topic of the debate?* (different energy sources) *What does the narrator need to do?* (The narrator needs to prepare for the debate.) *What information will the* *narrator have to learn about to prepare for the debate?* (consequences of using each energy source) *What is another word for consequence?* (effect)

COLLABORATE **Intermediate** Have partners describe what will happen at a debate using evidence from the text: At the debate, one team will talk about the benefits of one energy source. Then the other team will talk about issues and problems of using the energy source.

COLLABORATE **Advanced/Advance High** Have partners discuss why they think the teacher decided not to tell the students which side they will argue at the debate using evidence from the text. (Possible answer: I think the teacher didn't tell the students so they would learn about both sides. The narrator explains that students have to learn about both sides to be able to argue either side.)

Page 120

Paragraphs 1–2 Read the text with students and review the Vocabulary word *ancient. What is fossil fuel?* (a fuel made from ancient plant and animal remains formed over hundreds of millions of years) *What are problems with using fossil fuel?* (We use it faster than it forms, and we will run out of it; it pollutes the air.) *What are some ways we use fossil fuel?* (cars, factories)

Intermediate *What do geologists do?* (study earth) *Why are fossil fuels a nonrenewable resource?* (Fossil fuels are nonrenewable resources because when they are used, they cannot be replaced.)

Advanced/Advanced High *What are the benefits and drawbacks of fossil fuels?* (We use fossil fuels for gasoline and factories and cars, but fossil fuels are a nonrenewable source; they pollute the air.)

Sidebar: What Is Energy? Remind students that a sidebar gives additional information. Have students read the heading. *What information will you get from this section?* (information that tells what energy is)

COLLABORATE Have partners read and restate the information. The sidebar tells that energy is the ability to do work or make a change. It also tells how energy is produced. Some sources of energy are the wind, the sun, fossil fuels, and biofuels. Coal turns into heat. First, coal gets burned to make heat. Then the heat gets converted, or changed into electrical energy. Finally, people use the energy to light their houses.

Page 121

Paragraphs 1–2 Read the text with students and review Vocabulary words *renewable, converted, efficient, installed, consume, coincidence, entire, percent, and population.* Help students identify **relevant details** about wind energy. *What kind of energy is wind energy?* (renewable energy) *What does this mean?* (It will never run out.) *How efficient is wind energy?* (It is not as efficient as other energy sources. It would be expensive to install wind turbines.) Then help students state the **central idea**. *What is the most important idea about wind energy in paragraph 1?* (Wind energy has advantages and disadvantages.)

COLLABORATE **Intermediate** Have partners monitor their understanding of the text by taking turns asking and answering questions about the benefits and consequences of wind energy. What is one benefit of wind energy? One benefit of wind energy is that it is renewable. Wind turbines do not damage the environment. What is one problem with wind energy? One problem with wind energy is that it is not as efficient as some energy sources. Installing wind turbines is expensive.

COLLABORATE **Advanced** Have partners compare the benefits and drawbacks of using wind energy to fossil fuels. (Possible answer: Wind energy is renewable and will never run out, but we can run out of fossil fuels. Fossil fuels pollute the air. Wind energy does not harm the environment.)

FORMATIVE ASSESSMENT

STUDENT CHECK-IN

Have partners retell important ideas from the text. Then have students write the events in order using sequence words.

LEARNING GOALS

- **We can read and understand narrative nonfiction by identifying the central idea and relevant details.**
- **We can identify and use adverbs that tell where, when, and how.**

OBJECTIVES

Paraphrase portions of a text read aloud or information presented in diverse media and formats, including visually, quantitatively, and orally.

Demonstrate command of the conventions of standard English grammar and usage when writing or speaking.

LANGUAGE OBJECTIVES

Students will discuss the central idea and relevant details of a narrative text using key vocabulary.

Students will inquire about adverbs using complete sentences.

ELA ACADEMIC LANGUAGE

- *central idea, relevant details, adverbs*
- Cognates: *idea central, detalles relevantes, adverbios*

MATERIALS

Reading/Writing Companion, pp. 118–121, 122–123

Online Scaffolded Shared Read, "The Great Energy Debate"

Online Shared Read Writing Frames, p. 16

Online Language Development Cards, 50B

Online Language Development Practice, pp. 298–300

Online Language Transfers Handbook, pp. 15–19

"The Great Energy Debate"

Text Reconstruction

Focus on a single chunk of text to support comprehension and language development across the four domains.

1. Read aloud Paragraph 1 on page 120 in the **Reading/Writing Companion** while students listen.
2. Write the following on the board, providing definitions as needed: *geologist, remains, nonrenewable,* and *pollutes.* Instruct students to listen for them as you read the paragraph a second time.
3. Read the paragraph a third time. Tell students to listen and take notes.
4. COLLABORATE Have students work with a partner to reconstruct the text from their notes. Help them write complete sentences as needed.
5. Have students look at the original text. Ask them to tell what the paragraph is mostly about. (fossil fuels) Tell students that they are going to identify the relevant details that support the central idea.
6. *Where do fossil fuels come from?* (they formed from ancient plant and animal remains) *How long did it take for fossil fuels to form?* (hundreds of millions of years) *Why is using fossil fuels a problem?* (we use them faster than the time it takes them to form; burning them makes pollution) *What words help you understand what* nonrenewable *means?* ("If we keep using them, eventually there will be none left.") *What do the relevant details tell about the central idea?* (fossil fuels are an energy source but there are problems with using them because they create pollution and will run out eventually)
7. Have students compare their text reconstructions to the original text. Have them check whether they included the central idea and relevant details.

Beginning Have students follow along in the Reading/Writing Companion as you read the text aloud. Have them circle the words from Step 2 as they hear them.

Grammar in Context: Adverbs

Notice the Form Display the sentence from the text. Underline the adverb *never*.

> *For example, unlike fossil fuels, wind will never run out.*

Point to the word *never* and explain that it is an adverb. Discuss with students that adverbs tell when, where, or how an action happens. Point out that many adverbs end in *-ly* but some do not, such as *never*. *Does the word* never *tell about where, when, or how?* (It tells about when.) Discuss other examples of adverbs: *I walk quickly/slowly. Do the adverbs quickly and slowly tell about when, where, or how?* (They tell about how.) Generate other adverbs that tell when, where, and how. Have students copy and label the adverbs in their notebooks.

Apply and Extend Have partners write sentences using adverbs. Check their answers and provide corrective feedback.

For additional practice, see **Language Development Cards**, Lesson 50B, and **Language Development Practice**, pages 298–300.

Independent Time

Vocabulary Building Have students build glossaries.

Beginning/Early Intermediate Have students complete the Glossary Activities in the **Scaffolded Shared Read**.

Intermediate/Advanced/Advanced High Have students add the vocabulary from **Reading/Writing Companion** pages 122–123 and self-selected words they would like to learn to the chart.

Mixed Levels Have students at different proficiency levels work together to learn vocabulary: Beginning and Early-Intermediate students can teach each other vocabulary from their Scaffolded Shared Read glossaries. Intermediate and Advanced/Advanced High students can teach their self-selected words.

WORD/PHRASE	DEFINE	EXAMPLE	ASK
ancient	from a long time ago, very old	Fossil fuels formed from ancient remains.	What did ancient people use for energy?

COLLABORATE **Shared Read Writing Frames** Use the online leveled Shared Read Writing Frames for "The Great Energy Debate" to provide students with additional oral and written practice. Differentiated frames are available to provide support for all levels.

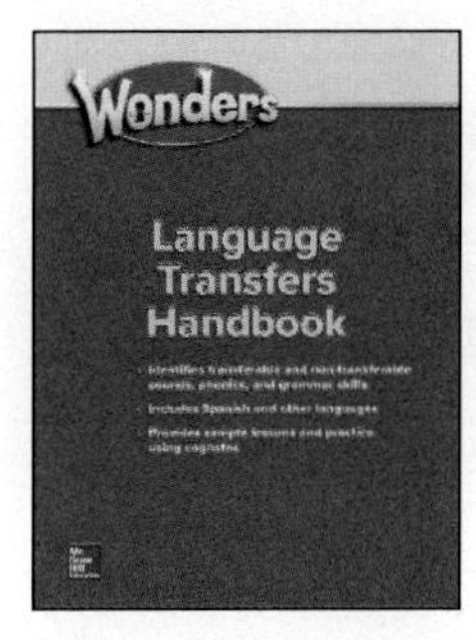

Language Transfers Handbook, Grammar Transfers, pp. 15–19

DIGITAL TOOLS

For additional support, use the online activities.

Grammar Video

Grammar Song

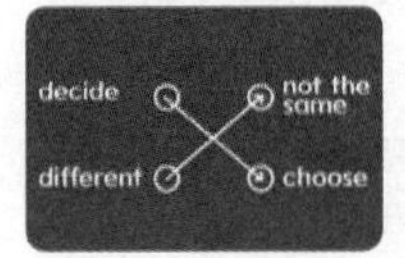

Vocabulary Activity

FORMATIVE ASSESSMENT

STUDENT CHECK IN

Text Reconstruction Have partners share their notes. Have students reflect on their work using the Check-In routine.

Grammar in Context Have students share their sentences. Have students reflect on their work using the Check-In routine.

LEARNING GOALS

- **Read** I can read and understand narrative nonfiction.
- **Reread** We can analyze text, craft, and structure.

OBJECTIVES

Refer to details and examples in a text when explaining what the text says explicitly and when drawing inferences from the text.

By the end of year, read and comprehend informational texts, including history social studies, science, and technical texts, in the grades 4-5 text complexity band proficiently, with scaffolding as needed at the high end of the range.

Review the key ideas expressed and explain their own ideas and understanding in light of the discussion.

Identify and classify Earth's renewable resources, including air, plants, water, and animals; and nonrenewable resources, including coal, oil, and natural gas; and the importance of conservation.

LANGUAGE OBJECTIVES

Students will inquire about the text by answering questions using key vocabulary.

ELA ACADEMIC LANGUAGE

- *repetition*
- Cognate: *repetición*

MATERIALS

Reading/Writing Companion, pp. 130-132

Literature Anthology, pp. 458-475

Visual Vocabulary Cards

Online ELL Anchor Text Support BLMs, pp. 39-41

DIGITAL TOOLS

Have students read along as they listen to the selection to develop comprehension and practice fluency and pronunciation.

Energy Island

Prepare to Read

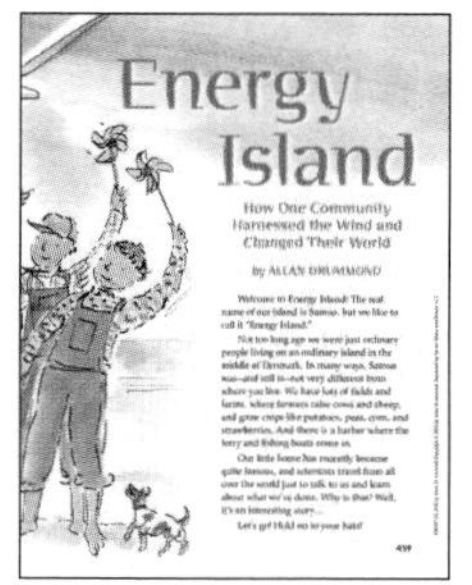

Literature Anthology, Lexile: 840

Build Background Discuss the ways students use energy, such as electricity for lighting and heat. Explain that most electricity is created using fossil fuels that can not be easily replaced. Guide students to tell whether using renewable energy is a good idea and why.

Vocabulary Use the **Visual Vocabulary Cards** to review the vocabulary: *renewable, converted, consequences, installed, coincidence, incredible, efficient, consume.*

Set Purpose Today we will read about how one group of people used renewable energy. As we read, think about how we can use different kinds of energy to save our resources.

Have students listen to the audio summary of the text, which is available in multiple languages.

Read

Literature Anthology, pp. 458–475

Use the **Interactive Question-Response Routine** to help students read and discuss Energy Island.

Beginning Help students discuss in complete sentences. Provide sentence frames: Samsø is an island. The people of Samsø found new ways to get energy.

Intermediate Ask students to respond in complete sentences and add details. Provide sentence starters as needed: Samsø is an island in Denmark. It is called Energy Island because they use only renewable energy.

Advanced/Advanced High Have students respond in complete sentences and add details.

COLLABORATE **Independent Reading Practice** Have mixed level pairs complete pages 39-41 of the **ELL Anchor Text Support BLMs** and share with the group.

Reread

Use the following prompts when working on **Reading/Writing Companion**, pages 130-132.

Literature Anthology, pages 460–461

COLLABORATE **Author's Craft: Repetition** Read the paragraphs with students, emphasizing the word "ordinary." Have students ask about words or phrases they don't know or understand. Note the repetition of "ordinary." Elicit that authors often repeat words or phrases to emphasize or show that something is important. Instruct students to listen to how the author uses this word as you reread the text.

Beginning Read the second and third paragraphs on page 460 with students. Restate and explain sentences as needed. *What is one thing that is ordinary about the island?* In the summer, they have fun at the beach. *What is one ordinary thing about the way they use energy?* They used hot water without even thinking. *What is not ordinary about the island?* (the wind)

Intermediate Have partners discuss what is described as ordinary. (what people do on the island, how they use energy, Mr Hermansen) *What is described as not ordinary?* (the wind) Discuss the meaning of "independent of nonrenewable energy." *What energy did the people on Samsø use that was nonrenewable energy?* (oil) *Will the people of Samsø use nonrenewable energy?* (no)

Advanced/Advanced High *What are the ordinary things that people at Samsø do and what will they do that is not ordinary?* (The way they use energy is ordinary, but their plan to become independent of nonrenewable energy is not.) *Why does the author repeat the word ordinary on these pages?* (The author wants to show that the island is like every other place and something not ordinary is going to happen with the wind.)

Literature Anthology, pages 462–463

COLLABORATE **Author's Purpose** Read page 462 with students. Have students ask about words or phrases they don't understand. *What does Søren Hermansen ask his students?* (to think of ways to make their own energy) *What did they suggest?* (ride bicycles instead of cars, get heat from the sun, use oil from crops, burn straw and wood) *What are some of the effects of making their own energy?* (oil tankers would not need to come to the island, electricity wouldn't need to come from the mainland, the island would have cleaner energy) Read page 463 with students. *What does Katherine suggest?* (to use energy from the wind) *Why does she make the suggestion?* (The island gets plenty of wind all the time.) Discuss the literal and idiomatic meanings of "Hold on to your hats!" *Why does the class say "Hold on to your hats"?* (because the island is windy)

Beginning Read the first paragraph and the speech bubbles with students and restate sentences. Have partners retell student's suggestions: People can use bicycles instead of cars. They can use heat from the sun and oil from crops. They can burn straw and wood.

Intermediate *What does the phrase "Hold on to your hats!" refer to?* (the wind on the island)

Advanced/Advanced High Have partners discuss the meaning of "Hold on to your hats!"

Literature Anthology, page 472

COLLABORATE **Author's Craft: Word Choice** Read the text with students. Discuss the meaning of the phrase "plenty going on" and elicit that it means that a lot of events are happening. *What happens at the learning center?* (People from all over the world come to learn about what the people of the island did and to share new ideas for energy.)

Beginning Read the paragraph with students. Help them restate challenging sentences. *Where is the narrator?* (top of turbine) *Which words tell you the narrator is looking down at the island?* ("Down there") *What does the narrator see?* (new learning center)

Intermediate *What did the author call the island at the beginning?* (ordinary) *What word tells the author's opinion of Mr. Hermansen?* (extraordinary) *Why does the author call Mr. Hermansen extraordinary?* (ordinary people in ordinary places did something extraordinary)

Advanced/Advanced High *Why does the narrator say "there is plenty going on"?* (The island has changed with wind turbines. People want to learn about how they did it.)

FORMATIVE ASSESSMENT

STUDENT CHECK-IN

Read Have partners tell each other important details from the text. Have them reflect using the Check-In routine.

Reread Have partners share responses and text evidence on **Reading/Writing Companion** pages 130–132. Ask students to reflect using the Check-In routine to fill in the bars.

LEARNING GOALS

- **We can read and understand narrative nonfiction by identifying the central idea and relevant details.**
- **We can compare using irregular adverbs.**

OBJECTIVES

Paraphrase portions of a text read aloud or information presented in diverse media and formats, including visually, quantitatively, and orally.

Demonstrate command of the conventions of standard English grammar and usage when writing or speaking.

LANGUAGE OBJECTIVES

Students will discuss the central idea and relevant details using academic vocabulary.

Students will discuss using adverbs to compare in complete sentences.

ELA ACADEMIC LANGUAGE

- *central idea, relevant details, adverbs, comparative*
- Cognates: *idea central, detalles relevantes, adverbios, comparativo*

MATERIALS

Literature Anthology, pp. 458–475

Online Language Development Cards, 53A–53B

Online Language Development Practice, pp. 313–318

Online Language Transfers Handbook, pp. 15–19

Energy Island

Text Reconstruction

Focus on a single chunk of text to support comprehension and language development across the four domains.

1. Read aloud paragraph 2 on page 462 in the **Literature Anthology** while students listen.
2. Write the following on the board, providing definitions as needed: *crops, power up, tankers, mainland, renewable resources,* and *think big.* Instruct students to listen for them as you read the paragraph a second time.
3. Read the paragraph a third time while students listen and take notes.
4. COLLABORATE Have students work with a partner to reconstruct the text from their notes. Help them write complete sentences as needed.
5. Have students look at the original text. Ask them to say what the paragraph is mostly about. (the benefits of using renewable energy on the island) Tell students they are going to identify the relevant details that support the central idea.
6. *What were the people of Samsø using to make energy?* (they used oil and electricity from the mainland) *What did they say they could use instead?* *(renewable resources, the sun, their crops, and their legs, or their own energy)* *What are some benefits of using renewable resources?* (they wouldn't need oil or electricity from the mainland, it would be cleaner, and they would save money.) *What do these details tell you about the central idea?* (It is good to use renewable resources.)
7. Have students compare their text reconstructions to the original text. Have them check whether they also included words that introduce the central idea and the relevant details.

Beginning Allow students to follow along in the Literature Anthology as you read aloud. Have them point to the words from Step 2 as they hear them.

Apply Author's Craft: Word Choice

Remind students that authors use descriptive language to help readers visualize ideas in the text. *On page 472, what does the author say people are doing at the Energy Academy? (people from all over the world come to visit) What else are the people in Samsø doing?* (Possible answers: creating, sharing) *What does the author want you to visualize?* (Possible answers: a lot of activity, excitement) Have students rewrite the paragraph in their own words.

Grammar in Context: Deconstruct a Sentence

Write this sentence from page 468 on the board: *Suddenly, all the electricity on the entire island went out!* Facilitate deconstructing this sentence for better comprehension.

- Point to the word *suddenly* in the sentence. *What kind of word is it?* (adverb) *What do adverbs do?* (They tell how, when, and where an action happens.) *What does the adverb suddenly tell about?* (how the electricity went out)
- Discuss that we can use adverbs to compare two or more actions. Write on the board: *I arrived late. Sue arrived later than me. Lee arrived the latest.* Point to *later* and *latest.* Point out that *later* compares when I and Sue arrived and latest compares when I, Sue, and Lee arrived.
- Discuss that *-er* and *-est* endings are added to most short adverbs to compare, such as: *fast/faster/fastest; easy/easier/easiest.* For long adverbs, we add the words *more* and *most*: *carefully/more carefully/most carefully.* Review the comparative forms for *well* and *badly*: well/better/best; badly/worse/worst.
- With students, generate sentences using adverbs to compare and have them copy the sentences in their notebooks.

For additional practice, see **Language Development Cards**, Lessons 53A-53B and **Language Development Practice**, pages 313-318.

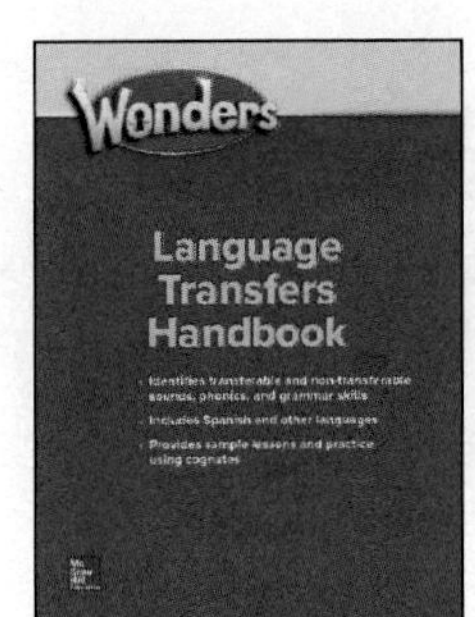

Language Transfers Handbook, Grammar Transfers, pp. 15–19

Independent Time

Vocabulary Building Have partners create an interactive word wall with energy-related vocabulary from the selection. Have students write the type of energy onto index cards. On the back of each card, have them describe where it comes from, and how people use it. Have pairs tape the index cards to the wall with the description facing out. Then have other students look at a card, guess the energy source, and turn the card over to confirm their answer.

Beginning Allow students to include drawings in the description.

Intermediate/Advanced/Advanced High Have students include some of the energy related self-selected words and content-area words they added to their glossaries.

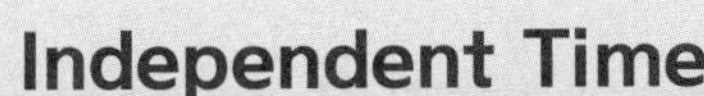

Compare with Adverbs Have partners select two or three animals and generate verbs and adverbs to describe each animal. Then have them use the chart to compare actions. Then have them write a sentence using the adverbs to compare. Check their sentences and provide corrective feedback.

ADVERBS	COMPARATIVE ADVERB	SUPERLATIVE ADVERB
high	higher	highest

FORMATIVE ASSESSMENT

STUDENT CHECK-IN

Text Reconstruction Ask partners to share their notes. Have them reflect using the Check-In routine.

Grammar in Context Have partners reflect on their deconstructions using the Check-In routine.

LEARNING GOALS

We can apply strategies and skills to read narrative nonfiction.

OBJECTIVES

Determine the central, or main, idea of a text and explain how it is supported by key details; summarize the text.

Use common, grade-appropriate Greek and Latin affixes and roots as clues to the meaning of a word.

Review the key ideas expressed and explain their own ideas and understanding in light of the discussion.

LANGUAGE OBJECTIVES

Students will explain the central idea and relevant details using simple and complex sentences.

ELA ACADEMIC LANGUAGE

- *visualize, prefix, central idea, relevant detail, sidebar*
- Cognates: *visualizar, prefijo, idea central, detalle relevante*

MATERIALS

Online ELL Genre Passage: "Energy from the Sea"

"Energy from the Sea"

Genre Passage
Lexile: 820L

Prepare to Read

Build Background Talk with students about using water as a source to generate power, such as electricity. Have students share what they know or learned about the ways people generated energy in the past, such as the waterwheel or dams.

Vocabulary Use the Define, Example, Ask routine to pre-teach difficult words or unfamiliar concepts, such as *waterwheel, force* and *hydroelectric* (cognates: fuerza, hidroeléctrico). Invite students to add new vocabulary to their glossaries.

Set Purpose *Today we will read "Energy from the Sea." As we read, think about how our energy resources have changed over the years.*

Read the Text

Page E1, Paragraph 1

What did the narrator see? (waves) *What idea did this give the narrator?* (using water for power)

Beginning Read the first paragraph. Restate the sentences as needed. *What words help you visualize, or picture in your mind, the waves?* The waves crash on the sand. The water splashed around me. *What can we use for power?* (water)

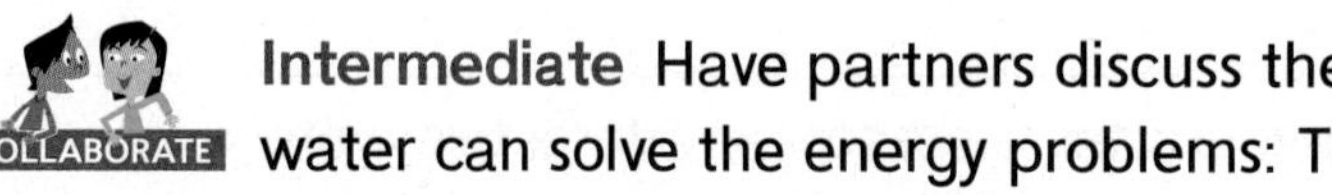

COLLABORATE **Intermediate** Have partners discuss the reason that the narrator thinks water can solve the energy problems: The author thinks that water is a solution because it is a renewable resource.

Advanced/Advanced High *How is water useful?* (It is a renewable source and can help to solve energy problems.)

Page E1, Paragraphs 2–3

Greek Prefixes Point out that the word *hydropower* has the Greek prefix *hydro-*, which means "water." *What does* hydropower *mean?* (power from water) *Who used waterwheels?* (people in ancient Egypt, Greece, and Rome) *What did people use waterwheels to do?* (to grind corn and run machines)

COLLABORATE **Beginning** Read the second paragraph with students and restate sentences as needed. Help partners take turns to ask and answer questions: *What is a waterwheel?* A waterwheel is a big wheel. *What does it do?* It runs machines. *Who used the waterwheel?* The ancient Egyptians, Greeks, and Romans used the waterwheel. The Pilgrims also used the waterwheel.

Intermediate *What could the first hydroelectric plant do?* (make energy to power a house and two paper mills) *What can they do now?* (produce enough power to light many homes)

Advanced/Advanced High Have partners describe how a waterwheel created power to run machines. (The wheel was connected to a machine. The force of the water turned the wheel. When the wheel turned, it ran the machine.)

Central Idea and Relevant Details Have partners describe the central idea on page E1 and identify relevant details: Waterpower is a renewable resource that has been used since ancient times. Water may help us solve our energy problems.

Page E2, Paragraphs 1–3

Why is using water as an energy source a problem? (It cannot be used in all places.)

Beginning Read the second paragraph with students and restate sentences as needed. *Why does the narrator go to the library?* The narrator wants to find out how much waterpower people use. Read the fourth sentence and clarify that "our energy" refers to the energy people use.

Intermediate Have partners describe the meaning of the phrase "I had hoped to see more power made from sources that can be reused": The author wanted to discover that more energy came from renewable resources like water and wind.

Advanced/Advanced High *Based on the text, what is the author's point of view about renewable sources?* (Possible answer: The author thinks that renewable resources are the energy sources people should use.)

Page E2, Sidebar

Dams hold water. What else can dams do? Dams can make electricity. *When the water is high, the pressure makes turbines turn. This generates, or makes, power. What can that power do?* It can *heat and light the houses nearby*.

Respond to Reading

Use the following instruction to help students answer the questions on page E3.

1. **Visualize** *Read the first paragraph in "Energy from the Sea." What does* the sea *refer to?* (water) *What does the water do?* (splash and pull shells)
2. *Look at page E1. What words or phrases signal time?* (many years, 2500 BCE, 1628, 1882, today) *How are the dates presented in the text?* (*in the order they happened*)
3. **Sidebar** *What is the title?* (How Dams Work) *How does the sidebar relate to the main text?* (It tells how dams use water to make power.)

Fluency Have partners take turns reading the passage.

Build Knowledge: Make Connections

Talk About the Text Have partners discuss how our energy resources have changed over the years.

Write About the Text Have students add their ideas to their Build Knowledge pages of their reader's notebooks.

STUDENT CHECK-IN

Have partners share their responses on page E3. Ask students to reflect using the Check-In routine.

LEVEL UP

IF students read the **ELL Level** fluently and answered the questions,

THEN pair them with students who have proficiently read the **On Level**. Have them

- partner read the **On Level** passage
- summarize the **main idea** and identify supporting **details**

LEARNING GOALS

We can apply strategies and skills to read narrative nonfiction.

OBJECTIVES

Refer to details and examples in a text when explaining what the text says explicitly and when drawing inferences from the text.

Pose and respond to specific questions to clarify or follow up on information, and make comments that contribute to the discussion and link to the remarks of others.

Read grade-level prose and poetry orally with accuracy, appropriate rate, and expression on successive readings.

LANGUAGE OBJECTIVES

Students will inquire about hydropower by asking and answering questions.

ELA ACADEMIC LANGUAGE

- *ask and answer, rate, accuracy*

MATERIALS

ELL Leveled Reader: *Planet Power*

Online Differentiated Texts: "Cooking Throughout History"

Online ELL Visual Vocabulary Cards

DIGITAL TOOLS

MULTIMODAL

Have students read along as they listen to the selections to develop comprehension and practice fluency and pronunciation.

Planet Power

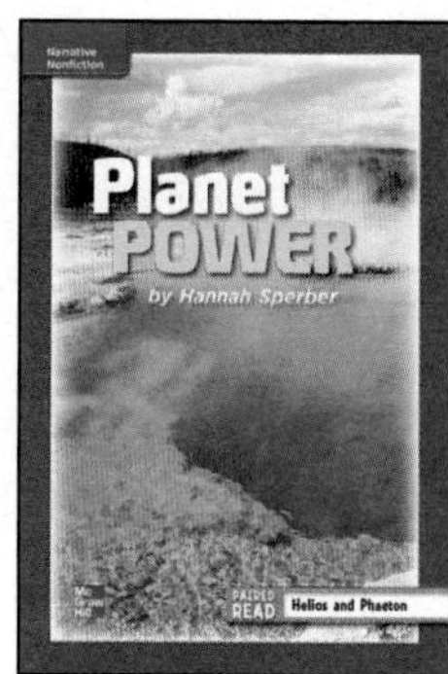

Leveled Reader
Lexile 770L

Prepare to Read

Build Background Read the title aloud. Discuss with students that the word *power* refers to energy. Then discuss with them what they think the text will be about. Preview *Planet Power* and "Helios and Phaeton": *Our purpose for reading is to learn about energy sources and how ancient Greeks thought of the sun.*

Vocabulary Use the routine on the **ELL Visual Vocabulary Cards** to pre-teach ELL Vocabulary *control* (Cognate: *controlar*) and *source*. Use the glossary definitions on page 19 of the text to define vocabulary.

Set Purpose *Today we will read a narrative nonfiction text called* Planet Power. *As we read, think about how our energy resources have changed over the years.*

Read the Text

Pages 2–3

COLLABORATE **Ask and Answer Questions** *Asking questions can help readers understand difficult ideas.* Demonstrate with these questions: What are fossil fuels? What are some examples of fossil fuels? How do people use fossil fuels? Have students reread the second paragraph on page 2 and answer the questions. Then have partners ask and answer questions about renewable energy.

COLLABORATE **Beginning** Help students talk about fossil fuels: Some examples of fossils fuels are oil, gas, and coal. People burn fossil fuels to release energy. Fossil fuels pollute the air. They can only be used one time.

Page 4

Beginning *What is an example of hydropower?* One example of hydropower is a dam. *What do dams make?* Dams make electricity.

Intermediate *What do dams use to generate electricity?* Dams use turbines to generate electricity. *How are turbines in a dam similar to waterwheels?* In a dam, moving water turns turbines. Moving water can also turn waterwheels.

COLLABORATE **Advanced/Advanced High** *How was water first used as a source of energy?* (Moving water turned waterwheels. The waterwheels pressed grains to make flour.) Have partners explain one way to generate electricity from water: First water moves through a dam. Then water turns turbines in the dam. Finally the movement of the turbines generates electricity.

Pages 7–8

COLLABORATE **Intermediate** Have partners describe how geothermal heat reaches the surface: Geysers and hot springs release hot water from under the ground.

Have partners discuss the source of geothermal energy and ways people use it: Geothermal energy comes from the heat inside Earth. People use it to cook, wash, and keep warm.

Pages 10

Beginning Help partners describe solar energy: Solar energy comes from the sun. People use it to heat homes.

Intermediate *What action words tell how the sun's rays are used?* (*trap; capture; convert*)

Advanced/Advanced High *How have uses for solar energy changed?* (People used it for heat. Now people also convert it into electricity.)

Respond to Reading Have partners complete their graphic organizers and discuss the questions on page 15.

Fluency: Rate, Accuracy

Read pages 12–13 with appropriate rate and accuracy. Read it again while students read along. For more practice, have students record their voices a few times and choose the best one.

Paired Read: "Helios and Phaeton"

Analytical Writing — Make Connections: Write About It

Use sentence frames to discuss the questions on page 18: *Why did ancient Greeks believe myths?* Myths explained natural events. *Reread the page 16. What does the sun create every morning?* The sun creates light and energy. *Reread paragraph 1 on page 10. Describe the sun's energy.* The sun's energy is clean and renewable.

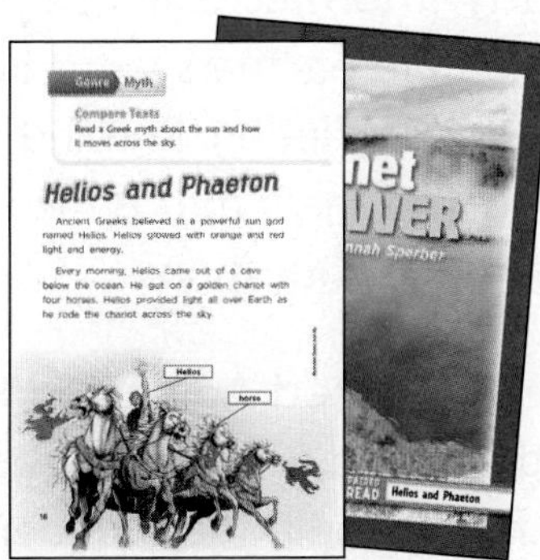

ELL Leveled Reader

Build Knowledge: Make Connections

Talk About the Text Have partners discuss how our energy resources have changed over the years.

Write About the Text Have students add their ideas to their Build Knowledge pages of their reader's notebooks.

Self-Selected Reading

Have students choose another narrative nonfiction from the online **Leveled Reader Library** or read the **Differentiated Text:** "Cooking Throughout History."

FOCUS ON SCIENCE

Have students complete the activity on page 20 to observe temperature changes using solar energy.

LITERATURE CIRCLES

Ask students to conduct a literature circle using the Thinkmark questions to guide the discussion.

FORMATIVE ASSESSMENT

STUDENT CHECK-IN

Have partners share their answers to Respond to Reading. Ask students to reflect on their learning using the Check-In routine.

LEVEL UP

IF students read the **ELL Level** fluently and answered the questions,

THEN pair them with students who have proficiently read the **On Level** and have students:

- read the **On Level** main selection aloud with their partners.
- list words they find difficult.
- discuss these words with their partners.

Access Complex Text

The **On Level** challenges students by including more **domain-specific words** and **complex sentence structures**.

LEARNING GOALS

I can read and understand historical fiction.

OBJECTIVES

Determine a theme of a story, drama, or poem from details in the text; summarize the text.

Use context (e.g., definitions, examples, or restatements in text) as a clue to the meaning of a word or phrase.

Engage effectively in a range of collaborative discussions with diverse partners on grade 4 topics and texts, building on others' ideas and expressing their own clearly.

LANGUAGE OBJECTIVES

Students will inquire about the theme of a historical fiction text using key vocabulary.

ELA ACADEMIC LANGUAGE

- *historical fiction, connotation*
- Cognates: *ficción histórica, connotación*

MATERIALS

Reading/Writing Companion, pp. 144–147

Online Scaffolded Shared Read, "A Surprise Reunion"

Visual Vocabulary Cards

Online ELL Visual Vocabulary Cards

DIGITAL TOOLS

MULTIMODAL

Have students read along as they listen to the selection to develop comprehension and practice fluency and pronunciation.

"A Surprise Reunion"

Prepare to Read

Build Background Explain that the Lewis and Clark expedition was a journey to cross and explore the western part of the United States. Sacagawea was a Native American woman who helped Lewis and Clark reach their destination and establish contacts with Native American populations. Display a map and show the journey to the Pacific Coast.

Vocabulary Use the **Visual Vocabulary Cards** to review the vocabulary: *intensity, honor, ancestors, forfeit, despised, irritating, endurance,* and *retreated.* Use the online **ELL Visual Vocabulary Cards** to teach additional vocabulary from the Shared Read: *adjusted, offered, provide, strength,* and *transport.* (Cognates: *ofreció, transporte*)

Set Purpose *We will read a historical fiction about Sacagawea and her brother Chief Cameahwait. As we read, think about how* traditions connect people.

Read the Text

Select the **Scaffolded Shared Read** or the Shared Read in the **Reading/Writing Companion**, based on students' language proficiency.

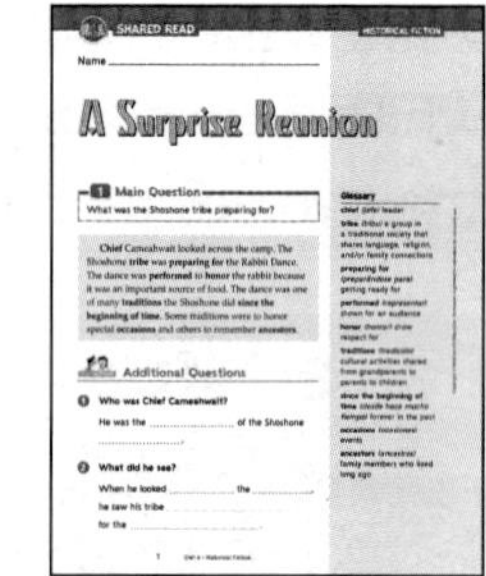

Scaffolded Shared Read, Lexile 460L

Beginning/Early-Intermediate Use the online Scaffolded Shared Read to help partners work together to read and understand historical fiction. Remind them to use the Glossary to help them read and the Word Bank to help them answer the Main and Additional Questions.

Intermediate/Advanced Advanced High Read the text with students and use the Interactive Question-Response Routine to help them understand historical fiction.

Reading/Writing Companion, Lexile 650L

Page 145

Paragraphs 1–2 Read the text with students and review the Vocabulary words *intensity, honor, ancestors,* and *forfeit.* Have students use visual and contextual clues to describe the Shoshone camp. *What visual and context clues tell you the meaning of* Shoshone*?* (The illustration, "Chief," and "camp" show that it is the name of a Native American people.) *What does the chief see?* (He sees the tribe prepare for the Rabbit Dance.) *Why do the Shoshone people honor the rabbit?* (It is the source of food and clothing.)

Paragraph 3 Read the text with students and review the words *despised* and *irritating. What does Chief Cameahwait remember about his childhood?* (playing with his sister) *What happened to his sister?* (she was kidnapped) *Does he know what happened to her?* (no)

Intermediate *What context clues help you understand the meaning of the word* despised? ("snatched...during a raid"; "those who had taken her")

Advanced/Advanced High *What clues describe how Chief Cameahwait feels?* (He feels pain, so he still misses her.)

COLLABORATE Have partners compare *smile* and *grimace* to help them understand **connotation**: People smile when they are happy, so smile has a positive connotation. The chief grimaces when he feels pain and anger, so grimace has a negative connotation.

Page 146

Paragraphs 1–2 Read the text with students and review the words *endurance, offered, strength* and *transport. What does Captain Lewis tell the Shoshone?* (He explains that his expedition is going to explore the land between the Missouri River and the ocean.) *What does Captain Lewis tell Cameahwait?* (Lewis needs help transporting supplies.) *What does Captain Lewis offer in exchange for Cameahwait's help?* (food and other goods)

COLLABORATE Have partners describe why Captain Lewis asks for help from the Shoshone: Captain Lewis needs help transporting supplies across the land during their expedition.

Paragraphs 3–5 Read the text with students and review the word *adjusted. What does Captain Clark suggest to Cameahwait?* (ways to help each other) *What does he tell Cameahwait?* (He is traveling with a woman who knows the language.) *What is the woman's name?* (Sacagawea)

Advanced/Advanced High *How can Sacagawea help in the meeting?* (Possible answer: Captain Lewis mentions that she knows the Shoshone language, so she can work as a translator.)

Page 147

Paragraphs 1–3 Read the text with students and review the words *retreated* and *provide. How does Cameahwait feel when he sees Sacagawea?* (He is surprised.) *How do you know?* (He "could not believe his eyes.") *What does he realize?* (Sacagawea is his lost sister.)

COLLABORATE **Beginning** Have partners describe the meaning of "could not believe his eyes." Cameahwait knew Sacagawea was his sister, but he needed to be sure.

Paragraphs 4–5 Read the text with students. *How did Lewis and Clark help Cameahwait and Sacagawea?* (They helped the brother and sister find each other.)

COLLABORATE Have partners discuss what new tradition Cameahwait will start for finding his sister. (singing and dancing each year to celebrate)

Intermediate *Does Cameahwait mean for the tradition honoring his sister to last a few years or many years?* (many years) *What phrase in the text supports your answer?* ("for generations to come")

Advanced/Advanced High *What word tells that Lewis and Clark did not know that they were going to reunite Cameahwait with his sister?* (*unwitting*) Have students use the word *unwitting* in a sentence.

Advanced High *How were Lewis and Clark "unwitting partners" in the reunion between Sacagawea and Cameahwait?* (Possible responses: They did not know that Sacagawea and Cameahwait were brother and sister.)

COLLABORATE Remind students that a **theme** is an important message the author wants to share. *How do Cameahwait and Sacagawea feel when they are reunited?* (*They are happy.*) *What does this tell about the theme?* (*Possible answer: Families are important.*)

FORMATIVE ASSESSMENT

STUDENT CHECK-IN

Have partners retell the events in the story in order. Then have students write the events in order using sequence words.

LEARNING GOALS

- **We can read and understand historical fiction by analyzing the theme.**
- **We can recognize and use prepositions.**

OBJECTIVES

Paraphrase portions of a text read aloud or information presented in diverse media and formats, including visually, quantitatively, and orally.

Form and use prepositional phrases.

LANGUAGE OBJECTIVES

Students will discuss the theme of a historical fiction text using key vocabulary.

Students will inform about prepositions using complete sentences.

ELA ACADEMIC LANGUAGE

- *theme, preposition*
- Cognates: *tema, preposición*

MATERIALS

Reading/Writing Companion, pp. 144-147, 148-149

Online Scaffolded Shared Read, "A Surprise Reunion"

Online Shared Read Writing Frames, p. 17

Online Language Development Cards, 56A-56B

Online Language Development Practice, pp. 331-336

Online Language Transfers Handbook, pp. 15-19

"A Surprise Reunion"

Text Reconstruction

Focus on a single chunk of text to support comprehension and language development across the four domains.

1. Read aloud the last two paragraphs on page 147 of the **Reading/Writing Companion** while students listen.
2. Write the following on the board, providing definitions as needed: *unwitting, reunited, beloved, honor,* and *generations*. Instruct students to listen for them as you read the paragraphs a second time.
3. Read the paragraphs a third time. Tell students to listen and take notes.
4.  COLLABORATE Have students work with a partner to reconstruct the text from their notes. Help them write complete sentences as needed.
5. Have students look at the original text. Ask them to tell what the paragraphs are mostly about. (It tells how Cameahwait will celebrate finding his sister.) Tell students they are going to analyze how this paragraph supports one of the story's themes: family is important.
6. *How did Lewis and Clark help Chief Cameahwait?* (they reunited him with his sister) *What words tell you about Cameahwait's feelings for his sister?* (she is a great gift; beloved) *How will people celebrate the reunion?* (they will sing and tell stories) *What does Chief Cameahwait say that future generations will do?* (they will remember and honor his reunion with his sister) *How do these details support the theme?* (It shows how important family is.)
7. Have students compare their text reconstructions to the original text. Have them check whether they also included words that support the theme.

Beginning Have students follow along in the Reading/Writing Companion as you read the text aloud. Have them circle the words from Step 2 as they hear them.

Grammar in Context: Prepositions

Notice the Form Display the sentences from the text, and circle the prepositions. Underline the nouns that are objects of prepositions.

> *"A slender woman with long, dark braids entered the tent. Her eyes adjusted to the dim light filtered through the thick cloth."*

What kind of words are the circled words? (prepositions) *What are the underlined words?* (nouns) *Which noun is the object of the preposition* with*?* (braids) *What is the prepositional phrase that begins with the preposition* with*?* (with long, dark braids) *What are the other prepositional phrases?* (to the dim light, through the thick cloth) Discuss with students the information each prepositional phrase provides: gives detail about the woman's hair; what her eyes did; the type of light the woman saw. Have students copy and label the prepositions in their notebooks.

Apply and Extend Have partners paraphrase and rewrite the sentences. Check their sentences and provide corrective feedback.

For additional practice, see **Language Development Cards**, Lessons 56A and 56B, and **Language Development Practice**, pages 331–336.

Independent Time

Vocabulary Building Have students build glossaries.

Beginning/Early Intermediate Have students complete the Glossary Activities in the **Scaffolded Shared Read**.

Intermediate/Advanced/Advanced High Have students add the vocabulary from pages 148–149 of the **Reading/Writing Companion** and self-selected words or phrases they would like to learn to the chart.

Mixed Levels Have students at different proficiency levels work together to learn vocabulary: Beginning and Early-Intermediate students can teach each other vocabulary from their Scaffolded Shared Read glossaries. Intermediate and Advanced/Advanced High students can teach each other their self-selected words.

WORD/PHRASE IN ENGLISH	DEFINITION IN ENGLISH	USE THE WORD/PHRASE IN A SENTENCE
mission	an important assignment or goal	The organization's mission is to end hunger.

COLLABORATE

Shared Read Writing Frames Use the online leveled Shared Read Writing Frames for "A Surprise Reunion" to provide students with additional oral and written practice. Differentiated frames are available to provide support for all levels.

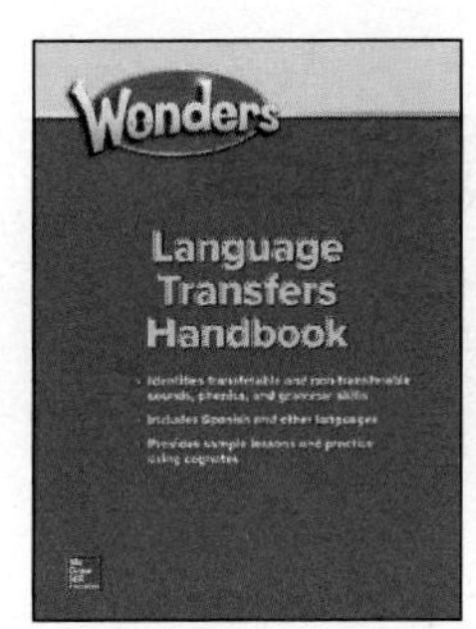

Language Transfers Handbook, Grammar Transfers, pp. 15–19

DIGITAL TOOLS

For additional support, use the online activities.

Grammar Video

Grammar Song

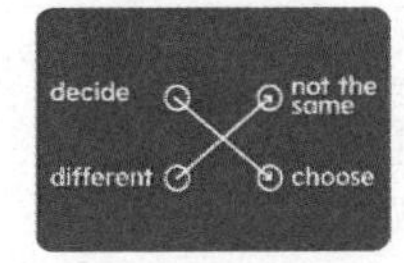

Vocabulary Activity

FORMATIVE ASSESSMENT

STUDENT CHECK IN

Text Reconstruction Have partners share their notes. Have students reflect on their work using the Check-In routine.

Grammar in Context Have students share their sentences. Have them reflect on their work using the Check-In routine.

LEARNING GOALS

- **Read** We can apply strategies and skills to read historical fiction.
- **Reread** We can analyze text, craft, and structure.

OBJECTIVES

Refer to details and examples in a text when explaining what the text says explicitly and when drawing inferences from the text.

Describe in depth a character, setting, or event in a story or drama, drawing on specific details in the text.

Engage effectively in a range of collaborative discussions with diverse partners on grade 4 topics and texts, building on others' ideas and expressing their own clearly.

LANGUAGE OBJECTIVES

Students will inquire by answering questions about the story using key vocabulary.

ELA ACADEMIC LANGUAGE

- *setting, describe*
- Cognate: *describir*

MATERIALS

Reading Writing Companion, pp 156-158

Literature Anthology, pp. 482-493

Visual Vocabulary Cards

Online ELL Anchor Text Support BLMs, pp. 42-44

DIGITAL TOOLS

MULTIMODAL

Have students read along as they listen to the selection to develop comprehension and practice fluency and pronunciation.

The Game of Silence

Prepare to Read

Literature Anthology, Lexile 900L

Build Background Tell students that *The Game of Silence* takes place in 1850. Explain that during that time, Native American groups were forced to leave their lands. This caused many problems for Native American tribes, or groups, such as the Ojibwe. On a map, point out the region of the United States where the story takes place, east of the Mississippi River near Lake Superior.

Vocabulary Use the **Visual Vocabulary Cards** to review the vocabulary: *intensity, honor, ancestors, forfeit, despised, irritating, endurance, and retreated.*

Set Purpose Today we will read a historical fiction story about a girl named Omakayas. As we read, think about how Omakayas learns that her way of life could change.

Read

Literature Anthology, pp. 482–493

Use the **Interactive Question-Response Routine** to help students read and discuss *The Game of Silence.*

Beginning Help students discuss in complete sentences. Provide sentence frames: The children play a game of silence. Omakayas pretends she is a stone.

Intermediate Ask students to respond in complete sentences and add details. Provide sentence starters as needed: The children play a game of silence. The adults discuss important matters. Omakayas wants the makazinan because her grandmother made them.

Advanced/Advanced High Have students respond in complete sentences and add details.

COLLABORATE **Independent Reading Practice** Have mixed level pairs complete pages 42–44 of the ELL Anchor Text Support BLMs and share with the group.

Reread

Use the following prompts when working on **Reading/Writing Companion**, pages 156–158.

Literature Anthology, pages 486–487

COLLABORATE **Author's Craft: Point of View** Read the text with students and review Vocabulary words *endurance, irritating,* and *forfeit.* Discuss the meaning of unfamiliar words or phrases. *Why does Omakayas pretend to sleep?* (to fool her brother and get her doll back) *Whose thoughts and feelings did you read about?* (Omakayas's) *Does something irritating make you smile or make you annoyed?* (annoyed) *What did Pinch do to irritate Omakayas?* (put a burning wand next to her leg) *What happened to the game?* (It was stopped because visitors arrived.)

Beginning Demonstrate making faces to show the meaning of *taunt*. Restate the sentences as needed. Have partners describe what Omakayas and Pinch did: Omakayas bit her lip. Pinch made a face at his sister.

Intermediate *How does Omakayas feel about her brother?* (very annoyed and irritated with Pinch) Have partners discuss why the author describes Omakayas's thoughts: It shows what she feels about her brother.

Advanced/Advanced High *How does Omakayas describe Pinch?* (He is clever and will try to annoy his sister on purpose to try to make her lose the game.) Have partners discuss what Omakayas's point of view of Pinch tells about the game of silence. (Possible answer: Her point of view tells me that it is very difficult for Omakayas because Pinch annoys her.)

Literature Anthology, pages 488–489

COLLABORATE **Author's Purpose** Read the text with students and review the Vocabulary words *retreated* and *despised*. *Who are the visitors?* (Omakayas's cousins and friends) *Why did Omakayas's family build an extra large lodge*? (so there is enough room for visitors) *Where did the venison soup come from?* (visitors) *Who came to see the visitors?* (Old Tallow) *What do these details tell about the community?* (everyone is welcome and they are family)

Beginning Read page 489 with students. Restate the sentences as needed. Guide partners to identify the words that describe the full lodge: The extra big lodge was packed entirely full. *What do people do in the lodge?* Everyone sits together. They eat venison soup. *Is there enough room for everyone in the lodge?* (yes) *What phrases in the text support your answer?* Help partners identify the text. ("...there was enough room for everyone.")

Intermediate Have partners identify the details that describe the lodge: The lodge is extra big and it is completely full. However, there is enough room for everyone. *What does everyone do?* They sit together and eat venison soup.

Advanced/Advanced High *What words describe how it feels to be in the lodge? ("squeezed into," "was extra big," "packed entirely full, but there was enough room")* Have partners discuss why the author describes the scene in vivid detail. (Possible answer: The author tells that it is important in Omakayas's culture to live and work together with others.)

Literature Anthology, pages 490–491

COLLABORATE **Author's Purpose** Read the text with students. Have students tell how the author describes the prizes. ("elaborately dressed," "tied together with split jack-pine root," "little roll of flowered cloth," "tipped with real brass points cut from a trade kettle") *What does this show about the Ojibwe?* (Prizes are important. Ojibwe value the children.)

Beginning Read page 491 with students. Restate the sentences as needed. Guide partners to identify and list the prizes. (marbles, makazinan, doll, knife, ribbon, cloth, bells, bow and arrows) Then have them describe some of the prizes. The doll wears britches and a leather coat. The arrows have tips of brass.

Intermediate Have partners take turns describing the prizes. Invite them to use the words *treasures, fancy, real, sharp, actual glass, elaborately*.

Advanced/Advanced High *Have students describe prizes and tell how they show that the Ojibwe value children.*

FORMATIVE ASSESSMENT

STUDENT CHECK IN

Read Have partners tell each other important details from the text. Have them reflect using the Check-In routine.

Reread Have partners share responses and text evidence on **Reading Writing Companion** pages 156–158. Then have them use the Check-In routine to reflect and fill in the bars.

LEARNING GOALS

- **We can read and understand historical fiction by analyzing the theme.**
- **We can identify and use negatives.**

OBJECTIVES

Paraphrase portions of a text read aloud or information presented in diverse media and formats, including visually, quantitatively, and orally.

Demonstrate command of the conventions of standard English grammar and usage when writing or speaking.

LANGUAGE OBJECTIVES

Students will discuss the theme of a historical fiction text using key vocabulary.

Students will inquire by answering questions about negatives in complete sentences.

ELA ACADEMIC LANGUAGE

- *theme, negative*
- Cognates: *tema, negativo*

MATERIALS

Literature Anthology, pp. 482–493

Online Language Development Cards, 54A–54B

Online Language Development Practice, 319–324

Online Language Transfers Handbook, pp. 15–19

Online Oral Language Sentence Frames, p. 7

The Game of Silence

Text Reconstruction

Focus on a single chunk of text to support comprehension and language development across the four domains.

1. Read aloud the paragraph on page 490 of the **Literature Anthology** while students listen.
2. Write the following on the board, providing definitions as needed: *gift, pile, impossible, attention, grown-ups, council, shush, degree, required, treats.* Instruct students to listen for them as you read the paragraph a second time.
3. Read the paragraph a third time while students listen and take notes.
4. COLLABORATE Have students work with a partner to reconstruct the text from their notes. Help them write complete sentences as needed.
5. Have students look at the original text. Ask them to tell what the paragraph is mostly about. (It tells when grown-ups were discussing something important and if the children kept quiet they would get a prize.) Discuss with students the theme that it was important for the tribe to work together. Students will analyze details that support the theme.
6. *Why did the children have to stay silent?* (the grown-ups needed to discuss something very important.) *How did the children know it was important to stay silent?* ("the degree to which their silence was required") *What does "without having to shush small children" mean?* (the grown-ups didn't want the children to make noise during their discussion) *What information did the grown-ups have to discuss?* (Possible answers: difficult questions and facts.) *What did the children get if they stayed silent?* (a gift; treats) *What do these details tell you about the theme?* (it was important for the tribe to work together.)
7. Have students compare their text reconstructions to the original text. Have them check whether they also included words about the theme.

Beginning Allow students to follow along in the Literature Anthology as you read aloud. Have them point to the words from Step 2 as they hear them.

Apply Author's Craft: Repetition

Discuss with students how the author uses repetition by discussing the example of what happens to Omakayas as she tries to stay silent. *In the first paragraph on page 484, the author repeats the word "stone" to show how difficult it is for Omakayas to stay silent. What other phrases tell you it was difficult? (closed her eyes, she kept her eyes closed, silent and more silent)* Have students rewrite the sentences in their own words using repetition.

Grammar in Context: Deconstruct a Sentence

Write this clause from page 486: *". . . but she didn't make a single sound; not a chirp, not so much as a mouse's squeak."* Facilitate deconstructing this sentence for better comprehension.

- *Which word is the subject of the clause?* (she)
- *What is the direct object of the verb* make*?* (sound)
- *Which words tell what she did?* (*did not make*) *Which word makes the verb* make *a negative?* (*not*) *What other words, besides* not, *can you use to form a negative sentence?* (*no, never, nothing*)
- Have students practice using one or more of these words. (She would never make a single sound; no chirp, and not so much as a mouse's squeak.)
- *Why does the author use three expressions to show what noises Omakayas did not make?* (Possible response: to show how determined Omakayas is to win the game)

For additional practice, see **Language Development Cards**, Lessons 54A and 54B, and **Language Development Practice**, pages 319–324.

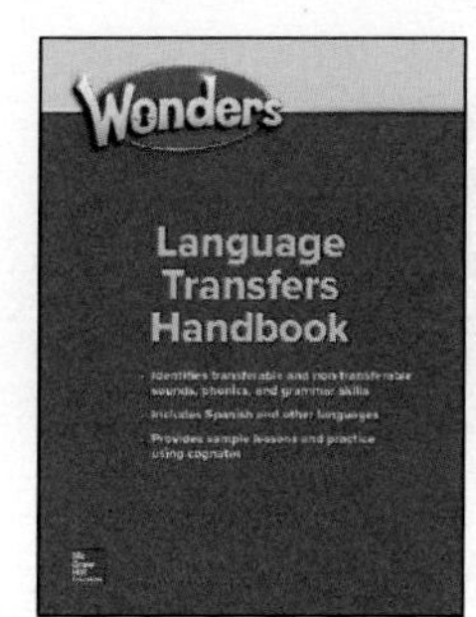

Language Transfers Handbook, Grammar Transfers, pp. 15–19

Independent Time

Vocabulary Building Invite students to create sentences using vocabulary from the selection. First, provide students with two sticky notes. Then have students select one noun and one adjective from the selection and write them on separate sticky notes. Next, have students mingle around the class to show their words. Students should pair their noun with another's adjective and vice versa. Finally, have pairs create and write sentences on a classroom poster.

Beginning Allow students to draw pictures as clues for the new words.

Intermediate/Advanced/Advanced High Have students include some of the self-selected words and content-area words they added to their glossaries.

COLLABORATE **Make Connections** Have partners connect the Essential Question to their own lives. Have small groups talk about special events or activities they do with their family to celebrate traditions and customs:

Beginning Provide sentence frames: Our family eats ____ when ____. We gather together to ____.

Intermediate Provide sentence starters: One tradition in my family is to ____ when ____. It is special because ____.

Advanced/Advanced High Encourage students to use descriptive details.

COLLABORATE **Engage in Dialogue** Have partners use the sentence frames on page 7 of the online leveled **Oral Language Sentence Frames** to discuss their opinions of *The Game of Silence*. Remind them to give examples from the text to support their opinions.

FORMATIVE ASSESSMENT

STUDENT CHECK-IN

Text Reconstruction Ask partners to share their notes. Have them reflect on their work using the Check-In routine.

Grammar in Context Have partners reflect on their deconstructions using the Check-In routine.

LEARNING GOALS

We can apply strategies and skills to read historical fiction.

OBJECTIVES

Determine a theme of a story, drama, or poem from details in the text; summarize the text.

Use context as a clue to the meaning of a word or phrase.

Engage effectively in a range of collaborative discussions with diverse partners on grade 4 topics and texts, building on others' ideas and expressing their own clearly.

LANGUAGE OBJECTIVES

Students will discuss the connotation and denotation of a word using clues in the text.

ELA ACADEMIC LANGUAGE

- *historical fiction, theme, denotation, connotation, connect, setting*
- Cognates: *ficción histórica, tema, denotación, connotación, conectar*

MATERIALS

Online ELL Genre Passage, "The Generation Belt"

"The Generation Belt"

Genre Passage
Lexile 730L

Prepare to Read

Build Background Have students share about things they learned from their parents, grandparents, or other relatives, such as customs or types of food. Tell students that "Generation Belt" is **historical fiction**. Review that historical fiction is set in the past and has realistic characters, events, and settings. As you read the text, help students point out these features.

Vocabulary Use the Define, Example, Ask routine to pre-teach difficult words or unfamiliar concepts, such as *heritage, dignified, mischievous, convince,* and *loom* (cognates: *digno, convencer*). Invite students to add new vocabulary to their glossaries.

Set Purpose *Today we will read "The Generation Belt." As we read, think about how traditions connect people.*

Read the Text

Page E1, Paragraphs 1–4

Beginning *What does Kanti's mom tell her?* (Her grandmother is going to teach her.) *How does Kanti react?* She is happy.

Intermediate H*ave partners describe Kanti's village:* The wigwams form a circle with a lake next to the village.

Advanced/Advanced High *Who does Kanti see in the village? What are they doing?* (one Ojibwe family repairing their home; her cousins playing in the lake) *What does this help you know about the people in the village?* (Families work and play together; many people there are in Kanti's family.)

Page E1, Paragraphs 5–7

Connotation and Denotation Have students use a dictionary to look up the word *dignified* and discuss examples, such as king and graduation, and the emotion it evokes. Help students identify the denotation and connotation: The denotation, or definition, of *dignified* is "serious and somewhat formal." The connotation, or emotion of a word, is "serious in a way that is worthy of respect."

Beginning Help partners talk about Kanti's lesson: Grandmother teaches about an important part of Kanti's heritage and culture. She teaches Kanti about weaving belts. The belts have purple and white beads.

Intermediate *What is Kanti's grandmother going to teach about?* (an important part of their heritage and culture) *Is the connotation of* dignified *positive or negative?* (positive)

Advanced/Advanced High Have partners discuss why the grandmother is dignified. (Possible answer: The grandmother is teaching about an important part of their heritage. She might want to show that it is a serious subject that deserves respect.)

Page E2

Theme *What is the belt's pattern? What does it represent?* (Squares connected by a line represent a peace agreement between nations or villages.) *"Connect" means to link together. How do the belts connect Kanti with her grandmother?* (Possible answer: Kanti's grandmother teaches Kanti how to make the belts.) *What is the theme, or big idea, of the story?* (It's important to learn about the history and traditions that connect people.) Help students identify other connections in the story.

Beginning *What is wampum made of?* Wampum is made of clams. They use clams to make the beads. *Which words tell what wampum is?* ("collect the quahog, or clams, the beads were made from.")

COLLABORATE **Intermediate** Have partners explain what Kanti's grandmother teaches her: Grandmother shows Kanti belts that have a beaded pattern of squares connected by a line. Kanti learns that the squares represent different nations and the agreement made to stop fighting each other.

COLLABORATE **Advanced** Have partners explain how the history of the belt teaches Kanti about what is important to her nation. (Possible answer: The belt shows an important agreement between the Five Nations to make peace. The belts will remind other generations about the agreement for peace.)

Advanced High *What will the belt be used for?* (to invite another village to come to a meeting about fishing) *Why do you think Kanti's grandmother wants to teach her how to create the wampun belts?* (Possible answer: So Kanti can carry on the tradition.)

Respond to Reading

Use the following instruction to help students answer the questions on page E3.

1. *Read the first paragraph in "The Generation Belt." When and where does the story take place?* (long ago, when the Ojibwe tribe lived in wigwams) *What is the story about?* (It is about how Kanti learns what wampum belts are and how to make one.) *How is the setting related to the plot?* (Kanti is learning a tradition from her grandmother.)
2. Have students reread the conversation between Kanti and her mother. *How does Kanti react when she hears her mother?* (she smiles) *What does this reaction tell about her relationship with her mother?* (Kanti is happy to hear her mother; this shows that she loves her mother.)
3. *What does Kanti learn from her grandmother?* (She learns from her grandmother how to make a belt, and she learns about the history of her people that appears on the belt.) *How does this affect Kanti?* (Kanti will make the belt to record the history she will experience, just like her grandmother did.)

Fluency Have partners take turns reading the passage.

Build Knowledge: Make Connections

Talk About the Text Have partners discuss how traditions connect people.

Write About the Text Have students add their ideas to their Build Knowledge pages of their reader's notebooks.

FORMATIVE ASSESSMENT

STUDENT CHECK-IN

Have partners share their responses on page E3. Ask students to reflect using the Check-In routine.

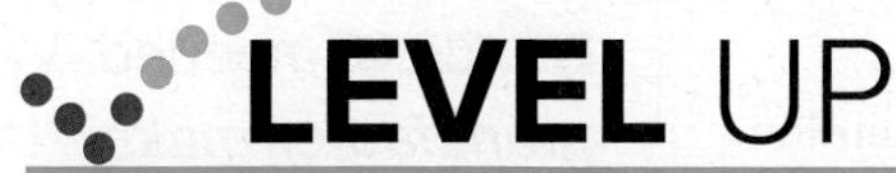

LEVEL UP

IF students read the ELL Level fluently and answered the questions,

THEN pair them with students who have proficiently read the On Level. Have them

- partner read the On Level passage.
- identify **theme**

LEARNING GOALS

We can apply strategies and skills to read historical fiction.

OBJECTIVES

Refer to details and examples in a text when explaining what the text says explicitly and when drawing inferences from the text.

Engage effectively in a range of collaborative discussions with diverse partners on grade 4 topics and texts, building on others' ideas and expressing their own clearly.

Read grade-level prose and poetry orally with accuracy, appropriate rate, and expression on successive readings.

LANGUAGE OBJECTIVES

Students will narrate a historical fiction story using key vocabulary.

ELA ACADEMIC LANGUAGE

- *reread, historical fiction*
- Cognate: *ficción histórica*

MATERIALS

ELL Leveled Reader: *Grandfather's Basket*

Online Differentiated Texts: "Connecting to the Past"

Online ELL Visual Vocabulary Cards

DIGITAL TOOLS

MULTIMODAL

Have students read along as they listen to the selections to develop comprehension and practice fluency and pronunciation.

Grandfather's Basket

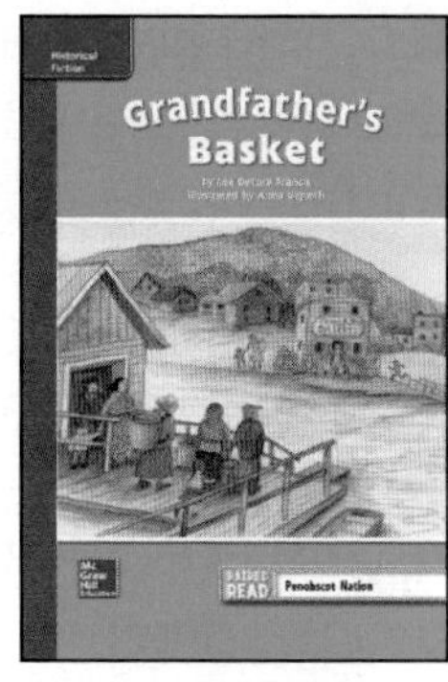

Leveled Reader
Lexile 540L

Prepare to Read

Build Background Invite students to talk about their family's traditions and describe ways they celebrate the traditions. Preview *Grandfather's Basket* and "Penobscot Nation." Ask students to tell how they think the Penobscot celebrate their traditions. *Our purpose for reading is to learn about how the Penobscot make baskets.*

Vocabulary Use the routine on the **ELL Visual Vocabulary Cards** to pre-teach ELL vocabulary *adopt, enthusiasm,* and *proper*. Have students discuss vocabulary in the context of the story and illustrations.

Set Purpose *Today we will read an historical fiction text called* Grandfather's Basket. *As we read, think about how traditions connect people.*

Read the Text

Pages 3–4

Beginning Read page 3 with students. Restate the sentences as needed. Help students describe how to make a *bundle*: I can tie together strips of the tree. *How does Rodney feel about his work?* Rodney enjoys his work.

COLLABORATE **Intermediate** Have partners describe what they think the relationship between Muhmum and Rodney is like: I think they have a good relationship because Muhmum stops working and talks to Rodney.

Advanced *How does Rodney feel about working with his grandfather? How do you know?* (Rodney enjoys working with him. He calls the uncut logs *beautiful.*)

Advanced High *Why did Muhmum remind Rodney that school is not far away?* (Possible answer: He knows that Rodney is worried about going to a new school.)

Pages 7–8

COLLABORATE **Beginning** Read page 7 with students. Restate the sentences as needed. *What do the men make?* (big baskets) *What does Rodney's grandfather make?* (laundry baskets, potato baskets, and pack baskets) *How do people use the baskets?* People put the baskets on their backs.

Intermediate *Why does Rodney prepare the ash?* (to make baskets) *Who makes the baskets?* (the women and men in the community) *Why are baskets important to Rodney's community?* (families sell them) *Where is Rodney's community?* (on an island)

COLLABORATE **Advanced/Advanced High** Have partners discuss how it feels to do something with enthusiasm. (Possible answer: When I do something with enthusiasm, I feel excited and ready.)

Page 14, Paragraphs 2–3

Beginning *Why is the pack special to Rodney?* Muhmum had the pack for many years. *What is the present tense of* wore? (wear) *What is the future tense of* wore? (will wear)

Advanced/Advanced High *What do you think Rodney will think about when he wears the pack?* (He will think about his family.)

Reread Have partners reread page 14 and discuss how Muhmum helped Rodney. (Possible answer: Muhmum gave a special pack to Rodney to help Rodney feel connected to home.)

Respond to Reading Have partners complete their graphic organizers and discuss the questions on page 16.

Fluency: Expression and Accuracy

Read aloud pages 4–5 with appropriate expression and accuracy. Read it again and have students read along. For more practice, have students record their voices a few times and choose the best one.

Paired Read: "Penobscot Nation"

Analytical Writing — Make Connections: Write About It

Before students write, discuss the questions on page 19. Guide students to find text evidence on page 19 that tells about the importance of the river to the Penobscot culture. The Penobscot culture is connected to the river. Have students reread page 9. *What did Rodney do when he was younger? What happened as Rodney got older?* Rodney used to watch his grandfather make baskets. Later Rodney helped make the baskets.

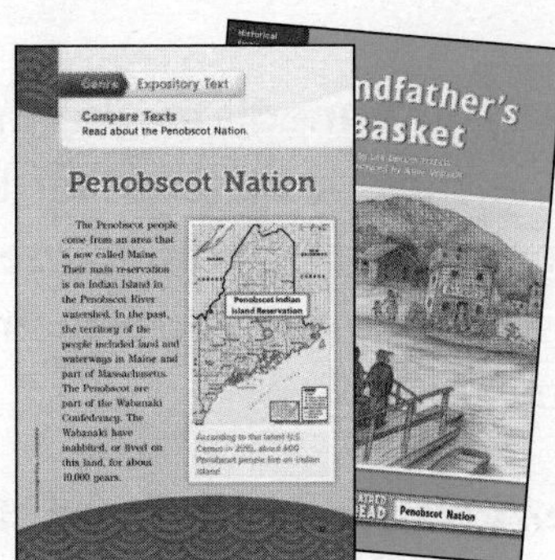

ELL Leveled Reader

Build Knowledge: Make Connections

Talk About the Text Have pairs discuss how traditions connect people.

Write About the Text Have students add their ideas to their Build Knowledge pages of their reader's notebooks.

Self-Selected Reading

Have students choose another historical fiction text from the online **Leveled Reader Library** or read the **Differentiated Text:** "Connecting to the Past."

FOCUS ON GENRE

Have students complete the activity on page 20 to tell a historical fiction story about a family member.

LITERATURE CIRCLES

Ask students to conduct a literature circle using the Thinkmark questions to guide the discussion.

FORMATIVE ASSESSMENT

STUDENT CHECK-IN

Have partners share their answers to Respond to Reading. Ask students to reflect on their learning using the Check-In routine.

LEVEL UP

IF students read the **ELL Level** fluently and answered the questions,

THEN pair them with students who have proficiently read the **On Level** and have students

- read aloud the **On Level** main selection with their partner.
- list words they find difficult.
- discuss these words with their partner.

ACT Access Complex Text

The **On Level** challenges students by including more **complex sentence structure.**

LEARNING GOALS

We can read and understand free verse poetry.

OBJECTIVES

Explain major differences between poems, drama, and prose, and refer to the structural elements of poems and drama when writing or speaking about a text.

Explain the meaning of simple similes and metaphors in context.

Engage effectively in a range of collaborative discussions with diverse partners on grade 4 topics and texts, building on others' ideas and expressing their own clearly.

LANGUAGE OBJECTIVES

Students will inquire about the theme of the poem using key vocabulary.

ELA ACADEMIC LANGUAGE

- *identity, describe, comparison, figurative language, metaphor, personification, imagery, theme*
- Cognates: *identidad, describir, comparación, lenguaje figurado, metáfora, personificación, imágenes, tema*

MATERIALS

Reading/Writing Companion, pp. 170-173

Online Scaffolded Shared Read, "Climbing Blue Hill," "My Name Is Ivy," and "Collage"

Visual Vocabulary Cards

Online ELL Visual Vocabulary Cards

DIGITAL TOOLS

MULTIMODAL

Have students read along as they listen to the selection to develop comprehension and practice fluency and pronunciation.

"Climbing Blue Hill," "My Name Is Ivy," and "Collage"

Prepare to Read

Build Background Explain to students that our identity refers to details about ourselves that make each of us special and unique. (Cognate: *identidad*) Say: *A person's identity is made up of many things, including family, culture, activities, and experiences.* Have students share details about themselves, such as an activity they do with their family or as part of their culture.

Vocabulary Use the **Visual Vocabulary Cards** to review the vocabulary: *gobble, individuality, mist, roots.* Use the online **ELL Visual Vocabulary Cards** to teach additional vocabulary from the Shared Read: *curiously, glimmer, intricate, scoff.*

Set Purpose *We will read poems about things that give people their identity. As we read, think about what shapes a person's identity.*

Read the Text

Select the **Scaffolded Shared Read** or the Shared Read in the **Reading/Writing Companion**, based on students' language proficiency.

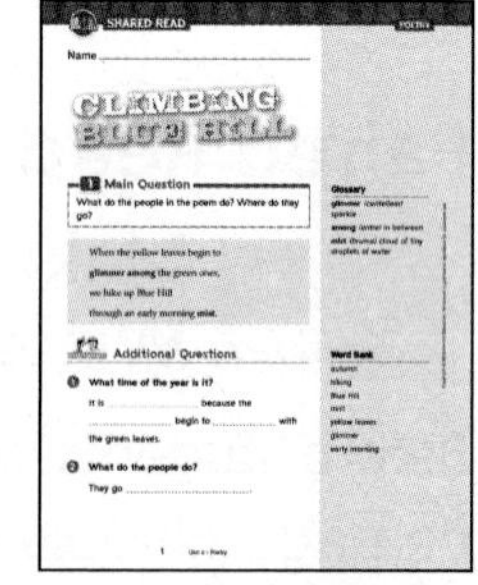

Scaffolded Shared Read, Lexile NP

Beginning/Early-Intermediate Use the online Scaffolded Shared Read to help partners work together to read and understand the free verse poems. Remind them to use the Glossary to help them read and the Word Bank to help them answer the Main and Additional Questions.

Intermediate/Advanced/Advanced High Read the text with students and use the Interactive Question-Response Routine to help them understand the free verse poems.

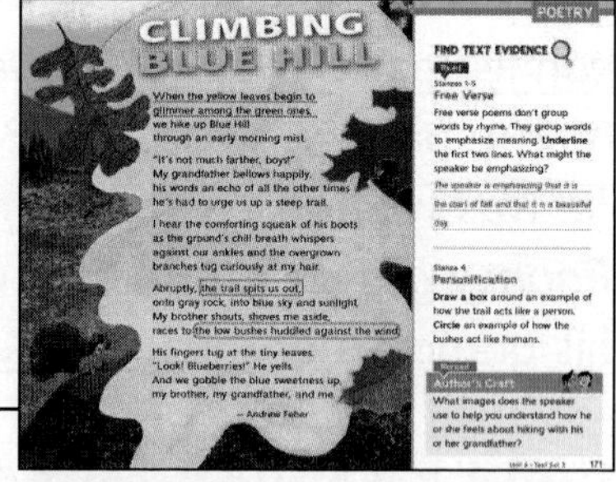

Reading/Writing Companion, Lexile NP

Page 171, "Climbing Blue Hill"

Stanzas 1–3 Read the text with students and review meanings of *mist, curiously,* and *glimmer. What is the speaker doing?* (climbing up Blue Hill) *What kind of place is Blue Hill? What words tell you?* (mountain, leaves, hike, hill) *What season is it?* (fall) *What tells you?* (yellow leaves) *What words show that the speaker has climbed with his grandfather before?* ("his words an echo of all the other times he's had to urge us up a steep trail")

COLLABORATE **Intermediate** Have partners describe what the last two lines in Stanza 2 tell about the speaker and his grandfather: The lines describe that they have climbed hills many times before. *What did the grandfather tell the speaker on other climbs?* The grandfather said they didn't have far to go.

Advanced/Advanced High *What words tell about sounds the speaker hears?* (bellows happily, echo, squeak of his boots) *What do the sounds help the speaker remember?* (other times he climbed up hills with his grandfather)

COLLABORATE Point out and discuss example of **personification** with students. *In Stanza 3, what words describe the mist?* ("the ground's chill breath whispers against our ankles") Have partners discuss why *breath* and *whisper* are human qualities. *How do the branches act human?* (They tug curiously at the speaker's hair.)

Stanzas 4–5 Read the text with students and review the Vocabulary word *gobble*. Point out that "Abruptly, the trail spits us out," describes the end of the trail. *Where did the characters arrive?* (onto a gray rock) *What can they see from there?* (sky and sunlight) *What does the brother do?* (finds blueberries)

COLLABORATE Review with students that theme is the main message or lesson that a poet wants to share with readers. Guide partners to discuss how the last stanza shows the theme of the poem: *What happens in the last stanza?* (The speaker eats blueberries with his brother and grandfather.) *How does the speaker feel? How do you know?* The word "sweetness" shows that the speaker feels happy. Have partners reread the poem and find other words related that give clues about feelings. ("glimmer," "bellows happily," "comforting squeak") *What might the poet want readers to remember?* (Possible answer: The speaker enjoyed the time he spent climbing hills with his grandfather and brother.)

Page 172, "My Name Is Ivy"

Read the text with students and review the Vocabulary word *intricate*. *What does the title tell you about the speaker of the poem?* (Her name is Ivy.) *What is* ivy? (a type of plant) *What does she want to know?* (why her mother named her after a plant) *What does ivy do?* (grip onto things, grow where it wants to go, climb over things and keep going)

COLLABORATE **Intermediate** Have partners identify action words that tell what the ivy plant does. (grip, grow, will find a way over walls, climbs, will touch)

COLLABORATE **Advanced/Advanced High** Have partners identify an example of personification in the fourth stanza. ("Will use its long skinny fingers to find a way over") Then have them discuss why they think the mother named the speaker Ivy. (Possible answer: The mother wants her daughter to be like the plant, strong and can keep going.)

Page 173, "Collage"

Read the text with students and review the Vocabulary words *scoffs* and *roots*. Discuss with students what a collage is. Ask: *How do you make a collage?* (use many different items) *How is a family like a collage?* (Each person is different, but together they form one family.) *What things does the speaker get from her family?* (eyes, nose, skinny toes, lopsided smile)

COLLABORATE **Intermediate** Have partners discuss why the speaker makes the comparisons: Grandma's eyes are like a panther's because she sees everything. Dad's toes seem to be from lemurs because his toes are skinny.

Advanced/Advanced High *Why do you think the poet includes comparisons?* (to create imagery and humor) *What is Grandpa's nose called?* (a bumpy, rocky road) *What kind of figurative language is this an example of? How do you know?* (It is a metaphor. The comparison says that one thing "is" another.)

COLLABORATE Have partners discuss what the speaker means by "I gave them my heart.": It means she loves them. Then have them discuss how the speaker is similar to a collage. (Her family makes her who she is.)

FORMATIVE ASSESSMENT

STUDENT CHECK-IN

Have partners retell the most important ideas in the poems. Ask them to reflect using the Check-In routine.

LEARNING GOALS

- **We can read and understand free verse poetry by identifying the theme.**
- **We can identify and use prepositional phrases.**

OBJECTIVES

Paraphrase portions of a text read aloud or information presented in diverse media and formats, including visually, quantitatively, and orally.

Form and use prepositional phrases.

LANGUAGE OBJECTIVES

Students will discuss the theme of a poem using key vocabulary.

Students will inform about prepositions and prepositional phrases in complete sentences.

ELA ACADEMIC LANGUAGE

- *stanza, theme, details, preposition, prepositional phrase*
- Cognates: *tema, detalles, preposición, frase preposicional*

MATERIALS

Reading/Writing Companion, pp. 170–173, 174–175

Online Scaffolded Shared Read, "Climbing Blue Hill"

Online Shared Read Writing Frames, p. 18

Online Language Development Cards, 56B

Online Language Development Practice, pp. 334–336

Online Language Transfers Handbook, pp. 15–19

"Climbing Blue Hill"

Text Reconstruction

Focus on a single chunk of text to support comprehension and language development across the four domains.

1. Read aloud stanzas 3–5 on page 171 of the **Reading/Writing Companion** while students listen.
2. Write the following on the board, providing definitions as needed: *squeak, chill, overgrown, tug, abruptly, trail, shoves, huddled, gobble.* Instruct students to listen for them as you read the stanzas a second time.
3. Read the stanzas a third time. Tell students to listen and take notes.
4.  COLLABORATE Have students work with a partner to reconstruct the text from their notes. Help them write complete sentences as needed.
5. Have students look at the original text. Ask them to tell what the stanzas are mostly about. (The speaker is climbing a trail with his family.) Tell students they are going to examine details that help them identify the theme.
6. *Who is the speaker hiking with?* (his brother and grandfather) *How does the speaker describe the sound of his grandfather's boots?* (comforting) *Why does the brother shout and shove the speaker aside?* (he is excited to find a blueberry bush) *What does "we gobble the blue sweetness up" tell you?* (they enjoyed eating the blueberries and ate them quickly) *What do these details tell you about the theme?* (Spending time in nature with family is fun.)
7. Have students compare their text reconstructions to the original text. Have them check whether they also included words that describe the theme.

Beginning Have students follow along in the Reading/Writing Companion as you read the text aloud. Have them circle the words from Step 2 as they hear them.

Grammar in Context: Using Prepositions

Notice the Form Display the sentence from the text. Circle the prepositions and underline the nouns as shown. Explain that there are three prepositional phrases.

> *When the yellow leaves begin to glimmer among the green ones, we hike up Blue Hill through an early morning mist.*

What kind of words are circled words? (prepositions) *What kind of words are underlined words?* (nouns) Review with students that prepositional phrases provide details such as location, direction, and time. *Where do the yellow leaves glimmer?* (among the green ones) *In which direction do the people hike?* (up Blue Hill) *When do they hike?* (through an early morning mist) Have students copy the sentences and label the prepositions and prepositional phrases in their notebooks.

Apply and Extend Have partners choose another sentence and label the prepositions and prepositional phrases. Check their work and provide feedback.

For additional practice, see **Language Development Cards**, Lesson 56B, and **Language Development Practice**, pages 334–336.

Independent Time

Vocabulary Building Have students build glossaries.

Beginning/Early Intermediate Have students complete the Glossary Activities in the **Scaffolded Shared Read**.

Intermediate/Advanced/Advanced High Have students add the vocabulary from **Reading/Writing Companion** pages 174–175 and self-selected words they would like to learn to the chart.

Mixed Levels Pair students together. Beginning and Early-Intermediate students can teach vocabulary from their Scaffolded Shared Read glossaries. Intermediate and Advanced/Advanced High students can teach their self-selected words.

WORD/PHRASE IN ENGLISH	DEFINITION IN ENGLISH	SENTENCE FROM THE TEXT
farther	More distant; comparative form of *far*	"It's not much farther, boys!"

COLLABORATE **Shared Read Writing Frames** Use the online leveled Shared Read Writing Frames for "Climbing Blue Hill" for additional oral and written practice. Differentiated frames are available to provide support for all levels.

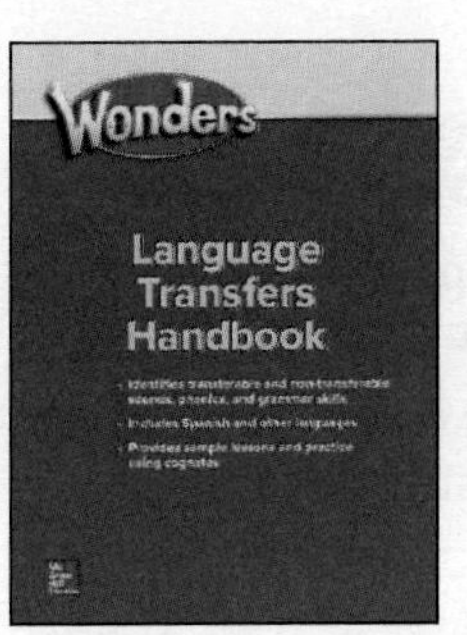

Language Transfers Handbook, Grammar Transfers, pp. 15–19

DIGITAL TOOLS

For additional support, use the online activities.

Grammar Video

Grammar Song

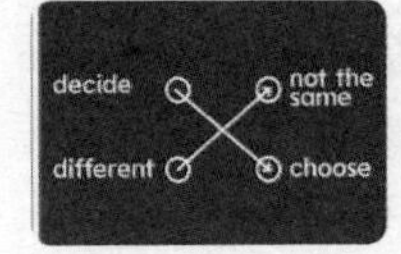

Vocabulary Activity

FORMATIVE ASSESSMENT

STUDENT CHECK IN

Text Reconstruction Have partners share their notes. Have students reflect on their work using the Check-In routine.

Grammar in Context Have partners share their sentences. Have them reflect on their work using the Check-In routine.

LEARNING GOALS

- **Read** We can apply strategies and skills to read free verse poetry.
- **Reread** We can reread to analyze text, craft, and structure and compare texts.

OBJECTIVES

Refer to details and examples in a text when explaining what the text says explicitly and when drawing inferences from the text.

Demonstrate understanding of figurative language, word relationships, and nuances in word meanings.

Engage effectively in a range of collaborative discussions with diverse partners on grade 4 topics and texts, building on others' ideas and expressing their own clearly.

LANGUAGE OBJECTIVES

Students will inquire by answering questions about the poems using key vocabulary.

ELA ACADEMIC LANGUAGE

- *personification, metaphor, imagery, details*
- Cognates: *personificación, metáfora, imágenes, detalles*

MATERIALS

Reading/Writing Companion, pp. 182–183

Literature Anthology, pp. 500–502

Visual Vocabulary Cards

Online ELL Anchor Text Support BLMs, p. 45

DIGITAL TOOLS

Have students read along as they listen to the selection to develop comprehension and practice fluency and pronunciation.

"The Drum," "Birdfoot's Grampa," and "My Chinatown"

Prepare to Read

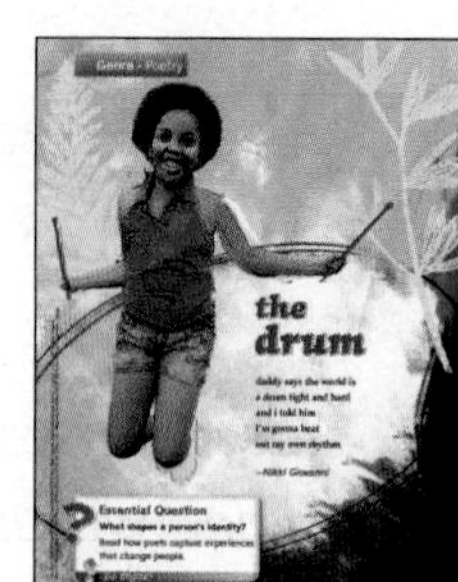
Literature Anthology, Lexile NP

Build Background Read the Essential Question: *What shapes a person's identity?* Explain that the phrase "shapes a person's identity" refers to details that make each of us special and unique. A person's identity is made up of many things, including family, culture, activities, and experiences. Invite students to share details about themselves that have shaped their identity.

Vocabulary Use the **Visual Vocabulary Cards** to review the vocabulary: *gobbles, individuality, mist, roots.* (Cognate: individualidad)

Set Purpose *Today we will read poems about things that give people their identity. As we read, think about what shapes a person's identity.*

Read

Literature Anthology, pp. 500–502

Use the **Interactive Question-Response Routine** to help students read and discuss "The Drum," "Birdfoot's Grampa," and "My Chinatown."

Beginning Help students discuss in complete sentences. Provide sentence frames: The first poem is a free verse poem. I know because it doesn't have a pattern. An example of imagery in the second poem is "live drops of rain".

Intermediate Ask students to respond in complete sentences and add details. Provide sentence starters as needed: The first poem is a free verse poem. The poem does not have a pattern. An example of imagery from the last poem is "the hum of the motor".

Advanced/Advanced High Have students respond in complete sentences and add details.

COLLABORATE **Independent Reading Practice** Have mixed level pairs complete page 45 of the ELL Anchor Text Support BLMs and share with the group.

Reread

Use the following prompts when working on Reading/Writing Companion, pages 182–183.

Literature Anthology, page 501

COLLABORATE **Author's Craft: Imagery** Read the poem with students. Restate the lines as needed and define words or phrases they do not know or understand. *What does the old man do?* (picks up toads on the road) *Why does* *he do that?* (it is raining; to save the frogs from cars) *What does the speaker tell the old man?* (can't save all the toads; stop picking them up; that they have places to go to) *How does he reply?* (He says that the toads have places to go to, too.) Have students discuss how the description of Grampa helps the readers care about what happens to the toads: Grampa cares about the toads, so this makes the readers also care about the toads.

Beginning Discuss the meaning of the words *gather* and *blinded.* Demonstrate to help students understand the meanings. Then reread the lines of the stanza. Help partners take turns asking and answering questions about the old man: *What does the old man do when he gathers the toads?* The old man holds the toads in his hand. *How do the toads get blinded?* The lights of the car blind the toads. *What does the speaker tell the old man?* The speaker tells the old man to stop getting the toads. *What does the old man tell the speaker?* The toads have places to go.

Intermediate Have partners use evidence to discuss the car ride: The car stops many times because the old man stops to pick up toads from the road. *What does the author compare the old man's white hair to?* (a mist) Have partners describe the metaphor: The metaphor compares the old man's white hair with mist. Both the white hair and mist are white.

Advanced/Advanced High *Who do you think the old man is? Why do you think he picks up toads on the road?* (Possible answer: I think the old man is the grandfather because the title mentions "Grampa." The old man probably wants to save the toads that can't see from the lights from the cars.) Have partners discuss the descriptions that help them visualize Birdfoot's Grampa. (his full, leathery hands; knee deep in the summer roadside grass) *What figurative language describes the toads in stanza 3?* (The toads are called "wet brown life") Recall the phrase *live drops of rain* in stanza 1. *Why do you think the author uses these words to describe the toads?* (It tells that Grampa respects them as living beings.)

Literature Anthology, page 502

Author's Craft: Details Read the text with students. Restate the lines as needed. *Who uses the sewing machine?* (the speaker's mother) *What does she make?* (pants, jackets, skirts, dresses) *How many hours a day does the mother work?* (twelve hours a day) *What does the speaker hear?* (noises from the sewing machine) *What does the speaker do?* (falls asleep) *What is the lullaby?* (noises from the sewing machine) *What words describe how the machine sounds?* (soft hum, soft chatter) *How does the speaker feel about her mother?* (she wants to be near her) *What kind of relationship do they have?* (they are close)

Beginning Read the last stanza and define the meaning of *lullaby* for students. Then read the stanza again with them. Have partners describe a lullaby: A lullaby helps babies fall asleep. *What is the speaker's lullaby?* The speaker's lullaby is the sound of the sewing machine.

Intermediate Have partners explain the *metaphor* in the second stanza: The speaker compares the sound of the sewing machine to a lullaby because she can fall asleep to it.

Advanced/Advanced High Have partners discuss how the speaker feels about the sounds from the sewing machine. (Possible answer: The speaker thinks the sounds are gentle because she falls asleep to the sound of her mother's work.) Explain the figurative language that describes her mother's work. (The metaphor calls the work a lullaby because it comforts her the way a lullaby comforts a baby.) *What does the sewing machine needle do? Identify the kind of figurative language the speaker uses to describe it.* (It gobbles up the fabric, turns miles of cloth, and is hungry. This is a personification.) *What details tell you why the speaker does this?* (Her mother works twelve hours a day, and the speaker wants to be near her.)

FORMATIVE ASSESSMENT

STUDENT CHECK IN

Read Have partners tell each other important details from the text. Have them reflect using the Check-In routine.

Reread Have partners share responses and text evidence on **Reading/Writing Companion** pages 182–183. Then have them use the Check-In routine to reflect and fill in the bars.

LEARNING GOALS

- We can read and understand free verse poetry by identifying the theme.
- We can identify and use prepositional phrases.

OBJECTIVES

Paraphrase portions of a text read aloud or information presented in diverse media and formats, including visually, quantitatively, and orally.

Form and use prepositional phrases.

LANGUAGE OBJECTIVES

Students will discuss the theme of a poem using key vocabulary.

Students will inquire by answering questions about prepositional phrases.

ELA ACADEMIC LANGUAGE

- *stanza, theme, details, preposition, prepositional phrase*
- Cognates: *tema, detalles, preposición, frase preposicional*

MATERIALS

Literature Anthology, pp. 500–502

Online Language Development Cards, 56A–56B

Online Language Development Practice, pp. 331–336

Online Language Transfers Handbook, pp. 15–19

"The Drum," "Birdfoot's Grandpa," and "My Chinatown"

Text Reconstruction

Focus on a single chunk of text to support comprehension and language development across the four domains.

1. Read aloud the poem "The Drum"on page 500 in the **Literature Anthology** while students listen.
2. Write the following on the board, providing definitions as needed: *tight, beat, rhythm.* Instruct students to listen for them as you read the poem a second time.
3. Read the poem a third time while students listen and take notes.
4. COLLABORATE Have students work with a partner to reconstruct the text from their notes. Help them write complete sentences as needed.
5. Have students look at the original text. Ask them to tell what the poem is mostly about. (playing a drum) Tell students they are going to examine how the text supports the poem's theme that people should live their lives their way.
6. *What does the speaker's father tell her?* (that the world is tight and hard) *What does he mean?* (Life is not easy.) *Read the fourth and fifth lines. What does "beat out my own rhythm" mean?* (She will live life her own way.) *How does her response reveal the theme?* (It describes the message that each of us should live our lives in our own way.)
7. Have students compare their text reconstructions to the original text. Have them check whether they also included text that supports the theme.

Beginning Allow students to follow along in the Literature Anthology as you read the text aloud. Have them point to the words from Step 2 as they listen.

Apply Author's Craft: Imagery

Review that authors use imagery to help readers visualize details. Help students write descriptive sentences using imagery. Model first: *In the last stanza on page 501, what word does the poet use to describe Grampa's hands?* (leathery) *How does the poet describe the toad he is holding?* (wet brown life) Have students rewrite the sentences in their own words using imagery.

Grammar in Context: Deconstruct a Sentence

Write the sentence from page 503 on the board: *After supper I sit beside my mother, listening to the hum of the motor, the soft chatter of the hungry needle.* Facilitate deconstructing this sentence for better comprehension:

- *What are the prepositions in this sentence?* (*after, beside, to, of*) *What do these prepositions begin?* (prepositional phrases) On the board, draw parentheses around the prepositional phrases.
- *Where are the* objects *of each preposition?* (*supper, mother, hum, motor, needle*) Draw arrows from each preposition to its object.
- *Which prepositional phrase tells* when? (after supper) *Which one tells* where? (beside my mother) *Which one tells* what *she hears?* (to the hum) *Which one* describes *the hum?* (of the motor) *Which one* describes *the soft chatter?* (of the hungry needle) *What does* soft chatter *mean?* (the quiet, rhythmic sound of the needle going up and down)
- Have partners restate the sentence in their own words. Check students' work and provide corrective feedback as needed.

For additional practice, see **Language Development Cards**, Lessons 56A and 56B, and **Language Development Practice**, pages 331–336.

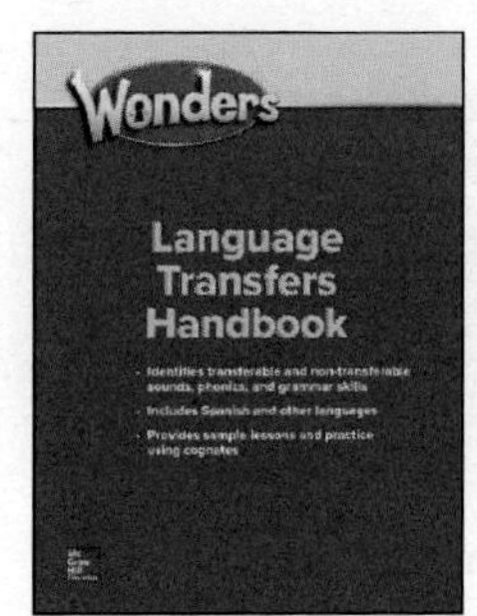

Language Transfers Handbook
Grammar Transfers, pp. 15–19

Independent Time

Vocabulary Building Create an interactive vocabulary display. First, assign one word from the selection to each student. Then, have each student write the word and draw a picture showing what it means. Next, have students use a dictionary to find another form of the word and copy and label it at the bottom of their drawing. Encourage students to post and share their drawings.

Beginning Allow students to work together.

Intermediate/Advanced/Advanced High Have students include some of the self-selected words and content-area words they added to their glossaries.

Use Prepositional Phrases in Sentences Have partners practice writing sentences using prepositional phrases. Have partners copy the chart. Encourage pairs to add other prepositions for additional practice. Have partners share their sentences and identify the preposition and prepositional phrases they used. Provide feedback.

PREPOSITION	PREPOSITIONAL PHRASE	SENTENCE WITH PREPOSITIONAL PHRASE
after	after the sunset	We arrived after the sunset.
beside		

FORMATIVE ASSESSMENT

STUDENT CHECK-IN

Text Reconstruction Ask partners to share their notes. Have them reflect on their work using the Check-In routine.

Grammar in Context Have partners reflect on their deconstructions using the Check-In routine.

LEARNING GOALS

We can apply strategies and skills to read poetry.

OBJECTIVES

Determine a theme of a story, drama, or poem from details in the text; summarize the text.

Explain major differences between poems, drama, and prose, and refer to the structural elements of poems and drama when writing or speaking about a text.

Explain the meaning of simple similes and metaphors in context.

Engage effectively in a range of collaborative discussions with diverse partners on grade 4 topics and texts, building on others' ideas and expressing their own clearly.

LANGUAGE OBJECTIVES

Students will discuss metaphor in the poem using key vocabulary.

ELA ACADEMIC LANGUAGE

- *metaphor, imagery, theme, free verse, speaker, compare, rhyme*
- Cognates: *metáfora, imágenes, tema, comparar, rima*

MATERIALS

Online ELL Genre Passages, "Me, As a Mountain" and "Quiet Room"

"Me, As a Mountain" and "Quiet Room"

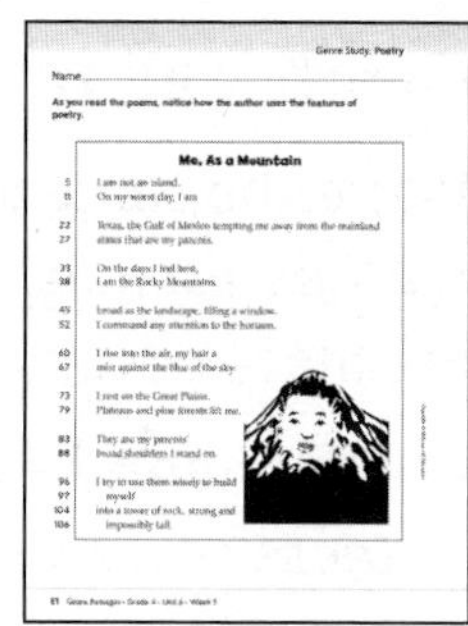

Genre Passage
Lexile NP

Prepare to Read

Build Background Read the title "Me, As a Mountain" aloud and discuss with students the characteristics of a mountain. Discuss with them what they think would be the characteristics of a person who calls themselves a mountain. On a map, point out the places in the poem: Texas, the Gulf of Mexico, the mainland states, the Rocky Mountains, and the Great Plains.

Vocabulary Use the Define, Example, Ask routine to pre-teach difficult words or unfamiliar concepts, such as *island, tempting, mainland, horizon, plateaus,* and *slightest* (Cognates: *isla, horizonte*). Invite students to add new vocabulary to their glossaries.

Set Purpose *Today we will read the poems "Me, As a Mountain" and "Quiet Room." As we read, think about what shapes a person's identity.*

Read the Text

Page E1, "Me, As a Mountain"

Metaphor Have partners identify a metaphor and tell what two things are being compared. (Possible answer: I am the Rocky Mountains; the speaker is compared to a mountain.)

Beginning Read the poem with students. Restate the lines as needed. *What does* worst *mean?* (very bad) *What does* best *mean?* (very good) *Do the words* worst *and* best *have the same or opposite meanings?* (opposite) Have partners describe what the poem is about: The poem tells the way a person feels on good and bad days.

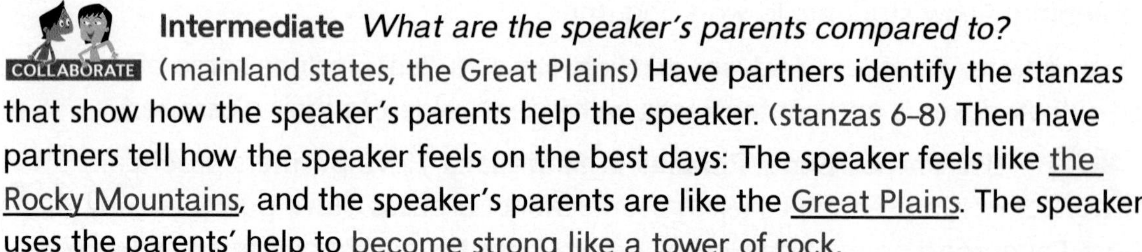

Intermediate *What are the speaker's parents compared to?* (mainland states, the Great Plains) Have partners identify the stanzas that show how the speaker's parents help the speaker. (stanzas 6–8) Then have partners tell how the speaker feels on the best days: The speaker feels like the Rocky Mountains, and the speaker's parents are like the Great Plains. The speaker uses the parents' help to become strong like a tower of rock.

Advanced/Advanced High *What does the speaker mean that he or she is not an island?* (The speaker is not alone.) *What does the speaker tell about the parents?* (The parents are like the Great Plains.) *What does the speaker try to do with the parents?* (The speaker tries to use the parents as rest and support. This helps the speaker be strong and successful.)

Respond to Reading

Use the following instruction to help students answer the questions on page E2.

1. **Imagery** *What does the title tell about the speaker?* (compares the speaker to a mountain) *What does the word* As *signal?* It signals a comparison.
2. *Have students read the poem aloud. Do the words rhyme?* (no)
3. **Theme** *How can a person be like an island?* A person who is alone is like an island.

Fluency Have partners take turns reading the poems.

Page E3, "Quiet Room"

Beginning Read the poem with students. Restate the lines as needed. *Why does the speaker want to stay in the quiet room?* The speaker likes to think. *How is the speaker different from some friends?* The speaker likes to think. The friends think a quiet room is boring. The friends think music is fun.

Intermediate *What does the speaker like?* (a quiet room) *What do the friends think about a quiet room?* (boring) *Why does the speaker like a quiet room?* (the speaker can think there) *What is an antonym of boring?* (fun)

COLLABORATE **Advanced/Advanced High** Have partners describe what the speaker's quiet room looks like. (Possible answer: The sunshine streams in.) Discuss why the speaker stays in the room. (Possible answer: The speaker likes the quiet, soft colors, streaming sunshine, and thinking.)

Theme Have partners describe the theme of the poem. (Possible answer: A quiet place is just as important as fun places.)

Respond to Reading

Use the following instruction to help students answer the questions on page E3.

1. *What do the speaker and the speaker's friends not agree about?* The speaker likes a quiet room, but the friends think the room is boring. The friends like music and fun.
2. **Poetry: Free Verse** Have students read the poem aloud. *Does the poem have words that rhyme?* (no) *What is one purpose for using free verse?* (to sound like someone is speaking in a way that is natural and free)
3. **Theme** *Which lines describe the reason the speaker likes a quiet room?* The speaker explains his reason in the last stanza. The speaker explains that the speaker can think freely in a quiet room.

Build Knowledge: Make Connections

Talk About the Text Have partners discuss what shapes a person's identity.

Write About the Text Have students add their ideas to their Build Knowledge pages of their reader's notebooks.

FORMATIVE ASSESSMENT

STUDENT CHECK-IN

Have partners share their responses on pages E2 and E3. Ask students to reflect using the Check-In routine.

LEVEL UP

IF students read the **ELL Level** fluently and answered the questions,

THEN pair them with students who have proficiently read the **On Level.** Have them

- partner read the **On Level** passage.
- summarize the details to infer theme.

LEARNING GOALS

We can apply strategies and skills to read realistic fiction.

OBJECTIVES

Explain major differences between poems, drama, and prose, and refer to the structural elements of poems and drama when writing or speaking about a text.

Engage effectively in a range of collaborative discussions with diverse partners on grade 4 topics and texts, building on others' ideas and expressing their own clearly.

Use context to confirm or self-correct word recognition and understanding, rereading as necessary.

LANGUAGE OBJECTIVES

Students will discuss the events in a realistic fiction story using key vocabulary.

ELA ACADEMIC LANGUAGE

- *theme, imagery, reread, realistic fiction*
- Cognates*: tema, ficción realista*

MATERIALS

ELL Leveled Reader *Homesick for American Samoa*

Online Differentiated Texts: "Life in a Mexican Village"

Online ELL Visual Vocabulary Cards

DIGITAL TOOLS

MULTIMODAL

Have students read along as they listen to the selections to develop comprehension and practice fluency and pronunciation.

Homesick for American Samoa

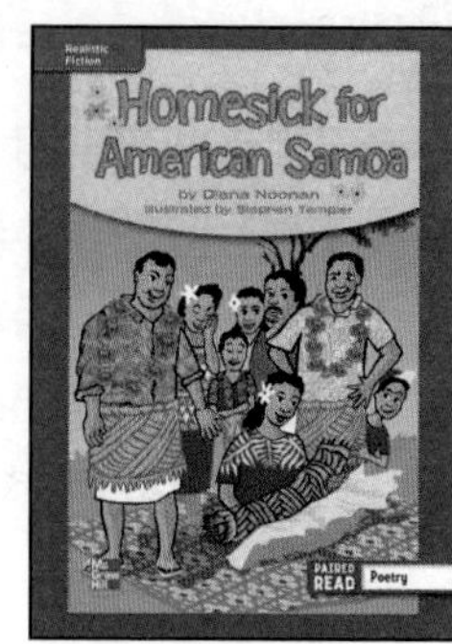

Leveled Reader
Lexile 570L

Prepare to Read

Build Background Ask and discuss with students: *Have you ever lived somewhere else? What was different? What did you miss?* Then preview *Homesick for American Samoa* by locating the island on a globe or map and explain that it is a tropical island. Discuss with students what life might be like for people on an island and use the illustrations in the **Leveled Reader** to discuss.

Vocabulary Use the routine on the **ELL Visual Vocabulary Cards** to pre-teach ELL Vocabulary *insisted, moped,* and *peculiar*. Have students discuss vocabulary labeled on the illustrations.

Set Purpose *Today we will read a realistic fiction text called* Homesick for American Samoa. *As we read, think about what shapes a person's identity.*

Read the Text

Pages 5–6

Beginning Read pages 5–6 with students. Restate sentences as needed. *What invitation did the parents receive*? The parents received a wedding invitation.

Intermediate Discuss with a partner why Salesi and Pele are going to Los Angeles instead of staying with their parents: Mom must take care of Grandma and Dad does not want to go without Mom.

Advanced/Advanced High *Why is Grandma sad?* (Possible answer: Many of her relatives visited California and they decided to live there. Grandma is worried the boys will want to live in Los Angeles.)

Page 8, Paragraphs 3–6

What shows how Aunt Vai and Rylan feel about going to Splash Out Fun? (The exclamations show they feel excited.) *What words describe the park?* (fun, amusement, new) Have students discuss what the author might want the readers to remember. (Possible answer: At first, new things can be fun and exciting.)

Beginning *What did Salesi notice on the freeway?* It was big. Things moved fast.

COLLABORATE **Intermediate** Have partners discuss imagery that describes Salesi's experience in Los Angeles. *What words help you imagine the sights and sounds?* (*ambulance raced past, giant trucks rumbled by*) *Why do you think Salesi felt like he was on another planet?* (Everything was different from home.)

Advanced/Advanced High *What does* peculiar *mean?* (strange, odd, unusual) *What makes Salesi feel as if he is "on another, peculiar planet"?* (The house, sights, and sounds are unfamiliar and different from those at home.)

Pages 13–15

Beginning *What word tells how Salesi felt?* (*homesickness*) *Why did Salesi feel sick?* Salesi missed his home. Have partners identify the names of Samoan clothing and food.

Advanced/Advanced High *How did Elisapeta feel about Grandma's present? How do you know?* (Possible answer: Elisapeta liked it, but it also made her feel homesick. She called it "amazing" and cried.)

Reread Have students reread to tell in detail how Salesi's feelings change: Salesi missed his home but the traditions at the wedding helped him feel better. *What is the author's message, or theme?* (Possible answer: The best things in life are traditions and home.)

Respond to Reading Have partners complete their graphic organizers and discuss the questions on page 16.

Fluency: Accuracy, Phrasing

Read page 15 with accuracy and appropriate phrasing. Read it again while students read along. For more practice, have students record their voices a few times as they read. Have them choose the best one.

Paired Read: "Fishing in the Supermarket"

Analytical Writing

Make Connections: Write About It

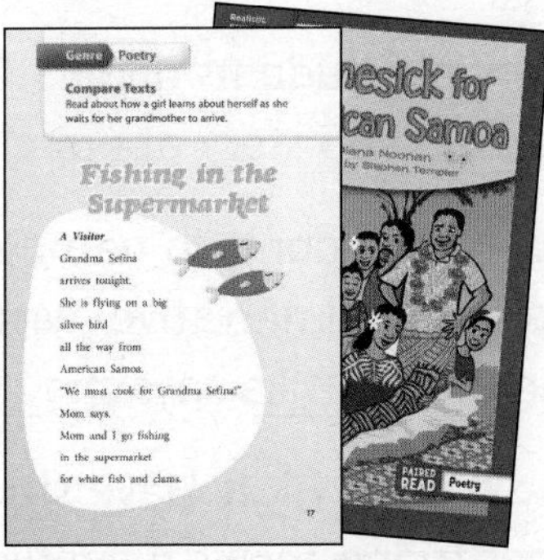

ELL Leveled Reader

Before students write, discuss the questions on page 19: *Reread the first paragraph on page 13. What makes Salesi's homesickness go away?* Before he saw the Samoan food, Salesi missed home. Then the homesickness almost went away. *Reread "Welcome" on page 19.* Like Salesi, Grandma Sefina is excited about the Somoan food.

Build Knowledge: Make Connections

Talk About the Text Have partners discuss what shapes a person's identity.

Write About the Text Have students add their ideas to their Build Knowledge pages of their reader's notebooks.

Self-Selected Reading

Have students choose another realistic fiction text from the online **Leveled Reader Library** or read the **Differentiated Text:** "Life in a Mexican Village."

FOCUS ON LITERARY ELEMENTS

Have students complete the activity on page 20 to use alliteration in a description of a special event.

LITERATURE CIRCLES

Ask students to conduct a literature circle using the Thinkmark questions to guide the discussion.

FORMATIVE ASSESSMENT

STUDENT CHECK-IN

Have partners share their answers to Respond to Reading. Ask students to reflect on their learning using the Check-In routine.

LEVEL UP

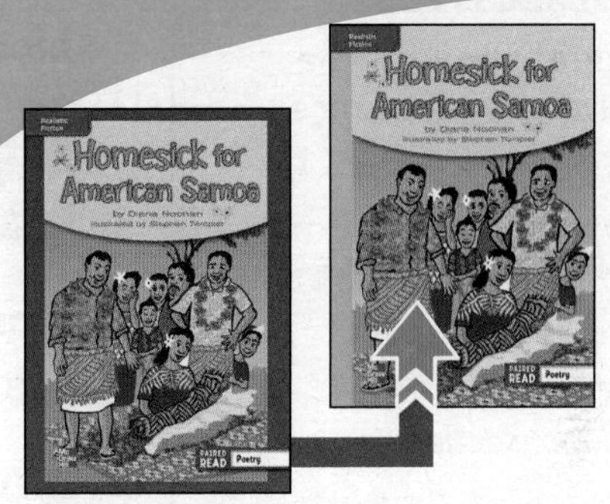

IF students read the **ELL Level** fluently and answered the questions,

THEN pair them with students who have proficiently read the **On Level** and have students

- read the **On Level** main selection with their partner aloud.
- list words they find difficult.
- discuss these words with their partners.

The **On Level** challenges students by including more **academic language** and **complex sentence structures.**

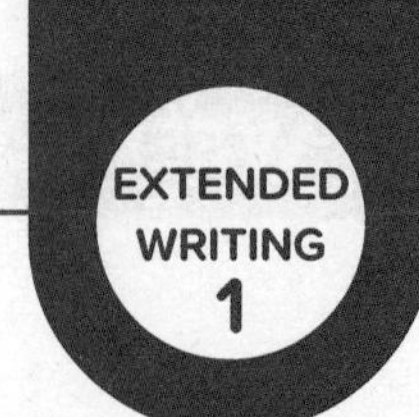

LEARNING GOALS

- **We can identify features of a fictional narrative.**
- **We can plan a fictional narrative.**
- **We can draft a fictional narrative.**

OBJECTIVES

Orient the reader by establishing a situation and introducing a narrator and/or characters; organize an event sequence that unfolds naturally.

Use a variety of transitional words and phrases to manage the sequence of events.

Use dialogue and description to develop experiences and events or show the responses of characters to situations.

LANGUAGE OBJECTIVES

Students will narrate by writing a fictional narrative using sequence words.

ELA ACADEMIC LANGUAGE

- *dialogue, features, characters, fictional, narrative, sequence*
- Cognates: *diálogo, secuencia*

MATERIALS

Online ELL Extended Writing Resources BLMs, pp. 82-83:

- My Writing Outline
- Draft: Dialogue

Online Graphic Organizer, 19

Online Language Development Cards, 27B, 28B, 88B

Online Language Development Practice, pp. 160-162, 166-168, 526-528

Reading/Writing Companion, pp. 192-195

Literature Anthology, p. 179

Fictional Narrative

Expert Model

Features of a Fictional Narrative

Review the features of a fictional narrative with students. Read "Aguinaldo" on page 179 of the **Literature Anthology** together. Use the first page of the story to discuss features and identify examples.

- *A fictional narrative is a made-up story about characters, settings, and events, and includes a conflict the characters must resolve. It seems real.*
- *Who is the narrator?* (Marilia) *What is the setting?* (It is December at a girls' school in Puerto Rico.)
- *Dialogue develops characters and plot. What does Marilia say in the dialogue?* (Marilia says she is not going to the nursing home.) *How does the dialogue develop the plot?* (The dialogue tells how Marilia feels. It shows a conflict.)
- *Sequence words tell the order of events. What are examples?* (*then, next, at first, in the end*)
- *Sensory details help readers picture what the characters experience. What is a sensory detail in the story?* (Marilia whispers to her friend.)

Have partners describe examples to identify features of a fictional narrative.

Beginning Confirm students understand what a fictional narrative is. A fictional narrative is a made-up story about characters, settings, and events.

Intermediate Ask students to name other features of a fictional narrative. For example: In a fictional narrative, writers use dialogue to develop characters and plot. The character Marilia says she does not want to go to the nursing home.

Advanced/Advanced High Have students discuss how the conversation between Marilia and her friend shows a conflict using terms *dialogue, characters, feelings.*

Plan: Choose Your Topic

Writing Prompt

COLLABORATE Confirm students understand the prompt: Write a fictional narrative. Write about a character who is nervous about trying something new. Ask partners to discuss: *What does it mean to be "nervous"? What is an activity that made you feel nervous the first time you tried it?*

Plan: Sequence of Events

Order the Events

Help students plan. Review that a fictional narrative tells events in a logical order and has a clear beginning, middle, and end. Help students orally share the events of their story using: First ___. Next ___. Then ___. Last ___. Have students use the online Sequence of Events **Graphic Organizer 19**. Once students have planned the sequence of events for their stories, they should plan what happens in the events.

Have partners use **My Writing Outline** to plan their writing.

Draft

Dialogue

Read the section of "Remembering Hurricane Katrina" on page 195 of the **Reading/Writing Companion**. Discuss meanings of any unfamiliar words and phrases like *possessions* or *temporary residents*. Point out that Aunt Lucia speaks a few sentences. Ask: *How does the author tell details about the story using dialogue?* (She explains what is happening. She tells about the other characters.) Write Aunt Lucia's dialogue on the board and read it with students. Ask: *What details can you find in Aunt Lucia's dialogue?* Underline the phrases the students point out. (Sample answers: New Orleans, Louisiana; homes and possessions; temporary residents of the Astrodome)

Beginning Help partners create more dialogue between Aunt Lucia and the narrator. Have students describe their dialogue: It shows the characters' feelings and personalities.

Intermediate Help students create more dialogue between Aunt Lucia and the narrator, and have the narrator speak more. Have students describe their dialogue: It shows the characters' feelings and personalities.

Advanced/Advanced High Have partners create dialogue between Aunt Lucia and the narrator in a new setting. Have them talk as if another big hurricane were coming.

Mixed Levels Have partners use **Draft: Dialogue** to practice adding dialogue in their narratives.

Language Development Practice For additional support using past tense verbs, see Lessons 27B and 28B. For additional support using sequence words, see Lesson 88B.

Write a Draft

COLLABORATE Have students prepare for writing a draft by orally sharing their narrative with a partner. Students should refer to My Writing Outline as they share.

Beginning My fictional narrative is about ______. In the beginning ______. Then ______. In the end ______.

Intermediate My fictional narrative is about ______. In the beginning ______. My character felt ______. Then ______. In the end ______. My character felt ______.

Advanced/Advanced High Have partners summarize their fictional narrative and discuss how their characters felt.

Have students work independently to write their fictional narratives.

TEACHER CONFERENCES

To help students write their draft, meet with each student to provide support and guidance.

Beginning Help students write about the events in order using signal words. Discuss ways they can add dialogue to their narratives.

Intermediate Have students describe and read the sentences they like and sentences they are struggling with. Provide suggestions to help them show the order of events and to add dialogue to their narratives.

Advanced/Advanced High Discuss with students what they like about their draft and what they want to improve. Have them focus on the order of events and the dialogue in their drafts.

FORMATIVE ASSESSMENT

STUDENT CHECK IN

Features of a Fictional Narrative Have partners name three features of a fictional narrative.

Plan Have partners share **My Writing Outline**.

Draft Have partners point out two examples of dialogue in their drafts.

Ask students to reflect using the Check-In routine.

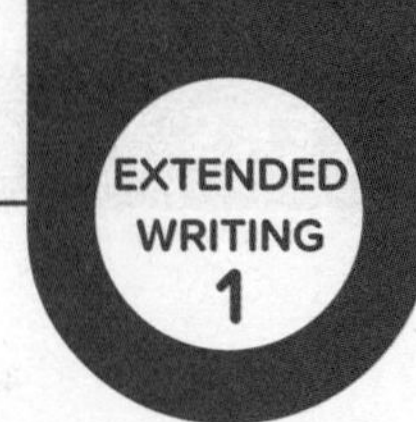

LEARNING GOALS

- We can revise a fictional narrative.
- We can edit and proofread a fictional narrative.
- We can publish, present, and evaluate a personal narrative.

OBJECTIVES

Use concrete words and phrases and sensory details to convey experiences and events precisely.

With guidance and support from peers and adults, develop and strengthen writing as needed by planning, revising, and editing.

Follow agreed-upon rules for discussions and carry out assigned roles.

LANGUAGE OBJECTIVES

Students will narrate using description and sensory details.

ELA ACADEMIC LANGUAGE

- *sensory, visualize, descriptive, feedback, edit, proofread*
- Cognates: *sensorial, visualisar, descriptivo, editar*

MATERIALS

Online ELL Extended Writing Resources BLMs, p. 84

- Revise: Description

Online Language Development Cards, 8A, 12A–12B, 42A

Online Language Development Practice, pp. 43–45, 67–72, 247–249

Reading/Writing Companion, pp. 196–199

Literature Anthology, p. 181

Fictional Narrative

Revise

Description

Refer to **Reading/Writing Companion** page 196 to discuss description. Remind students that description and sensory details can paint a picture for readers and allow them to visualize the characters, setting, and events of the story.

Description *One way to add description to your stories is to use descriptive adjectives and adverbs. Adjectives describe nouns, and adverbs describe verbs. These words can help your reader picture the characters and events in your story.* Use an example from "Aguinaldo" on **Literature Anthology** page 181: "'*Hola,* Señora Collazo,' I said, smiling sweetly." Discuss with them what the phrase *smiling sweetly* tells about how Marilia feels. Generate with them a list of words they could use to describe feelings.

Have partners find more examples of descriptive adjectives and adverbs on page 181 of "Aguinaldo."

Beginning Help students explain: Marilia describes her friends sitting on the polished tiles. Have partners write different words to describe the tiles.

Intermediate Help them explain using: The writer describes the friends playing jacks. In my own story, I can describe the friends excitedly playing a game of jacks.

Advanced/Advanced High Have students identify examples in "Aguinaldo" and describe how the words add to their understanding.

Sensory Details *Sensory details can help readers see, hear, smell, taste and feel.* Review the paragraph about Marcy and the kitten on **Reading/Writing Companion** page 196. *The paragraph about Marcy and the kitten tells you a few things about both characters, but it leaves out sensory details.* Ask: *What details would help you create a picture in your mind or visualize the characters?* (Sample responses: what Marcy looks like, what the kitten looks and sounds like and how they are acting together, how the garden looks and smells).

Ask students to look for ways to add sensory details. Help students choose a sentence about one of the characters in the story.

Beginning Help students revise their sentence: My character has dark brown, curly hair and wears glasses. My character feels nervous.

Intermediate/Advanced/Advanced High Help students revise by asking questions. For example: What does your character look like? What do you want to show about him or her? Help them add more sensory details.

Mixed Levels Have partners complete **Revise: Description** for support in improving descriptions.

Revise

Prepare students to revise their drafts. First have them work with partners, and then independently.

Discuss features of the genre, such as characters, settings, events, and conflict. Remind students they should be using dialogue to develop their characters and move the events of the plot along.

Remind students that as they revise, they should make sure the events in their narratives are in order.

Discuss other features about the genre, including that the made-up events in the story should be things that could happen in real life.

Review with students the strategies they learned to revise for description. Help them apply these strategies to their own writing. Have partners describe their revisions to each other.

Beginning Have partners describe their revisions. For example: I will add an adjective to describe the character's feelings.

Intermediate Have partners describe their revisions. For example: I will add an adjective to describe the character's feelings.

Advanced/Advanced High Invite partners to describe their revisions to each other.

Peer Conferencing

Partner Feedback

Review the Revising Checklist on Reading/Writing Companion page 197 with students. Have partners use the checklist to give feedback on each other's work. Help students provide feedback. For example:

Beginning There is/is not a logical sequence of events in your narrative. I can/cannot tell there is a beginning, middle, and end. I like how you used the word ____ to describe ____.

Intermediate When I read your narrative, there is a logical sequence of events. I like the dialogue in this part. You can add details to describe ______.

Advanced/ Advanced High After using the Revising Checklist with their partners, have students reflect on which suggestions were most helpful.

TEACHER CONFERENCES

To help students revise, meet with each student to provide support and guidance.

Beginning Help students add descriptions and identify sentences where they can add more sensory details.

Intermediate Help students add adjectives and adverbs to their writing. Provide suggestions for how they can add more sensory details in their narratives.

Advanced/Advanced High Help students add more description, sensory details, and dialogue to improve plot development in their narratives.

Edit and Proofread

Using the Editing Checklist

Discuss the items in the Editing Checklist on Reading/Writing Companion page 198 to make sure students understand what each one means.

Have partners edit and proofread each other's drafts using the Editing Checklist.

If students need more support with editing and proofreading, use **Language Development Practice** lessons: Common and Proper Nouns (Lesson 8A), Possessive Nouns (Lessons 12A and 12B), and Contractions (Lesson 42A).

Publish, Present, Evaluate

Evaluate

Tell students they will use the rubric on Reading/Writing Companion page 199 to evaluate their own writing. Explain the language in the rubric to make sure students understand what the terms describe. Have students first try to apply the rubric to their own writing, and then describe their thinking to a partner.

FORMATIVE ASSESSMENT

STUDENT CHECK IN

Revise Ask partners to share ways they added description.

Edit and Proofread Ask students to share the partner feedback they gave.

Publish, Present, Evaluate Ask partners to share the scores they gave themselves using their rubrics.

Have students reflect using the Check-In routine..

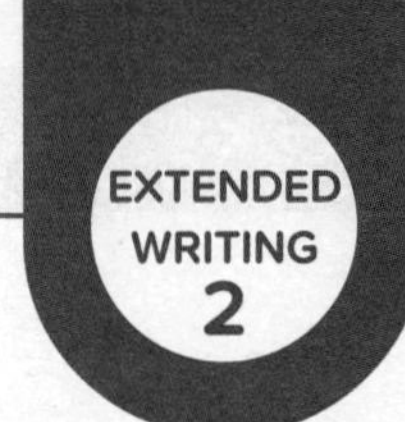

LEARNING GOALS

- **We can identify features of free verse poetry.**
- **We can plan a free verse poem.**
- **We can draft a free verse poem.**

OBJECTIVES

Explain the meaning of simple similes and metaphors in context.

Use concrete words and phrases and sensory details to convey experiences and events precisely.

Write routinely over extended time frames and shorter time frames for a range of discipline-specific tasks, purposes, and audiences.

LANGUAGE OBJECTIVES

Students will narrate by writing a free verse poem using figurative language.

ELA ACADEMIC LANGUAGE

- *free verse, alliteration, figurative language, prompt, metaphor, simile*
- Cognates: *literario, lenguaje figurado, metáfora, símil*

MATERIALS

Online ELL Extended Writing Resources, pp. 85–86:

- My Writing Outline
- Draft: Alliteration

Online Graphic Organizer, 20

Online Language Development Cards, 83A–83B

Online Language Development Practice, 493–498

Reading/Writing Companion, pp. 200–203

Literature Anthology, p. 501

Free Verse Poetry

Expert Model

Features of a Free Verse Poem

Review the features of a Free Verse Poem with students. Read the poem "Birdfoot's Grampa" on page 501 of the **Literature Anthology** with them and explain the words *rhythm, meter, rhyme*. Restate any difficult lines and use the poem to discuss the features and identify examples.

- *Free verse is a kind of poetry that does not use rhythm, meter, and rhyme. How can you tell that "Birdfoot's Grampa" is a free verse poem?* (It does not rhyme or have a specific rhythm or meter.)
- *A free verse poem may have figurative language. What simile or metaphor is in the poem?* (The metaphor of *live drops of rain* describes leaping toads.)
- *Sensory words may describe how things look, feel, taste, smell, or sound. What sensory words can you find in the poem? (blinded by our lights and leaping; leathery hands)*
- *A free verse poem uses alliteration, or the repetition of the same sounds at the beginning of words. What examples are in the poem? (lights and leaping, live)*

Have partners describe examples in "Birdfoot's Grampa" to identify the features of a free verse poem to each other.

Beginning Confirm students understand what a free verse poem is. A free verse poem does not have rhyme or rhythm. The poet tells about when his grandfather helped toads.

Intermediate Have partners name other features of a free verse poem: The poet uses figurative language and alliteration to help the reader picture images.

Advanced/Advanced High Have students discuss features using more examples from the poem "Birdfoot's Grampa."

Plan: Choose Your Topic

Writing Prompt

Confirm students understand the prompt: Write a free verse poem. Write about someone who is important to you. Ask partners to discuss and then share with the group: *What makes the person special to you? How does the person make you feel?* Help students use this discussion to select or revise their writing topic.

Plan: Metaphor and Simile

Figurative Language

Help students plan. Review types of figurative language they can use in their free verse poems. *Figurative language includes similes and metaphors. A simile compares two things using the words* like *or* as. *For example: My uncle is like a soft teddy bear. Metaphors compare two things without using* like *or* as. *For example: My uncle is a teddy bear.* Have partners find a metaphor in the first stanza of "Birdfoot's Grampa." (live drops of rain) Then discuss with them why this is a metaphor. Help students review the types of figurative language and fill in their Idea Webs or online **Graphic Organizer 20**.

Beginning Help partners write a simile using the words *like* or *as*: The boy jumped like a frog.

Intermediate Provide more models for using similes and metaphors. The busy street was a beehive. Have partners discuss why it is a simile or a metaphor.

Advanced/Advanced High Have students write one simile and one metaphor about the classroom.

Have partners use **My Writing Outline** to plan their writing.

Draft

Alliteration

Display **Reading/Writing Companion** page 203. Explain that poets use alliteration to make language more interesting. Alliteration is the repetition of the same beginning consonant sound in a line or verse. Ask: *What is the sound that the poet repeats?* (sound of "L") Have partners identify and say the alliterative words. Ask: *Why does alliteration make this verse more interesting?* (It adds a continuous sound as we read.)

Beginning Help students add words that start with *b* to this sentence: The big baboon hugged its baby before breakfast. Have partners read their sentences to one another.

Intermediate Have partners brainstorm words that begin with the same consonant. Have them write the words and read to each other using: The big balloon bounced before it burst by the bench.

Advanced/Advanced High Name some alliteration words that could be used in a poem. Help students add alliteration words to a word wall that students can refer to as they write.

Mixed Levels Have partners use **Draft: Alliteration** to practice using alliteration.

Language Development Practice For additional support with figurative language, see Language Development lessons 83A and 83B.

Write a Draft

Have students prepare for writing a draft by orally sharing their poem with a partner. Students should refer to **My Writing Outline** as they share.

Beginning My free verse poem is about ______. I use a simile to describe ______.

Intermediate My free verse poem is about ______. I use a simile to describe ______. I use a metaphor to describe ______.

Advanced/Advanced High Have partners summarize their free verse poem and discuss the figurative language they used.

Have students work independently to write their free verse poems.

TEACHER CONFERENCES

To help students write their draft, meet with each student to provide support and guidance.

Beginning Help students write a poem using figurative language. Help them choose the type of figurative language they want to use in their poem.

Intermediate Have students describe and read the sentences they like and sentences they are struggling with. Provide suggestions to help them add figurative language and alliteration.

Advanced/Advanced High Discuss with students what they like about their draft and what they want to improve. Have them focus on figurative language and alliteration in their drafts.

FORMATIVE ASSESSMENT

STUDENT CHECK IN

Features of a Free Verse Poem Have partners name three features of free verse poetry.

Plan Have partners share **My Writing Outline**.

Draft Have partners point out an example of alliteration in their drafts.

Ask students to reflect using the Check-In routine.

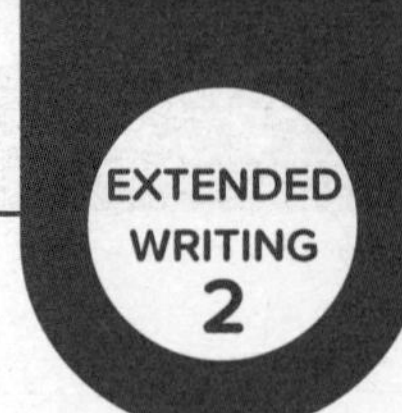

Free Verse Poetry

LEARNING GOALS

- **We can revise a free verse poetry.**
- **We can edit and proofread a free verse poetry.**
- **We can publish, present, and evaluate a free verse poetry.**

OBJECTIVES

Choose words and phrases to convey ideas precisely.

With guidance and support from peers and adults, develop and strengthen writing as needed by planning, revising, and editing.

Pose and respond to specific questions to clarify or follow up on information, and make comments that contribute to the discussion and link to the remarks of others.

LANGUAGE OBJECTIVES

Students will inform by using precise words in a free verse poem.

ELA ACADEMIC LANGUAGE

- *precise, figurative language, feedback, edit, proofread, publish, present, evaluate*
- Cognates: *preciso, lenguaje figurativo, editar, publicar, presentar, evaluar*

MATERIALS

Online ELL Extended Writing Resources BLMs, p. 87:

- Revise: Precise Words

Online Language Development Cards, 41A–41B, 56A–59A

Online Language Development Practice, pp. 241–246, 331–351

Reading/Writing Companion, pp. 204–207

Revise

Precise Words

Remind students that poets use precise words so readers will be able to clearly picture what the poet is writing about.

COLLABORATE **Use Precise Words** Review the poem on page 204 in the **Reading/Writing Companion,** and ask students if any of the words could be more precise. *Precise words refer to specific things rather than general things. For example,* bird *is a general word because it refers to all birds.* Heron *and* egret *are precise words because they refer to specific birds.* Generate with students precise words to replace or add to *day* and *girl* in the poem, such as: *sunny day, a happy little girl.* Discuss how the precise words affect the images and feeling in the poem. Elicit that the language creates a more vivid picture for the reader.

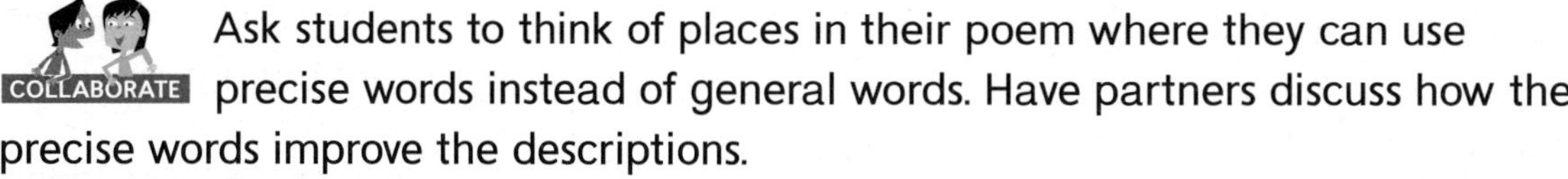

COLLABORATE Ask students to think of places in their poem where they can use precise words instead of general words. Have partners discuss how the precise words improve the descriptions.

Beginning Help students complete the frames to use precise words. For example: My older sister and I had a wonderful day. We played with Legos together and watched funny movies.

Intermediate Provide more models for using precise words. For example: My sister is five years older than me. She is always happy to let me go to the movies and the beach with her. Have partners explain to each other why these words are precise.

Advanced/Advanced High Have partners choose a sentence from their draft with general words and replace them with more precise words. (*rain; mist; white; kept saying; save*) Have partners discuss the difference in their writing.

Mixed Levels Have partners complete **Revise: Precise Words** for support in using precise words in their poems.

Revise

Prepare students to revise their drafts. First have them write with partners, and then independently.

Discuss features of the genre, such as figurative language, sensory words, and that it does not use rhythm, meter, or rhyme. Ask students to make sure they include details to help their readers picture images from their poems.

Remind students that as they revise, they should make sure their poem is about a person who is important to them, and includes details about how this person makes them feel and why this person is important to them.

Review other features of the genre, such as using alliteration, and making sure the writing is descriptive and interesting for the reader.

Review with students the strategies they learned to revise for precise words. Help them apply these strategies to their own writing. Have partners describe their revisions to each other.

Beginning Have partners describe their revisions. For example: I will change a general word to a specific word to add more feeling in the poem.

Intermediate Have partners describe their revisions. For example: I will change a general word to a specific word to add more feeling in the poem.

Advanced/Advanced High Invite partners to describe their revisions to each other.

Peer Conferencing

Partner Feedback

Review the Revising Checklist on page 205 of the Reading/Writing Companion with students. Have partners use the checklist to give feedback on each other's work. For example:

Beginning There are/are not precise words in your poem. I like how you used figurative language to describe ____.

Intermediate When I read your poem, there is/is not figurative language. I like this part because _____. You can add a precise word to describe _____.

Advanced/ Advanced High After using the Revising Checklist with their partners, have students reflect on which suggestions were most helpful.

TEACHER CONFERENCES

To help students revise, meet with each student to provide support and guidance.

Beginning Help students use specific words in their poems. Help them identify where they can replace general words with specific words.

Intermediate Have students add precise words to their poems. Provide suggestions to help them refer to specific things in their writing.

Advanced/Advanced High Help students add precise words to their poems. Discuss how they can make their poems more vivid and add feeling to their poems.

Edit and Proofread

Using the Editing Checklist

Discuss the items in the Editing Checklist on Reading/Writing Companion page 206 to make sure students understand what each one means.

Have partners edit and proofread each other's drafts using the Editing Checklist.

If students need more support with editing and proofreading, use Language Development Practice pages for additional practice: Pronoun-Verb Agreement (Lessons 41A–41B), Prepositions (Lessons 56A through 59A).

Publish, Present, Evaluate

Evaluate

Tell students they will use the rubric on Reading/Writing Companion page 207 to evaluate their own writing. Explain the language in the rubric to make sure students understand what the terms describe. Have students first try to apply the rubric to their own writing, and then describe their thinking to a partner.

FORMATIVE ASSESSMENT

STUDENT CHECK-IN

Revise Ask partners to share ways they used precise words.

Edit and Proofread Ask students to share the partner feedback they gave.

Publish, Present, Evaluate Ask partners to share the scores they gave themselves using their rubrics.

Have students reflect using the Check-In routine.

Summative Assessment

Get Ready for Unit Assessment

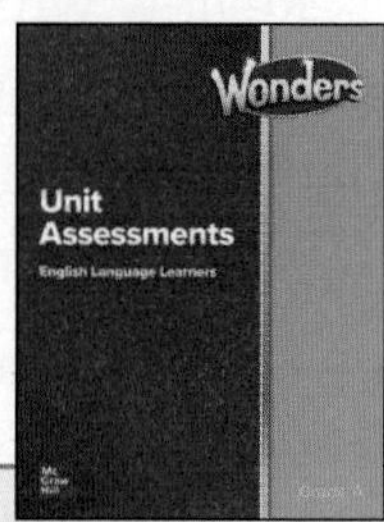

Unit 6 Tested Skills

LISTENING AND READING COMPREHENSION	VOCABULARY	GRAMMAR	SPEAKING AND WRITING
• Listening Actively • Comprehension • Text Structure • Cohesion	• Unit Vocabulary Words	• Prepositions • Adverbs • Condensing Ideas	• Presenting • Writing • Supporting Opinions • Retelling/Summarizing • Text Structure

Create a Student Profile

Record data from the following resources in the Student Profile charts on pages 320–321 of the Assessment book.

COLLABORATIVE	INTERPRETIVE	PRODUCTIVE

• Collaborative Conversations Rubrics
  • Listening
  • Speaking
	• Leveled Unit Assessment:
	  • Listening Comprehension
	  • Reading Comprehension
	  • Vocabulary
	  • Grammar
	• Presentation Rubric
	  • Listening
	• *Wonders* Unit Assessment
		• Weekly Progress Monitoring
		• Leveled Unit Assessment
		  • Speaking
		  • Writing
		• Presentation Rubric
		  • Speaking
		• Write to Sources Rubric
		• *Wonders* Unit Assessment

The Foundational Skills Kit, Language Development Kit, and Adaptive Learning provide additional student data for progress monitoring.

Level Up

Use the following chart, along with your Student Profiles, to guide your Level Up decisions.

LEVEL UP	If **BEGINNING** level students are able to do the following, they may be ready to move to the **INTERMEDIATE** level:	If **INTERMEDIATE** level students are able to do the following, they may be ready to move to the **ADVANCED** level:	If **ADVANCED** level students are able to do the following, they may be ready to move to on-level:
COLLABORATIVE	• participate in collaborative conversations using basic vocabulary and grammar and simple phrases or sentences • discuss simple pictorial or text prompts	• participate in collaborative conversations using appropriate words and phrases and complete sentences • use limited academic vocabulary across and within disciplines	• participate in collaborative conversations using more sophisticated vocabulary and correct grammar • communicate effectively across a wide range of language demands in social and academic contexts
INTERPRETIVE	• identify details in simple read alouds • understand common vocabulary and idioms and interpret language related to familiar social, school, and academic topics • make simple inferences and make simple comparisons • exhibit an emerging receptive control of lexical, syntactic, phonological, and discourse features	• identify main ideas and/or make some inferences from simple read alouds • use context clues to identify word meanings and interpret basic vocabulary and idioms • compare, contrast, summarize, and relate text to graphic organizers • exhibit a limited range of receptive control of lexical, syntactic, phonological, and discourse features when addressing new or familiar topics	• determine main ideas in read alouds that have advanced vocabulary • use context clues to determine meaning, understand multiple-meaning words, and recognize synonyms of social and academic vocabulary • analyze information, make sophisticated inferences, and explain their reasoning • command a high degree of receptive control of lexical, syntactic, phonological, and discourse features
PRODUCTIVE	• express ideas and opinions with basic vocabulary and grammar and simple phrases or sentences • restate information or retell a story using basic vocabulary • exhibit an emerging productive control of lexical, syntactic, phonological, and discourse features	• produce coherent language with limited elaboration or detail • restate information or retell a story using mostly accurate, although limited, vocabulary • exhibit a limited range of productive control of lexical, syntactic, phonological, and discourse features when addressing new or familiar topics	• produce sentences with more sophisticated vocabulary and correct grammar • restate information or retell a story using extensive and accurate vocabulary and grammar • tailor language to a particular purpose and audience • command a high degree of productive control of lexical, syntactic, phonological, and discourse features